BRITISH POPULATION IN THE TWENTIETH CENTURY

Social History in Perspective
General Editor: Jeremy Black

Social History in Perspective is a new series of in-depth studies of the many topics in social, cultural and religious history for students. They will also give the student clear surveys of the subject and also present the most recent research in an accessible way.

PUBLISHED

John Belchem *Popular Radicalism in Nineteenth-Century Britain*
Hugh McLeod *Religion and Society in England, 1850–1914*
N. L. Tranter *British Population in the Twentieth Century*

British Population in the Twentieth Century

N. L. Tranter

St. Martin's Press   New York

BRITISH POPULATION IN THE TWENTIETH CENTURY
Copyright © 1996 by N. L. Tranter
All rights reserved. No part of this book may be used or reproduced
in any manner whatsoever without written permission except in the
case of brief quotations embodied in critical articles or reviews.
For information, address:

St. Martin's Press, Scholarly and Reference Division,
175 Fifth Avenue, New York, N.Y. 10010

First published in the United States of America in 1996

Printed in Malaysia

ISBN 0-312-12940-8

Library of Congress Cataloging-in-Publication Data
Tranter, N. L.
British population in the twentieth century / N. L. Tranter.
p. cm. — (Social history in perspective)
Includes bibliographical references and index.
ISBN 0-312-12940-8 (cloth)
1. Great Britain—Population—History—20th century. 2. Great
Britain—Emigration and immigration—History—20th century.
3. Migration, Internal—Great Britain—History—20th century.
4. Mortality—Great Britain—History—20th century. 5. Fertility,
Human—Great Britain—History—20th century. I. Title.
II. Series.
HB3583.T67   1996
304.6'0941'09049—dc20   95-36424
                                                             CIP

TO HEATHER, RACHEL, SARAH AND ALAN

Contents

List of Tables		viii
Map 1	Britain	x
Map 2	Scotland	xi
Introduction		xiii
1	**Population Growth and Location**	1
2	**Internal and Overseas Migration**	19
3	**Mortality**	62
4	**Fertility**	83
Conclusion		126
Notes		128
Bibliography		162
Index		170

TABLES

1.1 The population of England, Wales, Scotland and Britain, 1801–1991 (thousands) — 3
1.2 The population of England, Wales, Scotland and Britain. Intercensal increase or decrease (% per annum, 1801–1991) — 4
1.3 Percentage share of the population of mainland Britain by region, 1751–1991 — 6
1.4 Intercensal rates of population growth in Britain by region, 1951–1991 (%) — 8
1.5 Average annual rates of population growth by type of district. England and Wales, 1961–1991 (per thousand population) — 16
2.1 Net migration as a percentage of natural increase. Great Britain 1871–1991 — 20
2.2 Net migration as a percentage of natural increase. Scotland, 1861–1990 — 22
2.3 Number of migrants by sea between the United Kingdom and non-European countries, 1913, 1920–1963 (thousands) — 26
2.4 Number of migrants into and out of the United Kingdom by sea and air, 1964–1990 (thousands) — 29
2.5 Net gain or loss by migration. England/Wales and Scotland, 1871/81–1981/91 (thousands) — 38

Tables

3.1 Annual average crude death rates, by sex.
England/Wales and Scotland, 1838/50–1981/90   64

3.2 Expectation of life at birth in years, by sex.
England/Wales and Scotland, c.1900–1988/90   65

4.1 Annual average crude birth rates.
England/Wales and Scotland, 1855–1990   86

4.2 Illegitimacy ratios. England/Wales and
Scotland, 1855–1990   89

4.3 Average annual crude marriage rates.
England/Wales and Scotland, 1855–1990   95

Map 1   Britain. Counties, planning regions and major towns, 1981
Source: Edward Royle, *Modern Britain. A Social History 1750–1985* (London, Edward Arnold, 1987), p. xii

Map 2 Scotland. Civil counties and regions, 1861–1939
Source: Michael Flinn (ed.), *Scottish Population History from the Seventeenth Century to the 1930s* (Cambridge, Cambridge University Press, 1977), p. xxiii

INTRODUCTION

At the beginning of the twentieth century the demography of each of the countries of mainland Britain was already an intriguing blend of the old and the new. In common with the experience of the preceding hundred years or so rates of population growth remained relatively high. A substantial proportion of each country's natural excess of births over deaths continued to disappear to overseas destinations. Changes in the internal geography of residence continued to favour England at the expense of Scotland and Wales, northern rather than southern counties of England, urban rather than rural locations, and core rather than more peripheral areas. Average expectations of life and variations in rates of mortality and life expectancy by region and socio-occupational class differed only moderately from those of a century earlier. Ages at marriage and percentages married and single had remained roughly constant for over 50 years. Crude birth rates were still only marginally lower than in the early nineteenth century and regional differentials in fertility were wider than ever. In these and many other respects the demographic structure of Britain around 1900 was little different from that of 1850 or even 1800.

At the same time, even before 1900, some of the demographic forms inherited from the past were beginning to change. In the course of the later decades of the nineteenth century the shift of population from south to north, rural to urban, and periphery to core started to slow. Regional, urban-rural and social class differentials in mortality began to narrow and average expectations of life to rise. Crude birth rates and levels of marital fertility began to decline and marital fertility replaced nuptiality as the principal demographic determinant of trends in overall fertility.

Compared with what was to happen in the twentieth century, it must be stressed, the changes which occurred in Britain's demographic structures in the decades before 1900 were modest. The late nineteenth century may have been the period in which the transition towards a modern demographic regime was initiated. But it was in the twentieth century that the bulk of the transformation was achieved.

Between 1800–9 and 1891–1900 average life expectancy at birth in England rose by about 11 years. Between 1891–1900 and the mid 1980s, chiefly in response to a decline in deaths from infectious disease and the displacement of communicable, infectious disease by non-communicable, degenerative disease as the main cause of death, it rose by over 26 years. In the half century before 1900 crude birth rates fell by just 15 per cent in England and Wales and 5 per cent in Scotland. In the course of the next 50 years they declined by 45 per cent and 39 per cent respectively. From around five among women marrying in the mid 1870s, the average number of births fell to around two among those marrying in the last quarter of the twentieth century. Accompanying this decline in fertility were marked reductions in regional and socio-occupational class fertility differentials and, in the later years of the century, unprecedented increases in the frequency of divorce, levels of extramarital cohabitation and rates of illegitimacy.

No less striking have been the changes that have taken place in patterns of migration and population growth. Between the 1930s and 1980s England and Wales together (though not Scotland), in sharp contrast to the experience of previous ages, gained far more people than they lost on balance of international migration. Despite this, rates of population

Introduction

growth fell to levels lower than at any time since the late eighteenth century. By the 1970s and 1980s, under the impact of persistently low levels of fertility, rates of population growth were negligible and even negative. The trend to lower rates of population increase was accompanied by major changes in the geography of residence within Britain. Although England has continued to increase its share of Britain's population and although, within England, the ranking of regions according to their share of the total population has remained largely unaltered, in contrast to what had happened in the nineteenth century the twentieth century has seen the re-emergence of a north to south drift in the balance of population location, a movement of people from core to geographically more peripheral regions, and a shift of people away from the largest urban communities towards smaller urban communities and rural areas.

In the demography of Britain at the beginning of the twentieth century there was still a great deal that generations born a hundred years or more earlier would have recognised. In the demography of Britain at the end of the twentieth century there is very little that would be familiar to them. What follows is an attempt to chart in more detail the progress of this transformation and to unravel some of the more important causes which underlay it.

1
POPULATION GROWTH AND LOCATION

One of the most striking characteristics of British population history in the decades since the end of the First World War has been the persistence of rates of population increase far below those achieved in the century or so prior to 1914. As Table 1.2 shows, at their peak during the early decades of the nineteenth century rates of population growth in mainland Britain as a whole averaged from 1.4 per cent to 1.8 per cent a year. Between the 1840s and the first decade of the twentieth century they slowed, to between 1 per cent and 1.4 per cent. But it was not until the decade 1911–20 that the decline became pronounced. From the 1910s to the 1960s annual rates of population growth slumped to around 0.5 per cent. In the course of the following twenty years they declined still further. By the 1970s growth rates were negligible and by the 1980s even the absolute size of the population had begun to decline.

Broadly the chronology of population growth in each of the mainland countries followed much the same pattern. In England growth rates peaked during the early decades of the nineteenth century before settling at slightly lower levels in the period between the middle of the century and the outbreak of the First World War. With occasional exceptions in the late sixteenth and late eighteenth centuries, at no time since at least the mid sixteenth century have rates of English population growth approached those recorded between 1801 and 1911.[1] Between 1911 and 1920 they suddenly fell to less than 0.5 per cent a year, at which level they remained for the following five decades. In the 1970s there was a further sharp fall. By the 1980s, for the first time since the years of demographic crisis in the late seventeenth and early eighteenth centuries, even the absolute size of England's population declined.

In Wales and Scotland too rates of population increase peaked in the early nineteenth century before stabilising at lower, though still historically high, levels between the mid nineteenth century and the First World War. In the century before 1914 the pace of population growth in Wales was only marginally below that in England and in several decades, notably 1901–11, even exceeded it. The postwar decline in rates of population increase, however, was greater in Wales than in England. In every decade from the 1920s to the 1960s the population of Wales grew more slowly than that of England and in the 1920s and 1930s it actually decreased. During the 1970s and 1980s, on the other hand, rates of population growth in Wales exceeded those in England. Of all mainland countries only Wales avoided an absolute decline in population in the 1980s and only in Wales did the pace of population increase in the 1970s and 1980s not fall below the levels recorded in any other decade since the beginning of the nineteenth century.

Rates of population growth in Scotland during the nineteenth century were consistently lower than in either England or Wales. Except in the 1920s and 1930s, when they compared favourably with the Welsh experience, they have remained relatively low ever since. Only in Scotland was the further deceleration in growth rates in the 1970s and 1980s accompanied by a decline in the absolute size of the resident population in both decades.

With few exceptions, rates of population increase in Britain since the First World War have been lower and less volatile than in other European countries. Generally, however, the recent evolution of Britain's population has followed a pattern common to much of continental Europe. As in Britain, rates of population growth in most European states since 1918 have

Table 1.1 The population of England, Wales, Scotland and Britain, 1801–1991 (thousands*)

	England	Wales	Scotland	Britain
1801	8305	587	1608	1 0500
1811	9491	673	1806	1 1970
1821	1 1206	794	2092	1 4092
1831	1 2992	904	2364	1 6260
1841	1 4868	1046	2620	1 8534
1851	1 6764	1163	2889	2 0816
1861	1 8780	1286	3062	2 3128
1871	2 1300	1412	3360	2 6072
1881	2 4403	1572	3736	2 9711
1891	2 7231	1771	4026	3 3028
1901	3 0515	2013	4472	3 7000
1911	3 3650	2421	4761	4 0832
1921	3 5230	2656	4882	4 2768
1931	3 7359	2593	4843	4 4795
1939	3 8995	2465	5007	4 6467
1951	4 1159	2599	5096	4 8854
1961	4 3461	2644	5179	5 1284
1971	4 6018	2731	5229	5 3978
1981	4 6226	2790	5131	5 4147
1991	4 6161	2799	4957	5 3917

* Excludes the Isle of Man, Jersey, Guernsey and associated islands.

Sources: Office of Population Censuses and Surveys (OPCS), *Census 1981. Historical Tables 1801–1981 England and Wales* (London, 1982), pp. 16–17. OPCS, *1991 Census. Preliminary Report for England and Wales* (London, 1991), p. 21.

fallen well below nineteenth-century levels and, apart from a handful of cases where the decline was reversed in the 1980s, fell continuously from the 1960s or 1970s onwards.[2] By the 1980s historically low rates of increase were the norm almost everywhere. In most countries population was growing more slowly than at any time since the early nineteenth century and in some rates of population growth barely exceeded the levels necessary for replacement.[3] Despite these broad similarities it bears emphasising that England and Scotland were the only European countries to experience absolute population

Table 1.2 The population of England, Wales, Scotland and Britain. Intercensal increase or decrease (–) (% per annum, 1801–1991*)

	England	Wales	Scotland	Britain
1801–11	1.43	1.47	1.23	1.40
1811–21	1.81	1.79	1.58	1.77
1821–31	1.59	1.39	1.31	1.54
1831–41	1.44	1.57	1.08	1.40
1841–51	1.28	1.12	1.03	1.23
1851–61	1.14	1.01	0.58	1.11
1861–71	1.27	0.94	0.93	1.27
1871–81	1.47	1.07	1.06	1.40
1881–91	1.10	1.20	0.75	1.12
1891–1901	1.15	1.29	1.06	1.20
1901–11	0.98	1.86	0.63	1.04
1911–21	0.45	0.91	0.25	0.47
1921–31	0.60	–0.24	–0.08	0.47
1931–9	0.53	–0.62	0.41	0.47
1939–51	0.46	0.45	0.15	0.43
1951–61	0.54	0.17	0.16	0.50
1961–71	0.57	0.32	0.10	0.53
1971–81	0.05	0.22	–0.19	0.03
1981–91	–0.01	0.03	–0.34	–0.04

* Excludes the Isle of Man, Jersey, Guernsey and associated islands.
Sources: See Table 1.1.

decline during the 1980s while rates of population increase in Wales were also among the lowest recorded. Since 1918, indeed, Scottish and Welsh growth rates have been consistently among the slowest in Europe.

Regional Distribution

The twentieth-century trend towards lower and, ultimately, negligible or negative rates of population increase has been accompanied by major changes in the spatial distribution of Britain's inhabitants. The most significant alterations in *regional* patterns of residence are summarised in Table 1.3.

In some respects, it is true, the regional structure of Britain's population over the last two centuries has displayed a remarkable continuity. The share of the mainland population resident in England, for instance, has risen continuously from at least as early as the middle of the eighteenth century while that of Scotland and, until the 1970s, of Wales has steadily declined. Within England, where the South East remained the largest population concentration, followed invariably in the same order by the North West, the West Midlands and Yorkshire/Humberside, the North and East Midlands and East Anglia, the ranking of regions according to their share of total population changed little between 1801 and 1991. Only the South West, whose share fell from second or third largest in the first half of the nineteenth century to fifth largest in the twentieth, significantly altered its place in the regional ranking.

Recognition of these broad continuities in regional population distribution, however, must not be allowed to obscure the existence of important changes in residential location that have occurred around them. Between 1801 and 1911, for example, the Western Lowlands region of Scotland more than doubled its share of the nation's population while that of all other regions of the country declined, moderately in the cases of the Eastern Lowlands and the North East, more substantially in the Far North, the Highlands and the Borders. At a lesser pace the trend towards residence in the Western Lowlands continued throughout the interwar period, largely at the expense of the Far North, the Highlands and the North East. Between 1801 and 1939 the pecentage of Scotland's population living in the Western Lowlands (the counties of Ayr, Lanark and Renfrew) rose from a fifth to almost a half.[4] Since the Second World War it has declined slightly. But even as late as 1971, 43 per cent of all Scotland's inhabitants still resided in Western Lowland counties.

In England the regional distribution of residence had already begun to shift from south to north in the second half of the eighteenth century. Between 1751 and 1801 the North West, Yorkshire/Humberside and West Midlands regions increased their combined share of the country's population from 19.4 per cent to 24.4 per cent. The share of the population living in the East Midlands, East Anglia and the South West, on the other hand, fell from 27.9 per cent to 24.9 per cent. This northward drift persisted throughout much of the nineteenth century. By 1851, 29 per cent of the population of England lived in the North West, Yorkshire/Humberside and West Midland counties: by 1901, 31.9 per cent. In contrast the share of East Midland, East Anglian and South West counties fell to 21.3 per cent and 15.4 per cent. Had it not been for a persistent increase in the proportion of the population resident in the South East the south–north shift of residence in the eighteenth and nineteenth centuries would have been even more marked.

At the same time as the geography of England's population was drifting northwards the pattern of residence was altering in favour of central rather than more peripheral parts of Britain. Except for a few areas like central Scotland, South

Table 1.3 Percentage share of the population of mainland Britain, by region, 1751–1991

	1751	1801	1851	1901	1951	1961	1971	1981	1991
England	76.8	79.1	80.5	82.5	84.3	84.7	85.3	85.5	85.6
South East	22.8	23.8	24.6	28.4	31.0	31.2	32.0	30.9	31.0
West Midlands	7.5	8.2	8.2	8.1	9.1	9.3	9.5	9.5	9.4
East Midlands	6.4	6.1	5.5	5.4	5.9	6.5	6.3	7.0	7.2
East Anglia	6.5	6.0	5.0	3.1	2.8	2.9	3.1	3.4	3.7
South West	15.0	12.8	10.8	6.9	6.6	7.2	7.0	8.0	8.5
Yorkshire/ Humberside	6.2	7.8	8.7	9.5	9.3	9.1	8.9	9.0	8.8
North West	5.7	8.4	12.1	14.3	13.2	12.5	12.5	11.8	11.4
North	6.7	6.0	5.6	6.8	6.4	6.1	6.1	5.7	5.6
Wales	6.1	5.6	5.6	5.4	5.3	5.2	5.0	5.2	5.2
Scotland	17.1	15.3	13.9	12.1	10.4	10.1	9.7	9.5	9.2

Sources: R. Lawton, 'Regional Population Trends in England and Wales, 1750–1971', in J. Hobcraft and P. Rees (eds), *Regional Demographic Development* (London, 1978), p. 36. OPCS, *1991 Census. Preliminary Report for England and Wales* (London, 1991), p. 33.

Wales and North East England where rates of population growth remained high, the regions of most rapid population increase before 1914 were located in a belt of core counties stretching from South Lancashire and West Yorkshire through the East Midlands to Greater London. Between 1851 and 1911 fewer than a third of all registration districts in England and Wales, most of them lying in central locations, had rates of population growth above the national average. In as many as a third of all English and Welsh registration districts, the majority situated in geographically more peripheral areas, the absolute number of inhabitants actually decreased.

Even before the outbreak of the First World War, however, the tendency for Britain's population to drift from south to north and from periphery to core was beginning to slacken. By the interwar period new patterns of regional population growth and distribution, involving a reversal of the south–north drift and a slowing down in the relocation of people from peripheral to core regions, had emerged. During the 1920s and 1930s the only regions of England to experience rates of population growth in excess of the national average were the South East and the West and East Midlands. Compared with the period before 1914 the pace of population growth in the North, North West and Yorkshire/Humberside regions was now relatively low and whereas many peripheral areas, particularly in remoter northern and western parts, continued to record some of the heaviest population losses, others, especially in East Anglia and the South West, experienced rates of population increase that differed little from those of the North, North West and Yorkshire/Humberside.[5]

The reversal of nineteenth-century regional patterns of population growth and distribution has persisted in the second half of the twentieth century. During the 1950s and early 1960s the continuing north to south residential drift was reflected in relatively high rates of population growth in all regions of the south and the midlands, including the South East (Table 1.4). Even as late as the period 1961–6 rates of population increase in the South East remained above the average for Britain as a whole and were only slightly lower than those in East Anglia, the South West and the East Midlands, the regions of most rapid growth.[6] Throughout the 1970s and 1980s, despite a modest contribution from the South East in the years 1977–84, the southwards shift of residence remained chiefly a redistribution towards East Anglia, the South West and the East Midlands. Between the First World War and the mid 1960s the drift south was predominantly a movement towards counties in the South East and the West Midlands. After the mid 1960s it was directed primarily at those in East Anglia, the South East and the East Midlands.[7]

As indicated by the persistence of relatively high rates of population growth in regions like East Anglia and the South West, the decades since the Second World War also experienced a moderate transfer of people from core to more peripheral parts of the country. By the 1970s and 1980s rates of population growth in many of the remoter parts of Britain – west, middle and north Wales, northern Scotland and the Scottish borders, Cumbria, north Yorkshire and elsewhere in

Table 1.4 Intercensal rates of population growth in Britain by region, 1951–1991 (%)

	1951–61	1961–71	1971–81	1981–91
England	5.6	5.7	0.5	−0.1
North	3.2	0.7	−1.4	−3.0
Yorkshire/Humberside	2.3	3.7	−0.1	−1.8
North West	1.9	2.6	−2.9	−4.3
East Midlands	7.6	9.4	4.8	2.5
West Midlands	7.6	7.4	0.5	−1.4
East Anglia	5.2	13.6	11.7	7.7
South East	7.5	5.9	−1.2	−0.1
South West	5.8	10.6	6.0	5.5
Scotland	1.6	1.0	−1.9	−3.4
Wales	1.7	3.2	2.2	0.3

Sources: A. G. Champion, 'Population Trends in the 1970s', in J. B. Goddard and A. G. Champion (eds), *The Urban and Regional Transformation of Britain* (London, 1983), p. 197. B. R. Mitchell and H. G. Jones, *Second Abstract of British Historical Statistics* (Cambridge, 1971), pp. 16–17. OPCS, *1991 Census. Preliminary Report for England and Wales* (London, 1991), pp. 3, 21.

northern England, Cambridgeshire, Cornwall, Devon, Dorset, Norfolk, Somerset, Suffolk and Wiltshire – were among the highest achieved anywhere.[8] Typical of what happened in many outlying areas was the experience of the Highlands and Islands region of Scotland where, after a century of persistent decline, the number of inhabitants increased in the 1960s and 1970s.[9]

Urbanisation

Changes in the regional distribution of residence have been accompanied by equally pronounced changes in the relative extent of urban and rural living.

The bulk of the transformation from rural to urban residence occurred in the nineteenth century. In Scotland the proportion of the population living in communities of 5000 inhabitants or more rose from 21 per cent in 1801 to over 58 per cent in 1911, with the Western and Eastern Lowlands accounting for more than four in every five urban dwellers.[10] In England and Wales the urban population rose from 24 per cent of the total in 1750 to almost 34 per cent in 1801 before accelerating to 54 per cent by 1851 and 79 per cent by 1911.[11] On the eve of the First World War Britain had already become the world's first extensively urbanised society. The trend towards urban living has continued ever since, though inevitably at a much slower pace. By 1981 the share of the British population in communities with at least 2000 inhabitants had risen to over 89 per cent.[12]

The most intriguing feature of the history of urbanisation in the twentieth century, however, is what has happened to the size of the very largest urban communities.

At the beginning of the nineteenth century London was the only place in Britain with a population in excess of 100 000. By 1851 the number of communities with populations of 100 000 or more had risen to 10, by 1911 to 39 and by 1951 to 59.[13] By this stage the density of urban concentration in certain parts of the country was sufficient to persuade the Registrar-General to distinguish seven conurbation areas – Greater London,

Merseyside, South East Lancashire, Tyneside, the West Midlands and West Yorkshire in England, and Clydeside in Scotland. As early as 1901 these together accounted for almost 40 per cent of Britain's total population. By 1961 the figure had reached 42 per cent. Thereafter it began to decline, to under 39 per cent in 1971, around 36 per cent in 1981 and under 35 per cent in 1991. The trend away from conurbation residence was common to all conurbations. In the case of South East Lancashire (Greater Manchester), with a brief interruption in the 1950s, it began as early as the second decade of the century: in Clydeside and Greater London from the 1930s: in Merseyside, Tyneside and the West Midlands from the 1960s. Only in the case of the Yorkshire conurbations of Leeds and Sheffield was it barely noticeable.

Indications of a growing preference for life in smaller, less densely populated settlements were already apparent in the 1950s. Although the populations of the inner, core districts of the largest urban communities continued to increase, their rate of increase was lower than that in surrounding suburban areas. In some instances, a few dating back to the early years of the century, the populations of inner city districts even declined absolutely. Though growth rates in metropolitan regions during the 1950s were still above those in non-metropolitan rural regions, where the number of inhabitants continued to fall, they were now no higher than the average for Britain as a whole and distinctly lower than those in non-metropolitan urban regions. For the first time the traditional, positive correlation between settlement size and rate of population growth in some cases began to give way to a negative correlation.[14]

Between 1961 and the mid 1970s the trend towards population deconcentration intensified dramatically.[15] As Table 1.5 shows, the main loci of population growth shifted from metropolitan to non-metropolitan, or freestanding, regions and, within each type of region, from urban cores to less urbanised surrounds.

In the 1960s the population of Greater London decreased at an accelerating rate and much more rapidly than that of other metropolitan regions in England and Wales, where numbers even rose slightly during the first half of the decade. In stark contrast the populations of non-metropolitan regions increased substantially. Within both metropolitan and non-metropolitan regions there was a steady drift of population away from the most densely settled areas. In the Greater London Metropolitan District the loss of population was more pronounced in inner than outer areas. In other metropolitan districts there was a marked distinction between the experience of the principal cities, whose populations declined,[16] and that of their surrounding areas, whose populations continued to grow. By the end of the decade the share of urban core populations in the total population of all metropolitan regions had been greatly reduced.[17]

A similar trend towards a less centralised pattern of residence occurred in non-metropolitan regions. In the course of the second half of the 1960s a modest increase in the size of non-metropolitan city populations gave way to a modest decrease. Throughout the decade rates of population growth in non-metropolitan cities fell well below those in other parts of the non-metropolitan regions. It was in new towns like Basildon and Stevenage and in medium-sized or small urban communities like Bristol, Leicester and Southampton that the highest rates of population growth in Britain were attained.[18] Rates of population increase in excess of the national average and comfortably above those in metropolitan regions and cities generally were also recorded in port, resort and retirement settlements and in industrial and remoter, largely rural parts of non-metropolitan regions. The demographic experience of the more remote, rural areas of England and Wales during the 1960s is particularly striking. In the 1950s these had continued to lose population. In some cases, in parts of Wales and along the Welsh and Scottish borders for instance, the decline in population persisted into the early 1960s. By the end of the decade, however, decline had been replaced by growth. In contrast to what happened elsewhere in England and Wales rates of population increase in remoter, largely rural districts were higher between 1966 and 1971 than between 1961 and 1966.[19]

The spatial redistribution of population which occurred in Britain between the 1950s and 1960s was essentially a flight from the cities or, more precisely, from their high-density, inner cores. The new pattern emerged first and proceeded most rapidly in the largest cities but ultimately affected all city populations. In the course of the 1960s the aggregate population of the seven principal cities of England and Wales fell by over 8 per cent and that of the ten large cities by over 1 per cent. The total population of the 16 smaller cities, on the other hand, rose by more than 2 per cent. Only five of the country's smaller cities experienced a decline in population between 1966 and 1971. Despite this the growth of even small city populations remained well below that of most other urban and rural communities.[20]

The process of decentralisation reached its peak in the early 1970s. Between 1971 and 1974 the drain of population from metropolitan regions and from the cities of non-metropolitan regions was as high or higher than at any time during the previous decade. By contrast rates of population growth elsewhere remained substantially positive. The result was that the difference between the demographic experience of metropolitan and non-metropolitan regions widened. Within the Greater London metropolis population losses were more severe in inner than outer boroughs; in other metropolitan regions more severe in the principal cities than elsewhere. Within non-metropolitan regions too rates of population growth were negative in the cities and, except in the new towns, lower in urban and industrial than in remoter, largely rural areas, the only type of district to boast higher rates of increase in the early 1970s than in the 1960s.[21]

Even in the early 1970s, however, there were signs that the pace of decentralisation was about to slow. In Greater London the acceleration in rates of population decline was more marked in outer than inner boroughs; in other metropolitan regions greater in 'other districts' than in the principal cities, while in non-metropolitan regions rates of population growth rose in remote, rural areas and stabilised in the cities but fell elsewhere. After the mid 1970s, although the process of decentralisation continued, it did so at a slower and generally diminishing pace. By the late 1980s variations in rates of population growth from one type of district to another were negligible.

From its peak in the mid 1970s the pace of population decline in the Greater London metropolis progressively lessened. Between 1984 and 1987, for the first time in over 30 years, the population of Greater London rose. Significantly, when it once more began to decline in the late 1980s, the decline was much less pronounced than that of the 1960s and 1970s. Population losses in other metropolitan regions during the late 1980s were likewise less severe than at any time since the early 1970s. In non-metropolitan regions, on the other hand, rates of population growth between 1974/7 and 1988/91 were lower than in the 1960s and early 1970s. As a result, over the period 1974/7–1988/91 the differential in rates of population growth between metropolitan and non-metropolitan regions steadily narrowed until by the close of the period the populations of both regions were declining at much the same pace.[22]

Further evidence of the recent downturn in the speed of decentralisation is provided by the changes that have occurred in the spatial distribution of residence *within* metropolitan and non-metropolitan regions. In the Greater London metropolis the contrasts between the demographic evolution of inner and outer boroughs were much less marked by the 1980s. By 1988–91, indeed, the population of inner London was falling no more rapidly than that of outer London. In other metropolitan regions, though losses of population from the principal cities continued to exceed those elsewhere, the differentials similarly narrowed after the mid 1970s and by 1988–91 were smaller than at any time since the early 1960s. In non-metropolitan regions the recent evolution of residential patterns has been more complex. But here too the general tendency has been towards a reduction in the pace of dispersal. Before the late 1980s the extent of the reduction was modest. Between 1974/7 and 1984/7 non-metropolitan cities continued to lose residents to all other types of settlement except the industrial. Broadly, however, the scale of the loss was smaller than in the 1960s and early 1970s. The extent to which rates of population growth in new town, other urban and remoter, largely rural areas exceeded the non-metropolitan average declined from the mid 1970s. Only in port, resort and retirement areas did rates of growth exceed the non-metropolitan average by a wider margin between 1981/4 and 1984/7 than in the previous 20 years. In non-metropolitan regions the trend away from residential dispersal suddenly and sharply intensified in the late 1980s. By 1991, in metropolitan and non-metropolitan regions alike, rates of population growth varied little from one type of district to another. Never before had there been such uniformity in the geography of population trends.[23]

Inevitably, as the rate of regional population dispersal slowed, so did the rate of counterurbanisation. Throughout the 1970s, it is true, the redistribution of people from larger to smaller urban communities and from urban to rural areas continued and there remained a strong, negative overall correlation between rates of population growth and settlement size. Population losses were still heaviest in the largest cities and diminished or gave way to population gains as the size of settlement decreased.[24] But a significant change was already beginning to occur. From the middle years of the decade the pace of population decline in London and other principal cities and of population increase in new town, port, resort, retirement and rural settlements started to slow. By the end of the decade variations in rates of population growth between settlements of different size had narrowed perceptibly.[25]

The pace of counterurbanisation slowed further in the 1980s. Although the populations of the cities and largest towns continued to decline, they did so at a noticeably slower rate than in the 1970s. The rate of decline in the population of the London boroughs fell from –10 per cent between 1971 and 1981 to less than –5 per cent between 1981 and 1991: in the principal cities of other metropolitan regions from –10 per cent to just over –7 per cent: in non-metropolitan cities from under –5 to around –2 per cent: and in non-metropolitan large towns from –5 to well under –4 per cent. By comparison, in most other types of settlement demographic circumstances worsened between the 1970s and 1980s. In non-metropolitan regions the growth rate of small towns fell from 3.5 to 0.3 per cent, of industrial districts from about 3 to –0.2 per cent, of new town districts from about 15 to 6 per cent, of other urban and mixed urban-rural districts from between 7 and 8 per cent to between 3 and 4 per cent and of remoter, largely rural communities from over 10 per cent to between 6 and 7 per cent. Except for cities and large towns the only settlement type to improve its demographic profile between the two decades was the resort, port and retirement districts where rates of population growth rose from just under 5 per cent in the 1970s to just over 5 per cent in the 1980s.[26] In the course of the period 1971/8–1978/84 the largest upward shifts in population growth rates occurred in the inner London boroughs, in other major cities like Birmingham, Glasgow, Liverpool and Manchester and in seaside resorts like Bournemouth, Hastings and Hove. New and expanded towns such as Cramlington, Cumbernauld, East Kilbride, Runcorn, Skelmersdale, Tamworth, Telford and Thetford and some of the more remote rural areas like Nairn, Radnor, Ross and the Shetlands, by contrast, experienced particularly sharp declines in rates of population increase.[27]

Despite its slackening pace the trend away from residence in the largest, most densely populated settlements persisted more or less throughout the 1980s.[28] As Table 1.5 shows, it was not until 1988–91 that variations in rates of population growth between different types of settlement practically disappeared. The effective culmination of the tendency towards residential deconcentration has been a very recent phenomenon.

Allowing for some variation in timing, extent and occasionally even direction, the changes that have taken place in the geography of human residence in Britain in recent decades have been shared by most countries of the advanced world. From the USA and Canada through the countries of non-Communist Europe to countries like Australia and Japan an established preference for life in densely populated urban areas gave way to a preference for less urbanised and more

Table 1.5 Average annual rates of population growth by type of district. England and Wales 1961–1991 (per thousand population)

	1961–6	1966–71	1971–4	1974–7	1977–81	1981–4	1984–7	1988–91
Greater London	−4	−9	−12	−12	−7	−2	1	−2
Inner London	−8	−19	−21	−19	−15	−5	0	−2
Outer London	−1	−2	−6	−7	−3	−1	−1	−2
Metropolitan Districts	2	−0	−4	−5	−4	−3	−3	−1
Principal cities	−8	−8	−11	−10	−7	−5	−3	−2
Other districts	7	4	−1	0	−3	−3	−2	−1
Non-Metropolitan Districts	13	10	8	4	5	3	6	−1
Cities	1	−2	−2	−4	−3	−3	−4	−1
Industrial	8	7	7	−7	−1	−1	−1	−0
With new towns	23	19	16	14	14	3	9	−0
Resort, port, retirement	14	10	9	5	5	7	13	−1
Other urban	23	17	9	9	−3	5	7	−0
Remoter, largely rural	8	10	15	9	6	6	11	−0
England and Wales	6	4	2	0	1	1	3	−1

Sources: A. G. Champion, 'United Kingdom: Population Deconcentration as a Cyclic Phenomenon', in A. G. Champion (ed.), *Counterurbanization. The Changing Pace and Nature of Population Deconcentration* (London, 1989), p. 91. C. Jones and Bob Armitage, 'Population Change within Area Types: England and Wales, 1971–88', *Population Trends*, 60 (1990), 25. OPCS, *1991 Census. Preliminary Report for England and Wales* (London, 1991), p. 6.

scattered patterns of residence. Throughout the developed world the 1970s was characterised by unprecedented rates of population deconcentration as people deserted the inner cities for the suburbs, large cities for smaller cities and towns, metropolitan for non-metropolitan locations, and urban for rural environments. By the 1980s, just as they did in Britain, so almost everywhere in the developed world the closely associated processes of decentralisation and counterurbanisation slowed down.[29] It follows that whatever factors were responsible for recent changes in the internal geography of Britain's population must also have been active elsewhere.

Summary

Perhaps the most striking contrast between the demographic structures of nineteenth- and twentieth-century Britain is the dramatic decline which occurred in rates of population growth after 1911. Almost the whole of this decline occurred in two decades – the 1910s, when rates of population growth slumped to less than half those of the decades immediately preceding the First World War, and the 1970s, when after half a century of relative stability rates of population increase fell to levels barely above and subsequently below replacement. High rates of population growth between the late eighteenth and early twentieth centuries were accompanied by a shift in the distribution of residence from peripheral to core regions and from south to north. Lower rates of population growth after the First World War, on the other hand, were accompanied by a redistribution of residence in favour of the periphery rather than the core and the south at the expense of the north. At the same time, although the nineteenth-century tendency for people to concentrate in conurbations continued throughout the first half of the twentieth century, the period since the 1960s and early 1970s has been characterised by a flight from conurbation residence and by a preference for less densely populated habitats – in non-metropolitan rather than metropolitan regions and in smaller urban and rural settlements rather than cities and larger towns. The pace of this residential dispersal, however, had already begun to slow down by the late 1970s and by the end of the 1980s had almost entirely ceased.

Underlying these changes in national and regional rates of population growth and residential distribution was a complex interplay of the forces of migration, mortality and fertility and the factors responsible for shaping them. The behaviour of these mechanisms and their determining influences will be examined in the subsequent chapters.

2
INTERNAL AND OVERSEAS MIGRATION

The trends in national and regional rates of population growth summarised in the previous chapter were the result of changes in rates of natural increase (defined as the relationship between numbers of births and deaths) and in the balance between in- and out-migration. The relative significance of each of these variables has varied greatly both over time and from place to place.

For England and Wales and mainland Britain as a whole rates of population growth from at least as early as the mid sixteenth century have been determined chiefly by fluctuations in levels of natural increase. Between the 1560s and 1640s net out-migration removed no more than a fifth of England's excess of births over deaths. Between the 1690s and 1710s the proportion rose to just over a quarter. From the 1730s to the 1860s it averaged less than a tenth. Only between the 1650s and 1680s and again in the 1720s did rates of English population growth prior to the middle of the nineteenth century owe more to the influence of net migration than natural increase.[1]

Natural increase has remained the predominant mechanism of overall English and British population trends ever since. Except for the occasional year, at no time from the 1870s to the 1980s did the net gain or loss of people on balance of migration play more than a minor role in altering the size of

Britain's population. In the 1870s, 1890s and 1950s rates of British population growth were determined almost entirely by variations in rates of natural increase. In the 1880s, 1900s, 1920s–1940s and 1960s the contribution of net migration, though never more than modest, was somewhat greater. Only during the 1910s, 1970s and 1980s, when the net loss on migration amounted to around one-third of the excess of births over deaths, was it more substantial. But even in these decades changes in the relative levels of fertility and mortality exercised the dominant influence (Table 2.1).[2]

In the case of Scotland, at least in recent times, the impact of net migration on rates of population growth has been more pronounced. Before the 1770s levels of net out-migration from Scotland were negligible and rates of population growth dependent almost entirely on variations in rates of natural increase. Even during the later decades of the eighteenth century, when the number of Scots leaving for overseas destinations rose, net out-migration reduced the excess of births

Table 2.1 Net migration as a percentage of natural increase. Great Britain, 1871–1991

1871–81	−6.6
1881–91	−19.8
1891–1901	−3.0
1901–11	−16.5
1911–21	−30.7
1921–31	−21.7
1931–51	+15.2
1951–61	+5.1
1961–71	−12.6
1971–81	−30.6
1981–91	+36.0

Sources: Registrar-General Scotland, *Annual Report 1971. Part II – Population and Vital Statistics* (Edinburgh, 1972), p. 43. Registrar-General England and Wales, *Statistical Review for 1971. Part II. Tables. Population* (London, 1973), p. 89. OPCS, *International Migration 1980. United Kingdom, England and Wales* (London, 1981), p. 11. OPCS, *International Migration 1991. United Kingdom. England and Wales* (London, 1993), p. 1.

over deaths by only 15 per cent. Between 1825 and 1853 the proportion of the country's natural surplus leaving Scottish ports for overseas destinations, the principal outlets for Scottish emigrants at the time, remained below a fifth. Beginning around the middle years of the nineteenth century the contribution of net out-migration to rates of Scottish population growth increased dramatically. Between the 1860s and the end of the 1930s over half of Scotland's surplus of births over deaths was lost on balance of migration, the ratio varying positively with fluctuations in the volume of emigration from as little as 10 per cent in the 1890s and about 20 per cent in the 1870s and 1930s, to between 40 per cent and 50 per cent in the 1880s and 1900s, 66 per cent in the 1910s and 111 per cent in the 1920s and generally reaching higher levels in the first half of the twentieth century than in the second half of the nineteenth. After the Second World War the contribution of net out-migration to Scottish population growth increased still further. Between the 1950s and 1960s the proportion of the country's natural surplus lost to net emigration rose from three-quarters to over four-fifths. By the 1970s the excess of emigrants over immigrants was two to three times larger than the excess of births over deaths: by the 1980s four to five times larger (Table 2.2).[3] Before the 1920s most Scottish emigrants went overseas rather than to other parts of the United Kingdom. During the interwar period this pattern was reversed, more than four-fifths of the net outflow, initially at least, departing for United Kingdom destinations. After the Second World War a preference for overseas destinations re-emerged and the number of Scottish emigrants going to other parts of the United Kingdom declined to between a third and a half of the total.[4]

Until well into the twentieth century rates of population growth within the different regions and settlement types of each country on the British mainland were also determined chiefly by the behaviour of natural increase. In Scotland this remained the case until the second half of the century. In no decade between the 1860s and 1930s did migrational balances raise or lower regional Scottish population totals by much

Table 2.2 Net migration as a percentage of natural increase. Scotland 1861–1990

Period	Value
1861–71	−28.5
1871–81	−19.9
1881–91	−42.9
1891–1901	−10.7
1901–11	−46.8
1911–21	−66.2
1921–31	−111.2
1931–51	−49.6
1951–61	−75.6
1961–71	−85.6
1971–81	−267.7
1981–90	−468.7

Source: Registrar-General Scotland, *Annual Report* 1990 (Edinburgh, 1991), p. 107.

more than a tenth, and typically by a good deal less.[5] In more recent decades, however, the contribution of net migration to changes in the size of the population in a number of Scottish regions has greatly increased. By the 1960s, as was the case in other remote, rural areas of Britain and elsewhere in the developed world, migration had already become the main determinant of population growth in the Scottish Highlands and Islands. By the 1970s it was the dominant force in the Borders, Fife, Grampian, Strathclyde and Tayside, as well as in the Highlands and the islands of Orkney and Shetland. In the Western Isles net migration and natural increase contributed more or less equally to population growth. Only in the Central, Dumfries/Galloway and Lothian regions were variations in the number of inhabitants still determined primarily by trends in rates of natural increase. By the 1980s natural increase remained the principal mechanism of population change in the Lothians and had become the dominant influence in Fife, Tayside and the Western Isles. Elsewhere – in the Borders, Central, Dumfries/Galloway, Grampian, the Highlands, Orkney/Shetland and Strathclyde – migration played the key role.[6]

In England and Wales too regional rates of population growth prior to the First World War owed far more to the influence of natural increase than to that of net migration. Thereafter the relative contribution of the two variables changed. As early as the 1920s net migration had become the main determinant of population growth in almost two-thirds of all urban and over three-quarters of all rural areas. By the 1950s and 1960s a clear distinction had emerged between the experiences of regions in the southern and northern halves of England. In the former, comprising the Greater London, Outer Metropolitan, Outer South East, East Anglian and South West regions, gains or, in the case of Greater London, losses on balance of in- and out-migration were the chief cause of variations in population size. In the latter, comprising the East and West Midlands, the North, North West and Yorkshire/Humberside, trends in natural increase exerted the dominant influence.[7] By the 1970s and 1980s, as levels of natural increase continued to decline, rates of population growth in almost all regions of the country, particularly in metropolitan areas, came to depend predominantly on the effects of net migration.[8]

Focusing solely on the contribution of net migration to rates of population growth within individual regions and settlement types, moreover, does not do adequate justice to its importance. In the absence of substantial differences in rates of natural increase between regions, migration has always taken the leading role in determining regional differentials in population growth rates and thus in determining the changes which have occurred in the spatial distribution of Britain's inhabitants.

Even before 1914 regional differentials in rates of population increase in most cases depended far more on variations in the balance between in- and out-migration than on variations in the relationship between numbers of births and deaths. Most of the more striking features of regional differentials in rates of population growth during the interwar period – the abnormally high rates of growth in parts of the English Midlands, on Severnside and everywhere in South East

England except Inner London, and the higher rates of growth in southern than northern Britain – were also largely the result of differentials in migration balances.[9] After the Second World War migration remained the principal mechanism of regional differences in growth rates. Occasions when differentials in natural increase exercised an equal or greater influence on the geography of Britain's population were rare.[10] In the main it was through the agency of migration that variations in rates of population growth from one area to another were brought about.[11]

If then we are to explain the processes of decentralisation and counterurbanisation which occurred in twentieth-century Britain, and the north to south shift in residential distribution which accompanied them, it is to migration, and the forces responsible for it, that we must primarily turn. Chronological changes in rates of population growth, on the other hand, have more often been determined by the behaviour of natural increase. Yet even here there have been times when alterations in the balance of migration had a not insignificant impact.

Overseas Migration

For the period before 1912, when for the first time travellers between the United Kingdom and countries outside Europe were required to state whether or not they intended a permanent change of residence, reliable data on the extent of migration into and out of Britain are difficult to provide. Down to the middle of the nineteenth century it is probably safe to assume that the number of genuine emigrants and immigrants equated reasonably closely with the number of passengers travelling to and from non-European destinations. If this assumption is correct, compared with what was to follow the volume of in- and out-migration was as yet moderate. Over the whole of the seventeenth and eighteenth centuries the total number of emigrants from mainland Britain barely exceeded one million. Between 1815 and 1850 the scale of the exodus increased. In the second quarter of the nineteenth century alone at least half a million natives of England and Wales and a further 174 000 who left from Scottish ports emigrated overseas.[12] Altogether, between 1815 and 1850 around three-quarters of a million people born on the British mainland moved to non-European destinations.[13]

Until late in the eighteenth century levels of immigration were probably even lower than those of emigration.[14] As in the case of emigration, however, in the course of the late eighteenth and first half of the nineteenth centuries immigrant numbers began to rise, largely as a result of a growing influx from Ireland.[15] Despite this the volume of movement to mainland Britain in the mid nineteenth century was modest compared with what was to follow.

Data on numbers of passengers between the United Kingdom and extra-European countries imply that the scale of both emigration and immigration increased enormously between the middle of the nineteenth century and the outbreak of the First World War, with especially dramatic surges in emigration during the years 1879–93 and 1903–14. Because of an increase in the amount of intercontinental travel for reasons of business or pleasure, made possible by improvements in methods of overseas transport, a close equation between numbers of passengers and numbers of genuine migrants can no longer be assumed. It follows that the absolute volumes of emigration and immigration in the half century or so preceding the First World War cannot be quantified with any precision. Fortunately, since the numbers of people moving into and out of the country for business or pleasure purposes were roughly similar the early passenger statistics can be regarded as a reasonably accurate guide to the balance between in- and out-migration.

A comparison of passenger statistics for United Kingdom citizens in the decades before 1913 with migration statistics for British citizens in subsequent decades suggests that in the years immediately following the First World War the scale of emigration reached levels not far short of those attained during the great prewar peaks of 1879–93 and 1903–14. In the second half of the 1920s rates of emigration fell to the much lower levels prevalent in the third quarter of the nineteenth century and between 1894 and 1902. They fell even more dramatically at the start of the 1930s and remained at very low levels throughout the decade. After the Second World War emigrant totals once more rose and have stayed at levels similar to those of the 1920s ever since. In every decade from

Table 2.3 Number of migrants by sea between the United Kingdom and non-European countries, 1913, 1920–1963 (thousands[*])

	In	Out	Balance
1913	85.7	389.4	−303.7
1920	86.1	285.1	−199.0
1921	71.4	199.5	−128.1
1922	68.0	174.1	−106.1
1923	57.6	256.3	−198.7
1924	64.1	155.4	−91.3
1925	56.3	140.6	−84.3
1926	51.1	166.6	−115.5
1927	55.7	153.5	−97.8
1928	59.1	136.8	−77.8
1929	56.2	143.7	−87.5
1930	66.2	92.9	−26.7
1920–30	691.8	1904.5	−1212.7
1931	71.4	34.3	37.1
1932	75.6	27.0	48.6
1933	59.3	26.3	33.0
1934	49.8	29.2	20.6
1935	46.2	29.8	16.4
1936	47.2	29.8	17.4
1937	42.6	31.8	10.8
1938	40.6	34.1	6.5
1931–8	432.7	242.3	190.4
1946	63.1	166.6	−103.5
1947	56.5	121.6	−65.1
1948	73.7	168.1	−94.4
1949	64.8	152.6	−87.8
1950	71.9	136.3	−64.4

Table 2.3 *Continued*

	In	Out	Balance
1946–50	330.0	745.2	−415.2
1951	76.2	169.6	−93.4
1952	82.2	181.8	−99.6
1953	77.8	155.1	−77.3
1954	92.3	148.4	−56.1
1955	84.8	128.1	−43.3
1956	73.8	140.9	−67.1
1957	63.4	162.9	−99.5
1958	66.9	113.0	−46.1
1959	71.6	101.4	−29.8
1960	84.7	93.2	−8.5
1961	83.7	91.0	−7.3
1962	68.0	91.2	−23.2
1963	47.1	107.2	−60.1
1951–63	972.5	1683.8	−711.3

* From 1 April 1923 the figures exclude passengers arriving at and departing from ports in the Irish Free State. Before 1948 the data are for British citizens only. Migrants are defined as persons claiming a permanent change in country of residence.

Source: B. Thomas, *Migration and Economic Growth. A Study of Great Britain and the Atlantic Economy* (Cambridge, 1954), pp. 276–7. Central Statistical Office (CSO), *Annual Abstract of Statistics 1958* (London, 1958), p. 43. CSO, *Annual Abstract of Statistics 1962* (London, 1962), p. 40. CSO, *Annual Abstract of Statistics 1965* (London, 1965), p. 19.

the 1950s to the 1980s around 2 million people have left the United Kingdom to take up permanent residence elsewhere.

Trends in the volume of immigration followed a similar if less volatile pattern. As with emigration, the scale of immigration was greater in the years before and immediately after the First World War than in the second half of the 1920s and throughout the 1930s. On the other hand, the decline in immigration during the interwar period, particularly during the 1930s, was less marked than that in emigration. Indeed, in contrast to the number of emigrants, immigrant numbers in the early 1930s exceeded those in most years of the previous decade. After the Second World War the volume of immigration, like that of emigration, considerably increased. Even allowing for the fact that earlier data exclude non-British citizens, the number of migrants coming to the United Kingdom by sea from countries outside Europe was greater between 1946 and 1963 than at any time since the early 1930s. After the mid 1960s it rose to levels greater than at any time since statistics on migration first began to be formally recorded.

Until 1914 migrants to Britain were drawn mainly from Ireland and Eastern Europe. Large-scale immigration from Ireland originated in the late eighteenth century and peaked in the 1840s and 1850s. From then until the outbreak of the First World War the volume of Irish immigration declined to a relative trickle and, though still the largest foreign-born group, the share of Irish-born in the total population of mainland Britain steadily decreased.[16] Immigration from Russia and other parts of Eastern Europe, predominantly of Jews, first became extensive in the early 1880s and reached its highest levels between 1899 and 1905/6. Between two-thirds and three-quarters of the 250 000 or so Jews resident in England and Wales in 1914, when Russian and Eastern European immigrants accounted for nearly one-third of all foreign-born inhabitants, had entered the country at some time during the previous 25 years. By comparison, the volume of immigration from other sources was as yet small: a handful of Chinese living in London and the principal sea ports; a small but growing number of blacks from Africa and the Caribbean; and slightly larger numbers of Americans, French, Germans and Italians and other white immigrants from Australia, Canada, New Zealand and South Africa.[17]

Throughout the interwar period Jewish immigrants, now drawn mainly from Germany and elsewhere in central Europe, continued to contribute substantially to United Kingdom immigration flows, particularly during the 1930s when at least 60 000 came to settle. But the chief sources of immigration in the decades between the two world wars were the Irish Republic, which supplied a net influx of over 239 000 immi-

Table 2.4 Number of migrants into and out of the United Kingdom by sea and air, 1964–1990 (thousands[*])

	In	Out	Balance
1964	214	273	−59
1965	211	288	−77
1966	222	304	−82
1967	236	322	−86
1968	237	281	−44
1969	222	299	−77
1970	226	291	−65
1964–70	1568	2058	−490
1971	200	240	−40
1972	222	233	−11
1973	196	246	−50
1974	184	269	−85
1975	197	238	−41
1976	191	210	−19
1977	163	209	−46
1978	187	192	−5
1979	195	189	6
1980	173	228	−55
1971–80	1908	2254	−346
1981	153	232	−79
1982	201	257	−56
1983	202	184	17
1984	201	164	37
1985	232	174	58
1986	250	213	37
1987	211	209	2
1988	216	237	−21
1989	250	205	45
1990	267	231	36
1981–90	2183	2106	77

[*] The figures are estimates devised from the International Passenger Survey, a sample survey covering the main air and sea routes between the United Kingdom and all overseas destinations except the Irish Republic. They include people subject to immigration controls as well as British citizens. Migrants are defined as persons who have lived either in the United Kingdom or abroad for at least one year and who declare an intention to live elsewhere for at least one year.

Sources: CSO, *Annual Abstract of Statistics 1971* (London, 1971), p. 21. CSO, *Annual Abstract of Statistics 1981* (London, 1981), p. 26. CSO, *Annual Abstract of Statistics 1992* (London, 1992), p. 19.

grants between 1924 and 1939, and, in the 1930s, 'New World' countries like Canada and the USA from which earlier British emigrants returned in large numbers. Coloured immigration from Africa, the Caribbean and the Indian sub-continent remained negligible.[18]

Apart from its increasing scale, the most striking feature of United Kingdom immigration in the second half of the twentieth century has been the emergence of the Caribbean islands and the Indian sub-continent as major immigrant sources.

The arrival of nearly 500 immigrants from Jamaica in 1948 is usually regarded as the start of the great postwar surge in coloured immigration. In fact, as late as 1952 and 1953 the annual inflow of migrants from the West Indies still barely exceeded 2000. In 1954, partly due to restrictions on West Indian migration to the USA following the McCarran–Walter Act of 1952, the number of West Indians migrating to Britain suddenly rose to over 9000. By 1961 it had risen to over 74 000. Between 1952 and 1961, when coloured immigration was dominated by people of West Indian origin, a total of almost 290 000 people came from the islands of the Caribbean to settle in Britain. In subsequent years both the absolute and relative volume of West Indian immigration decreased. By 1966 numbers had fallen to 15 000, by 1971 to 5000 and from 1976 onwards to no more than 3000 or 4000 a year.

Beginning in the early 1960s, immigrants from the Caribbean were replaced by immigrants from the Indian sub-continent as the main source of coloured immigration. First significant in 1953, the number of arrivals from the Indian sub-continent increased from around 11 000 in 1955 to between 70 000 and 100 000 a year by the early 1960s. As with West Indian immigration, the scale of the influx subsequently declined, to an annual average of about 27 000 in the mid 1960s and mid 1970s, and 25 000 or 26 000 between 1981 and 1986. Not even the arrival of over 111 000 Asian immigrants from Kenya and Uganda between 1968 and 1975 did more than temporarily halt the decline which occurred in the absolute and relative size of coloured immigration from its early 1960s peak.[19]

For all its size and novelty coloured immigration was by no means the only nor, except for brief periods, even the main type of immigration to Britain in the second half of the twentieth century. Between 1945 and the late 1950s more than a third of a million immigrants came from continental Europe, some from countries such as Austria, France, Germany, the Netherlands and Switzerland but the majority from Italy, Latvia, Lithuania, Poland, the Ukraine and Yugoslavia. The postwar period also saw the resumption of large-scale immigration from Ireland. From 1946 to 1959 a total of 352 000 Irish immigrants arrived in Britain. Throughout the 1950s, indeed, the Irish comprised the largest single immigrant group and levels of migration from Ireland to the British mainland reached heights not attained since the 1870s and 1880s. In the 1970s the growing prosperity of the Irish economy temporarily reduced the influx and for a time Ireland even gained on balance of migration with the mainland. By the 1980s, however, the volume of Irish immigration once more increased and the traditional net inflow of Irish to mainland Britain reasserted itself.[20]

Although relatively high levels of immigration in the 1950s and early 1960s owed much to growing numbers of coloured immigrants from the West Indies and the Indian sub-continent, they also owed a good deal to increasing levels of white immigration from countries outside the Caribbean, the New Commonwealth and Pakistan. Even excluding immigrants from the Irish Republic, as early as 1966 only 12 per cent of all United Kingdom immigrants came from Bangladesh, India, Pakistan and Sri Lanka and fewer than 7 per cent from the Caribbean. By comparison, over 16 per cent came from Australia, Canada and New Zealand, 16 per cent from other Commonwealth countries and more than 35 per cent from elsewhere. Twenty years later the respective shares of the Indian sub-continent and the Caribbean had fallen to around 10 per cent and 2 per cent, of Australia, Canada and New Zealand to 12 per cent and of other Commonwealth countries to below 12 per cent, while that of other parts of the world had risen to 58 per cent.[21] Between 1980 and 1990 immigrants from the New Commonwealth and Pakistan, which by this stage provided the bulk of coloured immigration, accounted for little more than a quarter of all migrants to the United Kingdom. Almost three-quarters were drawn from countries of predominantly white settlement – 15 per cent in the Old Commonwealth, 23 per cent in the European Union and 35 per cent in other parts of the world.[22] Much of the modest decline in levels of immigration during the 1970s and early 1980s stemmed from a drop in immigration from Australia, Canada and New Zealand while much of the increase in immigration during the second half of the 1980s came from European Union and white Commonwealth countries. By the late 1980s non-Commonwealth and particularly European countries had become the main sources of immigrant flows.[23]

Immigration to the United Kingdom persisted throughout the twentieth century despite increasingly stringent legislative attempts to restrict it. Apart from temporary restrictions imposed during the French Revolutionary and Napoleonic Wars and the 'French scare' of 1848–50 no attempt was made to curb immigration until the Aliens Act of 1905, an essentially racist measure designed to reduce the influx of poor Jews from Russia and Eastern Europe in response to native working-class resentment over rising unemployment and housing shortages in the East End of London where most of these immigrants had settled. Under the provisions of the Aliens Acts of 1914 and 1919, which remained in force until 1971, similar legislation was extended to all aliens. From 1920 onwards the immigration authorities were empowered to exclude all foreign nationals who had either not received official permission to enter the country or who lacked a completed landing and embarkation card. In practice this legislation was aimed primarily at undesirables like criminals, transient seamen, political dissidents and the diseased. These apart, very few of those who wished to settle in the United Kingdom were excluded. As yet, moreover, none of this legislation applied to British or Commonwealth citizens.[24]

For many Commonwealth citizens, however, the situation changed radically in 1962. Even before the Commonwealth

Immigrants' Act of that year restrictions on the issue of passports to uneducated or unskilled persons other than those who were dependants of existing immigrants had begun to impede immigration from a number of Commonwealth countries. Prompted in part by mounting concern over unemployment but mainly by worsening racial problems, with effect from July 1962 immigration was restricted solely to dependants of immigrants already resident in the United Kingdom and to people (and their dependants) in receipt of work permits for which, for the first time, Commonwealth citizens were required to apply in the same way as foreign nationals.

Difficulties in verifying dependent status, especially for applicants from the Indian sub-continent, together with the growth of Asian immigration from newly independent East African countries, led to the imposition of still more stringent immigration controls in subsequent years. Under the terms of the 1968 Commonwealth Immigrants' Act entry was limited to United Kingdom passport holders who had either themselves been born in the United Kingdom or whose parents or grandparents either lived in the United Kingdom or were naturalised and registered as United Kingdom citizens. For those failing to meet these criteria entry was controlled by a system of vouchers which, on the whole, were available only to applicants with special skills or professional qualifications. In 1969 an Immigrants' Appeals Act required dependants from the Indian sub-continent to justify their claim for unrestricted entry before leaving home. The 1971 Immigration Act, effective from January 1973, instituted a new category of immigrant – the patrial, which effectively restricted rights to United Kingdom citizenship, and therefore to free entry, to those with parents or grandparents of British origin.[25] Although in theory unrestricted immigration was also available to families and dependants of non-patrials already resident in the United Kingdom, in these cases it was not automatic and in practice was severely limited by requirements that were difficult to understand and often impossible to satisfy.

Further restrictive legislation, aimed specifically at curbing the immigration of Commonwealth non-whites, was passed in the 1980s. In 1981 a British Nationality Act established three categories of citizenship – British, British Dependent Territories and British Overseas. Only those included in the first of these were entitled to automatic entry. In 1985 and 1986, to cope with growing numbers of illegal immigrants and the practical problems involved in attempting to verify claims for access at ports of disembarkation, immigrants from Bangladesh, Ghana, India, Nigeria, Pakistan and Sri Lanka were required to obtain their visas in advance of departure. Beginning in 1988 husbands were required to prove their ability to provide the necessary financial support for immigrant dependants and, in the case of polygamous marriages, were permitted to bring over only one wife. Anticipating an influx from Hong Kong following its return to China in 1997, the 1990 British Nationality (Hong Kong) Act limited immigration from Hong Kong to 50 000 so-called 'key' workers and their dependants.[26]

With the exception of the 1905 Aliens Act which contributed significantly to the decline in Jewish immigration from Russia and Eastern Europe in the years leading up to the First World War,[27] until the Commonwealth Immigrants' Act of 1962 the impact of legislation on the flow of immigration was minimal. Thereafter its influence increased, especially for non-white immigrants from Commonwealth countries whose entry it was principally intended to restrict. Public debate of the issue of immigration controls and a growing realisation that the introduction of some form of limitation was inevitable clearly contributed to the sharp rise which occurred in immigration from Pakistan and New Commonwealth countries in the years immediately preceding the 1962 Act. Coupled with the relaxation of US immigration laws in 1965, the Act also helps to explain why in the course of the 1960s immigration from the Indian sub-continent came to dominate that from the Caribbean. Over the last several decades too there can be no doubt that levels of non-white immigration would have been higher and the trend towards non-Commonwealth and, particularly, European immigration less marked had legislative controls of the kind that were adopted not been introduced.[28]

At the same time the effect of legislation on the extent and ethnic composition of immigrant flows should not be exaggerated. Firstly, legislation was itself largely a response to the growth of racial tension and conflict in an increasingly ethnically diverse society. Secondly, variations in the scale and geographic origins of immigration were in any case chiefly the result of political or economic circumstances, the impact of which legislative controls merely modified.

Some of those who came to Britain were motivated mainly by a desire to escape political persecution: Russian Jews fleeing the repression which followed the assassination of Tsar Alexander II in 1881 and the revolution of 1905; Irish escaping the protracted campaign for independence which culminated in the Eastern Rising of 1916 and the 'troubles' preceding the establishment of the Irish Free State and whose principal alternative destination, the USA, was increasingly restricted by immigration controls; and Europeans fleeing the tyranny of Nazism in the 1930s and the turmoil that engulfed much of central Europe in the years immediately following the Second World War. More recent instances of politically motivated immigration include Hungarians in 1956, Czechoslovakians in 1968, Asians driven out of Uganda by Idi Amin in 1972–3, Chileans forced into exile following the collapse of the Allende government, Iranians fleeing militant Islam and Chinese 'boat people' from Vietnam.

In most cases, however, the decision to move to Britain was based overwhelmingly on economic considerations. Whether the push of economic deprivation at home or the pull of economic opportunity in Britain weighted most heavily in individual decisions to migrate is difficult to determine. Probably, in the period from 1945 to the mid 1960s or early 1970s the pull of the British economy predominated. Throughout the 1950s and early 1960s shortages of labour, caused by a combination of falling fertility in the prewar years and unusually high rates of economic growth, forced employers such as British Rail, London Transport and the National Health Service to actively recruit workers from the populations of the Caribbean islands. The result was that within the period 1955–74 variations in levels of West Indian immigration correlated closely and positively with variations in levels of British employment opportunities.[29] The fact that most non-white immigrants settled in the inner zones of conurbations, where losses of population had been heaviest, and in areas like the South East, the Midlands, the West Riding and those parts of the North West which had failed to retain adequate supplies of indigenous labour rather than in areas of higher unemployment like Scotland, Wales, Merseyside and the North may be taken as further indication of the primacy of pull factors.[30]

After the mid 1960s the push of economic hardship at home began to play an increasingly important role in determining levels of immigration from Commonwealth countries. As demonstrated by the existence of a negative correlation between levels of emigration and national income on each West Indian island during the early 1960s, even Caribbean immigration had always owed something to the push of overpopulation, unemployment and poverty. In the case of immigrants from the Indian sub-continent push factors had probably always predominated over pull. Levels of immigration from the Indian sub-continent and other parts of Asia have never correlated as closely with fluctuations in British employment levels as those from the Caribbean. Even before the mid 1960s immigration from India and Pakistan owed more to the push of unemployment and land hunger at home than to the lure of opportunities for work in the United Kingdom. By the late 1970s, if not earlier, push factors dominated pull factors in the economic motives for non-white immigration from all parts of the world.[31] While the persistence of a negative relationship between United Kingdom unemployment rates and numbers of work permits issued to aliens during the period 1969–87 confirms that pull factors continued to have some influence on immigration decisions, [32] these factors were probably of greater relevance to white immigrants from non-Commonwealth and European countries than to non-white immigrants from the Commonwealth and elsewhere in the world who responded largely to push forces. Given the more or less continuous rise in British unemployment levels since the mid 1960s and the coincidence between the mid 1970s and mid 1980s of severe economic recession and the arrival onto the labour market of the children of the 1960s 'baby boom', it is not surprising that the significance of pull relative to push impulses in migration to Britain has decreased in recent years.

In the final analysis, immigration was part of a world-wide process involving a transfer of people from countries where economic opportunities were few to countries where they were more abundant. It was one of the legacies of its Empire and of the unusually high dependence of its economy on international trade and investment that Britain was more prone to immigration from a wider mix of races and countries than most.

In spite of its attractiveness to immigrants mainland Britain and each of its constituent countries have invariably lost more people to emigration than they have gained by immigration. In the case of England net migration has been more or less continuously unfavourable since at least the middle of the sixteenth century.[33] Losses on balance of migration for England and Wales since the late nineteenth century were especially severe in the 1880s, 1900s and 1910s and more moderate in the 1870s, 1890s, 1920s, 1960s and 1970s (Table 2.5). Only during the periods 1931–65 and 1981–91 was the balance of migration positive. Scotland has been even more disadvantaged by migration than England and Wales, losing more people to emigration than it gained through immigration in every decade from the 1860s to the 1980s.[34]

Possibly the most surprising feature of British migration history in the twentieth century has been the re-emergence of substantial net losses on international migration in the later 1960s, 1970s and early 1980s. At various times between the 1950s and 1970s, by contrast, other European countries began to experience either net gains or steadily diminishing net losses on balance of migration.[35] In Britain, the occasional year apart, the phenomenon of large-scale net out-migration persisted until the mid 1980s.

Underlying the vast net exodus of people from mainland Britain in the decades prior to the First World War was a

Table 2.5 Net gain or loss (–) by migration. England/Wales and Scotland, 1871/81–1981/91 (thousands*)

	England/Wales	Scotland
1871–81	–164	–93
1881–91	–601	–218
1891–1901	–69	–53
1901–11	–501	–254
1911–21	–620	–239
1921–31	–170	–390
1931–51	757	220
1951–61	406	–282
1961–71	–106	–327
1971–81	–149	–151
1981–91	385	–103

* For both England/Wales and Scotland the figures relate to migration to and from all other destinations.

Sources: Registrar-General England and Wales, *Statistical Review for 1971. Part II. Tables. Population* (London, 1973), p. 89. OPCS, *Population Trends, Spring 1981* (London, 1981), p. 35. OPCS, *International Migration 1981. United Kingdom, England and Wales* (London, 1982), p. 2. Registrar-General Scotland, *Annual Report 1990* (Edinburgh, 1991), p. 107. OPCS, *International Migration 1991. United Kingdom. England and Wales* (London, 1993), pp. 1–2.

unique mix of demographic, economic and technological circumstances which, facilitated by improved methods of transport and communication and a growing awareness of conditions and opportunities overseas, combined to enhance the attractions of the New World relative to the Old. Mass emigration in this period, it should be stressed, was not the consequence of an absolute decline in the capacity of the British economy to generate opportunities for capital and labour. On the contrary, more opportunities for wealth-creation and work were available in late nineteenth- and early twentieth-century Britain than ever before. Had this not been so levels of emigration would undoubtedly have been higher. By transforming existing economic and social systems and disrupting traditional mentalities and ways of life economic development, at least in the short term, increases rather than decreases the impetus for migration. It is therefore no coincidence that variations in the onset of mass emigration from one country to another correlated closely with the date at which modern industrialisation began nor that Britain, the most developed economy, provided the largest number of emigrants to the New World.[36] Economic growth also ensures that potential emigrants have the financial resources necessary to meet the costs of emigration. Accordingly the majority of emigrants came not from areas of greatest economic backwardness and poverty but from areas most affected by the forces of economic development and change.[37] Typically it was not the very poorest who emigrated. On the whole emigration did not serve as a safety-valve for the destitute. Most British emigrants before 1914 were people seeking to transfer from at least a minimally adequate standard of life to what they hoped would be a better standard of life overseas. Whatever may have been the case at certain times and places elsewhere in Europe, the bulk of emigrants from late nineteenth- and early twentieth-century Britain were prompted more by a desire for advancement or a wish to avoid possible, *future* destitution than by a need to escape the immediate realities of pauperism.[38]

In addition to capital an ability to emigrate requires the fulfilment of two other conditions: firstly that there is somewhere with the necessary opportunities for personal improvement to which would-be emigrants can go: secondly that potential emigrants have knowledge of these opportunities and access to a transport system capable of bringing them speedily and cheaply within reach.

Down to the middle of the nineteenth century, for the majority of people, realistic alternatives to life in Europe were extremely limited. Not until the later decades of the century were the economies of New World countries sufficiently developed to allow them to assimilate an influx of immigrants on a mass scale, and methods of transport and communication capable of transmitting large numbers of people to the new opportunities overseas. To some extent, of course, improvements in the technology of transport and communications were themselves a consequence of the growth of intercontinental passenger and freight traffic. But, by increasing the safety and reducing the opportunity-cost of travel, they also acted as powerful stimuli to emigration in their own right.[39]

In accounting for mass emigration from Europe in the decades prior to the First World War and, in particular, for the marked regional variations in its extent, the role of information diffusion and the factors influencing it deserve special emphasis. One of the more instructive aspects of late nineteenth-century county by county variations in levels of English emigration is how little they were related to variations in the extent of urbanisation, the size and structure of populations, rates of fertility, distances from the main emigration ports, levels of income among the unskilled, rates of literacy or proportions of the workforce employed in agriculture. They were, however, closely and directly related to variations in the extent of previous emigration flows. Once established, it seems, emigration built up a self-sustaining momentum, a momentum which often persisted irrespective of changes in the economic circumstances of sending or receiving countries. Ties of kinship and community initiated by earlier emigrants, together with the financial assistance these gave to those who followed, considerably reduced the emotional and monetary costs of emigration and helped perpetuate movement even when the immediate material motives for relocation were less urgent than they had previously been. Supported by the promotional activities of overseas governments, railway and steamship companies, and by the work of the Emigrants' Information Office and the numerous, voluntary emigration societies, the information contained in letters from previous emigrants and in newspaper reports of their circumstances and achievements provided a vital, additional stimulus to continued movement overseas and the directions it took. Areas where the feedback of information was greatest were precisely those areas which became emigration-saturated soonest.[40]

Clearly, the wealth generated by economic growth coupled with innovations in transport and communications and an increased awareness of the opportunities emigration afforded were important, permissive agents in the mass exodus of people from Britain and other European countries to the countries of the New World in the decades before 1914. But they were not its fundamental cause. However easy it became to go, the fact is that people would not have left had they not had good reason for doing so. At root, the phenomenon of late nineteenth- and early twentieth-century mass overseas emigration was the result of the creation of an integrated international economic system in which regions with differing rates of natural increase and differing endowments of labour, capital and raw material resources grew at different rates and in different ways. Inevitably this created both a necessity and an opportunity for labour to seek out those regions where its efforts would yield the greatest individual and aggregative return. In countries like Britain, where the increase in the size of the labour supply caused by falling mortality more closely approximated to, and at times even exceeded, the requirements of the economy for labour, expectations of continued material advance could easily be seen to be under threat. In the New World, where demand for labour generally exceeded supply, such expectations seemed more likely to be met. Mass emigration was a response to circumstances new to the late nineteenth- and early twentieth-century world when what were considered inadequate or inadequately rewarded opportunities for labour at home coincided with more favourable opportunities for labour overseas. In the absence of sufficiently rigorous and extensive controls over fertility, and wherever domestic cultural, political and social arrangements permitted, emigration was an inevitable reaction to what, for large sections of the population, were unique differentials in employment and income levels between the Old World and the New.[41]

The reappearance of large-scale emigration and of a substantial loss on balance of overseas migration after the hiatus imposed on international mobility by the First World War suggests that the disparities of opportunity between the Old World and the New continued into the 1920s. Compared with the economies of New World countries, the British economy performed poorly throughout much of the immediate postwar decade. Wage restrictions and high unemployment, especially in the export industries, made emigration an attractive proposition. For the first time since the early nineteenth century the coincidence of labour surplus at home and labour shortage in the colonies and dominions with a desire to strengthen Empire and Commonwealth ties by increasing the number of British-born settlers persuaded British governments to introduce state-funded emigration schemes.

State financial support for emigration originated in the recommendations of the Dominions' Royal Commission published in 1917. In the interests of imperial economic and political unity the Commission urged that labour (and capital) should be redistributed from the United Kingdom, where it was underemployed, poorly rewarded and therefore a potential source of social disturbance, to countries like Australia, Canada and New Zealand, where it would reduce labour and thus production costs, increase the supply of cheap food and raw materials for the mother country and enhance the ability of consumers to buy British goods. In an era of widespread tariff protection and severe depression in international trade such recommendations appeared to make a great deal of sense.

The first tentative steps towards a programme of state-sponsored emigration were taken in 1919 when free passages to the Dominions were offered to ex-servicemen and their families. The scheme accounted for almost a fifth of all emigration from Britain to Commonwealth countries between 1919 and 1927. Its success helped to pave the way for the Empire Settlement Act of 1922. This Act, which remained in force until 1937, empowered British and Dominion governments to contribute to the passage costs of any migrant nominated by friends or relatives already resident in the Dominions or prepared to work in agriculture or domestic service on arrival. At £15 a head, of which the British government could provide no more than half up to a maximum outlay of £3 million in any one year, assisted passage money represented a significant proportion of the ordinary third-class steerage fare to Australia and New Zealand (£36–£40) and especially to Canada (£18) and must have been a considerable inducement to emigrate for unskilled workers whose annual earnings averaged around £70. Little wonder that between 1922 and 1931 more than £6 million was spent on assisting 400 500 people overseas.

In addition the Empire Settlement Act permitted the imperial authorities to share interest payments on loans raised on the London money market by the Australian government for the purposes of land settlement and development. In 1925 the amount that could be borrowed was increased to £34 million and the activities on which it could be spent were widened to embrace any public work likely to increase Australia's ability to absorb immigrants. Under the provisions of the scheme British governments were required to contribute £130 000 for every £750 000 advanced by the Australian federal government to state governments. It was anticipated that the 1925 agreement would assist the emigration of around 450 000 people in the course of the following ten years. In the event, despite an expenditure in excess of £7 million on the various immigrant-absorption schemes, between 1925 and 1932 the annual total averaged barely half the expected number. Even so, over one-third of all British emigrants to Canada and nearly two-thirds of those to Australia in the period 1923–9 received some financial assistance from the state.

Empirical analysis of the relative importance of push and pull factors on emigration from the United Kingdom in the 1920s indicates that, on balance, conditions in countries of destination exerted a greater influence than conditions at home. Variations in United Kingdom income levels had no noticeable effect on levels of emigration while variations in United Kingdom unemployment rates, though closely related to fluctuations in the volume of emigration to Australia, bore no obvious relationship to those in the number of emigrants to Canada or the USA. On the other hand levels of emigration from the United Kingdom to Canada and the USA did correlate closely with variations in the *differential* between United Kingdom and Canada/USA per capita incomes. There was also a close relationship between levels of unemployment in Australia and Canada and levels of immigration from the United Kingdom.

In view of the availability of state assistance for emigration to Commonwealth destinations and the extent of the dichotomy between the performance of the British and New World economies, it is surprising that levels of emigration in the 1920s were not higher than they were. If the Australian case is typical, this cannot be explained by the effect of high wartime mortality on the number of young adult males, a reduction in the supply of agricultural workers and domestic servants or, at least until the last years of the decade, any narrowing in income differentials between Britain and the New World. A more likely explanation was the rise which occurred in the real cost of emigration. In turn this was due to a combination of higher transport costs, a relative increase in the real cost of living in countries like Australia, rising unemployment in Britain, which increased the desire for emigration but decreased the ability to finance it, and rising unemployment in Commonwealth countries, which raised the costs faced by emigrants in finding a job and at the same time prevented governments from spending more on subsidising immigration.[42]

The problems confronting would-be emigrants from the United Kingdom in the 1920s were compounded by the introduction in many of the more important countries of destination of legislation to reduce immigration.[43] True, the restrictions imposed by the various quota acts were much less serious for Britain than they were for many other emigrant-sending countries. At no time during the interwar period did the number of British emigrants to restricted destinations reach the quotas allowed. It is possible, however, that the existence of quotas worked psychologically to deter some who might otherwise have gone. The increase in emigration in 1923, partly motivated by a desire to anticipate the USA Immigration Restriction Act of 1924, may be one indication of this.[44]

Even without the introduction of legislative restrictions the relationship between in- and out-migration would have altered radically in the 1930s. In part the sharp decline in levels of emigration and the emergence of a favourable balance on international migration was a result of modest improvements in employment prospects at home. In the main, however, it reflected the world-wide nature of the economic depression which occurred around 1930 and in the course of which the demand of primary-producing countries for additional labour collapsed and differentials in opportunities for labour between the Old World and the New largely disappeared.[45] In the case of the United Kingdom, where the severity of economic depression in the early 1930s was relatively muted and recovery began relatively early, these differentials disappeared almost entirely and, as a result, losses on balance of migration gave way to gains.

As noted above, in contrast to the experience of other western European countries, in Britain net losses on migration reasserted themselves in the decades following the Second World War and persisted more or less without interruption until the second half of the 1980s. The explanation lies in the performance of the economy. Measured against their own historical record, in the 25 years or so after 1945 rates of economic growth and advances in average standards of living in Britain were greater, and rates of unemployment lower, than in any previous period of comparable length. These were the circumstances chiefly responsible for the vast influx of migrants from the Caribbean and Indian sub-continent in the 1950s and 1960s. On the face of it the same circumstances might be expected to have discouraged emigration. That they did not stemmed from the fact that levels of output and standards of life rose less rapidly in Britain than almost anywhere else in the developed world. This had two consequences. First it meant that emigrants from less advanced parts of eastern and southern Europe would be more inclined to prefer countries in northern and western Europe to Britain: second that differentials in opportunity between the British economy and the economies of other developed countries, particularly those in the New World, once again became sufficiently pronounced to make emigration worthwhile. In the cases of Australia, Southern Rhodesia and New Zealand the effect of the latter was augmented by the introduction in 1953 of an Overseas Migration Board offering assisted passages of £10 a head in an effort to reinforce Commonwealth unity by increasing the share of its population that was of British descent.[46] Rising levels of unemployment from the mid 1960s and the onset of severe economic recession between the late 1970s and mid 1980s helped sustain the net loss on migration. Only with the modest recovery in rates of economic growth which occurred in the second half of the 1980s was a favourable balance on international migration restored. On the whole, however, the 1930s and latter half of the 1980s were the only peacetime periods since at least the middle of the sixteenth century to boast an economy whose attractions relative to some other economies were sufficient to ensure an excess of immigrants over emigrants.

Internal Migration

Before the middle of the nineteenth century movements of people from one county of England to another were dominated by the pull of London and high levels of mobility between a group of industrialising counties in the North and Midlands – Cheshire and Lancashire, Lancashire and Yorkshire, Staffordshire and Warwickshire. As yet there was no sign of a net south to north migrational flow nor of any marked change in a long-established pattern of movement in which people ebbed and flowed between areas with few predominant directional foci.

In the half century preceding the outbreak of the First World War geographically diffuse patterns of mobility were replaced by a tendency for migrants to gravitate towards a relatively small number of regions: in Scotland towards the Western Lowlands: in England and Wales towards London and the Home Counties, the East and West Midlands, the North West, North East and South Wales. Between 1851 and 1911 no more than one in four of all registration districts in England and Wales gained on balance of migration and no more than one in ten, the majority located in the South East, the North West and Yorkshire, did so in each decade. Almost three-quarters of all registration districts recorded net migrational losses. Especially heavy flows of emigrants went from rural areas in central, western and south-western parts of England to Glamorgan and Monmouth, from rural areas in eastern, southern and south-western England to London and the Home Counties, from everywhere in rural England to the county of Durham and, most noticeably of all, from rural to urban communities. The process, graphically described by Lawton as migration from periphery to core, peaked in the third quarter of the century. Thereafter, as the direction of migration began to shift in favour of the South East and to a lesser extent the West and East Midlands chiefly at the expense of northern industrial and coalmining regions, it slowed.[47]

Underlying these changing patterns of migration were regional disparities in the nature and pace of economic growth and thus in income levels and employment opportunities. For as long as manufacturing remained a small-scale, spatially scattered activity, agriculture the dominant occupation and urban settlements primarily service or market centres, the pattern of mobility remained circular, diffuse and short-distance. As manufacturing enterprises grew in scale and came to concentrate in fewer locations so the geography of mobility altered. Average migrant distances increased and both the direction of migrant flows and the process of urbanisation began to focus on London and the Home Counties, where the attractions of industry were aggregated by London's status as the capital and principal commercial centre, and on the rapidly industrialising regions of the North West and West Riding of Yorkshire (textiles), the North East (chemicals, coal, engineering and shipbuilding), the West Midlands (coal, copper, engineering and pottery), West Scotland (coal and iron-ore, steel, engineering, shipbuilding and textiles) and South Wales (coal, iron and steel). Outside the main industrial areas only resort, port and naval districts attracted immigrants and expanded their urban populations on a similar scale. When, in the course of the later nineteenth and early twentieth centuries, rates of economic growth in some of the older mining and manufacturing districts started to decline the direction of migration slowly shifted towards the more prosperous industrial and commercial parts of the South East and Midlands.[48]

During the 1920s and 1930s, with the further decline of agriculture as an employer of labour, the more remote, rural areas of Britain, in most cases more severely than before the First World War, continued to lose large numbers of people on balance of migration with more central, urbanised locations. There were, however, some significant changes in the direction of movement. Firstly, as the pace of suburbanisation accelerated, rural areas in the vicinity of London and the larger provincial cities and towns began to gain on the ebb and flow of migration. Secondly, the tendency of Inner London to lose on net migration, already apparent in the prewar decade, intensified. Thirdly, the net exodus of people from the older industrial regions of the English North East and North West, Yorkshire, Clydeside and South Wales to Greater London and the English Midlands and, generally, from north to south Britain greatly increased.[49] The causes of this lie in the sharply contrasting regional experiences of economic growth. In those parts of the country where economies were dominated by the depressed staple industries of coal, iron and steel, cotton textiles, shipping and shipbuilding, levels of prosperity were low and rates of unemployment high. In the South East and those parts of the Midlands where service activities and the 'newer' industries of electrical engineering, chemicals and motor vehicles were most heavily concentrated, levels of prosperity and employment opportunities were greater and rates of unemployment relatively low. Inevitably, as the share of the nation's employment and wealth-generating capacity gravitated towards the southern half of the country so too did more of its people.[50]

Throughout the 1950s and 1960s levels of interregional migration increased steadily and remained high until the mid 1970s. Between the mid 1970s and mid 1980s, in line with the experience of other developed countries, they fell. Between 1985 and 1988 they once more began to rise and, despite falling in 1989, remained higher than at any time since the start of the decade.⁵¹

Accompanying these variations in the frequency of interregional mobility were further changes in its direction. During the 1950s and 1960s, though more obviously in the former than the latter, prewar tendencies for migrants to move from north to south and from urban to more rural regions intensified. Migrational gains were greatest in the English South East and West Midlands and migrational losses heaviest in the older industrial and mining areas of the North, North West, Yorkshire/Humberside and South Wales and, with some exceptions, in the rural peripheries of northern England, southern Scotland, parts of the Scottish Grampians and southern and western Wales. But although the relationship between settlement size and the extent and direction of migrational balance remained generally positive (smaller settlements losing and larger settlements gaining on migration), the strength of the correlation was already weakening. Positive balances on migration were now being recorded in some of the small settlements in the remoter, rural peripheries of Scotland, Wales, East Anglia, the East Midlands, the North and the South West as well as in many of those surrounding the largest urban centres. Increasingly the trend of mobility was away from the largest cities and towns towards smaller urban and rural communities. By 1966–71 all non-metropolitan regions were experiencing migrational gains and all metropolitan regions with the exception of South Yorkshire migrational losses. Within metropolitan regions movements of people were increasingly favouring less urbanised districts at the expense of the more densely populated urban cores.

The drift of people from north to south temporarily halted in the early 1970s but speeded up again after 1973 when modest net gains on migration in much of Scotland, northern and north-western England, Yorkshire/Humberside and the western Midlands once more gave way to modest but growing deficits. Throughout the 1970s and 1980s the only English regions to gain consistently on balance of migration were East Anglia, the East Midlands and, until the end of the 1980s, all parts of the South East lying outside the Greater London area. Except for Greater London where migrational balances were always unfavourable, regions of persistent net migrational loss were concentrated in the northern half of the country – in the North, North West, the West Midlands and, before the late 1980s, Yorkshire/Humberside.[52]

Over the last twenty years or so heavy net losses on migration have persisted in all the main conurbations – Greater London, Greater Manchester, Merseyside, the West Midlands, Strathclyde and Tyne and Wear. Generally the larger cities and towns of England and Wales continued to lose population to smaller urban and rural communities. In Scotland net migrational losses in the most heavily urbanised regions of the Lothians and Strathclyde contrasted sharply with net migrational gains in almost all other regions.[53] Throughout mainland Britain net losses on migration in Inner and Outer London, the principal cities of other metropolitan regions and cities within non-metropolitan regions were countered by net migrational gains in New Towns, resort, retirement and other urban communities and among rural populations. The rate at which migrants flowed from north to south and away from the main urban-industrial centres slackened after the mid 1970s, hence the deceleration in the twin processes of decentralisation and counterurbanisation.[54] But it has not yet ceased entirely.

Considerable scholarly energy has been expended in attempting to explain why in the course of the second half of the twentieth century migrational balances shifted in favour of southern and less urbanised, more peripheral parts of the country and why in the final quarter of the century the pace of decentralisation and counterurbanisation slowed down.

The north to south drift of migration which effectively began in the interwar period and which, with temporary abatements in the years immediately following the Second World War and again in the early 1970s, has continued ever since, was the consequence of fundamental changes in the structure of the economy away from mining and manufacturing towards service activities and, within the mining and manufacturing sector, away from older towards newer industries.

The trend away from mining and manufacturing towards service occupations was already well underway by the interwar decades. Between 1920–1 and 1937–8 the number of United Kingdom workers employed in mining and quarrying fell by 413 000 and in manufacturing by 129 000. Employment in the distributive trades, insurance and banking, on the other hand, rose by 770 000, in other professional and miscellaneous services by 959 000, in building, contracting, transport and communications by 319 000 and in gas, water and electricity by 106 000. Beginning in the 1970s the pace of 'deindustrialisation' accelerated. After rising by 5 per cent in the 1950s and falling by a modest 4 per cent in the 1960s, total employment in British manufacturing industry decreased by almost a quarter in the 1970s and a further quarter between 1981 and 1988. By contrast, employment in public and private sector service activities rose by 7–8 per cent between 1971 and 1981 and by around 7 per cent between 1981 and 1988. Although similar trends also occurred in other advanced economies, nowhere did they proceed as far or as fast as in Britain where weaknesses in the competitiveness of manufacturing industry and the presence of an already relatively extensive service sector gave them an extra fillip.[55]

Accompanying the shift from manufacturing to service activities were changes in the relative prosperity of different industries within the manufacturing sector. While industries like coalmining, cotton textiles, iron and steel, mechanical engineering, shipping, shipbuilding and, since the 1970s, motor vehicles have performed poorly, industries like chemicals, electricals and electronics, man-made fibres and North Sea gas and oil have done much better. It is to regional variations in the composition of industrial activity as well as in the ratio of manufacturing to service occupations that we must also turn for an explanation of the geography of recent migration. In the southern half of Britain, where service activities and the more prosperous types of manufacturing were most heavily concentrated, employment opportunities generally increasing and unemployment rates lowest, conditions favoured a net influx of migrants. In northern Britain, except in the north of Scotland where employment opportunities were boosted by the development of the offshore oil industry, and Wales, employment levels fell, rates of unemployment were higher and the average length of time spent unemployed longer.[56] The result was a net outflow of migrants.

Variations in the relative prosperity of the manufacturing and service sectors and of different industries within the manufacturing sector also largely explain why the net flow of people southwards was less pronounced in the late 1940s, 1960s and early 1970s than in the 1950s and after the mid 1970s.

In the years immediately following the Second World War levels of net emigration from northern Britain were substantially reduced by the beneficial effects of postwar economic reconstruction programmes on the prosperity of the region's iron and steel, engineering, shipbuilding, coalmining and textile industries. By the 1950s, when most of the more urgent needs of reconstruction had been met and other economies had sufficiently recovered from the devastation of war to re-emerge as serious competitors to Britain in export markets, the prosperity of the north's staple industries diminished and rates of net out-migration accordingly rose. Aided by a moderate increase in manufacturing activity and a resurgence in the fortunes of the mining industry due to the oil crisis of the early 1970s, the temporary decline in levels of net emigration from north to south during the 1960s and early 1970s owed much to the introduction of government policies specifically designed to restrict the growth of employment in the more prosperous south and encourage investment in the relatively depressed industrial and mining regions of the north.[57] With the onset of severe economic recession in 1974 the ability of government policy to redress regional imbalances in employment opportunities effectively ceased. As Goddard points out, regional investment- and employment-generating programmes are much less likely to be effective when recession conditions are as deep and as prolonged as they were in Britain during the late 1970s and early 1980s. In part this is because severe recession decreases the supply of investable funds available for redirection; in part because as labour shortages in the more prosperous regions decline in the face of rising unemployment the incentive to divert investment towards regions of higher unemployment and greater labour surplus lessens. But the inability of regional development policy to have the same impact in the 1970s as in the 1960s also resulted from two other circumstances: first the fact that such limited investment in manufacturing as there was tended to be capital- rather than labour-intensive and was therefore, on balance, job displacing rather than job creating; and second the fact that British companies increasingly preferred to invest in newly industrialising countries overseas where, even after taking regional subsidies into account, labour and operating costs were lower than in assisted regions at home.[58] In any case, by the 1980s, partly in recognition of the failure of recent regional development policies and partly out of philosophical preference for a non-interventionist state role, Conservative governments largely abandoned the policies of the 1960s and 1970s, leaving the fate of regional economies and thus the volume and direction of migration to the ebb and flow of free market forces. Because the recession of the mid 1970s to mid 1980s was more severe in the north than the south and because recovery in the later 1980s was based chiefly on the growth of employment in the service sector, particularly that located in London and the South East, a further surge in the net flow of people southwards was inevitable.[59]

The factors responsible for the patterns of migration that underlay the postwar processes of counterurbanisation and decentralisation and for the slowing down of these processes since the early 1970s are less easy to unravel.

To some extent counterurban and decentralised patterns of migration were simply the continuance of a long-standing tendency for large urban settlements to overflow existing boundaries and spill over into an ever-widening circle of suburbanised communities in their immediate hinterlands.[60] But the importance of this factor should not be overstated. Suburbanisation was the dominant form of residential deconcentration only in the period before the late 1960s or early 1970s. Subsequently it was displaced by a genuine counterurbanisation phenomenon driven by motives much more complex than a simple desire for social segregation on which the process of suburbanisation was primarily based.[61] While it is difficult to determine the relative significance of suburban and counterurban influences on migration flows in regions bordering on urban cores, there can be no doubt that the net movement of people towards more distant, smaller urban and rural settlements, the novel feature of postwar human spatial redistribution, was motivated by factors other than mere suburban drift.

Among these factors were the forces of demographic change. Just as overpopulation and a lack of employment in rural areas had fuelled migration to urban areas in the nineteenth century, so by the middle of the twentieth century rural depopulation created conditions ripe for a reversal in the direction of net migrational flows.[62] That such a reversal occurred also owed something to the fact that by the 1950s and 1960s problems of overcrowding and housing shortage in the conurbations had become so serious that ever-growing numbers of people were compelled to find accommodation far beyond their orbit. The establishment of the New and Expanded Town programme was designed, at least in part, to reduce what were considered to be unacceptably high levels of population density in Greater London and other conurbations. It is surely significant that the period of most intense counterurban migration flow, the 1960s and early 1970s, coincided with a rise in levels of fertility to a postwar peak. Together with rising divorce rates and a growing tendency for young adults and the elderly to live separately from their families, this greatly intensified demands for additional housing space. By increasing the number of school-age and adolescent children in the household it also necessitated the construction of larger dwellings at a price that was affordable only in areas remote from the largest urban centres and their suburbs.[63]

Recent changes in the geography of net migration flows have also owed a good deal to a growing preference for life outside large urban conglomerations. Anti-urban sentiments, of course, were not unique to the postwar period nor to Britain. In all modern industrial societies, almost from the inception of mass urban living, the congestion, pollution, comparative lawlessness and stress of life in teeming urban communities have provoked a powerful reaction in favour of what was perceived to be the idyll of rural environments and their associated values. In the postwar era however, intensified from the late 1960s by a growing concern for ecological-environmental problems, dissatisfaction with urban lifestyles increased.[64] Surveys carried out in the early 1990s indicated that as many as two-thirds of all city dwellers would have preferred to live in a small town or village. Of those surveyed over half included dirt and noise among the reasons for their dissatisfaction with city life, nearly half cited the attractions of rural, open spaces and around a fifth the desire for a less stressful environment. Other, less frequently stated, concerns included overcrowding and crime, the lack of community spirit and the difficulty of bringing up children in urban areas.[65]

A preference for small town or rural residence was a particularly important stimulus to migration among the elderly and the retired who moved in growing numbers first to seaside and spa towns and from the 1970s, when property prices in established retirement areas reached prohibitive levels, increasingly to remoter, rural destinations. But it figured prominently in the motives for migration among males of all adult ages.[66] Thus data for 1983 indicate that for well over half of all non-Scottish migrants to the Highlands and Islands, whose average age was below the national average and considerably below that of the communities they joined, the search for a more pleasant environment was the prime motive for movement.[67] Clearly, for substantial numbers of people the scenic attractions, relative tranquillity, less polluted and more relaxed nature of life in rural areas were significant considerations and migrants of working age were often prepared to make considerable sacrifices of income and occupational status to satisfy them.

Since the Second World War, moreover, it has become easier for larger numbers of people than ever before to translate a desire to escape city life into reality. One reason for this was the further advances which occurred in methods of communication and transport (particularly the increase in motorway and trunkroad mileage and the extent of car ownership) which improved accessibility to large urban centres, increased the amount of information available on conditions in more distant places and facilitated contact between those who moved and the relatives and friends they left behind. Another was the improvement that occurred in the quality of the social infrastructure in rural communities (in, for example, education and health provision, electricity and water supply and standards of housing and home entertainment) which provided rural populations with many of the amenities hitherto only enjoyed by urban residents, and thus enhanced the attractiveness of rural life. A third was the growing familiarity of rural environments brought about by more leisure travel, the greater geographic mobility of employees during their working lives and an increase in the extent of second home ownership. A fourth was the decline in average ages of retirement and semi-retirement which reduced the length of time people spent tied to a specific place by their employment. But the factor which more than any other made it possible to translate residential ideals into reality was the dramatic postwar rise in levels of material affluence. In turn this was a combined result of several influences: rising real wages and the part played by technological innovation in increasing the share of the workforce employed in better-paid, non-manual occupations; higher state social security payments and a growth in the number of private occupational pension schemes; and the substantial rise in house prices, particularly in South East England.[68] Together these provided the levels of income and saving necessary to permit more of those disillusioned with city life to move to smaller urban and rural settlements. It is no coincidence that when, in the 1960s and early 1970s, the growth of affluence was most rapid, the processes of counterurbanisation and decentralisation were at their peak.

Probably the most important single cause of the tendency for net migration balances in the postwar period to shift in favour of less urbanised, geographically more diffuse locations was the growth of employment opportunities in the less densely populated regions of the country. Of the various factors responsible for this, special emphasis should be given to the development of the rural leisure and tourist industry, extensive investment in afforestation programmes and the support given by the European Union to British farming, the construction of nuclear power stations at sites remote from the main centres of population and, particularly in northern Scotland, the development of an offshore oil and gas industry and its ancillary activities.[69] The main cause, however, was the changes which took place in the location of manufacturing industry.

To some extent, it is true, these changes were as much a consequence as a cause of the new patterns of migration, a response to opportunities created by changes in the spatial distribution of residence that had occurred for other reasons.[70] Even so, there can be no doubt that the dispersal of manufacturing industry acted as a powerful stimulus to the emergence of counterurban, decentralised migrational flows. Beginning in the 1960s, the geography of manufacturing employment in Britain and other advanced economies increasingly shifted away from the conurbations and largest cities towards rural areas and the smaller cities and towns lying beyond the major urban populations.[71] In part this was a consequence of increasing concentration of ownership and control in industry; in part a consequence of an equalisation of production conditions caused by wider access to more standardised transport and communications networks, health and education services and public utilities; and in part the result of changes in technology which not only deskilled many jobs, thereby facilitating the employment of untrained labour, but also reduced the necessity for goods to be produced only in areas where they could be serviced by large workforces based on a single workplace.[72] Fielding argues that the new patterns of migration which underlay the processes of counterurbanisation and decentralisation can best be understood as a product of the transformation from an economy in which each place was involved in all aspects of the production of the goods it manufactured, to one in which each place came to specialise in particular aspects of the production function. Until the 1960s the former was the dominant characteristic, hence the net influx of people to urban areas. From the 1960s the latter has become more and more common. Increasingly the major cities came to focus on management activities and activities closely related to management decisions – marketing, banking, insurance and other financial services, taxation and other forms of legal advice. Prestige environments within easy reach of the major cities focused on research and development while smaller cities and towns and rural areas remote from the metropolitan cores and the older industrial centres took over the task of manufacturing.[73] The effect was an adjustment of net migration flows in favour of less heavily populated and more peripheral regions where the growth of employment was greatest.

The explanation for the emergence of this new spatial distribution of manufacturing is complex. Partly it was a consequence of the growing share of output taken by large national and multinational, multiplant organisations which lacked long-standing ties with particular communities and which were better able than smaller organisations both to recognise the advantages of spatially disaggregated production and to introduce it. Partly it reflected the emergence of high-tech industries which, because they required relatively small workforces, did not need to locate near to large labour markets and could therefore pay more attention to residential preferences in their location decisions. And partly it stemmed from the fact that the growth rate of new companies is greater in small towns because smaller businesses are more inclined to establish themselves in areas where the existing size of firm is small than in areas where it is large. Above all, however, it reflected the cost advantages that accrued from siting industry in areas where space was plentiful and therefore cheap, where an abundance of female or non-unionised labour kept labour costs down, and where labour relations were relatively good and, as a result, the productivity of labour likely to be higher. To varying degrees cost considerations of this kind were applicable to all advanced economies. In Britain, however, the comparatively poor performance of industry in terms of sales, profitability and general competitiveness rendered them especially crucial.[74]

In the period between the 1950s and early 1970s changes in the location of industry also owed something to the implementation of regional economic policies designed to combat problems of overpopulation and social deprivation in the inner cities and encourage the development of new or expanded towns in less heavily populated areas, and particularly in areas where older industries were in decay and employment opportunities too limited to prevent large-scale net out-migration. Though their influence should not be overstated, state-supported inner city slum clearance initiatives, coupled with the introduction of planning restrictions on suburban housing development and active programmes for the creation of new towns and the relocation of small industries to rural areas, certainly contributed to the new patterns of migration which underlay the particularly rapid rate of counterurbanisation and decentralisation characteristic of the period.[75]

Amendments to state regional economic policy also help to explain why the pace of counterurbanisation and decentralisation subsequently slowed down. By the mid 1970s policy preferences had changed in favour of inner city rejuvenation. The emphasis of inner city housing programmes switched from slum clearance, road construction and the replacement of housing by offices to the preservation and improvement of the existing housing stock and the redevelopment of previously cleared land with housing suitable especially for the elderly and young single-person or single-parent families. Simultaneously public support in the form of labour subsidies and capital investment for farming, forestry and local government services in rural and semi-rural areas was reduced, the new and expanded town programme wound up and efforts to attract investment back to older urban centres intensified.[76] All this helped to diminish the flight from the cities.

The main causes of the recent deceleration in the pace of counterurbanisation and decentralisation, however, lie in a combination of demographic and economic circumstances. Negligible rates of population growth in the 1970s and population decline in the 1980s ended the need for urban overspill. Declining household size – a product of falling fertility, rising numbers of divorced and single-parent families and an increased preference for the material benefits of a dual-income, no-child lifestyle – made it easier to provide suitable accommodation in crowded urban areas. Moreover, as the baby boom cohorts of the late 1950s and early 1960s reached young adulthood, the pressures in favour of a return to the cities in search of work and social recreation intensified. At the other end of the age scale declining proportions of the elderly in the population from the 1970s lessened the need for retirement migration at precisely the time when the saturation of many traditional retirement areas increasingly limited its feasibility.[77]

To the impact of demographic change must be added that of economic recession. During the second half of the 1970s and early 1980s, in Britain as in many other economies, prolonged recession drastically curtailed opportunities for migration. Recession meant fewer job vacancies, lower rates of job turnover, less need for new industrial sites in greenfield locations and lower levels of housebuilding. Higher rates of unemployment in hitherto prosperous small town and rural environments undermined their attractiveness to potential city emigrants and encouraged disillusioned migrants to return to the cities. Except for Hatfield, Letchworth, Stevenage and Welwyn Garden City in the South East of England, which remained prosperous until the cutbacks in defence and aerospace expenditure in the early 1990s, none of the new and expanded towns were able to offer opportunities for employment on a scale sufficient to maintain net immigration at the levels prevalent in the 1960s and early 1970s. Even during the brief interval of economic recovery in the second half of the 1980s, the fact that much of the new employment that was created lay in higher level service occupations merely served to reinforce the decline which has occurred since the mid 1970s in the rate of migrational drift from the largest urban centres. The effects of this were compounded by reductions in local authority spending. Just as the growth in public sector employment generated by local government reorganisation in 1974–5 worked temporarily to prolong the processes of counterurbanisation and decentralisation, so the progressive decline in local authority expenditure under the impact of government anti-inflationary and monetarist policies in the late 1970s and 1980s worked to curb them.[78] While these factors were not sufficiently powerful to entirely halt, let alone reverse, the postwar tendency for migration to favour counterurban, decentralised patterns of residence, they have certainly been strong enough to moderate its pace.

3

MORTALITY

Trends in average annual crude death rates (deaths per thousand total population) for England/Wales and Scotland since the middle of the nineteenth century are summarised in Table 3.1. Despite making no allowance for the influence of variations in the age and sex structure of populations, the story they tell is accurate enough for most purposes.

In both England/Wales and Scotland a substantial and generally continuous decline in mortality began around 1870 and accelerated during the opening decade of the twentieth century.[1] Similar early declines in mortality occurred elsewhere in Europe: in Austria, Belgium, European Russia, Germany, Hungary, Italy, the Netherlands, Poland and Switzerland also from the 1870s; in Yugoslavia from the 1880s; and in Bulgaria, Portugal, Romania and Spain from the 1890s or 1900s.[2]

In the case of England and Wales average decennial crude death rates for males and females together fell in each successive decade from 1871–80 to 1921–30 before stabilising at marginally higher levels in the 1930s and 1940s and declining sharply in the 1950s. Since then there has been little further improvement. During the 1950s and 1960s, indeed, death rates actually rose. Between the mid 1970s and mid 1980s, when slight reductions in age-specific mortality rates were offset by the effects of a rise in the average age of the population, crude death rates altered little one way or the other.[3] Only towards the end of the 1980s did levels of mortality in England and Wales once more begin to decline.

In the case of Scotland annual average decennial crude death rates for males and females combined fell in each successive decade from the 1860s to the 1950s, remained at the new low throughout the 1960s and then stabilised at a slightly higher level in the 1970s and 1980s. Overall, between 1871–80 and 1981–90 crude death rates fell by 46 per cent in England and Wales and 43 per cent in Scotland, the bulk of the decline occurring in the last quarter of the nineteenth and first quarter of the twentieth centuries. As in other advanced economies, most of the further reduction in mortality since the Second World War occurred in the 1950s.[4] Subsequent improvements in mortality rates were relatively modest everywhere.

Two other features of Table 3.1 deserve emphasis. Firstly, except during the third quarter of the nineteenth century, crude death rates have always been higher in Scotland than England/Wales, though the difference was barely discernible in the later decades of the nineteenth century and much greater between 1901–10 and 1931–40 than in the second half of the twentieth century. Secondly, mortality has always been higher among males than females. Both in England/Wales and Scotland, however, the differential narrowed considerably in the course of the 1980s.

The impact of death rates on trends in average expectations of life at birth is shown in Table 3.2. In the nineteenth century advances in life expectancy were relatively modest and confined mainly to the final quarter of the century.[5] The pace of improvement quickened dramatically from around the beginning of the twentieth century. In England and Wales life expectation at birth for males rose from about 50 years, for the cohort born 1900–4, to over 65 years, for the cohort born 1940–4, and an estimated 73 years for the cohort born 1988–90; for females from around 57 to over 72 and over 78 respectively. In Scotland it increased from under 45 (males)

Table 3.1 Annual average crude death rates, by sex. England/Wales and Scotland, 1838/50–1981/90

	England and Wales			Scotland		
	Male	Female	Both sexes	Male	Female	Both sexes
1838–50	23.2	21.6	22.4			
1851–60	23.1	21.4	22.2	21.7	19.9	20.8 (1855–60)
1861–70	23.7	21.4	22.5	23.1	21.2	22.1
1871–80	22.7	20.1	21.4	22.6	20.7	21.7
1881–90	20.3	18.1	19.1	19.7	18.7	19.2
1891–1900	19.3	17.2	18.2	19.0	18.0	18.5
1901–10	16.4	14.4	15.4	17.1	16.1	16.6
1911–20	16.0	13.0	14.4	16.0	14.8	15.4
1921–30	12.9	11.4	12.1	14.4	13.2	13.8
1931–40	13.1	11.5	12.3	14.1	12.7	13.4
1941–50	14.0	11.0	12.3	14.5	12.1	13.1
1951–60	12.4	10.9	11.6	12.9	11.3	12.1
1961–70	12.4	11.2	11.7	13.0	11.3	12.1
1971–80	12.3	11.4	11.9	13.0	11.8	12.3
1981–90	11.7	11.3	11.5	12.5	12.2	12.3

Sources: B. R. Mitchell, *British Historical Statistics* (Cambridge, 1988), pp. 57–9. Registrar-General Scotland, *Annual Report 1991* (Edinburgh, 1992), p. 19. OPCS, *Mortality Statistics. Area.* Series DH5, Nos. 8–17. OPCS, *Mortality Statistics 1991. Causes.* Series DH2, No. 18.

Mortality

Table 3.2 Expectation of life at birth in years, by sex. England/Wales and Scotland, c.1900–1988/90

England and Wales			Scotland		
Cohort born	Male	Female	Cohort born	Male	Female
1900–4	49.9	56.8	1891–1900	44.7	47.4
1905–9	53.1	59.8			
1910–14	55.7	61.9	1910–12	50.1	53.2
1915–19	58.8	65.7			
1920–4	60.1	66.8	1920–2	53.1	56.4
1925–9	61.9	68.7			
1930–4	63.4	70.3	1930–2	56.0	59.5
1935–9	64.9	71.3			
1940–4	65.4	72.3	1942–4	59.8	64.6
1950–2	66.4	71.5	1950–2	64.4	68.7
1961	68.1	74.0	1961	66.3	72.0
1971	69.0	75.2	1971	67.3	73.7
1981	71.0	77.0	1981	69.0	75.2
1988–90	73.0	78.5	1988–90	70.8	76.6

Sources: R. Schoen and J. Baj, 'Twentieth Century Cohort Marriage and Divorce in England and Wales', *Population Studies*, 38, 3 (1984), 442. CSO, *Annual Abstract of Statistics 1961* (London, 1961), pp. 36–7. T.Devis, 'The Expectation of Life in England and Wales', *Population Trends*, 60 (1990), 24. CSO, *Annual Abstract of Statistics 1993* (London, 1993), p. 42. Registrar-General Scotland, *Annual Report 1980* (Edinburgh, 1982), p. 270.

and over 47 (females) in the 1890s birth cohort to over 64 (males) and nearly 69 (females) in the early 1950s cohort and almost 71 (males) and over 76 (females) in the late 1980s cohort. As in other countries, advances in longevity in Britain have been predominantly a twentieth-century phenomenon.[6]

The relatively modest improvement in life expectancy achieved during the late nineteenth century stemmed chiefly from declining rates of mortality in the child, adolescent and young adult age groups (1–44), where chances of survival were already comparatively high around the middle decades of the century.[7] Substantial decreases of mortality among infants (0–1) and adults over the age of 45 did not effectively begin until the twentieth century.[8] In the case of infant mortality, however, the apparent discontinuity in trend around 1900 should not be overdramatised. In as many as 40 of the 55 counties and regions of Britain analysed by Lee, infant death rates peaked as early as 1861 or 1871 and, apart from a temporary increase in the 1890s, fluctuated around a steadily declining mean from then until the start of the twentieth century when a continuous decline became the norm everywhere.[9] Similar reductions in infant mortality in the decades before the First World War were recorded in most western European countries. In Belgium, France and, possibly, Italy, with a short-lived upsurge in the late 1890s, death rates in infancy fell from about 1890. In the Netherlands, Prussia and Sweden, where a temporary rise occurred in 1900, the decline began around 1880. Only in Britain was there an increase in national average levels of infant mortality between the 1880s and 1890s.[10]

Once underway the decline in infant death rates continued almost without interruption. In England and Wales levels of infant mortality fell from 154 per thousand live births in 1900 to 75 in 1925, 30 in 1950, 16 in 1975 and 8 in 1990, at least halving in each successive 25-year period. Before the First World War they were invariably higher than in Scotland. Between 1912 and 1977, by contrast, Scottish infant mortality rates exceeded those in England and Wales. Not until the late 1970s and 1980s was parity restored. Despite this generally less favourable record, in Scotland too death rates in infancy have plummeted in the twentieth century, from 128 per thousand live births in 1900 to 39 in 1950 and 8 in 1990.

Perhaps the most surprising feature of infant mortality trends in the present century has been their continued decline during the years of the two world wars and throughout the decades of severe economic depression between the wars. The decrease in infant death rates between 1914 and 1918 was unique to Britain and was especially marked in urban-industrial areas where, in the prewar period, levels of poverty, overcrowding and mortality in infancy had been greatest. Most of the improvement in infant life expectancy during and after the First World War was the result of falling death rates among infants aged between one and eleven months (post neonatal mortality). Death rates at ages up to one week (perinatal mortality) and from one to three weeks (neonatal mortality) fell more slowly.[11] At differing levels and rates, similar trends were apparent throughout Europe.

The greatest advances in life expectancy during the twentieth century have occurred in infancy (0–1) and childhood (1–4) and, to a lesser extent, among adolescents and young adults (15–24) and adults aged between 25 and 44. In each of these age groups the bulk of the improvement had been achieved by the middle years of the century. Rates of maternal mortality (defined as women dying during pregnancy or childbirth), which in England and Wales remained at around 4 per thousand live births between 1900–2 and 1936–7 and in Scotland rose from below 5 per thousand in 1900–2 to over 6 per thousand in 1930–2, had also already fallen to just 1 per thousand by the early 1950s.[12] In the age groups 45–54, 55–64 and 65–74, though mortality fell more or less continuously from the beginning of the twentieth century, most of the decline did not occur until the second half of the century. Death rates among men and women aged 80 and above did not begin to decline until the 1940s since when they have decreased slowly if erratically.[13]

Except in the case of males and females aged 15–44 during the latter half of the 1980s for whom death rates rose,[14] the only significant interruptions to the long-term decline in levels of mortality were those that occurred during the world wars. For both sexes and for all age groups above infancy death rates increased between 1914 and 1918. For obvious reasons the increase was especially pronounced among men aged between 17 and 36.[15] The impact of the Second World War on the life expectancy of civilians was less uniform and, on the whole, less detrimental. In Scotland mortality among males aged 15 and above was higher in 1940 than 1935 and for those aged 15–34 remained higher in 1945. Among females death rates between 1935 and 1940 fell in the age groups 0–1 and 15–54, changed little for those aged 1–14 and rose for those aged over 55. By 1945 death rates in all age groups of

Scotland's female population were lower than they had ever been before. In England and Wales mortality among males aged 15 and above increased between 1931–5 and 1940 while that of males under 15 either declined or remained stable. Between 1940 and 1945 civilian male death rates decreased in all age groups except 20–4. Among the civilian female population of England and Wales death rates between 1931–5 and 1940 rose for the age groups above 55 and either fell or remained unchanged for those below 55. Between 1940 and 1945 mortality declined for females of all ages.

Mortality by Region and Social Class

From the time when reasonably reliable data on rates of mortality first became available around the middle of the nineteenth century, expectations of life at birth have always varied substantially by region and socio-occupational class. In the case of the former the degree of variation has steadily diminished in more recent times. At the start of the twentieth century regional differentials in infant mortality ranged from under 100 per thousand live births in rural areas such as Dorset, Rutland, the Scottish Highlands, Westmorland and Wiltshire to between 150 and 170 per thousand in industrial and mining areas such as Durham, the East and West Ridings of Yorkshire, Lancashire, Northumberland, Nottinghamshire and South Wales. In the course of the period 1881–1921/31 regional differentials in infant death rates widened. Thereafter they gradually converged and by 1971 were less pronounced than at any time since the mid nineteenth century. Despite this the geography of regional infant mortality variation changed little throughout the first three-quarters of the twentieth century, with death rates in infancy in the southern half of England (the East, South East, South West, East and West Midlands regions), for example, remaining well below those in Wales and northern England (the North, North West and Yorkshire/Humberside regions). By the mid 1980s the regional geography of infant mortality levels in England had begun to change. Although the likelihood of surviving infancy was still lowest in the North West and highest in East Anglia, regions with relatively low infant death rates now included the North, the North East and Merseyside while the West Midlands had joined the North West as an area where the chances of surviving the perils of infancy were poorest.[16]

Regional variations in mortality in other age groups followed a broadly similar trend. Here too, though regional inequalities narrowed, the traditional ranking of regions by mortality level persisted largely unchanged. Around 1900 life expectation at birth in rural areas substantially exceeded that in non-agricultural and urban areas and was higher in commercial than in industrial or mining districts. Urban-rural inequalities in longevity, however, had already begun to decline. By 1911 a ten or eleven year advantage in the life expectancy of rural over urban dwellers had already shrunk to just three or four years.[17] By the mid 1920s differentials in life expectation in favour of agricultural over non-agricultural populations were only half those of a quarter of a century earlier. Thereafter, especially for males, they continued to decrease.[18] But they have never entirely disappeared. In Britain as elsewhere in northern and western Europe male longevity in the years 1969–77 was still lower in urban, dockyard, mining and heavy industrial areas than in suburban and agricultural districts. Albeit less noticeably, in the 1980s, as in the first decade of the century, rates of mortality increased and life expectancies decreased as one moved from South and East to North and North West England and on into Scotland and from rural to urban-industrial environments.[19]

Generally mortality has everywhere and always varied inversely with socio-occupational class. On the eve of the First World War socio-occupational differentials in death rates, though still considerable, were less extreme than at any time since at least the middle of the nineteenth century.[20] After the war, in contrast to trends in regional mortality differentials and despite the establishment of the National Health Service in 1946, variations in mortality by social class widened. In 1895–7 the lowest rates of infant mortality were found in social class

VIII (agricultural labourers). Otherwise death rates in infancy varied more or less negatively with social class, rising progressively from class I (professional occupations such as lawyers and physicians) through classes II (managerial and lower status professional occupations like teachers), III (skilled manual and clerical workers), IV (the semi-skilled), V (the unskilled), VI (textile workers) to class VII (miners). By 1910 infant mortality was lowest in social class I, followed in ascending order of severity by classes VIII, II, III, IV, V, VI and VII. On average, death rates among infants of unskilled workers were roughly twice as high as those with fathers in professional occupations. By the end of the interwar period, chiefly as a result of developments in the 1920s, class differentials in infant death rates were even more pronounced and by the 1970s and 1980s, when mortality among infants of the unskilled was at least twice as high as among those of professional people, as great as at any time since the beginning of the century.[21]

In other age groups too social class mortality differentials have widened in recent decades. Among males aged 15-64, for instance, standardised mortality ratios in social class V, where mortality was highest, exceeded those in social class I, where mortality was lowest, by 23 per cent in 1930-3, 37 per cent in 1949-53, 88 per cent in 1959-63 and 78 per cent in 1970-2. Differences in adult male standardised mortality ratios between social classes III and IV/V were likewise much greater by the early 1970s than fifty years or so earlier. In England and Wales by the beginning of the 1980s death rates at ages 1-4 were two to three times higher for social class V than social class I: at ages 5-9 about twice as high: and at ages 10-14 between one and a half and two times higher. In the course of the period 1930/2-1976/81 standardised mortality ratios for men aged 15-64 in social class V deteriorated from 11 to 24 per cent above the average for England and Wales while for those in social class I they improved from 10 to 34 per cent below the national average.[22] As these figures illustrate, in the main it has been the higher status social groups that have benefited most from the great improvement in life expectation during the twentieth century.

Between the mid nineteenth and mid twentieth centuries, when the bulk of the mortality decline occurred, falling death rates were predominantly due to the demise of communicable, infectious disease as the principal cause of death. As much as two-fifths of the decline in mortality between 1848/51 and 1971 stemmed from reductions in the incidence and fatality of airborne infections such as bronchitis, diphtheria, influenza, measles, pneumonia, scarlet fever, smallpox and, above all, respiratory tuberculosis. A further fifth was a consequence of reduced death rates from water-, insect- or foodborne infections such as cholera, diarrhoea, dysentery, typhoid and typhus. Other infections – convulsions, syphilis, puerperal fever and the like – together accounted for about one-eighth of the decline. Not more than a quarter of the dramatic improvement in life expectation between the mid nineteenth century and the early 1970s stemmed from a decline in mortality from causes of death other than viral or bacterial infections. Since death rates from infectious disease were greatest among infants, children and young adults, it is not surprising that these were the age groups to benefit most from the impressive advance in longevity that was achieved prior to the middle of the twentieth century.

By the second half of the century deaths from communicable infections had decreased to such an extent that they were replaced as the main causes of death by non-communicable, degenerative diseases such as ischaemic heart disease and cancers, the so-called 'diseases of affluence' which primarily affect the older age groups. Most of the relatively modest decline in death rates which occurred after the Second World War was due to a reduction in mortality from degenerative diseases, though mortality from the most significant of these – ischaemic heart disease and cancers of the lungs and bronchus – remained higher, and declined later, in England and Wales and particularly in Scotland, than in most other countries of the developed world.[23] Within Britain death rates from heart disease and cancers, as from many of the other main causes of death, were highest among the populations of the inner cities, the blue-collar suburbs and the industrial regions of South Wales, South West Scotland, Lancashire, Teesside and Yorkshire.[24]

In view of its importance to the unprecedented rise in human life expectancy during the late nineteenth and first half of the twentieth centuries it is surprising how little is known about the factors responsible for the decline in mortality from infectious disease. One possible explanation is that, in part at least, it was the consequence of either a natural reduction in the virulence of infectious disease organisms themselves or of a genetically-inspired rise in levels of human resistance to such organisms. Particularly through the impact they had on deaths from scarlet fever, smallpox and typhus, autonomous influences of this kind, it is suggested, may have accounted for as much as a fifth to a third of the overall decline in mortality during the second half of the nineteenth century and continued to play the major role in the further decline in mortality from streptococcal diseases such as scarlet fever, nephritis and rheumatic fever which persisted throughout the first half of the twentieth century.[25]

That forces independent of human action do have an effect on levels of mortality is clear from the events of the 1890s when a fortuitous sequence of hot, dry summers combined with the general unhealthiness of urban environments to raise death rates from diarrhoeal disease.[26] On the other hand, especially for that part of the modern mortality decline which occurred in the twentieth century, the significance of autonomous changes in the virulence of, and resistance to, disease organisms should not be overstated. Trends in the case-fatality rates of diseases like tuberculosis suggest that for most infectious diseases there was no long-term decline in virulence. Even the reduction in mortality from scarlet fever, considered the best example of a disease whose natural severity has diminished in recent times, owed something to the spread of isolation hospitals which helped to lessen the risks of transmission and reduce its fatality. While a decline in the virulence of the β-haemolytic streptococcus may have contributed to the continued decrease in maternal deaths from puerperal sepsis after the Second World War, it cannot easily account for the sudden, sharp drop in mortality from this infection which occurred around 1937.[27] As even the supporters of the autonomous interpretation acknowledge, the bulk of the explanation for the demise of infectious disease as the principal cause of death must lie somewhere within the realm of human activity. The difficulty has always been to determine which of the improvements made by man to his personal and environmental condition have contributed most to the prolongation of life.

One school of thought holds that special significance should be attached to man's success in raising his standards of nutrition, thereby increasing his resistance to infectious disease and enhancing the likelihood of recovery when infection did strike. Thus, according to McKeown and his co-authors, dietary improvement, particularly via its impact on mortality from tuberculosis and to a lesser extent typhus, probably accounted for as much as half of the increase in life expectancy between 1850 and 1900 and remained the major cause of falling death rates, especially from airborne infections such as tuberculosis and measles, throughout the first three-quarters of the twentieth century.[28] According to Winter, while other factors were *necessary*, improvements in nutrition were the only *sufficient* cause of the decline in infectious disease mortality between 1870 and 1950. Without significant advances in standards of diet, death rates from diseases such as bronchitis, influenza, pneumonia, scarlet fever, tuberculosis and whooping cough would not have declined as they did. Improved nutrition, Winter argues, was the chief reason for the continued reduction in infant death rates during the years of the First World War and one of the chief reasons for improvements in the health of mothers and babies even during the worst years of economic depression in the 1930s.[29]

Most historians, however, take a more conservative view of the contribution of nutritional improvement to mortality decline. Though none would deny that variations in diet played some part in accounting for secular, spatial and socio-occupational variations in life expectation, the role of nutrition is usually regarded, at best, as no more crucial than that of a number of other important influences or, at worst, as very much secondary to the contribution of other factors.

Even in the late nineteenth century, when its effect is likely to have been greatest, there are good reasons not to overstate the role of nutrition. That some advances in nutritional standards occurred before 1900, even among the poorest, is indisputable.[30] But for the majority of the working-class population these advances were modest, and some would say negligible.[31] The belief that working-class diets in the late nineteenth century were sufficiently superior to those of earlier times to have a significant impact on levels of resistance to infectious disease has still to be convincingly demonstrated. Furthermore, if nutritional standards were as vital as some have claimed why did females, who received a disproportionately small share of the family food supply, live longer than males, and middle-class infants, who probably consumed a disproportionately large share of less nutritious patent foods, experience lower mortality rates than working-class infants?[32] Given that improvements in diet were no greater for urban than rural populations, it is equally difficult to reconcile trends in nutrition with the fact that in the half century or so before 1914 death rates fell more quickly in urban than rural areas. Nor does the nutritional thesis adequately account for the pattern of late nineteenth- and early twentieth-century mortality decline. If diet was so important why at a time of general advance in dietary standards did death rates from some infectious diseases fall while for others – croup, diphtheria, measles and infant diarrhoea, for example – they rose? In reality, variations in the incidence of major diseases such as cholera, smallpox and typhus appear to have owed little to variations in nutritional status. Even in the case of tuberculosis, where cohort, class and regional differentials in mortality are clearly to some extent influenced by varying standards of diet, death rates began to decline long before the onset of widespread improvements in nutrition.[33]

Claims for the primacy of the nutritional factor are no easier to confirm for the period after the First World War. Although improved standards of maternal nutrition obviously contributed to the continued decline in rates of maternal mortality after 1945, their contribution to the initial downturn in maternal death rates in the late 1930s and to regional variations in levels of maternal mortality ever since is thought to be minor compared with that of medical innovation and of changes in certain other conditions associated with poverty.[34] Work on the causes of international differentials in life expectancy during the 1900s, 1930s and 1960s likewise suggests that the main causes of mortality variation lie in factors other than changing levels of income and food per head.[35] In so far as standards of nutrition are determined by levels of real income, unemployment and poverty, the relationship between these variables and death rates has never been close enough to confirm the predominance of nutrition among the factors responsible for shaping mortality trends. To judge from data on the strength of the correlation between rates of infant mortality on the one hand and the income and occupation of fathers on the other, rising levels of per capita real income and declining levels of poverty made at least some contribution to the reduction in infant death rates that occurred in England and Wales in the decade immediately prior to the outbreak of the First World War. But, as indicated by the persistence of above average levels of infant mortality among miners, a relatively high income group, and below average levels of mortality among the infants of agricultural labourers, a relatively low income group, other factors were probably more influential.[36] While Brenner's analysis of mortality in England and Wales between 1936 and 1976 suggests a significant correlation between mortality rates and levels of unemployment, analyses based on arguably sounder statistical techniques by Stern and McAvinchey show the strength of the correlation to be much weaker.[37]

In fact, rising incomes and the new patterns of diet and consumption to which these gave rise may even have worked to increase deaths from certain causes. Coupled with the effects of technological innovation, greater consumer purchasing power permitted an ever-growing proportion of the population to eat, drink and smoke to excess, to avoid physical exercise and, until very recently, to switch their preferences from natural, high-fibre foods to less healthy diets based on convenience foods with a high fat content and excessive amounts of salt, sugar and artificial additives. It is no accident that in areas like Scotland and northern England and among lower status socio-occupational groups, where the incidence of alcoholism, cigarette smoking and fat consumption is greatest, death rates from 'diseases of affluence' such as lung cancer and heart disease are relatively high. The rise of such diseases to prominence in the disease aetiology of the later twentieth century may have been mainly no more than a secondary consequence of the decline in mortality from infectious disease, itself partly a result of improvements in nutrition. Yet there can also be no doubt that deaths from cancers and heart disease would have been lower had it not been for the new consumption habits made possible by the emergence of a more affluent society. An increase in the incidence of cigarette smoking between the First World War and the early 1960s was accompanied by a steady rise in mortality from lung cancer; rising levels of alcohol intake from the 1950s by an increase in deaths from alcohol-related diseases between the mid 1960s and mid 1980s; and higher levels of meat and fat consumption up to the early 1970s by an increase in mortality from heart disease. With the decline in cigarette and alcohol consumption, from the early 1960s and mid 1980s respectively, and the gradual replacement from the early 1970s of saturated by polyunsaturated fats, full cream milk by semi-skimmed milk and red meat by vegetarian foods in the popular diet, death rates from lung cancer and heart disease have decreased.[38] But for much of the twentieth century a combination of relatively high levels of cigarette smoking and a diet unusually rich in fat ensured that mortality from the two diseases in Britain was among the highest in the developed world.

If the part played by nutrition is less crucial than some have supposed, does a more satisfactory explanation of the mortality decline lie in the advances that have been made in the supply of medical institutions and personnel and the range and effectiveness of medical therapy and surgical technique?

For that part of the decline which occurred during the second half of the twentieth century, subsequent to the discovery and application of chemotherapeutical drugs from the later 1930s, the answer must be yes. The initial, sharp decline in rates of maternal mortality in 1936–7, for example, stemmed chiefly from the use of protonsil, the first of the sulphonamide drugs, in the treatment of puerperal fever: and it was largely as a result of further advances in medicine – the use of penicillin to treat septic abortion, the growing practice of blood transfusion, higher standards of midwifery following the Midwives Act of 1936, a greater emphasis on gynaecology in the training of medical students and general improvements in the quantity and quality of maternity services – that rates of maternal mortality continued to fall after the Second World War.[39] Most of the decline in perinatal death rates in England and Wales between 1950 and 1973 and in Scotland during the 1970s was due to improvements in obstetric practice and clinical management.[40] Beginning in the 1940s or 1950s deaths from respiratory diseases, whooping cough, enteric fever and tuberculosis were greatly reduced by the use of sulphyridine, sulphonamides, chloramphemicol, streptomycin and BCG immunisation. Around one-third of the decline in mortality from cardiovascular disease in recent decades was the result of drugs which reduced levels of blood pressure and cholesterol, beta blockers and anticoagulants and coronary bypass surgery, while improvements in diagnosis, drugs, surgery and radiation therapy have significantly reduced deaths from certain types of cancer. Even today, of course, there remain many causes of premature death that medicine cannot effectively overcome. But this should not be allowed to obscure the fact that innovations in medical therapy and surgical technique, facilitated by the creation of a National Health Service, made an important contribution to the continuing decline in death rates during the second half of the twentieth century.[41]

For the more substantial part of the modern mortality decline which had already occurred by the middle years of the century the contribution of medicine is more debatable.

If the role of medicine is interpreted solely in relation to the effectiveness of specific medical therapies and surgical techniques its significance was limited. Improvements in medicine and surgery were important to mortality decline only in the cases of appendicitis, peritonitis, smallpox, syphilis and deaths from causes other than micro-organisms, none of which figured prominently among the main causes of death in the late nineteenth and early twentieth centuries. For those infectious diseases whose decline contributed significantly to the rise in life expectation before the Second World War, effective, specific medical and surgical treatments were not available until the mid 1930s at the earliest.[42] A comparison of death rates in six different socio-economic sub-groups of the population of England and Wales between 1851 and 1911 confirms the view that medical advance made only a minor contribution to the initial phase of mortality decline.[43] To suggest, as some have, that declining rates of infant mortality in the period immediately before and during the First World War owed much to improved facilities for antenatal and post-natal maternal and child care and rising standards of midwifery following the Midwives Act of 1902 is to understate the difficulties involved in translating intention into reality. Despite the obvious growth in concern for mother and child welfare, standards of obstetric practice and antenatal and post-natal care improved very little before 1914 while the decline in infant death rates between 1914 and 1918, it has been suggested, far exceeded anything that might have been expected from the extent and quality of wartime infant and maternity welfare services. As late as the 1930s levels of obstetric knowledge and technique were so poor that they were more likely to increase than decrease death rates in childbirth. Even allowing for the contribution of innovations to which insufficient attention is usually paid – the growing use of anaesthetic, antiseptic and aseptic procedures in surgery, the discovery and application of a diphtheria antitoxin and an antimalaria serum, immunisation against tetanus and the use of insulin in the treatment of hormone deficiency diseases – it is difficult to dissent from the view that declining rates of infectious disease mortality in the first half of the twentieth century owed relatively little to advances in specific medical and surgical practice.[44]

It has recently been pointed out, however, that by concentrating solely on the role of specific medical and surgical techniques we run the risk of understating the contribution made by the medical profession. If the role of medicine is extended to include the pressure exerted by its members in favour of improvements in standards of personal hygiene and public health the significance of medicine is considerably enhanced. Through their involvement in the campaign for better housing, purer supplies of food and drink, improved methods of sewage disposal, higher standards of cleanliness and the more widespread adoption of efficient quarantine procedures, medical researchers and practitioners were crucial to the discovery and implementation of a range of environmental improvements which together were probably the single most important set of causes of increasing human longevity between the late nineteenth and mid twentieth centuries.[45]

To judge from the existence of a close, positive correlation between the extent of urbanisation on the one hand and levels of mortality on the other and also from the fact that, once begun, the pace of mortality decline was greater in urban than rural areas,[46] the principal explanation for the rise in life expectancy during the first half of the twentieth century lay in the success of initiatives designed to reduce excessive urban population densities and resolve the worst problems of food adulteration, housing, sanitation and disease control which inevitably accompanied them.

Some scholars, it is true, insist that the extent of environmental improvement was too limited to have had a significant impact on death rates. Winter, for instance, concludes that, though improved sanitation played a major role in the decline in mortality from waterborne infections, and legislation to combat food and drink adulteration a major role in the decline in infant mortality, overall, improvements in public health conditions and in the quality of food and drink products were, like innovations in medicine, secondary to rising standards of nutrition among the causes of increased longevity before the Second World War.[47] McKeown, Record and Turner reach a similar conclusion. Improvements in the quality of infant foods, water and milk and rising standards of sanitation, they claim, together accounted for no more than a sixth of the total reduction in death rates during the first half of the twentieth century. Most of the reduction was due to the effect of advances in nutrition and, to a lesser degree, medical therapy on the prevalence of airborne infections and causes of death other than those carried by food or water.[48]

Arguably, these interpretations are too pessimistic. Few would deny that the pace of environmental improvement was slow, particularly before the First World War, and that much remained to be done even in the 1950s. As late as 1914, despite a considerable body of permissive and sometimes compulsory legislation, little in practice had been achieved to resolve many of the worst problems of air and river pollution, urban overcrowding and working-class housing. Nevertheless, some effective steps had already been taken towards improving the nature of the environment in which people lived. The quality of food, milk and water supplies had risen. Methods of waste disposal had been improved by the drainage of cesspools and the introduction of dry conservancy and waterborne sewage systems and modern infiltration and treatment plants. The adoption of early notification procedures and the establishment of larger numbers of isolation hospitals had begun to combat the spread of contagious disease, and improvements in working conditions to reduce the incidence of industrial accidents and disease.

After 1914–18 the pace and range of environmental improvement increased. Of all the principal determinants of environmental quality only the quality of the urban air supply failed to improve in the course of the interwar period. Coupled with the trend towards smaller family sizes which began in the later nineteenth century and which, by lessening the risks of disease transmission, helped to reduce deaths from infectious diseases like measles, advances in public health conditions between the late nineteenth and mid twentieth centuries contributed more to the rise in human life expectancy than it has sometimes been usual to suppose. Cholera and typhoid succumbed primarily to the development of a purer water supply made possible by improvements in sewage systems. Deaths from non-respiratory tuberculosis and childhood diseases like scarlet fever declined under the impact of more regular and efficient quarantining practices. Drier and better ventilated housing, aided by the effect of falling fertility on infectious disease transmission rates, made a significant contribution to the decrease in mortality from respiratory tuberculosis and other airborne infections. A combination of purer drinking water, improvements in housing and methods of refuse disposal, the pasteurisation of milk and the increasing use of dried, powdered and unsweetened condensed milk as infant foods and the replacement of animal by motor transport, which reduced the scale of the urban dung problem, played an important part in the decline in deaths in infancy and childhood from diarrhoeal and related gastro-enteric infections.[49] In tandem with the benefits for health which accrued from the decline in family size, environmental improvements of this kind were influential elements in the continuous advance in human longevity through the first half of the twentieth century.[50]

Currently, perhaps the only acceptable explanation for the dramatic decline in mortality in the last hundred years or so is that it was the result of a complex variety of factors. Among those given the greatest emphasis in the literature are autonomous reductions in the virulence of disease viruses themselves, innovations in medicine, rising standards of public health, personal hygiene and housing and improved levels of nutrition. Less often stressed, but no less crucial, were the many factors which made all but the first of these possible: improvements in the education of mothers; more enlightened, less fatalistic attitudes towards ill-health and death; the emergence of central and local governments with the necessary authority and capability to pass and enforce medical and public health legislation; acceptance of the germ theory of disease; declining family size; the substitution of manual by non-manual, middle-class lifestyles with their greater stress on healthier eating, recreational exercise and lower fertility; and, above all, the technology and higher per capita incomes which came with economic modernisation and made so many of the proximate causes of a longer life feasible.[51] Beyond agreeing that autonomous factors were less important than those which originated in the actions of man and that the relative significance of each of the latter varied considerably by time, region and socio-occupational group there is, however, no consensus on the precise mix of causation. This is not surprising. So closely intertwined is the relationship between the various determinants of mortality that both in theory and practice it is difficult, perhaps impossible, to be more specific.

4

FERTILITY

Although lacking the precision of more sophisticated methods of measurement, the crude birth rate data (births per thousand total population) set out in Table 4.1 give an adequate indication of the main trends in overall levels of fertility in recent times.

As late as the third quarter of the nineteenth century crude birth rates were higher than in any other period of comparable length since at least the middle of the sixteenth century.[1] In the course of the decade beginning around 1876 they started to decline and, except for a brief interruption in the years immediately after the First World War, continued to decline until the late 1930s. In little more than 50 years birth rates in mainland Britain more than halved. Average numbers of births fell from between five and six for women born around 1870 to just two for women born around 1920. Except in eastern and southern Europe, where the onset of the fertility decline began later and where birth rates were still falling in the late 1930s, a similar trend occurred in many European countries.[2] Before 1911 the rate of decline was greater in some parts of Britain than others and the extent of pre-decline regional variation in birth rates temporarily widened. After 1911 regional birth rate differentials narrowed.[3] The result was that over the period from the mid 1870s to the late 1930s as a whole the decline in birth rates from one region to another was remarkably uniform and patterns of regional variation at the end of the interwar period remained much the same as those at the beginning of the century.[4]

In the years immediately prior to the outbreak of the Second World War crude birth rates began to rise, though the rise was less pronounced in Britain than in a number of other European countries. Total period fertility rates (defined as the number of children a woman would have had if she experienced current age-specific fertility rates throughout her reproductive span) reached their lowest level, 1.72, in 1933. By 1939 they had increased to 1.83.[5] Despite the fact that the exclusion of the British army from Europe for much of the war period helped keep fertility higher than it would otherwise have been, birth rates fell during the early years of the war but from 1941, in Scotland, and 1942, in England and Wales, once more began to rise. In the case of Scotland crude birth rates in the final year of the war were lower than they had ever been before. In the case of England and Wales however, though lower than in 1943 and 1944, they reached levels higher than at any time between 1931 and 1942. The repatriation of servicemen at the end of the war was accompanied by a sharp rise in fertility in 1946 and 1947. But from then until the mid 1950s birth rates declined. Between 1950 and 1955 total period fertility rates in England and Wales were among the lowest in Europe.[6]

Sometime around the mid 1950s fertility decline gave way to a surprising if moderate and shortlived increase. In England and Wales, where levels of total period fertility rose from a low of 2.14 in 1951 to a high of 2.94 in 1964, crude birth rates increased in each successive year between 1956 and 1964. Women born around 1937 and married by the early 1960s were the most fertile cohort of women born since the 1920s.[7] A similar, albeit less regular, increase in birth rates occurred in Scotland. The baby boom of the late 1950s and early 1960s was common to almost all countries in the developed world, but nowhere was it as pronounced as in Britain. The result was that by the mid 1960s rates of fertility in England and Wales were no longer among the lowest in Europe.[8]

In the second half of the 1960s baby boom was replaced by baby bust. From a peak of 18.5 per thousand in 1964 crude birth rates in England and Wales fell to a trough of 11.5 per thousand in 1977. Only among females in the youngest adult age groups did fertility continue to increase through the latter half of the 1960s, and even this tendency ceased from the early 1970s.[9] From 1978 the fertility of all socio-occupational groups in the population of England and Wales once again began to rise, though as late as 1990 birth rates were still only slightly higher than a decade or so earlier.[10] In Scotland crude birth rates fell from 20 per thousand in 1964 to 12 per thousand in 1977. Here, however, the extent of recovery in the late 1970s and 1980s was even less marked and persistent.[11]

Nearly everywhere in the developed world the evolution of fertility since the mid 1960s followed much the same pattern as in Britain. In most other European countries too the baby boom ended around 1964 or 1965 and rates of fertility decreased until the mid or late 1970s. Subsequently, while in most cases the decline in fertility either slowed or, as in Britain, gave way to modest fertility increase, there was rather more diversity of experience.[12] Everywhere, however, the preference for a two-child family structure remained intact.

Throughout the second half of the twentieth century, although the direction of birth rate trends was similar in almost all regions of mainland Britain, there remained some regional differences both in levels of aggregate fertility and in the rate at which these levels changed. From the 1960s to 1990 total period fertility rates were invariably higher in Scotland and the northern and midland regions of England than in the southern half of the country, and higher in regions with conurbations than elsewhere. In general, however, the extent of variation was small and, as in other European countries, tended to decline over time.[13] The tendency for regional fertility differentials to converge in the second half of the century is particularly evident in the change which took place in the relative levels of crude birth rates in England/Wales and Scotland. Between the beginning of the century and the early 1980s Scottish birth rates

Table 4.1 Annual average crude birth rates. England/Wales and Scotland, 1855–1990

	England/Wales	Scotland
1855	33.8	31.3
1860	34.3	35.6
1865	35.4	35.5
1870	35.2	34.6
1875	35.4	35.2
1880	34.2	33.6
1885	32.9	32.7
1890	30.2	30.4
1895	30.3	30.0
1900	28.7	29.6
1905	27.3	28.6
1910	25.1	26.2
1915	21.9	23.9
1920	25.5	28.1
1925	18.3	21.4
1930	16.3	19.6
1935	14.7	17.8
1940	14.1	17.1
1945	15.9	16.9
1950	15.8	18.1
1955	15.0	18.1
1960	17.1	19.6
1965	18.1	19.3
1970	16.0	16.8
1975	12.2	13.1
1980	13.2	13.4
1985	13.1	13.0
1990	13.9	12.9

Sources: B. R. Mitchell, *British Historical Statistics* (Cambridge, 1988), pp. 42–7. CSO, *Annual Abstract of Statistics 1993* (London, 1993), pp. 27–8.

consistently exceeded those in England and Wales. From the late 1960s, however, the differential began to narrow and by the late 1970s was barely perceptible. By 1983–90, as had been the case through much of the second half of the nineteenth century, crude birth rates and rates of total period fertility in Scotland had fallen below those in England and Wales.[14]

Illegitimacy

Variations in levels of overall fertility are a product of variations in one or other of three demographic mechanisms – the number of births outside marriage (illegitimacy), ages at marriage and the proportions married (nuptiality), and the frequency of childbirth within marriage (marital fertility).

From at least as early as the middle of the sixteenth century levels of illegitimacy have varied considerably by social class, region and time. In the twentieth century, as in previous centuries, illegitimacy has been predominantly a working-class phenomenon. In 1983, for example, over three-quarters of all illegitimates were born to women in the manual occupational groups of the population, more than a third of the total to women in social class V.[15] Levels of bastardy in England throughout the period between the late sixteenth and late twentieth centuries were consistently higher in western and northern than southern and south-eastern counties.[16] Thus, in 1981, English illegitimacy ratios (illegitimates per hundred live births) ranged from 9.5 in East Anglia to 10.3 in the South West, 12.6 in the South East and East Midlands, 12.8 in the West Midlands, 13.2 in the North, 13.5 in Yorkshire/Humberside and 15.5 in the North West. In 1990 the range of variation ran from a low of 22.8 in East Anglia to 24.3 in the South West, 25.9 in the South East, 28.0 in the East Midlands, 30.6 in Yorkshire/Humberside, 32.5 in the West Midlands, 32.8 in the North and 34.5 in the North West.[17] In Scotland between the mid nineteenth and mid twentieth centuries illegitimacy ratios were always relatively high in midland, south-eastern and south-western counties, lowest in northern and north-western counties and, unusually, higher among rural than urban populations. Only after the mid 1950s did levels of bastardy in Scottish urban areas rise above those in rural areas.[18]

Trends in levels of illegitimacy since the middle of the nineteenth century are summarised in Table 4.2. Down to the middle of the twentieth century illegitimacy ratios in Scotland exceeded those in England and Wales. The differential narrowed in the years immediately following the Second World War and from the 1950s onwards was largely reversed. In every year from 1952 to 1990, with the exception of 1973, 1975 and 1976, bastardy ratios in Scotland were lower than in England and Wales.

Despite this, both countries experienced a very similar trend. In England levels of illegitimacy were already beginning to fall in the 1840s. In Scotland the decline began in the 1860s. By 1900 the proportion of live births born outside marriage was a third lower than half a century earlier. From then until the 1950s illegitimacy ratios fluctuated around a relatively unchanging trend. Sometime around 1960 they began to rise. The rise was particularly rapid between the late 1950s and late 1960s and in the 1980s. Between the late 1960s and late 1970s, perhaps because the easier availability of legal abortion made possible by the 1967 Abortion Act allowed the termination of some of the pregnancies that might otherwise have resulted in an illegitimate birth, it was more muted. The increase in illegitimacy during the 1980s, an increase shared by all regions and social classes, was quite extraordinary and greater in Britain than in all other European countries except France and the Republic of Ireland. By 1990 in excess of one in four children were born outside wedlock, a ratio more than twice that of a decade earlier.[19]

Broadly similar trends in illegitimacy occurred in most developed countries of the world. Between 1880 and 1940 levels of bastardy declined nearly everywhere in Europe.[20] From around 1960 they rose. In some countries, mainly located in eastern and southern Europe, the rise was negligible or, at most, small. In others, chiefly in northern and western Europe, it was more marked – in the cases of Belgium, Denmark, East Germany, France, the Irish Republic, the Netherlands, Norway and Sweden even greater than in Britain.[21] Actual levels of illegitimacy, of course, have

Fertility

Table 4.2 Illegitimacy ratios (illegitimate births per hundred live births). England/Wales and Scotland, 1855–1990

	England/Wales	Scotland
1855	6.5	7.8
1860	6.4	9.2
1865	6.3	10.0
1870	5.7	9.5
1875	4.8	8.7
1880	4.9	8.5
1885	4.8	8.5
1890	4.4	7.6
1895	4.2	7.3
1900	4.0	6.5
1905	4.0	6.9
1910	4.1	7.3
1915	4.5	6.9
1920	1.6	7.5
1925	4.1	6.5
1930	4.6	7.3
1935	4.2	6.5
1940	4.4	5.9
1945	9.3	7.7
1950	5.0	5.2
1955	4.6	4.3
1960	5.5	4.3
1965	7.8	5.6
1970	8.2	7.7
1975	9.0	9.3
1980	11.7	11.2
1985	19.2	18.5
1990	28.3	27.1

Sources: B. R. Mitchell, *British Historical Statistics* (Cambridge, 1988), pp. 42–7. Registrar-General Scotland, *Annual Report 1991* (Edinburgh, 1992), p. 19. OPCS, 'Tables', *Population Trends*, 68 (1992), 47. J. Cooper, 'Births Outside Marriage: Recent Trends and Associated Demographic and Social Changes', *Population Trends*, 63 (1991), 9.

continued to vary substantially from one country to another. Throughout the first half of the twentieth century illegitimacy ratios in the United Kingdom were comparatively low and as late as 1956–60 still lower than in 12 of 21 European countries.

By 1966–70 they were exceeded in only 7 of 23 European states and by 1990 only in the northern European countries of Denmark, Iceland and Finland.[22]

The causes of variations in bastardy remain obscure. The fact that trends in illegitimacy followed much the same pattern from one country to another has led some historians to presume the existence of a common explanation. But even if this presumption is justified there is as yet no agreement on what this common explanation, or common set of explanations, was. For the time being, therefore, the only sensible course to pursue in the search for causation is to proceed country by country. Why then did levels of illegitimacy in Britain decline between the mid nineteenth and mid twentieth centuries and rise in the second half of the twentieth century, with particular rapidity in the 1980s?

Some possible explanations can be speedily dismissed. Among these must be included variations in the extent of urbanisation and industrialisation, in the numerical balance between the sexes and in levels of material prosperity, nutrition and health and the effects these had on rates of fecundity, ages at menarche and the incidence of spontaneous abortion or stillbirth.[23] Nor, it seems, should too much significance be attached to the part played by variations in the extent of courtship activity and in the size of what has been called 'the sub-society of the bastard-prone'. Periods of relative economic prosperity, it is argued, were accompanied not only by higher rates of nuptiality and marital fertility but also by an increase in the extent of sexual intercourse among the unmarried and a substantially greater rate of growth in the fertility of women who bore children outside wedlock than in that of women who bore children within marriage.[24] Intriguing though this thesis is, it has to be said that for the twentieth century anyway it lacks consistent empirical support. While low and relatively constant illegitimacy ratios between the late nineteenth century and the 1930s conformed with a period of low and relatively constant rates of nuptiality and rising illegitimacy ratios between the late 1950s and late 1960s with a period of rising nuptiality, no such relationship between the two variables was apparent in the 1970s, and in the 1980s, when illegitimacy ratios increased dramatically, levels of nuptiality actually fell.

Other potential explanations are less easily dismissed. In their explanation for the emergence and persistence of low rates of bastardy between the late nineteenth and mid twentieth centuries, for instance, Tilly, Scott and Cohen stress the contributions made by declining numbers of sexually vulnerable female domestic servants, reductions in the flow of female migrants to towns and cities and, above all, the growth of working-class prosperity which worked to restrict illegitimacy by reducing the number of young women away from their families, facilitating marriage and reducing the population of highly mobile, propertyless men whose need constantly to move in search of employment had increased the likelihood that pregnancy would not be followed by marriage.[25] Admittedly, in this case too, the argument is offered as an hypothesis with little or no empirical confirmation and one aspect of it – the suggestion that illegitimacy ratios correlated positively with numbers of female domestic servants – receives no support from Crafts' analysis of interurban differentials in bastardy in England and Wales in 1911 where the presence of a large population of female domestic servants was accompanied by low, not high, levels of illegitimacy. On the other hand the fact that low levels of income and employment among women in 1911 correlated with high rates of illegitimacy, coupled with the fact that regional variations in illegitimacy in England and Wales 70 years later were positively related to variations in levels of male unemployment and the proportion of the labour force in unskilled occupations, suggests that what Tilly, Scott and Cohen have to say about the implications for bastardy of increased working-class prosperity should not be dismissed too readily.[26]

Long-term variations in levels of illegitimacy may also have owed something to a combination of changes in the nature of birth control technology and changes in attitudes towards pre-marital sex and the institution of marriage. According to this interpretation the two phases of abnormally high and rising rates of illegitimacy in modern times, the first in the late eighteenth and early nineteenth centuries and the second between the 1960s and 1980s, were chiefly the result of a dramatic increase in the extent of sexual promiscuity among the unmarried. During the first phase greater opportunities for employment, and thus for financial independence, liberated young, single women from the customary control of parents and community and allowed them to indulge in a degree of sexual licence never before possible. In the absence of effective, or effectively practised, birth control technologies the consequence was a sharp rise in the number of children born outside wedlock. When, between the late nineteenth and mid twentieth centuries, methods of birth control improved and the practice of birth control became more acceptable, levels of illegitimacy declined. A further increase in the extent of premarital sexual activity, this time prompted by the revolt of a new youth culture against parental authority and traditional norms of social behaviour, occurred in the 1960s. Because contraception was practised less efficiently by the unmarried than the married, this too was accompanied by another surge in rates of bastardy.[27]

The belief that secular trends in illegitimacy were essentially a function of changes in the incidence of extramarital sexual intercourse has been hotly disputed, principally on the grounds that the only evidence offered in support of variations in levels of sexual activity outside marriage is the variations which occurred in levels of illegitimacy themselves.[28] At least for the twentieth century, however, there is some reason to suppose that the rejection of what has come to be known as the Shorter thesis is premature and probably unjustified. Lower rates of premarital conception in the 1950s than in Victorian times, together with the continued rarity of extramarital cohabitation and divorce, imply that until well into the second half of the twentieth century commitment to the values of married life, a commitment reinforced by the psychological impact of the two world wars,[29] was too strong to permit widespread sexual intercourse outside marriage. The sudden surge in premarital conception rates in the late 1950s and early 1960s and rising levels of extramarital cohabitation and divorce from the 1960s and 1970s, by contrast, imply the recent emergence of more liberal attitudes towards nonmarital sexual intercourse.[30] Some confirmation of this is provided by the results of survey data on the extent of sexual intercourse among unmarried women. As late as the 1950s and early 1960s fewer than one in three women admitted to having had sex before marriage. By the end of the 1960s the figure had risen to 60 per cent and ten years later to between 80 and 90 per cent. In the space of little more than a decade sexual intercourse outside marriage had become the typical rather than the atypical experience.[31] As late as the early 1970s the usual outcome of a premarital conception was marriage. By the 1980s abortion or illegitmacy were the more likely consequences.[32] In part this stemmed from the emergence of a value system which attached more importance to the wishes and interests of the individual than to those of the family or the community and which therefore allowed greater individual freedom of choice in behaviour.[33] But, in part, it was also a secondary consequence of the decline in rates of nuptiality which occurred during the 1970s and 1980s, and the forces responsible for it. As the proportion of women living outside marriage increased, so too did levels of extramarital sexual intercourse and illegitimacy.[34]

Nuptiality

Before the last quarter of the nineteenth century temporal, regional and socio-occupational class differences in rates of fertility were mainly determined by differences in levels of nuptiality. Since the mid 1870s, though nuptiality has continued to have an influence, the behaviour of aggregate fertility has been determined chiefly by what happened to marital fertility.[35]

Between the middle of the nineteenth century and the early 1930s crude marriage rates (marriages per thousand total population), average ages at marriage and the proportions never married fluctuated around levels that had been typical of British and western European nuptiality experience since at least the seventeenth century. It follows that the nuptiality mechanism could have played no more than a minor role in the novel, long-term decline in rates of overall fertility which began in the mid 1870s.[36]

In stark contrast the period between the 1930s and the start of the 1970s saw the creation of 'a new marriage pattern... which had not been seen in the west for centuries'.[37] In all social groups ages at marriage and the percentages of men and women remaining unmarried in each age group declined and crude marriage rates rose. Similar increases in nuptiality occurred in many other industrialised countries of the European and non-European world.[38] Because of improvements in the ratio of men to women caused by changes in the balance and sex structure of international migration and the absence of male mortality rates on the scale of the First World War, the increase in nuptiality in the several decades leading up to the early 1970s was especially marked among females.[39] All scholars agree that this tendency towards earlier and more universal marriage contributed significantly to the baby boom of the late 1950s and early 1960s and perhaps accounted for as much as 30 per cent of the rise in aggregate fertility rates between 1930 and the mid 1960s.[40]

Since the early 1980s, in line with what happened in most industrialised countries, crude marriage rates have fallen, average ages at marriage have risen and, at least in the age groups 16–29, the proportions marrying have declined. Despite this, at the end of the 1980s Britain still boasted one of the youngest marital age patterns in western Europe and marriage remained the ultimate preference for the great majority of people.[41]

As Table 4.3 shows, from at least as early as the middle of the nineteenth century down to the outbreak of the Second World War, crude marriage rates were consistently higher in England and Wales than in Scotland. In two out of every three years between 1941 and 1990, by contrast, marriage rates were higher, and marriage earlier, in Scotland. A similar trend towards less regional diversity in nuptiality experience

Table 4.3 Annual average crude marriage rates. England/Wales and Scotland, 1855–1990

	England/Wales	Scotland
1855	16.2	13.2
1860	17.1	13.9
1865	17.5	14.8
1870	16.1	14.3
1875	16.7	14.8
1880	14.9	13.2
1885	14.5	13.1
1890	15.5	13.7
1895	15.0	13.5
1900	16.0	14.6
1905	15.3	13.6
1910	15.0	13.0
1915	19.4	15.2
1920	20.2	19.2
1925	15.2	13.3
1930	15.8	13.8
1935	17.2	15.3
1940	22.5	21.2
1945	18.7	18.9
1950	16.3	15.8
1955	16.1	16.9
1960	15.0	15.5
1965	15.5	15.6
1970	17.0	16.6
1975	15.4	15.1
1980	14.9	14.9
1985	13.9	14.2
1990	13.1	13.6

Sources: B. R. Mitchell, *British Historical Statistics* (Cambridge, 1988), pp. 72–4. CSO, *Annual Abstract of Statistics 1993* (London, 1993), pp. 22–3.

emerged in most European countries in the course of the twentieth century.[42]

Accompanying these changes in the incidence of and age at marriage were equally notable changes in the extent of divorce, remarriage and extramarital cohabitation.

Until the late 1950s rates of divorce remained negligible. Thereafter they began to rise, slowly at first and then, from the late 1960s, more rapidly. In England and Wales the number of divorces per thousand married couples increased from around two in 1961 to six in 1971, around twelve in 1981 and, following a period of relative stability in the early 1980s, around thirteen between 1985 and 1990. In Scotland, where divorce rates were always slightly lower, they likewise rose to a peak in 1985 (11.2) before settling at between 9.8 and 10.7 in the second half of the 1980s. These trends were repeated everywhere in the industrialised world.[43] Generally, levels of divorce have varied inversely with social class and, except for those in personal service, artistic, literary, sporting, security and selling occupations, have invariably been higher among manual than non-manual workers.[44]

Throughout the first half of the twentieth century, when rates of adult mortality were lower than they had ever been before, and divorce a rarity, the incidence of remarriage was low. Since the late 1970s, as a result of rising divorce rates, its incidence has greatly increased. Between 1965 and 1988 the proportion of marriages in England and Wales involving at least one previously married partner rose from 16 to 37 per cent.[45] As a proportion of all divorced men and women, however, rates of remarriage fell by a third in the 1970s and continued to fall in the 1980s.[46] The reason for this was that divorced people increasingly preferred cohabitation outside marriage. Until the early 1970s only about one in twenty married couples had lived together before marriage. Ten years later the figure had soared to over a quarter and by the end of the 1980s to half of all first-married couples and nearly three-quarters of all remarried couples. Simultaneously, the average length of time spent cohabiting increased from nine months in the 1970s to fifteen months in the 1980s.[47]

The persistence of relatively low levels of nuptiality in the period before the 1930s was the consequence of a complex mix of demographic and economic circumstances. One of the most important of these was the excess of women over men in the marriageable age groups, itself a product of higher rates of male than female mortality and of the disproportionate share of males in net overseas emigration flows in the decades immediately before and after the First World War. Housing shortages, high levels of male unemployment, restricted opportunities for the employment of married women and, to extend an argument advanced by Friedlander to explain the decline in nuptiality between 1873 and 1896, a general mood of economic insecurity provided additional reasons for postponing or even abandoning marriage.[48]

Economic circumstances also go some way towards explaining why in the course of the first half of the twentieth century regional differentials in nuptiality experiences narrowed. At the beginning of the century, when many local economies were still weakly integrated into national economic systems, spatial variation in nuptiality and other demographic characteristics was inevitable. In Scotland between 1861 and 1914, for instance, levels of nuptiality were always highest in regions where the pace of economic growth was greatest and opportunities for employment most abundant. Lower levels of nuptiality in Scotland than in England and Wales between the mid nineteenth and mid twentieth centuries likewise owed much to differences in economic conditions, in this case especially to the unusually high ratio of live-in farmworkers in the Scottish labour force and the relatively limited opportunities afforded by the Scottish economy for employment in mining and heavy industry.[49] Even in the late twentieth century regional variations in percentages married in England and Wales were partly determined by variations in male wage levels.[50] Of course, as Watkins reminds us, economic factors were not the only ones at work. In addition to the influence exerted by the forces of market integration, labour migration and transport improvement, the decline in regional nuptiality differentials also owed a good deal to the development of mass communications systems, the promotion of a stronger sense of national unity during the depression of the 1930s and the two world wars and the creation by central governments of more uniform, nation-wide institutions for education and welfare.[51]

The determinants of nuptiality trends since the 1930s are no less complex and the relative importance of each no less difficult to assess. Some were of only limited or short-lived significance. In this category might be included advances in state social welfare provision which facilitated marriage by alleviating the worse effects of unemployment and low incomes; further growth in the acceptability of 'artificial' contraceptive practices and the greater availability and lower cost of contraceptive technology which made it easier to control family size without having to postpone or deny the pleasures of marriage; improvements in the numerical balance between the sexes brought about by changes in the relationship between levels of in- and out-migration; increases in the stock of public sector housing in the 1950s and 1960s; and the role of wartime propaganda and psychology in reinforcing the traditional emphasis on woman's domestic function and the virtues of family life and in encouraging a desire for higher rates of fertility in the economic and political interests of Britain and her Empire.[52] All these, it has been argued, contributed in some measure to the unmistakable rise in nuptiality rates which occurred between the 1930s and early 1970s.

To some historians, however, rising levels of nuptiality in the 1950s and 1960s owed most to the fact that these were decades of unprecedentedly high incomes and full employment, particularly for teenagers and young adults. At precisely the time rising standards of health were acting to reduce the age of sexual maturity and thus the age at which the desire for a regular sexual relationship within marriage began, rising real incomes were acting to make this desire easier to fulfil.[53] When, in subsequent decades, levels of unemployment increased and the pace of per capita real income growth slackened, high rates of nuptiality became more difficult to sustain, marriage rates fell and ages at marriage rose.

If only because of its simplicity and apparent fit with the empirical evidence, this interpretation of nuptiality trends in the second half of the twentieth century is appealing. Arguably, however, it oversimplifies the nature of the relationship between variations in employment and prosperity on the one hand and variations in nuptiality on the other. Indirectly, by promoting individualism and greater levels of tolerance for individual nonconformity and by raising the real costs involved in searching out a suitable partner, rearing children and providing the goods and services essential for a satisfying family life, rising levels of prosperity in the 1950s and 1960s may have worked to discourage rather than encourage marriage.[54] Mindful of this most historians are inclined to believe that a more acceptable explanation of nuptiality trends after the Second World War lies in what happened to the relationship between the earning power of men and women.

In the period between 1945 and the early 1970s, partly because demographic changes increased the ratio of female to male workers and partly because most of the growth in employment opportunities was concentrated in the service sectors of the economy where women were in particular demand, women's wages decreased drastically in relation to those of men. As the relative earnings of women declined, the amount of income lost by women in preferring marriage and children to paid employment diminished, and marriage became an increasingly attractive proposition, all the more so since, in terms of income foregone, time spent on domestic duties is less costly when supplied solely by the no- or low-wage spouse. In the course of the first half of the 1970s, by contrast, the ratio of female to male wages rose and, despite periodic fluctuations, has remained higher than in the 1950s and 1960s ever since. As the relative earnings of women increased, the attractions of marriage lessened, ages at marriage rose and marriage rates fell.[55]

The recent decline in levels of nuptiality, of course, has not been entirely due to changes in economic circumstances. Rising rates of divorce and a growing preference for cohabitation outside marriage, and the forces responsible for them, have also played a part. One of the factors responsible for the recent increase in divorce rates in Britain and elsewhere in the developed world was the widespread liberalisation of divorce laws in the 1960s and 1970s which facilitated the legal dissolution of unsatisfactory marriages. The fundamental cause, however, was those forces which made the introduction of more liberal divorce legislation possible. One of these was falling mortality, which increased the average duration of married life and thus the likelihood of marital disharmony. Another was the Second World War which, by subjecting marriages to long periods of separation and increasing the number of marriages entered into with undue haste, enhanced both the potential for marital breakdown and the desire for easier divorce legislation. Reductions in male and female earnings differentials since the early 1970s have added a further impetus to the growing frequency of divorce. As their relative incomes rose, married women became less willing to continue in unsatisfactory unions and better able to withdraw from them. But perhaps the most influential force at work was the changes which occurred during the 1960s and 1970s in the underlying philosophies of individual and family life. The belief that the institution of marriage was inviolable was only one of the many facets of traditional social and cultural organisation and custom to fall prey to a system of values that increasingly emphasised individual free choice at the expense of the dictates of family, church and state.

Once divorce rates began to increase they exerted their own depressive impact on levels of nuptiality. Divorce is emotionally as well as financially draining. As its incidence grew, the expected gains from marriage diminished and a preference for extramarital cohabitation increased. For ever-larger numbers of people cohabitation was seen as an ideal vehicle for acquiring the additional information needed to minimise the risks of divorce and improve the likelihood that marriage would bring the benefits anticipated. In tandem with the effects of increasing sexual activity outside marriage, the availability of more effective methods of contraception which lessened the chances of nonmarital pregnancy and, in the 1980s, a resurgence of housing shortages and the introduction of less generous laws relating to mortgage tax relief, this attitude was sufficient to promote informal cohabitation at the expense of formal marriage.[56]

Marital Fertility

Allowing for some contribution from variations in nuptiality,[57] temporal, regional and socio-occupational differentials in aggregate fertility between the late nineteenth and late twentieth centuries were determined primarily by variations in the extent and frequency of childbirth within marriage. Down to the mid 1870s levels of marital fertility in England and Wales fluctuated around a more or less unchanging trend. In the ten years following 1876, at roughly the same rate in every region of the country, they began to decline and continued to decline until the 1930s.[58] In Scotland rates of marital fertility between the mid nineteenth century and the 1930s were higher than in England and Wales, but here too began to fall from the mid 1870s and more rapidly from the mid 1880s. Despite a growing tendency for childbirth to be compressed into an ever shorter time-span early in married life, from the mid 1950s to the mid 1960s, partly because of an earlier start to childbearing among married couples and partly because of a decline in the percentage of childless and single-child marriages, rates of marital fertility rose. Sometime around the mid 1960s, as a result of an increase in the number of permanently childless marriages but principally because of a reduction in the number of families with three or more children, rates of marital fertility once more started to decline. By the 1980s intervals between births were so protracted and the onset of childbearing so long delayed that in all socio-occupational groups a substantial divergence had emerged between the reproductive behaviour of females in their teens and twenties, whose fertility rates fell, and that of females in their thirties and early forties, whose fertility rose. The divergence was especially noticeable among females in social classes I and II. Similar trends in marital fertility since the Second World War were evident throughout western Europe and much of the rest of the developed world.[59]

Even before 1914 regional variations in levels of marital fertility in England and Wales were modest and steadily decreasing. By the early 1930s low rates of fertility within marriage were the norm almost everywhere. In Scotland, though less marked than on the continent of Europe, regional marital fertility differentials were more pronounced than in England and Wales and widened between the 1870s and the outbreak of the Second World War. In some of the more remote parts of the Scottish Highlands, indeed, levels of marital fertility remained high until well into the 1930s. After 1945, however, in Scotland as elsewhere in Europe regional variations in marital fertility rates markedly decreased.[60]

Differences in rates of marital fertility by socio-occupational class long pre-dated the onset of the modern fertility decline in the mid 1870s. During the initial stages of the transition to lower fertility, from the mid 1870s to the First World War, the differences probably widened. Since the First World War, as elsewhere in western Europe, they have narrowed. Until the middle of the twentieth century the fertility of married couples varied inversely with social class, rising from its lowest level in social class I (mainly the highest status professional occupations) to progressively higher levels in social classes II (managers, senior administrators and other professional occupations of intermediate status), IIIN (non-manual workers such as clerks and salesmen), IIIM (skilled manual workers), IV (the semi-skilled) and V (the unskilled). By the second half of the century rates of marital fertility in social class II had fallen below those in social class I and were lowest of all in social class IIIN. Otherwise, in broad terms at least, fertility differentials within marriage have continued to correlate negatively with socio-occupational status.[61]

Causes of Marital Fertility Decline

Why did rates of marital fertility decline between the mid 1870s and the 1930s and why have they remained low ever since?

At its most superficial level the explanation lies in the increasing awareness, acceptability, availability and application of ever-more effective techniques for limiting the frequency of conception. Birth control practices within marriage were not, of course, wholly new to the late nineteenth and twentieth centuries. What was new was an unprecedented growth in the willingness of married couples to resort to them. Spurred on by the publicity given to the Bradlaugh–Besant trial of 1877 and, subsequently, by the spread of more liberal attitudes to sex provoked by the First World War and the work of Marie Stopes in the immediate postwar years, popular appreciation of the aims and means of family planning increased dramatically. For the first time the advocacy and adoption of 'artificial' methods of contraception within marriage became publicly acceptable. By the 1930s, if only when it could be justified on health grounds, even those bastions of sexual conservatism, the Anglican church and the British Medical Association, were prepared to advocate birth control practices.[62]

Accompanying these advances in awareness and acceptability were advances in the accessibility and efficiency of birth control technology itself. Most of the innovations in contraceptive techniques before the First World War – the rubber condom, the Dutch cap, the douche and chemical spermicides of one kind or another – were expensive or difficult to utilise and therefore restricted mainly to upper- and middle-class sections of society. On the whole, those working-class couples who had already begun to reduce their fertility continued to rely on abortion, abstention or the less reliable method of *coitus interruptus*, a fact which goes some way towards explaining why social class differentials in fertility widened during the initial phase of the modern fertility decline. By the interwar period the new mechanical and chemical methods of contraception were less costly and more accessible and, as a result, working-class fertility began to decline more rapidly. After the Second World War innovations such as the female contraceptive pill, the coil and sterilisation further improved the cost-effectiveness of birth control technology and helped continue the progress towards narrower differentials in socio-occupational class fertility rates.

All scholars are agreed that improvements in birth control methods played some part in making the transition to lower levels of marital fertility possible. At the same time, given that traditional rather than modern techniques of contraception remained the dominant means of family limitation throughout the period down to the middle of the twentieth century when the bulk of the fertility decline occurred,[63] it would be unwise to accord them too much importance. According to Crafts, advances in birth control technology and reductions in the real cost of modern contraceptive devices accounted for no more than half of the decline in levels of fertility which occurred in England and Wales between 1895 and 1938, a view shared by most other students of the phenomenon.[64]

In any case, whether it involved the more widespread application of old methods or the adoption of new ones, contraception was merely the *instrument* by which lower levels of marital fertility were brought about. The crucial questions are why birth control techniques were more extensively adopted and why lower fertility norms became desirable.

From the outset attempts to answer these questions have focused on various aspects of the process of modernisation. This is not to deny that there have been occasions when reductions in fertility were designed to preserve rather than to destroy traditional values and customs. Interpretations of the fertility decline couched simply in terms of the effects of a transition from traditional to modern productive, attitudinal and behavioural systems can sometimes be misleading. In the case of the Sicilian peasantry, for instance, the adoption of lower fertility norms was intended to protect age-old traditions which, for various reasons, were becoming increasingly difficult to sustain.[65] Even in these cases, however, the achievement of lower fertility would not have been possible without at least some of the prerequisites for fertility control which originated in the process of modernisation. Generally there can be no doubt that the fertility transition was a corollary of modernisation, broadly defined, and would have been inconceivable without it.[66] The problem has always been to identify those facets of the modernisation process that were most responsible. Was the fertility transition chiefly a response to prior reductions in levels of infant and child mortality? Was it mainly a consequence of the changes in economic and social structures which accompanied modernisation and, if so, of which ones in particular? Or was it principally due to changes in ideational systems which emerged independently of the process of modern economic development?

In theory there is every reason to suppose a close relationship between levels of fertility and levels of mortality in infancy and childhood. The lower the rate of mortality in infancy and childhood the greater the need for parents to limit their fertility in the interests of ensuring that the financial and emotional costs of children do not exceed what they can afford. Lower infant and child death rates also reduce the necessity for couples to bear large numbers of children in order to ensure support in old age and, at the same time, increase the amount of emotional energy they lavish on children. A child-centred family culture of the kind that had emerged by the early twentieth century, it has been argued, is only feasible when infant and child survival rates are high enough to make it worthwhile for parents to invest considerable time and affection on their offspring.

In practice the extent to which the fertility transition depended on a prior decline in infant and child mortality has provoked much dispute. Chesnais has recently concluded that, though by no means the only factor involved, the reduction in mortality in infancy and early childhood should be given principal responsibility for the trend to lower fertility norms. Indeed, had it not been for the part played by overseas emigration in relieving Britain and other European countries of an excess population caused by falling mortality, the fertility transition may have begun even earlier, and proceeded more rapidly, than it did.[67]

Few scholars have been prepared to go quite so far, though most accept that declining infant and child mortality did make a significant contribution to the adoption of lower fertility schedules.[68] For some, however, even this is to claim too much. It has been pointed out, for instance, that variations in marital fertility by socio-occupational class in England and Wales in the period 1870–1914 were only partially related to variations in infant and child death rates.[69] Cross-sectional analysis of data for the urban populations of England and Wales in 1911 indicates only a weak correlation between fertility and levels of mortality in infancy and childhood, suggesting that the contribution of declining mortality to the decrease in marital fertility between the mid 1870s and the late 1930s was minimal.[70] Within each region of England and Wales, moreover, temporal fluctuations in fertility and rates of mortality in early childhood were so closely synchronised that it is difficult to see how couples could have been basing their subsequent reproductive decisions on the mortality experience of previous births. Throughout the late nineteenth and first half of the twentieth centuries national and regional trends in infant and child death rates were always more variable than those in marital fertility and, whereas in the course of the period regional differentials in mortality diminished, those in fertility did not. In at least one sub-period, 1885–98, while fertility rates fell in every region of England and Wales, rates of child mortality rose in some regions, fell in others and for England and Wales as a whole altered little. None of this suggests that the contribution of declining infant and child death rates to the fertility transition deserves special emphasis.[71] If survival rates early in life were as crucial to fertility decisions as some believe, why did the trend to lower fertility not begin earlier in rural areas, where mortality in infancy and childhood was relatively low, than in urban areas, where it was relatively high? The answer must be that there are determinants of reproductive behaviour more important than levels of mortality in the first year or so of life.

Among the most influential of these was the process of economic modernisation. Declining rates of infant and child mortality, of course, were themselves largely a consequence of the rising standards of nutrition, medical care and personal and public hygiene made possible by advances in education, technology and wealth. Of more direct and critical significance for trends in marital fertility, however, were the effects of modern economic growth on levels of real income, the extent and character of female employment, patterns of income distribution, the availability of consumer goods and the structure of the family economy.

The implications for marital fertility of rising levels of per capita real income depend on the nature of the environment within which the latter occur.[72] When not accompanied by changes in tastes, costs and knowledge, higher real incomes make it easier to support additional children and act to promote fertility. Where they help to widen the range of consumer choice and are accompanied by a need for children of improved quality and therefore greater cost, they work to alter patterns of parental expenditure in ways that are inimical to fertility.[73] As one scholar has put it, while the direct effects of economic growth tend to encourage procreation, the indirect, or social, effects of economic growth tend to discourage it.[74] In economies and socio-occupational groups where incomes are close to subsistence and the range of goods and services available as alternatives to children are relatively restricted, a rise in per capita income is more likely to increase than decrease fertility, hence the apparent rise in birth rates during the initial stages of the British Industrial Revolution.[75] By the late nineteenth century the economic environment within which fertility decisions were taken was very different. For the bulk of the population continued economic growth, assisted by the import of cheap food from the countries of the New World, had lifted incomes comfortably above basic subsistence levels and broadened the range of goods and services available for purchase as alternatives to children. The result was that more people than ever before were in a position to choose between expenditures on children and expenditures on material goods or leisure activities. Increasingly they chose the latter. Before the First World War the contribution of rising incomes to the decline in fertility in England and Wales was probably modest and in Scotland rates of marital fertility remained highest in regions where the pace of economic growth and opportunities for employment were greatest. By the interwar period, however, it was usually regions and occupations with the lowest per capita incomes and highest rates of unemployment, where additional children were less likely to be seen as a threat to improvements in living standards, that had the highest fertility levels.[76] To the extent that economic growth and rising real incomes were accompanied by increased rates of social mobility and a decline in regional, and especially rural-urban, income differentials, the range of conditions favourable to reductions in marital fertility widened still further.[77]

One of the features of economic modernisation given particular emphasis in recent explanations of the modern fertility decline is the changes that have taken place in the extent and character of women's employment. The explanation stems from the observation that socio-occupational differentials in fertility relate inversely to the proportion of women in paid employment outside the home; in coalmining populations, where women were rarely gainfully employed, fertility was relatively high; in the textile industries, where women were more extensively employed, fertility was relatively low.[78] Most of the increase in female employment opportunities in the first half of the twentieth century was confined to unmarried women. As the employment of single women in manufacturing industry, technical and clerical services and the professions increased while that in home-based occupations like domestic service decreased, so they became more independent and more exposed to the liberating influences of higher wages, more leisure time and the greater knowledge generated by increased contact with the media and other females. Together these influences ensured that marriage, when it came, was a more equal partnership between husband and wife than it had ever been before. One inevitable consequence was a reduction in the frequency of childbearing.[79]

Since the Second World War, and especially since the 1960s, the effect on marital fertility of growing opportunities for employment among unmarried women has been reinforced by a revolutionary increase in the extent of employment among married women, itself a product of the relatively rapid recent growth of the service sector of the economy. This produced a range of occupations and occupational environments so much more congenial to women than the physically arduous, repetitive, dirty and largely manufacturing work hitherto available that even married women, who usually have less need to seek employment than single women, were increasingly willing to forego childbirth in order to benefit from the additional income, independence and self-esteem they permitted.[80] Given that much of the modern decline in fertility had already been accomplished by the time married women first became extensively employed outside the home, the rise in labour participation ratios among married females was clearly less significant for the fertility transition than the growth of employment opportunities for unmarried females. Probably, too, neither influence was as important as the contribution made by the effect of economic modernisation on the nature of the family economy and, in particular, on the position of children within it.[81]

Three aspects of the changes which have occurred in the economic role of the family have been especially critical in reducing levels of marital fertility. The first was the transfer of support for elderly, infirm or unemployed parents from children to the state or private, commercial organisations, a transfer made possible by an unprecedented rise in levels of personal and community wealth. Even if this argument somewhat exaggerates the extent of the support provided by children in earlier times, there is no doubt that the emergence of alternative sources of succour for parents in crisis or old age has helped to undermine the necessity for high fertility norms.[82] More crucial to an understanding of the causes of the fertility transition, however, were two other changes in the nature of the family economy: the replacement of the family by large-scale, capitalist institutions as the principal producer of material goods; and the requirements of increasingly sophisticated forms of business organisation and technology for an ever more highly educated and competitively selected labour force.

In traditional economies, where the family was the main supplier of goods and most productive processes had little need for highly trained and formally educated labour, even if the net returns to children were slighter and less prolonged than is sometimes supposed, large numbers of offspring were an economic asset. Because children made a substantial contribution to family income and required little in the way of expenditure on training and education in return, the distribution of family resources favoured the adult male family head and the elderly at the expense of the young and other dependants. The resulting upward flow of wealth meant that men dominated the decision-making process and, coupled with the belief that children were a valuable source of labour and security, ensured that fertility norms remained high.

In modern economies the function of the family, and thus the distribution of resources and authority within it, differs. Partly because of the need for a more educated workforce, selected in the interests of efficiency on the basis of educational attainment rather than personal patronage, and partly because of the introduction of legislation against child employment, children are a net financial burden. At least until the second half of the twentieth century, when the employment of married women outside the home first reached significant levels, the result was a steady increase in the share of total family income contributed by the adult male breadwinner and a redistribution of family resources in favour of children. This gave husbands as well as wives a powerful incentive to limit fertility. Simultaneously, the authority of parents over their offspring was being eroded by the spread of formal systems of education which undermined the claims of parents to greater knowledge and wisdom, replaced success in domestic chores by success in schoolwork as the principal determinant of status and advancement and encouraged among the young a sense of egalitarianism, individualism and rationality and levels of expectation that were often at odds with those of parents and grandparents. As children's respect for parental authority declined and children became more demanding in terms of what they expected parents to provide, the emotional strains of parenthood intensified. On emotional as much as financial grounds having fewer children made sense.[83] Of course, since childrearing itself in many respects became easier in the course of economic modernisation, lower rates of fertility were only acceptable if there existed attractive alternatives to children that would otherwise have had to be foregone. It is no coincidence that only in the last hundred years or so, as a result of the higher incomes, more congenial employment opportunities and proliferation of consumer goods and leisure facilities made possible by economic modernisation, have such alternatives become available for sufficient numbers of people to permit reductions in fertility in all socio-occupational groups.[84]

Recently the search for a satisfactory explanation of the modern fertility transition has switched its emphasis from economic to ideational influences. Some scholars, it is true, maintain that changes in the latter are merely functions of changes in the former and should therefore be regarded as of only secondary importance.[85] Others, however, insist that ideational changes, at least in part, occur independently of economic forces.[86] Whichever view is the correct one, the contribution of ideational impulses to the long-term decline in marital fertility obviously deserves close scrutiny.

According to the ideationalist interpretation, changes in fertility schedules are more a response to changes in attitudes, motives and ideals than to changes in the structure of demographic, economic or technological systems. Ideational change, it is argued, facilitated fertility decline in two ways: first by encouraging attitudes more sympathetic to the use of birth control procedures and more inclined to regard birth control as beneficial; second by altering the definition of good fatherhood and motherhood in ways that persuaded fathers to become more aware of the burdens imposed on women by excessive childbearing, more involved in domestic duties and more willing to treat marriage as a partnership of equals, and mothers to measure success more in terms of the quality than the quantity of the children they bore. Prompted by the work of health visitors, infant welfare centres, school medical inspectors and care committees, the argument goes, from the early years of the twentieth century relationships between husbands and wives and perceptions of parenthood were redefined in ways inimical to frequent childbearing.[87]

Of all the changes that have occurred in western ideational systems in recent centuries two are considered especially critical to the adoption of lower fertility norms. The first was the trend away from beliefs which regarded procreation as the sole purpose of sexual intercourse and the environment as largely unalterable, towards more secularist, less fatalistic beliefs which encouraged sexual activity for reasons of affection or pleasure, and the notion that the environment was controllable, problems solvable and progress possible. The second was the emergence of a philosophy of individualism which freed the individual from communal and family control, thereby increasing his freedom of choice and action and fostering the pursuit of self-interest, self-respect and self-improvement. To a large extent these changes were a consequence of economic modernisation and the materialist values and aspirations which, particularly from the later decades of the nineteenth century, emerged with it. But they also owed something to the philosophers of the eighteenth-century intellectual enlightenment whose concern for the rights of the individual nourished both criticism of traditional customs and institutions, and the rise of new ideals of liberty and democracy. Together the forces of secularism, rationalism and individualism, complemented by rising standards of education, helped to raise the status of women and children to levels incompatible with the maintenance of high fertility rates.[88]

No one would dispute the truth of Chesnais' claim that explanations of the modern fertility transition must incorporate more than just economic factors. By themselves material circumstances cannot entirely account for what has happened to fertility norms since the late nineteenth century.[89] Some scholars continue to stress the primacy of economic determinants.[90] Others, more impressed by the apparently closer relationship between fertility and cultural, ethnic and linguistic traits than between fertility and economic circumstances, and by the great variety of economic environments within which the fertility transition occurred, prefer to emphasise the role of ideational systems, particularly during the initial stages of the transition.[91] All, however, are agreed that the causes of fertility decline were complex and multilayered. Clearly, some of the most important originated, directly or indirectly, in the process of modern economic growth; lower rates of infant and child mortality; higher real incomes and a wider range of attractive alternatives to children; increased employment opportunities for women; higher child costs; more generous state support for the elderly, infirm and unemployed; increased rates of migration which helped overcome regional cultural barriers to the spread of the small family ideal; and the impact on attitudes to family size of higher standards of material well-being in childhood which impelled future parents to sacrifice excessive childbearing in the interests of maintaining a standard of life they were reluctant to lose.[92] No less important, however, was the influence of more secular and individualistic mentalities and patterns of behaviour which, in part anyway, emerged independently of the process of economic modernisation.

In short, the modern fertility transition had no single cause nor even a single set of causes. Its determinants were so numerous, their mix so varied by time, class and place and their influence so difficult to quantify that many scholars feel it may never be possible to provide an accurate weighting of the relative importance of each of the agents involved, let alone an agreed, overall explanatory model of the phenomenon.[93]

The factors responsible for the variations which have occurred in levels of marital fertility since the Second World War are equally complex and difficult to unravel. Here too the similarities of experience between Britain and other developed countries strongly imply the operation of a common factor or common mix of factors.[94] But what this was has also still to be finally determined.

It is generally agreed that changes in levels of infant and child mortality were of little relevance. While the continued decline of infant and child death rates may have contributed something to the re-emergence of declining levels of marital fertility from the mid 1960s, the rise in marital fertility in the decade or so prior to the mid 1960s occurred at a time of falling, not rising, infant and death rates. The sequence of baby boom and baby bust which was shared by all developed countries in the third quarter of the twentieth century cannot easily be explained by reference to trends in survival rates during the earliest years of life.

Of greater significance was the legalisation of abortion and developments in the technology of birth control. Before the 1967 Abortion Act, which became effective in April 1968 and greatly extended the criteria under which terminations were permitted by law, abortion was legally permissible only when the life of the mother was thought to be at risk. The impact of the Act on abortion rates was spectacular. In England and Wales the number of legal abortions per thousand women aged 15–44 soared from 3.5 in 1968 to 11.4 in 1973. By 1976 it had fallen to 10.5. Thereafter, except in 1983 when there was a slight decline, it rose in each successive year to 15.5 by 1989, a level equivalent to about one abortion for every five recorded conceptions.[95]

In the absence of data on the frequency of illegal abortion it is unclear how much responsibility to attach to the legalisation of abortion for trends in marital fertility from the mid 1960s. Probably its contribution was limited. For one thing the culmination of the baby boom clearly long predated the implementation of the 1967 Act. For another the adoption of more liberal abortion laws was itself a consequence of the forces of economic and ideational change and therefore should not be accorded too independent or significant a role. Thirdly, however much the liberalisation of abortion legislation contributed to the downturn in marital fertility between the late 1960s and late 1970s, it was obviously of little relevance in the 1980s when, despite persistent increases in abortion ratios, fertility rates either stabilised or rose. As Coleman and Salt conclude, the introduction of legalised abortion probably accounted for no more than a fifth of the overall decline in levels of legitimate fertility after 1967–8.[96]

Until the mid 1960s the most common forms of contraception were withdrawal and the use of condoms and chemical spermicides. A female contraceptive pill first became widely available in the early 1960s and by the mid 1970s was the single most popular method of birth control. Among other birth control technologies to have grown in popularity since the 1960s are the intrauterine device and sterilisation. After 1976, as a result of the pill scares of 1970–2 and 1977–8 when higher than anticipated mortality among women using oral contraceptives encouraged those over 30 to switch to alternative methods, reliance on the pill declined and sterilisation, in particular, became increasingly common.

Before 1968 access to the contraceptive services offered by the National Health Service was restricted solely to women with proven medical reasons for avoiding pregnancy. Subsequently, under the terms of the 1967 Family Planning Act, local authorities were empowered, though not obliged, to supply contraceptives and contraceptive advice on social as well as medical grounds, and in practice most did so. From 1972 these powers included the provision of vasectomies for men and, from 1974, sterilisation for women. Beginning in 1974, in the case of contraceptives prescribed and dispensed through local authority NHS clincs, and in 1975, in the case of those supplied by general practitioners, contraceptive services were made available free of charge.[97]

If only because periods of rising or stable rates of fertility from the mid 1950s to mid 1960s and late 1970s to late 1980s were also periods of advance in the extent and efficiency of birth control practices, it is obvious that variations in the incidence and effectiveness of contraception cannot be given the primary responsibility for shaping postwar marital fertility trends. In any case, rates of fertility within marriage had already fallen to very low levels long before the widespread adoption of devices such as the pill, the coil and sterilisation, while similarly low rates of fertility within marriage were also achieved in countries where the most sophisticated methods of birth control were practised much less extensively than in Britain.[98]

Even so, the fact that the reappearance of fertility decline between the mid 1960s and late 1970s coincided with a period of abnormally rapid progress in the availability and application of more efficient, lower cost and easier to use contraceptives suggests that, during this period of least, improved birth control technologies did make some contribution to the reduction in family size.

In this context it is often argued that the female contraceptive pill played a particularly important role. Improvements in birth control methods, it has been suggested, may help to explain why Roman Catholics, whose fertility declined especially rapidly, increasingly denied a value system which discouraged all 'artificial' forms of family limitation.[99] According to Ni Bhrolchain, the greater ability of improved birth control devices to prevent unwanted pregnancies also helps to explain why the growth of female employment between the mid 1950s and early 1960s was accompanied by rising fertility, while its continued growth in the later 1960s and 1970s was accompanied by falling fertility.[100] Murphy goes even further. In his view the female contraceptive pill, adopted not in response to the forces of socio-economic or ideational change but simply because it was a more effective means of avoiding pregnancy than any previously available, was the *principal* determinant of British marital fertility trends between the mid 1960s and late 1970s. Significantly, Murphy claims, when concern over the health-risks of the pill in the early and late 1970s led to reductions in its use, the switch to less reliable methods of contraception was followed by a temporary increase in the number of conceptions.[101]

Yet, even for the period between the mid 1960s and late 1970s when the relationship between improved methods of contraception and falling rates of fertility appears strongest, the case for interpreting fertility trends in terms of changes in the nature of birth control technology should not be pressed too far. Fundamental to its validity is the assumption that the baby bust was a consequence not of a reduction in the number of children *desired* but of the success of improved contraception in reducing the number of *unwanted* conceptions. The flaw in this assumption is that decreasing numbers of unwanted pregnancies accounted for only a small part of the overall drop in fertility between the mid 1960s and late 1970s. Fertility fell because couples wanted fewer children, not because better contraceptive technology made it easier to avoid overshooting fertility targets which were as low during the period of the baby boom as during the period of the baby bust. Undue emphasis on the contribution of the pill also sits uncomfortably with the fact that a similar decline in fertility occurred in other European countries where the pill was not extensively used. Furthermore, although the temporary upturn in fertility in 1971 correlated reasonably neatly with the pill scare of 1970–2 and may well have been caused by it, fertility had already begun to rise before the second pill scare of 1977–8 and must have originated in factors other than a switch to less effective methods of contraception. While allowing new birth control technology some part in initiating the collapse of the late 1950s and early 1960s baby boom, it is surely more appropriate to regard this technology more as a means than a basic cause of the further decline in levels of marital fertility which began in the second half of the 1960s. In the main it is to changes in socio-economic and ideational circumstances that we should turn for an explanation of postwar fertility fluctuations.[102]

To some extent, it has been suggested, variations in levels of marital fertility after the Second World War were simply the result of variations in levels of general prosperity. In conditions like those of Britain before the mid 1960s, where few married women were employed outside the home, rates of fertility (and nuptiality) were partly a direct function of trends in the earning capacity of men. During the years of severe economic depression between the world wars, when levels of unemployment were high, housing relatively expensive and difficult to obtain, and male real wages much lower than they were subsequently to be, rates of marital fertility fell.[103] Once the brief postwar surge in marriage and fertility was completed, economic austerity and housing shortages in the late 1940s and early 1950s combined to reduce fertility rates to levels no higher than in the 1930s. In the decade or so beginning around the mid 1950s, by contrast, the pace of economic growth accelerated, unemployment largely disappeared, male real incomes soared and, thanks to extensive public and private sector building programmes, the problem of housing shortage was considerably alleviated. The result, achieved primarily through an increase in the numbers of first and second births, was an unexpected boom in marital fertility. The boom was intensified by the fact that economic depression in the interwar period, together with the demands made on resources by the needs of war and postwar industrial reconstruction, greatly reduced the standard of living expectations of consumers throughout the 1950s and early 1960s. Because this coincided with a period of dramatic improvement in the real wages of men, it widened the gap between incomes and expectations and thus increased the surplus available for spending on additional children. Frequent contemporary comparisons between the performance of the economy before and after the mid 1950s added another powerful, psychological impulse in favour of higher fertility. After the mid 1960s, the argument continues, declining rates of economic growth, increasing economic instability and rising levels of unemployment and inflation, coupled with the effect of higher standard of living expectations created during the years of prosperity in the 1950s and early 1960s, worked to force fertility down.[104]

For the period before the mid 1960s the association between periods of low fertility and low incomes–high unemployment, and periods of high fertility and high incomes–low unemployment is sufficiently regular to support the belief that temporal trends in levels of fertility were at least partly a direct response to variations in rates of economic growth. Since the mid 1960s, however, the nature of the relationship between fertility and economic growth has changed from positive to negative: whenever real incomes have risen and unemployment fallen, rates of marital fertility have decreased, not increased. Thus, rising per capita real incomes between 1970 and 1976 were accompanied by a decline in fertility, and falling real incomes in 1977 by a rise in fertility between 1978 and 1980. In most recent times, it seems, periods of rising income have increased the attractions of alternatives to childbearing and discouraged rather than encouraged conception.[105] A similar change took place in the nature of the relationship between fertility and housing. In contrast to the experience of earlier periods when levels of fertility correlated positively with the availability of housing, the decline in fertility after the mid 1960s occurred against a background of improving, not deteriorating, housing provision.[106]

The absence of a positive correlation between rates of fertility and rates of economic growth in the period since the mid 1960s has led some scholars to suggest that a more convincing explanation of postwar fertility trends lies in the changes which have occurred in the relationship between the incomes of parents and their children.

The explanation has been presented in two forms. The first, developed by Easterlin, sees the evolution of marital fertility chiefly as a result of changes in the relationship between the earnings and standard of living expectations of young adults of childbearing age, on the one hand, and the earnings of their fathers, on the other. If, on entering adulthood, the earnings of sons relative to those of their fathers are high, standard of living expectations fashioned in childhood and adolescence will be relatively easy to attain and fertility will rise. If, however, a son's earnings are low relative to those of the father, expectations established in childhood will be higher and more difficult to attain and fertility will decline in order to satisfy them.[107] In the alternative variant, developed by Oppenheimer, the 'relative income' (or 'relative economic status') of adult sons is determined not only by their earnings relative to those of their fathers, but also relative both to those of their mothers and to the size of the family in which sons spent their childhood and adolescence. Generally, the income and standard of living aspirations of adult sons compared to those of their parents varies inversely with the size of their birth cohort. For sons born during periods of low fertility, early adulthood is associated with abundant opportunities for education, employment and advancement and incomes sufficient to permit high fertility without sacrificing their material expectations. Sons born during periods of high fertility, on the other hand, face greater competition for work and training when they reach adulthood. Compared with those of their parents, earnings and prospects will be poor, and fertility has to be reduced to allow standard of living aspirations to be achieved. Thus, the argument goes, for children born during the low fertility decade of the 1930s and entering the labour market in the prosperous 1950s and early 1960s 'relative incomes' were sufficiently high to provoke a boom in births; for children born during the higher fertility era of the 1950s and early 1960s, who entered the more depressed and crowded labour markets of the 1970s and early 1980s, standard of living aspirations were harder to attain and baby boom accordingly gave way to baby bust.[108]

Empirical tests of the Easterlin–Oppenheimer variants of the 'relative income' interpretation of twentieth-century marital fertility trends have yielded mixed results. In the case of Germany the significance of the Easterlin variant has been described as 'weak', and even for the United States, for which it was initially devised, recent studies have failed to confirm its claims.[109] In the case of Britain, it seems to have some validity in the period down to the mid 1960s, when married women contributed little to family income, but not thereafter, when married women's contribution to family income increased. According to Crafts, trends in 'relative income' (as defined by Easterlin) go a long way towards explaining the decline in rates of fertility in England and Wales between 1877 and 1937.[110] As the Easterlin thesis predicts, rising levels of fertility in Britain between 1955 and 1964 coincided with, and were partly caused by, higher incomes relative to standard of living expectations among adult sons than among their fathers. Yet, as indicated by the lack of an obvious relationship between variations in fertility and 'relative income' during the years 1961–4, even within the period 1955–64 the correlation between the two variables was not always close. After the mid 1960s it almost entirely disappeared. Whereas fertility rates began to fall from 1964, the 'relative incomes' of childbearing age groups continued to rise into 1965–6. And, while declining rates of fertility coincided with declining 'relative incomes' in the later 1960s, the quickening pace of fertility decline in the 1970s occurred against a background of markedly improving 'relative incomes' among young adult males. At best, it seems, the Easterlin model is of only limited value as an explanation of postwar British marital fertility trends.[111]

Oppenheimer's variant of the 'relative income' hypothesis, in which rising levels of employment among mothers aged 35–44 in the 1950s and early 1960s increased standard of living expectations and thus depressed the 'relative income' of their adult children, has generally been considered a more satisfactory explanation for the downturn in fertility rates in the second half of the 1960s and 1970s. However, as Ermisch points out, its appeal owes much to the fact that it is difficult to subject to rigorous empirical testing. In the real world the effect of increasing female employment on the 'relative income' of children is especially difficult to quantify. Whether or not 'relative income' (as defined by Oppenheimer) did decline after 1964 remains unclear.[112] Supporters of the Oppenheimer interpretation can take little comfort from the findings of a recent analysis of the relationship between fertility and cohort size in 16 European countries since 1950 which shows that, with the *possible* and at best only partial exceptions of Belgium, England and Wales, Finland, France and Italy, temporal trends in rates of fertility have not been dominated by the workings of the 'relative income' variable.[113] No less disturbing is the fact that cohort studies carried out for Britain as a whole show a positive, not negative, correlation between a woman's fertility and the size of the family in which she grew up.[114] The implication is that neither the Easterlin nor the Oppenheimer variants of the 'relative income' hypothesis can safely be regarded as adequate explanations of fertility trends since the Second World War.

Of all the suggested explanations of postwar variations in marital fertility, the one currently seen as best fitting the pattern of boom and bust is the 'New Home Economics' thesis. This argues that the evolution of fertility in Britain and other developed countries in recent times has been determined primarily by changes in the proportions of married women employed outside the home, and thus in the ratios of women's to men's wages. The thesis is based on the premise that attitudes to procreation differ from household to household according to whether or not the woman is gainfully employed. In households where the man is the sole breadwinner rising real incomes lead to an increase in fertility. In households where both partners are employed, growing opportunities for female employment and increases in the ratio of female to male earnings encourage women to seek work and, by raising the opportunity costs of time of children, reduce fertility.[115]

Initially conceived for the United States, the 'New Home Economics' model has received widespread support as an explanation of postwar British marital fertility trends. Partly as a result of the growth of non-manual, service occupations after the mid 1960s, and partly in response to the passing of an Equal Pay Act in 1970, which required that women receive the same rate of pay as men for the same job and thus helped to raise the ratio of female to male wages from under two-thirds in the 1960s to around three-quarters by the mid 1970s, the proportion of economically active women in the age groups 20–64 rose from about one-third throughout the first half of the century to 42 per cent by 1961, 52 per cent by 1971, and 61 per cent by 1981.[116] On the eve of the First World War and throughout the interwar period fewer than one in ten married women were employed outside the home. By the mid 1960s the figure had risen to nearly four in ten and by the late 1980s to six in ten.[117] One authority has estimated that for a cross-section of British mothers in 1980 the income that would have been lost by having children amounted to as much as 43 per cent of a mother's lifetime earnings.[118]

The consequences for marital fertility, it is claimed, were unmistakable. Throughout the 1950s and early 1960s levels of employment among married women and the ratio of female to male earnings were not yet high enough to offset the effect of rising male real incomes and, as a result, rates of marital fertility increased. After the mid 1960s they were, with the result that first births were increasingly postponed, childbearing became increasingly concentrated on women in their late twenties and early thirties, and overall levels of fertility within marriage declined.[119] But for the increase in the ratio of female to male wages which followed the implementation of the Equal Pay Act the number of births registered in England and Wales between 1975 and 1978 may well have been as much as 8 per cent higher than it was.[120] When in the late 1970s the ratio of female to male wages and the percentage of families in which both partners were employed temporarily declined, fertility rates once more began to rise.[121] The fact that variations in the extent of female employment are also known to have been a significant determinant of regional and socio-occupational class differentials in fertility may be taken as further testimony to the validity of the 'New Home Economics' model.[122]

Precisely which aspect of this model exercised the greatest influence on fertility rates has still to be finally resolved. Arguably, rising levels of female employment *per se* were less important than other facets of the female work experience. Contrary to what the model predicts, low rates of fertility in postwar Japan coincided with unusually low, not high, ratios of married women in employment.[123] In Britain rates of marital fertility among upper-class females changed little after the Second World War despite a considerable increase in their labour participation ratios, while the fertility of working-class females, whose participation in gainful employment remained relatively constant, decreased.[124]

More important, perhaps, were the effects of changes which occurred in the timing of married women's employment. By encouraging women to shorten their birth intervals and increase the tempo of childbearing in the early years of married life, growing opportunities for female employment during the 1950s and early 1960s worked to raise overall levels of marital fertility.[125] By the 1970s, because they were now accompanied by a new tendency for married women to return to work between births, improved job prospects for females acted to lengthen birth intervals and thus to reduce aggregate marital fertility rates.

But the aspect of the 'New Home Economics' interpretation which probably exerted the greatest influence on marital fertility, at least in the 1970s, was the sudden and pronounced improvement which occurred in the ratio of female to male earnings following the 1970 Equal Pay Act. This alone goes a long way towards explaining why rates of fertility in Britain fell by 26 per cent between 1970 and 1975, compared with a fall of just 16 per cent between 1965 and 1970 and a *rise* of 6 per cent between 1976 and 1981.[126]

To interpret variations in levels of marital fertility in the second half of the twentieth century solely in economic terms, however, is unwise and misleading. The baby boom of the mid 1950s to mid 1960s, for example, was due to much more than the influence of economic forces alone. In part it also owed something to the fact that the men and women who were then of reproductive age retained some of the mentalities of an earlier value system which favoured higher fertility norms. In part it was the understandable reaction of a generation that had lived through the traumas of war and for which the attractions of a secure and full family life were particularly appealing. In part too it reflected the emergence of a more sympathetic attitude towards children, itself a combined result of wartime propaganda emphasising the importance of woman's role as mother and sexual comforter of man, growing concern over the potential economic and political dangers thought to be inherent in low rates of population growth, and the introduction of government initiatives to strengthen family values and reduce the costs of childrearing in response to this concern.

The subsequent baby bust likewise owed much to non-economic influences. Children born between the mid 1940s and mid 1960s, and especially those born in the prosperous 1950s and early 1960s, avoided the disappointments and traumas suffered by their parents and were therefore inclined to regard high fertility less sympathetically. In this they were encouraged by a radical re-evaluation of the population problem, which substituted a concern for too few people with a concern for too many people. Coupled with advances in education and science which further eroded traditional rationales for high fertility and the political uncertainties provoked by the Cold War and conflicts in Vietnam and elsewhere, attitudinal changes of this type contributed significantly to the downturn in fertility rates from the mid 1960s.

Fundamental to them all, however, was an accelerating transformation of values away from a primary concern with the interests of collective 'institutions' such as kinship networks, the church, the community and the state, which favoured high fertility, towards a primary concern with the interests of the individual, which favoured low fertility. When, as in the twenty years or so immediately following the Second World War, collective and individual interests happened to coincide, rates of marital fertility rose. When, as has increasingly been the case since the mid 1960s, these interests conflicted, rates of marital fertility declined. Under the impact of a value system which gave so much encouragement to ambitions for self-fulfilment and self-improvement it was inevitable that more importance would be attached to the quality than the quantity of children and that rates of fertility would once again start to decline.[127] When its ideational determinants are added to its economic determinants, it is clear that the causes of short-term variations in levels of marital fertility during the second half of the twentieth century are just as intricate and difficult to quantify as the factors responsible for the permanent reduction in marital fertility targets which began in the later decades of the nineteenth century.[128]

CONCLUSION

Perhaps because of the greater challenges afforded by the relative paucity of its source-materials and the partial and at times dubious reliability of the raw demographic data these yield, historians of population have always shown more interest in the demography of the more distant than the more recent past.

By improving our understanding of earlier trends in rates of population growth and the mechanisms of fertility, mortality and migration that were responsible for them, this preference has made it possible to better appreciate the dramatic nature of the changes which have occurred in demographic systems during the last hundred years or so. This is not, of course, to deny the existence of significant demographic changes in earlier times. The period between the late eighteenth and late nineteenth centuries, for instance, was characterised by wholly unprecedented innovations in rates of population increase, patterns of internal migration and residential distribution and levels of overseas migration. And, as we have seen, some of what were to become established features of twentieth-century demography – among them the persistence of high volumes of emigration and immigration and of net losses on balance of international migration, the decline in fertility and the rise in life expectancy – had already begun to emerge in the late nineteenth century, or in some cases even earlier. Generally, however, the startling differences between the demographic environments of present day

Conclusion

and late eighteenth-century Britain, outlined and analysed in this book, were a twentieth-century creation.

If the word 'revolutionary' can ever safely be applied to phases of population history, it is surely more appropriate to apply it to the period after rather than before the turn into our own century. Low and declining rates of population growth after the First World War were not in themselves a new phenomenon, but the fact that they were caused by falling fertility rather than rising mortality certainly was. Twentieth-century migrational and residential patterns favouring the south over the north, peripheral at the expense of core regions and smaller rather than larger communities, in nature if not in degree and causation reminiscent of pre-industrial times, differed fundamentally from the patterns of mobility and population location which prevailed throughout the later eighteenth and nineteenth centuries. The decline in rates of fertility and mortality, though already underway in the late nineteenth century, was likewise overwhelmingly a twentieth-century phenomenon, while levels of divorce, remarriage, extramarital cohabitation and illegitimacy in the later decades of the century reached heights unparalleled among previous generations. In these and numerous other respects the demography of Britain in the present century contrasts starkly with that of even the immediately preceding centuries.

It would be surprising, indeed, if it did not. Essentially, though not of course entirely, demographic systems are a function of the character of the economic environment within which they exist, and of the cultural, social and political circumstances which this environment helps to create. Until well into the second half of the nineteenth century the impact of the Industrial Revolution on the technology, scale and composition of economic activity, and thus on the demography of the society, was relatively muted. Beginning in the late nineteenth century the pace of technological and economic change accelerated dramatically. Inevitably this was accompanied by the emergence of a demographic system radically different from that which had persisted more or less unaltered in its broad fundamentals for centuries.

NOTES

1 POPULATION GROWTH AND LOCATION

1. E. A. Wrigley and R. S. Schofield, *The Population History of England, 1541–1871. A Reconstruction* (London, 1981), pp. 531–4.
2. The exceptions include Finland, Iceland, Northern Ireland, Portugal and the Irish Republic.
3. For example in Belgium, Denmark, Germany, Italy, Luxembourg, Sweden and the Irish Republic.
4. M. W. Flinn (ed.), *Scottish Population History from the Seventeenth Century to the 1930s* (Cambridge, 1977), p. 306.
5. R. Lawton, 'Population Changes in England and Wales in the Later Nineteenth Century: An Analysis of Trends by Registration Districts', *Transactions of the Institute of British Geographers*, XLIV (1968), 57, 62, 65. R. Lawton, 'Regional Population Trends in England and Wales, 1750–1971', in J. Hobcraft and P. Rees (eds), *Regional Demographic Development* (London, 1978), 32–3, 36–8, 40, 46, 52. D. Coleman and J. Salt, *The British Population, Patterns, Trends and Processes* (Oxford, 1992), p. 94.
6. A. G. Champion, 'Population Trends in the 1970s', in J. B. Goddard and A. G. Champion (eds), *The Urban and Regional Transformation of Britain* (London, 1983), p. 200.
7. S. Kennett and N. Spence, 'British Population Trends in the 1970s', *Town and Country Planning*, 48 (1979), 223. W. Randolph and S. Robert, 'Population Redistribution in Great Britain,

1971–81', *Town and Country Planning*, 50 (1981), 227. S. Robert and W. Randolph, 'Beyond Decentralization: the Evolution of Population Distribution in England and Wales, 1961–81', *Geoforum*, 14, 1 (1983), 81. Champion, 'Population Trends in the 1970s', 196–7, 200. A. G. Champion, 'Recent Changes in the Pace of Population Deconcentration in Britain', *Geoforum*, 18, 4 (1987), 383–6. M. Britton, 'Recent Population Changes in Perspective', *Population Trends*, 44 (1986), 34–5. Coleman and Salt, *The British Population*, p. 95. In the period 1971–4, when rates of population growth in the South East, South West and East Anglia barely exceeded those in the rest of Britain, the north–south drift of residence was temporarily halted. It re-emerged in the later 1970s. J. B. Goddard, 'Structural Change in the British Space Economy', in Goddard and Champion (eds), *Urban and Regional Transformation*, p. 15.

8. A. G. Champion, 'Population Trends in Rural Britain', *Population Trends*, 26 (1981), 22. Champion, 'Population Trends in the 1970s', 206. Champion, 'Recent Changes in the Pace of Population Deconcentration', 386. Coleman and Salt, *The British Population*, p. 89. Randolph and Robert, 'Population Redistribution', 228.
9. The region includes Argyll and Bute, Orkney, Shetlands and the Western Isles. Most of the growth was concentrated at Aviemore, Fort William, Invergordon and Inverness. H. Jones, J. Caird, W. Berry and J. Dewhurst, 'Peripheral Counter-Urbanization: Findings from an Integration of Census and Survey Data in Northern Scotland', *Regional Studies*, 20 (1986), 16.
10. Flinn (ed.), *Scottish Population History*, pp. 313–15.
11. Urban areas defined as settlements with a high degree of population density and a minimum of 2500 inhabitants. C. M. Law, 'The Growth of Urban Population in England and Wales 1801–1911', *Transactions of the Institute of British Geographers*, XLI (1967), 130. C. M. Law, 'Some Notes on the Urban Population of England and Wales in the 18th Century', *The Local Historian*, 10, 1 (1972), 18–19, 22. For details of the spatial evolution of urbanisation in England and Wales see D. Friedlander, 'The Spread of Urbanisation in England and Wales, 1851–1951', *Population Studies*, 24, 3 (1970), 422–43.
12. OPCS, Registrar-General Scotland, *Census 1981. Key Statistics for Urban Areas. Great Britain. Cities and Towns* (London, 1984), pp. 107–8.
13. From data in B. R. Mitchell with P. Deane, *Abstract of British Historical Statistics* (Cambridge, 1962), pp. 24–7.

Notes

14. S. R. Kennett, 'Migration Within and Between Labour Markets', in Goddard and Champion (eds), *Urban and Regional Transformation*, p. 217. Champion, 'Population Trends in the 1970s', 189. A. G. Champion, 'United Kingdom: Population Deconcentration as a Cyclic Phenomenon', in A. G. Champion (ed.), *Counterurbanization: The Changing Pace and Nature of Population Deconcentration* (London, 1989), pp. 83, 88, 90. Coleman and Salt, *The British Population*, p. 96.
15. Randolph and Robert, 'Population Redistribution', 88. Champion, 'United Kingdom', 89–90.
16. During the 1960s the population of Liverpool fell by over 18 per cent, of Manchester and Newcastle by over 17 per cent and of Birmingham by over 8 per cent, losses that were between two and three times greater than in the 1950s. Champion, 'Population Trends in the 1970s', 189.
17. Champion, 'Population Trends in the 1970s', 190. Kennett, 'Migration Within and Between Labour Markets', 217.
18. Coleman and Salt, *The British Population*, p. 99.
19. Robert and Randolph, 'Beyond Decentralization', 79, 90.
20. Principal cities – Birmingham, Leeds, Liverpool, London, Manchester, Sheffield. Large cities – Bristol, Cardiff, Derby, Hull, Leicester, Nottingham, Plymouth, Southampton, Stoke, Swansea. Small cities – Bath, Brighton, Cambridge, Cheltenham, Durham, Exeter, Gloucester, Lincoln, Middlesborough, Newport, Norwich, Oxford, Preston, Reading, York, Worcester. Coleman and Salt, *The British Population*, pp. 96, 102, 104. Robert and Randolph, 'Beyond Decentralization', 76, 80. Kennett and Spence, 'British Population Trends in the 1970s', 221. Kennett, 'Migration Within and Between Labour Markets', 217, 219, 221.
21. Coleman and Salt, *The British Population*, p. 105. Champion, 'United Kingdom', 91.
22. Kennett and Spence, 'British Population Trends in the 1970s', 222–3. Randolph and Robert, 'Population Redistribution', 228. Robert and Randolph, 'Beyond Decentralization', 83. Champion, 'Population Trends in the 1970s', 194, 204. Britton, 'Recent Population Changes in Perspective', 33, 35–8. Champion, 'Recent Changes in the Pace of Population Deconcentration', 379, 381, 389, 391. A. G. Champion and P. D. Congdon, 'An Analysis of the Recovery of Greater London's Population Change Rate', *Built Environment*, 13 (1988), 193–211. Champion, 'United Kingdom', 83, 90. A. G.

Champion, 'Introduction: The Counterurbanization Experience', in Champion (ed.), *Counterurbanization*, 13. Coleman and Salt, *The British Population*, pp. 83, 105, 107.

23. Randolph and Robert, 'Population Redistribution', 227–8. Robert and Randolph, 'Beyond Decentralization', 83. Britton, 'Recent Population Changes in Perspective', 38. Champion, 'Recent Changes in the Pace of Population Deconcentration', 386–7. Champion, 'United Kingdom', 92. C. Jones and Bob Armitage, 'Population Changes within Area Types: England and Wales, 1971–88', *Population Trends*, 60 (1990), 28. Coleman and Salt, *The British Population*, p. 107. Between 1971 and 1981 the population of inner London fell almost 18 per cent and that of outer London by 5 per cent: between 1981 and 1991 by 6 per cent and 4 per cent respectively. OPCS, *1991 Census. Preliminary Report for England and Wales* (London, 1991), p. 6.

24. See data in Robert and Randolph, 'Beyond Decentralization', 89–90.

25. Robert and Randolph, 'Beyond Decentralization', 82–3, 88–9. Champion, 'Population Trends in the 1970s', 208. Champion, 'Recent Changes in the Pace of Population Deconcentration', 391. Champion, 'Introduction: the Counterurbanization Experience', 13. Champion, 'United Kingdom', 87, 90–2. Coleman and Salt, *The British Population*, p. 105.

26. OPCS, *1991 Census*, pp. 5–6. See also Champion, 'Introduction: the Counterurbanization Experience', 13. Jones and Armitage, 'Population Changes within Area Types', 28, 30. Coleman and Salt, *The British Population*, pp. 105, 107.

27. Champion, 'Recent Changes in the Pace of Population Deconcentration', 386–7. See also Britton, 'Recent Population Changes in Perspective', 33, 38, 41.

28. Robert and Randolph, 'Beyond Decentralization', 79. Champion, 'Recent Changes in the Pace of Population Deconcentration', 388, 391. Champion, 'United Kingdom', 93. Jones and Armitage, 'Population Changes within Area Types', 27, 32.

29. Champion, 'Population Trends in Rural Britain', 20. Robert and Randolph, 'Beyond Decentralization', 76–9. Champion, 'Recent Changes in the Pace of Population Deconcentration', 379. Champion, 'Introduction: the Counterurbanization Experience', 1, 3–9, 11–13, 15–16. A. G. Champion, 'Conclusion: Temporary Anomaly, Long-Term Trend or Transitional Phase?', in Champion (ed.), *Counterurbanization*, pp. 230–3.

Notes

2 INTERNAL AND OVERSEAS MIGRATION

1. Wrigley and Schofield, *The Population History of England*, pp. 227–8.
2. See also Lawton, 'Regional Population Trends in England and Wales', 30, 48. Champion, 'Population Trends in the 1970s', 197–8. Britton, 'Recent Population Changes in Perspective', 33–5. Jones and Armitage, 'Population Changes within Area Types', 25.
3. Flinn (ed.), *Scottish Population History*, pp. 441–4, 446. See also Champion, 'Population Trends in the 1970s', 197–8. Registrar-General Scotland, *Annual Report 1980* (Edinburgh 1982), p. 281. Registrar-General Scotland, *Annual Report 1990* (Edinburgh, 1991), p. 109.
4. Flinn (ed.), *Scottish Population History*, p. 442. Registrar-General Scotland, *Annual Report 1990*, p. 107.
5. Flinn (ed.), *Scottish Population History*, pp. 461, 464–5.
6. H. R. Jones, J. B. Caird, W. G. Berry and N. J. Ford, 'Counterurbanization: English Migration to the Scottish Highlands and Islands', in H. Jones (ed.), *Population Change in Contemporary Scotland* (Norwich, 1984), pp. 73, 78. H. Jones, N. Ford, J. Caird and W. Berry, 'Counterurbanization in Societal Context: Long-Distance Migration to the Highlands and Islands of Scotland', *Professional Geographer*, 36 (1984), 438. Registrar-General Scotland, *Annual Report 1980*, pp. 281–3. Registrar-General Scotland, *Annual Report 1990*, p. 109.
7. Lawton, 'Regional Population Trends in England and Wales', 41, 45, 48, 61. In the case of the South East region the main mechanism of population growth changed between the 1950s and 1960s from migration to natural increase. See also Lawton, 'Population Changes in England and Wales in the Later Nineteenth Century', 60.
8. Jones and Armitage, 'Population Changes within Area Types', 29–30. Britton, 'Recent Population Changes in Perspective', 36. Champion, 'Recent Changes in the Pace of Population Deconcentration', 393–4. A. J. Fielding, 'Counterurbanization', in M. Pacione (ed.), *Population Geography: Progress and Prospect* (London, 1986), p. 226.
9. Lawton, 'Population Changes in England and Wales in the Later Nineteenth Century', 65. Lawton, 'Regional Population Trends in England and Wales', 46, 52, 56–7.
10. For examples see Robert and Randolph, 'Beyond Decentralization', 96. Champion, 'Population Trends in the

1970s', 198. Champion, 'Recent Changes in the Pace of Population Deconcentration', 392–3, 395. Jones and Armitage, 'Population Changes within Area Types', 38.

11. Robert and Randolph, 'Beyond Decentralization', 91–2. Champion, 'Population Trends in the 1970s', 198, 203. J. Stillwell, 'The Analysis and Projection of Interregional Migration in the United Kingdom', in R. Woods and P. Rees (eds), *Population Structures and Models. Developments in Spatial Demography* (London, 1986), p. 160. Champion, 'Recent Changes in the Pace of Population Deconcentration', 392–3, 395. Champion, 'United Kingdom', 93–4. Champion, 'Conclusion', 235. Jones and Armitage, 'Population Changes within Area Types', 28–30, 32. Coleman and Salt, *The British Population*, p. 411.

12. D. Baines, *Migration in a Mature Economy. Emigration and Internal Migration in England and Wales, 1861–1900* (Cambridge, 1985), pp. 49, 57, 300.

13. Mitchell with Deane, *Abstract of British Historical Statistics*, p. 47.

14. Baines, *Migration in a Mature Economy*, p. 57.

15. The number of Irish-born residents of mainland Britain rose from 20 000 in 1787 to 727 000 in 1851. J. G. Williamson, 'The Impact of the Irish on British Labour Markets During the Industrial Revolution', *Journal of Economic History*, XLVI, 3 (1986), 707.

16. Flinn (ed.), *Scottish Population History*, pp. 455, 457. C. Holmes, 'The Promised Land? Immigration into Britain, 1870–1980,' in D. A. Coleman (ed.), *Demography of Immigrants and Minority Groups in the United Kingdom* (London, 1982), pp. 5, 7. C. Holmes, 'The Impact of Immigration on British Society, 1870–1980', in T. Barker and M. Drake (eds), *Population and Society in Britain, 1850–1980* (London, 1982), p. 173. J. Walvin, *Passage to Britain. Immigration in British History and Politics* (Harmondsworth, 1984), p. 49. The number of Irish-born resident in England and Wales fell from 566 540 in 1871 to 375 325 in 1911. Walvin, *Passage to Britain*, pp. 61, 65.

17. Homes, 'The Promised Land?', 5, 7–8. Holmes, 'The Impact of Immigration', 173, 175. Walvin, *Passage to Britain*, pp. 62, 64, 68–9, 71–4. Flinn (ed.), *Scottish Population History*, pp. 455, 457–8.

18. Holmes, 'The Promised Land?', 6. Walvin, *Passage to Britain*, pp. 51, 82, 84–5. Coleman and Salt, *The British Population*, p. 455.

19. G. C. K. Peach, 'The Growth and Distribution of the Black Population in Britain, 1945–80', in Coleman (ed.), *Demography*

of Immigrants, pp. 26–8. Holmes, 'The Promised Land?', 3, 7. Holmes, 'The Impact of Immigration', 174. Walvin, *Passage to Britain*, pp. 97, 110, 117, 123. Coleman and Salt, *The British Population*, pp. 448–9, 451, 455, 464. I. Diamond and S. Clarke, 'Demographic Patterns Among Britain's Ethnic Groups', in H. Joshi (ed.), *The Changing Population of Britain* (Oxford, 1990), p. 179.

20. Walvin, *Passage to Britain*, pp. 105–6, 111–12. Holmes, 'The Promised Land?', 7. Holmes, 'The Impact of Immigration', 173–4. Coleman and Salt, *The British Population*, pp. 444–5, 455.
21. Diamond and Clarke, 'Demographic Patterns', 179.
22. J. Bailey, 'International Migration 1990', *Population Trends*, 67 (1992), 32.
23. Coleman and Salt, *The British Population*, pp. 442, 444. Diamond and Clarke, 'Demographic Patterns', 179. Holmes, 'The Promised Land?', 6–7.
24. The only exceptions were a few black Commonwealth seamen erroneously excluded by the 1925 Orders in Council. Holmes, 'The Promised Land?', 16.
25. The status of patrial was conferred by one or other of the following criteria: citizenship of self or parent or grandparent either by birth, adoption, registration or naturalisation in the United Kingdom: acceptance for settlement and residence in the United Kingdom for at least five years: Commonwealth citizens with a United Kingdom parent: spouses of patrials who were themselves Commonwealth citizens.
26. Holmes, 'The Promised Land?', 16. Holmes, 'The Impact of Immigration', 184–5. Walvin, *Passage to Britain*, pp. 66–7, 108–9, 117–21, 217. Diamond and Clarke, 'Demographic Patterns', 179. Peach, 'The Growth and Distribution', 30.
27. Walvin, *Passage to Britain*, pp. 66, 117–18. Coleman and Salt, *The British Population*, pp. 438–9. D. Feldman, 'The Importance of Being English. Jewish Immigration and the Decay of Liberal England', in D. Feldman and G. S. Jones (eds), *Metropolis London. Histories and Presentations Since 1800* (London, 1989), pp. 56, 58, 60.
28. Holmes, 'The Impact of Immigration', 175. Peach, 'The Growth and Distribution', 29–30. Walvin, *Passsage to Britain*, p. 111. Diamond and Clarke, 'Demographic Patterns', 178. Coleman and Salt, *The British Population*, pp. 439, 449, 451.
29. Peach, 'The Growth and Distribution', 27–8. Coleman and Salt, *The British Population*, p. 458. G. C. K. Peach, 'British Unemploy-

ment Cycles and West Indian Immigration, 1955–74', *New Community*, 7, *(1978/9), 40–4.*
30. Peach, 'The Growth and Distribution', 30, 34. See also Walvin, *Passage to Britain,* p. 108.
31. Holmes, 'The Promised Land?', 4–5. Walvin, *Passage to Britain,* pp. 110–12. Coleman and Salt, *The British Population,* p. 458.
32. Coleman and Salt, *The British Population,* p. 462. The continuing influence of pull factors is also attested by the fact that immigrant numbers were higher during the periods of relative economic prosperity in the 1960s and late 1980s than during the period of recession between the mid-1970s and mid-1980s.
33. Wrigley and Schofield, *The Population History of England,* pp. 219–22.
34. Between 1871 and 1931, 39 per cent of Scotland's total net emigration went to other parts of the United Kingdom and 61 per cent to overseas destinations. Flinn, *Scottish Population History,* pp. 441–2. Between 1931 and 1951 the share going overseas fell to under 5 per cent. In subsequent decades, as economic opportunities overseas improved relative to those in the United Kingdom, it rose, to 50 per cent in 1951–61, 48 per cent in 1961–71, 66 per cent in 1971–81 and 55 per cent in 1981–91.
35. J. -C. Chesnais, *The Demographic Transition. Stages, Patterns and Economic Implications* (Oxford, 1992), pp. 178–9.
36. D. S. Massey, 'Economic Development and International Migration in Comparative Perspective', *Population and Development Review,* 14, 3 (1988), 383–4, 386–8.
37. D. Baines, *Emigration from Europe, 1815–1930* (London, 1991), p. 32. Baines, *Migration in a Mature Economy,* pp. 67, 281.
38. C. J. Erickson, 'Emigration from the British Isles to the USA in 1831', *Population Studies,* 35, 2 (1981), 191, 194, 196. C. J. Erickson, 'Emigration from the British Isles to the USA in 1841. Part II. Who Were the English Emigrants?', *Population Studies,* 44, 1 (1990), 22–3, 28, 30, 39. Baines, *Migration in a Mature Economy,* pp. 74–5, 282. W. E. Van Vugt, 'Running from Ruin?' The Emigration of British Farmers to the USA in the Wake of the Repeal of the Corn Laws', *Economic History Review,* XLI, 3 (1988), 415–19, 426. M. Harper, *Emigration from North-East Scotland. Vol. I. Willing Exiles* (Aberdeen, 1988), pp. 344–5.
39. J. D. Gould, 'European Inter-Continental Emigration, 1815–1914: Patterns and Causes', *Journal of European Economic History,* 8, 3 (1979), 611–12, 614. J. D. Gould, 'European Inter-Continental Emigration the Road Home: Return Migration

40. from the USA', *Journal of European Economic History*, 9, 1 (1980), 51. Baines, *Migration in a Mature Economy*, pp. 127, 132.
40. Baines, *Migration in a Mature Economy*, pp. 166–77, 279–82. Gould, 'European Inter-Continental Emigration, 1815–1914', 614, 618, 650, 659–61. Harper, *Emigration from North-East Scotland*, pp. 343–8. Chesnais, *The Demographic Transition*, p. 159. Massey, 'Economic Development', 396–7. J. D. Gould, 'European Inter-Continental Emigration: The Role of Diffusion and Feedback', *Journal of European Economic History*, 9, 2 (1980), 281, 300. C. J. Erickson, 'Emigration from the British Isles to the USA in 1841. Part I. Emigration from the British Isles', *Population Studies*, 43, 3 (1989), 367.
41. Gould, 'European Inter-Continental Emigration, 1815–1914', 667. Chesnais, *The Demographic Transition,* pp. 154, 160, 165, 168–9, 178–9.
42. W. L. Marr, 'The United Kingdom's International Migration in the Inter-War Period: Theoretical Considerations and Empirical Testing', *Population Studies*, 31, 3 (1977), 574–6, 578. D. Pope, 'Some Factors Inhibiting Australian Immigration in the 1920s', *Australian Economic History Review*, 24, 1 (1984), 34–6, 38–52. Coleman and Salt, *The British Population*, p. 441.
43. For details of this legislation see N. H. Carrier and J. R. Jeffery, *External Migration. A Study of the Available Statistics, 1815–1950* (London, 1953), pp. 35, 37. Marr, 'The United Kingdom's International Migration', 573–4. Gould, 'European Inter-Continental Emigration, 1815–1914', 620. Baines, *Emigration from Europe*, pp. 71–2.
44. Marr, 'The United Kingdom's International Migration', 574.
45. Symptomatic of the economic problems faced by Commonwealth and other New World countries in the 1930s was the withdrawal of the £10 ocean passage rate by the government of Canada and the Australian government's decision to provide assisted passage only to relatives of existing settlers. Carrier and Jeffrey, *External Migration*, p. 37.
46. Coleman and Salt, *The British Population*, pp. 441, 443.
47. D. Friedlander and R. J. Roshier, 'A Study of Internal Migration in England and Wales, Part I', *Population Studies*, 19, 3 (1966), 251–66. Lawton, 'Population Changes in England and Wales in the Later Nineteenth Century', 57, 60, 62, 65. Lawton, 'Regional Population Trends in England and Wales', 32–3, 38. Flinn (ed.), *Scottish Population History*, pp. 461, 463.

S. Nicholas and P. Shergold, 'Internal Migration in England, 1818–39', *Journal of Historical Geography*, 13, 2 (1987), 163–4.
48. Baines, *Migration in a Mature Economy*, pp. 279–80. Nicholas and Shergold, 'Internal Migration', 164–6. Lawton, 'Population Changes in England and Wales in the Later Nineteenth Century', 57, 60, 62. Lawton, 'Regional Population Trends in England and Wales', 38, 40, 46, 66. Friedlander, 'The Spread of Urbanisation', 430. Law, 'The Growth of Urban Population', 132, 135, 138–9.
49. Lawton, 'Regional Population Trends in England and Wales', 32–3, 37–8, 56–7. Coleman and Salt, *The British Population*, p. 410. The interwar period also saw an increase in the average distance of migration. Friedlander and Roshier, 'A Study of Internal Migration', 266–8. Lawton, 'Regional Population Trends in England and Wales', 33–4.
50. Lawton, 'Regional Population Trends in England and Wales', 37–8, 56. Coleman and Salt, *The British Population*, pp. 93–4, 410. Tony Champion, 'Internal Migration and the Spatial Distribution of Population', in Joshi (ed.), *The Changing Population*, p. 121.
51. A. A. Ogilvy, 'Migration – the Influence of Economic Change', *Futures*, October (1979), 383–94. Champion, 'Population Trends in the 1970s', 186, 189, 203. A. A. Ogilvy, 'Population Migration Between the Regions of Great Britain', *Regional Studies*, 16, 1 (1982), 65, 67. Fielding, 'Counterurbanization', 224. Coleman and Salt, *The British Population*, pp. 414–15. I. Balusu, 'Internal Migration in the United Kingdom, 1989', *Population Trends*, 62 (1990), 33. M. Rosenbaum and J. Bailey, 'Movement within England and Wales during the 1980s, As Measured by the N.H.S. Central Register', *Population Trends*, 65 (1991), 25.
52. Coleman and Salt, *The British Population*, pp. 95, 99. Champion, 'Population Trends in the 1970s', 189–90, 201, 203. Stillwell, 'The Analysis and Projections of Interregional Migration', 170. Fielding, 'Counterurbanization', 224. Champion, 'United Kingdom', 83. Ogilvy, 'Population Migration', 62–71. Goddard, 'Structural Change', 15. Champion, 'Internal Migration', 110, 114. Not until the late 1980s did the rest of the South East join Greater London in losing population on net balance of migration. Rosenbaum and Bailey, 'Movement within England and Wales', 26–8.
53. See data in Registrar-General Scotland, *Annual Report 1980*, pp. 281–3 and Registrar-General Scotland, *Annual Report 1990*, p. 109.

54. Balusu, 'Internal Migration', 34–5. Coleman and Salt, *The British Population*, p. 109. Champion, 'Population Trends in the 1970s', 190, 210, 203, 210. Fielding, 'Counterurbanization', 224. Stillwell, 'The Analysis and Projection of Interregional Migration', 178. I. Stillwell, 'Migration between Metropolitan and Non-Metropolitan Regions in the UK', in P. E. White and Bert van der Knaap (eds), *Contemporary Studies of Migration* (Norwich, 1985), p. 22.
55. S. Pollard, *The Development of the British Economy, 1914–90* (London, 1992), pp. 41, 234, 236, 395–6, 398. Coleman and Salt, *The British Population*, pp. 378, 381, 383.
56. For data on regional variations in employment and unemployment levels see Pollard, *The Development of the British Economy*, pp. 279, 404. Coleman and Salt, *The British Population*, pp. 379, 382–4, 387–8, 391. Champion, 'Internal Migration', 115.
57. D. E. Keeble, 'Industrial Decline, Regional Policy and the Urban-Rural Manufacturing Shift in the United Kingdom', *Environment and Planning A*, 12 (1980), 945. Champion, 'Population Trends in the 1970s', 190. Champion, 'United Kingdom', 99–100. Coleman and Salt, *The British Population*, p. 412.
58. Goddard, 'Structural Change', 20.
59. Champion, 'United Kingdom', 90. Champion, 'Internal Migration', 114. Coleman and Salt, *The British Population*, p. 430. Pollard, *The Development of the British Economy*, p. 405.
60. Jones et al., 'Counterurbanization in Societal Context', 437. Jones et al., 'Counterurbanization, 73. Champion, 'Population Trends in the 1970s', 189.
61. C. Hamnett and W. Randolph, 'The Changing Population Distribution of England and Wales, 1961–81: a Clean Break or Consistent Progression?' *Built Environment*, 8, 4 (1982), 272–80. Fielding, 'Counterurbanization', 239–40.
62. Champion, 'United Kingdom', 83. It has been pointed out, however, that the turnaround in net migration between urban and rural areas occurred in rural areas with high as well as low population densities. Fielding, 'Counterurbanization', 241.
63. Champion, 'Recent Changes in the Pace of Population Deconcentration', 398. Coleman and Salt, *The British Population*, pp. 112, 411.
64. Jones et al., 'Counterurbanization in Societal Context', 442, Jones et al., 'Counterurbanization', 73. Fielding, 'Counterurbanization', 240. Champion, 'Recent Changes in the Pace of Population Deconcentration', 397.
65. Mintel, *Regional Life Styles 1992* (London, 1992).

66. A. M. Warnes and C. M. Law, 'The Elderly Population of Great Britain: Locational Trends and Policy Implications', *Transactions of the Institute of British Geographers*, New Series, 9, (1984), 37–59. Champion, 'Recent Changes in the Pace of Population Deconcentration', 397. Champion, 'Counterurbanization', 237, 239–40.
67. Jones et al., 'Peripheral Counterurbanization', 18, 23. See also Jones et al., 'Counterurbanization in Societal Context', 439.
68. A. J. Fielding, 'Counterurbanization in Western Europe', *Progress in Planning*, 17, 1 (1982), 5–34. Fielding, 'Counterurbanization', 240, 242. Goddard, 'Structural Change', 3. Jones et al., 'Counterurbanization in Societal Context', 440–1. Jones et al., 'Counterurbanization', 74–6. Champion, 'Recent Changes in the Pace of Population Deconcentration', 397–8. Champion, 'Conclusion', 235–7, 240. Champion, 'United Kingdom', 98–9. Coleman and Salt, *The British Population*, p. 111.
69. Champion, 'Population Trends in Rural Britain', 22. Champion, 'Recent Changes in the Pace of Population Deconcentration', 347. Jones et al., 'Peripheral Counterurbanization', 16. Jones et al., 'Counterurbanization', 71, 79. Champion, 'United Kingdom', 100.
70. Goddard, 'Structural Change', 7. Coleman and Salt, *The British Population*, p. 98.
71. For details see Keeble, 'Industrial Decline', 945, 948. D. Massey and R. Meegan, *The Anatomy of Job Loss* (London, 1982), p. 189. D. Massey, *Spatial Divisions of Labour* (London, 1984), p. 135. Champion, 'Recent Changes in the Pace of Population Deconcentration', 397. Champion, 'Conclusion', 236. Champion, 'United Kingdom', 96–7. Similar, though less pronounced changes occurred in the location of the service sector. Fielding, 'Counterurbanization', 245.
72. Fielding, 'Counterurbanization', 246. Champion, 'Internal Migration', 121.
73. Fielding, 'Counterurbanization', 244–6. Champion, 'Conclusion', 240.
74. M. F. Dunford, 'The Restructuring of Industrial Space', *International Journal of Urban and Regional Research*, 1 (1977), 510–20. D. E. Keeble, 'Industrial Decline in the Inner City and Conurbation', *Transactions of the Institute of British Geographers*, New Series, 3 (1978), 101–14. Keeble, 'Industrial Decline', 948, 953. S. Fothergill and G. Gudgin, *Unequal Growth. Urban and Regional Employment Change in the U.K.* (London, 1982), pp. 104–12. Fielding, 'Counterurbanization in Western Europe', 31. Fielding,

'Counterurbanization', 246. Goddard, 'Structural Change', 5. D. B. Massey and R. A. Meegan, 'Industrial Restructuring Versus the Cities', *Urban Studies*, 15 (1978), 273–88. D. B. Massey and R. A. Meegan, 'The Geography of Industrial Reorganisation', *Progress in Planning*, 10 (1979), 155–237. Champion, 'Recent Changes in the Pace of Population Deconcentration', 396–7. Champion, 'Conclusion', 240. Champion, 'United Kingdom', 99. Champion, 'Internal Migration', 122. Coleman and Salt, *The British Population*, p. 111.
75. Keeble, 'Industrial Decline', 955, 957. Fielding, 'Counterurbanization in Western Europe', 29–31. Fielding, 'Counterurbanization', 243–4. Goddard, 'Structural Change', 6. Champion, 'Population Trends in the 1970s', 190. Champion, 'Recent Changes in the Pace of Population Deconcentration', 398. Champion, 'United Kingdom', 98–9. Champion, 'Internal Migration', 121–2. Coleman and Salt, *The British Population*, pp. 95, 98, 111–12, 412. D. E. C. Eversley, 'Population Changes and Regional Policies since the War', *Regional Studies*, 5 (1971), 211–17.
76. Keeble, 'Industrial Decline in the Inner City', 101–14. Massey and Meegan, 'Industrial Restructuring', 273–88. Champion, 'Recent Changes in the Pace of Population Deconcentration', 391, 397–8. Champion, 'United Kingdom', 99–100. Champion, 'Internal Migration', 124. Champion, 'Population Trends in the 1970s', 213. Coleman and Salt, *The British Population*, p. 414.
77. Goddard, 'Structural Change', 14. Champion, 'Recent Changes in the Pace of Population Deconcentration', 398. Champion, 'Population Trends in the 1970s', 192, 194, 213–14. Champion, 'Internal Migration', 124.
78. Champion, 'Population Trends in Rural Britain', 22. Champion, 'Population Trends in the 1970s', 191–4, 213–14. Champion, 'Recent Changes in the Pace of Population Deconcentration', 397. Champion, 'United Kingdom', 100. Champion, 'Internal Migration', 123–4. Goddard, 'Structural Change', 14, 19–20. Coleman and Salt, *The British Population*, p. 414. Champion, 'Conclusion', 240.

3 MORTALITY

1. See also D. Friedlander, J. Schellekens, E. Ben-Mosche and A. Keysar, 'Socio-Economic Characteristics and Life Expectancies in Nineteenth Century England: a District Analysis', *Population*

Studies, 39, 1 (1985), 138, 140. T. B. Gage, 'The Decline of Mortality in England and Wales 1861 to 1964: Decomposition By Cause of Death and Component of Mortality', *Population Studies*, 47, 1 (1993), 53.
2. Chesnais, *The Demographic Transition*, pp. 54–5.
3. R. I. Armitage, 'English Regional Fertility and Mortality Patterns, 1975–85', *Population Trends*, 47 (1987), 19.
4. B. Benjamin, 'Variations of Mortality in the United Kingdom with Special Reference to Immigrants and Minority Groups', in Coleman (ed.), *Demography of Immigrants*, p. 46.
5. Average life expectancy at birth in England between 1551–75 and 1776–1800 varied from a low of 33 to a high of 39 years and then rose from 39 for the cohort born between 1801 and 1825 to 40 (1826–50), 41 (1851–75) and 46 (1876–1900). R. Woods, *The Population of Britain in the Nineteenth Century* (London, 1992), p. 29.
6. S. H. Preston, 'The Changing Relation Between Mortality and Level of Economic Development', *Population Studies*, 29, 2 (1975), 244.
7. Compared with other countries, the age pattern of early British mortality decline was unusual. S. H. Preston and V. E. Nelson, 'Structure and Change in Causes of Death: an International Summary', *Population Studies*, 28, 1 (1974), 19–51.
8. T. McKeown and R. G. Record, 'Reasons for the Decline of Mortality in England and Wales during the Nineteenth Century', *Population Studies*, 16, 2 (1962), 100–1. R. I. Woods, P. A. Watterson and J. H. Woodward, 'The Causes of Rapid Infant Mortality Decline in England and Wales, 1861–1921. Part I', *Population Studies*, 42, 3 (1988), 348–9. J. M. Winter, 'The Decline of Mortality in Britain, 1870–1950', in Barker and Drake (eds), *Population and Society*, pp. 103–4. Woods, *The Population of Britain*, p. 57. Gage, 'The Decline of Mortality', 53–4, 64.
9. C. H. Lee, 'Regional Inequalities in Infant Mortality in Britain, 1861–1971: Patterns and Hypotheses', *Population Studies*, 45, 1 (1991), 58–9, 61.
10. Woods et al., 'The Causes of Rapid Infant Mortality Decline I', 348.
11. J. M. Winter, 'Some Aspects of the Demographic Consequences of the First World War in Britain', *Population Studies*, 30, 3 (1976), 547–8. J. M. Winter, 'The Impact of the First World War on Civilian Health in Britain', *Economic History Review*, 30, 3 (1977), 489, 493–4. J. M. Winter, 'Infant Mortality, Maternal Mortality and Public Health in Britain in the 1930s', *Journal of*

European Economic History, 13, 2 (1979), 443. J. M. Winter, 'Aspects of the Impact of the First World War on Infant Mortality in Britain', *Journal of European Economic History*, 11, 3 (1972), 714, 716, 720. For the 1980s see OPCS, 'A Review of the 1980s', *Population Trends*, 62 (1990), 14. See also J. Hellier, 'Perinatal Mortality, 1950-73', *Population Trends*, 10 (1977), 13-15. J. F. Forbes, F. A. Boddy, R. Pickering and M. M. Wyllie, 'Perinatal Mortality in Scotland, 1970-9', *Journal of Epidemiology and Community Health*, 36 (1982), 282-8.
12. CSO, *Annual Abstract of Statistics 1993* (London, 1993), p. 39. Winter, 'Infant Mortality', 454. Winter 'The Decline of Mortality', 104. I. Loudon, 'Maternal Mortality: 1880-1950. Some Regional and International Comparisons', *Society for the Social History of Medicine*, 1 (1988), 183, 187, 189-90, 196. I. Loudon, 'On Maternal and Infant Mortality, 1900-60', *Society for the Social History of Medicine*, 4 (1991), 37-40. E. Fox, 'Powers of Life and Death: Aspects of Maternal Welfare in England and Wales between the Wars', *Medical History*, 35 (1991), 332.
13. A. R. Thatcher, 'Trends in Numbers and Mortality at High Ages in England and Wales', *Population Studies*, 46, 3 (1992), 419-20.
14. In part due to an increase in the percentage of the age group aged 40-4. Both in Scotland and England/Wales, however, mortality among males aged 15-24 and 25-34 was also higher in 1990 than in 1985. In Scotland death rates among females aged 25-34 and 35-44 fell between 1985 and 1990 but those among females aged 15-24 did not. In England and Wales the mortality rates of females aged 25-34 rose in the second half of the 1980s while those of females aged 15-24 and 35-44 remained unchanged. K. Dunnell, 'Deaths among 15-44 year olds', *Population Trends*, 64 (1991), 38-43.
15. Winter, 'Some Aspects', 545.
16. Lee, 'Regional Inequalities', 57, 60-1. Winter, 'The Impact of the First World War', 495. Winter, 'Infant Mortality', 446-7. Benjamin, 'Variations of Mortality', 49. Coleman and Salt, *The British Population*, p. 320. B. Botting and A. J. Macfarlane, 'Geographic Variation in Infant Mortality in Relation to Birthweight, 1983-85', in M. Britton, *Mortality and Geography. A Review in the Mid 1980s England and Wales, Series DS No. 9*, (London, 1990), pp. 647-51.
17. Woods, The Population of Britain, p. 58. Friedlander et al., 'Socio-Economic Characteristics', 139-40. R. Woods, 'The Effects of Population Redistribution on the Level of Mortality

in Nineteenth Century England and Wales', *Journal of Economic History*, 45, 3 (1985), 647–51.
18. Winter, 'The Decline of Mortality', 101, 103.
19. P. H. Curson, 'Mortality Patterns in the Modern World', in Pacione (ed.), *Population Geography*, p. 115. F. W. A. Van Poppel, 'Regional Mortality Differences in Western Europe: a Review of the Situation in the Seventies', *Social Science and Medicine*, 15D, 3 (1981), 341–52. P. L. Knox, 'Convergence and Divergence in Regional Patterns of Infant Mortality in the United Kingdom from 1949–51 to 1970–1', *Social Science and Medicine*, 15D, 3 (1981), 323–8. A. M. Adelstein and J. S. A. Ashley, 'Recent Trends in Mortality and Morbidity in England and Wales', in R. W. Hiorns (ed.), *Demographic Patterns in Developed Societies* (London, 1980), pp. 150–1. Armitage, 'English Regional Fertility', 1923. Coleman and Salt, *The British Population*, p. 320.
20. Friedlander et al., 'Socio-Economic Characteristics', 139. Social class differentials in infant mortality on the other hand widened between 1895–7 and 1910. Woods, *The Population of Britain*, pp. 58–9.
21. Woods, *The Population of Britain*, pp. 58–9. Winter, 'Infant Mortality', 451. Winter, 'The Decline of Mortality', 108. Benjamin, 'Variations of Mortality', 52–3. Curson, 'Mortality Patterns', 100–4.
22. Curson, 'Mortality Patterns', 98–9, 101. Benjamin, 'Variations of Mortality', 52. Coleman and Salt, *The British Population*, pp. 314–15, 318–19. E. R. Pamuk, 'Social Class Inequality in Mortality from 1921 to 1972 in England and Wales', *Population Studies*, 39, 1 (1985), 19, 27. Standardised Mortality Ratios allow for the effect on death rates of variations in a population's age structure.
23. Winter, 'The Decline of Mortality', 108–9. For further details see McKeown and Record, 'Reasons for the Decline of Mortality'. T. McKeown, *The Modern Rise of Population* (London, 1976). Preston and Nelson, 'Structure and Change'. S. H. Preston, *Mortality Patterns in National Population with Special Reference to Recorded Causes of Death* (London, 1976). T. McKeown, *The Origins of Human Disease* (Oxford, 1988). H. C. Trowell and D. P. Burkitt, *Western Diseases: Their Emergence and Prevention* (London, 1981). F. B. Smith, *The Retreat of Tuberculosis, 1850–1950* (London, 1988). W. P. D. Logan, 'Mortality in England and Wales from 1848–1947', *Population Studies*, 4, 2 (1980). Gage, 'The Decline of Mortality'. Benjamin,

'Variations of Mortality', 48–9. Coleman and Salt, *The British Population*, pp. 238, 274.
24. Curson, 'Mortality Patterns', 116, 118.
25. T. McKeown, R. G. Brown and R. G. Record, 'An Interpretation of the Modern Rise of Population in Europe', *Population Studies*, 26, 3 (1972), 349. T. McKeown, R. G. Record and R. D. Turner, 'An Interpretation of the Decline in Mortality in England and Wales During the 20th Century', *Population Studies*, 29, 3 (1975), 391, 421.
26. Lee, 'Regional Inequalities', 59. Woods et al., 'The Causes of Rapid Infant Mortality Decline I', 362.
27. Coleman and Salt, *The British Population*, p. 54. A. J. Mercer, *Disease, Mortality and Population in Transition. Epidemiology-Demographic Change in England Since the Eighteenth Century as Part of a Global Phenomenon* (Leicester, 1990), pp. 122, 167. Loudon, 'Maternal Mortality', 199–200.
28. McKeown and Record, 'Reasons for the Decline of Mortality', 120. McKeown et al., 'An Interpretation of the Modern Rise of Population', 357. McKeown et al., 'An Interpretation of the Decline in Mortality', 421–2.
29. Winter, 'Some Aspects', 547–8. Winter, 'The Impact of the First World War', 499–501. Winter, 'Infant Mortality', 462. Winter, 'The Decline of Mortality', 112, 114–16. Winter, 'Aspects', 727–8.
30. B. Supple, 'Income and Demand, 1860–1914', in R. Floud and D. McCloskey (eds), *The Economic History of Britain since 1700. vol. 2. 1860 to the 1970s* (Cambridge, 1981), p. 135. P. Thane, 'Social History, 1860–1914', in Floud and McCloskey (eds), *The Economic History of Britain*, p. 202.
31. D. J. Oddy, 'The Health of the People', in Barker and Drake (eds), *Population and Society*, p. 125.
32. Mercer, *Disease*, pp. 120–1, 169. A. J. Mercer, 'Relative Trends in Mortality from Related Respiratory and Airborne Infectious Diseases', *Population Studies*, 40, 1 (1986), 130, 132, 145. R. I. Woods and P. R. A. Hinde, 'Mortality in Victorian England: Models and Patterns', *Journal of Interdisciplinary History*, 18 (1987), 53.
33. Mercer, 'Relative Trends', 132.
34. Loudon, 'Maternal Mortality', 186, 196–8, 208, 222. Fox, 'Powers of Life', 333–4.
35. Preston, 'The Changing Relation', 237–8, 240, 244.
36. P. A. Watterson, 'Role of the Environment in the Decline of Infant Mortality: an Analysis of the 1911 Census of England and Wales', *Journal of Biosocial Science*, 18 (1986), 457, 468. P. A.

Watterson, 'Infant Mortality Decline by Father's Occupation from the 1911 Census of England and Wales', *Demography*, 25, 2 (1988), 300–3.
37. M. H. Brenner, 'Mortality and the National Economy: a Review of the Experience of England and Wales, 1936–76', *The Lancet* (1979), 568–73. J. Stern, 'The Relationship between Unemployment, Morbidity and Mortality in Britain', *Population Studies*, 37, 1 (1983), 73, I. D. McAvinchey, 'Economic Factors and Mortality. Some Aspects of the Scottish Case, 1950–78', *Scottish Journal of Political Economy*, 31, 1 (1984), 17.
38. Benjamin, 'Variations of Mortality', 48–9. Pamuk, 'Social Class', 28. Coleman and Salt, *The British Population*, pp. 258–9, 280–8, 295, 345, 350, 352–3, 355. R. T. Ravenholt, 'Tobacco's Global Death March', *Population and Development Review*, 16 (1990), 213–40.
39. Loudon, 'Maternal Mortality', 195, 197–9. Fox, 'Powers of Life', 331, 333, 335. Winter, 'Infant Mortality', 455–60.
40. Hellier, 'Perinatal Mortality', 13–15. Forbes et al, 'Perinatal Mortality', 282–8. Coleman and Salt, *The British Population*, p. 335.
41. Coleman and Salt, *The British Population*, pp. 54, 274, 279. Stern, 'The Relationship', 74. For evidence on the importance of variations in medical provision for regional and class differences in mortality see Coleman and Salt, *The British Population*, pp. 356–7, 363. Loudon, 'Maternal Mortality', 222. Curson, 'Mortality Patterns', 98–100. Pamuk, 'Social Class', 28–9. Brenner, 'Variations of Mortality', 52.
42. McKeown et al., 'An Interpretation of the Decline in Mortality', 421–2.
43. Friedlander et al., 'Socio-Economic Characteristics', 137–8.
44. R. I. Woods, P. A. Watterson and J. H. Woodward, 'The Causes of Rapid Infant Mortality Decline in England and Wales', 1861–1921. Part II', *Population Studies*, 43, 1 (1989), 129–32. Winter, 'Some Aspects', 548. Winter, 'The Impact of the First World War', 496–8. Winter, 'Aspects', 724–7. Woods, *The Population of Britain*, pp. 65, 67. M. W. Beaver, 'Population, Infant Mortality and Milk', *Population Studies*, 27, 2 (1973), 243. C. Dyhouse, 'Working Class Mothers and Infant Mortality in England, 1895–1914', *Journal of Social History*, 12, 2 (1978), 248, 250, 262. Loudon, 'Maternal Mortality', 185–6, 192. Fox, 'Powers of Life', 329, 339. Winter, 'The Decline of Mortality', 109. Coleman and Salt, *The British Population*, pp. 45–6, 53, 278–9.

45. Winter, 'The Decline of Mortality', 110–11. Preston, 'The Changing Relation', 240, 243–4. Mercer, *Disease*, pp. 168–9. Chesnais, *The Demographic Transition*, pp. 54–5, 76, 83.
46. Friedlander, 'Socio-Economic Characteristics', 141–2, 144, 146–7, 151. See also Woods, 'The Effects of Population Redistribution', 647–51. Increasing regional inequalities in infant mortality in Scotland between 1871 and 1921 were largely the result of the rapid growth of mining and heavy industry in particular regions. The relative importance of mining and heavy industry in the economy together with relatively high housing densities also help to explain why infant death rates in Scotland between 1912 and the 1970s were higher than in England and Wales. Lee, 'Regional Inequalities', 61, 63–4.
47. Winter, 'The Decline of Mortality', 109–17.
48. McKeown et al., 'An Interpretation of the Decline of Mortality', 422.
49. Mercer, *Disease*, pp. 94–5, 121–3. Friedlander et al., 'Socio-Economic Characteristics', 138, 151. Beaver, 'Population', 252–3. Watterson, 'Role of the Environment', 457–8, 468. Watterson, 'Infant Mortality Decline', 289, 300–2. Coleman and Salt, *The British Population*, pp. 53, 55, 57–60, 242, 289, 293. Winter, 'The Impact of the First World War', 501. For criticisms of the contribution of pasteurisation and new 'artificial' infant foods to the decline in infant mortality see Dyhouse, 'Working Class Mothers', 255–7.
50. Mercer, *Disease*, p. 168.
51. Preston, 'Changing Relation', 240, 243–4. Coleman and Salt, *The British Population*, pp. 57, 297. Chesnais, *The Demographic Transition*, pp. 78, 83. J. C. Caldwell, 'Education as a Factor in Mortality Decline: an Examination of Nigerian Data', *Population Studies*, 33, 3 (1979), 391, 395–6, 409–13.

4 FERTILITY

1. Woods, *The Population of Britain*, p. 29. C. Wilson and R. I. Woods, 'Fertility in England: a Long-Term Perspective', *Population Studies*, 45, 3 (1991), 403.
2. D. V. Glass, 'Fertility Trends in Europe since the Second World War', *Population Studies*, 22, 1 (1968), 103.
3. M. S. Teitelbaum, *The British Fertility Decline* (Princeton, NJ, 1984), pp. 86–9.

4. W. Brass and M. Kabir, 'Regional Variations in Fertility and Child Mortality during the Demographic Transition in England and Wales', in Hobcraft and Rees (eds), *Regional Demographic Development*, pp. 73–4. At the smaller unit of the registration district there was more variation in the pace of fertility decline. R. I. Woods and C. W. Smith, 'The Decline of Marital Fertility in the Late 19th Century: the Case of England and Wales', *Population Studies*, 37, 2 (1983), 215.
5. Coleman and Salt, *The British Population*, p. 115.
6. G. Calot and C. Blayo, 'Recent Course of Fertility in Western Europe', *Population Studies*, 36, 3 (1982), 350–1.
7. Coleman and Salt, *The British Population*, p. 117.
8. J. Simons, 'Developments in the Interpretation of Recent Fertility Trends in England and Wales', in Hobcraft and Rees (eds), *Regional Demographic Development*, pp. 117–18. M. Murphy, 'Economic Models of Fertility in Post-War Britain – a Conceptual and Statistical Reinterpretation', *Population Studies*, 46, 2 (1992), 235. J. Bourgeois-Pichat, 'The Unprecedented Shortage of Births in Europe', in K. Davis, M. S. Bernstam and R. Ricardo-Campbell (eds), 'Below-Replacement. Fertility in Industrial Societies. Causes, Consequences, Policies', *Population and Development Review*, Supplement to vol. 12 (1986), 10. S. H. Preston, 'The Decline of Fertility in Non-European Industrialized Countries', in Davis et al. (eds), 'Below-Replacement', 26. Calot and Blayo, 'Recent Course of Fertility', 349.
9. E. Overton, 'The Decline in Fertility since 1964: The United Kingdom by Population Groups', in D. Eversley and W. Kolmann (eds), *Population Changes and Social Planning* (London, 1982), p. 34.
10. B. Werner, 'Fertility Trends in Different Social Classes, 1970–83', *Population Trends*, 41 (1985), 8.
11. Recent estimates of fertility by Brass suggest that crude birth rate data somewhat overstate the trend from baby boom to baby bust. W. Brass, 'Is Britain Facing the Twilight of Parenthood?', in Joshi (ed.), *The Changing Population*, pp. 24–5. Total Period Fertility rates, a more satisfactory measure of fertility than crude birth rates because they are free from the effect of changes in age structure, confirm the modest nature of the recovery in fertility in the late 1970s. See data in Armitage, 'English Regional Fertility and Mortality Patterns', 16, 23. J. Craig, 'Fertility Trends within the United Kingdom', *Population Trends*, 67 (1992), 17. J. Craig, 'Recent Fertility Trends in Europe',

Population Trends, 68 (1992), 20. OPCS, 'A Review of the 1980s', *Population Trends*, 62 (1990), 6, 8–9.
12. Coleman and Salt, *The British Population*, pp. 118–9. Calot and Blayo, 'Recent Course of Fertility', 349–51, 353, 372. Bourgeois-Pichat, 'The Unprecedented Shortage', 3, 5, 13. Murphy, 'Economic Models', 235. Craig, 'Recent Fertility Trends', 20. S. Kendrick, F. Bechhofer and D. McCrone, 'Recent Trends in Fertility Differentials in Scotland', in Jones (ed.), *Population Change in Contemporary Scotland*, p. 35.
13. Simons, 'Developments', 122. Craig, 'Fertility Trends', 19. Calot and Blayo, 'Recent Course of Fertility', 353, 372. Kendrick et al., 'Recent Trends', 37. Armitage, 'English Regional Fertility and Mortality Patterns', 17, 23. J. Coward, 'Fertility Patterns in the Modern World', in Pacione (ed.), *Population Geography*, pp. 70, 75, 81.
14. Craig, 'Recent Fertility Trends', 17–19. Kendrick et al., 'Recent Trends', 35. Overton, 'The Decline in Fertility', 46.
15. Coleman and Salt, *The British Population*, p. 167. Werner, 'Fertility Trends', 11–12. For the socio-occupational structure of illegitimacy in earlier times see N. Rogers, 'Carnal Knowledge: Illegitimacy in Eighteenth Century Westminster', *Journal of Social History*, 23 (1989), 358. N. L. Tranter, 'Illegitimacy in Nineteenth Century Rural Scotland: a Puzzle Resolved?', *International Journal of Sociology and Social Policy*, 5, 2 (1985), 41. The percentage of children conceived before marriage also varied inversely with socio-occupational class. J. Haskey, 'Social Class and Socio-Economic Differentials in Divorce in England and Wales', *Population Studies*, 38, 3 (1984), 434.
16. P. Laslett and K. Oosterveen, 'Long-Term Trends in Bastardy in England: a Study of Illegitimacy Figures in the Parish Registers and in the Reports of the Registrar-General, 1561–1960', *Population Studies*, 27, 2 (1973), 276–7. Teitelbaum, *The British Fertility Decline*, pp. 147–9.
17. Craig, 'Fertility Trends', 20.
18. Teitelbaum, *The British Fertility Decline*, p. 149. T. Smout, 'Aspects of Sexual Behaviour in Nineteenth Century Scotland', in A. A. MacLaren (ed.), *Social Class in Scotland* (Edinburgh, 1976), p. 63. I. Carter, 'Illegitimate Births and Illegitimate Inferences', *Scottish Journal of Sociology*, 1 (1976), 125. Coward, 'Fertility Patterns', 84.
19. Coleman and Salt, *The British Population*, p. 135. Laslett and Oosterveen, 'Long-Term Trends', 260–3. B. Werner, 'Recent Trends in Illegitimate Births and Extra-Marital Conceptions',

Population Trends, 30 (1982), 9–10. Werner, 'Fertility Trends', 12. K. Kiernan, 'The Family: Formation and Fission', in Joshi (ed.), *The Changing Population*, pp. 27, 36–7. J. Cooper, 'Births Outside Marriage: Recent Trends and Associated Demographic and Social Changes', *Population Trends*, 63 (1991), 9–10. C. Jones, 'Fertility of the Over Thirties', *Population Trends*, 67 (1992), 13. Craig, 'Fertility Trends', 20. B. Werner, 'Trends in First, Second and Later Births', *Population Trends*, 45 (1986), 29–30.

20. E. Shorter, J. Knodel and E. Van de Walle, 'The Decline of Non-Marital Fertility in Europe, 1880–1940', *Population Studies*, 25, 3 (1971), 375.
21. Bourgeois-Pichat, 'The Unprecedented Shortage', 13, 15. Similar increases in illegitimacy occurred in Australia, Canada, New Zealand and the USA from the early 1960s. In Japan, by contrast, levels of bastardy declined. Preston, 'The Decline of Fertility', 35–6.
22. From data in Bourgeois-Pichat, 'The Unprecedented Shortage', 15. Cooper, 'Births Outside Marriage', 8. Kiernan, 'The Family', 40. Werner, 'Recent Trends', 9. Levels of bastardy were similar in Australia, Canada, New Zealand and the USA. Preston, 'The Decline of Fertility', 36. In the USA in 1989, for example, 27 per cent of all births were illegitimate. US Bureau of the Census, *Statistical Abstract of the United States 1992* (Washington, 1992), p. 69.
23. Laslett and Oosterveen, 'Long-Term Trends', 256. Shorter et al., 'The Decline of Non-Marital Fertility', 380. P. Laslett, *Family Life and Illicit Love in Earlier Generations* (Cambridge, 1977), pp. 105–6.
24. Laslett and Oosterveen, 'Long-Term Trends', 256, 286. Laslett, *Family Life*, p. 107.
25. L. A. Tilly, J. W. Scott and M. Cohen, 'Women's Work and European Fertility Patterns', *Journal of Interdisciplinary History*, VI, 3 (1976), 475.
26. N. F. R. Crafts, 'Illegitimacy in England and Wales in 1911', *Population Studies*, 36, 2 (1982), 329–31. J. Coward, 'The Analysis of Regional Fertility Patterns', in Woods and Rees (eds), *Population Structure*, p. 64.
27. Shorter et al., 'The Decline of Non-Marital Fertility', 382, 392–3. E. Shorter, 'Female Emancipation, Birth Control and Fertility in European History', *American Historical Review*, 78, 3 (1973), 612–33. E. Shorter, *The Making of the Modern Family* (London, 1977), pp. 86–124. M. S. Hindus, 'Pre-Marital Pregnancy in America 1640–1971: an Overview and

Interpretation', *Journal of Interdisciplinary History*, V, 4 (1975), 537–70. Kiernan, 'The Family', 30–1.
28. Laslett and Oosterveen, 'Long-Term Trends', 256.
29. See p. 97.
30. On trends in divorce and extra-marital conception see pp. 92, 96. Rates of premarital conception in England and Wales roughly halved between the late nineteenth and mid twentieth century, rose from around 13 per cent in 1955 to 22 per cent in 1967 and fell to around 16 per cent after the mid 1970s. See data in Coleman and Salt, *The British Population*, p. 154. D. J. Van de Kaa, 'Recent Trends in Fertility in Western Europe', in Hiorns (ed.), *Demographic Patterns*, p. 64. Werner, 'Recent Trends', 12. Simons, 'Developments', 121–2. Kiernan, 'The Family', 31.
31. Kiernan, 'The Family', 30–1.
32. Coleman and Salt, *The British Population*, pp. 136, 154.
33. See pp. 100, 112, 125.
34. Bourgeois-Pichat, 'The Unprecedented Shortage', 3, 14. Preston, 'The Decline of Fertility', 35. Cooper, 'Births Outside Marriage', 8–10, 12, 14–15, 17.
35. Wilson and Woods, 'Fertility in England', 399, 406–7. M. R. Haines, 'Fertility, Nuptiality and Occupation: a Study of British Mid-Nineteenth Century Coalmining Populations', *Journal of Interdisciplinary History*, VIII, 2 (1977), 278–80. Woods, *The Population of Britain*, pp. 48–9.
36. Coleman and Salt, *The British Population*, p. 62. Teitelbaum, *The British Fertility Decline*, p. 106.
37. Coleman and Salt, *The British Population*, p. 134.
38. D. A. Coleman, 'Recent Trends in Marriage and Divorce in Britain and Europe', in Hiorns (ed.), *Demographic Patterns*, p. 122. S. C. Watkins, 'Regional Patterns of Nuptiality in Europe 1870–1960', *Population Studies*, 35, 2 (1981), 214–15. Glass, 'Fertility Trends', 105, 107. Preston, 'The Decline of Fertility', 30. Coleman and Salt, *The British Population*, pp. 180, 182. J. Hajnal, 'Age at Marriage and Proportions Marrying', *Population Studies*, 7, 2 (1953), 111–23.
39. Coleman and Salt, *The British Population*, pp. 182, 185. Coleman, 'Recent Trends', 88.
40. Glass, 'Fertility Trends', 105, 110. Coleman and Salt, *The British Population*, p. 135. Simons, 'Developments', 123. Overton, 'The Decline in Fertility', 37. J. Busfield and G. Hawthorn, 'Some Social Determinants of Recent Trends in British Fertility', *Journal of Biosocial Science*, Sup. 3 (1977), 66. M. Ni Bhrolchain,

'Period Parity Progression Ratios and Birth Intervals in England and Wales 1941–71: a Synthetic Life Table Analysis', *Population Studies*, 41, 1 (1987), 120. S. M. Farid, 'The Current Tempo of Fertility in England and Wales', *Population Studies*, 28, 1 (1974), 83. J. F. Ermisch, 'The Relevance of the Easterlin Hypothesis and the "New Home Economics" to Fertility Movement in Great Britain', *Population Studies*, 33, 1 (1979), 48.

41. Summary of nuptiality trends based on data and discussion in Coleman, 'Recent Trends', 88, 122. R. Leete, 'Marriage and Divorce', *Population Trends*, 3 (1976), 3–8. Kiernan, 'The Family', 27–8, 33. Busfield and Hawthorn, 'Some Social Determinants', 66–7. S. Eldridge and K. Kiernan, 'Declining First Marriage Rates in England and Wales: a Change in Timing or a Rejection of Marriage?', *European Journal of Population*, 1 (1985), 327–8, 335, 344. S. M. Farid, 'Cohort Nuptiality in England and Wales', *Population Studies*, 30, 1 (1976), 150–1. J. F. Ermisch, 'Economic Opportunities, Marriage Squeezes and the Propensity to Marry: an Economic Analysis of Period Marriage Rates in England and Wales', *Population Studies*, 35, 3 (1981), 347. J. Haskey, 'Marital Status before Marriage and Age at Marriage: Their Influence on the Chance of Divorce', *Population Trends*, 64 (1991), 4, 6. Glass, 'Fertility Trends', 130. R. Schoen and J. Baj, 'Twentieth Century Cohort Marriage and Divorce in England and Wales', *Population Studies*, 38, 3 (1984), 447–8. C. F. Westhoff, 'Perspective on Nuptiality and Fertility', in Davis et al. (eds), Below-Replacement, 155. J. M. Winter, 'War, Family and Fertility in Twentieth Century Europe', in J. R. Gillis, L. A. Tilly and D. Levine (eds), *The European Experience of Declining Fertility. A Quiet Revolution, 1850–1970* (Oxford, 1992), pp. 300–2. Throughout the twentieth century ages at marriage have correlated positively with social class. Coleman and Salt, *The British Population*, p. 190.

42. Teitelbaum, *The British Fertility Decline*, pp. 97–103. M. Anderson and D. J. Morse, 'High Fertility, High Emigration, Low Nuptiality: Adjustment Processes in Scotland's Demographic Experience, 1861–1914, Part II', *Population Studies*, 47, 2 (1993), 319. Watkins, 'Regional Patterns', 215. S. C. Watkins, 'From Local to National Communities: the Transformation of Demographic Regimes in Western Europe, 1870–1960', *Population and Development Review*, 16, 2 (1990), 242, 247.

43. Figures from Kiernan, 'The Family'. 34, J. Ermisch, 'Divorce: Economic Antecedents and Aftermath', in Joshi (ed.), *The Changing Population*, p. 42. CSO, *Annual Abstract of Statistics 1993* (London, 1993), p. 24. See also Coleman, 'Recent Trends',

93–4. Coleman and Salt, *The British Population*, pp. 192–3, 196, 199. Schoen and Baj, 'Twentieth Century Cohort Marriage', 439, 448. Haskey, 'Marital Status', 4, 11. Haskey, 'Social Class', 419. J. Haskey, 'Social Class Differentials in Remarriage after Divorce: Results of a Forward Linkage Study', *Population Trends*, 47 (1987), 34. Preston, 'The Decline of Fertility', 33–4. Bourgeois-Pichat, 'The Unprecedented Shortage', 3. R. Lesthaeghe, 'A Century of Demographic and Cultural Change in Western Europe: an Explanation of Underlying Dimensions', *Population and Development Review*, 9, 3 (1983), 416.
44. Haskey, 'Social Class', 424–5, 430, 436–7. Coleman and Salt, *The British Population*, pp. 200–1.
45. Coleman and Salt, *The British Population*, pp. 203, 205.
46. Haskey, 'Social Class Differentials', 34. Except in West Germany the decline was more pronounced in western Europe. Lesthaeghe, 'A Century', 416–17.
47. A. Brown and K. Kiernan, 'Cohabitation in Great Britain: Evidence from the General Household Survey', *Population Trends*, 25 (1981), 4–10. Eldridge and Kiernan, 'Declining First Marriage Rates', 329. Cooper, 'Births Outside Marriage', 10. Kiernan, 'The Family', 27, 31. In spite of the increase the extent of cohabitation in Britain at the end of the 1980s was less than in a number of other western and northern European countries. Eldridge and Kiernan, 'Declining First Marriage Rates', 344. Kiernan, 'The Family', 32.
48. Van de Kaa, 'Recent Trends', 111–12. D. Gittins, 'Married Life and Birth Control Between the Wars', *Oral History*, III, 2 (1975), 57, 62. Winter, 'War, Family and Fertility', 292, 299. J. M. Winter, 'Britain's "Lost Generation" of the First World War', *Population Studies*, 31, 3 (1977), 452, 465. D. Friedlander, 'The British Depression and Nuptiality: 1873–1896', *Journal of Interdisciplinary History*, XXIII, 1 (1992), 29.
49. Anderson and Morse, 'High Fertility', 340–1.
50. Coward, 'The Analysis of Regional Fertility Patterns', 64.
51. Watkins, 'Regional Patterns', 206–11, 214. Watkins, 'From Local to National', 244–5, 251–2, 254–5, 257–9. S. C. Watkins, 'Demographic Nationalism in Western Europe, 1870–1960', in Gillis et al. (eds), *The European Experience*, pp. 270–90.
52. Glass, 'Fertility Trends', 105. Busfield and Hawthorn, 'Some Social Determinants', 70–1. Van de Kaa, 'Recent Trends', 115. Coleman and Salt, *The British Population*, p. 143. Ermisch, 'Economic Opportunities', 355. J. Ermisch, 'Investigations into the Causes of the Postwar Fertility Swings', in Eversley and

Kolmann (eds), *Population Change*, p. 153. Simons, 'Developments', 123–4. Winter, 'War, Family and Fertility', 306–8.
53. Van de Kaa, 'Recent Trends', 115. Coleman and Salt, *The British Population*, p. 138. Brass, 'Is Britain Facing the Twilight of Parenthood?', 16.
54. Ermisch, 'Investigations', 150. R. Lesthaeghe and D. Meekers, 'Value Changes and the Dimensions of Familism in the European Community', *European Journal of Population*, 2 (1986), 228, 262.
55. Ermisch, 'Economic Opportunities', 347–9, 352, 354–5. Ermisch, 'Investigations', 149–51, 155. J. F. Ermisch, 'The Labour Market in Historical Development', in Eversley and Kolmann (eds), *Population Change*, pp. 158–9, 171, 175, 177. Westhoff, 'Perspective', 159.
56. Ermisch, 'Economic Opportunities', 350–6. Ermisch, 'Investigations', 151. Lesthaeghe, 'A Century', 418–19, 430–1. Westhoff, 'Perspective', 155–7, 159. Preston, 'The Decline of Fertility', 33. Winter, 'War, Family and Fertility', 303. Bourgeois-Pichat, 'The Unprecedented Shortage', 3. Kiernan, 'The Family', 31–2.
57. For examples of the influences of nuptiality see Wilson and Woods, 'Fertility in England', 411, 414. D. Friedlander, 'Demographic Patterns and Socio-Economic Characteristics of the Coalmining Population in England and Wales during the Nineteenth Century', *Economic Development and Cultural Change*, 22 (1973), 39–51. Coward, 'Fertility Patterns', 77–80. Overton, 'The Decline in Fertility', 37–8. R. Lesthaeghe and J. Surkyn, 'Cultural Dynamics and Economic Theories of Fertility Change', *Population and Development Review*, 14 (1988), 30.
58. Brass and Kabir, 'Regional Variations', 73–4.
59. Summary of postwar marital fertility trends based on data and discussion in Farid, 'The Current Tempo', 82–3. Simons, 'Developments', 121–2. Overton, 'The Decline in Fertility', 39, 45. Werner, 'Trends', 28. B. Werner, 'Birth Intervals: Results from the OPCS Longitudinal Study 1972–84', *Population Trends*, 51 (1988), 29. Ni Bhrolchain, 'Period Parity', 120–1, 123. Armitage, 'English Regional Fertility and Mortality Patterns', 16. Coleman and Salt, *The British Population*, pp. 148, 151–2. Craig, 'Fertility Trends', 18. Craig, 'Recent Fertility Trends', 22–3. Jones, 'Fertility of the Over Thirties', 10–11, 14, 16. Glass, 'Fertility Trends', 110, 116, 118. Calot and Blayo, 'Recent Course of Fertility', 356.

60. Wilson and Woods, 'Fertility in England', 414. Teitelbaum, *The British Fertility Decline*, pp. 127–43. Coward, 'The Analysis of Regional Fertility Patterns', 58. Kendrick et al., 'Recent Trends', 33. Watkins, 'From Local to National', 242, 244, 246–7.
61. Woods and Smith, 'The Decline of Marital Fertility', 223–4. Glass, 'Fertility Trends', 118. Overton, 'The Decline in Fertility', 48. Watkins, 'From Local to National', 250. Murphy, 'Economic Models', 243. Coleman and Salt, *The British Population*, pp. 161–2. Haines, 'Fertility', 253. Kendrick et al., 'Recent Trends', 41, 43. Coward, 'Fertility Patterns', 71, 73–4. Werner, 'Fertility Trends', 6, 8, 9. T. H. C. Stevenson, 'The Fertility of Various Social Classes in England and Wales from the Middle of the Nineteenth Century to 1911', *Journal of the Royal Statistical Society*, 83 (1920), 431–2. M. R. Haines, 'Social Class Differentials During Fertility Decline: England and Wales Revisited', *Population Studies*, 43, 2 (1989), 307, 309, 315, 321. M. R. Haines, 'Occupation and Social Class during Fertility Decline: Historical Perspectives', in Gillis et al. (eds), *The European Experience*, pp. 196–202. R. I. Woods, 'Approaches to the Fertility Transition in Victorian England', *Population Studies*, 41, 2 (1987), 283–311.
62. J. A. and O. Banks, 'The Bradlaugh–Besant Trial and the English Newspapers', *Population Studies*, 8, 1 (1954), 22–34. Gittins, 'Married Life', 57–8. J. Lewis, 'The Ideology and Politics of Birth Control in Inter-war England', *Women's Studies International Quarterly*, 2 (1979), 33. J. Cleland and C. Wilson, 'Economic Theories of the Fertility Transition: an Iconoclastic View', *Population Studies*, 41, 1 (1987), 29. Woods, 'Approaches', 295–311.
63. As late as 1970 a quarter of all birth control practitioners in England and Wales still relied on the traditional withdrawal method. Van de Kaa, 'Recent Trends', 71.
64. N. F. R. Crafts, 'A Cross-Sectional Study of Legitimate Fertility in England and Wales, 1911', *Research in Economic History*, 9 (1984), 95, 105. N. F. R. Crafts, 'A Time Series Study of Fertility in England and Wales, 1877–1938', *European Journal of Economic History*, 13 (1984), 588–9. N. F. R. Crafts, 'Duration of Marriage, Fertility and Women's Employment Opportunities in England and Wales in 1911', *Population Studies*, 43, 2 (1989), 335. See also G. S. Becker, 'An Economic Analysis of Fertility', in National Bureau of Economic Research', *Demographic and Economic Change in Developed Countries* (Princeton, NJ, 1960) 227, 230. D. M. Heer, 'Economic Development and Fertility',

Demography, 3 (1966), 428. H. Liebenstein, 'An Interpretation of the Economic Theory of Fertility: Promising Path or Blind Alley?', *Journal of Economic Literature*, XII, 2 (1974), 459. Gittins, 'Married Life', 53–4. Woods, *The Population of Britain*, p. 49.

65. J. and P. Scheider, 'Going Forward in Reverse Gear: Culture, Economy and Political Economy in the Demographic Transition of a Rural Sicilian Town', in Gillis et al. (eds), *The European Experience*, pp. 146–74.
66. Chesnais, *The Demographic Transition*, p. 392.
67. Chesnais, *The Demographic Transition*, pp. 47, 138–51, 159, 332, 354, 513, 515–16. See also Teitelbaum, *The British Fertility Decline*, p. 222. D. Freidlander, 'Demographic Responses and Population Change', *Demography*, 6 (1969), 359–81.
68. Becker, 'An Economic Analysis', 227, 230. Friedlander, 'Demographic Responses', 360. Gittins, 'Married Life', 62. Cleland and Wilson, 'Economic Theories', 29. R. Freedman, 'The Sociology of Human Fertility: a Trend Report and Bibliography', *Current Sociology*, 10–11 (1961–2), 53–4. W. Seccombe, 'Men's "Marital Rights" and Women's "Wifely Duties": Changing Conjugal Relations in the Fertility Decline', in Gillis et al. (eds), *The European Experience*, p. 78.
69 Haines, 'Social Class', 307.
70. Crafts, 'A Cross-Sectional Study', 105. Crafts, 'A Time Series Study', 588.
71. Brass and Kabir, 'Regional Variations', 76, 78, 85. The failure of national average infant death rates in England and Wales to decline until after 1899/1900, a quarter of a century later than the onset of marital fertility decline, suggests that falling mortality made little or no contribution to the initiation of the fertility transition. For criticisms of the role of mortality see Woods, *The Population of Britain*, p. 50. Woods, 'Approaches', 293–5. Teitelbaum, *The British Fertility Decline*, p. 183. J. A. Banks, *Victorian Values. Secularism and the Size of Families* (London, 1981), pp. 122–3. Recent work by Lee, however, shows that in many parts of Britain a decline in infant death rates predated or accompanied the early decline in rates of marital fertility. Lee, 'Regional Inequalities', 55–65.
72. J. C. Simon, 'The Effect of Income on Fertility', *Population Studies*, 23, 3 (1969), 327–41. R. P. Beaujot, K. J. Krotki and P. Krishnan, 'Socio-Cultural Variations in the Applicability of the Economic Model of Fertility', *Population Studies*, 32, 2 (1978), 319–25.
73. Becker, 'An Economic Analysis', 227–8. J. Blake, 'Are Babies Consumer Durables?', *Population Studies*, 27, 1 (1968), 5–25.

Liebenstein, 'An Interpretation', 462–3, 465. Chesnais, *The Demographic Transition*, 356.
74. Heer, 'Economic Development', 427–8. D. M. Heer, 'Economic Development and the Fertility Transition', *Daedalus*, 97 (1968), 447–62.
75. Chesnais, *The Demographic Transition*, p. 356.
76. Crafts, 'A Cross-Sectional Study', 105. Anderson and Morse, 'High Fertility', 340. Gittins, 'Married Life', 58–61.
77. Liebenstein, 'An Interpretation', 459. A. T. Flegg, 'The Role of Inequality of Income in the Determination of Birth Rates', *Population Studies*, 33, 3 (1979), 457, 472. B. G. Zimmer, 'The Impact of Social Mobility on Fertility: a Reconsideration', *Population Studies*, 35, 1 (1981), 120, 122, 126, 130. M. S. L. Cook and R. Repetto, 'The Relevance of the Developing Countries to Demographic Transition Theory: Further Lessons from the Hungarian Experience', *Population Studies*, 36, 1 (1982), 111–28. A. K. Bhattacharyya, 'Income Inequality and Fertility: a Comparative View', *Population Studies*, 29, 1 (1975), 9. Gittins, *Fair Sex*, p. 182.
78. Haines, 'Fertility', 245–80. Gittins, *Fair Sex*, p. 185.
79. Gittins, 'Married Life', 55, 57, 61–3. Gittins, *Fair Sex*, p. 182. Crafts, 'Duration', 331, 335. Woods, *The Population of Britain*, pp. 50–1.
80. Simons, 'Developments', 125. N. Keyfitz, 'The Family That Does Not Reproduce Itself', in Davis et al. (eds), Below-Replacement, 140–1, 143–4, 148–9.
81. Freedman, 'The Sociology', 56.
82. Liebenstein, 'An Interpretation', 459. Keyfitz, 'The Family', 139–40, 146. Coleman and Salt, *The British Population*, pp. 64–5. L. H. Lees, 'Safety in Numbers: Social Welfare Legislation and Fertility Decline in Western Europe', in Davis et al. (eds), Below-Replacement, 310–25.
83. Liebenstein, 'An Interpretation', 459–60. Keyfitz, 'The Family', 141, 144, 146. Coleman and Salt, *The British Population*, pp. 64–5. Gittins, *Fair Sex*, p. 182. W. Minge-Kalman, 'The Industrial Revolution and the European Family: the Institutionalization of "Childhood" as a Market for Family Labour', *Comparative Studies in Society and History*, 20, 3 (1978), 454–68. J. C. Caldwell, 'The Mechanisms of Demographic Change in Historical Perspective', *Population Studies*, 35, 1 (1981), 9, 12, 19. D. Levine, 'Industrialization and the Proletarian Family in England', *Past and Present*, 107 (1985), 191–200. D. Levine, *Reproducing Families. The Political Economy*

of English Population History (Cambridge, 1987), pp. 162–214. According to Banks education contributes to the spread of family limitation in yet another way – through the effect of public examination systems in creating an historically unique state of mind in which individuals are encouraged to believe that equal efforts yield equal rewards. Banks, *Victorian Values*, pp. 132–7.
84. Keyfitz, 'The Family', 141, 144, 148.
85. Chesnais, *The Demographic Transition*, pp. 401–9.
86. R. V. Wells, 'Family History and the Demographic Transition', *Journal of Social History*, 9, 1 (1975), 6. Woods and Smith, 'The Decline', 208. Cleland and Wilson, 'Economic Theories', 25. Lesthaeghe, 'A Century', 413–14. Lesthaeghe and Meekers, 'Value changes', 225–7. Lesthaeghe and Surkyn, 'Cultural Dynamics', 2–3, 8.
87. Haines, 'Social Class', 322. Gittins, 'Married Life', 62–3. Seccombe, 'Men's "Marital Rights"', 66–84. J. R. Gillis, 'Gender and Fertility Decline Among the British Middle Classes', in Gillis et al. (eds), *The European Experience*, pp. 312–47. E. Ross, 'Mothers and the State in Britain, 1904–1914', in Gillis et al. (eds), *The European Experience*, pp. 48–65.
88. Wells, 'Family History', 6. Liebenstein, 'An Interpretation', 459. Lesthaeghe, 'A Century', 411–14, 429. Lesthaeghe and Surkyn, 'Cultural Dynamics', 4, 8, 15, 17. Cleland and Wilson, 'Economic Theories', 25, 28. Haines, 'Social Class', 306, 322. Coleman and Salt, *The British Population*, pp. 64, 66.
89. Chesnais, *The Demographic Transition*, p. 360. See also Liebenstein, 'An Interpretation', 470. Gittins, 'Married Life', 53. Gittins, *Fair Sex*, p. 187. Lesthaeghe, 'A Century', 411–15. Lesthaeghe and Meekers, 'Value Changes', 225–6. Lesthaeghe and Surkyn, 'Cultural Dynamics', 2, 8. Keyfitz, 'The Family', 139. Cleland and Wilson, 'Economic Theories', 5.
90. See, for example, Becker, 'An Economic Analysis', 210. Bhattacharyya, 'Income Inequality', 6. Crafts, 'Duration', 335. Anderson and Morse, 'High Fertility', 343.
91. For example, Cleland and Wilson, 'Economic Theories', 25, 27–8. Chesnais, *The Demographic Transition*, p. 360. Coleman and Salt, *The British Population*, p. 66. J. R. Gillis, L. A. Tilly and D. Levine, 'The Quiet Revolution', in Gillis et al. (eds), *The European Experience*, pp. 1–9.
92. Chesnais, *The Demographic Transition*, p. 392. Gillis et al., 'The Quiet Revolution', pp. 1–9. M. J. Maynes, 'The Contours of Childhood: Demography, Strategy and Mythology of Childhood

in French and German Lower Class Autobiographies', in Gillis et al. (eds), *The European Experience*, pp. 101–24.
93. Woods and Smith, 'The Decline', 207–9, 225. Chesnais, *The Demographic Transition*, pp. 409, 471. Coleman and Salt, *The British Population*, pp. 62–3. M. Segalen, 'Exploring a Cause of Late French Fertility Decline: Two Contrasted Breton Examples', in Gillis et al. (eds), *The European Experience*, pp. 227–47. Simon, 'The Effect', 331. Liebenstein, 'An Interpretation', 469–71. Teitelbaum, *The British Fertility Decline*, p. 218. Keyfitz, 'The Family', 141. G. B. Terry, 'Rival Explanations in the Work–Fertility Relationship', *Population Studies*, 29, 2 (1975), 191.
94. Simons, 'Developments', 117. Murphy, 'Economic Models', 235.
95. 'A Review of the 1980s', *Population Trends*, 62 (1990), 6. B. Botting, 'Trends in Abortion', *Population Trends*, 64 (1991), 19–20, 23, 26–7.
96. Coleman and Salt, *The British Population*, p. 126. See also Leshaeghe, 'A Century', 412. S. H. Preston, 'Changing Values and Falling Birth Rates', in Davis et al. (eds), Below-Replacement, 187. Of all industrialised countries only in Japan has abortion played a particularly important role in the further decline in fertility in recent decades. Preston, 'The Decline', 42.
97. Botting, 'Trends', 24–5. M. Murphy, 'The Contraceptive Pill and Women's Employment as Factors in Fertility Change in Britain, 1963–1980: a Challenge to the Conventional View', *Population Studies*, 47, 2 (1993), 227–8.
98. Simons, 'Developments', 127, 130. Ermisch, 'The Relevance', 42, 53. Coleman and Salt, *The British Population*, p. 123
99. Preston, 'Changing Values', 182–4.
100. Ni Bhrolchain, 'Period Parity', 122.
101. Murphy, 'The Contraceptive Pill', 221, 223–4, 229, 236–8. See also Murphy, 'Economic Models', 241–2.
102. E. de Cooman, J. Ermisch and H. Joshi, 'The Next Birth and the Labour Market: a Dynamic Model of Births in England and Wales', *IPPF Medical Bulletin*, 16/4 (1982), 2–4. Ermisch, 'Investigations', 141, 152. Lesthaeghe and Meekers, 'Value Changes', 231. Lesthaeghe and Surkyn, 'Cultural Dynamics', 32, 34. Coleman and Salt, *The British Population*, pp. 122–3, 126. Murphy, 'Economic Models', 250.
103. Glass, 'Fertility Trends', 103. Gittins, 'Married Life', 60–1. Simons, 'Developments', 123. Coleman and Salt, *The British Population*, pp. 115, 138. Winter, 'War, Family and Fertility', 292.

104. Coleman and Salt, *The British Population*, pp. 117, 143. Ermisch, 'The Relevance', 50, 53. Ermisch, 'Investigations', 146, 153. M. Ni Bhrolchain, 'The Interpretation and Role of Work-Associated Accelerated Childbearing in Postwar Britain', *European Journal of Population*, 2 (1986), 135–54. M. Ni Bhrolchain, 'Women's Paid Work and Timing of Births: Longitudinal Evidence', *European Journal of Population*, 2 (1986), 43–70. De Cooman et al., 'The Next Birth', 255. Winter, 'War, Family and Fertility', 292–3. Busfield and Hawthorn, 'Some Social Determinants', 65, 74. Data from the 1976 OPCS Family Formation Survey suggest that housing conditions were the single most important influence on social class fertility differentials. N. J. Murphy, 'Differential Family Formation in Great Britain', *Journal of Biosocial Science*, 19 (1987), 482. The nature of housing tenure also helped shape regional fertility variations in England and Wales. Coward, 'Fertility Patterns', 84.
105. Ermisch, 'Investigations', 154–5. De Cooman et al., 'The Next Birth', 261–3. Coleman and Salt, *The British Population*, pp. 138–9. Preston, 'Changing Values', 179, 184.
106. Ermisch, 'Investigations', 153. Murphy, however, argues that, because owner-occupiers have lower fertility than those who rent, part of the explanation for declining rates of fertility after the mid 1960s was the increase which occurred in the percentage of young couples owning their own houses. M. J. Murphy, 'Housing the People: From Shortage to Surplus', in Joshi (ed.), *The Changing Population*, pp. 100–1.
107. R. A. Easterlin, 'The American Baby Boom in Historical Perspective', *American Economic Review*, 51 (1961), 869–911. R. A. Easterlin, 'The Conflict between Aspirations and Resources', *Population and Development Review*, 2, 3 & 4 (1976), 417–25.
108. V. K. Oppenheimer, 'The Easterlin Hypothesis: Another Aspect of the Echo to Consider', *Population and Development Review*, 2 (1976), 433–58.
109. J. F. Ermisch, 'Time Costs Aspirations and the Effect of Economic Growth on German Fertility', *Oxford Bulletin of Economics and Statistics*, 42, 2 (1980), 125–43. Ermisch, 'Investigations', 144. Socio-occupational differentials in fertility in the USA between 1930 and 1960 likewise fail to conform to the Easterlin thesis. A. Sweezy, 'The Economic Explanation of Fertility Changes in the United States', *Population Studies*, 25, 2 (1971), 260–2.
110. Crafts, 'A Time Series Study', 584, 589.

111. Ermisch, 'The Relevance', 40, 45–8. Ermisch, 'Investigations', 143–4.
112. Ermisch, 'The Relevance', 47–9.
113. Robert E. Wright, 'The Easterlin Hypothesis and European Fertility Rates', *Population and Development Review*, 15, 1 (1989), 109, 117–18.
114. Coleman and Salt, *The British Population*, p. 140.
115. R. J. Willis, 'A New Approach to the Economic Theory of Fertility Behaviour', *Journal of Political Economy*, 81, 2, Part II (1973), 514–64. W. P. Butz and M. P. Ward, 'Will US Fertility Remain Low? A New Economic Interpretation', *Population and Development Review*, 5, 4 (1979), 663–89. Ermisch, 'The Relevance', 40–2, 50. Ermisch, 'Investigations', 144–6. Even Lesthaeghe, the main protagonist of ideationalist interpretations, accepts that increases in female employment made some contribution to the decline in fertility from the mid 1960s. Lesthaeghe, 'A Century', 415–16. Lesthaeghe and Meekers, 'Value Changes', 261.
116. H. Joshi, 'The Changing Form of Women's Employment Dependency', in Joshi (ed.), *The Changing Population*, p. 158.
117. Similar increases occurred in almost all industrialised countries. Ermisch, 'The Labour Market', 179–81. Coleman and Salt, *The British Population*, p. 141.
118. H. Joshi, 'The Cash Opportunity Costs of Childbearing: an Approach to Estimation Using British Data', *Population Studies*, 44, 1 (1990), 53.
119. Ermisch, 'The Relevance', 52. Ermisch, 'Investigations', 149. De Cooman et al., 'The Next Birth', 255–7. Wright, 'The Easterlin Hypothesis', 118–19.
120. De Cooman et al., 'The Next Birth', 260. For similar conclusions on the importance of increasing female employment for Scottish fertility rates since 1964 see Kendrick et al., 'Recent Trends', 44–5.
121. Ermisch, 'Investigations', 155.
122. H. Jones, 'A Spatial Analysis of Human Fertility in Scotland', *Scottish Geographic Magazine*, 91 (1975), 102–13. M. Wilson, 'A Spatial Analysis of Human Fertility in Scotland: Reappraisal and Extension', *Scottish Geographic Magazine*, 94 (1978), 130–43. Coward, 'Fertility Patterns', 18–19. Kendrick et al., 'Recent Trends', 44–5, 47. Murphy, 'Differential Family Formation', 463–4.
123. Preston, 'The Decline of Fertility', 26, 28.
124. Murphy, 'Economic Models', 243.
125. Ni Bhrolchain, 'Period Parity', 123.

126. Murphy, 'Economic Models', 250.
127. Simons, 'Developments', 131, 133–4. Lesthaeghe, 'A Century', 430. Lesthaeghe and Meekers, 'Value Changes', 226, 261. Lesthaeghe and Surkyn, 'Cultural Dynamics', 32–6. Preston, 'Changing Values', 180–1, 189. Coleman and Salt, *The British Population*, pp. 146–7. Murphy, 'Economic Models', 241. Winter, 'War, Family and Fertility', 293, 305–8.
128. Murphy, 'Economic Models', 250.

BIBLIOGRAPHY

This is a highly selective list of books and articles intended as a guide to further reading.

Books

Baines, D., *Migration in a Mature Economy. Emigration and Internal Migration in England and Wales, 1861–1900* (Cambridge, 1985).
Baines, D., *Emigration from Europe, 1815–1930* (London, 1991).
Barker, T. and Drake, M. (eds), *Population and Society in Britain, 1850–1980* (London, 1982).
Champion, A. G. (ed.), *Counterurbanization. The Changing Pace and Nature of Population Deconcentration* (London, 1989).
Chesnais, J.-C., *The Demographic Transition. Stages, Patterns and Economic Implications* (Oxford, 1992).
Coleman, D. A. (ed.), *Demography of Immigrants and Minority Groups in the United Kingdom* (London, 1982).
Coleman, D. and Salt, J., *The British Population. Patterns, Trends and Processes* (Oxford, 1992).
Davis, K., Bernstam, M. S. and Ricardo-Campbell, R. (eds), 'Below-Replacement, Fertility in Industrial Societies. Causes, Consequences, Policies', *Population and Development Review*, Supplement to vol. 12 (1986).
Eversely, D. and Kolmann, W. (eds), *Population Changes and Social Planning* (London, 1982).

Flinn, M. W. (ed.), *Scottish Population History from the Seventeenth Century to the 1930s* (Cambridge, 1977).
Gillis, J. R., Tilly, L. A. and Levine, D. (eds), *The European Experience of Declining Fertility. A Quiet Revolution, 1850–1970* (Oxford, 1992).
Gittins, D., *Fair Sex, Family Size and Structure, 1900–39* (London, 1982).
Goddard, J. B. and Champion A. G. (eds), *The Urban and Regional Transformation of Britain* (London, 1983).
Hiorns, R. W. (ed.), *Demographic Patterns in Developed Societies* (London, 1980).
Hobcraft, J. and Rees, P. (eds), *Regional Demographic Development* (London, 1978).
Jones, H. (ed.), *Population Change in Contemporary Scotland* (Norwich, 1984).
Joshi, H. (ed.), *The Changing Population of Britain* (Oxford, 1990).
Levine, D., *Reproducing Families. The Political Economy of English Population History* (Cambridge, 1987).
Livi-Bacci, M., *A Concise History of World Population* (Oxford, 1992).
McKeown, T., *The Modern Rise of Population* (London, 1976).
Mercer, A. J., *Disease, Mortality and Population in Transition. Epidemiological-Demographic Change in England since the Eighteenth Century as Part of a Global Phenomenon* (Leicester, 1990).
Pacione, M. (ed.) *Population Geography: Progress and Prospect* (London, 1986).
Shorter, E., *The Making of the Modern Family* (London, 1977).
Teitelbaum, M. S., *The British Fertility Decline* (Princeton, 1984).
Walvin, J., *Passage to Britain. Immigration in British History and Politics* (Hardmondsworth, 1984).
White, P. E and Van Der Knaap, Bert. (eds), *Contemporary Studies of Migration* (Norwich, 1985).
Woods, R., *The Population of Britain in the Nineteenth Century* (London, 1992).
Woods, R. and Rees, P. (eds), *Population Structures and Models. Development in Spatial Demography* (London, 1986).

Articles

Anderson, M. and Morse, D. J., 'High Fertility, High Emigration, Low Nuptiality: Adjustment Processes in Scotland's Demographic

Experience, 1861–1914, Part II', *Population Studies*, 47, 2 (1993), 319–43.

Becker, G. S., 'An Economic Analysis of Fertility', in National Bureau of Economic Research', *Demographic and Economic Change in Developed Countries* (Princeton, NJ, 1960), pp. 423–44.

Beaver, M. W., 'Population, Infant Mortality and Milk', *Population Studies*, 27, 2 (1973), 243–54.

Blake, J., 'Are Babies Consumer Durables?' *Population Studies*, 22, 1 (1968), 5–25.

Busfield, J. and Hawthorn, G., 'Some Social Determinants of Recent Trends in British Fertility', *Journal of Biosocial Science*, Sup. 3 (1971), 65–77.

Butz, W. P. and Ward, M. P., 'Will US Fertility Remain Low? A New Economic Interpretation', *Population and Development Review*, 5, 4 (1989), 663–89.

Caldwell, J. C., 'The Mechanisms of Demographic Change in Historical Perspective', *Population Studies*, 35, 1 (1981), 5–27.

Calot, G. and Blayo, C., 'Recent Course of Fertility in Western Europe', *Population Studies*, 36, 3 (1982), 349–72.

Cleland, J. and Wilson, C., 'Demand Theories of the Fertility Transition: An Iconoclastic View', *Population Studies*, 41, 1 (1987), 5–30.

Cooper, J., 'Births Outside Marriage: Recent Trends and Associated Demographic and Social Changes', *Population Trends*, 63 (1991), 8–18.

Crafts, N. F. R., 'Illegitimacy in England and Wales in 1911', *Population Studies*, 36, 2 (1982), 327–31.

Crafts, N. F. R., 'A Cross-Sectional Study of Legitimate Fertility in England and Wales, 1911', *Research in Economic History*, 9 (1984), 89–107.

Crafts, N. F. R., 'A Time Series Study of Fertility in England and Wales, 1877–1938', *Journal of European Economic History*, 13 (1984), 571–90.

Crafts, N. F. R., 'Duration of Marriage, Fertility and Women's Employment Opportunities in England and Wales in 1911', *Population Studies*, 43, 2 (1989), 325–35.

De Cooman, E., Ermisch, J. and Joshi, H., 'The Next Birth and the Labour Market: a Dynamic Model of Births in England and Wales', *Population Studies*, 41, 2 (1987), 237–68.

Dyhouse, C., 'Working Class Mothers and Infant Mortality in England, 1895–1914', *Journal of Social History*, 12, 2 (1978), 248–67.

Easterlin, R. A., 'The American Baby Boom in Historical Perspective', *American Economic Review*, 51 (1961), 869–911.
Easterlin, R. A., 'The Conflict between Aspirations and Resources', *Population and Development Review*, 2 (1976), 417–26.
Eldridge, S. and Kiernan, K., 'Declining First-Marriage Rates in England and Wales: a Change in Timing or a Rejection of Marriage?', *European Journal of Population*, 1 (1985), 327–45.
Ermisch, J. F., 'The Relevance of the Easterlin Hypothesis and the "New Home Economics" to Fertility Movement in Great Britain', *Population Studies*, 33, 1 (1979), 39–58.
Fielding, A. J., 'Counterurbanization in Western Europe', *Progress in Planning*, 17, 1 (1982), 5–34.
Fox, E., 'Powers of Life and Death: Aspects of Maternal Welfare in England and Wales between the Wars', *Medical History*, 35 (1991), 328–52.
Freedman, R., 'The Sociology of Human Fertility: a Trend Report and Bibliography', *Current Sociology*, 10–11 (1961–2), 35–68.
Friedlander, D., 'The Spread of Urbanization in England and Wales, 1851–1951', *Population Studies*, 24, 3 (1970), 423–43.
Friedlander, D. and Roshier, R. J., 'A Study of Internal Migration in England and Wales, Part II', *Population Studies*, 19, 3 (1966), 45–59.
Gage, T. B., 'The Decline of Mortality in England and Wales, 1861 to 1964: Decomposition by Cause of Death and Component of Mortality', *Population Studies*, 47, 1 (1953), 47–66.
Gittins, D., 'Married Life and Birth Control between the Wars', *Oral History*, III, 2 (1975), 52–64.
Glass, D. V., 'Fertility Trends in Europe since the Second World War', *Population Studies*, 22, 1 (1968), 103–46.
Gould, J. D., 'European Inter-Continental Emigration, 1815–1914: Patterns and Causes', *Journal of European Economic History*, 8, 3 (1979), 593–680.
Gould, J. D., 'European Inter-Continental Emigration the Road Home: Return Migration from the USA', *Journal of European Economic History*, 9, 1 (1980), 41–112.
Gould, J. D., 'European Inter-Continental Emigration: the Role of Diffusion and Feedback', *Journal of European Economic History*, 9, 2 (1980), 267–315.
Haines, M. R., 'Social Class Differentials During Fertility Decline: England and Wales Revisited', *Population Studies*, 43, 2 (1989), 305–22.
Hajnal, J., 'Age at Marriage and Proportions Marrying', *Population Studies*, 7, 2 (1953), 111–36.

Heer, D. M., 'Economic Development and Fertility', *Demography*, 3 (1966), 423–44.

Heer, D. M., 'Economic Development and the Fertility Transition', *Daedalus*, 97 (1968), 447–62.

Laslett, P. and Oosterveen, K., 'Long-Term Trends in Bastardy in England: a Study of Illegitimacy Figures in the Parish Registers and in the Reports of the Registrar-General, 1561–1960', *Population Studies*, 27, 2 (1973), 255–86.

Law, C. M., 'The Growth of Urban Population in England and Wales, 1801–1911', *Transactions of the Institute of British Geographers*, XLI (1967), 125–43.

Lee, C. H., 'Regional Inequalities in Infant Mortality in Britain, 1861–1971: Patterns and Hypotheses', *Population Studies*, 45, 1 (1991), 55–65.

Lesthaeghe, R., 'A Century of Demographic and Cultural Change in Western Europe: an Explanation of Underlying Dimensions', *Population and Development Review*, 9, 3 (1983), 411–35.

Lesthaeghe, R. and Meekers, D., 'Value Changes and the Dimensions of Familism in the European Community', *European Journal of Population*, 2 (1986), 225–68.

Lesthaeghe, R. and Surkyn, J., 'Cultural Dynamics and Economic Theories of Fertility Change', *Population and Development Review*, 14 (1988), 1–45.

Levine, D., 'Industrialization and the Proletarian Family in England', *Past and Present*, 107 (1985), 168–203.

Lewis, J., 'The Ideology and Politics of Birth Control in Inter-War England', *Women's Studies International Quarterly*, 2 (1979), 33–48.

Liebenstein, H., 'An Interpretation of the Economic Theory of Fertility: Promising Path or Blind Alley?' *Journal of Economic Literature*, XII, 2 (1974), 457–79.

Logan, W. P. D., 'Mortality in England and Wales from 1848 to 1947', *Population Studies*, 4, 2 (1950), 132–78.

Loudon, I., 'Maternal Mortality: 1880–1950. Some Regional and International Comparisons', *Society for the Social History of Medicine*, 1 (1988), 183–228.

Loudon, I., 'On Maternal and Infant Mortality, 1900–1960', *Society for the Social History of Medicine*, 4 (1991), 29–73.

Marr, W. L. 'The United Kingdom's Inter-Continental Migration in the Inter-War Period: Theoretical Considerations and Empirical Testing', *Population Studies*, 31, 3 (1977), 571–9.

Massey, D. S., 'Economic Development and International Migration in Comparative Perspective', *Population and Development Review*, 14, 3 (1988), 383–413.

McAvinchey, I. D., 'Economic Factors and Mortality. Some Aspects of the Scottish Case, 1950–78', *Scottish Journal of Political Economy*, 31, 1 (1984), 1–27.

McKeown, T., Brown, R. G. and Record, R. G., 'An Interpretation of the Modern Rise of Population in Europe', *Population Studies*, 26, 3 (1972), 345–82.

McKeown, T., Record, R. G. and Turner, R. D., 'An Interpretation of the Decline in Mortality in England and Wales during the 20th Century', *Population Studies*, 29, 3 (1975), 391–422.

Mercer, A. J., 'Relative Trends in Mortality from Related Respiratory and Airborne Infectious Diseases', *Population Studies*, 40, 1 (1986), 129–45.

Minge-Kalman, W., 'The Industrial Revolution and the European Family: the Institutionalization of "Childhood" as a Market for Family Labour', *Comparative Studies in Society and History*, 20, 3 (1975), 454–68.

Murphy, M., 'Economic Models of Fertility in Post-War Britain – a Conceptual and Statistical Reinterpretation', *Population Studies*, 46, 2 (1992), 235–58.

Murphy, M., 'The Contraceptive Pill and Women's Employment as Factors in Fertility Change in Britain, 1963–1980: a Challenge to the Conventional View', *Population Studies*, 47, 2 (1993), 221–43.

Ni Bhrolchain, M., 'The Interpretation and Role of Work-Associated Accelerated Childbearing in Postwar Britain', *European Journal of Population*, 2 (1986), 135–54.

Ni Bhrolchain, M., 'Women's Paid Work and the Timing of Births: Longitudinal Evidence', *European Journal of Population*, 2 (1986), 43–70.

Oppenheimer, V. K., 'The Easterlin Hypothesis: Another Aspect of the Echo to Consider', *Population and Development Review*, 2 (1976), 433–58.

Pamuk, E. R., 'Social Class Inequality in Mortality from 1921 to 1972 in England and Wales', *Population Studies*, 39, 1 (1985), 15–31.

Pope, D., 'Some Factors Inhibiting Australian Immigration in the 1920s', *Australian Economic History Review*, 24, 1 (1984), 34–52.

Schoen, R. and Baj, J., 'Twentieth Century Cohort Marriage and Divorce in England and Wales', *Population Studies*, 38, 3 (1984), 439–49.

Shorter, E., 'Female Emancipation, Birth Control and Fertility in European History', *American Historical Review*, 78, 3 (1973), 605–40.

Shorter, E., Knodel, J. and Van De Walle, E., 'The Decline of Non-Marital Fertility in Europe, 1880–1940', *Population Studies*, 25, 3 (1971), 375–93.

Simon, J. C., 'The Effect of Income on Fertility', *Population Studies*, 23, 3 (1969), 327–41.

Terry, G. B., 'Rival Explanations in the Work–Fertility Relationship', *Population Studies*, 29, 2 (1975), 191–205.

Tilly, L. A., Scott, J. W. and Cohen, M., 'Women's Work and European Fertility Patterns', *Journal of Interdisciplinary History*, VI, 3 (1976), 447–76.

Watkins, S. C., 'Regional Patterns of Nuptiality in Europe, 1870–1960', *Population Studies*, 35, 2 (1981), 199–215.

Watkins, S. C., 'From Local to National Communities: the Transformation of Demographic Regimes in Western Europe, 1870–1960', *Population and Development Review*, 16, 2 (1990), 241–72.

Watterson, P. A., 'Role of the Environment in the Decline of Infant Mortality: an Analysis of the 1911 Census of England and Wales', *Journal of Biosocial Science*, 18 (1986), 457–70.

Watterson, P. A., 'Infant Mortality Decline by Father's Occupation from the 1911 Census of England and Wales', *Demography*, 25, 2 (1988), 289–305.

Wells, R. V., 'Family History and the Demographic Transition', *Journal of Social History*, 9, 1 (1975), 1–19.

Willis, R. J., 'A New Approach to the Economic Theory of Fertility', *Journal of Political Economy*, 81, 2, Part II (1973), 514–64.

Wilson, C. and Woods, R. I., 'Fertility in England: a Long-Term Perspective', *Population Studies*, 45, 3 (1991), 399–415.

Winter, J. M., 'Aspects of the Impact of the First World War on Infant Mortality in Britain', *Journal of European Economic History*, 11, 3 (1972), 713–18.

Winter, J. M., 'Some Aspects of the Demographic Consequences of the First World War in Britain', *Population Studies*, 30, 3 (1976), 539–52.

Winter, J. M., 'The Impact of the First World War on Civilian Health in Britain', *Economic History Review*, 30, 3 (1977), 487–507.

Winter, J. M., 'Infant Mortality, Maternal Mortality and Public Health in Britain', *Journal of European Economic History*, 13, 2 (1979), 439–62.

Woods, R. I., 'Approaches to the Fertility Transition in Victorian England', *Population Studies*, 41, 2 (1987), 283–311.
Woods, R. I., Watterson, P. A. and Woodward, J. H., 'The Causes of Rapid Infant Mortality Decline in England and Wales, 1861–1921. Part I', *Population Studies*, 42, 3 (1988), 343–66.
Woods, R. I., Watterson, P. A. and Woodward J. H., 'The Causes of Rapid Infant Mortality Decline in England and Wales, 1861–1921. Part II', *Population Studies*, 43, 1 (1989), 113–32.
Wright, Robert E., 'The Easterlin Hypothesis and European Fertility Rates', *Population and Development Review*, 15, 1 (1989), 107–22.

INDEX

Abortion, 93, 103
   and marital fertility, 114, 158
Abortion Act (1967), 88, 114
Age – specific mortality rates, 62–3
Ages at marriage, xiii, 93–4
   and fertility, 87, 94
   by social class, 151
   determinants of, 99
Aliens Act (1905), 32, 34
   (1914), 32
   (1919), 32

Baby boom, 37, 84–5, 94, 114, 117, 120, 124
Baby bust, 85, 114, 117, 120, 124
Bastardy, *see* Illegitimacy
Birth control:
   and illegitimacy, 92
   and marital fertility, 102–4, 111, 114–17
   methods of, 103–4, 154
Birth rates, xiii–xv, 83–5, 126–7, 147
   by region, xiii–xiv, 83–5, 147, 159
   by social class, xiv, 85, 159
   in England and Wales, 84–7
   in Europe, 83–5
   in Scotland, 84–7
Bradlaugh–Besant trial, 103
Brenner, 75
British Medical Association, 103
British Nationality Act (1981), 34

British Nationality (Hong Kong) Act (1990), 34

Chesnais, 105, 112
Cohen, 91
Coleman, 114
Commonwealth Immigrants Act 1962), 32–4
   (1968), 33
Contraception, *see* Birth control
Conurbations, 9–10, 17, 36, 50, 54, 57
Counterurbanisation, *see* Population decentralisation
Crafts, 91, 104, 120

Death rates, 73, 77, 79–81, 127, 142
   and marital fertility, 104–6, 113–14, 155
   by region, xiii–xiv, 68–9, 79
   by social class, xiii–xiv, 69–70, 78, 143
   in England and Wales, 62–4, 67–8, 142
   in Europe, 62
   in Scotland, 62–4, 67–8, 142
   influences on, 71–82
   in infancy, 65–70, 75, 77–9, 81, 146, 155; influences on, 73–5, 77–9, 81

Index

maternal, 67, 72, 74–5, 77–8;
    influences on, 72–5, 77–8
Deindustrialisation, *see*
    Occupational structure
Disease:
    infectious, xiii, 71–81; determinants of, 71–81
    non-infectious, xiv, 71, 76–8; determinants of, 75–8
Divorce, xiv, 92–3, 95–6, 99–100, 127
    and marriage rates, 99–100
    by social class, 96
    determinants of, 99–100
    in England and Wales, 96
    in Scotland, 96
Dominions Royal Commission, 42

Easterlin, 119–21
Emigrants Information Office, 40
Emigration, xiii–xiv
    and the fertility transition, 105
    causes of, 37–46
    from Scotland, by destination, 21, 135
    nature of data on, 24–5, 29
    state aid for, 42–4, 136
    volume of, 24–9, 126
Emigration societies, 40
Empire Settlement Act, 42–3
Equal Pay Act, 122–4
Ermisch, 121
Expectation of life, xiv, 73, 75, 79–81, 126
    by region, xiii, 69
    by social class, xiii
    in England, 141
    in England and Wales, 63, 65
    in Scotland, 63, 65
    influences on, 71–4, 79, 82
Extramarital cohabitation, xiv, 92–3, 95–6, 99–100, 127
    and divorce, 100
    and marriage rates, 99
    in Europe, 152

Family planning, *see* Birth control
Family Planning Act (1967), 115
Family size, and mortality, 80–1
Fertility, *see* Birth rates; Marital fertility
Fertility transition, causes of, 102–13

Fielding, 57
Friedlander, 97

Goddard, 52

Illegitimacy, xiv, 89–93, 127, 149
    by region, 87–8, 91
    by social class, 87–8, 91
    determinants of, 90–3
    in England, 87–8
    in England and Wales, 88–9
    in Europe, 88–90
    in Scotland, 87–9
Illegitimacy ratio, definition of, 87
Immigrants Appeals Act (1969), 33
Immigration, causes of, 34–7, 45, 135
    legislative restrictions on, 32–4, 44
    nature of data on, 24–5, 28–9
    origins of, 28, 30–2, 34, 133
    volume of, 24–32, 126
Immigration Act (1971), 33
Internal migration, and settlement size, 49–50
    causes of, 47–8, 50–61
    direction of, 46–50, 127, 129, 137–8
    distance of, 137
    extent of, 48–52, 61, 126
International Passenger Survey, 29

Lawton, 47

Marie Stopes, 103
Marital fertility, xiv, 87, 93, 101–25
    and illegitimacy, 90
    and real income levels, 106–8, 111, 113, 117–18
    and the employment of women, 106, 108–9, 113, 121–4
    and the 'family economy', 109–10, 113
    and the 'the New Home Economics' thesis, 121–4
    and the 'relative income' thesis, 119–21
    and value systems, 105, 111–13, 117, 124–5
    by region, 101–2, 106
    by social group, 101–2, 106, 108, 123

Index

Marital fertility – *continued*
  determinants of, 102–25, 157, 159–60
  in England and Wales, 101–2, 107
  in Europe, 101–2
  in Scotland, 101–2, 107
Marriage rates, xiii–xiv, 93–4, 96–9
  and fertility, 87, 93–4
  and illegitimacy, 90–3
  by region, 94–5, 97
  by social group, 94
  determinants of, 94, 96–9
  in England and Wales, 94–7
  in Europe, 94–5
  in Scotland, 94–5, 97
McAvinchey, 75
McCarran–Walter Act, 30
McKeown, 73, 80
Midwives Act (1902), 78
  (1936), 77
Mortality, *see* Death rates
Murphy, 116

National Health Service, and marital fertility, 115
  and mortality, 69, 77
Natural increase, and population growth, 19–24
Net migration, and marriage rates, 97–8
  and population growth, 19–24, 132
  as a percentage of natural increase, 20, 22
  balance of, 45–6, 126
New Towns, 11–12, 14–15, 50, 54, 59–60
Ni Bhrolchain, 116
Nuptiality, *see* Marriage rates

Occupational structure, 51
Oppenheimer, 119–21
Overseas Migration Board, 45

Passenger statistics, 24–5

Population decentralisation, 10–15, 17–18, 54, 56, 59–61
  causes of, 53–61
  see also Urbanisation
Population distribution, 126, 129
  by region, xiii–xv, 5–7
  by urban-rural residence, xiv–xv, 9–15, 17–18
Population growth rates, xiii–xv, 4, 17, 126–7
  by region, 7–9, 17
  by settlement type, 9–18, 130–1
  in Britain, 1–2, 4
  in England, 1–2, 4
  in Europe, 2–4
  in Scotland, 2, 4
  in Wales, 2, 4
Population, size of, 1–4, 60
Premarital conception, 92–3, 150
  by social class, 148

Record, 80
Remarriage, 95–6, 127
  in England and Wales, 96
  in Europe, 152

Salt, 114
Scott, 91
Shorter, 92
Stern, 75
Suburbanisation, 10, 48, 53–4

Tilly, 91
Total period fertility rates, 84–7
Turner, 80

Urbanisation, definition of, 129
  extent of, 9–18
  see also, Population decentralisation
USA Immigration Restriction Act, 44

Watkins, 97
Winter, 79

DATE DUE

JUL 2 4 2001	

DEMCO, INC. 38-2931

PALESTINE:
RETREAT FROM THE MANDATE

The Making of British Policy, 1936–45

PALESTINE:
RETREAT FROM THE MANDATE

The Making of British Policy, 1936-45

Michael J. Cohen

HOLMES & MEIER PUBLISHERS, INC.
NEW YORK

In memory of my mother

First published in the United States of America 1978 by
HOLMES & MEIER PUBLISHERS, INC.
30 Irving Place, New York, N.Y. 10003

Copyright © 1978 by Michael J. Cohen

ALL RIGHTS RESERVED

Library of Congress Cataloging in Publication Data
Cohen, Michael Joseph, 1940–
  Palestine, retreat from the Mandate.

  Bibliography: p.
  Includes index.
  1. Palestine—Politics and government—1929–1948.
2. Mandates—Palestine.   I. Title.
DS126.C532 1978   956.94′04   78–933
ISBN 0–8419–0373–5

PRINTED IN GREAT BRITAIN

Contents

List of Maps	vi
Acknowledgements	vii
Introduction	ix

1	The Mediterranean Strategic Context, 1936–39	1
2	The 1936 Rebellion—Martial Law or Political Concessions	10
3	Partition, 1937–38: Doubts and Suspicions	32
4	Anglo-French Attitudes to Palestinian Arab Nationalism	50
5	The White Paper, May 1939	66
6	British Policy during the Critical Phase, 1939–42	
	The 'Constitutional Clauses'	88
	Negotiations for a Jewish Army	98
7	Zionist Leadership in Crisis	125
8	Palestine and Arab Federation	140
9	British Policy in Palestine, 1943–45	
	Strategic Considerations	151
	Political Reassessments	160
10	Conclusion	187

Notes	192
Bibliography	225
Index	231

Maps

The Middle East in 1936   2

The Peel Commission's partition proposal, 1937   36

The Cabinet Committee's partition proposal, 1944   176

The UN partition proposal, 1947   185

Acknowledgements

Over nearly a decade's research and writing I have incurred a vast number of obligations. Space permits me to mention but three here. I am indebted, first, to Professor Elie Kedourie, under whose subtle guidance I first entered the labyrinth of British policy in Palestine; and next, to Professor Y. Bauer and Dr I. Kollat of the Hebrew University, Jerusalem, who encouraged me to embark and advised me on the current work. Needless to say, none of the above is responsible for the views expressed below.

I should like to acknowledge the assistance afforded to me by the Staff of the Public Records Office, London, the Library of the London School of Economics, the Central Zionist and the Israel State Archives at Jerusalem, the Weizmann Archives at Rehovot, the Middle East Centre at St Antony's College, Oxford and the Centre for Military Archives at King's College, London.

I should like to express my thanks to the Editors of *The Historical Journal*, *The Journal of Contemporary History* and *Middle Eastern Studies* for permission to use material which first appeared in their Journals. Since then I have added and changed much, but my central theses remain unchanged.

I should like to acknowledge the kind permission of Alfred A. Knopf, Inc. and Penguin Books Ltd to base the map on page 2 on part of the map which appears on pages 2–3 of *Europe Leaves the Middle East, 1936–1954* by Howard M. Sachar (Copyright © Howard M. Sachar, 1972) published by Alfred A. Knopf, Inc. in 1972 and by Allen Lane (with revisions) in 1974; and of Cambridge University Press and the Editor of *The Historical Journal* to reproduce the other maps in this book, which first appeared with an article of mine in *The Historical Journal*, Vol. 19, No. 3, September 1976.

A substantial part of this book was written while I was engaged as a Research Fellow at the Institute of Contemporary Jewry, at the Hebrew University, Jerusalem, in a project financed by the World Zionist Organization.

All unpublished Crown copyright material from the Public Record Office appears by permission of the Controller of HM Stationery Office.

M.J.C.

Introduction

The events related in this book should be seen in the context of a wider process that has been called 'The Imperial Sunset'.[1] The historian of Britain's imperial decline dates the beginning of that process back to 1921, the year in which in the Middle East the Empire reached its apogee. 'The War had given a major impulse to anti-imperial feeling and weakened the self-confidence of the ruling élites. The desire to limit defence expenditure was a dominant factor in foreign policy . . .'[2] Among those concerned with imperial policy-making during the inter-war years, the real difference lay between those for whom 'foreign policy was a matter of securing the requirements of the nation at the minimal cost and recognizing the increasingly severe limitations that Britain had to accept, and those who were prone to believe that the incantations of the proper formulae would make foreign policy in the old sense a thing of the past.'[3] By 1939 the 'Jewish National Home' in Palestine would be placed on the list of 'imperial luxuries' that had to be sacrificed.

During the years 1936–45 Britain reassessed and redefined its attitude to the Zionist enterprise in Palestine. The five years prior to 1936 had been a period of almost uninterrupted peace and prosperity for both the Arab and Jewish communities in Palestine. But in 1936 the Mandatory administration lost control over events as the Arab community began a revolt which lasted intermittently until the very eve of World War Two.

Perhaps the most significant consequence of the Arab Revolt was the almost casual transformation of the Palestine issue into a pan-Arab affair. This occurred at a juncture when Britain, faced with the growing likelihood of a global conflict, had to ration strictly the resources at its disposal for maintaining imperial strong-points. In view of its insupportable imperial burdens, Britain decided in 1939 to make a radical departure from the established policy of fostering the Jewish National Home in Palestine.

Prior to 1936, the Palestine mandate had been the exclusive concern of the Colonial Office. The 'regionalization' of the issue in that year brought the active intervention in the policy-making process of the senior Department, the Foreign Office, as well as that of the Chiefs of Staff and the War Office. Events in Palestine now assumed a significance out of all proportion to their local geopolitical context. There soon arose a conflict of policy-goals, as was seen in the debate on the partition of Palestine in 1937, between the strictly Palestinian merit of the proposal advanced by the Colonial Office and the wider, regional implications which were the subject of Foreign Office warnings. Henceforth, policy in Palestine would have to be determined strictly, and if necessary callously, according to the goals of Britain's grand policy in the Middle East as a whole.

Ideological justification for the new doctrine was found with the 'rediscovery' of the MacMahon–Hussein correspondence[4] in 1938. The British had always maintained that the promises given by the High Commissioner to Egypt, MacMahon, to the Arabs in 1915 (that Britain would establish an independent Arab State after the war) had not included Palestine. Now Whitehall, displaying a classical loss of imperial resolve to rule Palestine, expressed its doubts, and admitted that the Arabs at the very least had good grounds for claiming that Palestine had been promised to them. Since the correspondence predated the Balfour Declaration of 1917, it had to take precedence. Therefore the two undertakings of the Balfour Declaration—to 'facilitate the establishment in Palestine of a Jewish National Home', *providing* nothing was done to harm the interests of the Arab community—must be reversed. The provision for the protection of Arab interests—as interpreted by the Arabs themselves—would now become the first call on British policy in Palestine. Some Whitehall officials believed sincerely that the conflicting promises distributed during World War One had gravely prejudiced Arab rights. But in the long run academic discussion of what the various negotiators had really intended twenty-five years before produced little more than red herrings – British policy was henceforth determined by one single hardheaded criterion, not liberal ideals, but economic and strategic interests.

In contradiction of the spirit, if not the letter, of the Balfour Declaration the 1939 White Paper placed a five-year moratorium on future Jewish development in Palestine, curtailing Jewish immigration and land-purchases drastically. It also fixed a definite constitutional process leading to the establishment within ten years of an independent Palestinian State.

In 1939, the Government believed that it had but to reach a modus vivendi with the Arab States on Palestine for most of its troubles in the Middle East during the approaching war to dissolve. This proved to be a miscalculation on several counts; because the Arab States did not perform the moderating role expected of them, and London found itself being propelled at a faster rate than it had intended towards Palestinian independence; because during the war military victories rather than paper promises were what impressed the Arab world; and because London could not have anticipated the fate of the Jews during the war, or the strength of their resistance to the new policy.

Whereas Palestine itself did not in fact see hostilities during the war, the constant threat of Axis invasion during the first half of the war and the physical presence of large British armies in the Middle East for the rest of it enabled the Mandatory power to keep in cold storage the constitutional development promised to the Palestinian Arabs in 1939. However, a policy of appeasement was pursued in the Middle East long after it had been abandoned in Europe, even after the Axis had been ejected from North Africa. Appeasement in the Middle East was indeed a different brand from that initiated by Chamberlain in Europe. The Arabs could not jeopardize the security of the British Isles, as Hitler did, but they could sabotage vital economic and strategic interests. Moreover, these interests could be protected much more effectively by the friendship of the indigenous peoples than by military occupation.

In 1943, with the war over in the Middle East, both Zionists and Arabs began an urgent lobby of Western capitals. In London, Churchill, a self-confessed Zionist sympathizer, hand-picked a new Cabinet Committee to draw up a long-term solution based on a Jewish State in a part of Palestine—a majority of the Committee's members had voted against the 1939 White Paper in the Commons. But the 1939 policy was not to be jettisoned easily. Although British arms dominated the Middle East, Britain turned a wary eye to its wartime Allies, each waiting in the wings to exploit any false move. During the war, the dramatic increase in American trade and oil exploitation in the Middle East had resulted in competition, and even direct conflict, with British interests. The Soviets, who had opened several new diplomatic posts in the area, would exploit any social unrest. Even Churchill, the arch-opponent of appeasement in Europe, who had replaced Chamberlain as Prime Minister in May 1940, proved unable or perhaps unwilling to overrule the unanimous advice of his experts and officials, that in order to safeguard its interests in the Middle East Britain must adhere to the 1939 White Paper as a bare minimum – notwithstanding the human tragedy which was unravelling in Europe, or the pressures of public (especially American) opinion.

Churchill himself must remain something of an enigma. He was evidently torn between the pro-Zionist sympathies he brought from his Colonial Secretaryship in the early 1920s (when he had written the first official interpretation of the Balfour Declaration) and the policies advocated by his experts in response to the radically different problems of the 1940s. Churchill was most liberal with promises of a Jewish State, made in confidence to the Zionist leader Weizmann, but for all that he never in fact compromised generally accepted British interests for the sake of Zionism. Churchill's own ambiguous attitude accounts perhaps for the many vacillations of British policy during this period, something approaching almost impotence either to enforce forthrightly all the provisions of the White Paper, or repeal it.

The issue became even more clear cut when in October 1944 a meeting of Arab Foreign Ministers in Egypt signed the Alexandria Protocol, laying the foundations of what in March 1945 would become the Arab League. It was only to be expected that Britain would attempt to move with the tide of pan-Arabism during the war, yet London was not so unambiguously sanguine about these developments as some observers have maintained. Following its abortive attempts to mobilize Arab support for the 1939 White Paper (and, indeed, the bitter experiences of Hashemite–Saudi conflicts during and after World War One), London could not view with any complacency the future policies of a united Arab world, most especially not on the question of Palestine. The Alexandria Protocol unexpectedly declared the 1939 White Paper to be 'the acquired rights' of the Palestinian Arabs. On the one hand, this was a welcome endorsement, at long last, of established policy; on the other hand, there could now remain little doubt in anyone's mind that any attempt to stray from that policy would bring down upon Britain the united opposition of the Arab world.

The end of the war found the Zionists desperately militant in their demand for a Jewish State in Palestine; the Arabs in Palestine in political disarray, their charismatic leader, the Mufti, having been incriminated for his wartime collaboration with the Nazis. Most of the elements of the 1947–48 conflict which was to lead to the creation of Israel were already present.

Britain emerged from World War Two almost bankrupt, mortgaged economically, and therefore to a large extent politically, to the United States. Her inability to control or defend single-handed her huge Empire was underscored by the immediate post-war bellicosity of the Soviet Union. The Palestine impasse took on an even more intractable dimension when American intervention—dictated by the electoral considerations of an unelected President—counterbalanced the weight of the Arab world. British dependence on the United States proved greater even than her essential interests in the Middle East, and there began a process of reversing the White Paper policy, beginning in August 1945 with President Truman's demand to settle 100,000 Jewish displaced persons in Palestine, and ending in November 1947 when the United Nations voted for the establishment of a Jewish State in a part of Palestine.

Few governments are clear in their collective mind about their basic purposes and foreign observers intent on understanding what they are about make the common error of ascribing consistency and rationality to a pattern of administration which owes more to chance, emotion and intuition.

David Vital, *The Making of British Foreign Policy*, 1968

1

The Mediterranean Strategic Context, 1936-39

From 1936 to 1939 events moved quickly in Palestine, crisis overlapping crisis. The Arab Revolt in 1936, the Royal Commission proposal to partition Palestine in 1937, the near loss of control by the British Administration coinciding in 1938 with the Munich crisis in Europe, combined to shake to their very foundations the premises upon which Britain had hitherto based its rule in Palestine. The consequent reversal of British policy cannot be fully comprehended unless these events are first placed in the wider context of British regional strategy during the years preceding World War Two.

i. British vulnerability in the Mediterranean
British policy in the Mediterranean was a function of imperial interest in India, and was determined largely by the need to control both exits from the inland sea—at Gibraltar and at the Suez Canal. The Italian invasion of Abyssinia in October 1935 gave a profound shock to British strategic thinking. Enquiries by the Chiefs of Staff showed that, while many harsh words were being spoken in support of sanctions against Italy, no other Mediterranean powers apart from Britain had taken steps to prepare for active military intervention. In the event of war with Italy, Britain must expect to bear the brunt alone, at least for the first few weeks.[1]

Britain was not prepared to 'go it alone' against Italy. The year 1936 was one of greater danger to the Empire, and greater need for economic planning. If international sanctions could not stop aggression, then Britain would have to take diplomatic initiatives unilaterally. Economic sanctions against Italy were dropped on 15 July 1936, and the way was open to British recognition of the conquest of Abyssinia and a diplomatic entente.

Eden[2] maintained that the blow to British prestige resulting from Italian successes must be redressed. Otherwise there might be grave consequences for British oil supplies, and for her political position—both very vulnerable. In Cabinet, he went on to propose what amounted to a unilateral promise of support for Turkey, Greece and Yugoslavia, in the uncertain period which would follow the ending of sanctions.[3]

The Chiefs of Staff were quick to quash such ideas:

It has been emphasized on more than one occasion that it is of paramount importance to British strategical interests that we should be free from commitments in the Mediterranean if our defence arrangements are to prove adequate to deal with . . .

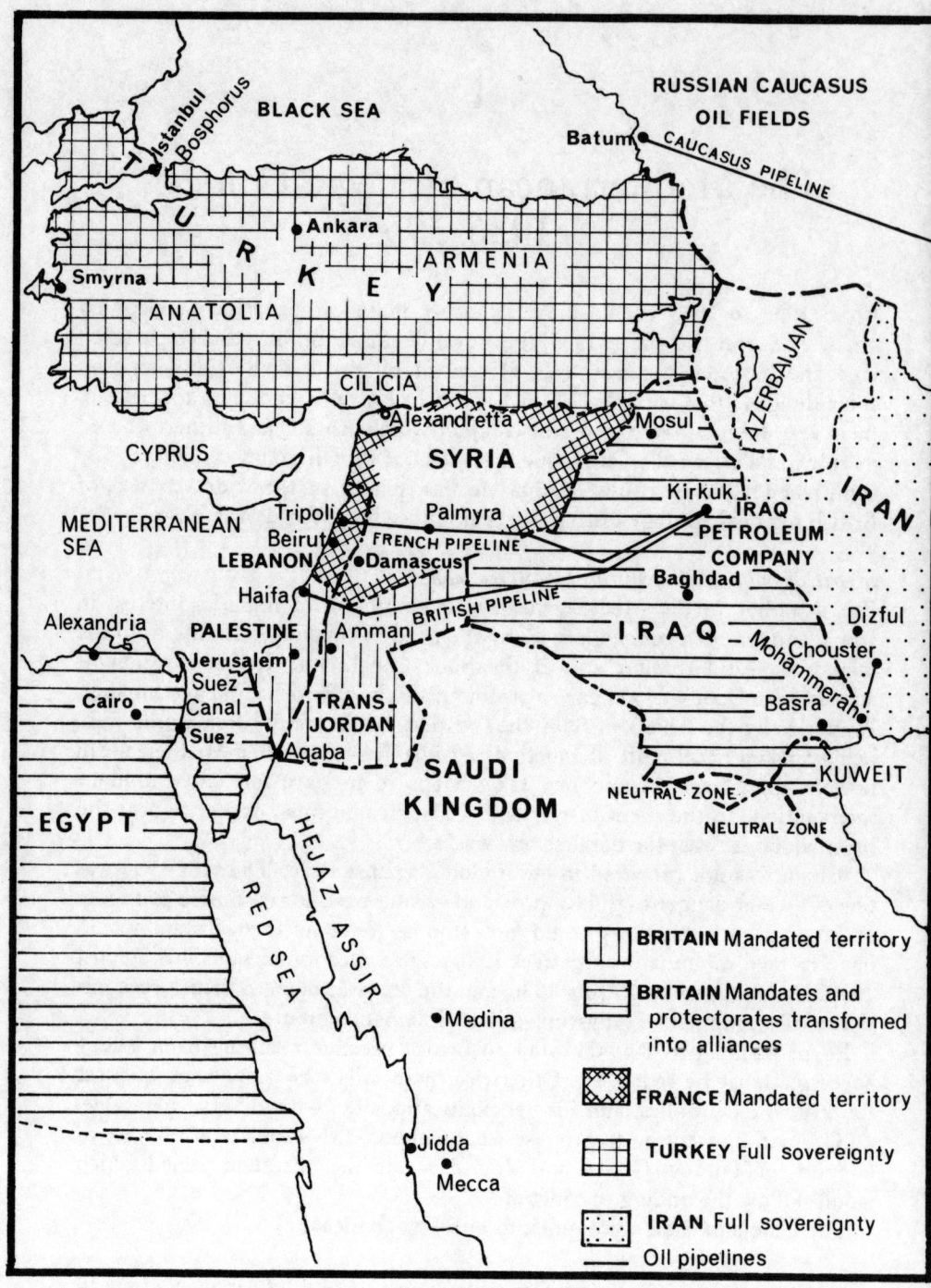

The Middle East in 1936

hostilites either in the Far East or at home, and to give us breathing space in which to recondition the Services.[4]

In their review of imperial defence for 1937 the Chiefs of Staff stated that in the event of a global conflict the Eastern Mediterranean Fleet would have to proceed to the Far East, the French Fleet being left to maintain command of the Western Mediterranean and, with the USSR, to prevent supplies reaching Italy, while Britain would try to hold on to its position at the Suez Canal. Some or all of Britain's Mediterranean possessions might come under siege, and it might be difficult to maintain forces in Egypt. But weakness in the Mediterranean would not be nearly so serious as the surrender of sea power in the Far East.[5]

The COS agreed that whereas it would be essential to keep control of Egypt and the Middle East in the event of war, it was conceivable that Britain might have to let Malta and the Mediterranean go for the time being, and rely on regaining ultimate possession after victory in the main theatres of war.[6]

The Foreign Office stressed that at least Egypt should be reinforced against the contingency of Italian aggression. On 20 October 1937 the Cabinet endorsed the Committee of Imperial Defence's conclusion that relations with Italy had not deteriorated to such an extent as to warrant departure from the earlier instruction to take 'no obtrusive measures . . . with the defence of Egypt, or in the projected movement of the Fleet'.[7]

The decision of 20 October 1937 put an end to Foreign Office attempts to include the Mediterranean in British global strategy. From the beginning of 1938 British strategic thinking on the Eastern Mediterranean revolved around two axes. First, the provision of a Middle East reserve force which, while acting as a police force in Palestine (where it was to be stationed in peacetime) if necessary, would have as its main task the defence of the Canal in the event of war. Second, Britain gave detailed consideration to the exploitation of its economic resources to win and secure the friendship of the minor powers and the Arab States in the Near East.

In February 1938 it was decided in Cabinet to create a holding force of brigade strength whose task would be to hold on to Egypt in the event of hostilites until Britain had won its major battles in Europe and in the Far East.[8] The new policy for Egypt was called 'self-sufficiency', as no reinforcements could be expected via the Mediterranean which, in view of the departure of the British Fleet, was expected to be dominated from its centre eastwards by the Italians. The Middle East Reserve Brigade was stationed in Palestine from the autumn of 1938 until July 1939 when, on the eve of war, it was transferred to the Canal Zone.[9]

The policy of relying on limited forces in the Eastern Mediterranean had obvious implications for British policy in the Middle East, and for Palestine in particular. Peace in Palestine itself was essential, not only to eliminate an issue which could lead to a general conflagration in the area, but for two other vital reasons. First, the troops stationed in Palestine had to be available to defend the Canal in time of war.[10] Second, in the event of Italy blocking the Red Sea entrance to the Canal, reinforcements from India would have to be brought to Egypt overland from the Persian Gulf, via Palestine. During the Munich crisis, part of the Mediterranean Fleet had to be diverted for escort duties to troop-carriers in the Red Sea. When the danger of thus diverting ships was pointed out by Sir Dudley Pound, Admiral of the Mediterranean Fleet, he was told that the situation in Palestine made it impossible to guarantee the safe transfer of troops across its territory.

In March 1938 the CID instructed its Sub-Committee on Middle Eastern problems to examine and report on the financial and economic measures which might be taken to influence the minor Powers and Arab States in the Near East. The Sub-Committee took for its terms of reference a COS memorandum written the month before:

The position in Palestine and Transjordan was uncertain; the government's partition policy had done nothing to lessen the hostility of the Palestinian Arabs; the possibility of a general war affording an opportunity for rebellion in Palestine would depend first upon the strength of the British forces in the country, and to some extent on the chance the Arab extremists thought they had of obtaining assistance from neighbouring Arab countries ... the Government's partition policy was not calculated to ameliorate the British military position in the Arab Near East. As for the Jews, whatever their feelings about partition, they were considered unlikely to take any violent action against Britain, but would probably, as before, try to gain their ends by propaganda and political pressure ... Moreover, in war time, much more vigorous action to suppress terrorism could be taken in Palestine than was possible in time of peace. It would be up to the sub-committee to devise financial measures to ensure the loyalty of the Arab States.[11]

In January 1939 the Sub-Committee submitted its report to the Committee of Imperial Defence.[12] The report laid out in detail various subsidies, loans and other 'remunerations' to be made by Britain to Turkey and the Arab States. However, the report was dominated by the warning given in its preface:

We feel it is necessary to point out at the outset ... the strong feeling which exists in all Arab States in connection with British policy in Palestine ... We assume that, immediately on the outbreak of war, the necessary measures would be taken ... in order to bring about a complete appeasement of Arab opinion in Palestine and in neighbouring countries ... if we fail thus to retain Arab goodwill at the outset of a war, no other measures which we can recommend will serve to influence the Arab States in favour of this country.[13]

The preface illustrated the disproportionate influence which events in Palestine had brought to bear upon British policy in the entire Middle East.

ii. The Zionist role in British strategy

The Zionists were naturally deeply interested in the course of British strategic thinking. What was to be their own role in the Mediterranean? If local military commanders in Palestine were at times glad to co-operate with Jewish forces, such as the Night Squads led by Capt. Wingate (see below), this did not indicate an official policy of support for the Jews against the Arabs. Tacit agreement to Jewish defence forces in 1936 gave way to open joint military operations under British command in 1938. But ultimately it was the home Government which decided how the British army acted, whatever the local military commanders thought. However valuable the Jewish forces proved themselves to be in Palestine, from mid-1937 the question was one of strategy in the Middle East as a whole. The intervention of the Arab States in Palestinian affairs from then on (see Chapter 2) effectively ruled out British co-operation with the Jews against the Palestinian Arabs. Military collusion in times of crisis gave way to political embarrassment once the emergency was over.

The military's desire to 'get the job done' conflicted with the politicians' intentions to appease those conducting the rebellion in Palestine. In Palestine itself, three successive commanders, Generals Dill, Wavell and Haining,[14] favoured the military suppression of the Arab rebellion, but their successor, General Barker,[15] arriving when it had petered out, favoured the disbanding of the Jewish forces which had helped the army curb it. Whereas the COS stressed the need to appease the Arab States, the Chief of the Imperial General Staff on the eve of war advocated the use of Zionist, rather than Arab, resources in the Middle East to form a Middle East Reserve. Hore-Belisha, Secretary of State for War,[16] hesitated to take a stand on the issue, fearing that, as a Jew, he would lay himself open to the same charges of bias as had the Colonial Secretary, Ormsby-Gore,[17] a pro-Zionist by reputation.

The question of Zionism's strategic value became an immediate issue in 1937, when the Peel Commission recommended the establishment in Palestine of a Jewish State. It now became the aim of the Zionists to convince the British that they should place their faith in a strong, viable Jewish territory; in return, the Zionists would look after British interests in the area.

They were encouraged in this aspiration by certain officers serving in Palestine. One in particular, Captain Orde Wingate,[18] was completely won over to Zionism and nurtured hopes of commanding the army of the Jewish State-to-be. Wingate told his Zionist friends that the War Office, though originally opposed to partition (see Chapter 3), had now come round to the idea and would help the Jews to obtain better frontiers, as they understood the requirements of Jewish defence and the benefit which a strong Jewish State would be to them from the strategic point of view. Wingate undertook to prepare a memorandum and circulate it among his friends at the War Office.

Even the veteran General Smuts,[19] an ardent Gentile Zionist, was not sure if, on strategic grounds, the Jews were well advised to opt for an independent State:

> Even with a more or less favourable partition, the position of the future Jewish State will be inherently unsound. The whole country is so small and your allotment of it will be so minimal and economic interest and transport communications are so inter-locked, that the Jewish State will continue to be at the mercy of the powerful Arab combination...[20]

Zionist talk of military and technical superiority over the Arabs quite missed the point. After their own frequent attacks on British policy, could they expect London to place all its faith in them, to rely on some half million Jews to counterbalance the possible enmity of the Arab States in the region? What point would there be in having a Middle East supply base in Palestine, or for that matter a British-fortified Zionist State, if Iraq were to sell its oil to Germany and allow Axis aircraft to land on its airfields? If Saudi Arabia were to collaborate with the Italians along the Red Sea littoral? If King Farouk were to welcome Italian forces across his borders? On the other hand, London made the cold assumption that with the future of European Jewry dependent upon the defeat of the Axis, the Zionists would not mount an all-out attack on the Mandatory.

The Cabinet's approval of partition in 1937 had been predicated on the reservation of certain areas of strategic interest to Britain:

> We cannot from the point of view of British interests relinquish effective control of 1) Jerusalem and the area around it; 2) Haifa and an area around it; 3) the southern triangle between the Gulf of Akaba and the Egyptian frontier.[21]

Foreign Office opposition to partition reflected its anxiety lest the implementation of partition against the wishes of the Palestinian Arabs provoke a rebellion by the Arab States. Even two million Jews as a garrison in Palestine could not offset the nuisance value of the Arabs. The Prime Minister[22] himself now questioned the fundamental precept of the Zionist thesis—that a Jewish State would guarantee British imperial interests in the Middle East; at an interview with Weizmann[23] he voiced doubts about the loyalties of future Jewish immigrants:

> Mr C. said that there was one question which he wanted to ask Dr Weizmann. The 450,000 who were in Palestine were fine people. Dr Weizmann now wanted to bring in another million. Would they be of the same sort? Would they be able to defend the country?[24]

The summer of 1938 witnessed a curious paradox. While London was preparing a political retreat from the Mandate and the partition proposal (see Chapter 5), military co-operation in Palestine with the forces of the Haganah[25] reached its zenith. But the use of Jewish forces under British officers against Arab guerrillas posed acute political problems for the proponents of appeasement in London. General Haining himself agreed that the Night Squads were doing well, but thought extreme care had to be taken about their extension.[26]

In London, the Colonial Office was concerned lest military policy in Palestine endanger the chances of political reconciliation:

> Hitherto Jewish assistance has only been enlisted in the capacity of supernumerary police for the *defence* of Jewish colonies. The moral strength of our position as holding the scales between Jew and Arab would be undermined and we should be placed in the position of having allied ourselves with the Jews against the Arab population of Palestine.[27]

Nevertheless, the security situation in Palestine during the summer of 1938, combined with increasing doubts as to the reliability of the Arab police, forced the Palestine Administration to enlist more and more Jews for the security forces, for use not only in the defence of Jewish areas but also, unprecedentedly, in purely Arab districts. The Administration's dilemma became most acute during the Munich crisis, when the Colonial Office seriously envisaged the contingency of raising a Jewish army to hold Palestine, in the event that war would necessitate denuding Palestine of British forces.[28]

However, with the Munich settlement, and the general belief that war had been averted, came a renewed determination to settle the Palestine issue by political concessions, even if meanwhile the rebellion itself had been to all intents and purposes subdued. The military policies of the summer of 1938 had by autumn become a political embarrassment:

> General Haining would deprecate any political announcement which went any way towards meeting the Arabs and enabling them, without loss of face or hopes, to cease the rebellion ... the military authorities in Palestine have insufficiently appreciated the policy of political appeasement preceding and accompanying the use of force ... unwittingly they have, in effect, a vested interest against that policy.[29]

Haining was alarmed at the possible consequences of the Round Table Conference sponsored by the Colonial Office at the end of 1938. He made a last-minute appeal that no concessions be made that might cancel out the advances made already by the military:

> Want to maintain pressure as an absolute necessity, and to add to it at my discretion as I consider situation demands ... I feel that I can ask in return that no concessions are now made in vain hope they may lead delegates to offer what they are not able to achieve. Any such action will inevitably weaken our position here, where we shall be accused of playing double game, pandering to rebels, failing to protect loyalty, which will set back settlement by producing lack of confidence just at time when we are beginning to obtain such confidence from those who desire peace.[30]

But it was not the Palestine Arabs whom the British Government were worried about principally—it was the Arab States, whose loyalty would be at a premium in the event of war. To meet this contingency, the Army's desire to finish off the job in Palestine would have to be checked, and Jewish proposals to provide a reserve of manpower and resources in the Middle East rejected.

Confirmation reached the Zionists from well-informed sources in London:

The General Staff circulated a memorandum a day or two ago about Middle Eastern strategy—in which they insisted that they *must* have a peaceful, friendly Arab world. The Jews are not even mentioned. They evidently discount them as a force.[31]

The Jewish Agency Executive (the Zionists' policy-making body—see Chapter 7) yet hoped to convince London that its strategic thinking was based on misconceptions. The Zionist delegates to the St James's Conference (which in February 1939 was convened to search for an Arab–Zionist compromise in Palestine—see Chapter 5) were briefed in advance on the points they would need to refute in debate: they were to stress that Hitler was not yet ready to tackle both East and West, that in any event there remained sufficient time in which to recruit a Jewish Force ... that they (the Jews) were better fitted to establish a war industry than the Egyptians, who lacked the technical experts and scientific ability. As to appeasing the Arabs ... they would in any case remain dissatisfied, and would turn against Britain at any moment of weakness. Pan-Arab policy only antagonized Turkey, which was more important than the Arabs as a military factor ... if the British appeared strong, supported by 50,000 Jews, the Arabs would not dare attack British interests in the Near East.[32]

Notwithstanding the politicians' disregard for their arguments, the logic of exploiting the Zionists' claimed war-potential was not lost on the War Office, which hoped to combine political appeasement of the Arab States with military co-operation with the Jews:

... Cabinet policy, as Mr MacDonald[33] is aware, is to make the forces in that area 'self-sufficient' for the first three months of the war ... The War Council are therefore forced to contemplate the employment of Palestinians ... [The] difficulty hitherto has been the necessity of holding an even balance between Arab and Jew, and the certainty that the enlistment of Jews would be regarded as a sign of favour towards that race. This difficulty, it might be hoped, would gradually lose its significance as more settled conditions became established in Palestine.[34]

Thus, War Office hopes of utilizing Zionist resources in the Middle East were based on the hope that the Jews would resign themselves to the implementation of the 1939 White Paper (see Chapter 5). This hope found its corollary in the Zionist war slogan that they 'would fight the war as if there were no White Paper, and fight the White Paper as if there were no war'. For their part, the Zionists hoped that their own military contributions would lead to a 'freezing' of the White Paper during the war. However,

General Ironside's[35] plans were blocked in 1939 by the Colonial Office, which in 1939 was the spokesman for Government policy in Palestine. It was the plan to raise a Jewish Force in Palestine—and not the White Paper—that was 'frozen'. The decision to allow the Jews to participate in what they regarded as a racist war against themselves was not taken until September 1944, well after the decisive battles of the Western Desert had been won, and Britain felt secure of her position in the Middle East.

In Palestine itself, during 1939—the year of the White Paper—the consequences of appeasing the Arabs were not slow to be felt. The Night Squads were disbanded, and Wingate, their once-praised leader, sent back to England. The Haganah, from whose ranks the members of the Night Squads had been hand-picked by the British, was now victimized. Forty-three of its members were arrested for illegal possession of arms.[36] The Zionists were not far off the mark in fearing that these arrests were the prelude to a general campaign to disarm the Yishuv, the Jewish community in Palestine. Barker concluded that the Haganah constituted a threat to the Mandatory itself—'There can be no doubt that the object of this military organization is based on the belief that they cannot trust the British Empire to produce the necessary force for the defence of Palestine. Secondly, a firm determination that the Jewish community will occupy Palestine by force of arms and hold it against any aggression from any power whatsoever'.[37] As will be seen below, there was to ensue an intermittent 'love-hate' relationship between the Army and the Haganah in Palestine—co-operation in times of crises for British arms in the Middle East, rejection and suppression once the immediate crisis had passed and long-term political planning took over from short-term military exigencies.

2
The 1936 Rebellion—Martial Law or Political Concessions

i. Arab hostilities and the Royal Commission

The Arab Rebellion began with sporadic outbrusts of violence. On 19 April 1936 these culminated with an attack by an Arab mob in Jaffa on Jewish passers-by which left behind it nine Jews killed and ten wounded. On that same evening a curfew was ordered and a state of emergency declared throughout Palestine. A coalition of the most prominent family-based political parties was on 25 April patched up into a Higher Arab Committee, which declared a National General Strike to gain three goals: the immediate cessation of all Jewish immigration;[1] a ban on all land sales to Jews; and the establishment of an independent, national government.

The National Strike took the form of a stoppage of trade and transportation facilities. Only partially observed, it did not succeed in paralysing the economic life of the country, since the Jews had already acquired a substantial part of the country's economic resources and enterprises. Jewish agriculture could supply the basic food requirements of the Jewish population, and the main industries were owned and operated by Jews.

Violent acts against Jewish life and property, particularly against outlying areas, vandalization of orange-groves and orchards, urban bomb outrages and shooting at British personnel in urban areas were the main features of the first months of the Rebellion. From the end of May, when British forces began to regain the initiative in the towns, the Rebellion's centre of gravity moved from Arab towns to country districts, where guerrilla bands attacked Jewish settlements, road and rail bridges, telephone lines, the IPC oil pipeline, and police and army installations. By June 1936 peasant bands were operating all over the country, and by mid-August, when the Rebellion reached its peak, they commanded many of Palestine's main communications arteries. Internal rivalries in villages encouraged the formation of bands, since when one clan formed a band the rival clan had to do likewise, to maintain its local standing. Activity decreased markedly in September, following the Government's announcement that it would dispatch a division to Palestine and restore order under martial law (see below). During the 1936 phase of the Rebellion some 80 Jews were killed and 400 injured, from a total casualty list of 300 killed, 1300 wounded.[2]

In April 1936 the Higher Arab Committee had brought together for the first time in uneasy coalition the two principal rival Arab families in Palestine —the Husseinis and the Nashashibis. The Husseini family had risen to prominence during the nineteenth century, when it had obtained large tracts of land in southern Palestine. Of Jerusalem's thirteen mayors between the city's incorporation in 1864 and the end of Ottoman rule in 1917, six had been Husseinis. The appointment of Haj Amin el Husseini, Mufti of Jerusalem, and current head of the family, as President of the Supreme Moslem Council in 1922 had brought to the family wide political powers, which went with the extensive patronage at the Council's command.[3] The Mufti's appointment had been a misconceived conciliatory gesture of the first High Commissioner, Samuel, an attempt to balance the political scales between the Husseini and Nashashibi families,[4] as well as to moderate the Mufti's radicalism by elevating him to high office and giving him the responsibilities of a post in the Establishment.[5]

The Council's members were never elected, as prescribed by law, and no legal limitation was ever placed on the President's powers. The results were in 1937 considered by the Peel Commission to be 'unfortunate':

... nothing will or can be done to reform the Supreme Moslem Council if such reform will have the effect of diminishing the power and position of the Mufti. The administration of Palestine is in fact in a vicious circle, which will have to be broken sooner rather than later. The existence of the Supreme Moslem Council need not, in itself, have led to the development of an Arab *imperium in imperio*, but the functions which the Mufti has contrived to accumulate in his person and his use of them have had that effect ...[6]

By 1936, the Mufti had fully consolidated his pre-eminent position and prestige inside the Arab community in Palestine. Rival Moslem landowning families, resenting the concentration of political and religious power in Husseini hands, had since the 1920s begun to organize themselves into an opposition, led by Ragheb bey Nashashibi. Ragheb had represented Palestine in the Ottoman Parliament, and held the mayoralty of Jerusalem from 1920 (when the Husseini mayor had been implicated in the riots of that year) until 1934. In the latter year, Ragheb Nashashibi formed the Defence Party, a generally moderate party, in contrast to the Mufti's recently formed, Husseini-dominated Palestine Arab Party.

But the Nashashibis never developed into a consistent, day-to-day opposition regarding itself as rival candidate for the responsibilities of government. They adopted a conciliatory attitude towards the Mandatory, preferring co-operation within the British administration to Husseini-dominated independence. The Nashashibis' initial agreement to the partition of Palestine in 1937 brought down upon them a wave of Husseini terror which resulted in more Arab victims than Jewish or British during this, the second phase of the Arab Rebellion. Ragheb himself fled Palestine for the more peaceful climate of Egypt, abdicating his place to his cousin, Fakhri Nashashibi. The latter's sudden claim to national leadership in 1938 was based less on the

Nashashibis' past record (indeed, Ragheb, from Egypt, disowned him) than on the people's despair with Husseini tactics.

The Arab parties had already, in November 1935, presented to the High Commissioner, Sir Arthur Wauchope,[7] the three demands that the Higher Arab Committee made in April 1936 when declaring the General Strike. Wauchope had enjoyed considerable success, since his appointment in 1931, in securing the rapid development of the country by productive co-operation with each community. His outlook now, and until his early retirement in 1938, would be dominated by the determination to avoid any step which might jeopardize his achievements during the early years of his regime. In 1935 Whitehall had refused to contemplate any reduction in Jewish immigration, but had acceded to Wauchope's proposal to introduce legislation to protect Arab small-holders, and to set up a Legislative Council on which both communities, under British aegis, would sit. When the Legislative Council scheme had been defeated in Parliament in March 1936 (owing largely to a successful Zionist lobby), the Government had invited an Arab delegation to London to present their demands in person. Internal bickering over the composition of the Arab delegation had delayed its departure until the outbreak of disorders in April had rendered its appearance in London untimely. If Parliament had turned down the Legislative Council scheme when peace reigned in Palestine, it was not likely that English public opinion would agree to the transfer of legislative power to what now appeared to be an aggressive Arab majority. Instead of diplomacy, pressure—in the form of a general strike—was applied.[8]

London feared that repercussions in the surrounding Arab States would be grave should repressive measures against the rebels be resorted to. The Foreign Office considered that the Jews had been forcing the pace of immigration, that it was unfortunate that German persecution had precipitated a flood of immigrants but that the Jews themselves must see that Palestine had to be related to the global picture. If British resources were overstrained, the Jews might find themselves under a different mandatory power, not so amenable.[9]

Since the Arabs now refused to come to London, the Government proposed to dispatch a Royal Commission to Palestine. Wauchope initiated the idea, and pressed it on the novice Colonial Secretary, J. H. Thomas, who meanwhile had been reassuring the Jews in London that no re-examination of the Mandate of any kind was contemplated.[10]

Quite apart from the unfortunate precedent of the 1930 Commission (whose recommendations had been accepted in the 'Passfield' White Paper of that year, claiming that Palestine was already rurally overpopulated and recommending that no further land be made available to Jewish settlers), the Zionists feared that a new Commission might call into question the fundamental premises (Jewish immigration and economic development) upon which the Mandate was based, and that tactically the appointment of a

Commission at present might be interpreted by the Arabs as a concession to their own pressure and violence.

However, Thomas brought Wauchope's proposal before the next Cabinet, not to task for specific decisions on the Commission's terms of reference or its composition, but for the Cabinet's agreement to a new Commission, in principle.[11] The Cabinet delayed its decision until 13 May 1936. During the interval, the Zionists learned of the initiative, and Lord Melchett,[12] a member of the Jewish Agency Advisory Committee in London, informed Thomas that in view of the latter's reassurances of a few days before, his current support for Wauchope must be regarded as a breach of faith. Melchett pleaded with Thomas to hold up the final decision, pending Weizmann's arrival in London from Palestine.

The Zionists mobilized Leo Amery[13] (formerly Colonial Secretary, now a leading Gentile Zionist), to 'head off' the Commission, at Prime Ministerial level. But Amery received the impression that the Prime Minister, Baldwin[14], 'had very great faith in Wauchope, and that it would take a lot to move him to oppose'.[15] The Zionists were worried by the apparent haste in which the decision was being rushed through. They arranged for a wide canvass of those Ministers concerned with Palestine, and of those Opposition leaders who could be relied upon to exert pressure on the Government.[16]

Thomas himself, in contrast to the adamant High Commissioner, was wavering under the onslaught of the Zionist canvass:

... while taking the view, as a matter of general principle, that it is better to follow the advice of the man on the spot, the Secretary of State for the Colonies felt some doubt whether ... in view of his own announcements about not capitulating to a threat of force, it would be wise to announce a Royal Commission at the present time, at any rate before seeing Dr Weizmann.[17]

Yet the Cabinet supported Wauchope against Thomas. There were two principal objections to waiting on Weizmann's arrival. Firstly, something should be done prior to 15 May when, according to Wauchope, the Arabs were to begin a taxes strike; secondly, if it became known—as seemed inevitable—that Weizmann, but not the Arabs, had been consulted prior to the Cabinet's decision, the good effects contemplated might be discounted. Agreeing that its decision must not seem like a concession to violence, the Cabinet decided to announce that the Government's first task would be to restore law and order, after which some form of inquiry would be undertaken.

Zionist disappointment at the decision, in contrast to their expectations based on their own canvass, was especially keen: 'He [Elliott][18] then said that he *alone* had fought against it, all the friends so lavish in assurances had given way, including Billy O.G. [Ormsby-Gore].'[19]

The Zionists viewed the decision with grave misgivings. Elliott saw the new line as tantamount to a declaration of war on the Zionists.[20] Melchett thought the issue serious enough for the Zionists to make a fight over it in the Commons—if the Government spokesman confirmed that a Commission had been appointed, their supporters might force a division. With the support of Churchill, Austen Chamberlain and a fair part of the Conservative party that was sympathetic to Zionism, the vote might go against the Government. Above all, Thomas's own personal vulnerability might be exploited.[21] But Sir Lewis Namier[22] and Mrs Dugdale thought the risks too great—there were limits to the expediency of parliamentary pressure groups. Labour leaders, Attlee in particular, advised against.

Weizmann arrived in London on the day before the Cabinet was due to ratify the draft announcement that had been drawn up by the Ministers concerned. On the morning of the meeting Weizmann rushed to Thomas, but it was too late—even had Thomas been amenable, his own deteriorating position rendered him unable to controvert a draft in the composition of which he had himself participated a few days before. The Cabinet gave its approval, and Thomas duly made the announcement in the Commons that same afternoon.[23]

Weizmann's visits to the Prime Minister and to the Colonial Office served merely to confirm his worst fears about the Royal Commission, and the continuing influence of Departmental officials upon the formulation of policy. This influence would be very hard to break, Weizmann believed, unless there was a change of Colonial Secretary, or even of the entire Government.[24] It was his impression that 'it is the policy of the Colonial Office definitely to use the Commission for the purpose of reducing the tempo of our immigration and development generally . . .'[25]

The Zionists considered boycotting the Commission, but once more the Labour leaders, especially Attlee, advised against. The net result could only be damaging. Weizmann himself hoped to persuade the Government to change its decision following the Arabs' refusal to call off their strike, pending the Commission's report.[26]

But Wauchope insisted that the Arabs' rejection of a truce was not a rejection in principle of the Royal Commission, but merely a refusal to accept the appointment of the Commission as a concession sufficient to warrant calling off the strike. What the Arabs wanted, he claimed, as a first step was the suspension of Jewish immigration.[27]

Ormsby-Gore's appointment in place of Thomas did not allay Zionist fears. The new Colonial Secretary, assuming office at the height of the Arab Rebellion, with a 'Zionist' past to live down in Arab eyes, was considered too weak to reverse the current trend towards a re-examination of Mandatory policy. Ormsby-Gore himself claimed later that he had found the Government too deeply committed to the Commission for him to be able to get out of it.[28]

Fundamentally, Ormsby-Gore remained a Gentile Zionist, whose political heritage included a deep sense of obligation to the Jewish National Home, as envisaged by the architects (including himself) of the Balfour Declaration. In time he was to grow almost to resent the Zionists for his own inability to free himself from them—unlike his successor, Malcolm MacDonald, Ormsby-Gore was to become involved in a losing struggle against the pro-Arab tendencies of the senior Department, the Foreign Office. To Weizmann, he would complain that the Foreign Office was staffed with 'new Pharaohs who knew not Joseph ... assimilated Jews, the same kind that had opposed the Balfour Declaration'.[29] Long before he was actually to leave the Colonial Office, Ormsby-Gore would bemoan his fate as intolerable, and threaten resignation.[30]

ii. Martial law—or suspension of immigration
In Palestine itself, where prospects of an early peace had not been improving, Wauchope debated with the GOC Palestine, Air Vice-Marshal Peirse, the advisability of instituting martial law in the country. In that event, executive authority would pass from the High Commissioner to the military, which increasingly had become frustrated by the administrative restrictions imposed on its military operations. For his part, Wauchope feared that the harsh consequences of martial law might doom all prospect of future peaceful development in the country.

The controversy between the civil and the military authorities was referred to London. Wauchope recommended piecemeal political appeasement (the Royal Commission), together with a show of strength in the form of troop reinforcements. In contrast, the military proposed an all-out repression of the rebellion under the powers of martial law.[31]

Wauchope's inability to alter the conception upon which he had based his policies during his first term of office—his fear of losing the Arabs' goodwill should he resort to stern measures against the rebels—later earned him universal contempt and castigation. In a sense, he was made the post-facto scapegoat for decisions taken (albeit upon Wauchope's advice) by the ministers responsible at the time. The Secretary of State for War at the time claimed later that he had insisted on Wauchope's recall, but Ormsby-Gore, who had initially agreed, had later opposed him.[32] In blaming Wauchope, the War Office itself shed all guilt:

... the conclusion cannot be avoided that the method adopted by the High Commissioner was entirely ineffective. Martial law and unfettered military control should have been exercised from the first. The behaviour and general conduct of the defence forces in very trying circumstances were admirable.[33]

Ormsby-Gore referred later to Wauchope as 'a dear little man, admirable while the going is good, but hardly the character to ride out a storm'.[34] This sentiment was echoed by a senior officer who was later to become GOC Palestine and subsequently Commander-in-Chief Middle East—'Sir Arthur

Wauchope loves greatly, administers with knowledge and imagination, but he does not rule'.[35]

Wauchope's policy, adopted in due course by London, did not fulfil the high hopes expected of it. The demands made by Palestine upon British military resources in 1936[36] came at a watershed of traditional British policy in the Mediterranean. It is doubtful whether such demands could have been met in later years.

The Colonial Office had to improvise new ideas that might possibly break the impasse in Palestine:

The situation has now developed in such a way that a continuance of the present measures of suppression, even if they are not as intensified as the Jews would like them to be, is likely to convert Arab goodwill into hatred for Great Britain. I am not in a position to express opinion as to the probability of this enmity spreading—nor whether this probability would justify HMG's effort *to alter Arab feeling by timely concession, for example by temporary suspension of immigration* . . .[37]

On 13 June Wauchope himself had proposed that the Government intimate to the Royal Commission that *it* might suggest the suspension of immigration. The Colonial Office had rejected this idea, for 'the natural reaction of the Royal Commission to any such suggestion would be to hand in their resignations at once'.[38]

As a political issue, the suspension of immigration was to become the source of various misunderstandings. Once the idea gained currency, Arab insistence led London—particularly the Colonial Office—to compromise its own declared policy. In the search for a mutually agreeable 'price' for ending the Rebellion, the Government would waive its own condition that law and order must be restored prior to any negotiation. Only when the Arabs, in their clandestine negotiations with the Mandatory, 'broke the rules' as London understood them, was martial law again considered as an instrument of policy.

Arab intransigence at this juncture was undoubtedly rooted in the confidence that they were masters of the situation in Palestine, and the conviction that combined Arab pressure at Whitehall was threatening the Zionists' traditional hegemony there.

The Foreign Office pressed for immediate steps to suspend Jewish immigration pending the Royal Commission's Report.[39] The Department was concerned particularly about possible repercussions of events in Palestine upon Ibn Saud, ruler of Saudi Arabia,[40] who may have already drawn the wrong conclusions from British inaction during the Italian conquest of Ethiopia. Since Arab pressure had yet to achieve full momentum, Eden decided to confine himself at the next Cabinet meeting to an oral recommendation (in lieu of a policy memorandum) that immigration into Palestine be stopped.[41]

Weizmann himself raised the question of a voluntary pause in immigration with the London Executive of the Jewish Agency.[42] The debate divided those Zionists who lived in Palestine from those in the Diaspora. Weizmann argued that whereas public opinion was clearly with the Zionists for the present, and they had a friendly Colonial Secretary in office who did not wish even to hear of a stoppage, it had to be remembered that public opinion was a fickle thing. Eden was worried about Egypt, and if the situation deteriorated there Egypt and Palestine together might prove to be more than Great Britain could manage:

If, then, Eden were to insist that something be done to relieve the situation in Palestine, we should be unable to resist, and might have lost the advantage of voluntarily making a gesture . . .[43]

But unrestricted immigration into Palestine was the lifeline of the National Home, the sine qua non for David Ben-Gurion[44] and his colleagues—the only thing that had kept the Jews from retaliating during the weeks of Arab attacks was the determination to do nothing which might prejudice future immigration. Notwithstanding the fundamental rift between them, Weizmann and Ben-Gurion attended a further interview with Ormsby-Gore.[45] The Colonial Secretary informed the two Zionist leaders that he was contemplating announcing in the Commons that as soon as the Royal Commission began its work immigration would be stopped, though the actual word 'suspension' would not be used. Ben-Gurion retorted that the Zionists had the strongest possible objection on principle to the suspension of immigration, even for a short period. However, Weizmann proposed that, if it would help matters, 'we might be prepared to postpone applying for the Schedule while the Commission was in Palestine . . .'[46]

But Weizmann was offering concessions that he would be unable to deliver. His own relations with Ben-Gurion did not permit even of mutual agreement on tactics prior to official meetings with Cabinet members. Weizmann was evidently arraigned before the Zionist Executive, for on the next day he sent a letter to Ormsby-Gore which read in stark contrast to his own statement at the interview:

. . . you contemplated the practical suspension of immigration (with the exception of independents) during the work of the Royal Commission. This means for us much more than the loss of a certain number of immigrants . . . we could only regard this as a retreat in the face of organized terrorism . . .[47]

But even had the Zionists been able to present a united front, it seems unlikely that the Government—under current circumstances—could have refused to consider concessions to the Arabs.

While Ormsby-Gore adhered to his policy of 'no bargaining with the rebels', he proposed to the Cabinet that the Government announce a suspension of immigration for the duration of the Commission's work, to be announced once law and order were restored and the Commission able to leave for Palestine.⁴⁸ The Cabinet approved his recommendation and reaffirmed its earlier decision not to adopt repressive measures.

The essence of the Government's dilemma, now and throughout the summer, would be the timing of that announcement—before, or after the disorders had been called off? Could there be an un-official intimation or promise to the Arabs that immigration would be stopped once they called off the disorders? Would the Arabs feel able to call them off without having first attained some demonstrable sign of victory?

iii. *The Arab States' mediation*

The answer to these questions was determined not only by the gravity of the situation in Palestine itself, but to perhaps a greater degree by the involvement of the surrounding Arab States during the course of the summer. The Palestinian Arabs had attempted at an early stage to mobilize the prestige and influence of neighbouring States as a lever with which to extract concessions from the British. The Mufti had turned first to Ibn Saud for aid, and the latter consulted the British Agent at Jidda. The latter strongly advised the Saudis against any intervention in Palestinian affairs, and pointed to the difference between independent Arab territories and mandated ones. The Saudi attaché reassured the Agent that Ibn Saud had no wish to intervene, and with that the matter was for the time being closed.⁴⁹

The Palestinians turned next to the Emir Abdullah, whom they asked to work for a suspension of immigration, prohibition of land-sales to Jews, and the establishment of a 'nationalist' regime. In response to the Emir's query, they replied that their minimum requirement was a temporary cessation of immigration. The Emir advised them to send their delegation to London.⁵⁰

On 6 June the Palestinians met the Emir at Amman once more. This time, the latter demanded that they cease the terrorism at once, in order that the Royal Commission (whose appointment had meanwhile been announced in the Commons) might proceed to Palestine.⁵¹ The Palestinians replied that the terrorism was itself in reply to the brutality of the Mandatory. When advised by the Emir of his recent talks Kirkbride, the British Resident at Amman, suggested to Wauchope: 'it should not be impossible to allow the Emir to say that the number of Jews shall never be brought up by immigration to a number which will put the Jews in a majority over the Arabs . . .'⁵²

Wauchope, evidently after consultation with London, asked his Chief Secretary. J. H. Hall, to

> explain very clearly to the British Resident the extraordinary position we should be put in had the British Resident told the Emir what he half suggests in his letter . . . It would form a definite pledge to all Arabs—a pledge which we have not the slightest justification in making. The British Resident must not think of making commitments of this sort, neither definitely, nor in conversation with the Emir.⁵³

Whereas Abdullah's intervention was stifled by Wauchope at Jerusalem, the Saudi initiative—quashed once at Jedda—now proceeded through Whitehall channels. The Saudi Minister at London, Sheikh Hafez Wahba, called at the Foreign Office to enquire about the situation in Palestine. On Colonial Office advice the Saudi Minister was informed that the Government would not be moved by threats of violence, and that Ibn Saud might employ his services best in persuading the Palestinians to give up their campaign of violence.[54]

This vague and seemingly harmless invitation to an Arab ruler to use his undoubted influence and prestige to help the British out of an awkward situation was to have far-reaching consequences. When informed of this step, the Colonial Office merely expressed its concern whether Ibn Saud's mediation would lead to delays, and if it might not be better for the Government itself to make a direct approach to the Arab rulers via its own embassies. It was also feared that Saud's proposed attempt to mobilize the King of Iraq and the Imam Yahya of Yemen might provoke inter-Arab jealousy. However, the Colonial Office was content to leave the final decision with the Foreign Office.

At a further meeting at the Foreign Office on 3 July, Oliphant informed the Saudi Minister that the Government would gratefully accept Ibn Saud's offer of mediation—together with the King of Iraq and the Imam Yahya— to secure a cessation of the armed rising in Palestine. The Saudi Minister reported that the Palestinian Arabs were now willing to call off the disorders at once, on three conditions: that all prisoners convicted since the outbreak were realeased; that the communal fines imposed recently on villages harbouring rebels were rescinded; and that all Jewish immigration was suspended forthwith.[55]

It was clear that the main problem was the question of immigration. The Foreign Office itself was in favour of conceding this to Ibn Saud, for use as a trump card in his mediation.[56] But Ormsby-Gore adhered to the view that any announcement on immigration prior to the restoration of law and order would be regarded as a surrender to violence, and his view was upheld by the Cabinet.[57] Lord Halifax[58] proposed that since Ibn Saud's offer to mediate had been accepted already, and that since he and his fellow Arab rulers would in all probability ask for a suspension of immigration, it might be best for the Government to anticipate them, and make its own announcement to that effect. Ormsby-Gore favoured a temporary suspension for the duration of the Commission's stay in Palestine. But since it had been agreed by all that the Commission would not leave for Palestine until the disorders had ceased, the Colonial Secretary asked that the decision as to when and whether a suspension be announced be left until a later date. This line was consistent with current advice from Wauchope, that to announce a suspension—at the same time as announcing the terms of reference and composition of the Royal Commission—would be regarded in Palestine as a surrender to violence.[59]

The Foreign Office was obliged to abide by the Cabinet decision. However, in acting as 'go-between' for the Arabs and the Colonial Office, the Department undoubtedly allowed its own attitude to influence its actions, adding confusion and ultimately compromising the negotiations.

It is of some historical interest to note that Ibn Saud's plan to include Egypt in his joint appeal to the Palestinians was opposed vigorously by Sir Miles Lampson, the High Commissioner at Cairo:

... better to avoid action which might bring Egypt directly into Palestinian and Arab affairs, which we have so far succeeded in avoiding...[60]

At a further interview with the Saudi Minister at the Foreign Office, it soon became apparent that London and Jedda were labouring under a misunderstanding.[61] The Saudi Minister reported that the Imam Yahya was prepared to co-operate in the appeal 'if the British Government promised first to suspend immigration'. King Ghazi of Iraq went so far as to ask for immediate talks on the Palestinians' grievances—immigration, land-sales and future government. As pointed out by the Saudi Minister himself, these latter demands were entirely out of place, as the Royal Commission had been appointed precisely to examine those very grievances.

However, the Saudi Minister did urge the desirability of a Government announcement on the suspension of immigration, pending the Commission's report. Moreover, he added, he did not think that he was asking for anything beyond the realms of feasibility, seeing that 'he himself had suggested this' when making his first representations to the Foreign Office.

Colonial Office officials were shocked when they received the report of the interview. Oliphant himself admitted that it was just possible that the Saudi Minister had 'thrown in a remark of this kind' as he was leaving, and that it might have been missed by the interpreter.

An embarrassed Foreign Office realized that it had allowed the Saudi initiative to begin on a completely false basis. Oliphant now had to pour cold water on the Saudi initiative, and at a further meeting he advised the Saudi Minister that the effect of Ibn Saud's efforts might be greater if they were confined to a letter from the King himself, rather than engagement in direct mediation.[62]

The next meeting of the Cabinet decided that it would be inadvisable to inform Ibn Saud of the existing decision to suspend immigration once the Royal Commission went out to Palestine. The Colonial Office now regretted the whole episode, based as it had come to be upon a straight trade of immigration certificates in return for the cessation of disorders.[63]

The Foreign Office was for the present outflanked. But in Palestine itself the refusal to impose martial law or instigate militant measures meant that the Rebellion continued out of control. Yet the longer the Rebellion continued the more reinforcements had to be brought in, the greater the loss to British prestige, and the harder it became for the Government to make concessions prior to the restoration of order, without loss of face.

By August, the Rebellion was getting so out of hand that the War Office—whose forces had been denied adequate powers and hampered by the inaction of the civil law courts[64]—added its voice to those demanding political concessions. So as not to appear to be yielding to violence, the War Office proposed that the Government should announce that the three Arab kings who had agreed to mediate with the Palestinian Arabs had themselves proposed the suspension of immigration, and that the Government had accepted the Arab rulers' proposals.[65]

Similar ideas prevailed at the Foreign Office, which was concerned more about the reactions of the neighbouring Arab States, and was anxious that their efforts (especially those of Ibn Saud) should be crowned with success. At the same time, the Colonial Office was concerned primarily for the prestige of its administration in Palestine, and with the long-term prospect of governing the country if the Rebellion was suppressed physically and the Arabs reduced to sullen passivity.

The factor which probably tipped the scales towards concessions was the conversion of Wauchope himself during August, following certain progress in renewed talks between Abdullah and the Arab Higher Committee.[66] Abdullah informed Wauchope that there were some moderates on the Committee, but that even these would do nothing without a prior announcement that immigration would be suspended for the duration of the Commission's stay in Palestine. Wauchope indicated the direction of his own thinking in a report to London:

... as for the cessation of immigration, I gave no promise, but I pointed out to His Highness that the terms of your statement on the subject in the House of Commons on 29 July might reasonably be interpreted as indicating that a temporary suspension may possibly be decided upon in due course ... .[67]

Thus hints dropped in the Commons, at Jerusalem and at Amman set the scene for meaningful negotiations at Jerusalem. After consultations between the High Commissioner, Hall (Chief Secretary of the Administration), Campbell (Commissioner for the Jerusalem District) and Dr Khaldi (Mayor of Jerusalem since 1934), a formula was arrived at.[68] Their draft agreement provided that the High Commissioner would give his word that immediately, or at the most one week after the strike was called off, immigration would be suspended until the Royal Commission recommended and the Government decided how immigration would be regulated in the future.

Wauchope forwarded the proposals to London, with his own recommendation to accept them. He argued that it might be wiser to make concessions now, while they might still prove effective, than later, when they would be unable to alter the course of events. Since it was the extremists who dictated Arab policy, concluded Wauchope, it was with them that the Government would have to deal.[69]

As on previous occasions, Ormsby-Gore adopted Wauchope's advice. He asked the Cabinet to adopt a drastic suspension of immigration, to be applied from 1 October, the day on which the Royal Commission was scheduled to leave England. He asked that Wauchope be allowed to announce this as soon as possible, in order to give due notice to would-be immigrants.[70] He wrote to Wauchope in this sense, making his recommendation to the Cabinet conditional on the High Commissioner first obtaining from the Arabs an unequivocal declaration on ending the disorders, as had been hinted.[71]

To all intents and purposes, it now remained only for Wauchope to obtain a formal assurance from the Higher Arab Committee, after which the Cabinet would be able—at its next regular meeting scheduled for 2 September —to confirm the new policy.

iv. The Nuri Said episode

At this juncture Wauchope's informal negotiations were overtaken by the much-publicized personal intervention at Jerusalem of Nuri Said, Foreign Minister of Iraq. Wauchope claimed later that Nuri's intervention had originated in 'higher quarters', at the Foreign Office.[72] This may explain why Wauchope now began discussions with Nuri, when he (Wauchope) had already made such progress in private with two members of the Higher Arab Committee. Not only were Foreign Office directives now involved, but Wauchope himself may have preferred to lean on the prestige of the Iraqi Foreign Minister.[73]

After meeting with the Higher Arab Committee in Jerusalem, Nuri reported back to Wauchope that he had hopes of ending the strike on the basis of a memorandum to be addressed by himself to the Committee.[74] This memorandum would 'express confidence that the informal mediation of Iraq would end the strike and disorders, in return for which Iraq would use its good offices to see that the Mandatory granted the legitimate demands of the Palestinian Arabs, whether they arose out of the present disorders or were connected with the bases of British policy in general, in Palestine'.

On 24 August, Wauchope informed the Colonial Secretary that the Higher Arab Committee, having gained the assent of local committees, would call off the strike on the basis of Nuri's memorandum. Wauchope urged the Government to accept Nuri's terms which, in Wauchope's opinion, did not go beyond the action contemplated originally by Ibn Saud. (In July, the Saudi Minister himself had admitted that it would be incorrect to prejudge the findings of the Royal Commission.—*MJC*.)

Only *force majeure* can explain why, on the very day that Wauchope telegraphed to London a simple scheme whereby he himself was to give his word that immigration would be suspended once the disorders had stopped, he should have in addition forwarded a much more involved Iraqi scheme, fraught with all the dangers of outside intervention in mandatory affairs.

Ormsby-Gore was quick to point out that Nuri Said had in fact gone further than Ibn Saud.[75] It had been made clear to the latter that the cessation of disorders must be unconditional and that no pronouncements on Arab demands could be made until then. Even more important, it had in no way been implied that if the Saudi mediation was successful, then Saudi representations would be entertained on behalf of the Palestinians.

If the Government agreed now to Nuri's mediation on his terms, it would be implied that it had (a) admitted that Iraq might properly intervene in the affairs of Palestine; and (b) committed itself in advance to meeting Arab demands. Above all, the Iraqi memorandum took no account of the much-publicized Royal Commission, whose recommendations would be an essential preliminary to the examination of grievances, or any change in policy.

Ormsby-Gore proposed alterations, to the effect that Nuri was confident that His Majesty's Government intended to effect a just and lasting settlement; that the essential preliminary was an impartial examination by the Royal Commission; and finally, that an Iraqi appeal be made to the Arab leaders to end their strike and thus enable the Royal Commission to begin its work.

But Wauchope insisted that Nuri's efforts were but the logical continuation of the course taken earlier by Ibn Saud. The High Commissioner pointed out that such was the mentality of the Arabs that it would have been impossible for Nuri to have intervened in a private capacity (as had been guaranteed by Nuri, originally) rather than in his official one. Matters had now reached such a pass that:

... if HMG reject the present offer of the Iraqi government to use its good offices with HMG for the grant of the legitimate demands of the Arabs ... [I] fear that every Arab will be firmly convinced that there is no intention to do anything for the Arabs ...[76]

Under pressure from the High Commissioner, Ormsby-Gore again gave ground and compromised further. If Nuri could persuade the Higher Arab Committee to call off the strike, he would now be prepared to allow the Iraqi Government to use its offices with His Majesty's Government with regard to those measures that the Royal Commission might recommend for meeting the legitimate demands of the Palestinian Arabs.[77] This was in contrast to Nuri's own formula, which claimed the right of mediation on *all* Arab demands. Yet it was in effect an admittance of 'formal' mediation by a foreign government in the affairs of the Mandate. In regard to the current disturbances, Ormsby-Gore proposed that Nuri's appeal read:

... the Government of Iraq, actuated by racial ties ... moved by the ties of friendship and alliance which bind them with Great Britain ... deem it incumbent on them to offer informal mediation with a view to ending the present disturbances in Palestine ...[78]

It remains a matter for academic conjecture what the ultimate difference would have been between 'informal' and 'formal' mediation. Whereas it remained for the Royal Commission—rather than the Iraqi Government—to propose measures to solve the Palestine problem, the Iraqi Government was explicitly to be allowed to 'ensure' that these measures were implemented.

But Ormsby-Gore's formula of 27 August proved unacceptable to the Higher Arab Committee. Nuri reported back to Wauchope that the Arabs had lost faith in the Government and that nothing less than his own original formula would now end the strike. To describe his mediation as 'informal' would of itself render his memorandum unacceptable. Nuri added that he, together with all the Arabs of Palestine, had interpreted the Colonial Secretary's speech to the Commons as meaning that immigration would be suspended after order had been restored, and it had been only in this just belief that he had offered his own mediation.[79]

Like Ibn Saud before him, Nuri Said ran into difficulties that were a product both of his own wishful thinking, and of British vacillation and timidity.

In desperation, Wauchope pleaded the necessity for political concessions. He advocated unconditional support for Nuri's formula, lest alteration should cause difficulties at the very moment when, in his opinion, 'victory was assured'. The immediate measures contemplated by Nuri Said and Wauchope were clemency towards those rebels who returned peacefully to their villages (a measure which, as Wauchope pointed out, was within his own prerogative); and the temporary suspension of immigration. Wauchope begged for a quick reply 'before it was too late'.[80]

Ormsby-Gore replied the next day that such a demand was beyond his own competence, and would have to come before the Cabinet on 2 September. Meanwhile, nothing should be done which could commit the Government to the suspension of immigration. While Ormsby-Gore now agreed to Nuri himself appearing before the Royal Commission, he made it clear that he would never agree to Nuri's intervention in matters of general policy in Palestine.[81]

On 31 August Nuri left Jerusalem for Constantinople, promising to return at short notice if needed. On his departure he reported to Wauchope that the Arabs, however foolishly, had definitely committed themselves to continue the strike until immigration was suspended.[82]

By this stage, the Foreign Office itself had turned against Nuri Said, appreciating from the outset that his ambition to attain some *locus standi* in Mandatory affairs was pregnant with future troubles. The Department was most concerned that Nuri Said should not be allowed to proceed along the very same course which had been denied Ibn Saud earlier. Nuri's own motives were also suspect:

It is obvious to us that Nuri is making the utmost use of the present situation to create maximum amount of elbow room for future Iraqi intervention in Palestinian affairs and to further his own Pan-Arab ideas . . .[83]

v. The ending of the first phase of the Rebellion

The blow which finally convinced the Cabinet that their pursuit of a negotiated settlement was in vain came on 1 September, with the publication in the *Palestine Post* of the alleged text of a provisional agreement between Nuri Pasha and the Higher Arab Committee. The alleged terms agreed provided for a general amnesty for all Arab offenders during the Rebellion, an immediate suspension of immigration to last until the Royal Commission published its report, and the provision that the Iraqi Government would represent the Palestinians before the Royal Commission.[84]

The Government was convinced that the Arabs were responsible for the leak. In fact it was the Zionists, whose intelligence kept them well abreast of the secret negotiations, who were responsible:

... when we discovered how the Arabs were using Nuri's mediation and what were the conditions he was ready to propose to them, we took care that it became published and reached London and that there the Government was asked to form its attitude towards this matter; either it should confirm the information, or it should deny it, and Weizmann got a denial which made a great impression on the whole East ...[85]

When Weizmann confronted Ormsby-Gore with the article, the latter had to agree to publish a written denial:

No such terms have been agreed to either by the High Commissioner or by His Majesty's Government. Moreover, there is no foundation for the suggestion ... that the High Commissioner has authorized Nuri Pasha to give assurances regarding measures, including the suspension of immigration, to be taken after the cessation of the disturbances ... no promises have been made to Nuri Pasha by the High Commissioner or by His Majesty's Government as regards either the suspension of immigration or his position as mediator in the affairs of Palestine ...[86]

Ormsby-Gore informed Wauchope that in view of recent events—the truculent attitude of the Arabs, their failure to reduce crimes and outrages during Nuri's mediation—he could not now agree to any apparent surrender to violence or recommend a date for the temporary suspension of immigration earlier than the date on which the Royal Commission would leave England.[87]

Furthermore, Ormsby-Gore would not recommend that the Royal Commission leave England until the Higher Arab Committee first declared publicly that the strike was over as far as they were concerned and until 'a more determined military effort' had been made to round up the 'gunmen' and 'murderers' and the authority of the Mandatory had been re-established sufficiently to enable peace to be negotiated. The Colonial Secretary's change in tone was a dramatic tribute to the success of Zionist counter-intrigue.

The Zionists had caught Ormsby-Gore 'red-handed', and exploited to the full their tactical and psychological advantage. However, Zionist tactics, if overplayed, could be counter-productive. The Colonial Secretary's public denial of the terms published in the *Palestine Post* served only to blacken his name further with those who discounted him on account of his pro-Zionist tendencies. Ormsby-Gore confessed to the Zionists that he

> was told that there would be no peace so long as he was at the Colonial Office; that he is reminded of his Zionist past; that there are cartoons depicting him as in the pocket of Weizmann, etc ...[88]

However, the Colonial Office blamed the Higher Arab Committee for the failure of the negotiations:

> ... the Palestinian Arabs are themselves entirely to blame for the failure of all those well-meant efforts at mediation. It was while mediation was actually under discussion with Nuri that they issued their intention to continue the strike until their aims were achieved ... when people behave like that, they obviously put negotiations out of court and leave us with no alternative but to proceed with stern measures...[89]

Wauchope suspected the veracity of Nuri Said's reports to himself, and held the Mufti personally responsible for the impasse created by the Press leak of the negotiations.[90]

The Palestinians themselves, for reasons connected with internal 'domestic' politics, had kept the negotiations a very loose secret. Whereas the Mufti had not agreed to the proposals brought back by Nuri from the Administration, Ragheb Nashashibi—who was eager to seize on the proposals as a way out of the strike—rushed to give the issue publicity in order to show the Arab public what a chance it was missing by following the Mufti.[91]

Iraqi intrigue had not helped matters. During Nuri's stay at Jerusalem, the Iraqi Prime Minister had informed the Saudi Minister at Baghdad that the Saudi initiative had failed because London did not trust Ibn Saud.[92] London had become involuntarily involved in the rival ambitions of the two most powerful independent Arab States. George Rendel, head of the Eastern Department at the Foreign Office, minuted—'Yasin [Pasha—the Iraqi Prime Minister] has been remarkably tortuous and dishonest over this.'[93]

Arab intransigence and Nuri Said's presumptuousness were the central themes at the Cabinet meeting on 2 September.[94] The consensus that emerged was a complete volte-face from the policy of agreeing to suspend immigration advocated in the Colonial Secretary's memorandum of barely one week before. Only the Secretary of State for India, the Marquess of Zetland, and the Foreign Secretary, Eden, were still in favour of concessions, while the Lord Privy Seal, Halifax, opposed the institution of harsh military measures, and found Nuri's intervention 'unobjectionable'. Viscount Swinton[95] believed that nothing less than a complete surrender by one of the sides could bring about a settlement. Duff-Cooper[96] argued that even were Britain to give way and make concessions, this would gain but an ephemeral peace—the Arabs would reject the Royal Commission's report unless it recommended a complete cessation of Jewish immigration.

THE 1936 REBELLION—MARTIAL LAW OR POLITICAL CONCESSIONS 27

In Baldwin's absence[97] the Home Secretary, Sir John Simon, took the Chair and decided the consensus to be against concessions. In his report to Baldwin, Simon interpreted Nuri's memorandum as a threat to the very foundations of the Mandate, and blamed Wauchope's vacillation for Arab intransigence.[98]

The Zionists made a more sophisticated analysis of Wauchope's vacillating role:

> ... the trouble is that he [Wauchope] is not contented with expressing his opinion, but, excepting the making of a formal announcement to the Arabs on the suspension of immigration—something which he cannot do without the consent of London—he has done everything he could to assure the Arabs that the cessation of immigration will come ... this is not the first time in these months that the roles of London and Jerusalem have interchanged ... now the High Commissioner holds on to Nuri like a lifebelt and he forces London to accept his judgement, emphasizing that if they do not accept Nuri's proposals and do not end the matter peacefully, the whole Near East is liable to rise up against Great Britain ...[99]

It was because the negotiations had become an Arab ultimatum that the Cabinet belatedly decided to reassert British authority in Palestine. Its announcement that it intended to send out to Palestine an extra division of troops which would operate under martial law had a most salutary effect on the country.[100] Consideration of a suspension of immigration was postponed, but not jettisoned.

Notwithstanding the Cabinet's decision, the Colonial Office acquiesced in one further 'unofficial' attempt at mediation, initiated this time by Lords Samuel and Winterton.[101] Their proposals contained in embryo some basic elements of future Government policy—a controlled rate of immigration to limit the Jews to 40 per cent of the total population; a partial, or in places absolute, prohibition of land-sales to Jews; and the institution of a process leading gradually to self-government.

When Samuel and Winterton visited Ormsby-Gore in order to obtain his official stamp of approval for their initiative, the latter emphasized that the Government could take no further steps until the disorders were called off and co-operation with the Royal Commission had been established. Their initiative would therefore have to be treated as private, not requested either by the Government or by the Zionists, with no guarantee that their proposals, even should the Arabs accept them, would be implemented.[102]

In the event, their meeting in Paris with Nuri Said proved fruitless.[103] The restriction on immigration that was to keep the Jews to a minority was no longer regarded as a concession—the Arabs confidently expected the Royal Commission to advocate this anyway. If the Commission let them down, the Arabs might then consider a voluntary restriction on immigration to be a concession, but not now. Samuel and Winterton's Legislative Council scheme, with membership in the proportions proposed, was quite unacceptable to Nuri. The formation of a Customs Union proposed by Samuel and Winterton was in fact already under discussion, as Nuri informed them, but the inclusion of Palestine was not contemplated, since the Jewish industrialists would then gain entry into a large, valuable 'protected' market.

In Palestine itself, Wauchope tried desperately to convince the Arab leaders that it was in their own best interests to call off the strike before force was resorted to. At a meeting with the Higher Arab Committee on 12 September, Wauchope was asked by the Mufti if London would object if the Committee itself asked the Arab kings to appeal to them to end their strike? Wauchope replied that they might approach whom they wished but would receive no support from London or from himself.

When approached by the Mufti for his mediation, Ibn Saud again took advice first at the Foreign Office.[104] The Saudi Chargé d'Affaires at London was advised by Rendel that—as stated by the Government recently—the first essential was the cessation of violence, and this could not be made subject to bargaining. Rendel remained adamant, even when urged that the concession might be regarded as having been made to Ibn Saud rather than to the Higher Arab Committee.

The Colonial Office was now quite aware of the Arabs' inferior tactical position following the Government's volte-face of 2 September, and prepared to exploit it to the full:

... we could have a settlement almost at once if we are prepared to pay the price ... the Committee say in so many words that they will do what the Arab kings tell them to do ... Ibn Saud is ready to move but he must have a concession (an amnesty for those imprisoned during the disturbances).[105]

The Higher Arab Committee turned next to King Ghazi of Iraq, asking him to publish a manifesto that would appeal for an end to the disorders on the condition that following a restoration of peace a general amnesty would be declared, Jewish immigration would be suspended and mediation would take place on the basis proposed by Nuri Said. By this stage not only the British Government, but also the Governments of the Arab States had tired of the Palestinians' protracted manoeuvres. Bateman, the Chargé d'Affaires at Baghdad, reported:

... new move appeared to be nothing more than another attempt to extract some promises in advance of cessation of disorders. This time, however, the Arab Committee were trying to put the onus on the shoulders of the kings who were being asked to make the appeal. These Governments would be assuming an unwarrantable responsibility and would be doomed to disappointment if they paid attention to further tiresome approaches of this kind ...[106]

The Higher Arab Committee was finally convinced that there was no hope of extracting last-minute concessions. The Mufti contacted the Iraqi Consul at Haifa and intimated that if an appeal was made by the Arab kings, his

Committee would call off the strike. Yasin Pasha arrived at an understanding with the Mufti that when the appeal was published:

> ... *no* (repeat) *no* statement will be made implying that any assurance concerning the future action of His Majesty's Government in Palestine has been received by the Arab rulers ...[107]

When informed of this development by the Foreign Office, Orsmby-Gore asked Wauchope how long he could delay the declaration of martial law, in order to give the Arab rulers time to issue their appeal.[108] Wauchope replied that the GOC Gen. Dill, would be ready by 11 October.[109] The Army was becoming impatient. Two days previously, Dill had telegraphed to London:

> ... am anxious as is also the High Commissioner that parleys with Arab kings should come quickly to an end. Appreciate political issues involved with Arab kings, etc., which are causing delays, but militarily it is highly desirable that 1st Division having arrived with great flourish of trumpets, strong action should immediately follow. The role of paper tiger for the army is neither dignified nor effective. Shall be grateful for anything you can do to force the pace, because unless greatly mistaken martial law will in any event be necessary to restore order here.[110]

However, Ibn Saud agreed immediately to the text of the appeal proposed by Iraq, and the Arab rulers agreed to issue it at once.[111] On 12 October Wauchope was able to inform Ormsby-Gore that the strike had been called off by the Arab Committee. The appeal proved to be so effective that many observers concluded that the strike had been kept going by its leaders alone. The order to impose martial law was in due course rescinded.

British encouragement of the Arab rulers' mediation in 1936 constituted a major shift in Mandatory policy. The Arab States' interventions had been welcomed by the Foreign and Colonial Offices in the naïve belief that London would be able to control the extent of their involvement in Palestine, and prevent future unsolicited interference.

But the departure from Mandatory convention was irreversible. The appeals—though made with the acquiescence of the Mandatory—had been made independently of London; the Arab States' appeal had been addressed to a population over which the former had no jurisdiction. One may assess the significance of this development by reference to an earlier official statement made by Harry Luke, Britain's representative to the Permanent Mandates Commission of the League of Nations, in 1931:

> ... it would be very difficult, and possibly even improper, for His Majesty's Government to invite foreign sovereigns to give advice ... It would be difficult, and possibly improper, to do so even if these sovereigns agreed with the advice that it was suggested they give. It would be infinitely more so if they disagreed with the advice ... It would also, he submitted, be improper for the rulers in question, even if not asked, to take the initiative in interfering – because giving such advice

would necessarily have the character of interference – with the political affairs of territories in no way under their jurisdiction.[112]

The immigration issue had yet to be settled by the Cabinet. While the Foreign Office had had to bow to the majority in Cabinet on 2 September, Rendel still viewed the question of suspending immigration as the 'test-case' for future policy in Palestine. A suspension would give the Arabs faith that Britain did not intend subjecting them to a Jewish majority. The Jews, who for their part made no secret of their intention to set up a Jewish State, had concentrated on averting a suspension for precisely the same reason. If no declaration were now made and no assurance given to the Arabs that their rights would be safeguarded, there was every reason to expect a strong reaction in the Arab and Moslem world.[113] It seemed to Rendel that the fates had combined to cloud the real issues:

... the Jews have played their cards extraordinarily well and made the most of the very considerable influence which they are in a position to exercise ... the Arabs have been so misguided in the conduct of their case that I sometimes wonder whether Jewish agents are not at work inside the Arab camp ...[114]

Prior to the next Cabinet meeting on Palestine, Eden asked Rendel for instructions—'was he right in thinking that he was to work for a temporary suspension of immigration once violence had ceased, and a "fair deal" from the Royal Commission?' Rendel replied that their aim should be to attain a decision *now* (i.e. before the disorders had ceased) on the suspension of immigration during the work of the Commission and to give assurances that whatever its findings, even if they were favourable to the Arabs, the Government would carry them out.[115]

With order being rapidly restored in Palestine, Wauchope had regained his nerve and now advised against any concessions—they would merely invite a recurrence of armed rebellion, as a method of gaining political ends.[116] Ormsby-Gore himself vigorously opposed any suspension of immigration. He recalled that of the two precedents for such a measure, in 1921 immigration had been suspended while the country was still in a disturbed state, and in 1930 the measure had been related to the problem of immigration in general. The maximum that the Colonial Secretary was now prepared to recommend was that Wauchope make 'a conservative estimate' of the economic absorptive capacity of the country.[117] This was in effect the first instance of implementation of a 'political high level' for immigration, predating the Peel Commission recommendation of July 1937.[118]

The Cabinet accepted the Colonial Office contention that any concessions now, when the disorders had already ceased, would create the impression that some 'deal' between London and the Arab rulers existed.[119] No self-respecting government could now make concessions. The Foreign Office might allude to 'risings' throughout the Middle East,[120] but Palestine itself was quiet, and after all, the Royal Commission itself had been appointed to examine Arab grievances, which would include undoubtedly the rate of Jewish immigration. The Colonial Office formula—'no change of policy, no suspension of immigration for political reasons', was amended by the Foreign Office to 'no *total* suspension of immigration'. It was agreed to announce that any change in the *status quo* with regard to immigration might prejudice the findings of the Royal Commission.[121]

Yet if concessions had for the time being been avoided, the manner in which the Rebellion had come to an end—under the threat, but not under the weight, of martial law—demonstrated that the policy of concessions was dormant, rather than defunct. Perhaps the most significant summary of the 1936 phase of the Rebellion was made by Military Intelligence:

The last rebellion was mainly raised and controlled by the Higher Arab Committee led by a gentleman called the Grand Mufti. The fact that the rebellion was not suppressed by military action and the institution of martial law, and that no direct measures were taken against the Grand Mufti and his Committee has left them with their power and prestige largely unimpaired.[122]

3

Partition, 1937-38: Doubts and Suspicions

i. The Peel Report

The Royal Commission headed by Earl Peel[1] left for Palestine on 5 November 1936. On the same day, the Colonial Office disclosed the award of 1800 entry permits under the Jewish labour immigration schedule for the half year ending March 1937. The Jewish Agency received the news with mixed feelings—gratification that the principle of immigration according to economic absorptive capacity was preserved, but dismay at the conservative estimate. The Higher Arab Committee had expected a suspension of immigration for the duration of the Commission's proceedings. Outraged by the new immigration schedule, it declared a boycott of the Commission's proceedings. Only in January 1937, following the proddings of Iraq and Saudi Arabia, did the Committee, including the Mufti in person, agree to give evidence. The long interval which elapsed before the Commission published its report in July 1937 created a tense climate in Palestine, in which rumours of the country being partitioned into separate Jewish and Arab States provided the population with its central debating point.

Meanwhile the Foreign Office, in the person of George Rendel, was taking its own private 'opinion poll' of the Arabs' views on Palestine.[2] With Foreign Secretary Eden preoccupied with European problems, the long-serving Rendel enjoyed exceptional influence in the Department. His minutes and memoranda usually formed the basis of Eden's policy on Palestine in Cabinet.[3]

On his own admission, Rendel developed close and cordial relations with Ibn Saud and admitted his predilection for the preserved, primitive character of Arabia, in contrast to his distaste for the 'brash modern look' that the Jewish colonists were giving to Palestine.[4] In many respects Rendel epitomized the 'romantic' school of British Arabophils, which counted among its more illustrious members such flamboyant characters as T. E. Lawrence and St John 'Abdullah' Philby,[5] not to mention Rendel's own counterpart at Cairo, the influential Ambassador, Sir Miles Lampson.

In April 1937, upon his return from the Middle East, Rendel circulated his impressions to the Colonial Office, stressing 'the need to solve the Palestine problem in a way which would placate the Arabs'.[6] Philby later confided to Ben-Gurion that Rendel had visited Jedda in order to ascertain the Saudi ruler's attitude to the Palestine problem.[7] Rendel warned against relying too much upon Ibn Saud's mistrust of Italy to keep him loyal to

Great Britain. He just might turn to Italy in despair, if driven to it by British policy in Palestine. Likewise with Iraq. If these two Arab States were to turn against Britain, it was difficult to see how Transjordan could then remain friendly. Lampson, whom Rendel had met at Suez, had expressed similar views regarding Egypt. Specifically, Rendel argued that the Arabs had to be given some guarantee that they would not become a minority in a Jewish State, 'as must happen if our present policy is continued'.

The Colonial Office was enraged at the proposal that Rendel's memorandum be submitted to the Peel Commission. The Department hotly denied that its policy would transform the Arabs into a minority in Palestine. Ormsby-Gore was incensed at such presumption on the part of a Civil Servant from another Department:

I realize that Mr Rendel is a sincere pro-Arab and anti-Jew and a critic of His Majesty's policy of carrying out the Mandate of the League of Nations, but that he has the right to submit to a Royal Commission his erroneous opinion of that policy is a right I cannot admit . . .[8]

The Foreign Office forecast of a chorus of Arab opposition to British policy in Palestine was broken only by the reports of reactions to be expected from Syria and the Lebanon. So long as Damascus continued to be the fountainhead of pan-Arabism, there was reason to be apprehensive of Syrian politicians. But the great mass of Syrians was more concerned with its own local problems than with the merits of the Peel Report. The Christians of the Lebanon, on the other hand, openly welcomed the prospect of a Jewish State on their southern frontier. This would break the hostile ring of Moslem Arabs which an independent Arab Syria and Palestine might otherwise form.[9] In June 1937 Weizmann met the Maronite Patriarch of Lebanon, Arida, and the Lebanese President, Emil Edé in Paris.[10] The Patriarch expressed his desire to see friendly relations established with the Jews. The President, on hearing from Weizmann that the Royal Commission had proposed a Jewish State, was visibly moved and asked Weizmann to promise that the first treaty of friendship to be made by the Jewish State should be made with the Lebanon. The only obstacle between the Zionists and the Lebanon remained the opposition of the French High Commissioner in Syria, M. de Martel.[11]

The Peel Commission submitted its report to the Cabinet in June 1937. It proposed certain 'palliative' measures to improve current conditions in Palestine, but concluded that the best hope of a permanent solution to the Palestine problem lay in 'the difficult and drastic operation of partition'.[12] Ormsby-Gore recommended Government endorsement of the report,[13] He saw in partition the most honourable way for the Colonial Office to extricate itself from an impossible position. Exasperated by attacks on Britain from both Arabs and Jews, he was inclined to tell both that 'this was the Government's proposal and they could either take it or leave it'.[14]

The Foreign Office objected on two grounds. Firstly, to the details of the partition scheme proposed by the Commission; and secondly, to the proposal that partition be strictly imposed, by martial law if necessary.[15] Bearing in mind the sensibilities of the Arab States, the Department proposed that instead of blaming the troubles on 'conflicting nationalisms', the Government should make the frank admission that the integral fulfilment of the Mandatory's obligations had proved impossible.

In Cabinet, Eden claimed that the Peel plan created a small Jewish State with unviable frontiers alongside an Arab State without access to the sea. The elevation of Abdullah to head Arab Palestine would arouse the resentment of Iraq and of Ibn Saud. The Secretary of State for India also thought that the Arabs had been given a 'raw deal'. Opposition was sufficiently strong for the Cabinet to decide not to commit itself to the details, but to confine itself to the approval only of the principle of partition.[16]

Rendel opposed the establishment of a Jewish State in any form. If Britain retained control over the proposed Jewish area, its obligations would not in fact be much greater than those involved in the policing of awkward British enclaves and the obligation to intervene between the Arab and Jewish States. His concept had the dual attraction—from the British point of view—of preserving the British position at Haifa, while at the same time assuaging Arab nationalism. Rendel particularly resented what he thought was the 'indecent haste' with which the Colonial Office sought to divest itself of all responsibility for Palestine at the earliest possible moment.[17]

When the Foreign Office tried to delete from the partition formula the benefit of national status for the Jews—on the grounds that this would preclude Britain from retaining Mandatory control—the Cabinet rejected the proposal because this in fact was the very essence of the appeal of partition for the Jews.[18] Oliphant, while agreeing with Rendel in principle, appreciated that to 'lop off' the Arabs while maintaining mandatorial relations with the Jews would only cause further trouble. Rendel's point was to be served by the decision of the Permanent Mandates Commission that both states should serve a probationary period under British tutelage.[19]

ii. The reception of partition—Zionist tactics misfire

The debate in the Commons on the Peel Commission's Report was regarded by the new Government's critics as a suitable occasion on which to pay off party and personal scores.[20] Opposition leaders drawn from all parties met with the Zionists, under the auspices of Sir Archibald Sinclair, in order to discuss their tactics in the coming debate.[21] Dr Weizmann favoured partition in principle, but contemplated a minimum immigration per annum of 50–60,000 in the meantime,[22] and stressed the need for adequate, defensible borders for the Jewish State.

Churchill,[23] who monopolized most of the conversation, expressed his emphatic disapproval of the whole scheme. He warned those present that the Government was untrustworthy:

... a lot of lily-livered rabbits. The Jewish State would not materialize ... the Arabs would immediately start trouble and the Government would run away again ... of course, if Dr W(eizmann) told him to shut up when the time came, he would shut up; he would stay at home, but he would be heartbroken about it ... .[24]

Mr Attlee was shocked by the partition proposal. Of course, if the Zionists agreed to the proposal he would not fight it, but it seemed to him a shame to put an end to a great experiment in co-operation between peoples; it represented a complete confession of failure in the working of the Mandate, and would be a 'triumph for Fascism'. He, Attlee, could not agree to the idea. Similar opposition was expressed by all present save Amery, who pragmatically asserted that it would be much easier to build up a Jewish State than to change the British Administration.

Mrs Dugdale warned the Zionists that partition must not be made 'the cat's paw of English politics'—these men were in no sense a team, and they knew little or nothing about the subject.[25]

Whether the Zionists could have exerted sufficient pressure on the Opposition to restrain it from 'overdoing' its attack on partition must remain a matter for speculation. But it seems that tactically the Zionists themselves were quite content for considerable criticism to be voiced of the Peel plan. One week prior to the Commons debate, Ben-Gurion discussed the issue with the Labour Party Executive.[26] When asked confidentially whether the Zionists wished the Party to oppose partition in principle, Ben-Gurion replied that they wanted the *alteration* of the plan, as they had lost faith in the administration of the Mandate, whose continuation might prove no less dangerous than partition.

Ben-Gurion himself felt some difficulty in manoeuvering between 'official' Zionist policy and 'internal directives' of the Zionist Actions Committee.[27] He was himself but a recent convert to partition and seemed unable to display an enthusiasm which he as yet lacked for the idea. The Zionist leaders in London agreed at quite an early stage that the best pragmatic approach would be to accept partition in principle, *faute de mieux*. On the other hand, the Zionists in Palestine equivocated in an alarming fashion. In March 1937 Shertok agreed at a meeting of the Zionist Executive in London that the scheme must be adopted, subject to modification of the area and to obtaining real autonomy.[28] Yet in June, Shertok sent a long letter to Wauchope listing Zionist objections to partition and pleading for a return to the proper administration of the Mandate.[29] Similarly Ben-Gurion, who did not formally agree (inside Zionist councils) to fight for partition until June,[30] was still making public declarations against the idea in July 1937.[31]

This equivocation stemmed from a deep suspicion of British motives on the one hand and, on the other, from a negotiating style which set unrealistically high goals in order to leave plenty of margin for bargaining down to actual goals. As Blanche Dugdale put it: 'their idea is to ask for everything as a "minimum" requirement'.[32]

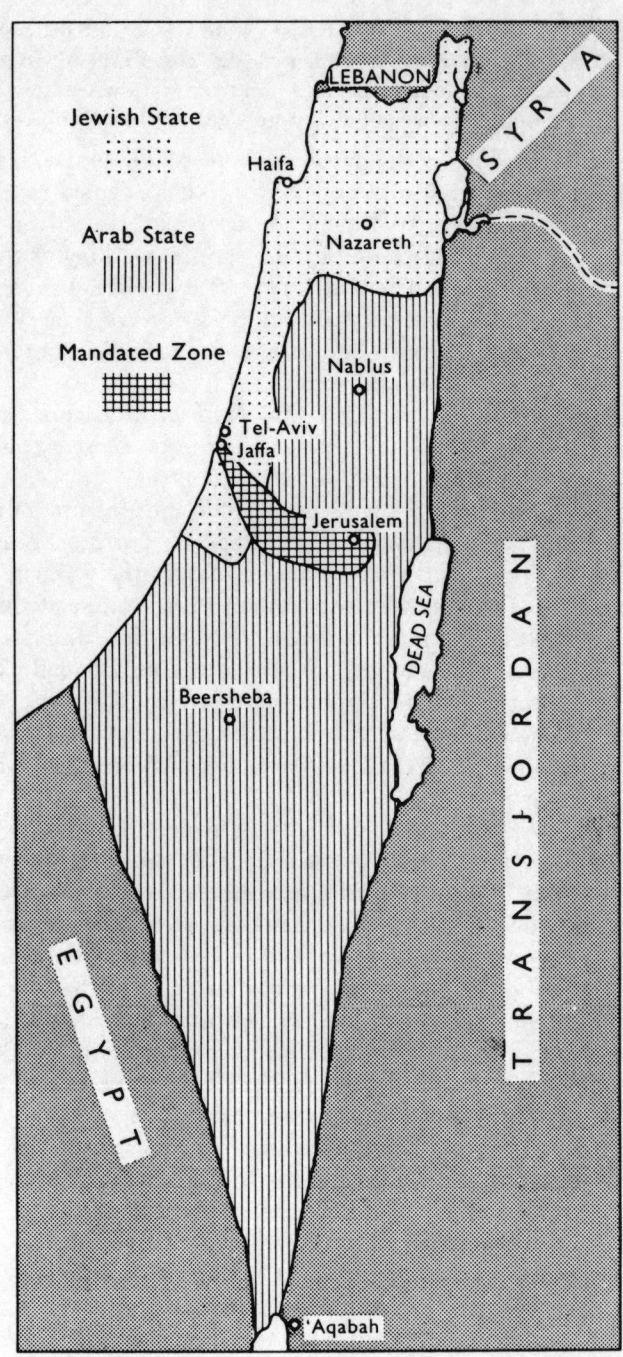

The Peel Commission's partition proposal, 1937

Typical was Ben-Gurion's assertion that the British must not be allowed to think they were 'doing the Zionists a favour', even if the Peel plan did contain many aspects favourable to the Zionists:

> ... this report ... gives us a wonderful strategic basis for our stand, for our fight ... the first document since the Mandate which strengthens our moral and political status ... it gives us control over the coast of Palestine; large immigration; a Jewish Army; systematic colonization under State control; the possibility of a large State loan; the chance of an ally on our northern border ...[33]

With the publication of the Report, the Zionists learned for the first time of the recommendation to impose a 'political high level' for immigration pending the partition of Palestine. At first, Ben-Gurion impetuously advocated a complete break with the British:

> If this was the method by which the Jewish State was to be established, he had no faith whatsoever that the Government would carry out that policy. This British Government was not going to get Haifa and Jerusalem by dirty tricks of this kind; they could return the Mandate to the League, or else they would have to fight for it ...[34]

Ben-Gurion's colleagues managed to dissuade him from this course. For the present, Ben-Gurion acknowledged Weizmann's superior judgement in the field of Anglo-Zionist relations and undertook to do nothing against the latter's will.[35]

In Parliament, the Government was surprised at the vehemence of the Zionist lobby against the Peel plan, which it had believed to be favourable to and favoured by the Zionists.[36] Sabotage of the Balfour Declaration was hinted at and the Government was accused of abdicating its responsibilities. The Labour Party proposed a Joint Select Committee of the House to examine the Report before committing itself. The Commons did not wish to be rushed into endorsing a scheme which a Royal Commission had taken six months to compile. A delaying amendment, first proposed by Churchill, was adopted without division. The partition scheme would be submitted first to the League of Nations' Permanent Mandates Commission. During the interim period the Government would be able to make adequate inquiries, so as to return to Parliament with a definite scheme taking into account the recommendations of the Royal Commission.

In fact, Zionist tactics had misfired badly. Their critical approach to the Peel plan, and their lack of enthusiasm, were undoubtedly seized upon by the opponents of a new Government, in order to make political capital. Zionist plaints were taken at their face value by their Gentile friends in Parliament. As one commentator has put it, 'the debate over partition offers the most striking example of the way the Zionists would often overstate their case and then, as a result, find themselves being outpaced by their Gentile supporters.[37] In retrospect, Weizmann claimed somewhat disingenuously that the Zionists' failure to display adequately their conversion to partition had been due to their having been denied an advance copy of the report.[38]

The debate on partition may be placed in logical sequence after the Parliamentary debates on the Legislative Council in Parliament during March 1936. The consequences of both debates, although each was dominated by pro-Zionist or Zionist-cued speakers, were counter-productive to Zionist interests in the long run. The Arab contention that whatever policy might be decided upon by the Cabinet, the High Commission at Jerusalem, or even by a Royal Commission could be ultimately undone by the Jews in Parliament began to win sympathizers even inside Parliament:

... He [Pickthorne] said that ... the Jews ... had overdone their case during the debate in Parliament after the Royal Commission's report ... the Government had been prepared at that time to carry out the Commission's proposals without much delay, but the Zionists and their powerful friends in Parliament had prevented it by their strong attacks in the debate ...[39]

iii. The Foreign Office sabotages partition

The Foreign Office attack on partition had been gathering momentum prior to the Parliamentary debate. But following the negative reactions of the Arab States during the summer of 1937, the Foreign Office began to advocate total abandonment of partition. It seems unlikely that the Department's campaign could have entered this second phase had the Government recommendation to implement partition been endorsed by Parliament in July 1937.

The first Arab State to react to the Peel Report was Iraq, whose Prime Minister issued an appeal to the Palestinian Arabs to oppose its findings. The Iraqi representative at the League of Nations' Permanent Mandates Commission caused considerable embarrassment for Great Britain when at Geneva he spoke up against partition. Ormsby-Gore suspected Foreign Office connivance and went so far as to warn Eden that unless the latter supported him on partition he would be forced to tell the Prime Minister that he could no longer take responsibility for Palestine.[40] This unprecedented attack on British Mandatory policy, by an ally of Great Britain, did little to enhance British prestige in the Middle East and created doubts about British sincerity over partition.

In Jerusalem, Shertok[41] expressed surprise at Iraq's public defiance of the Government's policy.[42] Wauchope retorted that if the Government left the Jewish leaders free to oppose its policy, it could not possibly deny the same freedom to Arab leaders, and referred to a Jewish Labour Party resolution opposing partition. Shertok pointed out that the Iraqi appeal had been issued by the Head of a State which was not only Britain's ally, but to all intents and purposes a vassal of hers. At a loss, Wauchope admitted that he himself had been most depressed by the Iraqi appeal, but: 'As there was, however, no doubt that the Foreign Office knew of what had happened, he did not think there was anything for him to do in the matter'.[43]

The Iraqi intervention, together with ominous reports from British representatives in Arab capitals, provided grist for the Foreign Office thesis that the implementation of partition would bring with it the risk of a general conflagration in the Middle East. The Foreign Office pursued the various alternatives to partition, and fired the opening shots in what was to be a bitter struggle with the Colonial Office.

The Department opposed any return to the *status quo ante*. If partition were abandoned due to Arab opposition and Jewish immigration resumed under the Mandate, regulated only by economic absorptive capacity, the ultimate result would still be a Jewish majority.[44] The Department therefore proposed that Britain openly admit that the task of implementing the Balfour Declaration had proved beyond its capabilities. Britain would offer instead to make an *amende honorable* by offering the Jews a free gift of British territory elsewhere.[45] Vansittart, the Permanent Under-Secretary, ruled out this approach, which would inevitably come up against Colonial Office opposition, and prove unacceptable to the majority of Jews.

Colonial Office officials were unable to comprehend their colleagues' objections to partition, which to them seemed to offer the only honourable exit from an ignominious episode in British colonial history:

... the falseness of our position hampered us at every turn; now at length we have a means of escape ... by which we can do substantial justice to both parties and clean our conscience of the odious imputation of breach of faith. We are ... in sight of shore after a prolonged buffeting in heavy seas. Are we to scuttle the lifeboat merely because the coast looks rocky and dangerous?[46]

It became clear that the appointment of the new (Woodhead) Commission which was to examine the technical feasibility of partition,[47] and the determination of its terms of reference, would be made the occasion for a complete reappraisal of the Government's policy in Palestine.[48]

The force of Parliamentary, League of Nations, and to some extent of British public opinion, now activated by new outrages against British personnel in Palestine, made it impossible for the Government to retreat openly from partition.[49] The Foreign Office therefore devoted its efforts to ensuring that the new Commission would be free not only to examine alternative schemes, but also to reject the idea of partition completely. This 'procedural' struggle was won in its essentials by the Foreign Office in December 1937.

The Foreign Office campaign was master-minded by Rendel, who claimed that the Middle East was one organic whole, which would react to whatever happened in one of its constituent parts. He argued that a 'local' solution between Arabs and Jews in Palestine would have been a relatively simple matter. The real problem was created by the annual introduction of alien immigrants from abroad. Palestine could never accommodate the masses of

European Jewry, a fact of which the Zionists themselves were perfectly aware. Moreover they, the Zionists, made no secret of their intention to use the new Jewish State as a base from which to expand into the Arab hinterland.[50]

Arab improvidence, disunity and indecision should not blind Great Britain to the growing importance of Arab nationalism. The creation of an insecure, expansionist Jewish State would ultimately involve the intervention of British troops. British obligations to the Jews depended to a great extent on a correct interpretation of the 'singularly ambiguous' Balfour Declaration —regarded as the 'Great Charter of the persecuted Jews of Central Europe'. No well-informed Zionist could really believe it was intended to turn the indigenous Arabs into a minority in a Jewish State.

The only way in which the Balfour Declaration could be made compatible with the various pledges made to the Arabs at the end of the First World War would be to assume that the Jewish National Home was to be a focus and centre for Jewish culture and civilization. The only solution would be to limit the Jewish population to a fixed ratio of the total population of Palestine. This might be as high as 40 per cent conceded Rendel.[51]

Rendel's memorandum was passed on to the Colonial Office, whose permission was asked to reassure the Saudi Minister in London that no definite decision on partition had as yet been taken. He also asked that Ibn Saud's views be laid before the new Commission.[52] Shuckburgh,[53] while pointing out that Ibn Saud had already been informed that his views would be taken into account, indicated that the '40 per cent ratio' proposal of Rendel was not reconcilable with the Government's declared policy of establishing a Jewish State in Palestine. Downie thought Rendel's scheme ludicrous. If this was the Foreign Office 'constructive alternative' to partition, the Colonial Office would have to retract its acceptance of the Peel Report and place itself in the unenviable position of having 'sold a pup' to Dr Weizmann, who had just fought for the acceptance of partition at the Zionist Congress.[54]

Rendel was anxious to avoid any recurrence of the 1936 dilemma, when political concessions had been cancelled in the face of Arab intransigence. The new wave of violence in Palestine, this time promptly dealt with by British action, threatened just such a situation. In Rendel's opinion, military measures were no subsitute for a just solution of the fundamental problem. In fact, the Jews would welcome the development of a situation in which the Arabs became open rebels and avowed enemies. Britain would then be committed to their suppression and, as a corollary, to 'unqualified and unhesitating support of the non-Palestinian Jews in their dreams of colonization'.[55]

Rendel despaired of the other departments concerned with Palestine. The Colonial Office would under no circumstances contemplate any change in policy. General Haining saw the latest outbreak of violence as a challenge to British rule by a band of criminals who did not represent the majority of Arabs. The Air Ministry also drew a sharp distinction between 'terrorists' and the bands of Arab nationalists who operated in the hills, and believed that the present troubles were incited from Syria.[56]

iv. The significance of the Woodhead Commission

For the Zionists, the announcement of the new 'technical' commission had come as a complete surprise. They had hoped to negotiate the details of the partition scheme in the more amenable climate of London.[57] However, Weizmann, with his long-standing faith in the British word, set great store by Eden's speech to the League Assembly, in which he had declared that the Government still saw in partition the best hope for a solution. Weizmann regarded the speech as the Jews' 'ace of trumps'.[58]

But in Palestine Shertok was less sanguine. The fact that the Commission was being sent to Palestine at all was cause for concern:

... it would fall straight into the arms of officialdom, and under the load of Arab pressure. It would see Galialee in another light from that seen only on a map.[59] ... His Majesty's Government is seeking to insert changes in the Peel plan to our detriment. This would have been difficult for them to do in London, for the majority of public opinion sees the plan as neglecting us, and also our pressure would be great ...[60]

These fears were confirmed and reinforced from Jerusalem:

... Some of the officials are freely expressing doubts as to the practicability of partition and some are most vigorous in proclaiming the impossibility ... of dividing up Jerusalem ...[61] unfortunately the Arabs have been persuaded that the High Commissioner is against partition and has gone to London to prevail upon HMG to abandon it ...[62]

The letter quoted evidence which indicated that much of the Arab opposition to partition was not genuine.[63] Above all, the Zionists were pessimistic, as they knew that the High Commissioner himself would not approve of any policy that he believed to be unpalatable to the Arabs. This meant in effect, the Zionists believed, to the Mufti.[64]

In London, Ormsby-Gore wished to clear up the uncertainties engendered by the delay in announcing the terms of reference to the new Commission. He wanted a policy statement which would display the Government's intention not to be shaken from its policy by a campaign of terror. Such a policy, it was hoped, would rally the moderates in the Arab camp to the Mandatory. He objected to the proposed association of the Arab States in the work of the Commission. Apart from Abdullah, the Arab rulers had shown themselves as hostile to partition as the Palestinian Arabs themselves. Uncertainty would only increase Arab intransigence and Ormsby-Gore remained convinced that partition remained the best solution.[65]

The Foreign Office gave notice that it intended to draft a reply, and Cabinet consideration of the issue was postponed for a week. Again, Rendel drew up the Foreign Office reply. Partition could now be imposed only by force, he claimed, rejecting the Colonial Secretary's central thesis that the Government's acceptance of partition in principle, irrespective of any risk involved, now precluded any alternatives. Rendel argued that the European implications of a hostile Middle East aligned with Britain's enemies must override the arguments in favour of partition. The terms of reference of the new Commission would have to be enlarged to ensure that they did not exclude all evidence other than that having a direct bearing on the partition scheme.[66]

Rendel urged that the Commission be directed to consider the '40 per cent' quota for Jewish immigration. But in Cabinet Eden confined himself to a brief reference to the scheme, and asked that the Commission be allowed complete freedom to consider whatever proposals it thought best suited to meet the new situation.[67] Ormsby-Gore replied that in effect this would reopen not only the Royal Commission Report, but also Government policy as embodied in its Statement of July 1937—if not the policy, now twenty years old, of the Balfour Declaration. Ormsby-Gore's main contention was that Britain would have to face up to an international odium of breach of faith if, after having accepted the impartial interpretation of the Royal Commission of its obligations to the Jews, it now repudiated that policy and offered the Jews instead a permanent minority status in Palestine.[68]

The Colonial Secretary had not discerned any evidence of permanent or widespread hostility among Arab rulers with regard to the Palestine question. Even if there were, concessions would not bring a solution:

... with such objections there can be no compromise. Either we must carry out our pledges to the Jewish people, as now interpreted by an impartial Royal Commission, or we shall have to tell the Jews that we cannot fulfil our frequently reiterated pledges, for fear of jeopardizing our relations with the Arab rulers outside Palestine ...[69]

No one in Government seriously questioned this view—the controversy between the Departments would be over the risks worth taking to fulfil British pledges to the Jews.

Were the Commission to be allowed to consider Ibn Saud's proposal to fix a set numerical ratio between the two races, the Government's acceptance of the Peel Report would be stultified.[70] Moreover, he knew of no precedent for inviting the representatives of foreign Governments to give evidence before a commission appointed to carry out investigations in territory under British administration.

It remained only for the Cabinet to adjudicate. On the eve of the decisive Cabinet meeting Foreign Office officials met to decide tactics.[71] The Department appreciated that if the Government from the outset inserted anything in the new Commission's terms of reference that enabled it to consider solutions other than partition, it would be exposed to the accusation of appointing a new Commission to go over the same ground. It would be difficult to convince Parliament that circumstances had changed sufficiently to warrant a change in policy. It might be better to leave the Commission free to report on the impracticability of partition, and take up the question of an alternative later. It was therefore decided rather to work for the excision of certain key clauses in the proposed terms of reference: the clause which confined the Commission to considering only those representations relevant to partition; that which declared the Balfour Declaration to be incompatible with the assignment to the Jews of a permanent minority position in Palestine; and that which declared the Government's intention to implement partition notwithstanding any lack of co-operation by either race, i.e. by force. All three points were deleted eventually by the Cabinet.

In Cabinet, the Prime Minister came down clearly on the side of the Foreign Office.[72] But even if it were assumed that partition would be too difficult to carry out eventually, the present moment was not propitious for announcing it. The impression might be given of a surrender to force. Chamberlain therefore proposed that the Government's statement make it clear that no action could be taken for a long time, pending the work of the Commission and the submission of its report to Parliament, the League, etc. If the Cabinet deemed it necessary to instruct the Commission that it was within their competence to find that there did not exist any workable scheme of partition, this might be done by way of a private communication to the Chairman.

MacDonald (then Dominions Secretary) was still not convinced that partition was not the least unobjectionable policy—even the pro-Arab MPs supported it. He agreed that it would be impossible to give the impression that the Government was running away from partition, but he was in favour of 'leaving the door open'. Ormsby-Gore was concerned not to let down his administration in Palestine. Partition would be acceptable only if Arabs and Jews were convinced that there were no alternatives, or that any that existed were worse. His defence of his own restricting terms of reference was weak.

In Whitehall there had occurred a total breakdown in communications between the Colonial and Foreign Office. The remarks of the First Secretary of the Middle Eastern Department summed up Colonial Office exacerbation:

... shocked by the levity with which the Foreign Office are prepared to throw partition overboard, without ... having any well-considered alternative to take its place. They seem to ... have no apprehension of the seriousness of the question or of the considerations on which the proposals of the Royal Commission are based.[73]

Ormsby-Gore advised Weizmann to exercise his own powers of persuasion at the Foreign Office, from whence Rendel—'a Papist who had done much harm to the Zionist cause'—had now departed.[74]

The Colonial Office was irritated particularly by dire warnings from the Middle East ambassadors,[75] which were studiously given Cabinet circulation by the Foreign Office. Typical was that from the Ambassador at Constantinople:

> ... I am far from underrating the importance of a friendly Jewry: but in the present state of effervescence in Asia ... the goodwill of Islam must at the lowest evaluation be a no less precious asset; and I cannot but feel that the Palestine problem, put in terms of compulsory partition, pins us down to a disagreeable and unprofitable choice between the two ....[76]

The Colonial Office did not question the Ambassador's assumptions but, in the light of its obligations assumed in Palestine, saw no alternative to current policy: 'either (1) to continue to attempt to work on a Mandate which experience as well as logic proves to be unworkable—a source of continual and probably growing friction with the Moslem and Jewish worlds; or (2) to yield to the extremist Arab demand and set up Palestine as an Arab State with a guaranteed Jewish minority—*a betrayal so dishonorable and a surrender to force so conspicuous as to earn us as much contempt as the gratitude of the Moslem world*.[77] So swift was the revolution in Government thinking that within eighteen months London proposed just that—the establishment of an independent State in Palestine.

Parkinson (Permanent Under-Secretary of State at the Colonial Office) thought it regrettable that ambassadors would not read the Royal Commission report before submitting views contrary to the policy of the Government. Ormsby-Gore gave instructions not to pass on the Ambassador's note to Palestine—'Sir Percy Loraine might be interpreting the views of the permanent officials at the Foreign Office, but *not* those of the Turkish Government.'[78]

The appointment of the Woodhead[79] Commission in January 1938 was regarded by the Colonial Office as an instrument with which the Foreign Office intended quietly and slowly to eliminate partition. Although a Cabinet appointment, the Commission was regarded by the Colonial Office as a Foreign Office creation, the secret instructions to be given it as a subversion of the Cabinet's earlier decision favouring partition in principle:

> ... I am extremely anxious about the whole position. It is indeed unique in my experience. Here we have a policy (good or bad is not the purpose) which was formally adopted by the Cabinet as a whole, but which the Foreign Office are doing their best—and encouraging their agents to do their best—to render nugatory.[80]

The Cabinet had decided ostensibly to go ahead with partition. Yet instead of announcing its determination to implement forthwith an equitable scheme, the Government announced it could take no steps towards partition for many months.[81] Its statement also specified that the large Arab minority which, under the Peel plan, would have found itself in the Jewish State would not be transferred by force. Lastly, and of key importance, was the confidential letter which Ormsby-Gore was instructed to send to the Chairman of the Commission.[82]

Eden complied with Ormsby-Gore's wish not to imply in the published terms of reference any hint of undue or premature readiness to abandon partition. As a *quid pro quo*, Ormsby-Gore agreed to clear up any doubts on this point in his letter to the Chairman.[83] The Colonial Secretary was placed in the somewhat humiliating position of having to produce for the Secretary to the Cabinet a letter indicating Eden's approval of his confidential instructions to the Commission.[84] Ormsby-Gore proposed that if the Commission judged partition to be unworkable, it should report back in a separate confidential note which would not be published.[85] This request in fact would have defeated the whole purpose of the Foreign Office, which was to have an 'independent' Commission publicly declare partition to be impracticable, and thus release the Government from its previous decision. On Foreign Office demand, Ormsby-Gore duly informed Sir John Woodhead that if his Commission was driven to the conclusion that partition was impracticable, it must obviously say so, duly setting out the grounds upon which its decision was based.[86]

The Foreign Office expected the Woodhead Commission to fail in its task. It viewed the Commission as a useful instrument with which to rubber-stamp its own views. Thus, there would be no point in appointing a body which would only be allowed to consider schemes which the Foreign Office thought impracticable.[87]

v. Zionist evaluation of Government intentions
How did the Zionists evaluate the Foreign Office attack at the time? They could only glean an incomplete picture from the scraps of information they received. The two Anglo-Zionists with Cabinet 'confidants' differed about the gravity of the situation.[88] Yet both agreed that the Generals' verdict on partition would be crucial. Mrs Dugdale was not too optimistic—'on this issue we cannot count on the Service Ministers—they want to keep peace in the Middle East as long as Britain keeps her hold on Palestine ...'[89]

Foreign Office representation of partition to the Arab States was not all that it might have been. In January 1938, Nuri Said visited London with an alternative plan for the Middle East and Palestine.[90] On meeting Viscount Cranborne,[91] Nuri expressed his conviction that partition was impracticable. Cranborne readily agreed:

... His Majesty's Government had adopted partition for the reason that, after careful study, no better policy had presented itself. They fully realized, however, that it was not a perfect solution and that its practicability still needed to be investigated ...[92]

Ormsby-Gore also met Nuri, and reports of what transpired between the two gave rise to Zionist speculation that the Colonial Secretary himself was weakening under Arab pressure.[93]

Foreign Office indiscretions and Colonial Office vacillation did not pass unnoticed by Nuri Said. He duly reported back to the Mufti, according to Jewish Agency Intelligence, with the remark—'hope for the abandonment of partition is not yet lost'.[94] Nuri's general impression from London was that the Government had grave doubts about the advisability of 'a Zionist policy' —due to the international situation, the efforts of the Italians and the Germans in the Middle East, and the attitude of official British circles in Arab countries. Although the Colonial Secretary had adhered to the official line that the Woodhead Commission was being sent out to devise a triple partition plan, Nuri received the definite impression that the Arabs might ask for part of Galilee, as the Royal Commission had 'given the Jews too much'. The Colonial Secretary had asked Nuri to persuade the Arabs to co-operate with the new Commission. The Arabs were free to oppose partition, but they should at the same time ask for their views to be taken into consideration, in the event that partition was ultimately decided upon. In reply to the Mufti's question whether the British reckoned with the Arab factor in Palestine, Nuri stated:

They reckon too much with it, for if it were not so they would never have hesitated in executing the partition scheme; nor would they appeal to us to assist them in stabilizing the situation in the Near East; nor would they instruct their representatives in the Arab States to explain to their Governments how difficult was Britain's position in view of the double obligation . . .[95]

On his return to London, Dr Weizmann placed his information on Nuri's talks before the Colonial Secretary himself.[96] Ormsby-Gore claimed that it had been the Foreign Office that had pushed Nuri on to him, that he personally had not wished to receive him. He vigorously denied that there was any truth in the report which Nuri had given the Mufti, and advised Weizmann to tell the new Commission that Galilee was essential for the security of the Jewish State—and they would get it. Ormsby-Gore categorically denied that there were any unpublished terms of reference. Weizmann warned of 'friends in Parliament', and of Zionist determination to 'fight to the last ditch' should the Peel plan not be improved upon, as Parliamentary opinion had favoured.

Before his departure from the Eastern Department Rendel did his utmost to ensure that the Woodhead Commission would reach the 'correct conclusions'. With the terms of reference settled to Foreign Office satisfaction, Rendel wished to ensure that the Commission's personnel would be of the 'right persuasion'—this meant selection by the Cabinet as a whole, and not by the Colonial Office alone.[97] However, Ormsby-Gore gained the Prime Minister's consent to exclusive selection by his Department alone.

Rendel therefore switched his tactics to ensuring that the Foreign Office point of view was placed in writing before the Commission.[98] In effect, he was asking that the substance of his own memoranda of the previous autumn be placed before the Commission as 'evidence'. But the views of the Foreign Office could hardly be submitted as the views of the Secretary of State, a member of the Cabinet that would later sit in 'impartial' judgement on the Commission's Report. Oliphant, Permanent Under-Secretary at the Foreign Office, feared that Ormsby-Gore might detect the handiwork of Rendel— as he had done in the past—even in memoranda submitted by Oliphant himself.[99] In face of Colonial Office objections, this proposal also had to be dropped. Otherwise there might have developed an undignified squabble of memoranda and counter-memoranda, which could not have enhanced Government prestige with the Commission.

Had the Zionists been fully aware of, or appreciated the gravity of the Foreign Office campaign against partition, they might well have mounted a campaign similar to that which in 1931 had secured the reversal of the Passfield White Paper policy. Mrs Dugdale had been kept current with only part of the Cabinet's discussions, and had conveyed what she knew to Weizmann only after the issue had to all intents and purposes been resolved in Cabinet.[100] Perhaps her own optimistic appreciation was influenced by her informer, Elliot. Although he issued dire warnings against placing too much reliance on British promises, Elliot still believed that partition had a chance, however feeble. He summed up the Cabinet's attitude to partition with an allegory:

... it was like the Gallipoli expedition – the orders were to try and force the Dardanelles. Winston took that to mean 'go on, heads down and force the Dardanelles'. But the others interpreted it to mean: 'Have a crack at the Dardanelles— but if you can't do it never mind—it wasn't a very good idea anyhow, and we will try something else!' And *that* is the spirit in which the Commission will go out.[101]

Mrs Dugdale concluded that provided the Jews gave no excuse for any breakdown, everything might still turn out well. She was responsible for allaying Zionist fears, and reassured Weizmann that there was no need for his presence in London. She advised him to remain in Palestine, where she would brief him when she arrived in January.[102]

The Cabinet decisions of late December on the terms of reference, and the report of Nuri Said's meeting with the Mufti in January 1938, took time to filter through to the Zionists. Elliot's appreciations became less sanguine:

... our opponents in the Cabinet are getting ready for a Hoare-Laval coup, but will put everything off as long as they can ... must make Chaim realize that the B(alfour) Declaration is no more – and that all we have is 400,000 in the Yishuv, and a few friends outside. We must make it suffice.[103]

Weizmann returned to London in February 1938. Like many Zionists, he suspected that behind the January White Paper there lurked a reversal of policy. In a report to the Jewish Agency Executive in London, Weizmann inferred that Foreign Office policy was influenced by Halifax's abortive visit to Hitler the previous November.[104]

Weizmann was received by the Colonial Secretary and the Prime Minister, but remained unconvinced by their reassurances.[105] On his return to Palestine, in order to prepare his evidence before the Woodhead Commission, he probed the Chief Secretary, who replied that he knew no more than had already appeared in public statements and documents. Weizmann rhetorically tried to reassure himself—'he took it that the Commission was indeed a partition commission; the High Commissioner had told him that their notepaper was headed "Partition Commission"—that must mean something!'[106]

The work methods adopted by the Commission during its stay in Palestine gave further cause for Zionist alarm. Shertok contrasted the approach of the present body with the historically-minded Peel Commission.[107] The members of the Royal Commission had been of a different calibre. Whereas they had analysed the situation in a statesmanlike manner, the attitude of the current commission was purely administrative:

... not what a Jewish State would be likely to give to the Jews, but what would be the fate of the Arabs left in the Jewish State ... not what the Jews needed, but what did they have already, and how would matters affect the Arabs.[108]

Moreover, the Zionists feared that the Commission would be influenced by the Palestine Administration, and the so-called 'Wauchope Plan'.[109] Zionist anxiety regarding this plan—which allotted Galilee to the Arab State—had increased following the report of Nuri Said's interview with Ormsby-Gore. Weizmann referred to the fact that the officials upon whom the Woodhead Commission would have to largely rely for assistance had already put up a scheme which they knew very well was utterly unacceptable to the Zionists.[110]

One of the Commission members, Mr Reid,[111] had leaked the news in Palestine that it would be open to the Commission to raise the whole question of partition *de novo*. On the boat home from Palestine, before the Commission's report had been drafted, Reid treated a Jewish Agency executive to a lecture on the 'Jewish Question':

... Zionism was not a wise movement for the Jews to foster. It was the same nationalism that we objected to in Hitler. The real solution of the Jewish problem was that adopted by the Bolsheviks – assimilation ... if they must have a State let them find a territory that was uninhabited. They had no right to displace the Arabs of Palestine ... the 450,000 Jews in Palestine could stay but they could not expect to establish a State in other people's territory. Of course, some of his best friends were Jews and he sympathized with them but they were pursuing a misguided policy by trying to set up a Jewish nationality and State ...[112]

The international situation, the calibre of the Commission, together with its terms of reference—all militated against it finding some 'practicable scheme of partition'. Colonial Office concessions merely helped the anti-partitionists in the Government.

Ormsby-Gore clung to the letter, rather than the spirit, of partition, eager to push it through in some form—however truncated—prior to his own departure from the Colonial Office and elevation to the Lords. His support assumed a negative character, partition became the means for extricating Britain—and in particular the Colonial Office—from an increasingly impossible position.

The conflict at Cabinet level between the two Departments during 1937–38 resulted in a tactical victory for the senior Department. The mutual suspicion and denigration subsided only with the appointments of a new head of the Middle Eastern Department at the Foreign Office, Lacy Bagallay, and a new Colonial Secretary, Malcolm MacDonald, in February and May 1938 respectively. Ormsby-Gore resigned from office a broken man, with Zionism the rock upon which his career had foundered. His efforts at steering a middle path between Jew and Arab had earned him the mistrust of the former without gaining him the sympathy of the latter. He turned against both:

... the Arabs are treacherous and untrustworthy, the Jews greedy and, when freed from persecution, aggressive ... I am convinced that the Arabs cannot be trusted to govern the Jews any more than the Jews can be trusted to govern the Arabs.[113]

His successor, Malcom MacDonald, soon gave official expression to Colonial Office submission on the question of partition.

4

Anglo-French Attitudes to Palestinian Arab Nationalism

i. British vacillation towards the Mufti

Wauchope's attitude to the Arab strike in 1936 had been conciliatory, despite strong evidence that the Mufti, through his paid agents, had been directly responsible for incitement to violence and rebellion against British rule.[1]

His attitude had changed with that of the home Government when harsh measures were decided on in September 1936. Wauchope then argued that Arab leaders outside Palestine held the Mufti responsible for the impasse into which the Rebellion had run, whereas in Palestine itself the Mufti's prestige was on the wane. This being so, and as the Mufti had proved himself unwilling to negotiate or co-operate with the Mandatory, Wauchope now recommended his deportation from Palestine.[2] Ormsby-Gore concurred with the advice but, following the end of the strike on 12 October, Wauchope began to have second thoughts. It might now prove difficult to justify the deportation, he claimed, seeing that the Arabs had 'of their own accord' called off their strike. London itself feared that should the Mufti be deported no viable negotiator would be found to replace him.[3]

The Mufti's position was discussed next in March 1937, during his absence on pilgrimage to Mecca.[4] It was the opinion of the GOC Palestine, General Dill, that law and order would not be restored in Palestine until the Mufti—whom he regarded as the main instigator of the previous year's rebellion—had been removed from his position. Battershill, the Chief Secretary of the Palestine Government, agreed that so long as the Mufti retained his influence there was unlikely to be any lasting peace in Palestine. Yet he opposed any action against him at this particular juncture, while the Mufti was engaged on his religious duties. To do this while the country was at peace would open the British Administration to charges of treachery and bad faith, and be liable to provoke disturbances from within and intrigue from without.[5] The Colonial Secretary supported the Administration's viewpoint, and Eden, concerned about possible unfavourable reactions from the Arab States, also opposed any measures against the Mufti.

Until the publication of the Peel Report in July 1937, there existed an uneasy truce in Palestine, likely to be broken once it became apparent that the new Commission was not going to respond adequately to Arab demands. The question of how to deal with the Mufti was central to any discussion on future Government action on the Royal Commission's recommendations. In July 1937, having completed his evidence before the Commission in Palestine,

Wauchope returned to London for consultations at the Colonial Office. Despite adequate evidence of 'undesirable activities' on the Mufti's part, the Government yet feared that the repercussions of arresting the community's religious leader might prove too serious, and the task of finding an alternative reputable Arab body with which to negotiate impossible. No clear-cut decision was therefore arrived at.[6]

The watershed of the Mufti's influence in Palestine came during the second phase of the Rebellion, which in the summer of 1937 gave expression to the Arabs' opposition to the partition plan. This phase was initially aimed principally against moderate Arabs (more than at the Jews or the British), especially the Nashashibis (who were suspected of supporting partition) or those who had co-operated with the British. The initial campaign of personal terror, which in September 1937 reached its climax with the murder of L. A. Andrews, Commissioner for the Galilee District, subsided under the weight of prompt British action (below, p. 53). But the rebels regrouped in the rural districts and by the summer of 1938 had gained control of most of the country's mountain districts, cut off most rail and telephone links, and reduced to impotency the civil administration throughout the country. Arab civil servants bought their lives by disclosing all official documents and secrets to the rebels, whose wounded were treated in Government hospitals. From the autumn of 1938, the Government adopted a policy of active retaliation, taking the fight into the bands' own hideouts in the hills, in commando operations carried out by Jewish-manned units—the so-called 'Night Squads'—led by Captain Charles Orde Wingate. A more punitive policy resulted in harsher deterrent penalites, including the hanging of over a hundred rebels between 1937 and 1939, compared with not a single instance in 1936. The military reinforcements which the Government was able to bring into Palestine after the Munich agreement of September 1938 soon tipped the scales against the rebels. At the end of October 1938 military rule was extended to the whole country, and harsh reprisals were executed against villages which resisted or continued to co-operate with the rebels. The vigorous nature of the Government's reaction encouraged the opposition to the Husseinis to come out into the open. Led by the Nashashibis, they organized their own 'peace' bands to resist Husseini-supported terrorists, and gave valuable information to the Government. During this period the family feuds deepened and crystallized, proving a fatal stumbling-block to attempts to re-build a unified political leadership after the war.

As rumours of partition filtered back to Palestine during the early summer of 1937, the Husseinis felt their supremacy to be threatened by the prospect that partition would place the Arab part of Palestine under the aegis of the Emir Abdullah of Transjordan. At a conference at Tiberias, the Mufti inaugurated a plan to win over to his party the Bedouin tribes of Transjordan.

The Nashashibis, finding in Abdullah a natural ally, began to revive their independent party organizations, which had lapsed in 1936 when the Higher Arab Committee had co-ordinated the activities of all Arab political groups. The mayors of Jaffa, Ramla and Nablus—all Nashashibi supporters—had spoken openly in favour of the kingship of Abdullah over Palestine. In mid-June, some 260 of the Mufti's opponents went to Amman to welcome Abdullah back from a trip to England.[7] But Nashashibi espousal of partition and sponsorship of Abdullah was short-lived and did not survive—at least not in public—the threat of Husseini reprisal.

Ragheb Nashashibi claimed that many Arabs preferred not to show their support for partition once they observed the Government's indulgent attitude towards the Mufti. Ragheb himself had been forced to recruit four bodyguards since his public pronouncement in favour of partition. Ragheb was warned by the British police in Palestine about threats from his political rivals.[8] For Ragheb, the sincerity of the Government's decision to implement partition was in doubt. At a meeting with British officers and officials, he explained the extent of the Mufti's power in Palestine. There did not exist a Moslem village in Palestine in which the Supreme Moslem Council did not have four officials—the keeper of the Mosque, the Imam (religious leader), the religious teacher, and an administrative official to deal with religious properties. If the teacher did not explain on Fridays the state of affairs in the country according to the way the Mufti saw them, he would be dismissed and condemned to remain without a living. Ragheb himself would be the first to elect the Mufti once more to the Presidency of the Supreme Moslem Council, unless adequate preparations were undertaken prior to any new elections. Ragheb proposed that the Government appoint a temporary manager for the Council, and fix a transition period during which its affairs could be 'cleaned up', after which fresh elections might be held.[9]

In July 1937 Wauchope had returned to his proposal to deport the Mufti, this time on the immediate pretext of a message sent by the Mufti to the Arab Kings, a message that had pleaded the necessity for 'rescuing the country from Imperialism and Jewish colonization and Partition . . .'[10]

The Colonial Office authorized the deportation on the same day,[11] but an arrest attempt by the Palestine Police proved abortive. They found eight members of the Higher Arab Committee in session, but not the Mufti.[12] The Government recoiled from breaking the sanctuary of the Haram area abutting the Al Aqsa Mosque, where the Mufti now took refuge.[13] Stripping the Mufti of his religious offices was also ruled out, for fear of a wholesale resignation of Sharia judges and officials.

With the Government impotent to execute its warrant for the Mufti's arrest, the cancellation of that warrant was soon justified. Downie, First Secretary at the Colonial Office, now argued that without the strongest possible case, the arrest of the 'head of the Arab cause' on the eve of possible negotiations on partition, would surely be regarded as an outrage, and wreck any prospect of an accommodation with the Arabs for a long while to come.

If the Mufti was indeed irreconcilable, he would soon reveal himself—if not, then why should the Government not resume negotiations with him? The resumption of relations would rescue the Administration from an embarrassing and ridiculous situation, and perhaps initiate a more moderate attitude, thus averting the danger of wrecking British relations with neighbouring Arab countries. As for a possible loss of face if the arrest warrant was cancelled, the Government had not in fact ever announced its intention to arrest the Mufti. Ormsby-Gore took his official's advice, and instructed Wauchope to cancel the warrant against the Mufti.[14]

But Ormsby-Gore's experiences at the League of Nations' Permanent Mandates Commission, in August 1937, finally convinced him that conciliatory policies in Palestine were counter-productive. Not only did he have to answer criticism of the Palestine Administration's policy during the 1936 Rebellion, but he had also to face an unprecedented critical outburst from the Iraqi delegate on the new plan to partition Palestine. In September 1937 the Mandates Commission censured the Government for having failed to declare martial law at an earlier stage of the rebellion. Ormsby-Gore's wrath focused on the Mufti:

... I still feel that we shall never get on top of this murder campaign and its inevitable consequences of counter-murder by Jews whom we are unable to protect, until we have eliminated the Mufti and his gang. He was the *fons et origo* of the murders in 1929, and as long as we appear to funk dealing with this black-hearted villain and allow him to disseminate anti-British propaganda throughout the Islamic world, and organize terrorism of any Arabs in Palestine not subservient to him and his Supreme Moslem Council, we cannot hope to maintain law and order or even be the *de facto* government of Palestine ...[15]

But mixed with Colonial Office determination to take firm positive action in Palestine were the traditional anxieties at not finding an alternative negotiating partner who would also be capable of implementing an agreed compromise, as well as fears at possible reactions from the Arab States. Ormsby-Gore's determination was therefore not translated into concrete measures until the murder of Mr Andrews at the end of September 1937.

The Colonial Secretary sought and obtained Cabinet authorization to arrest all the members of the Higher Arab Committee, including the Mufti— as soon as he could be lured from the sanctuary of the Haram area. Ormsby-Gore was also given the option to declare martial law in Palestine, without further reference back to the Cabinet.[16] It was decided also to divest the Mufti of his office as President of the Supreme Moslem Council, and of his Chairmanship of the *Wakf* funds committee. The dissolution of the Supreme Moslem Council, as at that time constituted, was gazetted in Palestine on 1 October.

Despite police surveillance the Mufti, dressed up as an old woman, soon made good his escape from the Haram area and from Palestine itself.[17] He was intercepted off the Lebanese coast by a French patrol boat and taken to Beirut. There the French High Commissioner, M. Martel, asked for instructions from Paris, regarding French policy.

ii. The Palestine problem and Anglo-French relations in the Levant
The treatment by the French Mandatory of its unexpected 'guest' provides a lens through which one may observe the respective attitudes of the French and British Governments towards a new brand of Arab nationalism upon which, as both Governments realized, would depend their respective positions in the Middle East in the future. Anglo-French rivalry in the Middle East had, since the First World War, been mitigated somewhat by the exigencies of their alliance in Europe. Whereas European security of necessity remained the first priority, mutual suspicions at the local level in the Middle East might on occasion involve the intervention of London and Paris. The arrival in the Lebanon of the charismatic leader of Palestinian Arab nationalism provided further occasion for the testing of an alliance which in Europe was soon to be tested in war with Germany.

The French believed their whole position and status in the Middle East to be at stake. Post-war bickerings over what the Sykes–Picot agreement of 1916 had actually promised to the Arabs, especially in Syria, were still fresh in the French memory. In 1937, the French feared that partition might be part of some British plot to extend her influence over the Middle East. They doubted whether they would be able to retain their hold over Syria once a new Arab State comprising Transjordan and part of Palestine was established. Such a creation in the British sphere of influence would soon extend its grip to Syria, leaving France with only the Lebanon. On the other hand, the French were prepared to support Arab nationalism to a degree, if only as a bid to mobilize Moslem opinion in French North Africa—at least as important for France as India was for Great Britain.[18]

In October 1937, the British Mandatory looked to the French to curb the Mufti's capacity to promote rebellion from the Lebanon. The French Administration was itself in a delicate position, however. The French Government was currently negotiating the details of a treaty whereby Syria was to receive independence, while safeguarding French interests in the country at the same time.[19] The measures desired by the British Mandatory in Palestine were precisely those calculated to further compromise the French with the Arab nationalist movement. With its entire position in the Levant at stake, the French decided first to test the serious intent of London, before taking any meaningful action against the Mufti.

At one extreme, the British Consul at Damascus, Colonel MacKereth, was convinced that if only the French would co-operate more, the Mufti could be rendered powerless and the rebellion in Palestine—'inspired and instigated by the Mufti from the Lebanon'—would collapse. At the other extreme, Rendel believed it mistaken to treat the rebels as 'thugs' when in fact they were idealists fighting for a cause. He believed that the solution lay not in the punishment of the rebels—though of course the murders and terror had to be stopped—but in the granting of their 'legitimate' demands. British approaches to the Quai d'Orsay consequently lacked the conviction and determination which alone might have persuaded the French to risk unpopularity by dealing firmly with the Mufti.

As the British Government could not cite its own secret Intelligence sources, it was unable to proffer charges against the Mufti to warrant his extradition back to Palestine. A proposal that he might be extradited on grounds of 'malversation of *Wakf* funds' was turned down by Battershill, who claimed that they did not have sufficient evidence for even a *prima facie* case.[20]

As the Mufti refused to go voluntarily into exile in France, the French promised the Foreign Office to keep him under strict surveillance in the Lebanon. While Eden thought the Government ought to thank the French, his Permanent Under-Secretary, Vansittart, thought the whole affair was a farce, and that the Mufti ought to be forced to go to France. The British Consul at Beirut reported that surveillance of the Mufti was minimal, and that the latter enjoyed a steady stream of visitors, including Syrian and Palestinian nationalists.[21]

The Mufti was in fact establishing an elaborate network of agents through whom he could raise funds, purchase arms, and dispatch men to Palestine to keep the revolt going. Evidence concerning this network was received at regular intervals from both the British consular staff at Beirut and Damascus as well as from Jewish Agency Intelligence reports.

Shortly after the Mufti's arrival in the Lebanon, the British Consul at Damascus telegraphed to London:

... French have lost control of the Police and I believe many Syrian gendarmes are unloyal to their French officers. It seems to me intolerable that rebellion in Palestine is being actively, almost openly planned in Damascus under the eyes of the Syrian Government and French authorities ...[22]

MacKereth concluded that the main anxiety of the French High Commissioner at Damascus was to avoid any trouble in Syria such as might hinder ratification of the Franco–Syrian Treaty in Paris.[23] On the other hand, the French felt that unless the British themselves declared some form of martial law in Palestine and assumed further control in Transjordan, they (the French) could not properly be called upon to employ armed forces on the frontier.

Rendel cast doubts on the practical value of the Consul's advice, based, as he believed it was, on false premises:

... MacKereth is still looking at the Palestine situation from the wrong angle. He thinks of it as a local rebellion against properly constituted authority ... but the causes of the trouble lie deeper, and cannot be dealt with by mere firmness of administration or by the kind of palliatives MacKereth suggests . . .[24]

Yet the fact that the rebellion in Palestine was currently being instigated from Syria was not in dispute:

. . . not only substantial traffic of arms going on from Syria to Palestine, but active preparations were being made to engage unemployed Syrians for service in bands to commit acts of banditry with the object of creating a general state of public disorder out of which the Palestinian irredentists hope to achieve their political aims . . .[25]

For their part, the French Mandatory authorities still remembered the 'inadequate sympathies' shown by the British authorities during the French difficulties in Syria in 1925.[26]

Yet MacKereth's representations to the Syrian Government did have some, albeit a temporary effect. He was soon able to report the 'comparative ease' with which the Syrian gendarmeries had been able to arrest some thirty young men attempting to enter Palestine to join the rebels. This could be explained only by the fact that the Syrian gendarmes no longer feared, as they certainly once had, that they might incur the displeasure of the Syrian Government.

Jewish Agency reports also reached the Colonial Office, from whence they were passed on to the Foreign Office. From these it appeared that the Mufti was allowed to meet in private, without the presence of the French Sûreté Publique, Shekib Arslan,[27] Muin al-Madi,[28] and Nabih al-Azmeh.[29] At one such meeting,[30] the Mufti berated his associates for not having raised a storm in the Arab and Moslem worlds. He was disappointed at the apathy of the Arab States to the 'repressive' measures adopted by the Mandatory power in Palestine. In Palestine itself, he did not hope for strong reactions for a number of reasons: tight military and police surveillance, English determination to 'cruelly suppress' any uprising, the opposition of the Nashashibis, and the fact that the people were still exhausted by the riots of 1936. But the Mufti had clearly hoped for a stronger reaction from the neighbouring Arab countries and was disappointed that they had confined their efforts to 'publishing some articles and sending a few protests and messages of sympathy'.

In London, the debate between the Foreign and Colonial Office on the consequences which the imposition of partition on Palestine might have on the Arab world was still raging. Rendel suspected the motives of the Colonial Office in forwarding the Jewish Agency report to them:

. . . it would be a mistake to regard this paper—as the Colonial Office would no doubt like us to regard it—as evidence that there are no strong feelings about Palestine in Arab countries, and that we need not trouble about reactions in the Middle East to our Palestine policy . . .[31]

Rendel believed that the Mufti was merely overstating his case in order to goad his audience into activity. He thought the Colonial Office inclined to overrate the part played by the Mufti. For Rendel, there was a universality about the Palestinian Arabs' cause, and he therefore saw no point in talking of individuals or groups who stood in the way of a settlement. Rendel failed to see that the Mufti's leadership condemned his own community to sterile extremism, preventing all compromise.

In February 1938, further reports came in, this time from British consular services, of the elaborate network established by the Mufti. They were dismissed by the Foreign Office as misguided and prejudiced. Terrorist statements provided ample evidence that not only did Syrians and Palestinians plan terrorist *coups* from Syria, but they also found ready refuge there on their return from raids in Palestine. When approached by the British Consul, the French High Commissioner was again unwilling to risk political trouble in Syria by taking direct action.

MacKereth recommended three alternative courses of action; first, an intensification of pressure on the French authorities; secondly, the closing, on grounds of public security, of the Syro-Palestinian and Syro-Transjordanian frontiers (this measure would soon force the Syrian Government to co-operate with the British, for Syrian merchants depended upon Palestine as a market for their goods); thirdly, the payment of a monthly subvention to key men, conditional on their complete and continued cessation of all political activity from Syria.[32]

Rendel treated the dispatch with derision. He reiterated his view that MacKereth had always tended to regard the Palestine rebellion not as a 'political movement due to our Zionist policy', but rather as an outbreak of crime instigated by ill-intentioned mischief-makers. If one regarded the issue as a major problem involving the entire relationship of France and England with the Moslem world, French caution and hesitation would be a good deal easier to understand. Yet, and not for the first time, Rendel's views were questioned by superiors such as Oliphant, who was inclined to give credence to the MacKereth's dispatches.[33]

Nevertheless, the Foreign Office agreed that 'in view of recent events here'[34] and the feelings of the French Government, no approach to Paris on the lines of MacKereth's dispatch should be made.[35]

A further Jewish Agency memorandum was treated with no more respect than had been that of the British Consul at Damascus. It appeared from this document that the Mufti had appointed a number of select men from among those who had worked previously for him in Palestine, to organize a new terrorist campaign in Palestine. Arms smuggling was made easier through the co-operation of Adel al-Azmeh, head of the Syrian gendarmerie. This was in contrast to the Lebanon, where the Palestinians had no comparable connections—there, one heard quite often of the seizure of arms intended for the Palestinian Terrorists' Committee.[36]

The Mufti also had an efficient propaganda machine, with agents throughout the Arab world—in Iraq, Egypt, Iran, the Lebanon, Syria, Saudi Arabia, even as far afield as Afghanistan. Propaganda was conducted on two lines; firstly, praising the terrorists and persuading the Arab world that terrorism was the most effective way of forcing Britain and the Jews to give in to Arab demands; secondly, praising the Mufti personally for his patriotism and devotion to the Arab cause, while vilifying his Arab opponents in Palestine as traitors who had sold themselves out to the British and the Jews.

The Italian Consul at Damascus supported the Nationalist press, the German Consulate at Beirut supported the Arab Club at Damascus, for which only persons educated in German schools were eligible. This club had a physical training course that was attended regularly by Syrian recruits for terrorist bands and most of the Palestinian exiles in Damascus. Some of the trainers were Nazis. The Club was in general used for spreading German influence in oriental countries. Baldur von Schirach, the Hitler Youth leader had recently paid a visit for consultation with the Director.

London decided not to forward the memorandum to Paris. Again, Rendel stubbornly discounted the importance, even the relevance of the information obtained:

... (n.b. This is a Jewish document) ... my only general comment is that one can easily overrate the importance of the part which the Mufti personally plays in the Palestine–Arab national movement. The Colonial Office and the Zionists are very much inclined to attribute the whole of the Palestine trouble to the Mufti personally, and to Italian funds. I am sure to do this is a dangerous mistake ... [37]

Rendel would not be moved from his *idée fixe*. Thus Intelligence reports, if contrary to his own entrenched conceptions, were discounted, regardless of whether they came from his own Government's accredited representative, from Jewish sources or, for that matter, from the High Commissioner in Palestine. At most, the Foreign Office would admit that there might be some truth in the allegations. If there were, the Mufti succeeded only because the Arab population of Palestine was still convinced that His Majesty's Government meant to insist at all costs on establishing either a Jewish State, or a Jewish majority in Palestine.[38]

Matters might have been allowed to rest there, had not renewed pressure been exerted from Palestine itself, where the Mandatory felt the blunt edge of the Mufti's activities. The new High Commissioner, Sir Harold Mac-Michael,[39] had no doubts as to who was the main inspiration behind the renewed wave of terrorism:

Among the many factors which continued to militate against the restoration of law and order there is none which operates more consistently and potently than the safe ensconcement of Haj Amin at Junieh, some ... two hours motor drive from Palestine, and the impunity with which he and other Palestinian emigrés in the Lebanon and Syria enjoy in plotting against this Government ...[40]

He pointed to the harmful psychological effect which the Mufti's apparent freedom of action was having on the people of Palestine, who argued that since the British and French were allies for all other purposes in a troubled world there must be some understanding between their respective Governments whereby Haj Amin and his entourage were to be left undisturbed. The motive behind this seemed obvious to them. The British Government, they claimed, did not wish to break finally with the Mufti, for it foresaw that no ultimate solution in Palestine would be possible without his goodwill, and therefore intended to bring him back at the appropriate moment.

MacMichael conceded that there was no proof against Haj Amin of the type which could be brought before a court of law, but contended that, armed as the Government was with an immense body of secret Intelligence reports, it had no need of such 'legal' proofs. All the more so, seeing that both Jews and Arabs agreed on the role which the Mufti was playing. On the Jewish Agency reports, MacMichael commented: '... Not to be despised, but require, and receive, checking in detail before acceptance on account of the element of special pleading for which some discount must be made ...'[41]

The continued unmolested presence of the Mufti in the Lebanon convinced Arab Opposition leaders in Palestine that the British Administration was not really determined to break his authority, or crush the rebels upon whom that authority now rested.

MacMichael proposed two alternative courses: either to remove the Mufti to some inaccessible part of Syria, with similar restraint being placed upon his supporters; or to deport him from Syria, either to Paris or the south of France. At the same time, his supporters also should be ordered to live outside Syria. MacMichael preferred the latter course, as 'the time had passed for half-measures'.[42]

MacMichael proposed two alternative courses: either to remove the Mufti that, in the event that the French High Commissioner should prove unco-operative, he advocated implementing MacKereth's plan to seal Palestine's frontiers with Syria. This would result in the practical cessation of all trade between the two countries. Palestinian merchants might in fact welcome a respite from Syrian competition, while the Syrians would be left with surplus goods on their hands.[43] No harm would be done to French interests, and Paris could claim that the British Mandatory had closed the frontiers without first consulting them. MacMichael therefore asked the Foreign Office to inform France that if the Mufti was not deported, His Majesty's Government would have no alternative but to authorise its High Commissioner to take action accordingly.

When the subject was broached with the French Ambassador in London, the latter replied that his Government felt unable to take any drastic action against the Mufti without making a martyr of him, thus exposing itself to criticism in the French Parliament. Therefore, his Government did not feel it could imprison the Mufti or prevent him receiving visitors.[44]

The Colonial Office was not satisfied with this reply, and MacDonald asked Lord Halifax, the new Foreign Secretary, for his views on implementing economic sanctions. Foreign Office advisers were prepared to approach the French Government about having the Mufti removed from the Lebanon, but did not entertain even the slightest doubt that the French would refuse to move him against his will. In that event, the Foreign Office was against the use of threats for the present.[45]

A meeting of the Departments concerned was held.[46] The Colonial Office thought that the French should be induced to bring the Mufti to Europe. Baxter, for the Foreign Office, repeated that the French would not do so against the Mufti's will—although they might yet be induced to ask him to leave the Lebanon. When Sir Grattan Bushe, legal adviser to the Colonial Office, proposed that the French be shown the Intelligence reports on the Mufti's criminal activities, Baxter pointed out that the French Government would want evidence that could be published, in order to satisfy public opinion. It was next proposed that an appeal be made on the grounds that European security was being threatened, in so far as the Mufti's activities were disturbing the whole Middle East and diverting troops from Europe, where vital French interests were at stake.

Yet from the security point of view, both the War Office and the Air Ministry representatives thought it would be preferable for the Mufti to remain in the Lebanon, rather than to be allowed to transfer to a place of his own choosing, especially—as was probable—if he chose Iraq.

The High Commissioner in Palestine was again referred to. MacMichael was still of the opinion that the removal of the Mufti would be invaluable, if only for its psychological impact. Otherwise, in the light of Britain's known association with France in matters of high policy, it must be assumed that the British did not genuinely object to the Mufti's presence in the Lebanon.[47]

Consequently, the Foreign Office instructed the Ambassador at Paris, Sir Eric Phipps, to approach the French Government with a view to having the Mufti removed from the Lebanon. At the same time, the Department instructed its representatives in Iraq and Egypt to ensure that, in the eventuality of the Mufti being deported, those countries would refuse him entry.[48] Sir Eric Phipps made no progress with the representative of the Middle Eastern Department at the Quai d'Orsay. He reported back to London that the French attitude seemed to show that the latter believed the British had deliberately allowed the Mufti to flee, in order to place the French in an awkward position.[49]

At the root of French lack of co-operation was their own vulnerability in the Middle East. In Paris the French explained that their inability to act against the Mufti was not due to any lack of goodwill on their part, but to the fact that the request had come at an inopportune moment. The general European situation had led them to cede to Turkey the Sanjak of Alexandretta, even at the risk of jeopardizing relations with the Arab world. To make matters worse, the French Parliament had now risen and the treaty with Syria could not be ratified for some time, a situation which naturally aroused Syrian suspicions. Any French action against the Mufti at the present juncture might well be 'the last straw'.[50]

Yet another meeting was held at Whitehall to review the situation.[51] The Colonial Office was still not satisfied and wanted further pressure put on the French. The Foreign Office vetoed this. Discussion switched to the desirability of moving the Mufti to a neighbouring Arab country. Mr Keith-Roach, Administrator of the Jerusalem District, at that time on leave in London, thought that any country would be preferable to the Lebanon, considering the degree of freedom he currently enjoyed there. The consensus was that Phipps should again be asked to approach the French, but that Iraq and Egypt should definitely be excluded as alternative places of exile. If the French remained adamant in refusing to deport the Mufti to France, they should be asked to transport him to a remote area of French Mandated territory.

But, working with a lack of conviction in what they were doing, Foreign Office representatives were not inclined to place too much pressure on the French:

... we are not really on strong ground; it was the local officials who let the Mufti escape, and this the French do not fail to rub in. I feel that such representations are a waste of powder.[52]

Action was postponed, in the hope that the authorities in Palestine might come up with further 'evidence', of the type which could be used against the Mufti. It was also hoped that the Colonial Secretary, then on a short visit to Palestine, might return with fresh proposals. But as a result of discussions with the men on the spot, MacDonald returned from Palestine convinced more than ever that the Mufti was the mainspring of the terrorist movement.[53]

The Foreign Office therefore reluctantly approached the French once more. The latter replied that they would decide after they had met with the Syrian Prime Minister, due shortly to visit Paris in connection with the ratification of the Franco-Syrian Treaty. For their part, the French claimed that their surveillance of the Mufti was effective.[54] The Foreign Office accepted defeat, and resigned itself to the limited goal of having the Mufti subjected to the most stringent precautions possible, in the Lebanon itself.

But such 'precautions' proved no more efficacious than before, and following the departure of the Syrian Prime Minister for Paris, the Mufti was able to resume full political activity with impunity.[55]

Only the higher priorities of World War Two persuaded the French authorities to tighten their grip on the Mufti. It took little less than one month for these measures to pay their first dividend. On the night of 14–15 October 1939 the Mufti fled to the 'freer' climate of Iraq, whence he was to conspire further against British interests in the Middle East.[56]

The attitude of the French towards the Mufti during his enforced stay in the Lebanon had been, at the least, ambiguous. Old 'scores' between the two Mandatories, in Palestine and in Syria, were laid aside only when the greater demands of global conflict prevailed. British Intelligence in the Middle East was alive to the anti-British tendencies of French Colonial officialdom, and the ever-present rivalry for the praises of the Arab world. It had leaked out to the British that the French Director of the Syrian Police, M. Columbani,[57] had taken a sum of £500 in return for removing the restrictions placed on the Mufti and thus facilitating his escape.[58] French liaison officers in Beirut were shamefaced about the whole affair. Yet the ambivalent attitude of French Colonial officialdom is revealed further in a document intercepted by British Intelligence:

... El Haj Husseini is a dangerous man, ready to play any role, whatever its aspect. England's enemy today, he may quite easily become ours tomorrow. His protestations of friendship are suspicious and show, to say the least, self-interest. *If his presence in Syria has been of use to us, it would appear to be with the greatest circumspection that we should employ him for our own political ends.*[59]

iii. The Mandatory's attitude to political alternatives in Palestine

The renewed outbreak of Arab terrorism which had begun in the summer of 1937 was characterized by internecine conflict. The increasing number of political assassinations would have sufficed to inhibit the growth of a strong, moderate Arab Party, even had there been such a demand. Yet by the close of 1938, when the British security forces were beginning to get the measure of the Arab bands, one branch of the Nashashibi family did make a bid for the leadership of the Arab community.

In November 1938, Fakhri Nashashibi[60] addressed an open letter to the Palestine Press, claiming to speak for Arab moderates, who, he claimed, represented more than half the Arab population of Palestine, and whose leaders represented more than 75 per cent of the country's economic interests. The letter expressed the Palestinian Arabs' satisfaction that partition had been abandoned and refuted the argument that the Mufti was the only person authorized to speak on behalf of the Arabs of Palestine.[61]

Ragheb Nashashibi hastened to denounce his cousin's letter,[62] and many telegrams poured into the High Commission at Jerusalem denying Fakhri's right to represent anyone. These denials seemed to confirm the view held in some Government quarters that the Mufti remained the only Arab leader of consequence. This viewpoint was all-important when the question of the Palestinian Arabs' delegation to the St James's Conference in 1939 (see Chapter 5) was discussed in London. At a conference at the Colonial Office, many had contended that if the Mufti himself was not invited he would terrorize anyone who attempted to attend in his place.[63] At a meeting of the Cabinet Committee on Palestine that was to prepare for the Conference,

Lord Dufferin[64] had advocated bringing the Mufti to the Conference, as he was 'the man who held the real power in Palestine'.[65] But the Committee decided against inviting him, a decision that was ratified by the Cabinet on 2 November 1938. This decision stood, notwithstanding further pleas from Lampson that if the forthcoming negotiations were to succeed, the Mufti must be invited and immigration be stopped immediately.[66]

Opposition to the participation of the Mufti at the St James's Conference was not due to conviction that the Fakhri Nashashibi initiative represented any significant change in Palestinian politics. It was due to traditional scruples about bargaining with terrorists and, in particular, to the vigorous opposition of the High Commissioner, MacMichael.

MacMichael himself did believe that Fakhri's move reflected dissension in Arab ranks, the first to be openly expressed since 1935, a dissension due in part to the country's weariness with terrorist methods. MacMichael was warned that if the Government proceeded to negotiate with that faction which practised terrorism, while snubbing that which did not, the Arabs of Palestine would draw their inevitable conclusion.[67] London surmounted its scruples by inviting members of the Husseini faction to London, but Mac-Michael's threat of resignation proved an insurmountable obstacle to inviting the Mufti himself.[68]

At an interview with MacMichael, Fakhri and five members of the Defence Party outlined their Party's policies.[69] Fakhri did not associate his party with the Husseini demand for the abolition of the Mandate and the creation of a Federal Arab State in treaty relations with Britain. Fakhri preferred amendments to the existing Mandate, with native participation in a Legislative Council and the *gradual* development of self-governing institutions. Another leader of the Defence Party, one of its two delegates to the St James's Conference, confided his own views to the District Commissioner of Nablus, on the eve of his departure for London:

... if the alternatives before the Arabs in London were to be 'independence with the Mufti', or 'British rule with the Jews', then the Defence Party would go all out for a British Administration with some form of local legislature, not necessarily with an unofficial majority ...[70]

The Palestine Administration did not quite know how to react to the Fakhri initiative and was unable to free itself from traditional acceptance of the Mufti as spokesman for the Arab community. Battershill warned his District Commissioners that whereas the emergence of a moderate movement among the Arabs was welcome to the Administration, they should not allow themselves to become involved in Arab domestic politics or, what was worse, in Nashashibi counter-terrorism. However, Battershill admitted that significant political changes were taking place, reflecting a revolt against the Mufti's extremism, and a desire to return to normalcy.[71]

But the British were unwilling to commit themselves to new political forces. At the end of 1938, after a year of widespread terrorism, there is no doubt that the Nashashibis would have found difficulty in rallying to themselves anything more than the passive support of the majority of Palestinian Arabs. What their chances might have been had the Mufti's activities in the Lebanon been curbed adequately and the terrorists in Palestine subdued earlier must remain a matter for speculation.

Following the Mufti's rejection of the concessions embodied in the White Paper of May 1939, dissension spread to the ranks of the Mufti's own immediate circle. Several leaders of the Rebellion signed a manifesto decrying the motives of those who sought to sustain the now-dying Rebellion. The manifesto claimed that the Higher Arab Committee's rejection of the latest proposals was due to the specific exclusion of the Mufti from Palestine, which had been announced together with the White Paper.[72] The document went on to condemn acts of terrorism perpetrated by the Mufti's henchmen against their fellow Arabs. It then elaborated upon and condemned the Mufti's own misappropriation of *Wakf* funds, and his land transactions with Jews.[73] The disenchanted rebels claimed that had the money which passed through the Mufti's hands[74] been devoted to the amelioration of conditions in Palestine, the country would have had no room left for a single Jew, and there would not have remained any land for them to purchase. The Husseini family's own land transactions were specified.[75]

In contrast to the rejection of the White Paper by the Higher Arab Committee (at the instigation of the Husseini party), the Defence Party gave clear indications, both in London and in Palestine, of their willingness to co-operate with the British authorities on the basis of the terms laid down by the White Paper. MacMichael himself was becoming convinced that the Defence Party, in its willingness to co-operate under the White Paper regime, was emerging as the true representative of the Arab community.[76]

Various prominent figures in the Arab world denigrated the Husseini party's policy. The veteran Syrian nationalist, Dr Shabbandar, told MacKereth that its rejection of the White Paper was mere bluff, designed to hide from the Jews Arab satisfaction with their gains. He added that the only person not contented was the Mufti, who was 'a menace to Arabism'.[77] Ibn Saud believed that the fundamental reason behind the Mufti's stubbornness was 'the fact that he seeks his own personal advantage so that whatever happens in Palestine is turned to his own profit'.[78] This was in contrast to the Iraqi view, which treated the Mufti as a powerful figure around which to focus nationalist and pan-Arab sentiments. The issue was intricately involved with the domestic and foreign policies of the Hashemite and Wahhabi dynasties respectively and their rivalry for the leadership of the Arab world.

With the outbreak of World War Two the Mufti offered, through Iraqi mediation, to rally the Arabs to Great Britain—if he were first requested to do so by Britain itself.[79] But the Mufti's offer was by now worthless currency.

The Rebellion in Palestine had to all intents and purposes petered out and the British were hardly likely to turn to a man who was now suspect of having liaison with Berlin.[80] London was not prepared to concede more than it had done already in the White Paper, and it was encouraged in its policy by the course of events in Palestine itself, where peace and order were slowly being restored and more and more Arabs co-operating with Government.[81]

Fluctuations in British policy regarding the Mufti of Jerusalem had stemmed from a genuine dilemma—could the Government associate itself with one who became progressively more implicated in a campaign of terrorism and violence, both against the Mandatory itself and against the moderates within the Arab camp itself? On the other hand, would the rejection and alienation of the community's single outstanding leader condemn the country to political and physical chaos? Even after the Mandatory acted against the Mufti and the Supreme Moslem Council in September 1937, the Mufti retained the capacity to terrorize Palestine from his place of 'house arrest' in the Lebanon. Whereas the High Commissioner vetoed the Mufti's presence at the St James's Conference in 1939, Government agreement to allow the Palestine Arab delegation to the Conference to consult with the Mufti in the Lebanon prior to and after the Conference meant that he controlled Arab policies in Palestine as effectively as if he had sat at the conference table himself.

The deterioration of the political status of the Husseini clan as a result of the 1936-9 Rebellion, and the Mufti's continued refusal to negotiate—even on advantageous terms—were to be followed by political embarrassment when the Mufti chose to support the Axis during the war. Husseini pre-eminence in Palestine was to be succeeded by the political chaos of quarrelling minority factions. The main victims in the breakdown of the political life of the Arab community in Palestine were the Palestinian Arabs themselves.

Seen in the wider context of Anglo-French rivalry in the Middle East, Anglo-French difficulties in exerting proper control over the Mufti during his stay in the Lebanon from 1937-9 fit naturally in the historical sequence which began with the Sykes-Picot 'share-out' in 1916, and ended with the involuntary exit of the French from the Middle East after the Second World War. Then all the darkest suspicions harboured by the French about British intentions in the Middle East seemed to materialize.

5

The White Paper, May 1939

i. The retreat from partition

The year 1938 proved to be one of crisis, both in Europe and in Palestine. Events reached their climax almost simultaneously in both areas. While Britain took emergency measures in view of the Munich crisis, the Palestine Government requested military reinforcements lest the Woodhead Report, awaited anxiously by the Government, provoke a new armed rebellion there.

Since 1937, the Foreign Office and the Chiefs of Staff had been stressing the need to settle the Palestine question in a manner 'satisfactory' to the Arab States. The Government was well aware that partition in any form was likely to weaken Britain's position in the Middle East. On the other hand, it was believed that the Jews—whatever their feelings—would be unlikely to resort to violent action, but be likely, as before, to try to gain their ends by propaganda and political lobbying. The main dangers were to be apprehended from the Arab States rather than from the Palestinian Arabs themselves. The actions of the latter were likely to be confined to acts of terrorism, rather than organized raids by disciplined bands. Moreover, in wartime much more vigorous action to counteract terrorism might be taken than was possible in peacetime.[1]

In May 1938, Malcolm MacDonald replaced Ormsby-Gore at the Colonial Office. The decision to set up a Middle East Reserve Force was three months old, the Middle Eastern Sub-Committee had already met several times. The opening moves in the Munich crisis were already being played out in London, where the English and French Governments had in April held talks designed to persuade the Czechs to make concessions to the Sudetens.[2] It is against this dynamic political background, and in relation to the increasingly serious security problem in Palestine itself, that the decision to abandon partition and to convene the Arabs and Jews at a conference in London has to be assessed.

MacDonald's experience at the Dominions Office had given him an insight into the vicissitudes of Colonial rule, but within the context of the global responsibilities of an Empire. The Zionists expected him to live up to his father's, and indeed his own, tradition of sympathy for their cause. But, as with his predecessor, the assumption of Ministerial responsibility cast a different light on the issue.

The new Colonial Secretary's familiarization with the problem proceeded against a backcloth of grave security problems in Palestine, such as could not fail to influence the ultimate direction of his own policy. The Chief Secretary of the Palestine Government, then on leave in London, reported back to the High Commissioner on the mood prevailing at the Colonial Office during the summer of 1938:

... it is clear that they are worried and somewhat stirred up over the security situation in Palestine. The general situation in the Colonial Office vis-à-vis the Palestine Administration is one of great helplessness ... Secretary of State wants to settle the security situation at once. I was asked how many troops and police it would take to do this ...[3]

Terrorist acts had continued unabated since October 1937, many crimes being committed by Arab against Arab. The High Commissioner and General Haining both agreed that whereas the Palestinian Arabs were in general hostile to the Jews, terrorism could not be defined as a national movement. The great majority of Arabs felt that it was pointless to continue to oppose the Mandatory. But the powers of intimidation wielded by the terrorists were such, and the moderates so lacking in leadership, that the extremists maintained the upper hand.

As martial-law powers had been consistently refused, the main security burden fell on the Palestine police. While the Jewish supernumeraries were in general considered to be reliable, the Arab police were not. It was difficult for them to act against so-called patriots, often harboured by, or a part of the very community in which they themselves lived. While owing their loyalty to the British administration for the present, the Arab police expected to have their services transferred soon to the new Arab State. If they now acted over-zealously against the terrorists—who were in the pay of the official Arab leadership—they would know what to expect from their future Arab masters.

Between June and September 1938 MacDonald took soundings on all sides, and paid a two-day visit to Palestine himself. Traditionally, the word of the man on the spot carried great, if not decisive weight. The advice of the Colonial Office, and from the Administration in Palestine, was now, owing to Arab opposition, against partition. Well before the end of this period MacDonald himself had arrived at the same conclusion.

From his several meetings with Dr Weizmann, MacDonald concluded that the Zionists would be unlikely to accept the token State the Woodhead Commission was likely to offer them.[4] In his report to the Cabinet, MacDonald also brought as evidence the views of Foreign Office representatives in the Middle East.

From Jedda came the reply that despite the efforts of the Ambassador to put the argument for partition forcefully to the Saudi authorities, the danger of alienating Ibn Saud if partition were to be pushed through was too great to be ignored.[5] This advice was crucial, for London regarded Ibn Saud as the most powerful and influential leader—if not the only one—in the Middle East. MacDonald openly admitted this to Weizmann:

> Syria was of comparatively little importance; as to the Arabs of Palestine, they were themselves intractable, intransigent, and pursuing their own aims by methods which could only be condemned. Iraq and Egypt, although they were lending a certain amount of support to the Arab nationalist movement, were really countries which, in the last resort, depended on Great Britain, and they could and should be brought into line ... Saudia was the one country which was of real importance. Ibn Saud was a man of high moral calibre; he was independent; he owed nothing to Britain; what he had achieved he had achieved for himself, without British assistance, and indeed, often against Britain, who had supported his enemy, Hussein ...[6]

From Egypt, the focus of British interests in the Middle East, came further warnings from the influential Ambassador. For an assessment of Lampson's role, we need not rely on the possibly suspect opinions of the Zionists, among whom he was regarded as the *eminence grise* behind British appeasement in the Middle East. We may turn to an appraisal written by MacDonald himself at the end of 1938, by which time no one would have accused the latter of pro-Zionist sentiments:

> ... in his private and personal conversations with all sorts of people, including Arab sympathizers, he has been out-Arabing the Arabs ... He was simply giving rein to his own preconceived ideas ... (I) have really got rather impatient with the way in which he has created actual difficulties for us by innocently encouraging Arab opposition ...[7]

Now Lampson warned London that the Arabs regarded the establishment of a Jewish State—to be used as a base for territorial expansion—as an even greater danger than unlimited Jewish immigration. Moreover, from the British point of view, it would be a mistake to hand over any part of Palestine in sovereignty to the Jews, for the present Zionist leaders were pro-British, but who could tell the inclinations of Polish and other Jews who would come in the future?'[8]

The Chargé d'Affaires at Baghdad, Bateman, was quite candid about the whole matter. If war were declared with Germany in the autumn, there would be no time to consider partition or any other 'quack' remedy for the troubles in Palestine. British interests must therefore come before those of either Arab or Jew and the search for the ideal solution must be abandoned at once. Instead, Britain should concentrate on placating the Arabs for the next year or two until the present European crisis passed. As for the Jews:

> ... they are anybody's game nowadays. But we need not desert them. They have waited two thousand years for their 'home' ... they can afford to wait a bit until we are better able to help them get their last pound of flesh ... the Royal Commissions for all the good they have done ... can be put aside—for the present.[9]

During his brief visit to Palestine, MacDonald sounded out the opinions of the Administration and of the military authorities.[10] He broached his own idea of an Arab–Jewish Conference, which might attempt to reach a compromise settlement.

MacMichael believed that no Arab would sit down with the Jews on the basis of partition. He was himself flirting with the idea of setting up a small Jewish State along the coastal plain, under a modified British Mandate. In five years' time the whole of Palestine, excluding this area and certain enclaves to be kept under permanent British Mandate, would be made into an Arab State. Other senior officials present thought that the Mandate should be continued, and saw no immediate prospects for partition.

By September 1938 events in Europe, combined with complications in Palestine, were dictating the pace for MacDonald. At the end of August, MacMichael and Haining had telegraphed for an extra division of troops, in order to keep matters under control. A meeting of Ministers convened on 31 August was compelled, in the light of the looming European crisis, to turn down the request.[11] MacDonald's proposal that the police be reinforced by more local recruits had been rejected as out of the question by the Palestine authorities. The CIGS, Viscount Gort, reported on the imminent dispatch of the Middle East Reserve Brigade and three battalions from India to the Middle East. MacDonald thought that this might meet the case, even though the reinforcements would not all arrive at once.[12] Inskip, the Minister for Co-ordination of Defence, doubted whether any reinforcements would stop the present terrorist campaign. On the other hand, the danger of tying up large bodies of troops in Palestine which, in the event of a war and the Mediterranean being closed, might be withdrawn only with great difficulty and delay, had to be considered.

Halifax asked whether it might be possible to obtain an advance summary of the Woodhead Commission's recommendations. MacDonald would not agree to renounce partition officially before the Commission's report was received, but agreed that it would do much to relieve the situation if the report proved unacceptable to the Jews and the Government was consequently forced to abandon partition.

MacDonald met Woodhead one week later. He confided to him that the Government had considerable evidence that the Arabs were planning a large-scale insurrection for the third week of October. If the Commission's report was liable to be of a nature which would take something of the sting out of Arab opposition, it should be published a reasonable time before that date. The end of the partition scheme would bring relief to the Arabs — and the sooner that relief was granted the better.[13]

Sir John was not so sure that the Jews would reject his Commission's proposals, when bearing in mind the alternatives. In any case, he could not agree to publishing conclusions before the detailed argument supporting them had been composed. He also refused to allow MacDonald to discuss the Commission's recommendations informally at dinner with its members.

On the same day, MacDonald met Weizmann. He informed him that while he still believed partition to be the best solution, he had recently been impressed by several facts; the inclusion of a substantial Arab minority in the Jewish State was dangerous, particularly when that State would be surrounded by powerful Arab neighbours in sympathy with the minority's aspirations;[14] there were inherent dangers in Italian and German support for the Arabs; lastly there was the conclusion from a recent study of the MacMahon papers that there might be a conflict between the dual policies of establishing a Jewish national home, and promoting the welfare of the indigenous Arabs in Palestine. He confessed frankly that it had been a great misfortune that during the past twenty years there had been a 'hopeless' Administration in Palestine—he himself did not believe the Mandate to be unworkable, but the officials had rendered it so.

It was now obvious to Weizmann that partition, a matter of convenience for the Colonial Office a year before, had since become a great nuisance.

MacDonald asked: 'What about a revival of the Mandate and the principle of absorptive capacity, of course applied cautiously?'

Circumstances had changed since the previous year, when Weizmann and his colleagues had reluctantly accepted partition in principle. The partition policy had been endorsed solemnly by the Government, on the basis of the Royal Commission's recommendations. But pressure had been exercised against that policy during the past year—if partition was dropped now, it could be interpreted only as a victory for Arab terrorism. As for the Mandate, would not the Arabs exercise the same pressure against it as at present?

Yet Weizmann's lifelong association with British statesmen was both his strength and his weakness. His inside knowledge of and free access to high circles in British politics made him an invaluable asset to the Zionists. On the other hand, his long and co-operative association with the British Government rendered him emotionally incapable of rebellion against it.

Thus, at the close of their interview, Weizmann could still assert his agreement to make another attempt with the Mandate, on MacDonald's terms—'if he could have a guarantee that MacDonald himself would remain in office for another five years'. His faith was placed not only in MacDonald personally, but in the country which he himself had adopted as an emigré some thirty years before—'whatever our complaints against the British Administration for its handling of Palestinian affairs, we could never lose sight of the fact that Britain was the only friend we had left in Europe'.

But Ben-Gurion had no such 'loyalties' to Great Britain. He drew different conclusions when MacDonald reiterated his arguments at a meeting with Weizmann and himself some days later. Ben-Gurion's personal account of the meeting reflects the suspicions harboured by the Palestine Zionists of Weizmann's 'weakness' for England:

It seems that he [Weizmann] hadn't grasped the meaning of MM's words . . .

Why has MM suddenly discovered, after twenty-two years, the MacMahon correspondence? For twenty years every British Government—coalition, Labour, Tory—had argued that Palestine had been excluded from the promises ... and only now has he (MacDonald) discovered that Palestine was promised to the Arabs and that the Palestinian Arabs were cheated ... why has he suddenly discovered that those who drafted the Balfour Declaration and the Mandate never intended a large immigration? It is difficult to guess whether this is a new development connected with the world situation ... or whether it is a well-thought-out policy ... England is now adopting a realistic policy like Hitler and Mussolini without using their terminology, and we are the victims of this change ...[15]

By late September 1938, a European war seemed inevitable.[16] The British Government was now prevented only by its own bureaucratic creation from announcing its policy—or rather, from renouncing its previous policy. Meanwhile, contingency plans were prepared. A Ministerial meeting decided that in the event of war partition would be summarily suspended pending the outcome of hostilities. All immigration would be stopped, on the grounds that all available shipping was needed for the war effort. A proclamation in this sense was drawn up and telegraphed to all Middle Eastern diplomatic posts, to be published in the event of war.[17]

In October MacDonald recalled for consultations the High Commissioner, together with some of his senior officials, from Palestine.[18] The Colonial Secretary summarized the position—the whole security system in Palestine was breaking down; lack of manpower gave no working margin for either troops or police; the Arab police had proved so unreliable that it had been found necessary to disarm them; they were reaching the political limit to which Jewish security forces might be used—in fact, there were already more Jews under arms than British troops and police combined.

MacDonald stated that the Jews would have to face the fact that if they failed to reach an agreement with the Arabs, then Palestine would be closed to further Jewish immigration and no Arab country would help out. MacMichael favoured the establishment of an Arab Federation, as no independent Arab Palestinian State would be able to afford to pay its own way. If the Arab States were invited to the proposed London Conference, Britain would have the opportunity to lead and guide the growing pan-Arab movement. But in order to win the confidence and assume the leadership of this movement, if would be necessary to abandon partition and announce the temporary suspension of all land-sales. MacDonald agreed.[19]

MacMichael proposed the immediate issue of a simple statement to the effect that partition had been found to be impracticable. But MacDonald, adhering to constitutional procedure, refused to prejudge the Commission's findings.

However, partition was to all intents and purposes already dead—all that was now required was a decent funeral. On 19 October, MacDonald told the Cabinet that while official policy remained partition, his own enquiries had some time ago led him to conclude that that was not the right policy.[20] The Commissioners reported back that upon a strict interpretation of their terms of reference they were unable to recommend boundaries for ... self-supporting Arab and Jewish States. However, the four commissioners did propose three alternative partition plans between them. Plan C, supported by two members against the serious reservations of the other two, reduced the boundaries of the Jewish State proposed in 1937 by the Peel Commission to a mere four hundred square miles of the coastal plain.[21] Considering Zionist dissatisfaction with the Peel boundaries, it was not difficult to predict Jewish reaction to the new plan. Upon reception of the Commission's report, the Cabinet appointed a Committee on Palestine to consider future policy. At its first meeting, the new Committee decided to publish the report, together with a Government White Paper rejecting partition.[22] This was done on 9 November 1938.[23]

ii. The St James's Conference
Meanwhile, MacDonald had begun to formulate a new policy for Palestine. Along with his Cabinet colleagues, he was quite clear that that policy would be determined ultimately by the degree of Arab acquiescence. The single principle to be adhered to rigidly was that Britain would not move out of Palestine—certainly not on the eve of war. The Government would make a display of its desire to reconcile the aspirations of Jew and Arab, by convening a 'round-table' conference in London. If no agreement between the parties themselves was forthcoming there, the Government would then be 'compelled' to implement a policy of its own. There was a view prevalent at the Colonial Office that both the Jews and Arabs had to be relieved of the responsibility for abandoning positions which each had taken up, through the good offices of His Majesty's Government. The round-table conference would in this sense be a good publicity exercise, demonstrating London's concern to reconcile the opposing parties, before having to impose its own policy.[24]

Justification for abandoning partition was summarized in a contemporary quasi-political assessment by Military Intelligence:

Had the European crisis of September 1938 developed into war, and had partition not been abandoned, we would probably have had to reckon with open rebellion in Palestine supplemented by contingents from outside, and repercussions in other Arab countries. Whatever their wishes may have been, the Arab Governments would have found it extremely difficult to fulfil their treaty obligations ... Owing to the abandonment of partition and the prospects that the rebellion in Palestine will have either been brought under control or will have subsided through appeasement by April 1939, the feeling of hostility to Great Britain ... should be no greater, and may be much less than at present.[25]

MacDonald envisaged for the short term a considerable degree of self-government in the Arab and Jewish areas of Palestine, with immigration allowed on a reasonable scale into defined areas. Ultimately, he envisaged a Middle East Federation of Arab States which would include Palestine. The Jews would be able, given Arab agreement, to expand within the Federation as a whole.[26]

The central Arab demands remained, since 1935, the cessation of all Jewish immigration, the prohibition of land-sales to Jews, and the creation of a constitutional Government. Jewish immigration had already been curtailed to the 'political high level' of 12,000 per annum recommended by the Peel Commission since July 1937. The Arabs now realized that in order to gain the last word on immigration they needed to become rulers of what they considered was their own country. Thus, by 1939, immigration and land-sales were subsidiary to the demand for 'constitutional government'.

The first draft policy submitted by the Colonial Office, at the end of 1938, provided for a revised Mandate, with Jews and Arabs in equal numbers assisting the High Commissioner on an Advisory Council. This Council would have to be consulted, but would not possess a veto on matters such as immigration, finance, etc. The Advisory Council would be superseded by an elected Legislative Council only when a two-thirds majority of both races agreed.[27] There was nothing revolutionary in these proposals. But it was hoped that the setting of a final limit to the expansion of the Jewish National Home might assuage the Arabs. According to various Arab sources, the number of Jews acceptable varied from a maximum of 300,000 to a minimum of 100,000.

The Government did not expect the London Conference to bring agreement between Jews and Arabs. Any final conclusion must either expose the Government to a charge of breach of faith with the Jews, or alternatively perpetuate hostility in Palestine and in the neighbouring Arab States. Of the two evils, the Government would choose the first.[28] The Foreign Office differed from its sister Department over the extent of the concessions it was prepared to make ultimately—'... the main point of difference ... between ourselves and the Colonial Office is that, though we are both agreed that the Arab demand for self-government should be refused, we should be prepared to go all the way to meet the Arabs as regards restricting Jewish immigration into Palestine'.[29]

Two alternative schemes of immigration were put to the Cabinet, for reference to the Conference. The first involved a rate of immigration calculated to bring the Jewish population in Palestine up to 35–40 per cent of the total at the end of a ten-year period—the question of subsequent immigration to be left open for decision by a further Conference.[30] The other alternative envisaged the same rate of immigration, but stipulated that subsequent entry after the ten-year period would have to be subject to Arab consent. The Colonial Office believed that the Arabs would probably reject the first scheme outright. If they did, the Government would then agree to an Arab veto on immigration after ten years, but hold out for the higher figure of 40 per cent when it came to determining the ratio of the Jewish to the total population. The Cabinet approved of this line, agreeing to take its final decision on the question once it became clear what stand the two sides at the Conference were adopting.[31]

The St James's Conference was opened formally on 7 February 1939. The British delegation, headed by the Prime Minister, gave its welcome to the Arab and Jewish delegations at separate sessions. The Arabs were represented by a Palestinian delegation, in which a small Nashashibi minority was dominated by the Husseinis, and delegates from Egypt, Iraq, Saudi Arabia, Transjordan and the Yemen. The Jewish delegation, headed by the Jewish Agency executive, also included heads of the Jewish communities from England and the United States.

At the Government's first working session with the Arab delegations, Jamal Husseini, acting as spokesman for the Palestinian Arabs, put their case at its maximum. He demanded an independent Palestinian Arab State, the abrogation of the Mandate, the end of the 'Jewish National Home experiment' and the creation of a sovereign State in treaty relations with Britain.[32] At their next meeting, MacDonald replied that while the Arabs should not be dominated by the Jews, neither should the latter be dominated by the former.[33]

The Arabs went on to attack the very premise of the British 'dual obligation'. At their demand, the Government agreed to lay open the MacMahon–Hussein correspondence for an Arab–British delegation to examine.[34] But MacDonald adamantly refused to consider the creation of an Arab State in Palestine, ostensibly on the grounds of protecting Jewish minority rights. He had used similar arguments with the Jews when he argued against any expansion of Jewish immigration.

At the first meeting with the Jewish delegation, Weizmann gave a masterly survey of the Jewish association with Palestine, in particular of its progress under the Mandate. He made great play with Britain's moral obligations under that international agreement:

I cannot believe that it is possible to conceive that the Government after twenty years is retreating from a moral and political position . . . the whole structure of the British Empire is such that a retreat from a great moral position as that . . . would mean a departure that would shake its very moral foundation . . .[35]

But Weizmann was playing into MacDonald's hand. The latter, in his reply, himself laid great stress on Britain's 'moral' obligations to the Arabs in Palestine who, he declared, had suffered owing to the 'vagueness' of the Balfour Declaration. While stressing to the Arabs the need to guarantee protection of the Jewish minority, he stressed to the Jews the need to take the Arabs in Palestine more into consideration. This was a subtle version of 'divide and rule'. MacDonald went on to insist that the Jewish right to Palestine must be conditioned by the consent of the Arab population already there—an assertion which in effect rendered nugatory the Balfour Declaration.[36]

Superficially, MacDonald's argument was incontrovertible. But just how far did British concern for Arab rights go? The Zionists saw through the tactics now employed by the Colonial Secretary. They believed that, as in Europe, the plea for self-determination for small nations was merely an instrument of propaganda in the hands of the Great Powers:

Did the question of consent apply only to those provisions of the Mandate which concerned the Jewish National Home or was the consent of the Arabs necessary also for the continuation of British rule in Palestine? Was the British Government ready to abandon Palestine if the Arabs did not consent to their remaining, or did they consider it necessary to remain in Palestine despite Arab opposition to foreign rule?[37]

When the Jewish delegation returned to the conference table they were faced with the second line of the British argument. MacDonald made a speech on the strategic importance of the Middle East for the British Empire. 'The position in that area depended upon the co-operation of the populations living there—if this assumption were incorrect, British armed forces in the area would have to be increased'. Arab hostility would have to be reckoned with and the readjustment made, if the Middle Eastern Arab States were 'tried too hard in the matter of British policy in Palestine'.[38] Even if the Jews did not appreciate British obligations to the Arabs, they must concede that sacrifices were necessary for the sake of the Empire.

The Jewish Agency had foreseen the 'strategic' attack and briefed its delegates in advance. The Zionist leadership believed somewhat naively that the Arabs' numerical and logistic advantages could be counterbalanced by the Jews' superior skills and financial resources. The Zionist memorandum advising the delegates took the line that during the initial, decisive campaign of the war, which it believed would take place in North Africa, there would be no immediate reinforcements of modern troops. The only possibility of raising local forces was from the Jewish potential in Palestine. As well as being available for service in Egypt if required, Jewish troops would be able to protect communications between Kantara (on the Canal), Haifa and Basra.

But the intricacies of Zionist logic were beyond the British mind. To hope that the British might rely on half a million Jews to police the Middle East was either wishful or desperate thinking. The Zionists were in effect being outmanoeuvred at every step—if they pleaded moral obligations, the British pleaded their own moral obligations to the Arabs; if they pleaded superior force of arms, this was in British eyes a doubtful hypothesis, to be weighed against the very real logistic advantages enjoyed by the Arabs.

In vain did the Jews argue at St James's Palace that the Arab danger was exaggerated, that the Arabs were exploiting the situation for their own benefit and that the Jews would make better, more reliable soldiers.[39]

MacDonald made no better progress with the problem of future Jewish immigration. He never broached to the Jews the first scheme put to the Cabinet, that which would have left open the question of immigration after the initial ten years.

MacDonald immediately put forward the harsher plan 'B', which envisaged the same rate of immigration as plan 'A' but gave the Arabs a veto on subsequent Jewish immigration. He stressed that the Jewish minority need not necessarily remain permanent—the potential Arab veto might act as an incentive to the Zionists to work for Arab goodwill in order to gain their consent to further immigration.[40]

But the Zionists saw these terms as condemning them to permanent minority status, and at their next meeting with MacDonald Weizmann rejected the formula.[41] At a private meeting the following day, MacDonald warned Ben-Gurion that the Conference looked like breaking up, in which case the British Government would have to impose its own policy:

... the Palestine Arabs are insisting on the immediate establishment of an Arab State and they are not going to budge from that position. I do not see any chance of an agreement with the Arabs. In these circumstances, it would perhaps be better not to have an agreement with you. Without an Arab agreement, an agreement with the Jews might only increase the opposition of the Palestine Arabs.[42]

MacDonald went on to define the terms of his plan for future Jewish immigration, in an effort to tempt the Jews with the immediate prospect of large-scale immigration—certainly on a larger scale than was currently being admitted into Palestine and more than some Zionist estimates of what the Zionist economy in Palestine would be able to absorb. If the Jews were restricted to 35 per cent of the total population during the next ten years, this would mean an annual immigration of 15,000—40 per cent would double that figure. But Weizmann again rejected the concept of an Arab veto on future immigration. The Zionists counter-claimed that the clause in the Balfour Declaration which protected 'the civil and religious rights of the non-Jewish communities' could not now be interpreted as investing the Arabs with the right to exclude Jews from Palestine.[43]

With the Arab delegations, MacDonald had to try first to establish the Jews' basic right to immigration into Palestine. He pleaded the case for immigration into already existent Jewish settlements, and reminded the Arabs that Jewish capital was a necessary stimulus for industry in Palestine.[44] But 'economic' arguments were of no avail. The Arabs insisted on the total cessation of immigration.

The Conference had reached a critical juncture. The Government's proposals had, not unexpectedly, been rejected successively by both the Jewish and the Arab delegations. MacDonald reported back to the Cabinet.[45] In view of the Palestinian Arabs' persistent demand for an independent State, some constitutional proposals would now have to be worked out. So long as the Arabs gained 'the form rather than the substance' of self-government they might concede something on immigration. But on no account could the Government allow itself to be 'landed' with the recognition of an independent *Arab* state. MacDonald hoped to secure at least the agreement of the Jews and the Arab States to his new constitutional proposals, hastily worked out at an ad hoc meeting of the Cabinet Committee on Palestine.[46]

The delegates of the Arab States agreed to meet informally with some of the Jewish delegation.[47] Weizmann welcomed the principles of independence and representative institutions—provided they were allowed to develop organically and were not imposed prematurely. Aly Maher Pasha offered the hospitality of the neighbouring Arab States to the Jews and suggested that only by co-operation and by peaceful penetration—rather than under the guarantee of promises and treaties—would the Jews acquire Arab friendship. But in response Ben-Gurion maintained the Jewish right to unrestricted immigration into Palestine, limited only by the economic absorptive capacity of the country—even if this did lead to a Zionist majority.

MacDonald intervened with his constitutional proposals. He proposed that in the autumn a further conference should meet in order to draw up the constitution for the proposed independent State in Palestine. Meanwhile, until the ultimate form of constitution was determined, the Palestinian Administration would take Palestinians on to the Executive Council, which would henceforth assume Ministerial status. In private, he reassured the Jews that those Palestinians now appointed to the Council would in effect be 'Ministers without Portfolio' and that for a long time all Ministries would be in British charge.[48] Weizmann showed some degree of acquiescence, provided a long transition period was agreed upon, during which time the provisions of the Mandate would remain in force. In that case, the Jewish Agency would continue to cater for the needs of the Jewish community. Provided the Jews were allowed to immigrate according to the economic absorptive capacity of the country, they might be in a majority[49] by the time genuinely representative institutions were created. Ben-Gurion, more closely involved with Palestinian domestic politics, stood out against the minority status implied by their representation on the Council, whether the British 'held the ring' or not.[50]

Matters came to a head over the weekend of 24–26 February, when two issues provided the Zionists with the concrete grounds on which to quit the Conference. First, the Zionists discovered from their own Intelligence that MacDonald—who had originally favoured equal representation of Jews and Arabs on the Executive Council—had now yielded to Arab pressure and agreed to a ratio of 3:2. The Zionist consensus on this development was that it was a 'sell-out'.[51]

Second, over the weekend, with the official Government minutes of its meetings with the Jewish delegation, the Colonial Office by mistake sent to the Jews a copy of its proposals as formulated for the Arab delegates' perusal.

The Zionists were shocked to see that the breathing-space of ten years' immigration before the Arab veto fell had been cut to five; and that after that period Britain would grant complete independence to Palestine.[52] The Zionists had been under the impression that these issues were still under negotiation. To make matters worse, the Arab Press in Palestine, to whom the proposals had been leaked, interpreted the British offer to mean the establishment of an Arab State in Palestine after five years.[53] Jewish extremists in Palestine reacted to the Press releases with bomb outrages that claimed numerous Arab victims.

MacDonald was naturally upset that his two-way diplomacy had been leaked to the wrong party. He had to convince the Jews not only that the communication was a clerical error, but also that his proposals were not the final word, but merely a basis for further negotiation. He was well aware of the divisions within the Jewish delegation, which he now approached at its weakest point—Weizmann. He rushed round to Weizmann's London home in person, to avert any rash reactions:

MM was in a great stew, put the blame on officials, etc. Chaim pointed out that whosever fault it was, the Arabs would now say that they had been cheated (as very likely they have been!).[54]

The Panel's discussion on whether to leave the Conference, held the next day, was interrupted by a personal telephone call from MacDonald to Weizmann, begging the latter not to break off negotiations. Weizmann answered with reserve that the Panel was at that moment deliberating.[55] Weizmann's close confidante, Blanche Dugdale, warned him that MacDonald's 'game was to detach him from the others'.[56]

Weizmann himself was against leaving the Conference, but found it impossible in the circumstances to argue for continuing any longer. Weizmann had retired to the country home of a friend to rest, leaving his colleagues to draw up the Jewish Delegation's letter of rejection. He was to confide later to R. A. Butler that 'Professor Namier was too logical and Ben-Gurion too emotional'.[57] Weizmann dutifully read out the statement of rejection at the Jews' next meeting with the British side.[58] Nevertheless, MacDonald managed to persuade the Jews to allow him to announce that informal discussions were to be arranged, at which he would bring forward new proposals.

At his informal meeting with the Jews on the following day MacDonald reassured them that his draft proposals as presented to the Arabs would be amended to acknowledge Jewish rights in Palestine as prescribed under the Mandate.[59] In a last effort to avert breakdown, he now offered to waive the Arab veto on future immigration—by the delaying tactic of a further Round Table Conference to decide the issue when the five years' transition period was up. But the Zionists would not commit themselves to yet another

Conference without first knowing upon what basis the discussions would be held.

MacDonald's concessions availed the Government little, for he had scarcely more success when he met again with the Palestinian Arabs. They also rejected the idea of a further Conference—how could an independent State have its constitution drawn up by a body of British, Jewish and Arab delegates? They demanded a provisional Government immediately, to act under a High Commissioner for a transition period of not more than three years. On the inception of the new State, an elected Legislative Assembly would then work out a constitution. Meanwhile, no further immigration, nor any land-sales to the Jews.[60]

The Arabs' plan embodied all the constitutional trappings of a Western liberal democracy. But was Palestinian society ready for such a jump into the twentieth century? From the British point of view, the plan amounted to the termination of their Mandate, and a swift end to their control over and presence in Palestine. Unable to reject the Arab plan on these grounds, MacDonald pointed to the evident fact that it ignored the Jewish National Home.[61]

MacDonald again reported back to the Cabinet.[62] The Jews had found it impossible to discuss an independent State until their position within it was guaranteed. Weizmann was having trouble with his delegation, particularly with Ben-Gurion. The Arab States had accepted the Government's proposals and were still trying to persuade the Palestinian Arabs. So far, the two representatives of the Defence Party and two of the Mufti's followers were in favour. But the rest, the majority, still wanted an independent State on the Iraqi model, within a maximum period of three years. MacDonald proposed that, if nothing changed within the next few days, he should close the Conference.

MacDonald now tried to make headway with his proposals for the development of self-government during the transitional period. But the Palestinian Arabs predictably rejected the idea of a Jewish veto over their ultimate independence, in much the same way that the Jews had rejected the Arab veto over their right to indefinite immigration.[63] The Western concept of 'give-and-take' had no place in Palestinian politics.

But MacDonald had never really believed he could gain the agreement of the Palestinian Arabs. He now arranged one last joint meeting between Jews and the Arab States' delegates, in order to gauge their opinion before he finally crystallized his own proposals.

Weizmann opened for the Zionist delegation.[64] He could not accept the idea of an independent Palestine State (which could arise only with Jewish consent) in the near future. He emphasized two principles—agreement on the nature of the regime, and the possibility of growth for the Jewish National Home. By the first point he meant non-domination of one people by another and by the second, immigration as of right.

Ben-Gurion went on to elaborate the Jewish case as he saw it.[65] He was not so concerned for the fate of those Jews already in Palestine—they could look after themselves, even without constitutional guarantees. But they, the Zionist Movement, were the guardians of the future of those Jews outside Palestine, yet to come.

Aly Maher, of Egypt, spoke next. He expressed deep respect for what the Jews had done in Palestine—they deserved a State of their own, and were Palestine empty they, the Jews, would be welcome to it. But it was not empty, and some 400,000 Jews had already entered Palestine and it was impossible to bring more in. He made one last appeal to the Jews to make a step towards peace, to give up something in order to win over the Arabs: 'Make a proclamation yourselves that for the sake of peace you are willing to stop immigration, or at least to limit it'.

Shertok's Diary reads: 'all at once a heavy atmosphere engulfed the room. Lord Dufferin nodded his head at what Aly Maher had said. Halifax and MacDonald kept quiet, but their faces were serious and concentrated. The English and the Arabs had united in one front.'

Ben-Gurion whispered to Shertok, 'See what they have called this meeting for—to tell us to give up.' To those assembled, Ben-Gurion replied that whereas he appreciated the 'spirit of peace' in which Aly Maher's appeal had been made, they, the Jews were sorry no less than others for what was happening in Palestine. They had not disturbed the peace and its return did not depend on them. He went on to compare the Arab appeal to stop immigration to an appeal to a woman in labour to stop birth.

Yet Weizmann did not dismiss the Egyptian leader's appeal so summarily. He now intervened:

I have listened with pleasure to the words of Aly Maher. For the first time in twenty years I have heard words of friendship and appreciation from a Muslim. In this spirit we could work. We are ready for negotiations with the Arabs on the basis of give-and-take. It is possible for 50–60,000 to enter Palestine each year. If it is said to us, we will make an agreement, slow down a bit – we will be able to find a common basis.

Shertok noted—'I thought, on hearing these words, that my hair had turned white. I felt as if an abyss had opened under us.'

MacDonald had remained quiet until now. He now seized on the straw apparently held out by Weizmann. 'The meeting has not been for nothing', he said, 'and it seems there is common ground for a slow-down of immigration, for some time. It seems necessary to continue the discussion tomorrow evening'. But Ben-Gurion was quick to correct the impression:

I am sorry to spoil people's pleasure, but I cannot yet see any common ground—we do not agree to a 'slow-down'. Dr Weizmann spoke of mutual concessions. Each one of us is ready for give-and-take negotiations, but there is no point in talking of a 'slow-down'—that is a one-sided conception.

MacDonald (with great reluctance) proposed once more that they resume their discussion the following day. Ben-Gurion asked whether it would then be possible to talk also of 'speeding-up'? MacDonald replied in the negative and to Ben-Gurion's query why not, he retorted that on the basis of 'speeding-up' there would not be any agreement. Ben-Gurion replied that on the basis of 'slowing-down' there would not be an agreement either. MacDonald now turned to Weizmann and asked if they would be able to get together again on the next day. Weizmann replied that he would be able to answer that question only on the morrow. This was as good as a rejection. The talks between the Zionists and the Arab States were not in fact resumed.

MacDonald still hoped that Weizmann might be able to bring his colleagues round—if he (MacDonald) was able for his part to get the Arabs to agree to drop their veto on immigration after the five-year period. With this point in mind, he again convened the representatives of the Arab States the next day, to ask their help in persuading the Palestinian Arabs to concede this point.[66]

Aly Maher thought it worth trying, if this would secure three-party agreement, but Fuad Hamza, the Saudi delegate, believed it would be impossible for the Palestinians to concede this, unless the British Government was willing to set a definite limit—say of five years—to the transititional period prior to independence. MacDonald agreed that if Arabs, Jews and British failed to agree on the proportions of further immigration after five years, the High Commissioner—if he were still in charge—would decide the issue together with the Colonial Secretary. If the new 'constitutional machinery' had been set up by then, then that body would decide.

Without the support of the Saudi Arabian and Iraqi delegates (Taufiq Suweidi of Iraq had supported the viewpoint of Fuad Hamza) it was inconceivable that MacDonald could succeed in getting the Palestinian Arabs to forgo the veto on immigration, which he himself had offered them. The issue was settled for him on the same day when a letter arrived from Weizmann, which made it clear that the latter had been overruled within his own delegation.[67] The letter made no mention of possible compromise, or of 'slowing-down', but related to what were, from the Jewish point of view, the unacceptable concessions made by MacDonald to the Arabs during the Conference.

The meeting of 7 March was in effect the last serious British attempt to mediate between Arabs and Zionists. With the last hope of compromise shattered, MacDonald set about making the best case he could for imposing the proposals which he now knew to be the minimum that would be acceptable by the Arab States. He brought these before the Cabinet, prior to submitting them to the Conference as the policy of His Majesty's Government.[68]

The Arabs were given their veto on immigration after the five years of limited Jewish entry. The Arabs, he reported, had suggested a figure of 50,000 Jews to be admitted during this period. MacDonald himself thought that, bearing in mind the concessions made in other spheres to the Arabs, the latter should accept a figure of 80,000.⁶⁹ Only the Minister of Health, Elliot, pointed to the discrepancy between the original 'minimum' acceptable to the Government,⁷⁰ and the figure now proposed by MacDonald.

The Cabinet's only qualm now concerned the danger of anti-British agitation which might possibly be worked up in America by its powerful Jewish community. But the potential dangers in the Middle East were considered to be greater than those to be anticipated from America. The Prime Minister supported MacDonald on this point:

... if it was necessary to face an outbreak of anti-British feeling in the United States ... it was better that this should happen at a time like the present, rather than at a time of acute international crisis ...⁷¹

On the next day, as expected, the Jewish delegation rejected categorically the Arab veto on further immigration after five years. In his reply, MacDonald accused Ben-Gurion and Shertok of 'clinging to Britain's skirt-tails'. They would never meet the Arabs half way while they had the British Government behind them.⁷²

With slight modifications, the Cabinet approved the proposals to be put to the respective delegations.⁷³ The modifications were again in the Arabs' favour. As the Jews had turned down representation on the Executive Council and the Arabs had been dissatisfied with their own representation, the ratio was now changed from 3:2 to 2:1 in the Arabs' favour. This was in fact a last attempt to stave off the Arab demand for full independence within a stated period.

Only the formality of official rejection of the Government's proposals by both sides remained. At the meeting with the Jews there was no discussion of MacDonald's last proposals, and Weizmann sent a letter of rejection on his delegation's behalf on 17 March.⁷⁴ The Palestinian Arabs reacted likewise, at two meetings on 15 and 17 March.⁷⁵

iii. Anglo-Arab negotiations after the Conference
The one outstanding crucial question for the Government was the attitude of the Arab States following the rejection of its proposals by the Palestinian Arabs. The Government proposed two alternative courses to the Arab States. Either they might endorse the Government's proposals—this would have the advantage of making them more binding on the Government; or they could agree to the Government making a unilateral declaration of policy and, for their part, appeal to the Palestinian Arabs to end their campaign of violence, on the grounds that the majority of their demands had been conceded. The Government believed that the Arab States were most likely to adopt the second course.

MacDonald and R. A. Butler held further meetings with the delegates from the Arab States after the official ending of the St James's Conference.⁷⁶ The Arabs now wanted to eliminate the probationary period the Palestinian

Ministers would serve under the High Commissioner; they wanted a definite time-limit of ten years, within which period the Palestinian State had to be set up—or, if it had not been set up by then, an undertaking that Britain would consult the Arab States on the future of Palestine.

The Cabinet Committee on Palestine discussed the Arabs' latest demands.[77] The nomination of certain Palestinians (in the ratio of two Arabs to each Jew) to head Departments once peace was restored was agreed to.[78] It was proposed that they should sit, with their heads of Departments as advisers, on the Executive Council. The number of Ministers would be increased until Palestinians sat at the head of all Departments, at which time 'consideration would be given to converting the Executive Council into a Council of Ministers'. The Committee conceded the time-limit of ten years for the establishment of an independent State and agreed, in the event of postponement, to first inform the League of Nations and the Arab States. Bearing in mind Jewish sentiment, it was to be noted that this independent State might be of a federal nature.

These proposals were forwarded to Cairo, where Lampson conveyed them to the representatives of the Arab States gathered there on their way home from London. The Arab States' delegates agreed to the 'evolution' of Palestinian ministerial responsibility, but vetoed any mention of the word 'federal'. They made it clear that they had not intended that they should be merely 'informed' of the Government's decision to postpone the establishment of an independent State—they had intended that the ten-year period should not be exceeded *without* their prior consent.[79]

The Cabinet Committee did not meet again until 20 April, when it agreed in essence to the Arabs' demands.[80] The question of Palestinian Ministers was taken as settled. MacDonald had qualms about leaving out all reference to the federal solution—an omission which would inevitably be noticed by the Jews. But the Government might get by if reference were made to it during the debate in Parliament. A diplomatic formula was devised for consulting the Arab States, which stated that Britain would not only consult them before deciding on any postponement, but would also 'invite their co-operation' in forming plans for the future.

The question of a possible postponement of the White Paper was discussed by the Cabinet Committee. It was feared that the security forces in Palestine, soon to be needed in Egypt, might prove insufficient to deal with the Jewish disorders to be expected upon the announcement of Government policy, MacDonald favoured immediate publication, notwithstanding the valid reasons for delay: the possibility that force would have to be used against the Jews; the prospect of opposition in the Commons and from the United States; the possibility that immigration would be stopped anyway in the likely event of war; and above all, the fact that the present scheme was 'admittedly the result of the need to placate the Arabs and would not have evolved had the Government not been under pressure'.[81] For MacDonald, there were reasons of overriding importance for publication now—the need to end the uncertainty and to avert the disappointment of the Arabs, whose benevolent neutrality was needed in the coming war. The Prime Minister again backed up MacDonald:

... we are now compelled to consider the Palestine problem mainly from the point of view of its effect on the international situation ... *if we must offend one side, let us offend the Jews rather than the Arabs.*[82]

Final agreement was now delayed, when the Egyptian Prime Minister invited the Mufti's supporters to Cairo to give their approval to the latest formula agreed to by themselves and the British Government. But this was the last thing that London wanted. In the White Paper of November 1938 that had announced the St James's Conference, the Government had taken upon itself to announce an independent policy of its own if the Conference failed. No open agreement could now be reached with only one of the parties to the dispute—at least not until after the Government published its own policy in London.[83]

Even worse, as feared, the Palestinians now added new conditions. With these, the last chance of the Arab States giving their full, if tacit support to the Government vanished. They had never really been willing to impose a British solution on the Palestinian Arabs.

The Palestinians now demanded that with the restoration of peace and order in Palestine a Palestinian Ministry (i.e. Cabinet) should be formed, with the British remaining in an advisory capacity only. Jewish immigration was not to exceed 75,000, and a regular census was to ensure that the Jews at no time exceeded one-third of the population. Lastly, the question of land-sales was to be determined by mutual agreement between the High Commissioner and the Palestinian Government.[84]

The Cabinet, if only because of British interests, could not accede to the demand for a Palestinian Ministry as soon as peace was restored—this would mean the ejection of the British themselves within a very short term. Neither could the Arabs be allowed to tie the hands of the High Commissioner over land-sales. The Cabinet agreed to the final immigration figure of 75,000, but decided that a census would be impracticable.[85]

When a Jewish Agency delegation called at the Colonial Office, Sir John Shuckburgh denied that anything in the nature of formal proposals beyond those placed before Jews and Arabs at the Conference had been made by the Government to the Arabs at Cairo.[86] When Shertok demanded the right to be informed of any indications which might be given to the Arabs of British readiness to modify the proposals made at St James's Palace, Shuckburgh reserved the Government's right 'to obtain information from whatever source it chose'.

Shertok called a second time at the Colonial Office, and questioned MacDonald in person on the post-Conference 'negotiations'. The Colonial

Secretary admitted that whereas the Government had not resumed conversations with the Palestinian Arabs, there was possibly some contact between them and the representatives of the Arab States, at Cairo. Shertok observed that there was no doubt that the Mufti was kept informed and added:

... it seems the Arabs had it both ways ... on the one hand they were the poor oppressed majority, on the other they were in a privileged position in being able to talk to Britain as an independent state.[87]

MacDonald closed the interview by expressing the 'hope' that before making any statement he would be able to give the Zionists an indication of the Government's proposals. This 'hope' was not realized.

Malcom MacDonald had been a 'favourite son' of the Zionists when his father had been Prime Minister. Weizmann had then specifically asked that he be included in the Cabinet Sub-Committee that was to formulate the Government's pro-Zionist interpretation of the Passfield White Paper. Weizmann had then written of him—'He has our complete confidence and if you will allow me to say so our most sincere affection and respect ...'[88] But the *realpolitik* of appeasement, as implemented by MacDonald at the Colonial Office, brought down the Zionists' wrath upon him. MacDonald himself professed later that he had foreseen this development:

When the Prime Minister appointed me to the Colonial Office, a misguided friend of mine offered me warm congratulations. I replied that his sentiments seemed hardly appropriate, since whatever policy the government pursued in Palestine, within twelve months I should be the most bitterly critized Colonial Secretary of modern times. My calculation was wrong by two days. It was one year and two days after my assumption of my present office before the White Paper, which the House is to discuss today and tomorrow, was published.[89]

The Zionists now inferred that he was a hypocrite and worse—'so anti-Semitic as to be almost demented'.[90] As with his two predecessors in office, MacDonald's own career and personal standing were not enhanced by his stay at the Colonial Office. Churchill's own animosity to MacDonald was well known,[91] and when he became Prime Minister he removed MacDonald from the Colonial Office, and not long after, from the Cabinet.[92]

iv. The significance of the White Paper
The terms of the White Paper on Palestine were published in London on 17 May 1939. They were essentially those agreed between the Arab States, the Palestinian Arabs and the British at Cairo. Certain key differences between the White Paper and the proposals put to the final sessions of the St James's Conference by the British were noted by, among others, the State Department at Washington.[93] The White Paper provided for the establishment within ten years of an independent Palestinian State in treaty relations with Britain,

as had been proposed at St James—but in addition the White Paper provided that in the event that circumstances should make postponement necessary Britain must consult not only with the Council of the League of Nations, but also with neighbouring Arab States; according to the St James' proposals, the regulation of Jewish immigration after five years was made subject to Arab consent and the establishment of an independent Palestine upon Jewish consent—now the White Paper omitted the Jewish veto on the establishment of the independent state in Palestine; whereas the final St James' proposals had proposed the establishment of an Advisory Council, to be replaced possibly by an elected Legislative Council after two years, the White Paper left the option of election to a Legislative Council, and added that the process of permitting both sections of the population to participate in the machinery of government 'will be carried on whether or not both sides availed themselves of it'. The restrictions on immigration (75,000 'labour' certificates over five years—of which 25,000 refugees were to be allowed 'free entry' regardless of the current economic absorptive capacity of Palestine) and on land-sales remained essentially those proposed by the Government at St James.[94]

In the Commons, the Government came under harsh criticism from all sides of the House. Herbert Morrison[95] spoke of the Jews being sacrificed to the Government's incompetence; the Liberal leader, Sir Archibald Sinclair, declared that the good name of Britain would be tainted if Parliament accepted the White Paper; Churchill warned that the White Paper—a betrayal of British promises to the Jews—would cast the country, and all that it stood for, one more step downward in its fortunes.[96]

The St James's Conference was an exercise in British colonial diplomacy from which the Government knew exactly what it wanted, well before the first session began. The participation of both Jews and Arabs at the Conference would allow Britain to place on their shoulders the responsibility for any failure to come to an agreement. At an interview with Sir John Chancellor, a former High Commissioner of Palestine, MacDonald did not contradict the following thesis:

[he] doubted if [the Conference] would result in any agreement – both Jews and Arabs must be relieved of responsibility of abandoning positions which they have taken up, and this could only be done through decisions of His Majesty's Government ... [he] appreciated incidental advantage of holding conference would be to show that, before taking their own decision, His Majesty's Government had gone to utmost limit in endeavouring to reconcile the opposing parties ....[97]

Whitehall also miscalculated its chances of success in winning over the Arab States to its side. Downie of the Colonial Office noted in retrospect:

... at an early stage in the London Conference the British delegation (more particularly the Foreign Office representatives) were anxious to achieve by all possible means a settlement which would be accepted, if not by the Jews and the

Palestinian Arabs, at least by the Arab States, and they were perhaps rather too optimistic as to the prospects of obtaining such a settlement ...[98]

Of the three delegations invited to the Conference the most important, in British eyes, was that from the Arab States. Once the Government felt reasonably certain that they would not rebel against British proposals, it had no further use for serious discussion with either the Jews or the Palestinian Arabs. Although the Conference did not break down 'officially' until 17 March, all serious negotiations with the two parties mainly concerned in Palestine had ceased over a week before that. From 8 March, the only serious consultations held were those between the British and the Arab States (in effect, with only the three most powerful, Egypt, Iraq and Saudi Arabia—the Yemen and Transjordan were left out).[99]

The May White Paper adumbrated future British policy in Palestine at a time when all members of the Cabinet, including Chamberlain, had accepted the inevitability of war in Europe. Yet, while measures for war were being concerted on a global scale, the Middle Eastern theatre remained of low military priority and appeasement remained the order of the day there, the White Paper its principal instrument.

The White Paper reflected a dramatic change from prior British policy in the area, in particular from the British attitude towards the Zionists, which previously had been at worst bureaucratically neutral and at best openly sympathetic. The White Paper was the result of diminishing options in the Arab Middle East on the eve of war and of a growing recognition of, if not respect for, the growth of a militant and increasingly anti-British brand of Arab nationalism in Palestine. The White Paper aimed at preventing it from becoming contagious.

6

British Policy during the Critical Phase, 1939-42

During the first stages of the war, many Zionists hoped and believed that the revival of the military co-operation that had existed between the Haganah and British forces in Palestine during 1936-38 might be the best way to undermine the provisions of the White Paper.[1] While Zionist demands in London centred—particularly during the critical phases of the war in the Middle East—on the demand for a Jewish Army, Arab agitation regarding Palestine centred on the implementation of the so-called 'constitutional clauses' of the White Paper. There was a certain consistency at least in the British conception which, from the autumn of 1940, linked the respective Zionist and Arab demands as concessions with which Jew and Arab might be played off one against the other. At St James's Palace in 1939 MacDonald had attempted to 'trade' Arab acquiescence in long-term Jewish immigration against Jewish acquiescence in Palestinian independence. During 1940-41, London contemplated trading the appointment of Palestinian Ministers against the raising of a Jewish Army.

THE 'CONSTITUTIONAL CLAUSES'

According to the 1939 White Paper, the first step in the projected constitutional progress of Palestine was to be the appointment of 'a few Palestinian Heads of Department', in the proportion of two Arabs to one Jew. Those appointed would sit on the High Commissioner's Executive Council, a purely advisory body.[2] Although this step would not have fundamentally altered the authority of the Mandatory, the date upon which the appointments were made would mark the inception of a five-year period during which a representative body was to be established in Palestine 'to review the working of the constitutional arrangements during the transitional period and to consider making recommendations regarding the constitution of the independent Palestinian State'.

Whereas one might regard the 1939 White Paper as the result of the three-year rebellion waged by the Palestinian Arabs themselves, the agitation for the implementation of the 'constitutional clauses' during the period under discussion is marked by the almost absolute absence of domestic Palestinian agitation. Rather, it was the Arab States—in particular Iraq and Saudi Arabia—whose constant prodding caused London repeatedly to consider this question. British willingness or reluctance to answer the demands of the

Arab States was a factor more of its military position in the Middle East as a whole rather than of any innate concern to abide by this particular section of the 1939 White Paper.

During the war years the Mufti himself helped organize the pro-Axis forces in Iraq. After the failure of Rashid Ali's coup in 1941 he made his way to Berlin, where he became an instrument of Axis propaganda.[3] Several of the exiled leaders of the now truncated Palestine Arab Party were allowed to drift back into Palestine. They discussed the formation of a new Party that might either remain independent of the Defence Party, or perhaps partially or totally absorb it. While none of these discussions gave birth to any substantial Arab political body, they do illustrate the dislike and jealousy of the Husseini clan (still not openly admitted, but freely expressed in private), as well as recognition of the advantages for the Arabs in the 1939 White Paper.[4] Fear of a possible return to influence of the Husseinis caused many of these splinter groups to attempt first to gain Government support for their party or programme. These inhibitions were perhaps the main obstacle to further political experiments by the Arabs in Palestine, for naturally the British Administration could not furnish the guarantees asked for.

The Mandatory did not receive any direct representations from any group of Palestinian Arabs regarding the constitutional clauses during this period. Within British officialdom, the main opponent of the clauses was MacMichael himself, who advocated the rejection of any such demands—should they be unexpectedly received.[5] In MacMichael's opinion, the reign of 'peace and order' upon which the implementation of the clauses had been made preconditional had yet to materialize. MacMichael did not envisage such conditions coming about for a long time:

> ... whether or no in any case 'peace and order' can be held to have been restored while a war is in progress and its course is uncertain, a temporary phase due to adventitious circumstances can hardly be said to constitute the new order of things which is surely envisaged by the White Paper as a condition precedent to taking the first steps towards new constitutional measures ... [6]

The High Commissioner's attitude was questioned by the Foreign Office, which considered it important to reiterate, whenever necessary, the determination of the Government to carry out the White Paper policy. Yet, like MacMichael, the Foreign Office regarded this part of the White Paper in terms of British expediency—one might reap the propaganda value of a declaration of adherence to the White Paper, even if one did not actually intend putting those declarations into practice. Foreign Office anxiety over possible repercussions in the Arab world due to the Palestine problem was still mixed with exacerbation with the Arab States' lack of co-operation on this question, particularly at the St James's Conference:

> The better-informed Arabs ... realize that they have no absolute guarantees for

the fulfilment of the White Paper policy by this country. They had their chances, at the time of the Conferences on Palestine, for an *agreement between Great Britain and the Arab States which would have been binding on all future Governments*. By refusing to accept the White Paper they missed their chance. But this does not mean that they would not regard it as a breach of faith if the present Government went back on the solution which they have indicated in the White Paper to be the most just which is possible in all circumstances . . .[7]

The Department had vivid memories of the complications caused by the seemingly conflicting promises given by Britain during the First World War.[8] While London had not accepted the Arab contention that they had supported Britain then on the strength of promises never fulfilled, if the Arabs were later able to claim that they supported Britain in two wars because of promises never fulfilled the effects would be lasting and fatal.[9]

With the outbreak of war in 1939 the Zionists had proposed to London that it 'freeze' any further implementation of the White Paper for the duration of the war. But despite the vigorous opposition of Churchill, the Cabinet decided to implement the Land Regulations envisaged by the White Paper, in February 1940. In some deference to Churchill's anxieties about the effect of anti-Zionist measures upon American Jewry, and consequently upon the American Administration, the British Ambassador at Washington was instructed: 'whilst we have not withdrawn from the policy stated in the White Paper, we are anxious not to arouse fresh controversies by a public reassertion of our position which might be considered provocative.'[10]

The apparent contradiction between this advice from Washington and the policy advocated by the Eastern Department of the Foreign Office was solved by simultaneous instructions to the Middle East Ambassadors that they should leave no enquirer in doubt as to London's intention to proceed with the White Paper policy—though they themselves were to avoid, as far as possible, all reference to the subject and leave the actions of the Government to speak for themselves.[11]

In this context, the legislation of the new Land Laws for Palestine was seen as a political gesture to divert possible Arab agitation from the constitutional clauses, to which the Mandatory itself had strong objections. Bagallay who had replaced Rendel as head of the Eastern Department at the Foreign Office, noted:

The issue of the Land Regulations in a few days ought to keep the Arab States and the Arabs of Palestine quiet for a while. After that, the demand for something to be done in the constitutional line may grow stronger, and unless some further sop can be found, e.g. some extension of what has already been done in the way of pardoning offenders, or some further measures to put down illegal immigration, we may have to press the Colonial Office to do something under the constitutional head.[12]

This procedure worked well enough for a few months, until German military successes began to erode Arab confidence in the Allies' ability to protect them, or even win the war. German progress, culminating in the drive on the Channel ports in May 1940, added extra lustre to Axis propaganda in Syria and in Palestine.

In May 1940, Nuri Said asked the British Ambassador at Baghdad for a clear-cut, unambiguous statement from London guaranteeing immediate (or at least at the end of the war) execution of promises already given for the organization of self-government in Palestine and French-occupied Syria,[13] where the three-year period before the implementation of independence promised by the French in 1936 had now overrun owing to the war. Foreign Office policy during June 1940 fluctuated violently as British military prospects in the Middle East plummeted. Initially, the Department adhered to the line set out in the instructions to Lord Lothian[14] the previous February. Expediency was again the main motive force in Bagallay's policy note:

Great Britain and France will not help themselves . . . by making further declarations about Palestinian Arab independence. Beyond an affirmation that the White Paper remains the policy of His Majesty's Government (if it does) there is no further declaration they could sincerely and honestly make, and if they did make one it would not really satisfy Arab aspirations. It might, on the contrary, merely confirm the Arabs in their sense of their own importance and of the present opportunity. *The only way in which the two countries can help themselves effectively is to re-persuade the Arabs that they are going to win the war. The best way of achieving this object is to have actual military successes. The second best is propaganda about coming military successes.*[15]

But the Italian declaration of war on 10 June, and the French surrender on 22 June 1940, radically limited—in the opinion of the Foreign Office—the options now open to London. With Britain now standing alone against the Axis, and a new front opened in the Middle East, Bagallay conceded that whereas a noncommittal reply to Nuri Said might have been sufficient a few days previously:

since then the acceptance of the German armistice terms by France has made it more important than ever that we should leave no weak joints in our armour in the Middle East. Arab doubts about our Palestine policy is the weakest of all these joints . . . It seems to me that the reiteration of our intention to abide by our policy is a small price for the Zionists to pay for the terrible risks we are now running as a result of establishing their national home.[16]

Halifax argued for a more 'conciliatory' line. The Arabs should be reassured that Palestine was being administered according to the immigration and land-sales regulations of the White Paper. With regard to Nuri's enquiry, London should declare that it did not consider peace and order to have been sufficiently restored for the first steps in the constitutional developments envisaged by the White Paper to be taken. The Government did not think it likely that this step could be taken while the present war continued, but they hoped and expected that 'when the war is ended conditions in Palestine will quickly permit the various stages of constitutional development to follow one another on the lines which the White Paper lays down'.[17]

With regard to anticipated Zionist reactions to a statement that would for the first time indicate that the White Paper was more than just a wartime measure, Halifax believed it would be 'kindest' to the Zionists in the long run to tell them the truth, 'finally and plainly'.[18]

The views of Halifax came under fire from the newcomers to Churchill's recently formed Coalition Cabinet (on 7 May). The declaration proposed by the Foreign Office was modified, specific undertakings being replaced by vague assertions.[19] The new Lord Privy Seal, Attlee, stated that he had always opposed the White Paper policy, and was not yet satisfied that it would be desirable to reaffirm that policy publicly at present—especially in view of the dangerous repercussions it might have on American opinion. Churchill himself saw no reason for any reply whatsoever to Nuri Said, seeing that Iraq had done nothing for the Allied war effort. Chamberlain, now Lord President of the Council, sought a compromise by avoiding any explicit statement of policy. He proposed an amendment to the declaration, to the effect that the policy of the White Paper had not changed and the Government hoped that when the war was over 'steps' would follow in orderly succession. The Foreign and Colonial Office agreed to consider the amendment.

The Colonial Office believed the main issue to be not whether Nuri received one reply or another, but that if Nuri or anyone else asked whether the White Paper was still in force he should receive an unequivocal affirmative. Indeed, seeing that Iraq had until now refused to break off relations with Italy when the latter had declared war on Britain, the Foreign Office itself belatedly saw the advantage in such a noncommittal reply.[20]

The final Cabinet decision was a compromise between those anxious to avoid any public statement specifically re-endorsing the White Paper policy, and those who insisted it would be impossible to revise that policy during the war.[21] The Cabinet decided that Nuri would be told simply that the Government 'did not see any reason to make any change in policy for Palestine as laid down in May 1939, and it remains unchanged'. If pressed, British representatives in the Middle East were authorized to state that they hoped and expected that when the war was over conditions in Palestine would permit the various stages of constitutional development to follow one another on the lines already laid down.

Objections to the Cabinet decision came from the venerated Ambassador at Cairo.[22] Lampson pointed out that the French collapse[23] had raised hopes of Syrian independence and—owing to British weakness in the Middle East —of Palestinian independence also. The military authorities in the Middle East thought it undesirable to weaken Vichy's hold on Syria, lest Britain herself be forced to fill the vacuum. If Britain herself adopted any action too favourable to the Arabs of Syria—such as recognition of their independence—the French there might turn against Great Britain. But if concessions were ruled out as regards Syria, then something should be done in Palestine, especially, in Lampson's opinion, in view of the strong movement towards confederation in the northern Arabic world, i.e. in Iraq, Syria, Transjordan and Palestine. Thus Lampson urged reconsideration of London's decision not to implement the constitutional clauses during the war.

Lampson's intervention brought an immediate response from MacMichael:

There is a vast nucleus of variegated intrigue afoot throughout the Arab countries. To speak of it as 'a strong movement for some confederation of independent states' suggests a unity which is very far from existing.[24]

In MacMichael's view, the French collapse did not extend to their military position in Syria or to their will to keep order there. With regard to Palestine, the High Commissioner remained firm in his opposition to any 'constitutional' experiments, not only on domestic Palestinian, but also on general Middle Eastern grounds:

I regard it as a fallacy to suppose that to give a few Heads of Departments to Palestinians is likely to turn the politicians of Egypt, Syria and Iraq into likely allies or do more than convince them that we are on the run. The only thing that will achieve the end desired is success in the field of war which will open their eyes to the fact that our friendship is worth cultivating.[25]

The Foreign Office, for its own reasons, was no more amenable to Lampson's promptings than MacMichael had been:,

... so long as we have to maintain our position in Egypt and Iraq and Palestine and to support the Jewish National Home there, we *are* against Arab aspirations, and I do not think that any attempts to get round this hard fact by pleasant phrases or half measures will do us any good in the long run ... If we had something really striking to offer the Arabs, such as some assurances regarding the future of Palestine going far beyond the terms of the White Paper, and saying that the Jewish National Home would never be greater than at present, or, better still, could join this with some promise about the independence of Syria, the propitiation might be real and the attempt worth making. But what Sir Miles Lampson's recommendations really boil down to is that we should go a little further than we have already about promising to bring about one bit of the White Paper, i.e. the constitutional proposals, into force even while the war is on ...[26]

On the other hand, any apparently unsolicited statement about Palestine might encourage the idea that Britain *was* less secure militarily than it had hitherto boasted. Bagallay concluded:

Until reinforcements can reach the Middle East, our whole position is rather in the nature of a gigantic bluff. That bluff to succeed must be consistent ... tinkering about with minor questions arising out of (the White Paper) policy is not going to have a decisive effect in the face of much greater issues upon which opinion in the Middle East will ultimately depend . . .[27]

Further promptings from Lampson, and continued Axis military successes, necessitated reconsideration of the issue. On the day that British forces withdrew from British Somaliland in the face of Italian attack, Lampson again urged the immediate implementation of paragraph 10 (4) of the White Paper, in order to 'keep the Arab world quiet'. Lampson did not see why this step should lead to increased difficulties in Palestine, and warned that failure to act now incurred the risk of increased demands in the future.[28]

Upon being asked for his comment, MacMichael agreed that the stakes were now rising.[29] He himself had learned that Nuri Said now insisted on a Council of Ministers (instead of a few Heads of Departments) and a constitution on the Iraqi model, within an Arab Federation. But MacMichael was unconvinced that British concessions now would avert increased demands later. On the contrary:

Not only would the pan-Arab appetite be whetted but our action would be attributed to fear and uncertainty . . . Palestine itself would exchange its present comparative placid preoccupation with domestic issues for intense political excitement.[30]

The Foreign Office agreed with MacMichael, especially since Palestine itself might soon become involved in military operations. If that happened any administrative or constitutional changes would be 'impracticable'.[31] The fact that the whole of the Middle East might soon become a battlefield was sufficient to justify delay, the more so since there had been no political demands from the Arabs of Palestine itself.

The Ambassador, as on previous occasions, gave up the struggle with a warning that future events might prove him right.[32] But the approach of the Axis armies towards the Middle East in the autumn of 1940 prompted the Colonial Secretary, Lloyd, to propose a reversal of standing policy:

In light of recent developments, particularly in the Balkans, unsatisfactory state of Arab opinion in Middle Eastern countries gives occasion for grave anxiety . . . the question of Palestine is of the first importance . . . Palestine has now enjoyed a lengthy period of internal peace and I do not think it possible any longer to maintain with conviction that peace and order have not been sufficiently restored for the purpose of implementation of para. 10 (4) of the White Paper . . . I feel bound to invite the Cabinet to reconsider their opinion of last July in favour of shelving appointment of Palestinian Heads of Department until after the war . . .[33]

Lloyd merely wanted MacMichael's opinion as to whether any Jew would be likely to accept appointment as a Head of Department, and if not, whether the third vacancy should be filled by another Arab or left vacant?

MacMichael now bowed to *force majeure*, agreeing that it would be desirable to remove the existing general impression that the constitutional clauses were more or less a dead letter. MacMichael admitted that his own negative attitude to the proposals *per se* had been responsible for his previous opposition, and stated that he would have been far happier to set up an Advisory or Consultative Council. He reported that there was no hope of securing a Jewish delegate to the Council, and proposed to leave the place vacant for the time being.[34] The Colonial Office itself emphasized that the present initiative was due not to the internal situation in Palestine—which was comparatively satisfactory—but rather to the general situation in the Middle East as a whole. It was because pressure was strongest from Iraq, Saudi Arabia and Egypt—rather from Palestine itself—that the Colonial Office now asked that their proposal be brought to the Cabinet under the joint aegis of themselves and of the Foreign Office.[35]

Their joint memorandum to the Cabinet laid great emphasis on the current weakness of the British position in the Middle East:

The situation in Iraq, where there are no British troops, is particularly unsatisfactory, and the Chiefs of Staff fear that serious military consequences may result unless a better atmosphere is created. In Egypt also, there is sympathy with Arab discontent, which might at any time express itself in a manner highly inconvenient to us in the Nile Valley. The Arab leaders in Syria and Palestine are in close contact with those in Iraq . . . but in spite of this tendency to turn towards the Axis there is still widespread dislike of Nazism and a bitter hatred of Italy and distrust of Italian ambitions . . . all our Arab friends, Ibn Saud in particular, are constantly urging us, in our own interests, to make a definite effort to rally Arab opinion to our side . . . in view of the increased gravity of the situation, we feel bound to invite the Cabinet to reconsider their conclusion of last July. Until we implement the paragraph 10 (4) our good faith will remain suspect in Arab and Moslem eyes, and their criticism will not be easy to rebut . . .[36]

Since the Government had recently given its general approval for the raising of a Jewish Army,[37] it now had at hand a ready counter-concession with which to counteract possible Zionist protests at the further implementation of the White Paper.[38]

But one of those unpredictable twists of fate now delayed the Cabinet decision. On 25 November 1940 a refugee ship in Haifa harbour, the 'Patria', was blown out of the water, causing the death of some 240 refugees and a dozen British policemen.[39] The emotional tide-wave of sympathy that swept the Jewish world made it impossible to 'pour salt into the wound' by adding 'constitutional' changes to Zionist troubles.[40] The opportune moment had been missed. The pendulum of military fortune in the Middle East now swung towards the British, with successful operations in Libya and in Greece. When the Colonial Office brought up the issue once more in February 1941, the Foreign Office saw fit to delay consideration pending the return of its new head, Anthony Eden, from a visit to the Near and Middle East.

On 24 February 1941, MacMichael himself—now fully converted to the idea—recommended implementation of the constitutional clauses, if only to correct the existing impression that they were a dead letter.[41] One might presume that since the correspondence of the previous November, Mac-Michael had been canvassing the idea in Palestine, and had perhaps hinted at forthcoming Government action. But the Colonial Office and the High Commissioner had now reversed their roles, and a perplexed MacMichael was now informed by the Colonial Secretary, that nothing should be done for the present:

... the main consideration at the present juncture is our general military position in the Middle East and from that point of view we must I feel avoid any action entailing risk of political excitement or disturbances whether Arab or Jewish ...[42]

One may detect Foreign Office influence on this decision. The fact that Nuri Said's name was connected with the original Arab initiative did the Arab cause no good at this particular juncture, when events in Iraq were confounding the predictions of the architects of the 1939 White Paper.[43] The Rashid Ali coup in Iraq was precisely that contingency which the concessions now under discussion had been designed to prevent. Britain could not compete with Germany in making promises to the Arabs—Germany could always offer more.[44]

The one discordant note again came from Cairo, where Lampson was not sure whether 'pro-Zionism in London does not constitute the major difficulty as regards Palestine'. In a private letter he maintained that the British failure to continue with the implementation of the White Paper and to deal satisfactorily with illegal immigrants had encouraged the general Arab belief that Zionist sympathies in London and the United States would prevent the execution of the White Paper, and that a British victory would eventually mean the domination of Palestine by the Jews.[45]

Following the grant of landing facilities in Vichy Syria to German aircraft en route to aid Rashid Ali, in May 1941, the British decided to invade Syria, to pre-empt the possible establishment there of a German base. The Anglo-French declaration of Syrian independence in June 1941 was designed to win over the Syrian Arabs. The declaration forced the reconsideration of the future of Palestine, from whose Arabs pressure for their own further constitutional progress might now be expected.[46] Renewed agitation in the Arab world itself in the direction of federation gave rise to the hope that the Jewish problem in Palestine would shrink in proportion to the size of the Arab union that eventually emerged.[47]

MacMichael, evidently anticipating imminent change in Palestine, set out his own alternatives for the future of the country.[48] His first preference would be for a 'clean-cut' solution—the creation of a token Jewish State, either independent, or possessing some kind of Dominion status within the Empire. This idea was ruled out by the Foreign Office, mindful of Zionist criticism of the State proposed by the Peel Commission, and of anything that resembled a 'ghetto' State.[49]

As a second choice, MacMichael advocated 'controlled' constitutional development similar to that normally followed in Crown Colonies, by gradual progression from Advisory to Legislative Council, and ultimately responsible government. Yet, as Lord Lloyd[50] pointed out, it had been just these 'controls, that had led the Arabs to reject the original terms of the 1939 White Paper' and to demand the immediate appointment of Palestinian Ministers. Lloyd insisted further that the Government was now bound to implement paragraph 10 (4), and would be free to propose such alternatives as MacMichael now brought up only if the Arabs as well as the Jews of Palestine refused to work it.

MacMichael's third alternative proposed that Britain take the opportunity of the war to abolish the Mandate and declare Palestine a Crown Colony. The Foreign Office rejected this last idea as 'a piece of the most spectacular and shameful chicanery'. The Department took MacMichael's second proposal—that of the Advisory Council—more seriously. Certain members of this Advisory Council might sit on the Executive Council, which in turn might be converted—as soon as circumstances permitted—into a Council of Ministers. This Council would thus, by a stroke of the pen, 'be turned into the Heads of Department of paragraph 10 (4) of the White Paper' whenever the time was ripe.[51]

But the Foreign Office now looked to a solution of the Palestine problem within the context of some form of Arab Federation. It was known that Weizmann himself believed that the solution lay in the establishment of an independent Jewish State within an Arab Federation.[52] The Department's one concession to MacMichael was its agreement that he proceed—if he wished—to establish a mixed Advisory Council.[53]

In a further dispatch, MacMichael pressed his own preference for the termination of the Mandate, arguing this time principally on the grounds of Britain's strategic requirements.[54] As MacMichael pointed out, when these requirements had been met, and Britain had further ensured the protection of the Holy Places and of foreign interests, '... not much scope will be left for the practice of independence as distinct from a measure of local autonomy ...'[55] Britain could remain in Palestine only if she eliminated 'the twin causes of the trouble'—the Mandate, which had created the antagonism, and the Jewish Agency, which conjointly kept it alive.

London ruled out MacMichael's advice, on grounds of opposition anticipated from both Jews and Arabs. The former would not countenance any curtailment of the authority of the Jewish Agency, whereas for the latter any revision of the Mandate would be regarded as a betrayal of the promise to give Palestine its independence.[56] MacMichael's proposals were discussed further at a joint meeting between the Colonial and Foreign Offices.[57] Battershill, now legal adviser to the Colonial Office, pointed out that the High Commissioner's schemes were based on the false presumption that the Syrian Mandate had been abolished by the joint declaration of independence, adding that in fact there had been no agitation in Palestine of late for any revision or abolition of the Mandate. The meeting agreed that there could be no retreat from the 'Heads of Department' scheme, although there would be no objection to the establishment of an Advisory Council—provided it was clearly understood that this was not in substitution for the constitutional clauses of the White Paper.

Fortunately for London, this particular issue never reached crisis point, as Arab leaders now concerned themselves with various schemes for Arab union. Neither they nor the Arabs of Palestine itself renewed the agitition for the implementation of paragraph 10 (4) of the White Paper.[58] Nor, contrary to the expectations of many, did promises to Syria and the Lebanon stimulate any Palestinian demand for the termination of the Mandate. This may perhaps be attributed to three factors. Firstly, to Arab disbelief in French pledges to Syria and the Lebanon; secondly, to the expectations in Palestine that their future lay in the wider frame of Arab union; and last, but by no means least, to the uncertainties of the British military situation in the Middle East during 1942, and to British dominance of the area after Arab procrastination on the eve of Britain's crises lost for Palestine the opportunity of wringing concessions from London. Britain saw no point in making concessions when she was already engaged in military operations. Once Britain had on her own overcome the worst of her crises in the Middle East, the whole logic of concessions in Palestine assumed a different complexion.

NEGOTIATIONS FOR A JEWISH ARMY

i. British and Zionist military needs
On the eve of World War Two, Dr Weizmann wrote to Chamberlain on behalf of the Jewish Agency offering the services of the Jewish people in every sphere of war activity. He added the pious hope that differences which had arisen over the White Paper might give way to 'the greater and more pressing necessities of the time'.[59] The Jewish Agency Executive at Jerusalem issued a similar statement on 3 September 1939. From the outset, Zionist offers of military assistance were linked to political expectations, and treated by the British Government accordingly.[60] London—concerned primarily with the reaction of the Arab world to a British-trained army in Palestine—was unable ever to divorce its assessment of the Jewish military potential from likely political repercussions. The conflict between political appeasement and military exigency at times led to disputes between the respective British authorities.

Shortly after the close of the St James's Conference, the War Office had approached the Colonial Office with a request to recruit more Jews in Palestine in order to fill those gaps in the regular British forces occasioned by the transfer of troops from Palestine to guard the Canal Zone.[61]

Notwithstanding the definite bias against Jewish military forces held by the military authorities in Palestine, some 86,000 Jewish men and 50,000

Jewish women in Palestine had registered for 'national service' by the end of September 1939. The Jewish Agency offered to place these recruits at the disposal of the authorities in Palestine, but in 'recognized Jewish units'. The offer, with its political implications, was turned down by the military authorities.[62] Government policy of 'balance' between the two races expressed itself in the somewhat naive idea of mixed Arab–Jewish units for the defence of Palestine.

In October 1939, Orde Wingate—presumably after consultation with the Zionists—submitted to Churchill a plan for the mobilization of a Jewish Army in Palestine.[63] The plan envisaged Government training in England for 1000 Jewish officers, who in turn would organize a Jewish force of 20,000 which might assume responsibility for internal security in Palestine within four months. The plan also outlined a scheme for the formation of Jewish desert units which would fight in the Western Desert; also the training of a further 1000 Jewish officers to lead a Jewish Division (of 15,000 men) in whichever theatre of war the Government decided upon.

Bracken[64] saw the Wingate–Cazalet approach as an attempt to by-pass the Colonial Office and advised Churchill that it would take the whole War Cabinet to overcome Colonial Office opposition.[65] Churchill in fact raised the question in Cabinet just a few days after receiving Wingate's plan, although not in the terms proposed by the latter.[66] Churchill advised the Cabinet that better use might be made elsewhere of the Regular battalions then stationed in Palestine if that manpower already available in Palestine were properly exploited. Churchill went on to make a proposal that was to handicap Jewish military initiatives for years to come. He suggested that each community in Palestine might 'keep watch' on the other, if the separate units set up by Arabs and Jews were balanced against each other. This seems to have been the origin of the 'parity' proposal.[67] Despite MacDonald's own warning that the Arabs might fear that the Jews were being armed for action against themselves, the Colonial Secretary was instructed by the Cabinet to explore—together with the War Office—all possibilities of raising local Palestinian forces, with a view to enabling the regular British garrison in Palestine to be reduced.

MacDonald reported back to the Cabinet in February 1940. He informed his colleagues that notwithstanding the desirability of reducing the Palestine garrison, the position in Palestine following several years of civil war was as yet too delicate to entrust internal security to purely Palestinian forces. The withdrawal of the British garrison would mean an outbreak of trouble between the Arab and Jewish elements in those forces which would, within a very short time, necessitate the return of the British garrison.[68]

Churchill made a swingeing attack on the Chamberlain Government's policy in Palestine:

It might have been thought a matter for satisfaction that the Jews in Palestine should possess arms, and be capable of providing for their own defence. They were the only friends we had in that country, and they were much more under our control than the scattered Arab population ... the sound policy for Great Britain at the beginning of the war would have been to build up, as soon as possible, a strong Jewish armed force in Palestine. In this way we should have been able to use elsewhere the large and costly British cavalry force, which was now to replace the eleven infantry batallions hitherto locked up in Palestine. It was an extraordinary position that *at a time when the war was probably entering its most dangerous phase, we should station in Palestine a garrison one quarter of the size of the garrison of India* – and this for forcing through a policy which, in his opinion, was unpopular in Palestine and Great Britain alike.[69]

Halifax reminded the Cabinet that the problem, in contrast to the impression given by Churchill, was not confined to Palestine alone, but had repercussions throughout the Moslem world. The Prime Minister, while regretting the 'policy which had brought us to the present pass', did not for the present see any solution to current difficulties and concurred with MacDonald that the Government certainly could not give the Jews alone freedom to arm. The Cabinet concluded that only when the last vestiges of the Rebellion in Palestine had been finally eliminated, and its police force re-organized,[70] would it be possible to begin reducing the British garrison there.

Churchill's appointment as Prime Minister in May 1940 gave rise to renewed Zionist expectations from London. Yet in his new capacity Churchill faced not only the traditional attitudes of Whitehall, but also the opposition of the Chiefs of Staff to his own conception of Palestine's place in imperial grand strategy.

Two days after the formation of his Cabinet the new Prime Minister received a new offer to raise a Jewish Army, this time from Jabotinsky, on behalf of the Revisionists.[71] Churchill passed on the scheme to his new Colonial Secretary, Lloyd, who, contrary to Zionist expectations, displayed fundamental opposition to any such scheme:

... it is clear that proposals of this kind, whether emanating from the New Zionists or from the Zionists, have as their prime object the recognition of the Jewish people as a nation, with a standing in the War Councils of the Allies and ultimately in the discussions of terms of peace. In both cases the conversion of Palestine into a Jewish State as a reward for Jewish military assistance is the objective ... [72]

Lloyd therefore recommended that for the present Jewish and Arab Palestinians should be enlisted into British units already serving in Palestine.[73]

Churchill himself did not accept the contention that the raising of a Jewish force would necessarily endow the Jews with a seat at the Peace Conference, since his intention was that the Jewish Force should fight solely in Palestine.[74] His primary motive remained to release the eleven battalions of regular troops stationed in Palestine, and to prepare the Jews for their own self-defence by the time these troops were moved. Churchill did not fear Jewish attacks on the Arabs, which Britain could effectively prevent or suppress with a maritime blockade.[75]

Following German advances in the Low Countries,[76] Churchill stressed to his Chiefs of Staff the vital role in home defence to be played by troops then locked up in Palestine:

> I cannot feel that we have enough trustworthy troops in England, in view of the very large numbers that may be landed from air-carriers preceded by parachutists ... the transports which brought the Australians to Suez should bring home eight battalions of Regular infantry from Palestine, properly convoyed, even at some risk, by whatever route is thought best. I hope it will be possible to use the Mediterranean ...[77]

The Chiefs of Staff opposed Churchill's proposal on grounds of general strategy in the Middle East. The regular battalions then in Palestine formed the only reserve of trained and equipped troops in the Middle East. Their removal would seriously prejudice the British position in Egypt and have a detrimental effect on British allies in the Middle East, particularly on Turkey. Such a move would correspondingly encourage Italy. The Chiefs of Staff also ruled out troop movements through the Mediterranean for the present.[78] But Churchill insisted on the return of the battalions:

> It is no use talking about a strategic reserve for the Middle East when we are in our present position at home. Even if these troops go round by the Cape, they could be here in six weeks.[79]

At a further meeting of the Chiefs of Staff, the Vice-CIGS, General Percival, outlined the underlying principles of current imperial strategy. It was essential to secure both the Middle East and Singapore rather than concentrate on the defence of the United Kingdom alone. If large numbers of troops were moved about during the following critical weeks, the result would be that they would be unavailable to fight anywhere. The decisive consideration during the next few weeks would be the effect of such a withdrawal on Italy's decision to enter the war.[80]

The issue was briefly discussed in Cabinet on 29 May, when Churchill reiterated his opinion that the eight battalions then stationed in Palestine were vital to home defence. The High Commissioner had informed London that in the event of the troops' withdrawal, he would want an assurance either that the Australians would remain, or that an equivalent force would be brought to Palestine.[81] The entry of Italy into the war on 10 June changed matters. The Prime Minister and the Chiefs of Staff now agreed to move the Middle East Reserve from Palestine to Egypt, the defence of which was the Reserve's principal purpose. But the Jews in Palestine would now require some means of self-defence not only against conceivable Arab attacks, but possibly against Italian invasion also.

Weizmann wrote to the Colonial Secretary asking that the Jews of Palestine be allowed 'to organize as many military units as they could, and to train their men, as far as possible with the help of British forces in the country'. Weizmann further asked for authorization of the Jewish Agency in England and in the United States to launch a campaign to provide all possible financial and military aid to the Jews of Palestine.[82] As Weizmann pointed out, the Jews in Palestine were not able—like the British—to evacuate:

The British forces now in Palestine may be required elsewhere ... Delay may mean the annihilation of the half-million Jews in Palestine, and the destruction of all our work ... If we have to go down, we are entitled to go down fighting, and the Mandatory Power is in duty bound to grant us this elementary right.[83]

The Colonial Secretary somewhat disingenuously laid responsibility for Government opposition to the Jewish Army scheme at the door of the War Office.[84] Lloyd warned Weizmann that the War Office saw 'certain practical difficulties in any scheme to form purely Jewish units of the British Army', and himself proposed that Jewish recruits be incorporated in the British Army. For this purpose, Jews might enlist in any country where permissible and practicable, though *not in Palestine*.[85]

In a private letter to Churchill, Lloyd elaborated on his own objections:

I need hardly emphasize the objections to this Zionist plan for arming the Palestine Jews ... the political and military consequences would be so grave that any disadvantages would count as nothing in the scale ... the arming of the Jewish community in Palestine under British auspices would undoubtedly be interpreted by Arab and Moslem opinion, not only in the Middle East but in India, as a step towards the subjection of Palestine to Jewish domination ...[86]

Appended to Lloyd's signature were those of Halifax and Eden. Undaunted by the combined views of his colleagues, Churchill in his reply again derided the Palestine policy he had inherited from Chamberlain:

The failure of the policy which you favour is proved by the very large numbers of sorely-needed troops which you have to keep in Palestine ... more than 20,000 men. This is the price we have to pay for the anti-Jewish policy which has been persisted in for some years. Should the war go heavily into Egypt, all these troops will have to be withdrawn, and the position of the Jewish Colonists will be one of the greatest danger. Indeed I am sure we will be told that we cannot withdraw these troops, though they include some of our best ... I had hoped you would take a broad view of the Palestine situation, and would make it an earnest objective to set the British garrison free ... I could certainly not associate myself with such an answer as you have drawn up for me. I do not at all admit that Arab feeling in the Near East and India would be prejudiced in the manner you suggest ...[87]

After consultation with Palestine, Lloyd informed Churchill that from the point of view of internal security in Palestine itself, most of the infantry could be realeased for Egypt. But, added Lloyd, both the High Commissioner and the GOC Palestine adhered emphatically to the opinion that the difficulty of the situation would be aggravated by the recruiting of a Jewish Military Force under British supervision.[88]

ii. The Palestine Buffs

Since the entry of Italy into the war in June 1940, the need to organize local self-defence forces in Palestine, exploiting indignous resources there, became both urgent and obvious. At the end of July 1940 the Cabinet Committee on Military Policy in the Middle East decided to raise six Palestine Companies, three Jewish and three Arab, from those members of each community already serving with British Forces in Palestine. The new companies, some 1000 from each community, would be independent and self-accounting, each allotted definite combat responsibilities, while still bearing the name of a British infantry corps (the East Kent Regiment—'the Palestine Buffs'). For 'political reasons', recruiting was to be in approximately equal numbers from each community, even if this meant restricting Jewish recruiting because of poor Arab response.[89]

Naturally, the Zionists were disappointed that their self-defence efforts should be limited by the Arabs' effort, particularly following Italian advances into British Somaliland in August 1940.

At a meeting with Churchill on 9 August, Weizmann put forward two specific proposals as alternatives for getting round the 'parity' restriction.[90] First, each race might be given equal, generous quotas. The result would be that Jews would enlist in large numbers, and the Arabs would have no grounds for complaint if they did not reach their own quota. Alternatively Weizmann proposed that the Jews of Palestine be recruited freely and that any recruits in excess of the quota be transferred to Egypt as part of the general defence forces of the Middle East.[91] These proposals were forwarded by the Prime Minister to the Colonial Office,[92] while Churchill turned his own attention to the mobilization of maximum forces by Middle East Command to withstand the expected invasion of Egypt:

I do not consider that proper use is being made of the large forces in Palestine. The essence of the situation depends upon arming the Jewish colonists sufficiently to enable them to undertake their own defence, so that if necessary for a short time the whole of Palestine can be left to very small British forces . . .[93]

On 16 August 1940, Churchill issued his General Directive to the War Office and to Wavell, ordering the latter to make arrangements to move most of the Commonwealth forces, together with the Polish Brigade and French Volunteer Unit, out of Palestine to the Delta at short notice.[94]

In the face of mounting pressure from the Prime Minister on the one hand and from the Zionists in Palestine, London and the United States on the other, the Colonial Office was forced to reconsider its policy. Pressed by the Prime Minister, Lloyd received Weizmann on 23 August 1940.[95] Whitehall seems to have concluded that it would perhaps be preferable to channel Jewish military aspirations on to the 'grand theatre' of global war rather than concentrate Jewish military forces in Palestine, with unpredictable political consequence. Lloyd now warned Weizmann that Jewish recruitment in Palestine would have to be restricted to battalion strength (i.e. up to five hundred, as against the previously agreed one thousand) on the grounds that the Arabs were unlikely to enlist in substantial numbers, and that there was insufficient equipment for more troops. On the other hand, Lloyd agreed to Weizmann's proposal (originally Bevin's)[96] that those Jews in Palestine who recruited in excess of the quota might join a Jewish Force to be raised *outside* Palestine.

Lord Lloyd added however that there would be obstacles to overcome, for instance from the War Office, where some Jewish officials opposed the scheme.[97] Weizmann gained an interview with Eden,[98] who confirmed the Government's decision to restrict recruiting in Palestine to a battalion from each community. Weizmann remarked that it was grotesque that the Czechs, the Poles and the French should be allowed to fight, while the Jews were debarred from doing so because the Arabs did not wish to. Eden added that there were political considerations to be taken into account, and that he had yet to consult Halifax and Lloyd. Dill, also present at their meeting, agreed with Weizmann's proposal that Wingate organize a striking force of some three thousand Jews, on the pattern of the Night Squads.[99] Eden interjected that, considering the Colonial Office knew nothing of this idea, the political implications would have to be examined.

As Italian activity in the Middle East increased (Weizmann himself believed that the bombing of Haifa by Italian aircraft in September 1940 had a great effect upon Whitehall), so the pace of negotiations in London quickened, often without full consultation between the various political and military bureaucracies involved. Ultimately, proposals approved at Ministerial level were to be frustrated by Whitehall officials, well supported by British representatives in the Middle East.

iii. The Jewish Division proposal

Despite War Office acceptance of Wavell's recommendation that no grander scheme for recruiting Jewish Forces should be proceeded with before the Middle East Command had had time to assess the effects of recruiting the six companies of Buffs in Palestine, and to assess the military capacity of the Palestine human material,[100] the Government now proceeded to negotiate formally with Weizmann on the grander scheme for a Jewish Division to participate in the Allied war effort.

On 13 September 1940, Eden informed Weizmann that the Zionists' proposals[101] had now been accepted in their entirety by all the Departments concerned. The Cabinet had yet to give its approval, but opposition was not likely once those Departments concerned had agreed. In answer to

Eden's enquiry, Weizmann proposed a Jewish Force of ten thousand initially, three to four thousand of whom would come from Palestine, the remainder from the United States. Eden proposed that the men be trained in England, to where they could be shipped conveniently in vessels returning empty from the Middle East. Lloyd injected the only note of disharmony, by insisting that the scheme should have no political implications and that all recruits should be guaranteed the right of return to their country of origin (i.e. that participation in the force would not give any right to settle later in Palestine). Weizmann ignored this remark.[102]

But it was precisely on the issue of possible political implications that the scheme was to founder. The Zionists themselves had variegated motives for mobilizing their own 'national' force. First, the multiple instinct of self-preservation tinged with emotions of vengeance—the need to protect the Jewish community in Palestine against Arab violence or Axis invasion, combined with the desire to fight as Jews against the Nazis in what they, the Jews, considered to be a war primarily against their own people. Secondly, the political, undeclared motive—the hope that a Jewish force might add political weight to Zionist claims at the Peace Conference.[103]

Within Zionist councils there was an evident rift between Weizmann, with his 'Anglo-saxon entourage', and the Jerusalem Executive as represented by Ben-Gurion.[104] When Weizmann triumphantly reported back to his Executive in London that he now awaited only the formal Cabinet confirmation of the Army scheme, Ben-Gurion pointed out that unless the Jewish units served in the Middle East it would be difficult to get men to leave Palestine, particularly since the invasion of Egypt.[105] Weizmann pointed out that in all their recent discussions it had been agreed to leave open the question of the location of the units. Ben-Gurion agreed that recruits from England and the United States might fight wherever needed, but insisted that Jews recruited from Palestine be used in the defence of their country. Weizmann disingenuously replied that it had been for this reason that he had mentioned a unit of 3–4,000 men from Palestine (he had in fact already accepted the British offer to raise battalions of 5–600 men). But Professor Namier indirectly confirmed Ben-Gurion's fears when he pointed out that should Major Wingate's proposals for a desert unit be accepted, that force might be used either in the Eastern or in the Western Desert, and he did not think they would be able to lay down more precise conditions than that.

At a further meeting of the Zionists two days later, relations between Weizmann and Ben-Gurion reached breaking-point.[106] Weizmann first announced the news that Wingate had received instructions to join General Wavell's staff in Egypt, and would not be available for the present to organize the Jewish force in Palestine as expected. Weizmann regretted the loss of Wingate, but argued that it would be inadvisable to fight the War Office on this point, and that they could not make the whole issue dependent on one man.

But Ben-Gurion differed with Weizmann on fundamentals. He understood their policy to be based on two demands; primarily that the Jews of Palestine be allowed to defend themselves, together with, of course, the British position in that part of the world; and secondly, that the Jews be given the right to fight as Jews against Hitler, irrespective of Palestine. Now, before he left England for the United States, Ben-Gurion had to know where Weizmann stood.

Mrs Dugdale thought Ben-Gurion was confusing two issues—the Jewish Army, and the Jewish Home Guard in Palestine. Dr Weizmann had obtained a promise of a Jewish Army, but the Yishuv's desire to raise a Home Guard for the defence of Palestine had yet to be discussed. Dr Weizmann interjected that they had attained Government agreement to train a group of some ten thousand men who would be sent to the Middle East. He had been commissioned to negotiate on these lines and had done so. They had all demanded that the Jews of Palestine be mobilized and trained for the defence of Palestine, but Lord Lloyd feared Arab opposition. They had now to decide whether to reject what was offered them until they received safeguards that Jewish manpower would be used in Palestine, or to take what was given them and ask for more afterwards. While not in agreement with the parity principle, he had had no choice but to accept it, as the final decision had lain with the Government.

Ben-Gurion agreed that they had to accept what they could get, but at the same time, he claimed, they should not relinquish their major aims. Mrs Dugdale's suggestion for a Home Guard for Palestine did not meet the case. He wanted the Jews in Palestine to be in the Regular Army. For him the crucial question remained whether the Jewish units to be raised would fight anywhere, or in Palestine and in the Middle East?

Weizmann's impression was that the Jews from Palestine and from other countries would be dispatched to the Middle East—whether to Palestine or to Libya he could not say. He thought they should cheerfully accept what they had been offered, and do whatever they could to implement the scheme. Even if their men were to fight in France, as a Jewish Army they would be fighting for Palestine. Lastly, concluded Weizmann:

... it was in the hands of Mr Ben-Gurion to make or mar the scheme ... if Mr Ben-Gurion would not do it, then he would have to consider coming to Palestine himself ... if they quibbled now, it would show lack of vision and confidence which in present circumstances would be deadly.[107]

Ben-Gurion replied that he was now going to the United States because it was there that units outside Palestine could be built up. He would try to mobilize a Jewish unit to fight wherever the British High Command might decide to send it. But he could not go to Palestine to ask Jews there to join an army not destined to fight in Palestine.

While Weizmann realized that the raising of Jewish units in Palestine—upon which the success of the whole scheme depended—would need Ben-Gurion's active support, he may have hoped that those members of the Jerusalem Executive remaining in Palestine would set about implementing the scheme while Ben-Gurion himself was still in the United States.[108]

Meanwhile, on 10 October 1940, the Cabinet decided in principle to accept Weizmann's proposals.[109] The Government authorized the Jewish Agency to recruit ten thousand Jews for incorporation as Jewish units within the British army, not more than three thousand of whom were to be Palestinians, with the remainder to come from wherever the Jewish Agency decided upon. Each recruit was to produce a guarantee that he would be accepted back in his country of origin; the units would be trained in Britain, and no guarantee would be given as to the theatre of war in which they would eventually serve. But the Cabinet decided that any practical measures to implement the decision were to be delayed until after the American Presidential election on 5 November 1940. Meanwhile no action was to be taken and no announcement issued by either party. As with the partition proposal in 1937, delay was to prove fatal to the scheme.

On the eve of the American elections, Weizmann again approached the Prime Minister's office, arguing that even if no publicity were given to the scheme, he might be allowed to begin discussions at the War Office on the organizational problems. He also asked for a Government announcement on the morrow, as soon as the elections were concluded.[110]

The Departments concerned now claimed that it had been agreed that once the elections were over, the Cabinet would have to consider the exact nature of the announcement to be made. It soon became apparent that the Foreign, Colonial and War Office were all against specific reference to a *Jewish* army. Furthermore, recent setbacks in the Middle East made the present moment inappropriate for such an announcement from the point of view of reaction in the Moslem world, and in particular in Turkey (whose neutrality was being severely tested by Axis gains in the Balkans).[111]

Nevertheless, if the announcement was delayed, Weizmann's pressure via the Prime Minister did move the War Office to begin consideration of the technical details of the scheme. On 15 November 1940, Eden gave Weizmann permission to begin discussions with the General Staff—though the timing, content and manner of any announcement would remain subject to further Cabinet decision.[112] On 22 November 1940, Weizmann was informed by General Haining that a General Leigh had been appointed Staff Officer to discuss details of the scheme with the Jewish Agency.[113] At a further meeting with Haining at the end of the year, Weizmann was informed that the scheme was being held up by the problem of how American Jews could enlist without forfeiting their citizenship. But Haining was able to announce the appointment of a commander for the Jewish force, Brigadier L. A. Hawes, reputedly a first-class organizer, who had been responsible for the trans-shipment of the

British Expeditionary Force to France. Hawes was to take up his new post on 4 February 1941.[114]

But there remained Whitehall's fundamental opposition. Weizmann did not always assess correctly the gravity of this opposition, but at times behaved as if re-living his role—as Zionist-inventor—of the First World War.

This anachronistic approach expressed itself during a further meeting with Lloyd on 17 December 1940.[115] Lloyd claimed that some thirty years hence American oil would dry up and the only sources available to Britain would be Iraq, Iran and the newly discovered wells in Arabia. All these sources were outside the Empire and mainly under Arab control—hence London's concern about Arab opposition to Zionist aspirations. Weizmann was ready with his answer—for some years he had been working on the problem of producing oil from sugar, and he believed he could 'make the Empire flow with oil'. But this time there would be no ambiguity—'he wanted Palestine'. Lloyd replied that if he could really do this, he might have whatever he wished.

The Foreign Office again expressed its opposition to the scheme, in particular to 'Zionist' sponsorship:

... there are strong objections to the present scheme, whatever the War Office may feel about the general principle ... the fundamental objection to the present scheme is that it is to be run by the Jewish Agency for *Palestine* ... It is to be operated by Dr Weizmann and his little clique of Palestine Zionists and by them alone ... The fact that the Palestine Zionists are taking the lead in this matter will be regarded as evidence that the scheme has a direct connection with Palestinian affairs. The Arabs will believe that, somehow or other, the scheme is to benefit and strengthen the Jewish National Home in Palestine, presumably at the expense of Arab interests ...
... Dr Weizmann ... wishes to establish a claim on British gratitude in order that at the end of the war he may be in a stronger position to induce His Majesty's Government to relax their restrictions on Jewish immigration into Palestine ...[116]

In anticipation of Churchill's objections to any move likely to incur American displeasure, the Foreign Office claimed that the Jewish Army scheme would merely set the stage for later misunderstandings and ill-feeling towards Great Britain. After Jews all over the world had 'come to the help of Great Britain in the hour of her need' it would be incomprehensible to Americans if London did not reward services rendered with suitable concessions. There might also be immediate resentment when it was realized that Jewish recruits were not being sent to the Middle East in order to defend Palestine, but to other theatres of war. The Department stressed the importance of not connecting the scheme with 'Dr Weizmann and his Palestine Zionists'.[117]

The Foreign Office succeeded in having all mention of the Jewish Agency removed from the proposed announcement, which Lloyd forwarded—together with amendments suggested by the Foreign and War Office—on 2 January

1941.[118] In reply Weizmann specifically insisted that since the offer had been made by himself, in his capacity as President of the Jewish Agency, and accepted as such by the Government, specific mention should be made of the Agency in the official announcement. Weizmann also demanded that specific mention be made of the 6,500 Palestinians already serving with British forces in the Middle East; and that the Government's intention to use the force in the Middle East should be stated—even if no guarantee of such use could be given.

At a meeting to clarify the issue on 24 January 1941,[119] Eden—now Foreign Secretary—denied any previous commitment to use the force in the Middle East, and refused emphatically to insert any such undertaking in the announcement. On the other hand, Eden himself thought that the request to have the Jewish Agency accredited with the origin and direction of the scheme was reasonable.[120] The most heated argument arose over the question of guarantees that non-Palestinian recruits would be allowed re-entry to their country of origin. Weizmann accused the Government of 'shooting at a non-existent target', of suspecting that the Army was to be used as a 'back door' into Palestine. The Zionists had no intention of using back doors, claimed Weizmann, but would go for the front door once the war was over. It would not be the ten thousand Jews of the Army who would clamour for Palestine, but sixteen million. With Weizmann carried away by his own rhetoric, Eden shrugged his shoulders in despair. Yet despite Eden's obvious distaste for Zionism, Weizmann left the meeting with the impression that the Foreign Secretary would honestly implement the scheme imposed upon him. Eden promised to try to settle the question at a conference of the Departments concerned due to be called the following week.

But opposition was mounting all the time. A further fusillade now came from the Ministry of Information.[121] The Director of Middle East propaganda at that Department, Professor Rushbrook-Williams, who also liaised on questions concerning the Foreign, Colonial and India Offices, expressed great unease about the probable repercussions of any announcement of a Jewish Army at the present juncture. He believed any such announcement would be seized upon by enemy propaganda as a further example of British subservience to Jewish interests. The effect upon the Palestinian Arabs and upon the Middle East in general would be little short of disastrous. However the announcement was worded, the Arabs would believe that the Government's real intention was to pave the way for Jewish domination of Palestine at the end of the war. Explaining why he had not raised any objection until now, the Professor argued that only in recent weeks had Axis propaganda concentrated itself to a special degree on alleged Jewish influence over the Government. He asked that the announcement be either postponed—lack of equipment could be given as the reason—or, at the very least, delayed for a week to ten days, during which time he and his agents might attempt to prepare the ground. The Colonial Office thought that postponement was no longer a practical proposition, but considered the request for a 'breathing-space' not unreasonable.

The manner in which the Director of Middle East propaganda intended to 'prepare the way' for the announcement on the Jewish Army was set out in a memorandum circulated on the day following his interview at the Colonial Office:

> Since the announcement will be regarded as a concession to the Jews, it is highly desirable that a 'counter-concession' should be made to the Arabs. Such a 'counter-concession' might take the form *either* of an announcement of the intention of HMG to implement paragraph 10 (4) of the White Paper *or* a declaration in precise terms that the policy laid down in the White Paper remains the policy of HMG, that it will be put into effect, and that it is in no way altered.
>
> If for reasons of high policy such a counter-concession cannot be made, the announcement must be drafted in such a fashion as to ensure that the Axis cannot exploit it as proof that HMG have abandoned the White Paper policy; in other words, *it must be specifically, and not merely by implication, divorced from the Palestine problem.*[122]

The critical phase into which the Middle East was then entering gave added force to the Ministry's request for delay, a fact duly noted at the Foreign Office:

> If in the course of those weeks the Germans sweep down through the Balkans to the Mediterranean, our position in the Middle East will be difficult enough. If, in the meantime, we have published the announcement, we shall merely be giving the Arabs an added inducement to throw in their lot with the Axis.[123]

MacMichael did not place much value on the *quid quo pro* stratagem:

> ... By publishing both declarations together we should naturally create an assumption in the Arab mind that they were closely connected and ... that it was intended to send the Jewish Army here while simultaneously making a childish attempt to placate the Arabs by offering a verbal sop.[124]

The general consensus was summarized by the Eastern Department—either to agree to raise the Jewish Army and to implement the constitutional clauses, or to decide that if the timing was unfavourable for the one, it was also unfavourable for the other.[125]

Yet Departmental opinion alone did not move Churchill from his determination to push through the Jewish Army scheme. The Prime Minister relinquished the scheme, against his own will, only when the appeal of General Wavell weighed in with the chorus of Whitehall's opposition:

> Vitally important that for next six months at least I should be free from anxiety and commitments in Palestine, Iraq and Syria, all at present targets of Axis propaganda ... if Jewish contingent [is] to be raised I consider it essential that para. 10 of the Palestine White Paper be first implemented and that raising of contingent should be dependent on Jewish acceptance and implementation of this. If any

contingents are to be raised in Palestine, must be trained outside the Middle East, and in no circumstances sent to the Middle East. Best not to raise contingent at all in view of shortage of equipment.[126]

This dispatch, forwarded also to the Prime Minister, was brought by the War Office to a fresh meeting of the Departments involved.[127] The new Colonial Secretary[128] advised the meeting that, having studied all the relevant papers, he would recommend to the Prime Minister either a drastic modification of the scheme, or else a six-month postponement. Moyne in fact proposed three alternatives to the Prime Minister:

1. To publish the declaration and to implement paragraph 10(4) of the White Paper.
2. To modify the declaration by:
   a) cutting out all recruiting from Palestine on the grounds that Jewish and Arab Palestinians already have facilities to join the Army in the locally raised companies;
   b) mentioning that the proposal came from the Jewish Agency, but making it clear that application from suitable recruits will be considered independently of their recommendation;
   c) the Secretary of State for War answering a supplementary question to the effect that while he could not bind himself to the theatre of war where the contingents would be sent, there was no intention that they should go the Middle East; or
3. To put off the announcement for six months in the hope that by then the Middle East situation may be less critical.[129]

Churchill was evidently disappointed with Moyne's unsympathetic attitude and remained totally unconvinced by Departmental attitudes. However, he felt he must concede the point to a much-pressed commander in the field, for whom he had as yet no substitute:

General Wavell, like most British military officers, is strongly pro-Arab. At the time of the licences to the shipwrecked illegal immigrants being permitted, he sent a telegram no less stong than this, predicting widespread disaster in the Arab world, together with the loss of the Baghdad–Basra–Haifa route ... I overruled the General ... all went well and not a dog barked.[130]

It follows that I am not in the least convinced by all this stuff. The Arabs, under the impression of recent victories, would not make any trouble now. However, in view of the 'Lustre' (the Greek expedition) policy, I do not wish General Wavell worried by lengthy arguments about matters of no military consequence to the immediate situation. Therefore, Dr Weizmann should be told that the Jewish Army project must be put off for six months, but may be reconsidered again in four months. The sole reason given should be lack of equipment.[131]

When he received Moyne's official notification of the postponement, Weizmann seems to have swallowed the official reasons offered (shortage of equipment), or at least he tried to convince his colleagues in Palestine that they were genuine.¹³² But he became aware very soon that there were other political motives behind the postponement. While appreciating some of the political and military influences on the decision, Weizmann as yet tended to place responsibility on individuals within the policy-making establishment, rather than on circumstance:

... Lord Lloyd died suddenly; Lord Moyne, quite fresh to the problem, became his successor. Halifax, who was on the whole a supporter of this scheme, left the Foreign Office to come here;¹³³ his place was taken by Eden, who when he became Foreign Secretary almost forgot what he did when he was War Secretary ... But as Lord Moyne has proved to be very friendly and sympathetic and accessible, the matter began to look as though we were coming to a definite favourable conclusion ... apparently on the instance of General Wavell ... the implementation of the whole project has to be postponed for four to six months ... Wavell's attitude and probably the attitude of the local administration in Palestine is dictated by the desire to appease the Arabs ... though the lack of equipment may have played some part in this decision, the political aspect of the problem was the second decisive cause ...¹³⁴

At Washington, Isaiah Berlin admitted to Revisionist leaders that 'lack of equipment' was just a formula of convenience, calculated not to alienate the Jews, among whom the idea of a Jewish Army was rapidly gaining support and sympathy. At the same time, the formula stressed the real need for equipment, in the hope that the United States might make extra efforts in that direction. But the essential reason for delay was British unwillingness to do anything which might anger the Arabs, admitted Berlin, adding that the centre of resistance now seemed to be no longer the Colonial or Foreign Office, but the Middle East Command.¹³⁵

iv. The fight against parity
But May 1941 was a disastrous month for British arms in the Middle East, ushering in a desperate phase for British policy-makers. British forces evacuated Greece, abandoning its inhabitants to Axis forces; Rashid Ali menaced the British garrison in Iraq; and Rommel continued with his relentless first offensive across the Western Desert. Whereas the physical position of the Yishuv in Palestine became daily more imperilled, the 'political' reasons for not arming the Jews—i.e., doubts about Arab loyalty—became ever more cogent. The result was a compromise of sorts.

In May 1941, the 'parity' ruling in Palestine itself was waived, in order to allow maximum mobilization of the Yishuv in its self-defence. But, notwithstanding the urgent needs of the Middle East Command itself, political objections prevented the expansion of Jewish mobilization beyond that needed for defence of Jewish settlements in Palestine.

As Rommel's spring offensive mounted, the Jewish Agency approached the new GOC Palestine and persuaded him to support their scheme for a maximum expansion of the Jewish Settlement Police.¹³⁶ When approached by the GOC, the High Commissioner, MacMichael, reluctantly concurred with the scheme and recommended to the Colonial Office that the Jewish recruiting programme be extended up to seven companies, irrespective of the rate of Arab enlistment.[137] The High Commissioner specifically added that the present scheme for the expansion of 'existing organizations of the Jewish Police and Special Constabulary' would do much to meet 'the Jewish demand for self-protection within the framework of the general scheme for the defence of Palestine'.

At an interview with Lord Moyne on 6 May 1941, Namier (Weizmann was then absent in the United States) was told of the Colonial Secretary's agreement to increased Jewish enlistment, regardless of parity. Moyne added that Jewish settlements were to be turned into military strongholds, and the supernumerary police were to be fully mobilized and enlarged and given intensive military training. The whole expansion programme would be limited by the amount of equipment available.[138]

Wavell thought that the Jewish initiative was '... merely another form of Jewish attempt to raise (an) Army in Palestine which will be available (at) end of war to take over Palestine.'[139]

Wavell asked the CIGS to stop the proposal getting past the Cabinet. In London, the Colonial and War Offices agreed between them that the new departure would apply strictly to Jewish self-defence in Palestine itself. The decision was kept under such a shroud of secrecy that Wavell's successor, Auchinleck, was apparently not even aware of it.[140]

Within a week of his arrival in Egypt, Auchinleck urged the War Office to step up the recruiting of Palestinian Jews in order to form fourteen new infantry companies to guard aerodromes and installations in Palestine and Egypt. The new companies would release regular British combat troops for front-line duties in the Western Desert. Auchinleck complained that the 'parity rule' was holding up Jewish recruitment, as Arab recruiting was very slow.[141]

MacMichael objected to the removal of ten companies of regular troops from Palestine, as being likely to lead to trouble among the Arabs. Auchinleck retorted that his urgent need of those units in Egypt outweighed by far the Arab danger in Palestine.[142] But the main obstacle remained the Foreign Office and its representatives in the Middle East. At the beginning of August, the War Office informed Auchinleck that the raising of four companies of Palestine Buffs for static duties in Palestine had been approved, 'provided equal opportunity (was) given to Arabs and Jews to enlist'. As regards the raising of the ten companies for aerodrome defence in Egypt, this was under consideration by the Foreign Office, and a final decision would have to await its verdict.[143]

The Foreign Office made its agreement conditional upon the agreement of the Cairo authorities. The ex-attaché at Baghdad faithfully predicted Lampson's reply:

... Sir M. Lampson *will* see an objection. The Oriental Secretariat in Cairo are very pro-Arab and anti-Jew. What is to happen if Sir M. Lampson sees objections and the military insist? Does not Mr Lyttelton [Minister of State at Cairo] settle the difference?[144]

However, Lampson's influence, if anything, had grown during the war, as he 'outlived' many Ministerial careers. As the 'doyen' of British representatives in the Middle East, his influence seems to have exceeded—in certain spheres—that of the Minister of State at Cairo, appointed first in June 1941. The new Minister, with a seat in the War Cabinet, was intended to be a 'political supremo', to relieve the military command of extraneous responsibilities.[145]

Lampson's influence was due not only to his own stature, but to Foreign Office resentment at direct Cabinet intervention at Cairo. The Department preferred to deal with its own diplomats and maintain a monopoly over information emanating from the Middle East. The appointment led to some dispute over the distribution of authority with the Foreign Office.[146]

When approached by the Foreign Office with Auchinleck's request, Lampson duly objected. Lampson claimed that the employment of Jewish forces in Egypt would have unfortunate political reactions in the country, where anti-Jewish feeling was already strongly on the increase. Eden supported the Ambassador.[147]

Auchinleck urged the Foreign Office to put off any final decision, pending his own appeal to Lampson.[148] His appeal led to the first open clash between British military needs and the political frigidity bequeathed to the area by the 1939 White Paper:

The point at issue ... has been the formation of these [Jewish] companies [of the Palestinian Buffs] without forming an equal number of Arab companies ... if we are bound by the parity rule we cannot make the best use of the available manpower ... The effect of your decision is that a source of local manpower will not be used to the full, since I cannot propose to raise these units for use in Palestine ... .[149]

The Minister of State supported Lampson's objections, especially in view of the delicate situation with which he himself had to deal in Syria.[150]

But the War Office in London felt bound to support its new C.-in-C. Middle East. Margesson minimized the political repercussions—the total number of Jews involved would be about two thousand, who would be scarcely noticeable in Egypt; at least some of the companies would be stationed in desert aerodromes remote from the Delta and existing centres of population; above all, there was the necessity to reorganize and train the regular troops in the Middle East for the coming offensive in the Western Desert.[151] Following this appeal, the Foreign Office urged Lampson to reconsider his objections.[152]

Yet the final decision was left to the better judgement of the Cairo authorities which, at a meeting of the Middle East War Council, decided 'for practical reasons' to leave the issue in abeyance.[153] Undoubtedly, improving military prospects influenced the decision.

v. The rejection of the Jewish Division scheme

Meanwhile, the four-month period after which the grander scheme for a Jewish Division was to be considered had drawn to a close. At the beginning of July, Moyne had asked Eden's advice in preparing his reply for the expected Zionist return to their former demands.[154] Moyne himself advocated a simple repetition of the former pretext, notwithstanding his own prediction that this would no longer satisfy the Zionists.

The Foreign Office agreed that nothing had occurred during the previous four months to diminish the political objections to the scheme. Although the crisis in Iraq had been settled, Britain was by no means freed from anxiety in that country. Moreover, Syria had been promised her independence, whereas nothing had been announced in Palestine about the implementation of the constitutional clauses—until that was done, any announcement about a Jewish Army would have the worst effect on Palestine. The Department therefore advised that should the Jewish Agency make fresh enquiries, it should be informed that current stresses on shipping and on other resources made it impossible to bring over and train Jewish recruits.[155]

Back in London to take up the negotiations halted five months previously, Weizmann found himself shuttled from Department to Department. Moyne disingenuously told him at the beginning of August that the Colonial Office saw no political objection to restarting the scheme, and encouraged him to tackle the War Office.[156] At the War Office, the liaison officer for the Jewish Division emphasized his reluctance to become involved in the 'political' side of the scheme, and told Weizmann that once the so-called 'political' problems had been clarified, the War Office for its part would be ready and willing to begin discussion on technical details.[157]

After consulting Churchill, Moyne informed Weizmann that the scheme would have to remain in cold storage, but might be reconsidered once more after a further three months.[158] Noticing the change in Moyne's tone since their meeting at the beginning of the month, and fearful of being compromised within the Zionist movement, Weizmann now pressed for a definite answer.[159]

The decision that Weizmann demanded could be taken only at Cabinet level. While Moyne himself considered the political objections to have receded since the previous February, Lyttelton had advised in August that political objections remained strong and that it would not be worth awakening Arab fears for the sake of a measure which would have little military value for Britain.[160] Moyne therefore proposed that the issue be decided solely on military grounds.[161] Agreeing with Moyne, the Foreign Office deemed it necessary to controvert Weizmann's assertions concerning the potential influence of American Jews on their country's war effort—a question on which Churchill was known to be sensitive. An internal minute shows an acute awareness of the potential vulnerability of American Jewry at that time:

> There is a considerable class of prosperous Jews [in the United States] which is aware of its unpopularity and is very alarmed at the Jews being denounced as warmongers ... There is just enough in the Hitler cry that America is being run by a Judean plutocracy to make the Administration anxious that American Jews, as Jews, should not be a leading war party ... the feelings of the American Jews should not be a first-rate consideration ...[162]

Moyne informed the Cabinet[163] that on purely military grounds the War Office now opposed the scheme, being doubtful of the military value of ten thousand Jews, and fearful of the repercussions in the Arab world. The Foreign Office was not opposed on political grounds—provided the public announcement reassured the Arabs that the force would not be used in the Middle East. But, continued Moyne, if this latter point were conceded, Weizmann might reject the whole project. Moyne himself agreed with Eden that it would have to be made quite clear from the outset that the Jewish Force would *not* be used in the Middle East.

The Cabinet decided against the formation of the Jewish Army, and Moyne duly informed Weizmann, again basing the Government's refusal on the supply problem, made more acute since London had undertaken large-scale assistance to Soviet Russia.[164] The Cabinet had however stressed the necessity to utilize Jewish military potential in the Middle East, and Moyne asked Weizmann to meet him to discuss 'various other possibilities'.

At their meeting on 23 October 1941, to which Weizmann brought Ben-Gurion, Moyne proposed to employ Jewish personnel as experts and technicians.[165] Weizmann turned down this idea as a substitute for a Jewish Army—experts had been supplied already, and would be in the future. For Weizmann, the only satisfactory alternative would be to organize existing Jewish companies in Palestine (the Buffs) with their own distinctive badge, under the Jewish name and flag. Ben-Gurion stated that the Jews regarded it as an insult to their racial pride that although they were organized in companies separately from the Arabs, they were not formed into larger Jewish units or given the status of a national force, and consequently the full extent of the Jewish war effort was obscured.

With the tide turning in favour of the British in the Middle East, Auchinleck's pressure for Jewish units subsided and traditional opposition to arming the Jews revived. Until this stage, MacMichael had played a relatively minor role during negotiations. But his warnings now placed the whole issue on a different level. The Jewish Army was seen by him as a sinister instrument which would one day be turned against the Mandatory itself:

> ... Situation foreseen by political Zionists is that by the end of the war they will have many thousands of Jews in Palestine trained to arms. Simultaneously HMG will be faced with the task of carrying out a policy regarding Palestine. If that

policy is not one commending itself to political Zionists (and nothing short of Palestine as a Jewish State will satisfy them) they are confident they will be able to defeat it because in the last resort no British Government would dream of taking extreme military measures against the Jews and nothing short of such measures will induce the Jews, organized and prepared as they will be, to give way ... Hence the present intensive campaign for a Jewish Army with Jewish emblems, insignia, etc ... [the] primary objects of political Zionists are thus clearly revealed as:
a) to obtain recognition for Jews as a State by their recognition of a 'national army',
b) to concentrate this army in Palestine in order that Jewish post-war demands may be backed by ultimate sanction of force ...[166]

This time, MacMichael's views fell on attentive ears at Whitehall.

vi. The Palestine Regiment

The next Jewish initiative came some six months later, on the eve of Rommel's second offensive in the Western Desert. Jewish appeals for the elementary right to self-defence in Palestine now reached a crescendo both in Palestine and in the United States. London was particularly worried about the campaign conducted in the United States, with its possible repercussions on Anglo-American relations.

The campaign for a Jewish Army there had first gained real momentum following Weizmann's public announcement of London's final rejection of the Army scheme.[167] Weizmann's confession of failure on 9 November 1941 had removed the curbs previously exercised by himself and the moderates in the Zionist movement. Shortly after Weizmann's announcement, a Jewish Army Committee was formed in New York, led by a nucleus of Revisionists. The Committee's campaign, conducted through full-page advertisements in leading American newspapers—to which prominent figures in American public life had been persuaded to lend their signatures—took the form of two demands: a) the demand for a greater mobilization of the manpower available in Palestine, and b) the demand for the formation of a Jewish Division composed of Jewish volunteers both from Palestine and the rest of the world. The campaign had been successful in its simple appeal that the many thousands of Jews anxious to fight and die in a war against Hitler were being deprived of that elementary right by His Majesty's Government.

The Revisionists' activities later prompted Eden to circulate a memorandum to the Cabinet to the effect that Zionist propaganda in the United States was responsible for increased tension in the Middle East, a situation exacerbated by the lack of caution of certain members of the Administration itself. Eden proposed that a formal warning be given to the American Administration with regards its support for Zionist propaganda.[168] But the Embassy at Washington doubted whether the American Administration would risk losing an appreciable section of the Jewish vote, or alienating influential Jewish groups, by attempting to curb the campaign.[169] On the contrary,

Weizmann himself, on a further visit to the United States, attempted to bring further pressure to bear on London by lobbying prominent members of the Administration.[170]

Thus the 'American dimension' had to be considered when Weizmann again approached the Foreign Office, in January 1942, to plead once more that those Jewish units already serving in Palestine be granted their own badge and insignia.[171] In April 1942 Shertok urged Auchinleck to allow the Palestine Buffs to be trained as fighting battalions, from which might be built a Jewish Division. He also requested an increase in recruiting into the Jewish Auxiliary Police, up to fifty thousand.[172] In reply, Auchinleck asked what forces were available in the Yishuv for the war effort.[173] Shertok gave a detailed reply on 19 May, but was informed by Auchinleck on 25 May that the issue involved some questions of high policy, and an authoritative answer could not be given before reference to London. On the day after Auchinleck's reply, Rommel began his offensive in the Western Desert, and Shertok never heard from Auchinleck again.

Auchinleck had in fact forwarded Shertok's information to London where, at the beginning of May 1942, the War Office—in conjunction with the Colonial Office—prepared a comprehensive scheme for a Palestine Regiment. The scheme was intended on the one hand to satisfy Zionist demands in Palestine and thus neutralize the publicity campaign in the United States; on the other hand, the regiment would facilitate the proper organization of all available forces in Palestine on the eve of the offensive in the Western Desert.[174] The proposed regiment was to consist of separate Jewish and Arab battalions, incorporating the companies of the Palestine Buffs. The insignia of the regiment would be common to both the Jewish and Arab battalions.

This draft was opposed by the Foreign Office, which did not believe that the scheme proposed would meet Jewish requirements.[175] The Foreign Office believed that the Jews would not be interested in 'Palestinian' battalions, but only in a Jewish fighting force serving under its own flag, which could be used later to support the argument that they were a nation on the same footing as other Allied nations. The Jews' next step would be to demand a distinctive badge for their own battalions, and then to demand that the Jews —who greatly outnumbered the Arabs—should be formed into a separate regiment. The Government would then be back where it had started, except that it would have taken one more step towards the formation of a Jewish Army.

The British retreat to El Alamein on 28 June 1942 gave added urgency to Zionist demands that the Yishuv be allowed maximum scope to organize for its self-defence. Once more, Weizmann made a personal appeal to Churchill:

... Today again, the Jews of Palestine are facing a period of supreme danger. It is not only the annihilation of our work but the actual physical existence of nearly

600,000 Jews in Palestine which is at stake ... if we go down in Palestine, we are entitled to go down fighting ... the refusal to grant this right will never be understood ...[176]

A further dimension now entered British calculations, after the Biltmore Conference in May 1942 (which demanded the establishment of a Jewish Commonwealth in all of Western Palestine—see next chapter) had divided the Zionist camp into 'moderates' and 'extremists'—at least in British eyes. Weizmann's message for Churchill was transmitted to London via the British Embassy at Washington, whence Halifax added his own comment and recommendations:

... The Revisionists and their 'Committee for a Jewish Army' set up a great agitation directed at the Prime Minister ... and Weizmann no doubt felt that he must also weigh in with an appeal of his own, if he was not to appear too moderate altogether. *Weizmann's moderation is of great value to us here and it is our impression that he is fighting a difficult battle.* His dignity and experience have had a steadying effect and have raised his prestige among Zionists; but moderation seldom appeals to Americans unless it produces visible results ... If, therefore, any concession in the direction of a Jewish Fighting Force should be contemplated, *we think it would be to our interest that the concession should be made to Dr Weizmann personally so that he can gain credit for it and show that modernation pays*.[177]

At Washington, Weizmann made further appeals to Halifax that London should recruit forty thousand more Jews in Palestine, and appoint Wingate to organize Jewish commandos.[178] Churchill was concerned at the possible repercussions in the United States resulting from a policy which he himself was condoning with some reluctance:

... The strength of opinion in the United States is very great, and we shall suffer in many ways there by indulging the British military authorities' and Colonial Office officials' bias in favour of the Arabs against the Jews. Now that these people are in direct danger, we should certainly give them a chance to defend themselves ... Wingate should not be put on one side, but given a fair chance and proper authority.[179]

This outburst did little to help the matter in hand, and Cranborne (Colonial Secretary, February–November 1942) was quick to rebut the accusations levelled at his own Department:

I could not for a moment accept the suggestion that the officials of the Colonial Office or the Colonial Service are anti-Semite, any more than I am myself. We are all engaged in carrying out a policy which Parliament approved. Zionist leaders have never accepted that policy, and have been engaged, quite frankly, in pressing for a Jewish Army as a step towards a Jewish State. This would lead to serious trouble, as well as being inconsistent with British policy. This does not mean that I would not do all in my power to give the Jews of Palestine means to defend themselves against Nazi invasion ...[180]

Cranborne's was a candid statement of the British dilemma—the reasonable probability that if they now helped the Jews in their current emergency, the forces thus trained would one day be used at the very least as a lever to propel British policy in a pro-Zionist direction.

At London's request, the situation was reviewed at Cairo.[181] At a conference especially called, it was agreed that while the fullest possible use should be made of Jewish manpower, it was essential that the British authorities—and not the Jewish Agency—should remain the judge of the way in which these men were employed, and retain full effective control of them. The Conference proposed that the Jewish Agency offer of ten thousand further recruits for the Palestine Buffs be accepted—at the rate of five hundred per month—from which would be formed a Palestine Regiment. The Jewish demand for ten thousand additional urban special police for the 'active defence' of Jewish settlements was rejected, on the grounds that the Yishuv was already so well armed and organized secretly that it was in no danger from any possible Arab rising. In the event of a German invasion, no residual Jewish force—even if armed—could have any effect on events. On the other hand, such a force would constitute a grave political menace, looking as it did to the Jewish Agency and those who controlled the Haganah rather than to British authorities. The Conference therefore agreed to raise only 1,500 additional Jewish rural special police. All these proposals precluded 'Jewish direction of the forces concerned, use of Jewish flags or insignia, or Jewish political objectives'.[182]

The War and Colonial Offices added the proviso that the Palestine Regiment should henceforth be given combat rather than static duties, a limitation that had been regarded by the Jews as humiliating.[183] Perhaps most important was the Department's proposal that the 'parity' principle now be abandoned. The role to be assigned the new regiment led to controversy between the Departments concerned (in particular with the Foreign Office). The Cabinet finally accepted the Colonial Office compromise that the announcement on the regiment should avoid all details of its duties. The Colonial Secretary's announcement in the Commons merely stated that 'normally the regiment will be employed in Palestine or adjacent countries for the defence of Palestine'.[184] The Zionists' request that Wingate be placed in command of the Jewish force was ruled out once and for all by the War Office, on the grounds of the latter's professed sympathy for Zionism.[185]

The vagueness of the Government announcement left ample room for the Middle East authorities to interpret the new scheme according to their own lights. The Jewish Agency was informed by the new GOC Palestine, General McConnell, that the role of the new Regiment would be similar to that of the existing companies of the Buffs, i.e. defence of vital points and the provision of local mobile forces.[186] The Jewish Agency was unable to reconcile this interpretation with their own view of the Commons announcement. Jewish apathy to the new force increased once its functions became known. The target figure of five hundred recruits per week was never reached apparently bearing out MacMichael's opinion that in fact there did not exist any large untapped sources of Jewish manpower in Palestine. Government hopes that the announcement of the regiment would allay agitation in Jewish circles proved unfounded.

Moreover, Auchinleck, engaged as he was with all his forces against Rommel, felt unable to equip the new battalions—as yet an unknown quantity —as front-line troops. The War Office accepted this argument, but attempted to salvage something of the political value of the regiment scheme by asking that at least it should be allowed to announce that combat duties for the new regiment were not ruled out, emphasizing the propaganda motive behind the scheme:

Object of Palestine Regiment was to sidetrack agitation for Jewish Army and unless we convince Jewish opinion here, in Palestine and in United States that we are giving Palestinian Jews a real opportunity to fight in the defence of Palestine we shall be not better off than before.[187]

The War Office request was considered at a meeting of the Middle East Council at Cairo.[188] The Minister of State, supported by his deputy, Lord Moyne, thought that the role of the regiment should be decided by the Middle East Command alone, solely according to military requirements. General Alexander[189] was strongly opposed to a Jewish force, on military grounds. He did not want any more separate armies—there were quite enough in the Middle East already. The equipment needed to establish the regiment as a front-line formation was anyway much more than could possibly be provided by the Middle East Command. Alexander did not wish to see in Palestine an independent, strong Jewish force which might start fighting the Arabs—although he admitted his need for all the skilled labour he could obtain. The fact that Jewish recruits were releasing British regular front-line troops for combat was in itself most important. The Council therefore advised the War Office to reject any proposal to alter the regiment's role.

The Secretary of State for War, Grigg, reported back to the Cabinet on the disappointing reception of the regiment scheme in Palestine.[190] It was agreed that he would make a statement in the Commons stressing the integral role which the regiment currently played in the defence of the Middle East. On 15 December 1942, after stressing the Government's appreciation of the anxiety of the Jewish communities throughout the world to ensure that their kinsmen in Palestine were afforded every opportunity for self-defence against possible Axis invasion, Grigg explained to the House of Commons that the regiment's duties must be related to Middle East defence requirements as a whole, and that a combat role in the future was not ruled out.[191] In reply to a question by Victor Cazalet, Grigg confirmed that the parity ruling would not be applied in the case of the regiment.[192]

vii. *The Jewish Brigade, 1944*

As the front receded from Palestine during the winter of 1942–3, relations between the Zionists and the military authorities in Palestine deteriorated. In January 1943 a Jewish battalion was shipped out of Palestine—in contravention of an assurance given in 1940 to the Jewish Agency that the Palestine Buffs would be employed solely in the defence of Palestine. The Jewish Agency rightly interpreted the move as political in intent, designed to weaken the Yishuv by removing its reservoir of trained soldiers.[193] In July 1943, a second battalion was shipped from Palestine, without the Jewish Agency being consulted first. Excessive sentences on Jewish arms-smugglers in September, and heavy-handed arms-searches of Jewish settlements during October–November 1943, brought public resentment to a peak. The Palestine Administration was warned that its actions against the Haganah might precipitate the very contingency they were intended to prevent—a Jewish revolt against the Mandatory. Shertok's warnings to the High Commissioner and to London caused Whitehall to intervene to prevent further army operations of the same kind. The Haganah remained unbroken, but it adopted henceforth a distinctly anti-British disposition.[194]

With the Allied invasion of Europe from Italy in September 1943, the question of a Jewish fighting force—dormant for nearly a year—was again discussed in Zionist councils.[195] Shertok pressed the scheme again at a meeting of Zionist leaders in London in February 1944. The political value of such a force had not been lost sight of. Moreover, there could not be the same objections to a Jewish army in Europe as to one serving in the Middle East. Shertok stressed the West's moral obligation to the Jews, for whose sufferings there existed a great reservoir of sympathy:

> ... This is a politico-moral question, and not a military-technical one. We have got to bring it before the highest authorities as a moral obligation of the democratic world to the stricken Jew ...[196]

On 28 March 1944, Weizmann wrote to both Churchill and Grigg pleading for the formation of a Jewish fighting force within the British Army, to participate in the liberation of Europe.[197] Weizmann observed that concern for Arab objections would not be relevant to the European theatre of operations.

The War Office again rejected the Zionist proposal.[198] From the purely military point of view there would be great difficulty in replacing the three Jewish battalions then serving in Palestine, Egypt and Cyrenaica; a Jewish force would need some six to twelve months to train, whereas it was hoped that Germany would be defeated by the beginning of 1945; there was little surplus manpower in Palestine, and it was doubtful whether the Jewish Agency would be able even to raise the recruits required; there remained also the genuine shortage of equipment. But most important, as before, were the political considerations. It was currently estimated that the Haganah had a potential strength of 100,000 men, of whom some 25,000 were armed, first-line troops. The War Office treated Weizmann's proposal as a ruse whereby the Zionists would receive military training at British expense, with the prospect that if the British Government failed later on to establish in Palestine a Jewish National Home, that very same force would establish a *fait accompli* in Palestine while British Forces were still engaged in operations against Japan.

In Cabinet, Churchill bowed to War Office objections, and acquiesced in the rejection of the Jewish Division scheme. But he insisted on an examination of the possibility of mobilizing a Jewish Brigade Group.[199] This time, Churchill would not tolerate departmental procrastination:

... When the War Office say they will carefully examine a thing, they mean they will do it in. The matter must be set down for an early meeting of the War Cabinet ...[200]

On the following day Weizmann made a specific appeal to Churchill that the 24,000 Palestinian Jews who had so far volunteered for military service be allowed to form a division of their own, carrying their own flag—with the Star of David—on to the European battlefield.[201]

The War Office encountered opposition from those commanders in the field who would be required to implement the scheme. General Paget feared that the return of even a brigade to Palestine after the war might lead immediately to widespread disturbances; General Wilson thought the project should be on a sufficiently long-term basis to allow new Jewish recruits to be mobilized to replace those selected for the Brigade Group, *before* its formation.[202] In face of Prime Ministerial pressure, the War Office was forced to ignore warnings as to possible political consequences, although it did insist that the Jewish Agency undertake to find 350 officers and 6,500 other ranks to replace those units intended for the Brigade. The War Office stipulated further that the Brigade be made available for service in any theatre of war, and that its demobilization be governed entirely by military considerations. Those Jews enlisted outside Palestine would not qualify automatically for residence in Palestine, and there should be no separate Jewish flag.

Churchill conceded most of the War Office conditions, except for that concerning the flag. He discussed this issue personally with the King, and obtained the latter's assent. Churchill instructed the War Office to commission Dr Weizmann to produce a design,[203] and urged that the Brigade be formed as soon as possible and dispatched to Italy.[204] But the War Office adhered to its precondition that the Government retain the right to demobilize and disperse the Brigade outside Palestine when the time came,[205] and the issue had to be brought to Cabinet once more.[206]

The Cabinet agreed that there should be no limitation on the service of the Brigade, although Churchill intimated that it would not serve in the Far East. This stipulation would have to be dealt with in a confidential letter, as any specific public announcement on this point might prove embarrassing to the United States. Churchill agreed also that the Brigade would neither serve nor be demobilized in Palestine. The Cabinet yielded to Churchill with regard to the flag.

It remained only to attain the consent of Roosevelt, which was received by the end of the month.[207] The Cabinet endorsed the design for the flag proposed by the Jewish Agency on 4 September, and on 18 September 1944 drafted a press announcement for the next day.[208]

It had taken the Jewish Agency five years to obtain nominal recognition of the Jewish war effort. In the twilight of the European war, Churchill—defeated in his efforts to satisfy Jewish aspirations to self-defence in Palestine—succeeded in affording the Jews a minor role (however important to the Jews themselves) in the final operations against their oppressors. The decision of September 1944, pushed through against universal Departmental opposition, was characterized by the determination of a Prime Minister long frustrated in his desire to effect some concrete expression of his deeply rooted sympathy for the Jewish people and the Zionist cause.

The Jewish Brigade saw action in Italy and Germany, and after the war it did valuable work among Jewish Displaced Persons. Many of its personnel went on to form the cadres of 'Tzahal', Israel's defence forces. But the fact that Jews fought in a separate unit, under their own chosen national insignia, did not endow the Jewish nation with added political punch at the post-war peace councils. The Jews reaped military (albeit curtailed by the British) rather than political fruits from their contributions to the Allied war effort.

7
Zionist Leadership in Crisis

i. The machinery of Zionism

The primary function of Palestine, stated the Zionists' platform, was to solve the 'Jewish Problem' by reconstituting the Jewish National Home in its ancestral homeland.[1] This would be effected once the Jews became a majority in Palestine and were able to determine the form of its government. In order to avoid arousing Arab fears, Zionist spokesmen refrained from making this claim openly, although in effect this doctrine never ceased to guide Zionist strategy. From the inception of the Mandate, faith in the ultimate establishment of a Jewish State led the Zionists to insist on the management of their own affairs. For this purpose they created administrative machinery which, since it was not sovereign, yet quasi-governmental, developed under the Mandate into an 'imperium in imperio'.[2]

A special relationship was created between the National Home and the Jewish Diaspora. Zionist claims did not base themselves upon the community currently resident in Palestine, but rather on the millions of Diaspora Jews who would eventually settle there. The apparatus for the participation of world Jewry in Palestinian affairs was in the Zionist Organization and the Jewish Agency. This division, or duplicity of policy-making, would continue until the Yishuv attained its ultimate goal, statehood.

Under the Mandate the Zionist Organization, according to article 4 of the Mandate, was alone made responsible for the administration of the National Home. The President of the World Zionist Organization, Dr Chaim Weizmann, sat in London, whence he directed the affairs of the Jewish National Home for the first eleven years of the organization's existence, until 1931, when he resigned from office following a vote of no confidence at the 17th Zionist Congress. It was an anomaly that Diaspora leaders, sitting in a western capital thousands of miles away from Palestine, should direct the affairs of their brethren, provincial pioneers who, separated by a physical and mental divide from their mentors, were translating their diplomacy into a new reality.

Weizmann's political reputation and international prestige developed while the future leaders of Zionism and Israel were still immersed in the formidable problems of developing from nothing a Jewish workers' economy in Palestine. Weizmann's own position in the Zionist movement rested on his reputed contribution to the diplomatic campaign which had attained for the Zionist movement the Balfour Declaration.[3] As such, and for as long as London interpreted the 1917 Declaration in a positive fashion, Weizmann was the undisputed leader, Zionism's natural choice for its liaison with the Mandatory power.[4] The Yishuv's tendency to by-pass an often hostile Administration in Palestine by negotiating directly with London served to strengthen Weizmann's position—but thereby heavily mortgaged his career to the continued productive co-operation between Zionism and the Mandatory.

During Weizmann's absence from the Zionist helm (1931–35), labour leaders in Palestine completed a process of asserting control over the Movement. At the Zionist Congress held in Prague in 1933, the Labour parties identified with the *Histadruth* (Trade Union Federation), led by *Mapai*, the party headed by Ben-Gurion, gained 138 of the 318 seats and a majority on the Jewish Agency Executive.[5] In 1935, Ben-Gurion became Chairman of the Agency Executive, and other members of Mapai, Shertok and Kaplan, became heads of the Agency's Political Department and Treasury respectively.

Having secured the key portfolios on the Agency Executive, the leaders of Mapai became world Zionist leaders overnight, in addition to their roles as political partisans in Palestine itself. Weizmann and his London circle would now have to give greater consideration to their views and, on occasion, take them along to his interviews in Whitehall and Downing Street. Ben-Gurion, little known outside the context of the Palestinian labour movement until 1933, now emerged as the leader of political Zionism in Palestine, and was to use his new position as Chairman of the Agency Executive as a power-base from which to challenge Weizmann's leadership of the world movement.[6]

iii. Weizmann—symbol of the London–Jerusalem Axis

So long as Jerusalem retained its faith in the partnership with the Mandatory, Weizmann remained the undisputed chief negotiator in London. But during the critical period preceding World War Two, the Jerusalem branch of the Executive began to see its mission as the close surveillance of Weizmann, in order to ensure his strict adherence to orthodoxy. As Shertok put it:

> As for Weizmann, we knew his weakness. That was one of the reasons we thought it vital that our people should be next to him in London. That was the reason why Ben-Gurion had to return there immediately ...[7]

It seems that as early as 1936 Ben-Gurion considered ousting Weizmann from the leadership of the movement, but was restrained by his colleagues, who dreaded both the internal and external repercussions of such a move.[8] But whatever their reservations about Weizmann's political leanings, the Palestinians were in need of his diplomatic skills, to which even a veteran member of the House of Lords had occasion to pay tribute:

> ... absolutely no one like him: his power and personality in dealing with individuals and the manner in which he controls affairs in this country is unrivalled ...[9]

But the Palestinian Jews could not help differing with Weizmann on Zionism's ultimate goals, or the methods by which to attain them. When Weizmann strayed from the Jerusalem 'line', he would be branded Anglophile. In 1936, he wrote to a confidant: '... they (the Actions Committee) will argue with me thinking I am the Mandatory Power. In due course I shall be called a traitor ...'[10]

Some Palestinian leaders were aware that their 'supervision' of Weizmann was not subtle enough. Again, Shertok seems to have been concerned about possible negative repercussions:

... Weizmann thinks the initiative is not in his hands, but in Jerusalem ... He argues that two types of telegram come from Jerusalem; either we tell him that such and such a danger is pending and we propose he takes such and such steps – in fact, a complete programme of action. That arouses in him an internal opposition, and he doesn't do what he is supposed to do ... or telegrams come to the effect that what he is about to do will spoil things ... *we have to learn how to treat Weizmann*, we have to encourage him so that he should feel he has some freedom.[11]

But the gap between Weizmann and his Palestinian colleagues was intrinsically unbridgeable.[12] Weizmann felt, and was indeed held to be, personally responsible for the political setback embodied in the White Paper of 1939. Yet until 1941 the main mission of Zionist diplomacy remained the exertion of pressure on Whitehall (primarily for the establishment of a Jewish military force), with Weizmann its indispensable instrument. When the Zionists' campaign for a Jewish Division ended in public failure in November 1941, Jerusalem turned from Great Britain to the United States, and Ben-Gurion initiated a series of frontal attempts to depose Weizmann from the leadership of the Zionist movement.

That this struggle ensued on a personal level was due partly to the circumstances in which the Zionist Movement found itself during the war, when the German conquest of Europe altered beyond recognition the complexion of the Movement represented by the delegates to the last Zionist Congress, held at Geneva in August 1939. The elected—those that had survived—were without an electorate. This demographic metamorphosis was described by Weizmann:

There is one large community in the Americas; a few small communities in the British Empire; and an important community in Palestine which, though numerically much smaller than the American, differs from it in quality and is in many respects superior to it. But in spite of the obvious differences, these two communities have a great deal in common ... both are young and without traditions; both are more or less provincial; both are excitable, and apt to overplay their hands. In the past this lack of balance has always been counteracted by the Europeans, who had traditions, who were inured to suffering, and who with it had learned patience ...[13]

The highest political authority in the Movement during the war remained the Smaller Actions Committee, composed of the thirty or so residents in

Palestine nominated by the parties represented at the 1939 Congress according to their numerical strength then. Yet, with the paralysis of the great centres of Jewry in Europe during the war, the centre of gravity of the Movement moved, especially with the Americans' entry into the war, to the United States. It was Ben-Gurion's mistake to believe that he could extrapolate his prestige and tactics inside the Yishuv on to the plane of world Zionism, firstly in London, and then in New York.

It is appropriate at this point to examine the ideological differences, such as they were, that lay behind the clash between Weizmann and Ben-Gurion.

iii. Ben-Gurion—advocate of the rift with Britain

The Zionists regarded the 1939 White Paper as a breach of the articles of the Mandate, and as such it annulled in their eyes the *de jure* legitimacy of British rule in Palestine. After 1939, one school of thought in Zionism—that of Weizmann—moved away from the concept of a National Home under British Mandate, towards the conception of Jewish independence, in a State which might take its place either in an Arab Federation or perhaps as a Dominion within the British Empire. It was in this sense that Weizmann interpreted the Biltmore programme of 1942. Typifying this approach was Weizmann's belief in the Philby plan, whereby a Jewish State would be established in the whole of Palestine west of the River Jordan, and Palestine's Arabs resettled in neighbouring Arab countries—all under British and American aegis. Weizmann, and certain officials at the State Department, undoubtedly hoped that he would be able to repeat the success he had enjoyed with the Emir Feisal[14] in 1919, this time with the Hashemites' successor, Ibn Saud.

Neither Ben-Gurion nor his colleagues entertained such illusions. Prior to the war, Ben-Gurion remained true to two traditional alternatives—either partition, or a bi-national regime within the mandatory borders of Palestine.[15] Ben-Gurion made his mental break with Britain after the promulgation of the 1939 White Paper. This break became final once it became apparent that not even the Churchill Government would repeal the White Paper during the war—nor even allow the Yishuv to mobilize for its own defence.

The promulgation of the Land Laws in February 1940 provoked bitter dissension within the Agency Executive at Jerusalem. Ben-Gurion proposed that the fight against the White Paper take precedence over all else, arguing that only force would bring London to rescind its policy—'the only hope for Zionism is if it becomes a fighting Zionism, there is no future for a talking Zionism'.[16] But the great majority of his colleagues, Shertok included, rejected a course of conflict with Britain during its mortal struggle against Germany. Ben-Gurion's colleagues warned that such a policy would not be understood by world opinion, and the Yishuv would destroy itself in the process.[17]

On 29 February 1940 Ben-Gurion resigned as chairman of the Agency

Executive, without prior warning. His resignation was not accepted. In fact, Ben-Gurion never ceased to attend Executive meetings and in April 1940 was induced to withdraw his resignation.[18]

With the entry of Italy into the war in June 1940 Palestine became a potential theatre of war, and Ben-Gurion's line changed with the circumstances, to one of co-operation with Britain in their common struggle. Long-term solutions—whether there was to be a Jewish State in a part, or in the whole of Palestine—must take second priority to the organization of the Yishuv in its self-defence, and the final defeat of Hitler.[19] The Zionists' secret radio transmitter (*Kol Israel*—the Voice of Israel) made its last broadcast on 11 June, with a call to the Yishuv to suspend its struggle with Britain over the White Paper and to pool all its resources to defend Palestine.[20] Ben-Gurion anticipated favourable changes on the part of the new Government in London, headed by Zionism's long-standing friend, Winston Churchill.

Ben-Gurion blamed Weizmann for the failure of the Jewish Army negotiations. He blamed him for not having sufficiently emphasized the need for Jewish units in Palestine, and claimed later that Weizmann had not consulted him enough before negotiations. He also accused Weizmann of being afraid to exploit the full publicity value of the issue.[21]

If Weizmann remained inhibited in his actions and utterances against the Government, it was largely because Churchill himself was repeatedly reassuring him that once the war was over he would implement in Palestine a solution favourable to the Zionists. Weizmann was embarrassed particularly during his visits to the United States by Revisionist publicity campaigns for a Jewish Army, which threatened the harmony of Anglo-American relations. It was this identification with Great Britain which was attacked by Ben-Gurion, and about which Weizmann, a naturalized citizen who had adopted Britain as his home, was most sensitive, as may be seen from the following extract from his letter to an American colleague:

... as a British subject I have to be extremely careful not to contribute to the strain in Anglo-American relations ... Perhaps Ben-Gurion does not feel it, but I do, chiefly for one good reason: we have one great friend in England, the Prime Minister. Just as you would be extremely careful not to alienate the sympathies of the President, I find myself, especially on foreign soil, in an extremely delicate position ...[22]

The letter illustrates also Weizmann's tendency to rely on Western statesmen, rather than on Zionist action, to gain a Jewish State in Palestine.

Spellbound by the mammoth scale of American war preparations, and by the relatively untapped resources of the five-million-strong American Jewish community, during his stay in the United States during the winter of 1940–41, Ben-Gurion returned to Palestine in February 1941 with his own version of Weizmann's Jewish State programme. Prior to his departure, Ben-Gurion in fact published his views in the internal organ of the American Zionist Organization, *New Palestine*.[23] Ben-Gurion's central thesis was that Palestine must be rendered capable of receiving millions of Jews through its establishment as a Jewish Commonwealth. Ben-Gurion did not expect the immediate abolition of the White Paper, but he did expect the White Paper policy to be put into 'deep freeze' for the duration of the war. After the war, the Jewish people must be given an opportunity to have and govern their own land, in Palestine. No foreign power, however friendly to Zionism, would in his opinion be willing to carry out such a programme.[24]

Like Weizmann, Ben-Gurion did not rule out adherence of the Jewish State to an Arab Federation. But, as in the case of partition, Zionist acceptance of a new concept preceded its willingness to publicly adopt a new programme. Upon his return to Jerusalem, Ben-Gurion brought his ideas before the Agency Executive. His new concept was accepted in principle, although the words 'Jewish State' were exchanged for the milder-sounding 'Jewish régime'. Furthermore, the Executive thought that the time was not yet ripe for publication of the new platform, and the Jewish public would need to be prepared first.[25]

Ben-Gurion returned to London during the summer of 1941, before continuing in the winter to the United States. During his stay in London, relations between him and Weizmann deteriorated further over the Jewish Army negotiations. Ben-Gurion's demand that he should accompany Weizmann to all his meetings with British officials—regarded by Weizmann as improper, and in effect a vote of no confidence in his leadership—was flatly rejected. Had Weizmann accepted Ben-Gurion's dictate, it would have meant submission to the directives of the Agency at Jerusalem, and of its Chairman, Ben-Gurion. After twenty years of unchallenged, productive leadership Weizmann's ego did not take criticism or competition lightly.[26] In London he was surrounded by an entourage of like-minded associates. Ben-Gurion therefore preferred to delay their open confrontation until they both met in the United States during the summer of 1942.

Most of the Zionist forces in the United States were concentrated in the American Zionist Emergency Council, where vital roles were played by men close to Weizmann in approach—Rabbi Dr Stephen Wise, Nahum Goldmann, Louis Lipsky[27] and others. In January 1942, in an article in the prestigious *Foreign Affairs*, Weizmann made the first *public* Zionist demand for a Jewish Commonwealth in the whole of Western Palestine. Weizmann laid stress also on the millions of refugees who would need to make their new home in Palestine after the war.

At the beginning of 1942 Meyer Weisgal, one of Weizmann's closest aides, agreed to supervise arrangements for an American Zionist Conference to determine the goals of Zionism and to mobilize American Zionists for extensive political and fund-raising activity. The programme and draft resolutions for the Conference, held at the Biltmore Hotel in New York in

May 1942, were prepared in their essentials by Weisgal, who based his ideas on Weizmann's article. The Biltmore Programme, as adopted by the Conference, contained three main provisions: a) that Palestine be opened to immigration; b) that the Jewish Agency be vested with control of immigration and with the authority necessary for developing the country; and c) that after the war Palestine be established as a Jewish Commonwealth integrated in the structure of the new democratic world.[28]

Ben-Gurion's public differences with Weizmann were later to centre on the orthodox interpretation of Biltmore. Initially, Biltmore remained only a local resolution of American Zionists that did not necessarily bind the world movement. Until virtually the eve of his departure from the United States, Ben-Gurion gave first priority to the Jewish Army issue. It was on the grounds of Weizmann's failure in this field that Ben-Gurion now challenged the former's right to lead the Movement.

iv. Ben-Gurion challenges Weizmann's leadership

Shortly after the Biltmore Conference, Ben-Gurion wrote to Weizmann giving him clear warning, for the first time, of the 'constitutional consequences' of not co-operating fully with himself:

Since you came here you have acted entirely on your own ... I do not think that this is in the best interests of our movement, not merely because our Constitution does not authorize you to act in this way. I wish I were convinced that you could conduct our political affairs and guide the movement alone. I am sorry to say that I am not, and it seems to me that some of the things you have said and done so far are not very helpful to our cause ... unless the Executive and the Emergency Committee with your wholehearted support can assure the necessary and united action, I really don't see how our work can properly be done, or what use I can be here, or how I can share in the responsibility.[29]

Weizmann professed ignorance of the charges levelled at him,[30] and put them down to 'the result of a temporary mood, dictated not by calm judgement but rather by an imaginary grievance caused undoubtedly by the many hearthbreaking disappointments which all of us must face in this crucial hour'. Weizmann expressed his conviction that Ben-Gurion might be of more use to Zionism in Palestine than in the United States, and if anything it had been Ben-Gurion himself, by his own absences from meetings, who had been unco-operative.

Ben-Gurion referred the issue to Dr Wise, asking him to convene an informal meeting of American Zionist leaders and members of the Jewish Agency Executive then in the United States, in order to discuss Weizmann's leadership.[31] With Weizmann's acceptance of the gauntlet thrown down by Ben-Gurion,[32] American Zionism was being asked to chose between the two leaders—an impossible choice, upon which in any case no American Zionist body was competent or authorized to decide.

Before the meeting could be arranged, the fall of Tobruk (on 21 June) and the immediate threat to Palestine itself injected a new sense of urgency into Zionist affairs. Despite Wise's request,[33] Ben-Gurion did not agree to postpone the 'showdown'.

At their meeting,[34] Ben-Gurion accused Weizmann of having negotiated the Army scheme, as indeed other Zionist affairs, on his own, without consulting his colleagues. He expressed concern at Weizmann's inability to say 'no' to an Englishman, and at Weizmann's habit of reporting regularly on his activities to the British Ambassador in Washington. Ben-Gurion proposed the creation of adequate machinery to ensure that Weizmann never negotiate alone again.

These tactless remarks undoubtedly upset the emotional balance of the ageing leader (now almost 68 years old) whom recurring illness and family loss had aged prematurely. Weizmann reacted sharply to and rejected the humiliating demand that he be placed under constant supervision:

If in most cases I choose to see people alone, or sometimes go with another, that must be left to my discretion. *There is no constitutional law to follow the prescription of Ben-Gurion.*[35]

Weizmann warned that if Ben-Gurion's views were those of the Jerusalem Executive, he would resign. He would not be subject to 'the particular strictures or whims of a man, or men, who are trying to frame up a case out of imaginary grievances for political assassination'.

Wise tried to pacify the parties, and asked Weizmann to strike from the minutes his remarks about 'political assassination'. But warnings against the dangers of internal conflict were of no avail and Ben-Gurion, sensing that the meeting was turning against him, walked out in a huff.[36]

Weizmann now concurred with Wise's proposal for the establishment in New York of an office of the World Zionist Executive, distinct from the faction-ridden Zionist Emergency Council. Weizmann wished to concentrate in this office—which he himself intended to run—all the authority of the World Zionist Movement. Weizmann proposed also that a considerable fund be placed at his disposal, to be disbursed at his own discretion, without the usual reference to committees and sub-committees. Advance knowledge of Weizmann's plans may have prompted Ben-Gurion to bring the leadership crisis to a head.[37]

The confrontation seems to have thrown all Weizmann's plans into the melting-pot. A consensus was apparently reached at a further meeting between the two,[38] yet Ben-Gurion failed to turn up for a third, conclusive meeting simply because it was scheduled to be held at Weizmann's private office rather than on the neutral ground of the Emergency Committee office.

Many of Weizmann's colleagues were concerned at the effect upon him of the conflict with Ben-Gurion. In August, he received official notice that his pilot son Michael—missing on a mission since the previous February—

must be presumed dead. This, on top of the trials and demands of his stay in New York, brought about a further breakdown in health. Weizmann was hospitalized in New York for two weeks at the end of August, after which he went for two months' convalescence to the country. His close aide and confidant Weisgal was concerned that he might abandon his Zionist work.[39]

As one commentator has put it, a statesman remains a symbol of an attitude long after the attitude has passed away.[40] Weizmann's career traversed two political eras, and the 'elder statesman' was unable to comprehend, let alone adjust to the contrasting demands of an inevitable conflict with Britain. Whereas his diplomatic skills and prestige remained at a premium during the war years, Weizmann's credit within the Yishuv was eroded by the failures of 1939 and 1941, and was to be destroyed completely by the disillusion with the post-war Labour Government's policy, as represented by Ernest Bevin. From the Zionist viewpoint, Weizmann's continued leadership would have diminished the very credibility of the Yishuv's determination to fight. Meanwhile, Weizmann was tantalized by the hints and assurances of British statesmen regarding the 'rosy' post-war period. It was perhaps less painful for him to indulge in illusory day-dreams than to reject the premises upon which a lifetime's diplomacy had been based.

Weizmann was undoubtedly at times closer in outlook to the British Establishment than to his Palestinian colleagues. Despite his denials, he was in the habit of reporting back to Ambassador Halifax, perhaps seeking British support for his own moderation, when recalling his own clashes with Ben-Gurion. If this was his intention, he gained the full co-operation of the Ambassador:

Our latest information suggests that Ben-Gurion wishes to return to Palestine principally in order to obtain increased influence for himself from the Zionist Executive in Jerusalem as against Weizmann whom he regards as having 'appeased' HMG too much. His (BG's) plan is to return to the United States after a brief visit, in order to try and interest the United States War Department in the creation of a Jewish Fighting Force, leaving Weizmann hopelessly negotiating with the British. *Weizmann told me today that Ben-Gurion had been pretty difficult with him and Weizmann, I have no doubt, would be glad to get him away.*[41]

Ironically it was the very attack by Ben-Gurion on Weizmann's pro-British tendencies, and the split of the Zionist camp into moderates and activists, which would revive Weizmann's value for London. During Weizmann's convalescence, Ben-Gurion made a last attempt to arraign him, in his absence.[42] Ben-Gurion wanted Wise and a small group of American Zionist leaders to hear his own proposals regarding future policy. Wise refused to attend any but a formal meeting of the Emergency Committee. He deplored the fact that Ben-Gurion should wish at a time when Weizmann was unable to defend himself, to reopen the issue before a group which would have no authority to do anything more than just listen. Wise reminded Ben-Gurion that even the Jerusalem Executive had no authority to pass judgement upon the President of the World Zionist Organization. Wise asserted confidently that the only competent body, the full Actions Committee, would, if convened, reject Ben-Gurion's charges out of hand.

On 18 September 1942, Ben-Gurion left New York by air for Palestine. Having failed to induce Wise to call a meeting, Ben-Gurion himself convened a few of the Office Committee of the Emergency Committee.[43] He informed the gathering that both at the Jerusalem Executive and at the Actions Committee meetings he would be demanding Weizmann's resignation. With the exception of Robert Szold,[44] the meeting was solidly against Ben-Gurion. At the same time, Ben-Gurion attacked Weizmann's political philosophy. Although in January Weizmann had estimated that two million Jewish refugees would seek a home in Palestine after the war, he had not determined any particular time-scale—he seemed to be willing to consider an annual target of a hundred thousand, but regarded Ben-Gurion's conception of a one-time transfer of two millions as 'sheer fantasy'. Ben-Gurion attacked the Weizmannist 'gradualist' school. After the war, the Movement would need to obtain 'Governmental support for a mass immigration or transfer of perhaps two million Jews in one great operation'.[45]

On his return to Jerusalem, Ben-Gurion stressed that the transfer of the two millions would not only solve the problem of the refugees themselves, but in the process would transform the Yishuv from a minority into a majority.[46]

But Weizmann had not intended to revolutionize Zionism at the Biltmore Hotel. The vague wording of the resolutions suited Weizmann's goal—the formulation of a broad political platform suited to the American arena, from which could be negotiated any solution offering mass immigration and settlement in Palestine, whether via partition or as part of a Middle Eastern Federation. In either of these, the link with Britain remained a vital feature of Weizmann's philosophy. Ben-Gurion had now introduced into the formula a specific meaning not originally intended. Since it was obvious that Britain would never contemplate the scheme now adumbrated by Ben-Gurion the latter's proposals were, at least in their implication, if not overtly, an attack on the Weizmannist doctrine of co-operation with London.

Weizmann, in a letter to his close friend, 'Baffy' Dugdale, contemptuously treated Ben-Gurion's interpretation as demagogic political manoeuvering:

... It [the Biltmore Declaration] has become, so far as I can see, a new Decalogue, a new Basle programme,[47] and one would have thought that it has emerged out of deliberations which occupied months of serious study ... it is nothing of the kind. The Biltmore Declaration is just a resolution, like the hundred and one resolutions usually passed at great meetings in this country. It embodied, in somewhat solemn terms, the chief points as laid down in my article in the *Foreign Affairs*. But Ben-Gurion, after his stay here of eight or nine months, had absolutely nothing to show by way of achievement, and so he stuck on to the Biltmore Resolution, more or less conveying the idea that it is the triumph of his policy as against my moderate formulation of the same aims . . .[48]

Yet, however utopian it may have sounded at the time, Ben-Gurion's version of the Biltmore programme was responsible for converting a local American resolution into a prophetic, even Messianic, slogan for the whole Zionist movement. Unlike Weizmann, Ben-Gurion grasped that the Yishuv could never develop freely under Mandatory rule and that sooner or later Zionism would have to break with London. This remained true even after published details of the Holocaust made it evident that the millions of Jews on whose behalf the demand for a Jewish State was being made had not in fact survived the war. The rupture between Zionism and the Mandatory was delayed only by the greater exigencies of the common war effort against Nazism.

Thus, during the autumn of 1942, Ben-Gurion gave Zionism its ideological lead. While London embarked upon further exploration of partition, leaving Weizmann waiting in eager anticipation in the wings, Ben-Gurion ploughed Palestine in a political campaign to win over the Yishuv to his own interpretation of Biltmore, with all its consequences. His single-minded determination eventually swamped the initial opposition of his own colleagues, who until now had shied away from the idea of open revolt against the British.[49] As Weizmann had been the determining influence in Zionism at the inception of the Mandate, so it would be Ben-Gurion who would be the architect of the break with the Mandate and the establishment of the Jewish State, Israel.

Weizmann ostensibly maintained his authority in the United States, consulting there with an Executive composed solely of American Zionists. Thus, during the period when London began a reassessment of the White Paper policy, the Zionist movement suffered from 'lack of co-ordinated authority, duplication and confusion'.[50] The British authorities seemed more aware of inner Zionist dissension than the rank and file of the movement itself. The following extract of a speech by Ben-Gurion reached Whitehall via British Intelligence:

. . . during the past two years he [Weizmann] has been hesitant on the subject of our maximum demands. He considers that there are tremendous difficulties facing us in America, England and Palestine. He is an old man who has suffered much through the death of his son, and he would like to live to see the creation of a Jewish State. His political activity today, therefore, is still based on the old Partition Plan, and in this lies our difference of opinion. I see the same difficulties as he does, but he has lost all personal feelings for the Yishuv. He is not impregnated with the Zionist ideals of our Jewish youth in Palestine. He sees problems where we see facts . . .[51]

There is circumstantial evidence at least that the revival of partition was, in part, a British attempt to sustain Weizmann at the head of the Zionist movement. In November 1943, Smuts told Weizmann that Churchill was thinking of partition, and that the Government wanted to retain his (Weizmann's) leadership.[52] Halifax pleaded repeatedly that any concessions made to the Zionists should be made to Weizmann personally, in order to strengthen his position.[53]

At the beginning of 1943, Ben-Gurion elaborated on his objections to Weizmann's continued leadership in a long memorandum presented to the Agency Executive.[54] The document was little more than a personal slander, with hardly a word on Weizmann's past achievements. Any achievements of the Zionist movement had been attained because 'Weizmann had never had a chance to speak with anyone by himself or to do anything on his own opinion'. Weizmann, according to Ben-Gurion, had no talent for talking on concrete issues, but only for 'after-dinner' talk on abstractions, and Weizmann alone, apparently, was the one jeopardizing the Zionist cause in the United States. Once again, Ben-Gurion threatened resignation should he discover that decisive negotiations were being conducted by Weizmann himself on behalf of the Executive.

The Jerusalem Executive determined to try to settle the conflict before Weizmann returned to London and possibly to further negotiations. In March 1943, Shertok went to New York. On good personal terms with Weizmann, Shertok was able to explain calmly the 'constitutional' side of the issue.[55] He informed Weizmann that as President of the World Zionist Organization he did not have the authority to organize his own Political Department. Weizmann retorted that all his own efforts to organize such a political instrument during the previous eight months had failed, and that the Agency's vacillations were severely hampering political work. Added to this, the demoralization and undermining of authority brought about by Ben-Gurion had created a situation in which Weizmann had found it intolerable and impossible to continue. Consequently, he asked Shertok to have the Agency relieve him of all his responsibilities for political work.[56]

As with Ben-Gurion's resignation of 1941, we hear no more of Weizmann's in 1943—perhaps because on his return to London Weizmann was immediately given high hopes that a new partition plan was brewing. Weizmann in turn challenged Jerusalem's right to carry on with its own policies regardless—'a form of isolationism which fails to take into account the fact that what happens in Palestine affects the whole of world Jewry and the hopes of thousands of Jews to make Palestine their home'.[57] The dispute over sovereignty between the Yishuv and the Diaspora was irresolvable within the framework of the Zionist constitution then in existence. It would be resolved finally only with the assumption of full sovereign rights by the first Government of Israel.

Shertok's report back to Jerusalem confirmed in substance Ben-Gurion's views on Weizmann, even if it was tinged with Shertok's own patronizing sympathy.[58] The danger signals were clear for the British Government, which once more obtained a report of Shertok's 'secret' speech:

I met Dr Weizmann. I hardly recognized him. He is much older. His intensive scientific work and sorrow over the loss of his son depressed him so much that he had a nervous breakdown and was ordered away to the hills for a rest ... we cannot ignore him, however. His influence among Jews and Gentiles is strong and his scientific achievements may be able to help us in our aims. He has one big fault; he can easily be influenced. He is in complete agreement with the Biltmore Resolutions, but he cannot forget his Partition Plan. If we were given any part of Palestine for a Jewish State I think he would accept it. Those close to him, including Louis Lipsky, told me that he dreams of being the President of an independent Jewish State and that he is ready to concede much if his dream can be realized. Although he agrees with the terms of the Biltmore resolutions, he believes them far removed from any chance of being realized. I think he suffers from an inferiority complex as a result of his observance of British policy in Palestine ... His personal opinion is that the Biltmore resolutions should be completely revised, so that Britain will be able to do something for us and so that the Arabs will be pacified ...[59]

At the end of June 1943, Weizmann returned from the United States to London. Ben-Gurion warned that he would resign if Weizmann continued his political activity in London.[60] The crisis was delayed throughout the summer of 1943 by a promise to Ben-Gurion that his colleagues would ensure that a 'clarification' took place soon in Jerusalem. Yet Weizmann did not intend to change his mind about appearing 'in the dock' at Jerusalem:

... (he) Ben-Gurion attacked me in New York for my sins in London, choosing for his battleground a place where there was no one else from London who could either confirm or refute what I had to say. Now he wants me to come to Palestine, where he will attack me for sins committed in America—again in a place where there will be nobody from America who can join in the discussion.[61]

On 26 October 1943, without prior warning, Ben-Gurion resigned yet again from the Executive of the Jewish Agency.[62] Ben-Gurion, believing himself to be irreplaceable, evidently hoped thereby to force Weizmann's own resignation, and thus impose his own will upon the movement. Weizmann remained adamant in his refusal to come out to Palestine—in addition to his wife's poor health, there was now added a further, crucial factor, discussions at top Governmental level, for which he must remain on hand in London.[63] Weizmann might physically have been very glad to be relieved of the burdens of leadership, but it now appeared to him that the new discussions on partition might afford him a chance to crown his long career with a Jewish State. The impasse was settled when in February 1944 Shertok went to London at the head of a Jerusalem Executive delegation to negotiate.

Discussions between the two sides in London—in the absence of a head-on clash between the two protagonists—were conciliatory, with the Jerusalem delegation trying clearly to appease Weizmann. However, many 'emotional' hurdles remained to be overcome.[64]

The delegates from Palestine from the start expressed their regret at Ben-Gurion's resignation, and their confidence in Weizmann's leadership. They stressed the need for co-operation between Weizmann, 'the central figure in the Zionist movement', and Ben-Gurion, 'the father of the Yishuv'. All the participants were conscious of the disastrous repercussions of a split between the two leaders.

Contrary to Ben-Gurion's earlier predictions, London was again becoming a political focus for Zionism. Partition was again being considered by the Cabinet (see Chapter 9), and Weizmann would be indispensable in any negotiations that ensued. Shertok himself was now convinced that there would be no escape from partition.[65]

But Weizmann was in need of mollification. At their second meeting, Weizmann made a lengthy reply to Ben-Gurion's charges, as transmitted by Shertok. Weizmann despaired of ever being able to work again with Ben-Gurion, and announced his intention of remaining at his post for another few weeks, until the situation clarified with the visit of the Dominions Prime Ministers—after that he would resign and cede his position to Ben-Gurion. In response to the unanimous plea to reconsider his position, Weizmann asked for time to consult his London 'circle'.

After a week of further consultation, Weizmann informed the Palestinians that he and his colleagues 'were ready to see Ben-Gurion in London whenever he wished to come', although Weizmann himself was of the opinion that it might be better to wait a while, until it looked as if something were going to happen. Weizmann was praised for his statesmanship, and all expressed gratification that an internal crisis had been averted.

As a result of Shertok's report,[66] the Jerusalem Executive decided to maintain a member permanently in London. Ben-Gurion withdrew his resignation on 27 February 1944, and the Agency Executive endorsed the decisions of the London talks.

The agreement was more a 'cease-fire' than the 'constitutional' settlement needed. One might speculate that the need for Weizmann's skills in London in 1944 was largely responsible for the *ad hoc* agreement reached there.

Weizmann finally made his first wartime visit to Palestine in November 1944, arriving just after a new wave of Jewish terrorism had culminated in the assassination of Lord Moyne, the Minister of State at Cairo (see Chapter 9). Weizmann discovered to his chagrin that many important developments, especially in the field of security and underground activity, had progressed without his having been consulted. Weizmann attacked the Jerusalem Executive, particularly Ben-Gurion, for having worked on its own initiative, leaving himself in the dark.[67] The wheel thus turned full circle—Weizmann in Palestine accused Ben-Gurion of the same personal rule that the latter had accused him of in the Diaspora. Although Weizmann's warnings against the political consequence of terrorism were heeded, his influence over the Yishuv had in effect evaporated. Even had Weizmann managed to travel to Palestine in 1942 to fight for his own interpretation of Biltmore, it is highly doubtful whether his Zionist credo—co-operation with Britain—could have survived among a people who were in many respects practically at war with the Mandatory.[68]

The removal of Weizmann from the Presidency of the Zionist Movement, at its Congress in January 1946, was historically an inevitable reaction to the anti-Zionist turn taken by Bevin and his colleagues. Even so, Weizmann's diplomatic skills could not be as easily dispensed with as his political philosophy ostensibly was. At each crisis of the many that were to plague the Zionist campaign for a State, Weizmann's prestige and power of exposition were called upon. Moreover the Jewish Agency itself now moved inevitably towards the very partition solution which Weizmann had supported unwaveringly for ten years. Thus the removal of Weizmann in 1946 was a symbolic, defiant act against Britain, ironically at the very time when the Zionist movement was pragmatically resigning itself to Weizmann's programme.

Weizmann ultimately realized his dream of becoming President of a Jewish State—but not perhaps in the fashion that he would have wished. Whereas he was given full credit for his role in the diplomatic campaign for the State, no room was left on the Scroll of Independence for his signature (he was in New York on a diplomatic mission at the time). Of the twelve persons who signed after the official ceremony at Tel Aviv, ten were in Jerusalem at the time, and one, like Weizmann himself, was in New York. All were left their place on the scroll, and in history—but not Weizmann. The elder statesman of Zionism was deeply wounded by what he took to be a political slight.[69]

8
Palestine and Arab Federation

i. Britain's 'Pan-Arab' policy

It has been a central thesis of this book that Britain's Palestine policy was to an ever-increasing extent a factor of her Middle Eastern policy as a whole. It would therefore be appropriate, before turning to the evolution of her Palestine policy during the closing stages of the war, to examine Britain's 'Pan-Arab' policy—if such a coherent, stable thing indeed existed.

The British attitude to Arab federation during the period under discussion here was ambivalent. However improbable it considered the prospects of Arab union, London had to pay lip-service to it, and give its public blessing to what was becoming for the Arabs themselves a central political aspiration. British policy-makers intended that should such a union—however tenuous—in fact materialize, it should look primarily to Britain for guidance and aid.

It was the interest displayed since 1936 by the Arab States themselves, particularly by Iraq, that led to the first serious Foreign Office study of the Pan-Arab movement since World War One. A contemporary report from Damascus—the 'cradle' of Arab nationalism—provides a fair summary of the British view:

... the Pan-Arab movement ... is in reality, in its extreme form, only 'the idea of dreamers and food for philosophers' ... what is believed to be a more practical possibility, and what the more enlightened Arab politicians hope to see, is an alliance or Confederation of independent Moslem States. But all stress independence as the *sine qua non* of such a Confederation ... As an idea the Pan-Arab movement exists; *as a vital force it is destroyed by the weakness inherent in a feudal patriarchal system, jealousy and distrust* ... The Syrian Arab regards the Iraqi as inferior to him in culture, in fact as little better than the Bedu whom he despises, except when he can make use of him for his own political ends. The Saudi Arab he considers a poor, unenlightened person to be treated with tolerant condescension. The one possible cementing factor – the Moslem religion – in itself provides elements of further disruption. Sunni hates Shiah, both despise the Ismaili, whilst the Wahhabi considers himself the only real true follower of the prophet ...[1]

The military intervention of Iraqi irregulars in the Palestinian rebellion during 1936 had prompted War Office consideration of the contingency of a unified Arab military revolt against the British in the Middle East. The appreciation was both realistic and prophetic.[2] The War Office agreed with the Foreign Office that the Arab national movement was 'more theoretical than practical'. While agitation over Palestine had produced a universal sentiment—which might in certain circumstances be translated into action against British interests—the Arabic-speaking countries would be unlikely to take such action during peacetime. However, the dangers and extent of Arab hostility were Britain at war with any of the Great Powers might be greatly increased. As for the current leaders of the Arab world, it was the War Office view that 'many with local influence, such as the Mufti and Nuri Said, lacked power, while Ibn Saud—who had more power and prestige than most—was not prepared to hazard these for the will-o'-the-wisp leadership of the militant Arab world. Egypt was unwilling to risk her newly acquired independence by offending Britain, whereas Syria was preoccupied with the French delay in the ratification of the Franco–Syrian Treaty'.

The outbreak of World War Two led to a reappraisal of the potential of Arab federation, written this time by Foreign Office experts for Cabinet consideration.[3] The Department concluded that despite 'a growing sense of solidarity among the Arab people's, there remained as yet formidable obstacles in the path of Arab unity.

Firstly, there was contention between the Arab rulers themselves. The strongest and most influential among them—Ibn Saud—was determined that if any Arab ruler was to emerge predominant, it should be himself. On the other hand in Egypt, and in recent years in Iraq also, there were genuine, separatist national movements. Secondly, there was the implacable opposition to Pan-Arabism of the French, who suspected British interest in federation to be a conspiracy to rob her of the spoils of the last war. Thirdly, despite repeated claims that she had no territorial ambitions in the area, Turkey's recent absorption of Alexandretta cast doubt on Turkish disinterest in the area, and consequently on Turkish acquiescence in Arab union in any form. Lastly, Bagallay turned to consider Britain's own interests:

Great Britain has managed until now to maintain its position as the predominant power in the Middle East. It is impossible, in pursuing any policy, 'consistent' or otherwise, to please all the Middle Eastern countries and peoples equally. When one can only be pleased at the cost of displeasing another, all that can be done is to balance the major against the minor interest ... there is much to be said for the contention that a number of minor states can be managed better than a large federation, and *it is unlikely that His Majesty's Government would ever of her own accord seek to promote Pan-Arabism*, even if the French attitude allowed, and they could support unity under one ruler without offending other Arab rulers ... But Pan-Arabism is a phenomenon in the Middle East which has probably come to stay, and any attempt to oppose it would be unwise. Thus, *while His Majesty's Government would be unwilling to take any initiative, if (the) point arose they would try not to show opposition, but guide the movement along lines most favourable to Great Britain*.[4]

In short, Britain would simply attempt to exploit to its own best purposes those trends which emerged to the fore, even if they were not trends that Whitehall itself would have wished to see developing.

From 1941, all discussion on Arab Federation became inextricably linked with the Palestine problem. In that year the Cabinet Committee appointed to examine the feasibility of Arab federation was asked to estimate also how such a union might affect Palestine. Likewise, the committee appointed by Churchill in 1943 to reconsider long-term policy in Palestine was asked to search for a possible solution in the context of Arab union. Various Arab statesmen—in particular Ibn Saud—persistently warned London not to diverge from the White Paper in the 'Zionist direction'.

The Rashid Ali crisis in Iraq in May 1941—and, in its wake, the Anglo-Free French invasion of Syria—not only posed a serious threat to British positions in the Middle East, but also led to the first major blow to the Mandatory system there. With the German Air Force allowed by Vichy to use Syria as a staging-base on the way to Iraq, London took the view that France had forfeited its Mandatory rights in the Middle East. On the eve of invading Syria, London decided that the inhabitants of that country must be won over to the Allies by the promise of independence. Propelled along by a rapidly developing military situation, London was precipitated into a propaganda war for the sympathies of the peoples of the Middle East. If the Free French could not be persuaded to join the British in their declaration, London would have to go it alone.[5]

Thus Foreign Office policy towards the Arab States moved into a new phase. Eden also referred in May 1941 to the thesis that the Palestine problem might find its solution in the context of Arab federation:

Many people have suggested that the only practical solution of the Palestine problem would be a Federation of Middle Eastern States, in which a Jewish State should have a place as one of the component units. We have never opposed such a federation. Our attitude has been that it is for the Arabs to decide what they want. I fear, however, that an Arab federation is not for the moment practical politics ... Nevertheless, the Arabs generally agree that some form of 'Arab federation' is desirable, and I think that *we should not only refrain from opposing such vague aspirations, but even take every opportunity of expressing publicly our support for them* ...[6]

Eden took his opportunity only two days later, *before* the Cabinet had had time to even consider or agree to it. Even so, too many observers then and later read too much between the lines of Eden's Mansion House speech on 29 May 1941, the critical phrases of which ran:

It seems to me both natural and right that the cultural and economic ties between the Arab countries, and the political ties too, should be strengthened. His Majesty's Government, for their part, will give full support to any scheme that commands general approval.[7]

Thus Britain gave the 'green light' to the Arabs to proceed on their own.

London thereby gained full propaganda value from its support for Arab aspirations, while at the same time she carefully avoided all concrete commitment.

While military events worked themselves out during the summer of 1941, London began an initial study of Arab federation. A memorandum was prepared for the Foreign Office by its Middle Eastern expert, H. A. R. Gibb, working in an advisory capacity at the Royal Institute of International Affairs.[8] He saw the usual obstacles to Arab union, classified into 'internal' and 'external'. In the former category were the development of regional economic and national interests in the post-1918 units, political inexperience and economic weakness. In the second category—which was of most concern to London—were the mandates in Syria and Palestine, and French, Italian and Spanish rule in North-West Africa. Gibb asserted that no progress in internal Arab affairs could be expected until the settlement of the Arab world's relations with the Western world. The removal of all obstacles to Syrian independence must be the first step to any practical accommodation with Arab nationalism.

The question of the Jewish National Home was more complicated. There was a 'basic incompatibility' between support for a movement in the direction of Arab federation, and the 'fulfilment of obligations assumed in 1917 towards the Jewish people'. Gibbs correctly foresaw that those Jews who supported partition would favour federation, while those opposed to partition would resist federation. Arab nationalists, while in general prepared to accept the existence of the National Home, thought in terms of cantonization rather than of partition. Nonetheless, Gibb was of the opinion that Jewish and Arab claims might be reconciled within the framework of a general settlement of the Greater Syrian problem. This concept was adopted later by important sections of the decision-making bureaucracy, but rejected, decisively, by the Foreign Office.

While Nuri Said was otherwise engaged in Iraq, picking up the pieces following the Rashid Ali débacle, the Saudi Minister in London (without, apparently, the knowledge of Ibn Saud himself) approached the Foreign Office to ask about 'British plans for Arab federation'.[9] Concurrently, Churchill himself was giving consideration to a scheme for Arab federation under the leadership of Ibn Saud, to be supported by Britain on condition that the latter first signed a treaty guaranteeing the Jews an independent State in Palestine. Churchill, and later Roosevelt also, believed that Arab fears of a Jewish State would be reduced to more digestible dimensions within the wider frame of a larger Arab unit.[10] However, the scheme for a Zionist treaty with Ibn Saud, promoted unsuccessfully by Saud's one-time confidant St John 'Abdullah' Philby, was pathetically anachronistic, drawing its inspiration from Weizmann's meetings and abortive treaty with the Emir Feisal after World War One.[11]

The Foreign Office, with more political commonsense in this instance than either Churchill or Roosevelt, quickly exposed the impossibility of imposing Saudi rule on the more advanced Arabs of the Fertile Crescent or Egypt. The Department repeated its view (four months after Eden's celebrated Mansion House speech) that any spontaneous attempt by the Government to promote Arab federation—from whatever motive—would be a risky experiment.[12] However, the Foreign Office view was overruled by a meeting in September 1941 of the Departments concerned with policy in the area, which invited the Middle East (Official) Committee of the CID to 'examine forthwith the various forms which a scheme of Arab federation might take and to report on their advantages and disadvantages, as well as their practicability, paying special attention to the Palestine problem'.[13]

Guided by the Foreign and Colonial Office, the Committee once more warned the Government: 'this is not the time for endeavouring to formulate and carry through a scheme of political federation'. It was feared that

The Arab desire for a closer union ... is in effect a wish to form a bloc of Arab States which will be strong enough to secure what are considered Arab rights in Palestine and Syria, and to present a united front to foreign powers, especially Great Britain and France ...[14]

However, the Committee advised against the adoption of a purely negative policy. The old formula was repeated—Britain should show sympathy for Arab aspirations and guide them, as far as possible—along lines consistent with British interests in the area. It also endorsed the proposals sent in by the Middle East Ambassadors regarding the encouragement of closer economic and cultural ties between the Arab States.

ii. Arab initiatives

The British victory at El Alamein and the flight of the German armies before Anglo-American forces in North Africa at the close of 1942 led to a spate of rumour and lobbying by both Arabs and Zionists on the political future of the Middle East. When Eden was asked in the Commons on 24 February 1943 whether any steps were being taken by Britain to promote greater co-operation between the Arab States, he replied quite innocently:

Clearly, such an initiative would have to come from the Arabs themselves, and so far as I am aware no such scheme which would command general approval has yet been worked out.[15]

The Arab States took the latest British reference to themselves as an invitation to produce a scheme for British approval. Nuri Said now approached the Egyptian Prime Minister, Nahhas Pasha, for his view on the convention of a conference of Arab States. The latter informed the Egyptian Parliament that, following a careful study of Eden's speech, he had decided to take steps to ascertain and as far as possible unify the points of view of the Arab Governments.[16] In view of Nuri's activities in 1936, the Foreign Office was troubled by his current foray into the Pan-Arab arena:

> ... his past dabblings in Pan-Arabism and his desire to offer the Mufti asylum in Iraq should have taught him that he cannot control these sort of movements as he likes ... we should impress on Nuri that he is setting his foot on a very slippery slope ...[17]

Foreign Office fears abated when Nahhas Pasha turned down Nuri's invitation to call a conference at Cairo, at which Palestine would have been the first item on the agenda. The Department relished the fact that its own predictions about Arab disunity were materializing: 'Like little Black Sambo, we can sit up a tree and watch the tigers tearing themselves to pieces.'[18]

While in Cairo, Nuri had met also with the British Minister of State, Casey, with whom he discussed the future of the Arab States. At Casey's invitation, Nuri followed up their conversation with a long memorandum,[19] in which he asked that in view of 'recent activities of the Zionist Organization in England and in the United States', Britain and the United States should make some declaration regarding the future of the Arab territories which formerly formed part of the Ottoman Empire. Nuri quoted Weizmann's article in *Foreign Affairs* (of January 1942) urging the creation of a Jewish State in Palestine after the war, and expressed concern at Zionist agitation to create a Jewish Army in Palestine and elsewhere, to fight against the Axis. Nuri warned that if there was any intention of recruiting such an army in Palestine or using it there or in neighbouring Arab countries, the Arabs would regard it as a Jewish attempt to coerce the Allies into acceptance of a Jewish State, and the ultimate purpose of such an army as being to fight the Arabs for possession of Palestine. In his opinion, if the United Nations immediately made a definite pronouncement, that they would not support the creation of a Jewish State in Palestine, but would adhere to the policy laid down in the White Paper of 1939, the Zionists would protest, but accept that decision as final.

At the same time, Nuri proposed that the United Nations guarantee the future of the Jewish National Home in its present form, with all the possibilities of normal semi-autonomous development within the fabric of a Greater Syria and an Arab League. According to Nuri's scheme, Syria, the Lebanon, Palestine and Transjordan would unite in one State, in which Palestinian Jewry would be given a semi-autonomous status—resting on international guarantees—though subject to the general supervision of the Syrian State. Once this 'Greater Syria' had been formed, an Arab League would be created to which Syria and Iraq would adhere at once, as well as any other Arab State that so wished. Nuri's plan was adopted in its essentials by Lord Moyne (Deputy Minister of State at Cairo), and in November 1943 was brought before the Cabinet Committee on Palestine.[20]

At the Foreign Office, the usual vacillation between outright support for, or rejection of the White Paper policy prevailed. The Department claimed that the scheme would not be acceptable even to the moderate Zionist camp, and neither could London make such a declaration regarding a Jewish State as desired by Nuri. Nuri was also overlooking Churchill's pledge to de Gaulle that the influence of France in Syria and in the Lebanon would predominate over that of other European countries. Finally, there were the usual inhibitions about 'betraying' Abdullah, who of all the Arab leaders had proved himself the most loyal during the war.[21]

One of the principal obstacles to plans for Arab unity, whether originating in Baghdad or Cairo, remained the opposition of the highly respected and much-wooed Ibn Saud:

Ibn Saud repeats the warnings given regarding dissentient Arab leaders who are at present agitating for Arab Congresses ... he trusts none of them as they are all playing their own hands in order to strengthen their positions in their own countries ... His Majesty is as always a sincere supporter of all legitimate Arab aspirations but he prefers to keep aloof from all these intrigues ...[22]

Ibn Saud's suspicions conformed to the Foreign Office assessment of the situation and also dovetailed neatly into the plans of British policy-makers, whose principal fear now was that any unified Arab bloc would be reduced to discussing the one problem on which all could agree—Palestine. A platform would thus be provided for undesirable public discussion of a problem that London preferred to 'freeze' until the end of the war. Palestinian extremists would probably set the pace, leaving the Arab States to vie with each other in support of demands that would most likely go beyond the limits set by the 1939 White Paper. This fear materialized in February 1944, when Nahhas Pasha announced the convention of an all-Arab Conference, to be held in Alexandria that autumn.[23]

iii. The formation of the Arab League

The Foreign Office view of Nahhas' initiative was hardly less cynical than that held of Nuri Said's efforts on previous occasions:

Nahhas' tendency to balance his internal instability by Pan-Arab stunts seems liable to become embarrassing. While it is we who keep him in power, we may hope that he will not shout too loud about official Palestine policy; but this is a tiresome tendency and may turn out awkwardly for us. We want *friendly* Arab leadership from Egypt, more like Ibn Saud – and more of his dignity and reserve too ...[24]

The Foreign Office devoted its efforts during the summer of 1944 to ensuring, as far as possible, that the impending Arab gathering should not debate Palestine in a contentious manner. Cornwallis (the Ambassador at Baghdad) was instructed to tell Nuri Said that London did not want the Palestine question raised until after the war. Nuri reassured the Ambassador that he saw no reason why the conference should not pass a resolution postponing consideration of the Palestine question until after the war.[25] At Cairo, Nahhas was persuaded to concentrate on such matters as could be agreed upon—mainly in the economical and cultural spheres. Nahhas agreed not to raise such contentious matters as Palestine and the Levant States, or only in a very 'uncontentious' manner (whatever that meant). If the Palestinian Arabs could not be represented, the whole issue would be shelved. The Syrians also promised to 'keep off' Palestine.[26]

On 12 July 1944, the Egyptian Government announced its invitation to the Governments of Iraq, Syria, the Lebanon, Transjordan, Saudi Arabia and the Yemen, to participate in a preliminary general meeting, to take place after Ramadan, which in that year ended in the third week of September.[27] No mention was made of Palestinian representatives, as they had so far failed to reach agreement among themselves. The interval between the Egyptian announcement and the first meeting of the Conference witnessed further difficulties.

From Cairo, Killearn reported that Nahhas was having regrets over his initiative, the results of which were rapidly slipping out of his control. At the same time, having rather rashly launched the scheme, Nahhas was now finding it very difficult to retreat. If he did, there were others quite ready to pick up the threads, oust Nahhas from the leadership of Pan-Arabism, and hold the meeting elsewhere. From London's point of view, the transfer of the Conference to another Arab capital was not desirable, for nowhere else would London be able to 'exercise some degree of tacit control and restraint upon the proceedings'. Killearn regarded the participation of Ibn Saud as another safeguard and brake upon 'intemperate or unwise discussion'.[28]

On the eve of the Conference the Foreign Office, as yet wallowing in its own complacency, patronisingly surveyed the Cairo scene, as sketched from the reports of its Ambassadors:

The stage is now set. The Arab leaders are all at sixes and sevens. The Iraqis are jealous of Nahhas. Nahhas hates Nuri. The Amir of Transjordan wants to be King of Syria and has recently quarrelled with Shukri Quwatli, the President of Syria, who apparently wants to include Transjordan in the Syrian Republic. Ibn Saud is backing Shukri because he hates all Hashemites ... The Palestinian Arabs can't agree on a delegation to represent them in the absence of the leaders in Germany, or under lock and key ... there are all the elements of an unedifying dog-fight, but we really dare not crash in and tell them to put it off – they would then at least agree about our opposition to Arab unity. Our tactful efforts to dissuade Nahhas and to get Ibn Saud to dissuade him have not succeeded. I don't think there is anything more we can do in that direction. We have already got undertakings from those participating to the effect that they will treat any references to Palestine with special discretion in view of the importance of not increasing tension while the war lasts.[29]

The Foreign Office—not for the first time—miscalculated the outcome of a conference in which the Arab States were involved, although British pressure on Arab leaders on the eve of the Conference paid off handsome dividends as regards Palestine. At the end of its deliberations, from 15 September to 7 October 1944, the Conference issued five resolutions, which became known as the 'Alexandria Protocol'.[30]

The first four resolutions dealt with the formation of an Arab League, and the political, social and economic relations between its members. The fifth resolution dealt with Palestine, noting that it was 'an important element of the Arab countries and that the rights of the Arabs could not be infringed in Palestine without danger to the peace and stability of the Arab world'. At the same time it stated that the engagements assumed by Great Britain (i.e. the 1939 White Paper) constituted the 'acquired rights' of the Arabs. These 'engagements' were listed as the stoppage of Jewish immigration, the protection of Arab lands and the preparation of Palestine for independence. While expressing sympathy for the plight of European Jewry, the Conference declared that this problem must not be confused with the question of Zionism.

The Middle East Ambassadors—who had so recently discounted the formation of any Arab unified bloc—were now quick to point to the advantages in it for Great Britain—if she 'played her cards right'. It was even claimed that the aim of the Conference had been to 'unite the Arab world in co-operation with Great Britain'.[31] Cairo regarded the Protocol as an achievement that would have to be nurtured carefully:

It is not impossible that this solidarity of the Egypt–Arab world may be conciliated with our essential interests ... provided we are able to adapt ourselves to the new conditions quickly enough. If however ... we have also in the interests of our world policy to adopt local policies in Syria and Palestine unacceptable to the Arabs, there is little likelihood of our being able to bring a consolidated Middle East into friendly co-operation.[32]

The resolution on Palestine thus provided yet another occasion for a protest from the Middle East that London must adhere to the White Paper policy. According to confidential reports, the resolution had been so phrased in order to find a formula which would be acceptable to Jamal Husseini, who had allegedly—despite the Mufti's remonstrances—initialled the 1939 White Paper, together with Musa el-Alami,[33] in Nuri Pasha's house in May 1940. Typical was the comment of Cornwallis, the venerated Ambassador in Baghdad:

... this acceptance of Britain's last official statement of policy by and on behalf of the so-called extremist Palestine party, and its endorsement by the conference, is very significant. It means on the one hand that the Palestinian Arabs are now committed to an acceptance of the White Paper, and that we have the general support of the Arab world for the policy it enshrined. But, on the other hand, it means equally that *any serious divergence from that policy will confront His Majesty's*

Government not only with the hostility of the Palestinian Arabs, but with that of all the signatories to the Alexandria Protocol...[34]

London was being swept along, not entirely of its own volition, by a movement which it felt powerless to stifle but which at the same time was narrowing its options in the Middle East. Naturally, the Foreign Office made a virtue of necessity—'policy of seeing what they (the Arab States) can themselves agree on and encouraging them gently in that direction is the right policy and not one of imposing from without any sort of unity which the peoples would regard as a new and devilish interference with their independence and a crafty imperialistic way of creating a new Dominion'.[35]

The Pact which formed the Arab League on 22 March 1945—although following the general lines laid down at Alexandria the previous October—was in many respects a less binding document, making special reservations to guarantee the independence and sovereignty of member States.[36] There was also an important change in the provisions on Palestine. Whereas the Alexandria Protocol had based itself on the status quo in Palestine as established by the White Paper of 1939, the League Pact now took for its point of reference the First World War, when the Arab countries—including Palestine—had been detached from the Ottoman Empire. Although Palestine had then not been in a position to settle its own affairs, stated the Pact, '*the Covenant of the League of Nations of 1919 settled her régime on the basis of the acknowledgement of her independence*'.[37] Moreover, continued the Pact, owing to the peculiar circumstances of Palestine, and until that country enjoyed effective independence, the Council of the Arab League would undertake the selection of an Arab delegate from Palestine to participate in its work.

London was contented with the emasculation of the federation idea into that of a League—this was but the appreciation of the real difficulties in the way of federation, which the Foreign Office itself had consistently warned against. There was, however, general agreement on the necessity to avoid any serious rifts within the League so that it might, as a unit, be guided in the direction desired by Great Britain—'*Divide et impera* may be a risky motto for us in the future, for others may well profit by the divisions for their own ends.'[38]

The policy followed by the British Foreign Office during the war—that of 'balancing major against minor interests'—would have to be reconsidered. Whereas the prospect of Arab union had been feared as an 'anti-foreign' instrument, the British position had been eased considerably during the war by the removal of France as a major factor of influence in the Levant. However, whereas London could now be more generous as regards Arab aspirations in the Levant, Britain herself was left as the sole focus of Arab resentment in the area. Henceforth, if London could not please all the Middle Eastern countries at one and the same time, it must try not to displease those which held sway in the Arab League.

In this context, established policy on Palestine—adherence to the White Paper of 1939—received the strongest possible support—'the development of the League certainly makes it more than ever necessary that we should not evolve for Palestine a settlement which is too great an offence to Arab interests and hopes . . .'[39]

9

British Policy in Palestine, 1943-45

STRATEGIC CONSIDERATIONS

The Government's debate on a long-term solution for Palestine, renewed in 1943, was affected by factors extraneous to Palestine itself: (a) by a new awareness of her strategic vulnerability in the Middle East, whose oil-reserves assumed an increased importance during the war; (b) by British anxiety, from as early as 1943, regarding American and Soviet penetration into an area which between the wars London had regarded as its own private hegemony;[1] and (c) by the weighty objections of Britain's strategic planners to the idea of partitioning Palestine, an idea that had remained since 1937 the basis of Governmental plans for Palestine's future.

Britain became most aware of its own vulnerability in the Middle East during 1941.[2] In the spring of that year, General Wavell's forces were spread across the battlefields of Greece, Tripoli and East Africa. His decisive victories over Italian forces in December 1940 had not been pressed beyond Egypt's western borders, so as to maintain a capacity to intervene against the Axis in the Balkans. This capacity was called on when in April 1941 Berlin issued ultimatums to Greece and Yugoslavia. The removal of 60,000 troops from the Middle East in an attempt to save Greece from conquest by the Germans left the British vulnerable to rapid advances by Rommel in the Western Desert. This, followed closely by the British debacle in Greece, gave Rashid Ali his opportunity to stage a pro-Axis coup in Iraq. Heavily outnumbered by Iraqi forces, Britain owed its survival in that country not only to London's sang-froid and determination to demonstrate British military might to the Arabs (in contrast to Wavell's defeatist vacillation), but also to Germany's pre-occupation with its June invasion of the Soviet Union.[3]

The German invasion of the Soviet Union prompted a reassessment of their potential threat to the Middle East, in the contingency that they defeated Russia swiftly and turned to sweep southwards via the Caucasus, perhaps in combination with a renewed offensive by Rommel into Egypt.[4]

The Middle East, in its capacity as a land-link from Suez to the Indian Empire, was now considered to be of equal importance to the Atlantic sea-route. If Germany broke through to the Persian Gulf and gained access to the Indian Ocean, British communications to the East would be broken, and 'the development of the maximum war effort of the British Commonwealth, and indeed its very existence, would be called into question'.[5] The present British position afforded strategic hinterland to the north of the shores of the Persian Gulf and the Indian Ocean.

In their debate on priorities between the southern (Western Desert) and northern (Balkans–Caucasus) flanks of the Middle East, the Chiefs of Staff gave top priority to the security of the Anglo-Iranian oilfields and the Abadan refinery, the loss of which would make it difficult—if not impossible —to pursue the war. Military needs had brought an awareness not only of the need to possess oil reserves, but also to have them immediately available. Whereas alternative oil resources to those of the Middle East were available in North America, at least 270 additional tankers—then non-existent—would be required for their transportation. A recent report by the Oil Control Board had concluded that the loss of Abadan and Bahrein 'would be calamitous in as much as it would enforce a drastic reduction on our total war capacity, and probably the abandonment of some of our present fields of action'.[6]

In March 1942, the Minister of State at Cairo and General Auchinleck informed London categorically that with the present resources available 'the Middle East could not be held against attack from the North.'[7] In reply to their plea for reinforcements, the Chiefs of Staff advised:

> The best way in which we can both safeguard our own oil and help Russia to keep the Caucasian oil is to fight the Axis where we can. For the Middle Eastern theatre this is at present in Libya.[8]

British strategy in the Middle East in the summer of 1942 had therefore to rely on two factors: (a) effective Russian resistance to Germany; and (b) maximum offensive action by Britain in the Western Desert, to take the weight off Russia. Because of the paucity of British resources, it was at this juncture that the local command in Palestine considered training Jewish guerrilla units to sabotage and work behind the lines of any German advance through northern Palestine.

The psychological effect on Britain of the challenge to its position in the Middle East undoubtedly accounts to a great extent for its extreme sensitivity to developments in the area during the second half of the war, after the Axis had been ousted from North Africa. The British reaction to the pan-Arab movement has been described in the previous chapter it remains to consider here British anxiety in the face of American and Soviet wartime penetration of the area.

i. *The American and Soviet challenge to British hegemony*

By the autumn of 1942 Britain was preparing to seize the initiative in the Mediterranean, from Egypt by land, and from French North Africa— together with American forces—by sea. Montgomery's October offensive at El Alamein was successful, and the German armies never stopped their retreat until their final surrender in May 1943. By January 1943, Churchill could write to his Chief of Staff, Ismay:

Account must be taken of the complete change in conditions in the Middle East since August 1942. The decisive victories in the Western Desert and the immense comeback of the Russians in South Russia and the Caucasus have removed for an indefinite period the principal dangers we then faced...[9]

But despite this very evident fact, there were no sudden or dramatic changes in British policy in Palestine. The established policy of appeasing the Arab States continued to hold sway, owing to British fears that any alienation of the Arabs would be exploited eagerly by either the United States or the Soviet Union, anxiously waiting in the wings, watching for their opportunity to exploit British mistakes.

Throughout World War Two, Washington tended to regard the region—notwithstanding American interest in Saudi Arabia and Palestine—as a British sphere of strategic and political responsibility.[10] However, once the United States took an active role in the war, particularly in the Middle Eastern theatre, mutual suspicions arose between her and Britain. Friction focused essentially on two major issues: on the American suspicion that Britain was exploiting her resources to protect her own imperial interests in the area; and on the question of post-war exploitation of Middle Eastern oil and markets.[11]

During the period between the two world wars, the pattern of oil ownership and development in the Persian Gulf had undergone a radical change, and British domination was challenged by American companies. The British maintained their exclusive control over the Iranian oilfields, and domination of the Iraqi Petroleum Company (IPC). But American companies had acquired nearly a one-fourth holding in IPC, half of the Kuwait concessions and exclusive ownership of the Bahrein and Saudi Arabian concessions. The Middle East had become for the United States more closely interlaced with issues of national defence and international status.[12]

Friction between the Allies increased when, in March 1943, an American Presidential Committee on International Petroleum Policy reported that future American demand for oil—both for defence and for essential economic requirements—would be in excess of American domestic production.[13] At the end of 1943, Secretary of State Hull proposed to Halifax in Washington that the two Governments enter informal and preliminary discussions towards an agreement on Middle East oil reserves.[14] In a memorandum to the Cabinet, in February 1944, Lord Beaverbrook, then Lord Privy Seal, objected vehemently to any division of Middle Eastern oil—'Britain's greatest asset'—with the United States.[15] Beaverbrook rejected American 'allegations' that their own oil reserves had been depleted for the benefit of Great Britain, that American interests had been providing a disproportionate share of the oil needed for the war effort, and that American reserves were now down to fourteen years' supply.

Under American pressure, talks on the reallocation of Middle Eastern oil finally took place during the summer of 1944. In August, the two Governments confirmed their 'mutual respect for valid concessions and lawfully acquired oil rights'. The 'agreement' recognized the new status quo, one now weighted heavily in American favour.[16]

The United States also played a vital wartime role in the operation of the Middle East Supply Centre at Cairo. Without American exports and shipping, the civilian economy of the region would have foundered in chaos. Yet at the same time, the Americans gained entry into a huge market which in peacetime might have been better 'protected'. The American demand for an 'open door' for its exports to the Middle East conflicted with British plans to project the regional planning of the Middle East Supply Centre into the post-war period.[17]

For their part, the British believed that the Americans were not above 'pushing post-war trade through the lever of wartime supplies which ought to be dictated by the interests of the general war effort'.[18] A meeting of British diplomatic representatives in the Middle East after the war was informed that approximately 50–60 per cent of Middle Eastern trade had been captured by the Americans during the war.[19]

On the other hand, Whitehall nurtured hopes that American economic interests would make the United States more amenable to British plans for political stability in the area—'by making our explanation of our political interests in the area coincide with a proposal for the maintenance and development of the economic partnership now existing at the Middle East Supply Centre, and thereby recognizing American interest in this respect, we stand a reasonable chance (a) of controlling the fierce economic rivalry that might otherwise break out between the two countries after the war, and (b) of taking the sting out of the assertion of our predominant political interest'.[20]

The Foreign Office was particularly concerned that 'inept' handling of the Palestine problem by London might facilitate further American penetration of the Arab Middle East. In May 1943, Eden circulated a Cabinet paper advocating that London warn its Washington ally that Zionist propaganda there—at times encouraged or endorsed by members of the Administration—constituted a danger to the joint war effort in the Middle East. Before this proposal could be considered in Cabinet, Washington itself proposed a joint Anglo-American declaration that would 'freeze' the status quo in Palestine until after the war. But in July 1943, following a fierce Zionist lobby in Washington, the American Government withdrew its initiative, ostensibly because of the improved military position in the Middle East.[21]

When in September 1944 the Cabinet Committee on Palestine recommended—against Foreign Office opinion—the partition of Palestine, Eden issued a specific warning regarding the potential American challenge in the future:

... whatever American sentiment may be, we run the grave risk, if we embark on a policy of partition, of losing to America the pre-eminent place we have always held, and which in our own strategic interests, including oil, we ought to continue to hold, in the Arab world. There is no doubt in my mind that the Americans have thoughts of usurping that place, beginning with Saudi Arabia ....[22]

London had come to regard her responsibilities in Palestine, especially to the Jews, as an intolerable burden, leading inexorably towards a clash with the Arabs. The desire to end the system whereby London assumed sole responsibility for the Palestine Administration, and to involve the United States in some way, was to remain a central factor in Foreign Office thinking on Palestine.

Whereas Russian interest in the so-called 'northern tier' of the Middle East was traditional, most historians of Soviet foreign policy date active Russian involvement in the Middle East itself as beginning somewhere in the 1953–55 period.[23] But as with the United States, the war facilitated Russian advances that would not have been so readily acquiesced in by Britain in peacetime. The joint Anglo-Russian occupation of Iran in August 1941, the subsequent demonstration of the strategic utility of the Iranian trunk line, the Tripartite Treaty (Britain, Russia, Iran) of January 1942, and the Teheran Declaration by Churchill, Roosevelt and Stalin in December 1943 were all decisive in re-establishing Russia as a Near Eastern Power. During the course of the war, Russia gave expression to her new interest in the area by opening diplomatic missions in Cairo, Baghdad, Damascus and Beirut.[24]

Well before the end of the war, British policy-makers studied the potential Russian challenge to British interests in the Middle East. Being sensitive to any questioning of its own right to exploit Middle Eastern oil, Britain appreciated the attraction which the Middle East held for other Great Powers, including the Soviet Union.[25] Firstly, Russian dependence on the oil resources of the Caucasus made her suspicious of any foreign interest or military approach—even by her allies—to the 'northern tier'. With the development of modern communications the geographical inaccessibility of those areas separating British interests in Iraq and Persia from those of Russia in the Caucasus had in effect ceased to be of consequence. Military or air activities by either side in its own area might become the source of mutual suspicions. Soviet domestic oil requirements were expected to increase rapidly and, like the United States, the Soviet Union might think it desirable for strategic reasons to conserve the oil resources in its own territory. The Soviets might be especially interested in Middle Eastern oil during the immediate post-war period, when drops in their own coal and power production were likely to cause serious bottlenecks in industrial expansion. Following its wartime experience, the Soviet Union was also expected to show a permanent interest in the Trans-Persian railway, and in the warm-water ports of the Persian Gulf.

Further threats to British strategic interests were foreseen in Turkey, where Soviet policy might result in detaching Turkey from the Western orbit and bringing her under predominant Russian influence—which in turn could lead ultimately to a threat to British Middle East oil supplies and Mediterranean communications; and in the rise of the Soviet Union as a first-class naval power.[26]

The British 'answer' to the potential Soviet threat would be, on the one hand, to agree to 'any reasonable demands' by the Soviets, provided they did not conflict with vital British interests; and to endeavour to maintain friendly relations but, in the event of a Soviet threat developing, to insure against it by close collaboration with the United States;[27] to maintain adequate naval superiority and certainly not less than parity in the air, and to so organize the British strategic reserve that it could be rapidly concentrated in any vital area, particularly in the Middle East.[28]

Neither was the potential threat of socialist revolutionary expansion discounted. As one Foreign Office expert put it:

... those we are associated with in the Middle East are predominantly of the wealthier classes, while the Russians' friends are more likely to be among the have-nots. If you try and exclude the Russians from consultation, they will intrigue with the lower classes against our friends.[29]

While the Soviet Union was not yet considered to be aggressive or deliberately unfriendly to Britain, its policy was considered to be 'suspicious, opportunist, and ready to spread the leaven of her political and economic evangel in any quarter of the Middle East which shows signs of social maladjustment or unrest'.[30] If Britain itself did not tackle these problems, concluded the Minister of State at Cairo:

There will be no security for us in the Middle East, whatever forces we maintain in it, if we fail to guide its governments into some reasonable measure of our own regard for social justice, education, and the elementary claims of health.[31]

With the end of the war, British unease regarding future Soviet designs on the Middle East was transformed into concrete grievance. The Soviet Union—by violating the treaty deadline for the withdrawal of its forces from Iran;[32] by actively promoting the dismemberment of Iran through the establishment of the 'autonomous Republics' of Azerbaijan and Kurdistan; by its pressure on Turkey to revise the Montreux Convention of 1936 governing the Straits; and by its forward oil policy—gave ample warning to the West of the character of its future policy in those parts of its borders flanking the Middle East.[33]

Thus, during the second half of the war, with the Middle East albeit safe from Axis military threat, Britain had to an ever-increasing extent to look over its own shoulder in an attempt to assess the challenge developing from its current Allies. Having been in the area for some thirty years, Britain had to look to its image in Arab eyes, and to convince the Arab world that past 'sins' were but aberrations, not to be repeated.

ii. Some strategic aspects of partition

As early as December 1942, the Joint Planning Staff Committee of the War Cabinet was commissioned to undertake a study of Britain's post-war strategic requirements in the Middle East.[34] In dealing with each country in the Middle East, they envisaged that mandates would be replaced by independent régimes in treaty relationship with Great Britain. In the event of any change in the mandate for Palestine, British strategic needs there would focus on Haifa. Facilities would be required to protect those sections of the Haifa–Baghdad road and the Haifa–Kirkuk oil pipeline, as well as the oil installations at Haifa itself. Britain would need to develop a naval base at Haifa, and to control the Haifa–Qantara railway. To guarantee and protect all these interests and facilities would require air and troop bases.

The views of the Chiefs of Staff were sought frequently by the Cabinet Committee appointed in July 1943 to consider a long-term solution for the Palestine problem. General Wavell, not normally a member of the War Cabinet, was invited to give his views, based upon his long experience of Palestine and of the Middle East.[35] Wavell predicted that the Jews, if left to themselves, would defeat the Arabs in Palestine, although this would be a disaster if Britain allowed it to happen. Whereas Wavell considered that the pledges given to the Arabs had created a situation of real difficulty, he feared more that 'the present Jewish aspirations in Palestine constituted a danger to the security of the British Commonwealth and Empire'.[36]

In Cairo, the Middle East War Council debated the Palestine question in May 1943.[37] Apart from external factors—such as the 'problematical role which Russia may seek to play in the future'—the Council envisaged two principal threats to the peace and stability of the Middle East; (a) from the presence in the Middle East itself of two discordant elements—the Jews in Palestine and the French in Syria and the Lebanon, and (b) from the danger of economic disorder and collapse.

With regard to Palestine specifically, the Council resolved that in order to make a resort to force unprofitable for either party, one division would have to be stationed in the country, with a further division—including its armour—on short call. Before April 1944—the date on which the White Paper immigration provisions would expire—this force would have to be increased by a further division. The British police force in Palestine would have to be brought up to its full complement, and a British gendarmerie created; efforts to seize hidden arms and stop the illegal arms traffic would have to be made; and London was advised to issue a clear public warning that it would not permit any attempt to alter the Palestine Administration by force.

The Council concluded that none of these measures were likely to be effective unless accompanied by a full statement of policy—preferably supported by the United States—reaffirming the status quo. Any deviation from the principles of the 1939 White Paper, asserted the Council, would almost inevitably provoke a new outbreak of violence.

The Cabinet Committee on Palestine commissioned a report of its own on British strategic needs in Palestine after the war.[38] The Chiefs of Staff echoed the Foreign Office thesis that Palestine could not be treated in isolation, but only as part of the 'hub' of the Middle East. The assessment concluded that a peaceful and secure Palestine would remain of the utmost importance to imperial strategy, and that 'the continued occupation of Palestine by British forces and the control of air-bases and means of communication in that country after the war are essential'.[39] The views of the General Staff on Palestine were ultimately to bring them into conflict with the politicians after the war.

When the Cabinet Committee on Palestine produced its first report, in December 1943, its proposal to partition Palestine was brought under the scrutiny of the Chiefs of Staff, who could hardly find a good word to say for the Committee's plan:

... Partition of a small country like Palestine is bound to complicate military control ... frontiers give difficulty, due to length of common Jewish frontier with Arabs and difficulties in movement of forces from one end of Palestine to the other ... trouble is brewing in Palestine, and we may in any case be faced with a commitment in the first half of the year, which we should be unable to meet unless C.-in-C.s concerned are allowed to use Indian Divisions for internal security in Palestine and Middle East. *We have to consider whether to attempt to lessen trouble by an immediate attack on Jewish secret organizations.*[40]

The Chiefs of Staff recommended that the proposed partition frontiers should be reconsidered; that the local commanders should be asked for their appreciation of the situation likely to develop, and that any implementation of the scheme should be deferred until after the defeat of Germany.[41] Meanwhile, no leakage of the proposal should occur.

Churchill rejected the Staffs' assessment.[42] He believed it to be based on the false assumption that partition would arouse Jewish resentment whereas in fact, claimed Churchill, it was the 1939 White Paper that had alienated the Jews. It was from the Arabs, claimed Churchill, that they might expect a violent reaction. This would be countered by the Jews who, as Wavell had pointed out, would on their own beat the Arabs. Thus, there would in fact be no need for British resources with which to impose partition.

But the Chiefs of Staff remained adamant.[43] They pointed out that whereas partition might indeed prove acceptable to Dr Weizmann and the moderates in the Zionist camp, it was not certain that he would manage to prevail over the Jewish Agency, whose leaders had recently reaffirmed their uncompromising support for the Biltmore programme and had explicitly rejected partition. It was this 'extremist' section of the Jewish Agency, claimed the Staffs, that controlled the Haganah. Should the Zionist Organization reject partition—a possibility that could not be ruled out—it might resort to force, a risk sufficiently likely to compel the Staffs to evolve necessary counter-measures. They concurred with Churchill that the Palestinian Arabs alone did not constitute any serious military threat, but pointed to the possibility of serious external repercussions in response to British action to suppress Arab opposition.

In September 1944, the Cabinet Committee on Palestine decided nevertheless that partition—'to be implemented as soon as the necessary arrangements could be made'—remained the sole viable long-term solution for Palestine. The Chiefs of Staff were once more asked to examine the strategic implications of the plan now proposed. They replied categorically:

... it would be impossible, taking into account the manpower allocation to the Services, to provide for the war against Japan, the occupation of Europe, and an increased security commitment of the above order in the Middle East simultaneously.[44]

The Staffs concluded that the earliest time by which they would be able to muster the forces necessary to deal with the widespread disorders expected—without serious consequences elsewhere—would be some nine to twelve months after the defeat of Germany. In support of their conclusions, they outlined the military implications of a wholesale search for the secret arms-caches suspected to be held by the Haganah—a measure necessary if the Jewish military potential were to be neutralized.[45] Such a search-operation was likely to escalate into a full-scale conflict with the Haganah, now believed to have over fifty thousand trained and armed men. It was estimated that a further British infantry division would be needed in Palestine before any such search could be attempted. It was also emphasized that the defection of Jewish labour that would result from widespread disorders would cause acute embarrassment to the installations and workshops of all three Services, as well as to the oil refineries at Haifa. All in all, any such search for arms would 'entail a military commitment which could only be met at the expense of operations against Germany'.[46]

Churchill accepted the consensus that nothing could be done before the defeat of Germany, and informed Weizmann so.[47] Unfortunately for the Zionist interest, the final surrender of Germany preceded by only a short period the electoral defeat of Churchill and his replacement by Attlee.

Even after the cessation of hostilities the military commitment involved in the pronouncement of any departure from the 1939 White Paper was to remain a major consideration.[48] The demand for general demobilization and the need to face the economic costs of the war were issues which the politicians would ignore at their peril. The appointment of the Anglo-American Commission on Palestine, in November 1945, must also be seen in this context:

The chief *military* consideration is that an outburst over Palestine should not occur until some of our other military commitments have been liquidated. The proposal for a full enquiry into the Jewish problem will make for delay, and is therefore satisfactory...[49]

When Attlee resuscitated the Cabinet Committee on Palestine, it was again inundated with 'strategical' arguments. The Minister of State at Cairo predicted that Britain's post-war presence in the Middle East would depend upon four strategic areas[50]—Egypt, Palestine, Transjordan and Iraq.[51] Grigg's 'quadrilateral' security system was incompatible with the partition of Palestine, which would remain the sole territory (apart from Cyprus) where Britain would retain absolute administrative control and unlimited facilities even in peacetime. On the other hand, relations with other sovereign Arab States would have to be based on mutual defence treaties, with British forces remaining inconspicuously in the background. Therefore, Palestine would have to remain under exclusive British control:

The worst political feature of partition, namely, its alienation of the whole Arab world, is almost equalled by its military defects, which are the alienation of the Palestine coast, the dependence upon treaty rights for the defence of Haifa and the pipeline, and the reduction of British tenure to a land-bound Jerusalem State possessed of highly controversial frontiers and surrounded on all sides by uncertain friends if not by positive enemies. It is indispensable to imperial security in the Middle East, as also for the discharge of our responsibilities in this region to the new world order, that *Palestine should be administered by Britain as an undivided whole* ... that there should be no armed forces in it but those which the British Administration controls ... the Middle Eastern Defence Committee is unanimous in the opinion that *the partition of Palestine would, from the military standpoint, spell irremediable disaster* ...[52]

When, in May 1946, the Chiefs of Staff agreed to place political expediency before all else and offer to evacuate British forces from Egypt, they did so in the firm belief that alternative Middle East bases were available, and that Palestine was destined to become one of two main substitutes for the Suez Canal bases.[53]

POLITICAL REASSESSMENTS

The 1939 White Paper remained the basis of British rule in Palestine during the first three years of the war. The military crises that erupted in the Middle East in 1940–42 did not allow consideration of any alternatives—if only because Britain could not be certain that it would still be in the area at the end of the war. Since his appointment to the War Cabinet Churchill had tried, in vain, to halt the further implementation of the White Paper. In February 1940, when the Land Transfers clause of the White Paper was promulgated, Churchill had had to content himself with having his opposition recorded in the Cabinet minutes.[54] But even when Churchill became Prime Minister he did not feel free to impose pro-Zionist measures against the opinions of those Ministers involved directly with Palestine, backed as they were by powerful Departmental bureaucracies. Nor did he feel able, during the years of military crisis in the Middle East, to oppose the opinions of the civil and military administrations in the Middle East which, in almost complete unanimity, warned against the dire consequences of not proceeding along the lines of declared Government policy.

The winter of 1942–3 was a turning-point in many senses. It was clear that once the threat to Britain's position in the Middle East was repulsed, long-term proposals that had been held up owing to the military situation would be actively canvassed by the various parties which saw their own future as lying in the area. Particularly embarrassing for London was the publicity campaign waged by the Zionists in the United States since the winter of 1941–2. This campaign, initially for a Jewish Army and later for a Jewish State in Palestine, attracted the public support of central figures in an Administration that was relatively new to the Middle East. American sympathy for the Zionist cause increased when in the autumn of 1942 the first authentic reports of Nazi mass exterminations filtered through to the West.

The Zionist publicity campaign in the United States did not go unnoticed in the Arab States. In December 1942, Nuri Said instructed his Ambassador at Washington to protest at an advertisement in the New York Times urging the recruitment of a Jewish Army. Iraq was particularly concerned that the statement in the Press had appeared above the signatures of Senators Hoover and Stimson, the latter being Secretary of State for War. Nuri Said told London that such public declarations by American notables might commit the United States to a pro-Zionist policy.[55]

London was agitated further by Weizmann's statements in the United States, citing Churchill as the sponsor of a scheme whereby, by negotiation between the Zionists and Ibn Saud, Palestine was to be transformed into a Jewish State.[56] Weizmann had kept London abreast of developments on this issue by his reports to the British Embassy in Washington.[57] Sumner Welles[58] apparently believed that Ibn Saud would settle with the Zionists in return for a substantial loan or contribution and on 26 January 1943, proposed that Weizmann himslf visit Saudi Arabia to negotiate. Weizmann reported that Welles seemed to accept the official Zionist programme, 'Jewish State and all'. Weizmann was apparently prepared to go to Saudi Arabia provided he first received the backing of both Churchill and Roosevelt. The Foreign Office was appalled at the Embassy report:

'On the one hand, the policy of HMG *approved* by Parliament—the White Paper. On the other, Dr Weizmann is discussing with the State Department another policy, described apparently by the State Department themselves as 'Mr Churchill's idea'.[59]

The Foreign Office thought the scheme unrealistic, and advised warning the State Department that what the British Prime Minister said off the record should not be accepted even as an unofficial proposal from the British Government. Prior to Churchill's departure for the United States in March 1943, Eden brought to his attention Weizmann's claims regarding the 'Ibn Saud' scheme, and asked what he really had said to the Zionist leader. Churchill replied that while Weizmann had no authority to speak for him, it was 'sufficiently well known that the views which Weizmann expressed were in fact substantially those of Mr Churchill'.[60]

The Department decided that it could not, on the grounds of Mr Churchill's reply, issue any *démenti* in Washington, and that in view of 'the dangerous interaction between Zionist propaganda and Arab unrest' it should draw up a Cabinet paper which, if nothing else, would serve as a warning. The Department's anxieties were only increased by further pronouncements by Churchill.

In April 1943, Weizmann wrote to Churchill[61] protesting against recent Ministerial statements in Parliament that had referred to the White Paper as 'the firmly established policy' of the Government.[62] In Jerusalem also, claimed Weizmann, the authorities missed no opportunity to 'nail down the White Paper as permanent and immutable'. The White Paper, Weizmann claimed, was the application to Palestine of the unhappy principle of appeasement, and he expressed the hope that with the abandonment of that principle, and the recent accretion of British strength and prestige, the Allies might deal 'boldly and generously' with the Jewish problem by assigning Palestine to the Jews.

The letter evidently served as a prick to Churchill's conscience, and he warned his colleagues that he would soon circulate it to the Cabinet:

I cannot agree that the White Paper is 'the firmly established policy' of the present Government. I have always regarded it as a gross breach of faith committed by the Chamberlain Government in respect of obligations to which I personally was a party . . . it runs until it is superseded.[63]

This was a clear warning that the political status quo in Palestine was not sacrosanct for Churchill. It was also a blow to the sensibilities of those Ministers whom Churchill had kept on from the Chamberlain Government,[64] who were now clearly informed that their retention under Churchill had not signified the latter's acquiescence in their Palestine policy.

As promised, Churchill elaborated on his views of the White Paper before the Cabinet, emphasizing that he personally remained a supporter of the Balfour Declaration, as modified by 'his own' White Paper of 1922.[65] Churchill expected full American support for a new policy on Palestine, to be declared after the war. He advocated an investigation into the possibility of making Eritrea and Tripolitania into Jewish colonies that might be affiliated to the Jewish National Home. As for Arab claims, Churchill asserted that apart from the loyal Ibn Saud and Emir Abdullah, the Arabs had been virtually of no use to the Allies in the present war. The only fighting they had done was against the British, in Iraq. Unlike after the First World War, the Arabs would have no claims on the victorious Allies.

The Foreign Office, already engaged in drafting a Cabinet paper on this subject, reacted sharply to Churchill's views which, they believed, missed the whole point:

The question is ... not whether we owe the Arabs a debt of gratitude, but whether we have important interests centring in the Arab world. The answer must be emphatically that we have; and in particular our oil interests ...[66]

In view of British interests in the area, the Foreign Office was opposed to giving to the Jews in Palestine any more than was already offered under the 1939 White Paper. The Middle Eastern section of the Department wanted a new, public declaration reaffirming the White Paper as Britain's post-war objective, but this was vetoed by warnings from the American section about American sensibilities. The Foreign Office, which blamed the American Administration for most of the recent agitation over Palestine, proposed that the Government convey a warning that American indiscretions risked creating a serious handicap to the Allied war effort.[67]

Viscount Cranborne, taking a more balanced view, pointed to the dilemma in the situation. The Government had to face the fact that in March 1944 the immigration provisions of the White Paper came to an end and, even if the long-term settlement was left over until after the war, some provision would have to be made for the Jewish future:

... If Jewish immigration is not brought to an end next year, wide sections of Arab opinion are likely to charge Great Britain with a breach of faith. On the other hand it is surely impossible, especially in view of the unhappy situation of the Jews of Europe, to close one of their main channels of escape during the war ...[68]

Cranborne's advice was that, pending the long-term solution, the Government should seek to 'freeze' the status quo, so that Jewish immigration might continue at the permitted rate beyond the five-year period allowed for by the White Paper. Ultimately, he agreed with the Prime Minister that the Government could not in the long term maintain a policy of 'absolute cessation of immigration into Palestine at the discretion of the Arab majority'.[69]

Added to this complex situation were the danger signs from Palestine itself.[70] The Palestine Administration reported that the Zionists had been engaged for some years in actively alienating the Jews of Palestine from the Mandatory, with the objective of securing the abandonment of the White Paper policy. The Zionists had adopted a maximalist programme, which aimed at gaining Jewish Agency control over immigration in order to create a Jewish majority in the country. This in turn had led to counter-claims, equally maximalist and nationalist, by the Palestinian Arabs, supported—for whatever motives—by Arabs in neighbouring countries. This situation, concluded the Administration, was likely to erupt in armed disorders unless something were done to remove the danger of a direct clash between Jews and Arabs, particularly if any substantial concession were made to either of the parties.

The Administration expected these disorders either at, or near the end of the war—but in any event, the crucial period would occur at the end of the spring of 1944, when the White Paper time-limit for immigration elapsed. Before that date, the Government must make both communities understand that it would not grant the maximalist demands of either, and that their differences would have to be settled by mutual compromise and partnership. The Middle East War Council endorsed the Administration's report, adding that 'any deviation from the White Paper principles would almost inevitably provoke an outbreak'. The Council recommended a public reaffirmation of the White Paper policy, supported if possible by the United States Government.[71]

To all these warnings was added that of the Minister of State Resident at Cairo:

Every informed observer ... is convinced ... that the country is heading for the most serious outbreak of disorder and violence which it has yet seen, and that the explosion is timed to go off as soon as the war ends, or possibly a few months earlier.[72]

Casey proposed that the United Nations should grant Great Britain a new mandate for the safeguarding of the entire Middle East area, including the Levant States. Britain would guarantee that the White Paper policy was upheld in Palestine, and that France was turned out of the Levant. This idea was predictably ruled out by the Foreign Office. A string of British military establishments throughout the Middle East could only harm the British image, while a United Nations Trusteeship would appear to derogate from the nominal independence already enjoyed by some Arab States. The Foreign Office aimed at placating the Arab States by stopping short of making Palestine a Jewish State, and by reducing the French position in the Levant to one corresponding to Britain's own position in Iraq.[73]

i. Partition revived

This then was the background to the Cabinet's consideration of the Palestine question when it finally came up for discussion in July 1943.[74] The Cabinet agreed that in the short term Jewish immigration should be permitted beyond the White Paper termination point of 31 March 1944—up to the 75,000 limit stipulated by that document. As regards the long term, Churchill reiterated his view that his Government was not tied to the White Paper, and that when the time arrived the Government would continue to carry out its solemn undertakings towards the Jewish National Home. Attlee (who was

Secretary of State for the Dominions at the time, without an official seat in the Cabinet) agreed that it would be impolitic to reopen the question for the present, but thought it important to begin consideration of long-term policy without delay, in order to be in a position to implement it immediately after the war. The Cabinet agreed on this point, and decided to set up a subcommittee 'to consider and report to the War Cabinet on the long-term policy for Palestine'. The Committee was guided to take the Peel Commission's plan of partition as its starting-point, and to consider whether it, or some variant of it, could not be adopted. Membership of the Committee was left to Churchill's discretion.

Churchill's personal choice caused pessimism at the Foreign Office:

... I am absolutely certain that we won't be able to get the Foreign Office view through this particular Committee. Every single member of it, with the exception of the Colonial Secretary (and they could hardly keep him out) voted against the White Paper in 1939.[75]

Dissatisfied with the Committee's leanings,[76] Eden attempted to have the pro-Zionist Amery removed, but he was rebuffed by Churchill:

... it is quite true that he has my way of thinking on this point, which is no doubt to be deplored, but he has great knowledge and mental energy ... anyway, the Report is only for the Cabinet to consider.[77]

Eden later attempted to console his officials:

... there is going to be much trouble on this subject, internal as well as external, before we are through. It is a comfort to reflect that Mr Amery has never been right on any subject that I can recollect from Palestine to the League of Nations ...[78]

The Committee's secretariat was bombarded with a variety of memoranda, arguing—as stated in the Committee's terms of reference—the feasibility of partition, based on the Peel plan. The main advocate of partition was Amery, intimately involved with the subject since 1937.[79] He argued that partition had been rejected by the Woodhead Commission in 1938 for the wrong reasons.[80] The Peel Commission had based its scheme on those areas in which Arabs and Jews already preponderated, whereas fulfilment of the Mandate would necessitate assigning to the Jews an area large enough to allow substantial immigration. The Woodhead Commission, continued Amery, had taken their instructions 'to include the fewest possible Arabs and Arab enterprises in the Jewish area, and vice versa', to mean in effect that the Jewish area was to include nothing beyond the area covered by existing Jewish settlements. The Woodhead Commission had further taken their instruction 'to delineate self-supporting Arab and Jewish States' as implying that the 'self-supporting Arab State' must continue to enjoy those amenities that Jewish enterprise and taxation had brought to undivided Palestine. Under these assumptions, of course no scheme had been found practicable.

Amery himself believed that the area assigned to the Jews by the Peel Commission—including most of inland and predominantly Arab Galilee—was less suitable than a mainly coastal area extending down to the Egyptian border, which would include the Negev, with access to the Dead Sea and to the Gulf of Akaba. The Arabs would then have all of northern Galilee, and most of the inland, hilly Samaria and Jerusalem districts.

Yet Amery was alone in advocating such a clear-cut solution. Opposition to any 'generous' scheme of partition came also from a surprising quarter, from Victor Cazalet.[81] Cazalet reported on his own personal experience of 'the intense unpopularity of the Jews, and in particular of the Zionist Organization, that prevails over the whole Middle East'. Cazalet put forward two alternatives. First, that Britain, together with the United States, should 'take over and run Syria, Lebanon, Palestine and Transjordan for an indefinite period—until the Jews, Arabs and Lebanese were prepared to form a federation between them, with or without our help'. Second, if this proved impossible, Cazalet advocated offering the Jews a token State, smaller than that under the Peel scheme, together with another territory elsewhere, as a refuge for the Jews. This latter proposal was really a gesture of despair, for Cazalet concluded 'there is no scheme you could offer them unless we are prepared to give them the whole of Palestine'.

The predominant tone of the Cabinet Committee's first meeting was pro-partitionist.[82] The Colonial Secretary opened the discussion by stating that they would have to accept the fact that the Arabs and Jews would not, at least for a generation, be able to live together peaceably in Palestine. This left two alternatives: (a) continued British administration over the whole country under some form of colonial system, or (b) partition. Colonel Stanley agreed with Amery that partition would have to be considered now on principles other than those that had guided the Peel Commission. Areas now predominantly Jewish or Arab would not necessarily remain so, and the Jews would have to have unfettered control over immigration into their area. Morrison proposed that they extend their enquiry to include Transjordan.

The Foreign Office, which had reserved its opinion until the various plans for partition were put forward, was alarmed at the bias of the Committee's deliberations. The Department was particularly concerned that certain Ministers were 'leaking' the news that partition was again under consideration.[83] This was in contrast to Cabinet instructions that they dissuade Nuri Said from accompanying the Regent of Iraq on a visit to London—expressly in order to avoid discussion of Palestine.[84]

On 25 October 1943, Weizmann was received by Churchill in London, with Attlee also present. Churchill informed Weizmann that he had been thinking about partition, and that he did not take for granted all the information that he received from the Near East, although he would not be able to say in public what he was telling the Zionist leader now. As if to console Weizmann for the behaviour of his own Conservative colleagues, Churchill assured Weizmann that Attlee and the Labour Party were committed to partition—to which Attlee nodded his agreement. The Prime Minister also took this occasion to inform Weizmann—two weeks before the official announcement in the Commons—that the balance of immigration certificates would be carried over past the White Paper deadline in March 1944.[85] Churchill's warnings not to expect his public support for the Zionist cause did not prevent Weizmann using his name in the United States later on. The Foreign Office later complained that Ministerial remarks were being 'bandied about in Washington as gossip', and that the Prime Minister was being widely committed to a pro-Zionist change of policy as regards Palestine.[86]

The Cabinet Committee did not meet again until November 1943. In the interim the Foreign Office, among others, prepared its attack on Amery's plan of partition.[87] Criticism focused especially on the assignment of the Negev to the Jews, for three reasons: (a) a Jewish-held Negev, combined with the Gulf of Akaba, would interpose a barrier between Egypt and the rest of the Arab world; (b) reports indicated that the Negev was hopeless from an agricultural point of view; and (c) to give to the Jews so large an area would be bound to cause repercussions among the Arabs against any new proposals for a Palestine settlement. In short, 'why go out of the way to invite trouble, when the advantage, from the Jewish point of view, seemed negligible?'

In reply, Amery argued that there was no reason to suppose that Egypt and Syria were worried about physical contiguity.[88] On the contrary, Amery argued that the nearer the Jews were brought to the Canal the better—so as to secure in that area a developed State bound to Britain by ties of gratitude, and even more, by practical interest. The reason for giving the Negev to the Jews was not so much for its agricultural value (though he did not rule this out) but for the access it gave to the Dead Sea minerals and their export via Akaba. Amery concluded with a direct gibe at the Foreign Office:

... if we are precluded from doing anything which could in any way offend Arab susceptibilities ... then surely our enquiry is superfluous.[89]

But it was exactly on this premise that the Foreign Office prepared—as it had done in 1937—its main attack on the very principle of partition:

... the solution to the Palestine question should be capable of fitting in with our general Middle Eastern policy. Any suggestion that ... (it) should be determined solely on the basis of world sympathy with the sufferings of the Jews, as contrasted with the alleged failure of the Arabs to assist the war effort, is to be deprecated...[90]

British policy in the future, continued the memorandum, could not be based on expected gratitude from the Arabs for having defeated the Axis. On the debit side of Britain's account with the Arabs would be the failure to remove the French from the Levant, the increased demands for military facilities that would have to be made from Iraq (to guard the Persian Gulf), and probably from Egypt. All this would outweigh any credit balance, and 'to put extra strain by the Palestine problem would endanger the stability of our Middle East policy'.[91]

Yet, as was not the case in 1937, the Foreign Office had now to take into account the weight of opinion inside the Cabinet Committee in favour of partition, and of the influence of the Prime Minister himself. Therefore, while arguing with all its power against partition and the creation of a Jewish State in Palestine, the Department pleaded that 'if Jewish State there must be, it should be confined to a "token" State considerably less extensive than the Peel plan'.

The Minister of State at Cairo, while accepting that it would be in Britain's own best interest to adhere to the White Paper, conceded that in the changed political context brought about by war this would clearly be impossible.[92] The Government was therefore thrown back on partition, *faute de mieux*. The Minister's scheme of partition was contrived from an idiosyncratically British sense of logic:

Partition, on any conceivable terms to us, is acceptable to neither party ... [it] should be possible to draw a boundary which, while not acceptable to either party, would not be so utterly unacceptable as to involve us in the strife and bitterness of the past twenty-five years ...[93]

Such a scheme, believed Casey, would have to follow the narrow lines of Woodhead, rather than the generous ones of Amery. He therefore proposed to exclude from the proposed Jewish State most of Galilee—including the fertile, settled areas of the Beisan–Nazareth–Tiberias triangle—together with the Huleh valley; Jaffa, with 66,000 Arabs as against 26,000 Jews, should remain an Arab port, even if this meant the clumsy expedient of a corridor to Arab territories in the interior.

The Colonial Secretary had come closer to the Foreign Office line since the summer. He reverted to the 'Peel' principle of drawing the partition lines according to extant Jewish and Arab settlements.[94] Reports from the Middle East during the summer had drawn his attention to the 'fact' that even the moderate plan of partition recommended by Peel had led to an Arab revolt. Since then, Arab national aspirations had been stimulated by promises made in the White Paper. Stanley now asserted that if Britain were to go back on her undertaking it could be only on the basis of a partition somewhat resembling the Woodhead Committee's plan 'B'. This would give the Jews the fertile plains of Esdraelon and Beisan running east from Haifa, and the coastal plain from Haifa to a point south of Tel Aviv, including Jaffa. In this State the Colonial Office calculated that the Jews would enjoy a bare majority, 386,000 to 306,000 Arabs. Under Stanley's modified plan the Arabs would retain all of Galilee (given to the Jews by Peel), including the Huleh salient, and the hilly 'spine' of Palestine—the Samaria, Ramallah and

Hebron sub-districts; also the northern Negev, including the Gaza and Beersheba districts. Stanley proposed that the question of the main area of the Negev should be left open until experts had shown whether development was practicable or not. The Colonial Office scheme would give the Jewish State 80 per cent of the Jewish population, and 78 per cent of the Jewish-owned land of Palestine; also the major towns of Tel Aviv, Jaffa and Haifa (with its important industrial area), and all the Jewish industries, except for the Dead Sea potash works.

A new element was introduced by the Deputy Minister of State at Cairo.[95] Lord Moyne, while in agreement that such a 'reduced' partition plan might be practicable, believed it would have no chance of success unless both the Jewish and Arab areas were linked to a Greater Syria. Lord Moyne proposed the creation of four 'Levant' states—Greater Syria (to comprise Syria, Transjordan and the Arab areas of the Lebanon and Palestine), Christian Lebanon, the Jewish State and a British-protected Jerusalem state.

The second meeting of the Cabinet Committee[96] witnessed general support for the Colonial Office scheme, from Casey, Moyne and the Palestine Administration. The Colonial Secretary, summing up the principles that had guided him, claimed that as no reasonable scheme would be acceptable to either party, the Government would have to impose its own, equitable scheme —one that would be practicable, and not lead to lasting resentment. Such pre-conditions meant conforming as far as possible to the existing demographic patterns of Palestine.

The Foreign Office concentrated its efforts at this stage on making the proposed Jewish State—if one must be created—as 'palatable' as possible for the Arabs. Its objections to even the modified Colonial Office scheme were based on three points: (a) the Jewish State would have as many Arabs as Jews—in itself a provocation; (b) the plan concentrated all the best land and industry in the Jewish State; and (c) the Arab hinterland was to be deprived of any port facilities south of Acre, unless, or until a new port could be built at Gaza.[97]

At the Cabinet Committee meeting, Law therefore asked for the exclusion from the Jewish State of the Beisan–Nazareth–Tiberias triangle, the Huleh salient, and Jaffa—all predominantly Arab in population. Stanley pointed out that this would involve the transfer to the Arab State of the important Jordan hydro-electric works, that supplied all Palestine with its electricity. Law retorted that the Jewish State would still be left with most of Palestine's industry and 80 per cent of its citrus area. But the Committee decided to leave the triangle in the Jewish State, on account of the 24,000 Jewish settlers already there. The Committee also rejected Law's proposal to transfer Jaffa to the Arab State, but instead agreed to guarantee reasonable port facilities to the Arabs. Against Law's objections, the Huleh salient (an area of projected Jewish development) was also left in the projected Jewish State—although its inclusion was now made dependent upon the agreement of the

Palestine Administration. Decision on the Negev was left over to the next meeting.

At its third meeting, the Committee concentrated on the two outstanding points—the Huleh salient, and the Negev.[98] The predisposition of the Committee became evident when, despite warnings of disturbances or even civil war conveyed in the meantime by the High Commissioner of Palestine, and over the objections of Law and Stanley, the Committee nevertheless confirmed the inclusion of the Huleh in the Jewish State. There was no clear-cut consensus concerning the Negev. Stanley advocated that it remain under the Mandate until its economic potential was examined. Cranborne suggested it remain permanently mandated, while Moyne advocated that it go to the Arab State, though he added that MacMichael should be asked what effect the exclusion of the Negev from their State would have on the Palestinian Arabs. Law expressed the opinion that the effect of partition on the Arabs outside Palestine might be less serious if the Negev remained under Mandate. The Committee finally agreed that—subject to MacMichael's agreement—the Negev would remain provisionally under Mandate until an impartial committee reported on its economic potential. Meanwhile, there would be no announcement on its allocation to either State, although development rights might be given to a chartered company.

The Committee also gave its general agreement to Moyne's scheme for the creation of a Greater Syria although, if necessary, partition was to proceed without it. The Committee decided to press ahead with working out the details of the scheme, in order to have it ready for implementation at the right psychological moment. This would be preferably after the defeat of Germany, although Moyne warned that it might have to be earlier, as one of the means by which to persuade the French to reduce their own rights in the Levant.

Having failed in its attempt to 'modify' the extent of the proposed Jewish State, the Foreign Office reverted to its original policy of outright opposition to partition, in principle. The Department expected violent Arab opposition to the new partition scheme because (a) it now allowed for unlimited immigration, whereas the 1939 White Paper had established the principle that the Jewish population of Palestine would remain at 33 per cent of the total; (b) the scheme was similar to plan 'B' of the Peel Report, and even if Galilee were now excluded from the Jewish State, Jaffa and other Arab lands were not; (c) the whole scheme rested on the principle that every possible area, except those wholly or almost wholly Arab in respect of population and land, was to be given to the Jews; and (d) for the Arabs, the scheme was a breach of good faith:

When we wanted to keep them quiet, in 1939, we produced the White Paper, but when, after the war, our international difficulties were eased, we decided to betray Arab interests by reverting to our original ideas of partition . . .[99]

The Department remained adamant in its opposition to leaving the Negev indefinitely under Mandate, which would only arouse Jewish hopes and Arab fears—and therefore proposed that the Negev be allotted to the projected Greater Syrian State. The Department also opposed the cession of the Huleh salient to the Jews, merely on the grounds of the concession granted them. In Jewish hands, the Huleh would form a barrier between Arab Galilee and Greater Syria, and create vulnerable frontiers.

But the Committee was by its very composition weighted against the traditional Foreign Office line, and at its fourth meeting—against Foreign Office objections—decided by majority on its Report, which summarized the conclusions of its previous meeting.[100] Casey registered his dissent from the main report in a separate paper,[101] advocating, like the Foreign Office, that the Huleh salient, the Beisan–Nazareth–Tiberias triangle, and the Negev should go to the projected Arab State. Cairo's opposition to the Jews' receipt of the Negev might have been connected with growing fears of the Jewish military potential, and its proximity to the Canal.

The Prime Minister expressed his approval of the Committee's report, even in the face of added opposition from the Chiefs of Staff.[102] But there was a general consensus that no announcement could be made prior to the successful conclusion of the war with Germany. Again, as in 1937, the Foreign Office was granted an interval between a policy decision and its execution, in which to work for the reversion of the original decision.

ii. The Foreign Office again attacks partition

In view of the fact that its traditonal objections had been overruled, the Foreign Office did consider for a time a 'secondary' line of attack—on the question of the effects, legal and social, of the establishment of a Jewish State in Palestine upon those Jews resident outside that State.[103] The Department was testing the 'weak link' in the Zionist case—the anxieties of those well established Jewish communities who, as had happened in 1917, might fear for their own well-being in their present country of residence.

The Department surmised that those Jews remaining outside the new State might be faced either with expulsion, or the loss of their existing nationality. Even in Britain and in the United States—the most 'tolerant' of nations—the possibility of anti-Semitism could not be ruled out, for the Jews might be regarded primarily as nationals of the Jewish State, rather than British or American. As nationality was usually based upon residence, the creation of a Jewish State would probably place most Jews in the dilemma of having to opt for one or the other. The large majority of Jews who remained outside the Jewish State would probably be frustrated, and might prefer that there should be no Jewish State rather than one of which they would not be citizens. The Foreign Office might explain the position to 'responsible' bodies in the United States and in Britain, in a published statement, and ascertain their feelings.

Such a statement would have bordered on being an actual warning, if not a veiled threat as to the consequences of the establishment of a Jewish State. Eden advised the Department not to go ahead with the idea until he had spoken with Morrison. The author has found no record of that consultation but, following the Cabinet's endorsement of partition in January 1944, Eden apparently rejected this line, reverting once more to the tactics that had worked so well in 1937-8—the mobilization of the chorus of British officialdom in the Middle East. Without doubt, the increasingly frequent publications of the extent of the Holocaust made it an acutely inappropriate moment at which to urge the solution of the Jewish 'problem' in German-occupied Europe. On the contrary, the White Paper immigration time-limit was to expire in the same month that German seizure of power in Hungary threatened to obliterate the last sizeable Jewish community (one million) in Europe.[104]

The Cabinet gave its general endorsement to the Palestine Committee's report—'as good as any that could be devised'.[105] The meeting agreed that any scheme would meet with strong protests, and that once the Government had taken a decision in favour of a particular solution, it should not allow itself to be deflected by opposition. The Chiefs of Staff's objections were overruled, although all agreed that the scheme be kept secret until the defeat of Germany. Eden asked for a suspension of any final decision, pending reports from his Ambassadors in the Middle East.

Churchill himself was convinced of the need to delay any decision on Palestine, not only until the successful conclusion of the European war but, more specifically, at least until after the American Presidential elections due to be held in November 1944.[106] It seems that Amery was the only one who saw, as he had in 1937, the danger in delay.

He discerned the need for swift, decisive action on what he regarded as an 'irreducible minimum', and argued allegorically:

The one thing that can make a Solomon's judgement possible is the swift and clean cut. What we cannot afford to do is to saw slowly away at a squealing infant in the presence of two hysterical mothers and amid the ululations of a chorus of equally hysterical relatives in the Arab and Jewish world.[107]

The Ambassadors' verdicts on partition were not hard to predict, especially in view of the lead given by Eden:

You may be surprised that the Committee, in the light of their past knowledge of the history of Palestine, should have recommended what is essentially a return to the Peel Plan, which was responsible for so much opposition and bloodshed in the years before the war ...[108]

Eden explained to his Middle East envoys that the change in Government policy was due to two factors: firstly, the change in the political balance of the

Cabinet effected by Churchill; and secondly, the difficulty in carrying out the latter stages of the White Paper provisions in a world radically changed from that of 1939.

By March 1944, the Government had to decide whether to 'close the doors' of Palestine to further Jewish immigration, or not. If it did not—and American opinion made Ministers all the more reluctant to do so—then the White Paper could be regarded as defunct. The question then became whether to 'return to the old pernicious system of absorptive capacity', or to return to the partition of Palestine—which would at least place the responsibility for future Jewish immigration on the Jews themselves. The Jews' suffering during the war had strengthened their case for establishing a Jewish State somewhere, and it could hardly be other than in Palestine. The Cabinet Committee had felt, explained Eden, that if partition was accompanied by an offer to terminate the mandates for Palestine and Transjordan and to facilitate the creation of a Greater Syria, this might be regarded as a 'new contribution' to offset any detrimental effects.

Eden asked the envoys specifically whether Arab opposition—if expected—would be materially reduced by giving the Huleh salient to the Arabs instead of to the Jews? If the Negev were definitely promised to the Arabs? If the plan were linked to the creation of a Greater Syria? Although Eden's enquiry referred to the details, rather than to the principle of partition, the Ambassadors' replies addressed themselves first and foremost to warnings as to the consequences of partition *per se*.

Lord Killearn[109] forecast bitter opposition from Egypt, which currently aimed at the leadership of the Arab States. The creation of an independent Jewish State in Palestine would be regarded as a 'torpedo' to that dream. He did not believe the inclusion or exclusion of the areas mentioned would mitigate Arab opposition, though if partition did go through he would advocate the inclusion of the Huleh in the Arab State, on the grounds of contiguity between Galilee and the rest of the Arab State. Killearn's own proposal was brutally simple:

... scrap the White Paper and Mandate and come out boldly with a decision to keep Palestine ourselves as a vital link in our defence system ... our physical control should be definite and unlimited ... both sides would squeal ... but would eventually submit to *force majeure* ...

This advice was not only contrary to Britain's supposed concern for its international obligations—but it also made nonsense of the Ambassador's oft-repeated warnings about the repercussions in the Arab world of British policy in Palestine. Killearn's attitude can perhaps be understood in the context of British military strength in the Middle East at that period, and the readiness with which Killearn himself was willing to display it.

From Baghdad, Cornwallis was not quite so unequivocal.[110] He believed that the announcement of partition was unlikely to produce any immediate violent reaction, provided sufficient force was shown. However, the Jewish State would become the *terra irredenta* of the Arabs, to be recovered when a favourable moment presented itself. Iraq itself would regard the abrogation of the White Paper as a gross breach of faith, and the establishment of a Jewish State as a betrayal. If there were riots in Palestine one might expect hostile demonstrations in Iraq, attacks on Jews and possibly on individual British subjects. At the very least, 'Iraq would leave the list of countries in which Britain had friendly interest', and the maintenance of British oil and other interests would become precarious. Cornwallis did not believe that the creation of a Greater Syria would 'soften the blow'—the Arab leaders already took such a development for granted. As regards the details of the scheme, he was against the cession of the Huleh to the Jews, as that area, largely populated by Arabs, might then be expected to become the source of a special grievance. He also warned against Britain acting alone, without the backing of its Allies, otherwise their influence would rise as that of Britain fell.

During this period, a new proposal, emanating from Roosevelt, was conveyed to London by his emissary to the Middle East, Colonel Hoskins.[111] Roosevelt advocated that Palestine be turned into a Permanent Trustee State, administered by a High Commissioner responsible to the United Nations, guided by a Council representing Jews, Christians and Moslems. Jewish immigration might continue, but within the limits of a fixed ratio to the Arab population.

The scheme—later resurrected by Eden —was ably disposed of for the moment by the Colonial Secretary.[112] Under trusteeship, claimed Colonel Stanley, Palestine would be left for ever under a mandatory system, with all the attendant evils inherent in it prior to the war. The scheme would shatter for ever Jewish hopes of nationhood; control of their own immigration would be denied them; and the Jews of Palestine would remain doomed to permanent minority status. On the other hand, the plan satisfied none of the Arab demands—independence, closer union with neighbouring Moslem countries, and the complete stoppage of Jewish immigration. It did not even have the advantage of partition, which ensured that in the future a large portion of Palestine would form part of an independent Arab State. Churchill agreed with Stanley, and repeated his determination to abide by the pledges given to the Jews by past British Governments.[113]

Additional support for partition now came from an unexpected quarter— from MacMichael. In his final dispatch before leaving Palestine for good, the High Commissioner also advocated partition, *faute de mieux*.[114] He had come to the conclusion, from his own experience, that the Government would not and probably could not effectively control Jewish immigration which, if it continued on any considerable scale into an undivided Palestine, would be 'disastrous for British imperial interests, to the security of the Middle East, to the Arabs, whose fear of a Jewish deluge is not without justification, and to the Jews themselves, for whom a process of gradual percolation in an atmosphere of qualified receptivity offers a far brighter future than does the attempt to obtain by force what is not theirs to take nor ours to give'. Under partition, Jewish immigration would lose much of its terror for the Arab, being confined to a defined area—and much of its attraction for the Jew.

With the exception of MacMichael, all British representatives in the Middle East warned against the consequences of partitioning Palestine. Such warnings had been expected, even solicited by the Foreign Office. But not even the Colonial Office or the pro-partitionists on the Cabinet Committee could have failed to be impressed.

iii. The Cabinet adopts partition

In August 1944 the Cabinet agreed that consideration of the Palestine problem should be resumed at an early date, and deputed the Colonial and Foreign Office to collaborate in working out a final scheme.[115] But whereas the Colonial Office produced a document entitled 'possible modifications to the partition scheme', the Foreign Office put 'The Case against Partition'.

The Colonial Secretary reported back to the Cabinet Committee (with the same membership as before, and still chaired by Morrison) on the objections of the Ambassadors at Cairo and Baghdad, and the opposition expressed by Middle East representatives (apart from MacMichael) at a conference called by Lord Moyne at Cairo, on his return from London.[116] The conference had advised against proceeding with Moyne's Greater Syria scheme for the time being, but had recommended the initial creation of a Greater Transjordan, to be known as Southern Syria—comprising Transjordan and Arab Palestine. Military representatives in the Middle East had made it clear that a policy of bi-nationalism in an undivided Palestine under British rule was preferable to the creation of independent States. The Chiefs of Staff had been asked for their opinions of the proposed frontiers.

But Stanley thought it inadvisable to suspend further action until the report of the Chiefs of Staff. He believed that no strategically defensible frontier was possible, but that partition should nevertheless proceed along the lines of the principles already agreed upon—on the basis of existing Jewish settlement, and avoiding the inclusion of too large an Arab element in the Jewish State.

The 'modifications' proposed by Stanley were minor. With the postponement of the Greater Syria scheme, it was now proposed that Galilee should form part of the new 'Southern Syria', to be administered from Amman. Special prominence would be given to the Jerusalem State, in which the High Commissioner would be personally responsible for the Holy Places. Some minor border rectifications were proposed (probably after consultation with the Palestine Administration), the most notable of which was the exclusion of Mount Tabor—the traditional site of the Transfiguration—from the Jewish State; as also the potash works at the southern end of the Dead Sea.

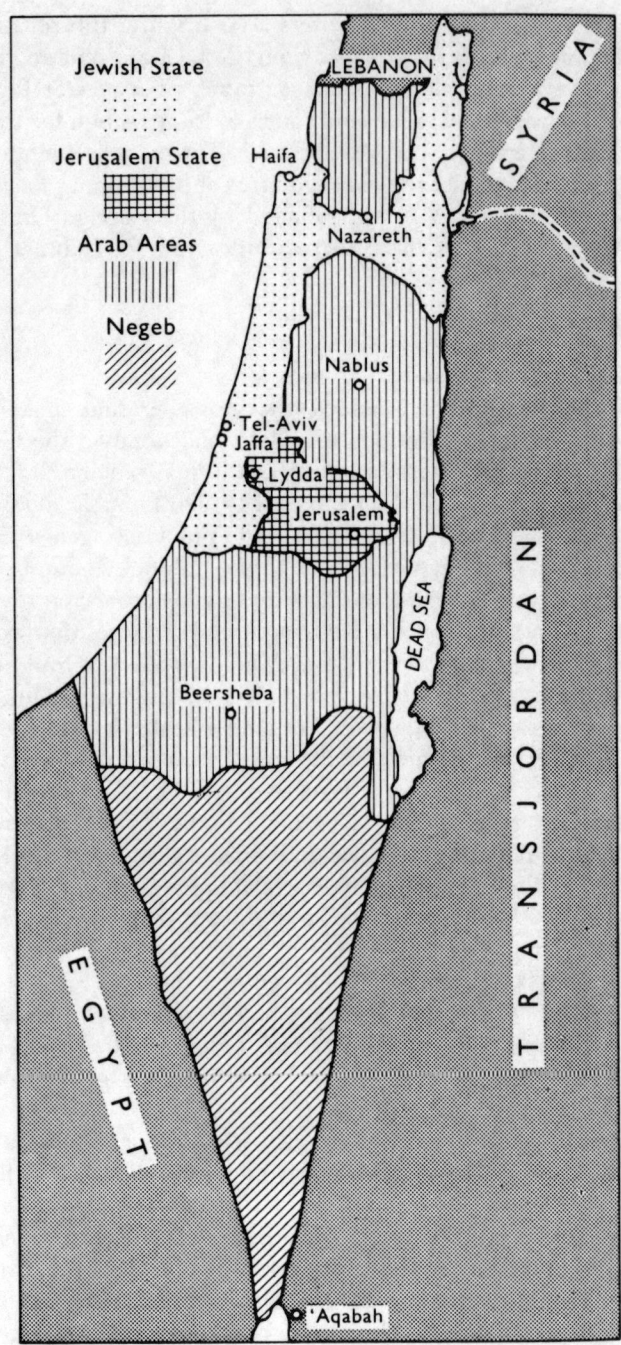

The Cabinet Committee's partition proposal, 1944

The Foreign Office rejected the whole thesis that partition would make for a final settlement in the area and predicted that:

> ... The Zionists will not be deterred by the small size of the Jewish State from filling it up with immigrants beyond its capacity. They will think of the Jewish State merely as a stepping-stone towards the realization of their wider hopes for a larger Jewish State covering the whole of Palestine and Transjordan. The Arabs will be kept in a continual state of tension. There will continually be disorders and bloodshed ...[117]

Eden, in a memorandum which summarized Foreign Office thinking since partition was first proposed in 1937, accused the Committee of making four major errors; (a) in underestimating the upheaval that would be caused in the Middle East by the creation of a Jewish State in any part of Palestine; (b) in placing too much emphasis on American opinion, when that opinion could not properly be assessed; (c) in giving undue consideration to the opinion of the Jewish extremists, whose views might not be endorsed by the bulk of their co-religionists outside Palestine; and (d) in believing that partition would bring finality, when in effect it would only transfer control from the Colonial to the Foreign Office and Service Departments.

The Foreign Office now took up Roosevelt's proposal to create a new Palestinian State under the aegis of the United Nations, with executive powers devolving on a British High Commissioner or Governor. The Department feared that any policy embarked upon by Britain alone, especially if it were partition, would involve the grave risk of ceding British pre-eminence to the United States. In contrast to its opinion of partition, the Department believed that the statute constituting the new State *would* be definitive, rendering Jewish immigration possible 'perhaps to within 100,000 of the Arab population', which would mean a further 300–400,000 Jews. The memorandum was a poorly patched-up motley of alarms and wishful thinking.

At the first of the second series of Cabinet Committee meetings,[118] Amery and Stanley opposed the Foreign Office attempt to reopen discussion on the issue of partition itself, and advocated adherence to the December scheme. Morrison agreed to defer discussion until Eden, then abroad, returned.

For the first time, Eden himself attended the next Committee meeting, on 26 September,[119] in order to put the Foreign Office case against partition. Amery, in his Ministerial capacity (as Secretary of State for India), sympathized with Eden's case—any alteration to the White Paper policy would greatly affect the Moslems of India, and he was certain that the Viceroy of India would oppose partition. But in Amery's opinion this view did not take into account the fact that unless the problem were handled decisively the position would grow worse, and both sides might commit themselves irrevocably to extremist policies. The Foreign Office scheme meant permanent denial of the self-government that both Arabs and Jews were determined to have. Amery also rejected the Foreign Office theory on 'Jewish expansionism'. When responsible for their own State, he argued, the Jews would be wary of the dangers arising from overpopulation, and would themselves take measures to control it.

Stanley asserted that the Foreign Office objections applied equally to any departure from the White Paper. The dangers risked by partition were a matter of opinion—his own advisers considered the risks less than those of any other alternative. Stanley, as in 1943, did not believe that an Anglo-American condominium held out any better prospect than did partition, whereas any scheme that envisaged a further immigration of 400,000 Jews would constitute a more serious departure from the White Paper than partition. The plan would be no more welcome to the Jews, since it ruled out a Jewish majority, a Jewish State, and self-government. No responsibility would be accepted by the United States or Soviet Governments and in the end it would be left to Britain alone to implement the plan. The Foreign Office attempted to put the argument that European Governments might bring pressure to bear on their Jews to migrate to the Jewish State, but this was countered by the Colonial Office view that the creation of a Jewish State might in fact have a stabilizing effect on the Jews who, without any need for political agitation, might become more welcome in those countries where they were.

Morrison summed up: the majority of the Committee clearly saw no reason to depart from the broad principles of its first report, and saw partition as the lesser of two evils. Eden gave notice that he would continue his opposition in Cabinet.

What in fact were the differences between the Committee's first and second reports, and what were the motivations behind the modifications proposed?[120] The linking of partition to the plan for a Greater Syria had been dropped, and the Greater Syria scheme postponed. It was concluded that any such scheme would have to await the clarification of the French position in the Levant; also, London's obligations to Abdullah precluded the attachment of Transjordan to Syria against his will—and Abdullah would not agree to such an amalgamation unless he himself were the ruler, which the Syrians in their turn would not accept.

The second report stressed the importance of the Jerusalem State, which would justify British presence in Palestine as guardian of the city sacred to three religions. Minor frontier rectifications had removed som 42,000 acres from the Jewish State, though this was compensated for by not taking—as had been intended at one time—48,000 acres from the Huleh area. On the two major points of contention, Galilee and the Negev, the Committee impressed by assessments received from Middle East posts, had swung towards the Arab interest. Galilee was now to go to Southern Syria, whereas the future of the Negev was left open—its northern border was to be adjusted so as to transfer the potash works at the southern end of the Dead Sea to the

Southern Syrian State. On the latter issue, no difficulties in transit were envisaged for the Jewish operating company from Transjordan.

iv. Partition shelved

On 6 November 1944, three days after the Secretary to the Cabinet prepared the Committee's report for Cabinet discussion, Lord Moyne was assassinated by Jewish terrorists at Cairo. Churchill issued a stiff personal warning to the Zionists in the House of Commons:

If our dreams for Zionism are to end in the smoke of assassins' pistols and our labours for its future to produce only a new set of gangsters worthy of Nazi Germany, many like myself will have to reconsider the position we have maintained so consistently in the past ... .[121]

Churchill gave instructions that Cabinet discussion on the committee's report should be held over, it being impossible to discuss plans for the future of Palestine while such outrages continued.[122]

There is some irony in the fact that an offshoot of the Revisionists—whose campaign for a Jewish Army in the United States had been so material in prompting British reconsideration of the White Paper policy—was now responsible for the delay of Government measures that would have displaced the White Paper principles as the basis for British policy in Palestine.

Zionist leaders appreciated the damage done, even if they remained unaware of how close they had been to a change in the status quo. The Jewish Agency agreed, for the first time, to co-operate actively with the British authorities in stamping out terrorist groups, although the Stern Group—responsible for Moyne's murder—ceased activity of its own accord, until the summer of 1945.[123]

In February 1945, as the White Paper immigration quota gradually exhausted itself,[124] the need for some Government decision became urgent. Stanley urged Morrison to convene a further meeting, in order to reach a decision as soon as possible.[125] The Colonial Office linked the decision on future immigration with that on partition.[126] The White Paper quota was not expected to last out beyond September, which meant that some new policy must be published by June at the latest. Stanley appreciated that, as usual, time had not worked in favour of partition—the recent Conference of Foreign Ministers of the Arab States at Cairo had not improved prospects; nor did the fact that Dr Weizmann—following his visit to Palestine—was allegedly moving away from partition towards full support of the Biltmore programme, which demanded Jewish Agency control of immigration into Palestine, which should be established as a Jewish Commonwealth. The Colonial Secretary's strongest argument in favour of partition was simply that it remained the only available option. He therefore challenged the Cabinet: it must choose partition, unless presented with a suitable alternative. In the meantime, he accepted the proposal made by the new Minister Resident at Cairo, Sir Edward Grigg (allegedly supported by Nuri Said as well) that a monthly quota of 2000 immigrants (or a compromise figure of 1500 if necessary) should be allowed, pending the final settlement of the Palestine question at the Peace Conference.

But the balance of forces had now tipped in favour of the 'anti-partitionists'. The second report of the Cabinet Committee had enjoyed the support of both the Minister Resident at Cairo and of the High Commissioner in Palestine. The new incumbents of both posts—Sir Edward Grigg and Viscount Gort respectively—now added their opposition to partition to that of the other British representatives in the Middle East.

Sir Edward Grigg produced his own proposal, a revision of the existing Mandate that would remove those defects that had brought about the current situation.[127] Grigg claimed that the constitution of the Arab League since the Cabinet decision of the previous September had fundamentally altered the prospects for partition, which the new body could now be expected to resist *à outrance*. Furthermore, as Mandatory of the new Jerusalem State, Britain would be committed to greater military and financial commitments than those undertaken during the previous twenty-five years in undivided Mandated Palestine. Grigg therefore proposed that the international body which the Committee had intended to set up to supervise and guarantee the three new States in Palestine should instead be entrusted with framing a new Mandate or Trust for an undivided Palestine, with Britain retaining its present responsibility for the administration and security of Palestine as a whole—but on new terms, which she herself would propose. In outlining these terms, Grigg made a profound analysis of the problems built in to the Mandatory constitution.

Grigg pinpointed three defects. Firstly, Britain bore sole responsibility for deciding on Jewish immigration—this was exploited in agitation in the United States, it embroiled Britain with the Arabs and had driven her to the surrender involved in the White Paper; immigration, proposed Grigg, should in future be decided upon by a suitable international body, in which a balance might be struck between Jewish pressure and Arab opposition. The second defect was the recognition of the Jewish Agency on terms that, combined with the weakness of the Mandatory, had enabled the Jews to set up a 'shadow' Government with its own armed forces; the main purpose of the new trusteeship over Palestine would be to institute a single system of government which would promote the development of both communities, and make the two peoples responsible in due course for their own government. Thirdly, some way would have to be found for financing Palestine for the benefit of both communities, under official control—without discouraging Jewish capital; Grigg proposed that Britain and the United States should establish a 'Palestine Development Fund' with an initial capital of £20 million.

Grigg's recommendations aimed at bringing the administration of Palestine within the frame of developing Anglo-American relations, and accordingly he recommended that responsibility pass from the Colonial to the Foreign Office.

Grigg took the opportunity to sound out the Middle East Ambassadors on his proposals, at an economic conference held in Cairo.[128] The meeting agreed unanimously with Grigg's critique of partition, yet realized that for reasons of high policy the Government might have to depart from the 1939 White Paper policy. However, if a departure was necessary, and even if American approval of future policy in Palestine had to be sought, the Ambassadors stressed that since Palestine played such an essential role in the strategic defence plan of the Middle East it must remain under effective British administration and control. The meeting concluded that any major policy changes should be deferred for as long as possible, in order to avoid disturbances at a time when Britain was in no position to deal with them, and that every effort should be made to adhere to the central principles of the White Paper.

Amery, the main proponent of partition in the Cabinet Committee, was by now on the retreat. In his last contribution to the debate, he stated that if partition had to be abandoned in deference to opposition (although he was not convinced that it should) it could only be on the basis of laying down the full equality of the two communities as the fundamental principle of future political development in Palestine. For the rest, Amery confined himself to a critique of Grigg's proposals, without putting forward any further alternatives of his own.[129] However, at the same time, Amery forwarded one further, lethal attack on partition from the pen of Wavell, now the Viceroy of India:

India contains 90 million Muslims who would deeply, perhaps actively, resent a solution of the Palestine problem which was against the interests of the Arabs. Agitation on an external Muslim grievance of this kind can quickly become formidable and can easily be exploited by anti-British Hindus for their own purposes ... Any serious estrangement between His Majesty's Government and the Muslim countries west of India would affect India's interests ... Indian troops cannot be used for police work in Palestine, and it is most important to avoid a situation in which there is any possibility of their being so used.[130]

Colonel Stanley believed Grigg's proposal to be simply a return to the White Paper, but for the fact that immigration policy—which would still remain Britain's executive responsibility—would now be decided upon by an international commission.[131] He proposed that Grigg be invited to London to participate in final Cabinet debate on the problem, and that if no decision were forthcoming by September—the date by which the immigration quota was expected to run out—Grigg and Gort should take steps to secure the temporary continuation of immigration, pending the long-term solution.

But before the Cabinet had the opportunity to consider Palestine again the war with Germany was brought to a successful conclusion, and Churchill formed a 'caretaker' Conservative Ministry pending the General Election.

As Prime Minister, Churchill had adopted a pro-Zionist stand on every issue that arose during the war—from the Land Transfers Bill in February 1940 and the various schemes for raising a Jewish army to discussion of partition itself. The reason why such a powerful Prime Minister failed to dislodge the White Paper does not lie in Churchill's infidelity to Zionism, but rather in the complex of bureaucratical and military circumstances in which he had to conduct the war.

Churchill faced overwhelming opposition from the Departments responsible for policy in the Middle East, even from those of his own friends whom he had himself brought into the Cabinet. Apart from his success in pushing through the decision on the Jewish Brigade, in September 1944, Churchill did not pursue to a successful conclusion any pro-Zionist measure. Neither did he seriously contemplate the dismissal of any colleague because of their differences over Zionism.[132]

Foreign Office fears that he would create something analogous to Lloyd George's Garden Suburb, 'of the most awful people including Brendan Bracken', soon proved illusory.[133] The Foreign Office preserved a much stronger position during the Second World War than it had under Lloyd George in the First. By debate or circumstance it triumphed on every major issue regarding British policy in the Middle East. Churchill himself remained consistent in his proviso that any decision on Palestine would have to await implementation until the end of the war, regardless of any appeal, or tragic event.[134]

From 1940 until the end of the war Churchill worked a 120-hour week, the conduct of the war absorbing all his time and energy.[135] The implementation of Government directives had to rest to a large extent on officials who were able to frustrate the implementation of decisions they had been unable to prevent being taken, simply through protracted delays and rigid adherence to technicalities. Officialdom at Whitehall was backed by the Administration in Palestine. During the war, the White Paper had become an integral part of the Administration's policy. There grew around it 'an official doctrine, an official practice, and official reputations and interests'. Officialdom in Palestine remained unmoved in the face of the known negative attitudes of Churchill and other, chiefly Labour, members of the Cabinet, and were unable to disguise their contempt for the 'ignoramuses in London'.[136]

Had Churchill tried to fight it out with these 'realists' it would have meant a continuous internal struggle. Just as he tried to avoid clashes over Palestine with Lloyd, Eden and Wavell, so he also avoided becoming involved in a permanent controversy with 'the mighty machinery of the Administration'.[137]

v. The Labour Government and Palestine

On 27 July 1945, following Labour's landslide victory at the polls, Clement

Attlee formed the first Labour Cabinet for twenty-four years. On 22 August, Attlee reconstituted the Cabinet Committee on Palestine, this time weighted more with those Departments directly concerned with the Middle East.[138]

Despite the Labour Party's numerous pro-Zionist declarations during the war,[139] the Labour Cabinet's Palestine Committee was less 'pro-partition' than its Coalition predecessor. Gone was Amery, the Gentile Zionist[140] upon whose participation in the Committee Churchill had insisted, and from whom Churchill had received his regular reports. Gone also was Colonel Stanley, if not an avid Zionist, then at least a reasonably unprejudiced Minister who —under the influence of his long-serving High Commissioner—had come to see in partition the best way out of a difficult situation. Gone also was Sinclair, a member of that small circle of Opposition Parliamentarians who in 1937 had been converted to partition by the Zionists.[141] Above all, there was the loss of the grey eminence behind the Committee's proceedings, Churchill himself. Churchill had hand-picked his Committee in defiance of Foreign Office objections. He was prepared to back, and capable of backing their findings against the combined bureaucracies of the great Departments involved, and personally against the combined views of the Chiefs of Staff. Perhaps only a Churchill, with his vast experience of the 'corridors of power', and with such a strong sympathy for the Jewish National Home, could have overcome the dead weight of established policy in Palestine.

The men who succeeded Churchill possessed none of his qualities. Bevin at times regarded the Arab–Jewish conflict as just another problem that required the brand of negotiating skill that had made him a powerful Labour leader. Although Labour's 'Big Three'—Attlee, Bevin, Morrison—had, as members of the Cabinet since 1940, had continuous access to all Cabinet papers regarding the Middle East, none of them had had direct Ministerial responsibility for the Middle East, or for the immediate conduct of the war effort. It is to be doubted whether the Labour Ministers in Churchill's Coalition assumed full responsibility for all of the decisions of the Cabinet in which they sat. Party and personal frictions survived the exigencies of war. Attlee was among that select group of Ministers whose 'wisdom' Churchill respected, but whom he would not chose as a 'boon companion'. Churchill could never really bring himself to like Morrison—though he greatly preferred him to Dalton.[142] Some Labour Ministers felt that their Conservative colleagues unduly interfered with their Ministries. Dalton had occasion to complain to Attlee that 'unless Labour Ministers were better treated each must consider his position'.[143]

Such frictions might in part explain the anomaly that successive Labour Party Conferences passed resolutions against the White Paper policy of the Government in which its own leaders sat.[144]

Prior to 1945, no Labour Minister had been exposed to the direct influence of the Middle Eastern Departments' bureaucracies. Within a few months of his entry into the Foreign Office, the previously indifferent Bevin was turning against the Zionist cause.[145] The new Labour Cabinet was overwhelmed immediately by domestic and international post-war problems and, unable to agree upon fundamental principles for a new policy in Palestine, it tended to rely more and more upon Bevin's faculty for improvisation. However, Bevin's own novel contribution to the debate—a Federal Union of Palestine and Transjordan, with Abdullah as its King—was received no more favourably than the Colonial Office brainchild, a scheme for Arab and Jewish Provinces, which was in fact, in another guise, the Cantonization scheme rejected by the Peel Commission in 1937.[146] The Cabinet was soon reduced to seeking interim measures that would somehow satisfy both sides until such time as conditions in post-war Europe settled and crystallized, perhaps enabling the Government to bring forward some compromise before the new United Nations.

However, the public intervention of President Truman in the Palestine problem[147] brought the Government to opt for the time-worn device of a Commission of Enquiry. This would not only provide reasonable grounds for further delay in tackling the problem seriously, but, as Bevin hoped, it might involve the United States responsibly with British policy in Palestine.[148]

However, Bevin's tactics misfired. Sensing correctly that public agitation in the United States was swept along on an emotional wave of sympathy for the plight of the remnants of European Jewry, Bevin intended initially that the Joint Commission should deal exclusively with this problem, inquiring into possible refuges in Europe, the British Dominions and the United States —everywhere but Palestine. However, owing to domestic electoral considerations, the American Administration was to insist, successfully, that the Commission's first task should be to examine the possibilities of Palestine's absorbing the Jewish refugees.[149]

The final terms of reference were thus in a sense a tactical victory for Zionism, which had for decades tried in vain to establish the link between the Yishuv, in Palestine, and those Jews living in the Diaspora. On the other hand, the Anglo-American Commission served two *British* purposes also. Firstly, it legitimized a much-needed delay for a war-weary country as yet unprepared for any large-scale conflict in the Middle East. Secondly, if only for the following six months, the Commission met Bevin's goal of working in tandem with the United States in a Soviet-threatened post-war world—at least in the Middle East.

However, Bevin's hopes for the long term that the Commission would inaugurate a new era of Anglo-American co-operation in Palestine were to be shattered on the rocks of American domestic politics. While continuing in its refusal to share the military consequences of the policy it was proposing for Palestine, the United States would continue to insist that more room be provided in Palestine for the victims of the Holocaust.

Truman and Attlee (not to mention Bevin) failed to achieve the close understanding and mutual respect attained by their predecessors. Britain

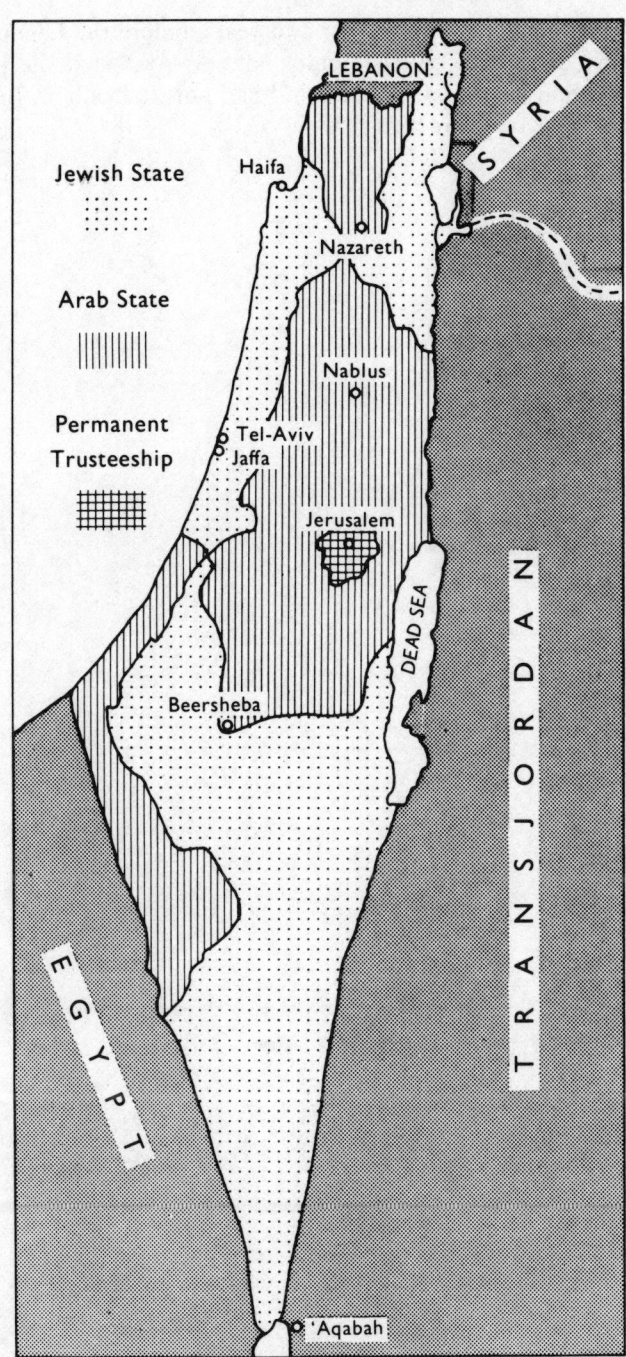

The UN partition proposal, 1947

was left to limp on alone for a further two years, before the Labour Government—against the advice of its military advisers—referred the problem to the United Nations, in order, as Churchill had put it already in July 1945, to 'let someone else have their turn'.[150]

10

Conclusion

It has been contended that none of the three parties—Britain, the Zionists and the Arabs—most closely involved in Palestinian political life during the period under review possessed a monolithic policy-making machine. Not only did the force of circumstances dictate changes in traditional, entrenched policies, but more often than not they were accompanied by the departure, or eclipse, of those leaders who had been most closely associated with the now discarded policies. In London, the Colonial Office school of thought which in 1937 had regarded partition as the most honourable way out of a Mandatory burden that had become insupportable had been superseded during 1938 by the Foreign Office school of thought which argued that Britain had already redeemed her obligations to the Jewish people under the Balfour Declaration. The Foreign Office maintained sincerely that the Jewish problem in Europe must be divorced from Palestine, a small country that was already over-inhabited and anyway could never hope to accommodate any meaningful proportion of the Jewish people.

With the dramatic, though not unanticipated, reversal of the British Government's traditional sympathy for the Zionist Movement, came the eclipse of the Anglophile school of Zionism which Weizmann in his own person epitomized and dominated. The clash between Britain-oriented 'diplomatic' Zionism and the militant 'Messianic' Zionism of Ben-Gurion found its expression in a bitter personal struggle between the doyen of the international movement and the Palestinian leader who, having risen to prominence within his own 'local constituency', went on to challenge the wisdom of the course mapped out for the World Zionist Movement by Weizmann. On the personal plane, the ageing leader, broken by personal grief and political frustration, was no match for a dynamic Ben-Gurion in his prime. Although Weizmann's standing and past record enabled him to withstand Ben-Gurion's onslaught on his leadership in 1942, Ben-Gurion had come to stay. The course of consequent events made his point for him, as Weizmann's almost involuntary attachment to Great Britain became increasingly anachronistic.

By the same token that the 1939 White Paper alienated the Zionist Movement, it might have been expected that the Palestinian Arabs would gratefully seize upon the rewards of their long struggle against the Jewish National Home. That this did not happen was due perhaps to two interconnected circumstances. First, Haj Amin el-Husseini—whose power to terrorize out of existence any challenge to his own political hegemony was adequately and repeatedly demonstrated—was specifically excluded from Palestine by the very same White Paper. Secondly, the Arabs lacked any notion of the type of political finesse taken for granted by British diplomacy. Tactically, they missed opportunities to come to terms at the moment of their adversary's maximum vulnerability. Repeatedly the Arabs misjudged the price they would be able to extract from the Mandatory power and got down to real bargaining only when the crises which the British had hoped to avert by timely concessions had in fact erupted.

What conclusions may be drawn therefore regarding British policy in Palestine during the years 1936–45? First, by the mid-1930s two new factors, unforeseen by British statesmen in 1917, dominated the Palestinian scene: on the one hand, the rapid acceleration in the rate of immigration into Palestine from anti-Semitic Europe; on the other hand, and largely in reaction to the former, the growth of a radical Arab nationalism that regarded the Jewish National Home as the main obstacle to its own constitutional advance as prescribed under the Mandate. The Arabs of Palestine suspected that the main reason why they had not achieved the same degree of political autonomy as their cousins in Iraq and Egypt (to whom they considered themselves intellectually superior) was that the Mandatory power intended to 'hold the ring' between the Jews and Arabs in Palestine until the former became a majority. At that point, the appropriate 'democractic' procedures would be promulgated in order to subject the Arab community in Palestine to a Jewish Government.

The first and perhaps only objective study of the Palestine problem in its new dimensions—that made in 1937 by the Peel Commission—made the revolutionary proposal to admit the Mandate's inability to provide sufficient political outlet for the two conflicting nationalisms. Although London held on to its trust for a further decade, the very fact that the Commission had pronounced the Mandate unworkable helped to make it so.

Under partition, the creation of a sovereign Arab State in the Arab-populated areas which as yet covered a majority of Palestine's territory could have liberated the Arabs from the prospect of eventual Jewish domination and given them a taste of the self-government they anticipated with much relish. The Zionists would have gained the first Jewish State since the destruction of the Second Temple some 1900 years before. It was hoped by the British that statehood would bring with it a higher degree of political responsibility than had been displayed by each community under Mandatory rule. Arab radicalism might be tempered by the burdens of office, and the 'token' Jewish State would have to restrict immigration of its own volition to the numbers it was physically able to absorb. London also hoped that each community would be sufficiently preoccupied with its own affairs and sufficiently interested in British support in the event of possible aggression on the part of its neighbour to concede the continued tenure by Britain of 'strategic enclaves' around Haifa, Akaba and the Jerusalem–Jaffa corridor.

It is not for the historian to conjecture how well partition would have worked out in practice. The fact was that in 1937 neither the Zionists nor the Arabs were prepared to make the compromises demanded by the Peel plan of partition. The Zionists were prepared to accept a Jewish State in part of Mandatory Palestine (though not as small a part as proposed by the Peel Commission) only as a tactical first step in obtaining a sovereign base from which they might expand later. Haj Amin el-Husseini, inspired and encouraged by the precedent of Iraqi 'self-rule', was no more ready on his part to relinquish his aspirations to rule over all of Palestine west of the River Jordan. But the Zionists' political strategy—acting the wronged party which had to be wooed by London with substantial improvements on the Peel Plan—proved to be too clever by half. Had the Zionists in 1937 been possessed of sufficient vision to press unreservedly for partition, their influence in London might just have brought immediate Parliamentary approval. In the event, various Opposition groups close to the Zionists—partly in their own narrow party interests—took up the cause of their 'betrayed' protégés, accusing the Government of abandoning its Mandatory trust. Thus that invaluable political instrument, the independent commission, was utilized by Whitehall to prepare the ground for the discarding of partition in 1938.

The decision to abandon partition was taken in a totally different international context from that in which the Government had dispatched the Peel Commission to Palestine in 1936. In September 1936, London had dispatched a division of troops to Palestine to suppress the Rebellion there under martial-law powers. But in September 1938, with the Munich crisis at its peak, London was unable to answer a plea from Palestine for troop reinforcements to avert an anticipated attempt by Arab irregulars to wrest control of Jerusalem and all of southern Palestine from the Mandatory. Furthermore, the Mufti of Jerusalem and Foreign Office representatives in the Middle East had by 1938 succeeded in involving the Arab States actively in Palestinian affairs. Ormsby-Gore might fume at Iraqi castigation of the Peel Plan at the League of Nations in 1937, but his successor, Malcolm MacDonald, clearly regarded the Palestinian problem as a pan-Arab one, and was himself instrumental in inviting the Arab States to discuss it at the St James's Conference in 1939.

On the eve of World War Two, Britain had to guarantee by political means the friendship, or at least the benevolent neutrality of the Arab world, whose territories, natural resources and airspace would be crucial to Britain's successful conduct of the war. However discredited appeasement might be in Europe, London still hoped that strict adherence to the White Paper in Palestine and open sympathy (accompanied by official restraint behind the scenes) for Arab initiatives towards federation would keep the Arab world within the British political orbit.

The decision taken by the Palestine Cabinet Committee in 1943 to revert to partition was due more to an entrenched sympathy for Zionism and the contemporary fate of European Jewry than to any logical assessment of British needs in the Middle East, as defined with monotonous regularity by the Foreign Office. Yet while the Foreign Office failed to sway the 'packed' Cabinet Committee against partition, it did succeed in having the proposed Jewish State cut down so much in area that one may safely presume that it would have been rejected by the Zionists.

Again, it must remain a matter for conjecture whether Churchill's Government would in fact have ultimately revoked the White Paper and imposed partition once the war was over. The scheme for raising a Jewish division had been rejected owing to fears that after the war it would be used to establish a Jewish State in Palestine by force of arms. Yet it is a matter of historical fact that the Foreign Office doctrine on Palestine and the Middle East was never accepted by Churchill and was seriously challenged by him and certain of his colleagues (primarily Amery) during the war. It seems at least probable that his Cabinet were in September 1944 about to prepare the machinery to establish the three new States in Palestine. However, cynics may assert that the assassination of Lord Moyne in November 1944 provided a welcome pretext for shelving a policy which, according to all the officials and experts, would have been harmful to British interests in the Middle East. Undoubtedly the formation of the Arab League at this juncture introduced an added and important dimension into Arab–British relations.

Given Britain's increasing awareness of her own vulnerability as possessor of an Empire which she no longer had sufficient resources to hold on to, her growing anxieties about future competition in the area from her current allies—the United States and the Soviet Union—and the realization in 1944 of the first, albeit halting steps in the direction of Arab unity, it would have been inconceivable for any politician who put British interests first to favour the establishment of a Jewish State in the middle of an area hostile to any such concept. Official caution regarding future British moves in the area was well expressed in a contemporary study by Chatham House:

The interests and the feelings of the Middle East countries themselves constitute the remaining factor in the situation and in many respects it is the most important factor of all. They naturally expect to be treated in a manner appropriate to their status as sovereign States. They expect attention to be paid to their views and interests alike and recognition to be given to them as partners in the task of maintaining stability. Any attempt to treat them either as poor relations or as wards would be unacceptable. Such an affront to their dignity or infringement of their sovereign rights would provoke violent resentment and might lead to the Middle Eastern countries shutting themselves in behind a ring fence of reaction trying to exploit the rivalries of the Great Powers with interests in the area to their own advantage ...[1]

The Government was caught on the horns of an insoluble dilemma. It was unable to create the State desired by the Zionists for fear of losing its hegemony to one of its many rivals waiting eagerly in the wings; yet unable either to redeem its promises to the Arabs to create an independent Arab State in Palestine and thus knowingly close the doors to hundreds of thousands of wretched Jewish refugees in Europe awaiting repatriation. With no obvious policy presenting itself, Britain under the new Labour Government drifted along aimlessly, improvizing on the White Paper policy, giving no satisfaction to either party, yet arousing the ire of each.

The immediate aftermath of the war for Britain was a period of confusion, during which a new Government, faced with the stupendous costs of global war and the traditional demand for demobilization, was only gradually brought to appreciate that it could no longer maintain the Empire intact. For although with the end of war Britain relinquished her Indian Empire, she continued to maintain forces 'east of Suez', and the implications for strategical thinking on the Suez Canal—traditionally the imperial road to India—took time to digest.

It was no coincidence that the long-overdue decision to return the Palestine Mandate to the United Nations in February 1947 came one month before the issue of the Truman Doctrine. The American promise of economic and military aid to States threatened by communism bolstered the British position in the Middle East, by bringing the Balkan flank, Turkey and Greece, under American aegis. In contrast to the great British imperial expansion in the Middle East after World War One, accompanied by an American withdrawal from international affairs, the Second World War was followed by a rapid reduction in the British imperial commitment, and the eventual involvement of the United States in a common front along the lines which demarcated Western from Soviet interests in the Middle East and Asia Minor.

Notes

INTRODUCTION

1. Max Beloff, *Britain's Liberal Empire, 1897–1921*, i, *The Imperial Sunset* (London 1969).
2. Ibid., p. 18.
3. Ibid., pp. 354–5.
4. An exchange of letters between the British High Commissioner in Cairo, Sir Henry MacMahon, and the Sharif Hussein Ibn Ali (1856–1931), the Emir of Mecca, who was negotiating future Arab independence on behalf of the Arabs. Although the correspondence was inconclusive, Hussein went on in 1916 to raise a revolt against the Turks. In 1924 he was defeated in the struggle for hegemony over the Arab peninsula by Ibn Saud, ruler of Saudi Arabia.

1 THE MEDITERRANEAN STRATEGIC CONTEXT, 1936–39

1. COS Sub-Committee, 13 January 1936, in Cab. 53/27/426.
2. *Sir Anthony Eden* (First Earl of Avon, 1961), 1897–1977: Foreign Secretary, December 1935–February 1938, 1940–45; Secretary of State for War, 1940.
3. Memorandum of 11 June 1936, CP 165, Cab. 24/262.
4. CP 174, 19 June 1936, in Cab. 24/262.
5. CP 273, 22 February 1937, in Cab. 24/268.
6. CID meeting, 5 July 1937, in CP 183, Cab. 24/270.
7. CP 248, 20 October 1937, Cab. 24/271; meeting of Cabinet, 20 October, Cab. 23/89.
8. Cabinet meeting of 23 February 1938, in Cab. 23/92.
9. Cabinet meeting of 24 May 1939, in Cab. 23/99. The opportunity of a worried Egypt herself asking for more troops than were stipulated by the 1936 Treaty to be stationed in Egypt, was too good to miss.
10. In August 1938 High Commissioner MacMichael pleaded for urgent reinforcements for Palestine. The Cabinet agreed, but before they could be dispatched the Munich crisis broke, and the troops had instead to be rushed to Egypt.
11. Mediterranean and North-East Africa Appreciation, 21 February 1938, COS sub-committee (Chatfield, Newall, Gort), in WO 33/1507.
12. For this and following, see ME(O) 292, 24 January 1939, in Cab. 51/11.
13. Ibid.
14. *Lt.-Gen. Dill:* CIGS, May 1940–December 1941; was GOC Palestine, 1936–37.
    Gen. Sir Archibald Wavell (first Earl, 1947): GOC Palestine, 1937–38; C.-in-C. Middle East, 1939–41; C.-in-C. India, 1941.
    Maj.-Gen. Haining: Director of Military Operations, 1936–38; GOC Palestine, 1938–39; Vice-CIGS, 1940–41; Intendant-General, Middle East, from 1941.
15. *Lt.-Gen. Barker:* GOC Palestine, 1946.

16. *Leslie Hore-Belisha* (First Lord, 1954): Secretary of State for War, 1937–40.
17. *W. G. A. Ormsby-Gore* (4th Lord Harlech, 1938): Secretary to the Cabinet in 1917, one of the drafters of the Balfour Declaration; British Liaison Officer to Zionist Commission to Palestine, 1919; Colonial Secretary, 1936–38.
18. *Maj.-Gen. Orde Wingate*, 1903–44: On duty as Captain in Palestine, 1936–39; organized special Night Squads of Jewish commandos that defended IPC pipeline against Arab bands. Ordered back to England in May 1939 on suspicion of collusion with the Zionists. See Christopher Sykes, *Orde Wingate* (London, 1959).
19. *Gen. Jan Smuts*, 1870–1950: Prime Minister and Minister of Defence of South Africa, 1939–1948. Served in the British War Cabinet which in 1917 decided to issue the Balfour Declaration.
20. Smuts to Weizmann, 21 October 1937, in Weizmann Archives (WA).
21. Ormsby-Gore to Chamberlain, 29 November 1937, 75730, CO 733/354.
22. *Neville Chamberlain*, 1869–1940: Chancellor of the Exchequer, 1931–37; Prime Minister and Leader of Conservative Party, 1937–40; Lord President of Council, 1940.
23. *Dr Chaim Weizmann*, 1874–1952: President, World Zionist Organization and Jewish Agency for Palestine, 1921–31, 1935–46; First President of State of Israel.
24. Weizmann–Chamberlain interview, 10 March 1938 (WA).
25. The unofficial Jewish defence force, the Haganah, deriving from the early Jewish settler-guards in Palestine, was consolidated into a centralized force through the 1930s—especially during the Arab revolt.
26. Report by Haining for period 20 May–31 July 1938, in 75523/74, CO 733/379.
27. Minute by Downie, 26 May 1938, in 75156/1, pt. 1, CO 733/367.
28. MacDonald–MacMichael, 22 September 1938, 75156/1, pt. 1, CO 733/367.
29. Minute by J. Sterndale-Bennett, 17 November 1938, in 75156/1, CO 733/367. The Minute is crossed through.
30. Haining reports, for period 1 November 1938–31 March 1939, and of 19 January 1939, in 75528/74, CO 733/379.
31. Dugdale Diaries (DD), 18 January 1939 (WA). The memorandum accurately referred to was a COS sub-committee report on the strategic importance of Egypt and the Arab Middle East—CP 7, of 16 January 1939, in Cab. 24/282. Blanche Dugdale (1880–1948) was a niece of A. J. Balfour, whose heritage she felt was continuing in her single-minded devotion to Zionism. Her best source of inside information was Walter Elliott (Minister of Agriculture, of Health, and at the Scottish Office in the years 1936–40); Dr Weizmann's aide, Meyer Weisgal, has written the following, in his introduction to the edited volume of her Diaries— 'She breathed into our lives, through her inexhaustible range of family and social and political contacts, the atmosphere of a world which was vital for our survival but which obstinately remained remote from our grasp' – *Baffy, The Diaries of Blanche Dugdale, 1936–1947*, ed. N. A. Rose (London 1973), p. vii. The Ambassador at Cairo later wrote of her—'The most ardent Zionist and apparently travels about in the pocket of the Weizmanns propagating the doctrine'. *Killearn Diaries*, ed. T. E. Evans (London 1972), p. 85.
32. Telegram of 13 February 1939, in S25/7626, Central Zionist Archives, Jerusalem (CZA).
33. *Malcolm MacDonald*, 1901– : Colonial Secretary, 1935, 1938–40; Minister of Health, 1940.
34. War Office to Colonial Office, 20 March 1939, 75929, CO 733/414.
35. *Field Marshal Sir Edmund Ironside*, 1880–1959: CIGS, March 1939–May 1940.
36. The men, sentenced to terms of from ten years to life imprisonment, were in fact released in February 1941. In that year, many of them were used on Intelligence

missions in Vichy-occupied Syria. On one such mission, Moshe Dayan lost his eye.
37. Memorandum by Gen. Barker, 10 November 1939, 75156/141, CO 733/398.

2 THE 1936 REBELLION—MARTIAL LAW OR POLITICAL CONCESSIONS

1. In 1935 a record 61,000 Jews entered Palestine, compared with 4000 in 1931.
2. See Y. Porat, *The Palestinian–Arab National Movement*, ii, *1929–1939* (London 1977).
3. See Y. Porat, *The Emergence of the Palestinian–Arab National Movement, 1918–1929* (London 1973).
4. See E. Kedourie, 'Sir Herbert Samuel and the Government of Palestine', *Middle Eastern Studies*, v, 1, 1969.
5. Porat, op. cit., ch. 4.
6. The Royal Commission (Peel) Report, Cmd 5479, p. 181.
7. *Lt.-Gen. Sir Arthur Wauchope*, 1874–1947: High Commissioner for Palestine and Transjordan, 1931–38.
8. See note of meeting on 22 April 1936 between G. Antonius and D. Ben-Gurion, in D. Ben-Gurion, *Talks with Arab Leaders* (Tel Aviv 1967), pp. 50–60.
9. Minute by L. Oliphant (Deputy Under-Secretary of State at Foreign Office), 9 June 1936, in FO 371/20110.
10. See Lourie-Brodetsky, 7 May 1936, in S25/6325, CZA.
    J. H. Thomas, 1874–1949: Colonial Secretary, November 1935–May 1936.
11. CP 132, in Cab. 24/262; also minutes of Cabinet meeting on 11 May, in Cab. 23/84.
12. *Henry Mond*, 1898–1949: Managing Director of ICI; Member of House of Lords, and of Jewish Agency Advisory Committee in London.
13. *Leopold Amery*, 1873–1955: Colonial Secretary, 1924–29; Secretary of State for India, 1940–45. A leading Gentile Zionist.
14. *Stanley Baldwin*, 1867–1947: Prime Minister, 1923–24, 1926–29, 1935–37.
15. Lourie-Shertok, 13 May 1936, S25/6325, CZA.
16. Ministers canvassed included Swinton, Elliott, Ormsby-Gore, MacDonald, Runciman, Halifax, Kingsley Wood, Stanley; also Margesson (Government Chief Whip), Attlee, Cecil, Churchill, Austen Chamberlain.
17. Minutes of Cabinet meeting on 13 May 1936, in Cab. 23/84.
18. *Walter Elliott*, 1888–1958: Minister of Agriculture and Fisheries, 1932–36; Minister at Scottish Office, 1936–38; Minister of Health, 1938–40.
19. D.D. 14 May 1936 (WA).
20. Ibid.
21. Lourie-Shertok, 13 May 1936, in S25/6325, CZA. Thomas was involved in a financial scandal, involving his (seemingly inadvertent) leakage of budget secrets. An Exchequer Court of Inquiry found him guilty of inadvertent disclosure. See *The Times*, 3 June 1936. Thomas resigned office before the Court's decision.
22. *Sir Lewis Namier*, 1880–1960: The prominent English historian, a Zionist, was to be a Member of the Jewish Agency Political Department during World War Two.
23. Minutes of Cabinet meeting on 18 May 1936, in Cab. 23/84; for Commons announcement, see *HC Deb.*, vol. 312, 5th series, cols 837–8.
24. On 19 May, Weizmann saw Baldwin, Maffey, Parkinson, and the Earl of Plymouth (Under-Secretary of State at the Foreign Office, 1936–39). See Lourie-Shertok, 20 May 1936, in S25/6325, CZA. For a closer examination of the roles

played by the various Departments in the formulation of Palestine policy, see the author's 'Direction of Policy in Palestine, 1936–45', in *Middle Eastern Studies*, xi, 3, October 1973.
25. Lourie–Shertok, ibid.
26. For account of meeting between Zionists and Labour leaders, see Lourie–Shertok, 28 May 1936, in S25/6329, CZA.
27. Wauchope–Thomas, 16 May 1936, in Appendix 1 to meeting of Cabinet on 18 May 1936, in Cab. 23/84.
28. Account of Ormsby-Gore–Dugdale conversation on 6 July 1936, in Lourie-Shertok, 7 July 1936, S25/6326, CZA.
29. Weizmann–Ormsby-Gore interview, 25 February 1938, in S25/7563, CZA.
30. Interview with Weizmann, 7 July 1937, in WA.
31. Wauchope to CO, 3 June 1936, in CO 733/297, 75156, pt. 11; also Peirse Report on 1936 Disturbances, in WO 32/4177. For a detailed review of this debate, see my 'Sir Arthur Wauchope, the Army and the Rebellion in Palestine, 1936', in *Middle Eastern Studies*, ix, 1, January 1973.
32. Weizmann–Duff-Cooper interview, 18 June 1937, WA.
33. Minute by C. J. Wavell, 31 December 1936, in WO 32/4177.
34. Ormsby-Gore–Chamberlain, 22 July 1937, in Prem. 1/352.
35. John Connell, *Wavell: Scholar and Soldier* (London 1964), p. 188, quoting a letter written by Wavell in October 1936.
36. At a time when Britain was committed to dispatch two divisions to France in the event of war, the equivalent was tied up in Palestine. See W. K. Hancock and M. M. Gowing, *History of the Second World War, The British Economy* (London 1949), p. 14.
37. Minute by O. G. R. Williams, 24 June 1936, in CO 733/314, 75528/8. My emphasis.
38. Ibid. Wauchope got the idea from the Manager of Barclays Bank at Jerusalem, who was no doubt concerned at the commercial disruption caused by the disturbances.
39. Minute of 18 June 1936, in FO 371/20021.
40. *Abdul Aziz Ibn Saud*, 1880–1953: King of Hejaz, Sultan of Nejd and Dependencies from 1926; King of Saudi Arabia from 1932.
41. As 39.
42. Meeting of Political Advisory Committee, 25 June 1936, WA. At a meeting with Nuri Said (Foreign Minister of Iraq) on 9 June, Weizmann had offered a unilateral suspension of immigration. He was rebuffed by his colleagues on the Agency Executive. See Shertok, op. cit., p. 394.
43. Meeting of Political Advisory Committee, ibid.
44. *David Ben-Gurion*, 1886–1973: Chairman, Jewish Agency Executive, Jerusalem, 1935–48; Prime Minister of Israel, 1948–53, 1955–63.
45. For following, see notes of meeting of 30 June 1936, in CO 733/297, 75156, pt. 111; also Z4/17068, CZA.
46. Ibid. The (Labour) Schedule was a four-monthly quota of immigration certificates issued by the Palestine Administration, calculated according to the work vacancies forecast by the Commissioner of Immigration. Those immigrants with private capital of at least £1000 – 'capitalists' – were allowed unrestricted entry, without certificates.
47. Weizmann–Ormsby-Gore, 1 July 1936, WA.
48. Ormsby-Gore memorandum, CP 190, in Cab. 24/263, and Cabinet meeting on 4 July 1936, in Cab. 23/85.
49. Sir A. Ryan–FO, 30 April 1936, in CO 733/314, 75528/44, pt. 1. Also Secret Jewish Agency Report, 'History of the Intervention', WA. This report quotes

verbatim entire passages from official British dispatches, and telegrams.
50. Note of meeting at Amman on 1 May 1936, in *Secret Report* . . ., ibid. *Abdullah Ibn Husayn*, 1882–1951: Emir of Transjordan from 1921; King of Transjordan from April 1946 until assassinated in 1951.
51. *Secret Report* . . ., ibid.
52. Kirkbride–Wauchope, 13 June 1936, quoted in ibid.
53. Wauchope–Hall, 7 July 1936, ibid. The delay of nearly one month in Wauchope's reaction suggests consultation with London, and perhaps reference to the Cabinet meeting of 4 July.
54. See Olihpant–Parkinson, 23 June 1936, in CO 733/314, 75528/44, pt. 1.
55. Minutes of meeting, in ibid.
56. Minute by Sterndale-Bennett, 7 July 1936, in FO 371/20021.
57. Minutes of meetings on 9 and 15 July 1936, in Cab. 23/85.
58. *E. F. L. Wood* (Viscount Halifax, 1934), 1881–1959: Lord Privy Seal, 1935–37; Lord President of the Council, 1937–38; Foreign Secretary, 1938–40; Ambassador to the United States, 1941–46. As Lord Privy Seal, he stood in for the absent Foreign Secretary at the meeting on 9 July.
59. Wauchope–Ormsby-Gore, 11 July 1936, in CO 733/295, 75113, pt. 1.
60. Lampson–Vansittart, 8 July 1936, in CO 733/314, 75528/44, pt. 1. *Sir Miles Lampson* (Lord Killearn, 1943), 1880–1964: High Commissioner of Egypt and the Sudan, 1933–36; British Ambassador to Egypt, 1936–46.
61. Oliphant–Hafez Wahba interview, 14 July 1936, ibid.
62. Ibid.
63. Minute by Parkinson, 16 July 1936, in CO 733/314, 75528/44, pt. 1.
64. Of particular notoriety were the pro-Arab sympathies of the Lord Chief Justice, Sir Michael MacDonnell. After he had made a particularly singeing attack on Wauchope from his Bench, during the course of the Rebellion, the Cabinet took the highly irregular course of recommending the Judge's transfer. See CP 194 in Cab. 24/263; also meeting of 15 July, in Cab. 23/85.
65. Conversation between Sterndale-Bennett and Gen. Sir R. Adam (DMO, 1936; Deputy CIGS, 1938–40), on 14 August 1936, in FO 371/20023.
66. Abdullah met the Higher Committee on 26 July and 5 August 1936 – see *Secret Report* . . ., op. cit.
67. Wauchope–Ormsby-Gore, 21 August 1936, ibid. The speech referred to by Wauchope was the Colonial Secretary's, announcing the terms of reference and the composition of the Commission. This speech (*HC Deb.*, 5th Series, vol. 315, col. 1511) was in direct contradiction to his speech of 9 June, when he had undertaken *not* to appoint or publish the terms of reference of the Commission until order was restored in Palestine. See Parkinson minute, 13 August 1936, in CO 733/294, 75113, pt. 1.
68. See Dr Khaldi–Hall, 26 August 1936, in S25/10335, CZA.
69. Wauchope–Ormsby-Gore, 22 August 1936, in CO 733/297, 75156.
70. Ormsby-Gore memorandum of 26 August 1936, CP 225, in Cab. 24/263.
71. Ormsby-Gore–Wauchope, 26 August 1936, in CO 733/297, 75156.
72. Wauchope–Shertok interview, 2 September 1936, in S25/4314, CZA.
73. Whereas the negotiations with Dr Khaldi and Auni Abdul Hadi (Istiklal) are filed in Colonial Office file 75156, Nuri's intervention is to be found in file 75528/44 – even though both sets of negotiations were about essentially the same issue, and at times proceeded simultaneously. Nuri Said was flown to Jerusalem by RAF aeroplane, and stayed at Government House as guest of the Administration.
74. Wauchope–Ormsby-Gore, 22 August 1936, in CO 733/314, 75528/44, pt. 1. When approached by the Zionists, Wauchope denied any knowledge of the Nuri

mediation – see interview with Shertok on 24 August 1936, in S25/19 CZA.
75. Ormsby-Gore–Wauchope, 25 August 1936, in 75528/44, pt. 1, ibid.
76. Wauchope–Ormsby-Gore, 26 August 1936, ibid.
77. Ormsby-Gore–Wauchope, 27 August 1936, ibid.
78. Ibid.
79. Above, p. 30, n. 2.
80. Wauchope-Ormsby-Gore, 28 August 1936, in CO 733/314, 75528/44, pt. 1.
81. Ormsby-Gore–Wauchope, 29 August 1936, ibid.
82. Wauchope–Ormsby-Gore, 31 August 1936, ibid.
83. Minutes in E5539/E5691/E5695/94/31, in FO 371/20024, 20025. Also *Secret Report* . . ., op. cit.
84. Ormsby-Gore–Wauchope, 1 September 1936, in CO 733/297, 75156, pt. 4.
85. Shertok report to Mapai Central Committee, 11–12 September 1936, in *Shertok*, op. cit., pp. 302–9. *Mapai:* majority party in the Labour coalition.
86. Ormsby-Gore–Weizmann, 2 September 1936, in CO 733/314, 75528/44, pt. 1; also in S25/6329, CZA.
87. Ormsby-Gore–Wauchope, 1 September 1936, in CO 733/297, 75156, pt. 4. There existed evidence that the Arabs were mounting one last guerrilla effort before entering negotiations. Fawzi Kawakji, a Lebanese officer then conducting a course at the Military School at Baghdad, arrived in Palestine on the same day as Nuri Said. From that date, guerrilla activity became better organized, and reached a peak between 27 August and 4 September. See Peirse, report on the Rebellion, in WO 32/4177.
88. Interview between Ormsby-Gore, Maffey and Weizmann, Namier, on 30 September 1936, in Z4/17068, CZA.
89. Shuckburgh–Rendel, 10 September 1936, in CO 733/314, 75528/44, pt. 11.
90. Wauchope–Ormsby-Gore, 12 September 1936, 75528/6, ibid.
91. Shertok report, in Shertok, op. cit., pp. 308–9.
92. Rendel, interview with M. Zada, Saudi Minister in London, 1 September 1936, in CO 733/314, 75528/44, pt. 11.
93. Rendel, minute of 9 September 1936, in FO 371/20025.
94. Minutes in Cab. 23/85; also Ormsby-Gore memorandum of 26 August 1936, in CP 225, in Cab. 24/263.
95. *Sir Philip Cunliffe-Lister* (Viscount Swinton, 1935), 1884– . Colonial Secretary, 1931–35; Secretary of State for Air, 1935–38.
96. *A. Duff-Cooper*, 1890–1954: Secretary of State for War, 1935–37; First Lord of the Admiralty, 1937–38; Minister of Information, 1940–41.
97. Baldwin, on the verge of a nervous breakdown, had in August been ordered by his doctors to take a complete rest for three months. See K. Middlemass and J. Barnes, *Baldwin, a Biography* (London 1969), pp. 962–65.
98. Simon–Baldwin, 2 September 1936, in Prem. 1/352.
99. Shertok speech, 31 August 1936, in Shertok, op. cit., p. 285.
100. Once the Cabinet decision became known in Palestine, lawlessness there dropped by 50 per cent. See Peirse Report, in WO 32/4177.
101. See the proposals in 75528/58, CO 733/315; also in the *Samuel Papers*, in the House of Lords Library, London.
Lord Herbert Samuel, 1870–1963: First High Commissioner to Palestine, 1920–25; Chairman of the Liberal Party, 1931–35; Member of House of Lords.
Earl Winterton, 1883–1962: Chairman of recently formed 'Unofficial Committee to defend Arab interests in the Commons'. Friend of Nuri Said.
102. Note of meeting on 8 September 1936, in CO 733/315, 75528/315.
103. Note of their meeting on 19 September 1936, ibid.
104. Interview between Rendel and M. Zada, 15 September 1936, in CO 733/314,

75528/44, pt. 11.
105. Minute by J. M. Martin, 18 September 1936, ibid.
106. Bateman–FO, 27 September 1936, in ibid.
107. See Clarke-Kerr–FO, 2 October 1936, in FO 371/20026.
108. Ormsby-Gore–Wauchope, 7 October 1936, in CO 733/314, 75528/44, pt. 111.
109. Wauchope–Ormsby-Gore, 8 October 1936, ibid.
110. Dill–War Office, 6 October 1936, in *Secret Report* . . ., op. cit.
111. Clarke-Kerr–FO, 8 October 1936, in CO 733/314, 75528/44, pt. 111, also *Secret Report* . . ., op. cit.
112. Minutes of 17th session of Permanent Mandates Commission, p. 77; quoted in memorandum by J. Stoyanovsky, in *Leo Kohn Papers*, LK 27, Israel State Archives. *Sir Harry Luke:* Assistant Governor of Jerusalem, 1920–24; Chief Secretary of Palestine Government, 1928–30.
113. Rendel minute of 14 September 1936, in FO 371/19983.
114. Rendel minute of 17 September 1936, in FO 371/20025.
115. Minutes of 17 September 1936 in FO 371/19983.
116. Wauchope–Ormsby-Gore, 1 October 1936, annexe to CP 269, Cab. 24/264.
117. Ormsby-Gore memorandum of 1 October 1936, CP 269, in Cab. 24/264.
118. See Chapter 3, note 22.
119. Minutes of Cabinet meeting on 28 October 1936, in Cab. 23/86.
120. Rendel minute of 21 October 1936, in FO 371/20028.
121. Minutes of Cabinet meeting on 4 November 1936, in Cab. 23/86.
122. Lecture of 22 June 1937, by MI2 (Military Intelligence), in WO 106/1594B.

3 PARTITION, 1937–1938: DOUBTS AND SUSPICIONS

1. W. R. W. Peel (1st Earl, 1920), 1867–1937: Secretary of State for India, 1922–24, 1928–29.
2. Rendel's expertise on the Middle East was welcomed gratefully by Ministers, who did not 'interfere' in the Eastern Department as they did in others. (Personal communication to author from Sir George Rendel.) Rendel had been instrumental in 1935 in arranging the visit to London of Ibn Saud's two sons, when he acted as their chaperon. He was invited back for a private visit with his wife in March 1937, when he toured the whole Middle East.
3. See, for instance, p. 30.
4. Sir George Rendel, *The Sword and the Olive* (London 1957), pp. 99, 109.
5. *T. E. Lawrence*, 1888–1935. British Liaison Officer with the Arab Revolt, 1916–18, later acclaimed as 'Lawrence of Arabia'.
   Harry St John Philby, 1885–1960. British explorer and Orientalist; for many years a close adviser to Ibn Saud; converted to Islam.
6. Memorandum of April 1937 in 75550/69b, CO 733/348.
7. See David Ben-Gurion, *Talks with Arab Leaders* (Tel Aviv 1967 – in Hebrew), p. 138.
8. Ormsby-Gore minute of 14 April 1937, in 75550/69b, CO 733/348. The Colonial Secretary's sentiments were reciprocated. Rendel believed Ormsby-Gore to be a dedicated Zionist who wanted all of Palestine to be Jewish, or at least, 'he kept the idea at the back of his mind always' (personal communication from Sir George Rendel).
9. See minutes in E4416/4418/22/31, FO 371/20810.
10. Weizmann met Arida on 6 June and Edé on 22 June 1937, WA.

11. See Weizmann meeting with Léon Blum (French Premier) on 27 January 1937, WA.
12. See Royal Commission Report, 7 July 1937, Cmd. 5479.
13. Ormsby-Gore memorandum to Cabinet, CP 166, in Cab. 24/270.
14. Ormsby-Gore minute to Lord Dufferin in 75718, CO 733/351.
15. See Rendel minute of 28 June 1937, in FO 371/20808. The Department was particularly concerned about the proposed transfer (by force if necessary) of the Arab population of the new Jewish State to the proposed Arab State.
16. See minutes of meeting of 28 June 1937, in Cab. 23/88.
17. See Rendel memorandum of 2 July, in FO 371/20808; also minute of 15 July regarding inter-departmental meeting with the Colonial Office, in E4297/22/31, FO 371/20810.
18. Minutes of meeting of 5 July 1937 in Cab. 23/88.
19. See minutes in E3630/22/31, FO 371/20808.
20. Chamberlain had formed his Cabinet on 28 May 1937.
21. See notes on dinner party held on 8 June 1937, in S25/4418, CZA. Present were Sinclair, Churchill, Amery, Attlee, J. Wedgwood, Victor Cazalet, James de Rothschild and Weizmann. *Sir Archibald Sinclair*, 1890– : Secretary of State for Air, 1940–45. Liberal Leader.
22. The Peel Report was to recommend a 'political high-limit' of 12,000 per annum during the interim period.
23. *Winston Spencer Churchill*, 1874–1965: First Lord of the Admiralty, September 1939–May 1940; Prime Minister and Minister of Defence, 1940–45.
24. Notes on dinner party of 8 June, ibid supra.
25. D.D., 9 June 1937, WA. Both Churchill and Attlee subsequently attacked the Peel plan in the Commons debate.
26. For Ben-Gurion's meeting with seventeen members of the Executive on 15 July 1937, see his diary notes in S25/10.066, CZA. Among the members mentioned are Greenwood, Wedgwood and Hopkins.
27. The Zionists' 'official' stand was to reject the finding that the Mandate was impossible to carry out, and to insist on its retention. Confidential instructions were to take every opportunity to improve on the Peel plan, without committing the Zionist Movement to accept it. See note of speech of 29 July 1937 to the World Congress of Poalei Zion, in David Ben-Gurion, *Bama' aracha* (Tel Aviv 1947) (in Hebrew), p. 115.
28. For note of meeting of 15 March 1937 see D.D. of same date, WA. Present were Weizmann, Shertok, Dugdale, Namier, Brodetsky, Lourie, and Stein.
29. Shertok–Wauchope, 21 June 1937, in S25/31, CZA.
30. He was apparently persuaded by Weizmann, Melchett and Mrs Dugdale. See D.D., 9 June 1937, WA.
31. See Wauchope–Parkinson, 19 July 1937—'Ben-Gurion and Ussishkin have openly declared they are against partition', in 75156, CO 733/332.
32. D.D., 14 June 1937, WA.
33. Ben-Gurion–Shertok, May 1937, in S25/10066, CZA.
34. See minutes of meeting of 7 July 1937, WA. Present were Weizmann, Ben-Gurion, Dr N. Goldmann, Dov Hos, Brodetsky, Namier, Dugdale, Stein, Lourie.
35. Ibid.
36. For debate of 21 July 1937, see *HC Deb.*, 5th series, vol. 326, cols. 2235–2367.
37. See Rose, op. cit., p. 222.
38. See Weizmann–Martin interview, 13 October 1937, 75156/30, CO 733/333.
39. See note of Bonne–Pickthorne (Unionist MP for Cambridge) interview of September 1938, in S25/7565, CZA.

40. See Ormsby-Gore–Eden, 15 July 1937, in FO 371/20809.
41. *Moshe Shertok* (later Sharett): Head of Jewish Agency Political Department, 1936–48; Israel's first Foreign Minister and later its Prime Minister.
42. For this and following, see Shertok–Wauchope interview of 13 July 1937 in A245, N/167, CZA.
43. Ibid.
44. The 'political high level' of 12,000 per annum recommended by Peel for the interim period was supposed to be a temporary measure. It was on this condition only that the Permanent Mandates Commission acquiesced in September 1937.
45. See Bagallay memorandum of 13 August 1937 in FO 371/20811.
46. See minute by Downie of 6 December 1937 in 75732, CO 733/354.
47. The announcement of this new Commission (eventually headed by Sir John Woodhead) was made by Eden while attending the League Sessions on Palestine in September 1937.
48. Minute by Rendel of 1 November 1937 in FO 371/20819.
49. On 26 September 1937 the British District Commissioner for Galilee, Andrews, was murdered. On 29 September the Cabinet approved the arrest and deportation of the Higher Arab Committee, and deprived the Mufti of his offices. See also Sir Alec Seath Kirkbride, *A Crackle of Thorns* (London 1956), pp. 98–112.
50. For this and the following, see Rendel minute of 14 October 1937, FO 371/20816.
51. Ibid. The '40 per cent ratio', advocated originally by Sir Herbert Samuel, was now championed by Ibn Saud.
52. Rendel–Shuckburgh, 5 October 1937, in 75718/ CO 733/351.
53. *Sir John Shuckburgh*, 1877–1953: Indian, then Colonial Office official; Assistant Under-Secretary at Colonial Office, 1921–31; Deputy Under-Secretary, 1931–42.
54. Downie minute of 20 November 1937, ibid.
55. Rendel memorandum of 27 October 1937, in FO 371/20818.
56. Rendel memorandum of 30 October 1937, in FO 371/20819.
57. See Shertok Diary for 14 September 1937, in S25/10066, CZA.
58. D.D., 14 September 1937, WA.
59. The insertion of Galilee in the proposed Jewish State by the Peel plan became a focus of Arab objections—understandably, as 90 per cent of its population was Arab.
60. Shertok Diary, 14 September 1937, in S25/10066, CZA.
61. The new Jewish suburbs of Jerusalem housed a greater population than the old Arab quarters. The Zionists aspired to obtain Jerusalem for the Jewish State.
62. B. Joseph–Weizmann, 22 September 1937, in S25/5168, CZA. The letter was forwarded to the Colonial Office, where it appears in 75156, pt. 1, CO 733/332.
63. The 'evidence' was a photostat of letters showing that the Mufti had arranged for protests to be sent in to the Government. This method should not have shocked the Zionists—they were not above applying it themselves at times.
64. Joseph's letter was written prior to the dismissal of the Mufti from his offices. The fact that he was deposed as a direct result of a new outbreak of terrorism is sufficient indication of his status in the eyes of the Mandatory. The Zionists did not yet know that Wauchope was in fact to be replaced.
65. See Ormsby-Gore memorandum of 9 November 1937, CP 269, in Cab. 24/272; also Cabinet meeting of 17 November 1937, in Cab. 23/90a.
66. See Rendel memorandum of 11 November 1937 in FO 371/20820.
67. See Eden's memorandum of 19 November 1937, CP 281, in Cab. 24/273. In essentials, it embodied those points made by Rendel in his note of 11 November.
68. Ormsby-Gore memorandum of 1 December 1937, CP 289, in Cab. 24/273.
69. Ibid.
70. Ormsby-Gore's successor, MacDonald, later defended the 'fixed ratio' idea,

before the Permanent Mandates Commission in July 1939—the majority of that body ruled that the concept conflicted with British obligations under the Mandate.
71. See note of meeting of 7 December 1937, in FO 371/20822. Present were Eden, Vansittart, Cranborne, Oliphant and Rendel.
72. See minutes of Cabinet meeting of 8 December 1937, in Cab. 23/90a. A student of the period has recently commented that Chamberlain had acquired or assumed a dominance over his Cabinet that had scarcely been approached in the interval between Gladstone and Lloyd George. Anyone who showed signs of independence was disposed of—the most conspicuous victims were Swinton, Eden and Ormsby-Gore. See Robert Rhodes James, *Churchill, A Study in Failure, 1900–39* (London 1970), p. 325.
73. Minute by Downie, 6 December 1937, in CO 733/354, 75730.
74. Weizmann–Ormsby-Gore interview, 25 February 1938, in S25/7563, CZA.
75. The Ambassadors to Egypt and Iraq respectively.
76. Dispatch from Sir Percy Loraine, 28 December 1937, in CO 733/354, 75730.
77. Minute by J. M. Martin, 21 January 1938, ibid. My emphasis.
78. Minutes of 24 January 1938, ibid.
79. *Sir John Woodhead*, 1881– : Indian Civil Servant since 1904.
80. Minute by Sir John Shuckburgh, 31 March 1938, in CO 733/354, 75730/6.
81. See White Paper of 5 January 1938, Cmd 5634.
82. Elliot had kept Mrs Dugdale abreast of the Foreign Office attack on partition—on condition that she did not pass on the information any further. But he does not seem to have informed her about the confidential note. D.D., 8 December 1937, WA.
83. Eden–Ormsby-Gore, 17 December 1937, in FO 371/20822.
84. Cabinet decision of 22 December 1937, in Cab. 23/90a.
85. Ormsby-Gore–Halifax, 14 March 1938, in FO 371/21862.
86. Bagallay minutes of 16 March 1938, ibid.; also Ormsby-Gore–FO, 22 March 1938, ibid.
87. Personal communication from Sir George Rendel.
88. Mrs Dugdale obtained information from Walter Elliot, and Lord Melchett from Hore-Belisha. Mrs Dugdale told Weizmann that Melchett's pessimism stemmed from his recurring heart trouble and from business anxieties.
89. See D.D., 27 November 1937, WA.
90. His plan envisaged an Iraqi-led Arab Federation, of which an Arab Palestine would form part. The Jews would be guaranteed minority rights inside Palestine, and the right to emigrate to any country within the Federation. See Sasson–Shertok, 19 December 1937, in S25/2966, CZA.
91. *Vt Cranborne*, 1893– : Under-Secretary at the Foreign Office, 1935–38; Colonial Secretary, February–November, 1942; Lord Privy Seal, 1942–45.
92. See minute of their interview of 21 January 1938 in FO 800/296.
93. Ormsby-Gore now believed that the only way in which partition might be forced through would be by amelioration of the terms from the Arab point of view.
94. See Jewish Agency Secret Report of 7 February 1938, recording Nuri's meeting with the Mufti on 4 February, in Z4/17.312, CZA.
95. Ibid.
96. See note of interview of 25 February 1938 in S25/7563, CZA.
97. See Rendel minute of 20 December 1937, in FO 371/20823; also minutes of Cabinet meeting of 22 December 1937, in Cab. 23/90a.
98. Rendel minute of 15 February 1938, in FO 371/21862.
99. Minute of 18 March 1938, ibid.

100. See D.D., 9 December 1937, WA.
101. Ibid.
102. Ibid. Mrs Dugdale was due to visit Palestine with Victor Cazalet, MP, on 5 January 1938.
103. Résumé of Elliot's letter to Mrs Dugdale, 22 December 1937, D.D., WA.
104. See his report to meeting of 19 February 1938. Present, apart from Weizmann, were Ben-Gurion, Brodetsky, Goldmann and Lourie. WA.
105. Weizmann met Ormsby-Gore on 25 February 1938, and Chamberlain on 10 March 1938; see S25/7563, CZA and WA respectively.
106. Minute of Weizmann–Battershill interview of 21 April 1938, in FO 371/21862.
107. Shertok report to Political Committee, August 1938, in S25/444, CZA.
108. Ibid.
109. The Plan aimed to balance out the respective populations of the Arab and Jewish States by removing Galilee and the Arab-dominated area south of Jaffa from the Jewish to the Arab State. Whereas the Peel plan would have placed 259,000 Arabs as against 296,000 Jews in the Jewish State, the Administration's plan reduced the Arab minority to 150,000. The plan was actually the product of D. G. Harris, of the Palestine Government—see 75730/4, CO733/354. Weizmann was told by Ormsby-Gore that the existence of the plan had led him to delay the dispatch of the Commission to Palestine until after Wauchope finally departed—see their interview of 25 February 1938, in S25/7563, CZA.
110. Weizmann–Ormsby-Gore, 28 February 1938, WA.
111. Mr Reid was the sole member to report that there existed *no* scheme of partition which might lead to an equitable and practicable solution.
112. B. Joseph–Shertok, 7 August 1938, in LK/21, ISA.
113. Ormsby-Gore–Chamberlain, 9 January 1938, in FO 371/21862.

4   ANGLO-FRENCH ATTITUDES TO PALESTINIAN ARAB NATIONALISM

1. Palestine Police Report, by H. P. Price, 27 October 1936, in FO 371/20028.
2. Wauchope–Ormsby-Gore, 12 September 1936, in 75528/6, CO 733/311.
3. See telegrams of 1 and 13 October 1936, ibid.
4. Minutes of Cabinet meeting on 3 March 1937, in Cab. 23/87.
5. See Battershill's telegram, attached as annexe to minutes of Cabinet meeting on 3 March 1937, ibid.
6. Meetings of 2 and 3 July 1937, in 75718, CO 733/351.
7. See A. H. Cohen report, June 1937, ibid.
8. For this and following, see A. H. Cohen report, 18 July 1937, in S25/10.097, CZA.
9. Secret Report by Ben-Zvi (head of *Va'ad Leumi* – National Committee of Palestinian Jewry), 4 September 1937, in S25/10.097, CZA.
10. Wauchope–Ormsby-Gore, 16 July 1937, in 75718/9, CO 733/352.
11. Ormsby-Gore–Wauchope, 16 July 1937, ibid.
12. The police later discovered that in their search of the Committee's offices they had overlooked a coal entrance. See Wauchope–Ormsby-Gore, 19 July 1937, ibid.
13. See minutes of Cabinet meeting of 21 July 1937, in Cab. 23/89.
14. Ormsby-Gore–Wauchope, 30 July 1937, 75718/9, CO 733/352.
15. Ormsby-Gore–Battershill, 8 September 1937, in 75718, CO 733/352.
16. See minutes of Cabinet meeting of 29 September 1937, in Cab. 23/89. Andrews had been murdered on 26 September 1937.
17. The Mufti escaped during the night of 14 or 15 October 1937. The Colonial Office ordered a police inquiry into the circumstances of his escape.

18. See extract from 'Palestine Post', 8 October 1937, reporting interview between the Editor of the Lebanese newspaper, 'Ad Difaa', and a high-ranking French official, in MacKereth (British Consul at Damascus) dispatch, FO 371/20818.
19. In March 1936, after a protracted general strike in Syria, the French Mandatory had surprisingly agreed to grant Syria independence within three years. The Syrians had already assumed control of domestic life (including the police), but delicate negotiations were proceeding regarding the grant of full independence, i.e. control of the Army, foreign affairs, etc.
20. The proposal was made by Lord Melchett, a member of the Jewish Agency's Political Advisory Committee in London. See communications of 20 and 21 October 1937, in FO 371/20817.
21. Harvard–Foreign Office, 23 October 1937, and minutes, in FO 371/20817.
22. MacKereth–Foreign Office, 17 October 1937, in FO 371/20817.
23. Talks were actually deadlocked over the 'role' to be played by the French Army in Syria after 'independence'.
24. Minute in E6078/22/31, FO 371/20817.
25. MacKereth–Foreign Office, 19 October 1937, in FO 371/20818.
26. Among the measures taken by the French against the Druse Revolt of 1925 had been the aerial bombing of Damascus. In 1925, the French Administration had accused the British Mandatory—particularly in Transjordan—of giving succour to the Druse rebels.
27. Syrian nationalist, known to be in receipt of Italian subsidies in return for which he furthered Italian interests in the Middle East.
28. Member of Palestine Istiqlal Party, which he represented in Iraq, and later in Syria.
29. Syrian nationalist, once exiled by the French to Palestine. His brother, Adel-al-Azmeh, was Director-General of the Syrian Ministry of the Interior.
30. For following, see Jewish Agency Secret Report of 23 October 1937, in FO 371/20820.
31. See Rendel minute of 13 November 1937, in ibid.
32. MacKereth dispatch of 5 February 1938, in FO 371/21873.
33. Minute by Sir Lancelot Oliphant of 23 February 1938, ibid.
34. Possibly reference to the Cabinet crisis and to Eden's resignation as Foreign Secretary, due to Chamberlain's decision to enter into conversations with Italy over Mediterranean and Red Sea questions.
35. See E862/10/31, FO 371/21873.
36. For this, and following, see Memorandum from Jewish Agency, 7 January 1938, in FO 371/21873.
37. Minute by Rendel, 11 February 1938, ibid.
38. Bagallay (First Secretary at the Foreign Office) minute, 3 February 1938, in FO 371/21873.
39. Sir Harold MacMichael, High Commissioner from 1938–44. Wauchope's second term had been cut short following the murder of Andrews in September 1937. The move reflected the final failure of his conciliatory policies.
40. For this and following, see MacMichael–Ormsby-Gore, 12 May 1938, in FO 371/21877.
41. Ibid.
42. Ibid.
43. Trade figures for 1937 had shown that the trade balance between the two countries had been in Syria's favour, to the extent of £P749,192.
44. Interview between Baxter and M. Cambon, on 20 May 1938, in FO 371/21876.
45. Baxter minute of 31 May 1938, FO 371/21877.
46. For minute of meeting on 2 June 1938, see ibid. Present were Shuckburgh (for

the Colonial Office), Baxter and Brennan (Foreign Office) and representatives of the War Office and Air Ministry.
47. See MacMichael–MacDonald, 13 June 1938, in FO 371/21877.
48. See Foreign Office–Phipps, 28 June 1938, in ibid.
49. Phipps–Halifax, 2 July 1938, in FO 371/21877.
50. Interview between Campbell (Counsellor at British Embassy in Paris) and M. Léger (Secretary-General of the Quai d'Orsay), on 13 July 1938, in FO 371/21878.
51. For minutes of meeting on 19 July 1938, see FO 371/21879.
52. Minute by Oliphant of 25 July 1938, ibid.
53. Minutes by Bagallay, 15 August 1938, in FO 371/21879.
54. Minutes in FO 371/21880.
55. Despatch of 27 October 1938, in FO 371/21883.
56. For data on the circumstances of the Mufti's escape, see E7036/6/31, FO 371/23240.
57. Columbani was a disreputable figure, once dispatched back to France due to his unsatisfactory record; he had procured his return to Syria owing to the evidence he had acquired of a scandal involving high Government officials.
58. See report by Major D. A. L. Mackenzie, 22 October 1939, in FO 371/23241.
59. Report by French Liaison Officer in Cairo to General Noguès in Algiers, forwarded to the Foreign Office by Major Cawthorn of British Intelligence, on 12 November 1939; see FO 371/23241. My emphasis.
60. Fakhri Nashashibi was a cousin of Ragheb's who had assumed leadership of the Defence Party during Ragheb's self-imposed exile in Cairo. Fakhri was murdered by the Mufti's agents in Baghdad in November 1941.
61. MacMichael–MacDonald, 16 November 1938, in 75872/12, CO 733/386.
62. MacMichael–MacDonald, 19 November 1938, ibid.
63. For minutes of Conference on 8 October 1938, see FO 371/21864. Among those present were Battershill and Harris of the Palestine Administration, General Pownall of the War Office, and MacDonald.
64. Parlimentary Under-Secretary of State at Colonial Office, 1937–40.
65. Minutes of meeting of 24 October 1938, in FO 371/21865.
66. Lampson–Foreign Office, 5 November 1938, in FO 371/21882.
67. Fakhri Nashashibi–MacMichael, 24 December 1938, in FO 371/23221.
68. See minutes of Conference at Colonial Office, in E5151/1/31, FO 371/21863.
69. For the following, see minute of interview of 24 January 1939 in FO 371/23221.
70. Report of meeting with Suleiman bey Toukan, in MacMichael–MacDonald, 7 February 1939, in 75872/11, CO 733/406.
71. Battershill–District Commissioners, 29 December 1938, in FO 371/23221.
72. See text of manifesto, enclosed in Colonial Office–Foreign Office, 10 July 1939, in FO 371/23238. The manifesto was signed by Section Commanders of Jaffa, Ramle, Nablus, Tiberias and Lydda, and the 'Secretary' of the Rebellion, all currently refugees in Syria.
73. In 1937, during his evidence to the Peel Commission, MacKereth recalled instances when the Mufti had acted as broker in sales by Arabs to Zionists, note of which might be found easily by reference to the Palestine Land Registers. See note of conversation of 7 January 1937, in FO 371/20804.
74. An estimated £P1 million from *Wakf* properties, and £P2 millions from contributions to Rebellion funds and for the upkeep of the Al Aqsa mosque.
75. See text of manifesto, op. cit.
76. MacMichael–MacDonald, 30 May 1939, in 75872/12, CO 733/406.
77. MacKereth–Foreign Office, 20 May 1939, in FO 371/23236.
78. Extract from secret Saudi document, in E6488/6/31, FO 371/23240.
79. Sir B. Newton (Ambassador at Baghdad)–Foreign Office, 15 September 1939, in

FO 371/23240.
80. Already in July 1937 the Mufti had contacted the German Consul at Jerusalem, to enlist his aid against the Partition plan. He pointed out the common aims of the Germans and the Arabs, and proposed sending an agent to Berlin. In a further interview in December 1937, the Mufti offered to promote the German cause. Both offers were turned down, the Germans not wishing on the one hand to offend Britain, and on the other hand being unwilling, as yet, to promote the Arab cause which, in their opinion, was neither defined or united. See *G.D. 1914–18, Series D.*, vol. 5, pp. 755, 766–7, 778–9. See also Lukacz Hirszowicz, *The Third Reich and the Arab East* (London 1966).
81. Minute by Bagallay, 18 September 1939, in FO 371/23240.

5 THE WHITE PAPER, MAY 1939

1. See 'Mediterranean and North-East Africa Appreciation', 21 February 1938, by COS Sub-Committee (Chatfield, Newall, Gort) in WO 33/1507.
2. See Anglo-French conversations of 28–29 April 1938, in *Documents on British Foreign Policy*, Third Series, vol. 1, no. 164 (HMSO), quoted by A. J. P. Taylor, *Origins of the Second World War* (London 1961), pp. 160–61.
3. See Battershill–MacMichael, 6 July 1938, in the *MacMichael Papers*, at the Middle East Centre, St Antony's College, Oxford.
4. For notes on meetings of 22 June, 4 July and 17 July 1938, see MacDonald's Cabinet memorandum, CP 190, 21 August 1938, in Cab. 24/278.
5. See Bullard–MacDonald, 3 August 1938, in ibid. Bullard's half-hearted advocacy of the Government's Palestine policy had precipitated a row between the Foreign and Colonial Offices—see 75730/6, in CO 733/354.
6. Minute of MacDonald–Weizmann meeting on 14 September 1938, in S25/7563, CZA.
7. MacDonald–Halifax (private), 14 December 1938, in FO 800/321.
8. Lampson–MacDonald, 2 September 1938, in Prem. 1/351.
9. Bateman–Oliphant, 30 August 1938, in FO 371/21881.
10. See MacDonald's report on his visit of 6–7 August, in FO 371/21863.
11. See minutes of Ministerial meeting of 7 September 1938, in Prem. 1/352. Present were MacDonald, Halifax, Inskip, Hore-Belisha, Gort, Stewart (Under-Secretary at the India Office), Oliphant and Shuckburgh.
12. In the event, two infantry battalions and an armoured car regiment, 'borrowed' from Egypt, had to be rushed back there at the height of the Munich crisis, on 26th September 1936. See 75156/1, pt. 1, CO 733/369.
13. See notes of meeting of 14 September 1938 in FO 371/21863; MacDonald had made an earlier attempt to obtain an intimation of what the Commission's report would be like—also in vain—on 16 August 1938. See CP 190 of 21 August 1938, in Cab. 24/278.
14. MacDonald pointedly cited to Weizmann the current case of the Sudeten Germans.
15. See note of meeting of 19 September at Weizmann's house, in Ben-Gurion, *Letters to . . .*, pp. 231–2.
16. On 26 September a State of Emergency was declared by Order in Council. The Fleet was mobilized and 50,000 Territorials called up.
17. See note of meeting of 23 September 1938 in FO 371/21864. Present were MacDonald, Downie and Grattan-Bushe from the Colonial Office, and Bagallay of the Foreign Office.

18. For following, see minutes of Conference of 7–10 October 1938, in E5723/1/31, FO 371/21864; present were MacDonald, Bagallay, and General Pownall (War Office), MacMichael, Battershill and Harris.
19. Yet, as recently as 2 September, MacDonald had denied the rights of the Arab States to any formal intervention in Palestinian affairs. See his interview with Weizmann, in Prem. 1/352.
20. For Cabinet meeting of 19 October 1938, see Cab. 23/96.
21. For details of the Woodhead Report, see Cmd. 5854. Each of the other two members produced his own plan, with an even smaller State allotted the Jews.
22. The Cabinet Committee included the 'Big Four'—Chamberlain, Halifax, Hoare and Simon—as well as MacDonald, Elliot and Zetland. For its debate on the Woodhead Report, see meeting of 24 October 1938, in FO 371/21865.
23. Cmd 5893. A Statement of Policy by His Majesty's Government (November 1938).
24. See for instance interview between ex-High Commissioner Sir John Chancellor and MacDonald, 17 September 1938, in Prem. 1/352, cited below, p. 86.
25. 'Appreciation of the situation in the Middle East from the Intelligence aspect in the event of Great Britain and France becoming involved in war against Germany and Italy in April 1939'—memorandum of 9 November 1938, in WO 106-1594B, MI 2A.
26. MacDonald memorandum of 20 October 1938, in FO 371/21865.
27. See memorandum by H. F. Downie, 2 December 1938, in FO 371/21868.
28. Ibid.
29. Foreign Office minute of 19 December 1938, in FO 371/21869.
30. This idea originated with J. L. Magnes in Palestine. It was publicized by Lord Samuel in the House of Lords, and dubbed the '40–10' plan, i.e. 40 per cent of the population after ten years.
31. See minutes of Cabinet meeting of 1 February 1939, in Cab. 23/97.
32. Meeting of 9 February 1939, in FO 371/23223.
33. Meeting of 11 February 1939, in ibid.
34. Meeting of 14 February 1939, in FO 371/23224.
35. Meeting of 8 February 1939, in FO 371/23223.
36. Meeting of 10 February 1939, in ibid.
37. See Ben-Gurion speech to the Panel (the Jewish delegation to the Conference), on 12 February 1939, WA. At an interview of 13 October 1938, MacDonald had told Weizmann—'... the British would govern Palestine. The Arabs might dismiss from their minds the idea of a national government'. See WA.
38. Meeting of 14 February 1939, in FO 371/23224.
39. Ibid.
40. Meeting of 15 February 1939, ibid. There is no evidence that MacDonald asked for or received Cabinet assent prior to dropping the planned first line of approach.
41. Meeting of 17 February 1939, ibid.
42. Meeting between MacDonald and Ben-Gurion on 18 February, 1939, WA.
43. Memorandum of 20 February 1939, in FO 371/23225.
44. The Woodhead report had warned that an economic depression might ensue in Palestine if Jewish immigration was stopped.
45. See minutes of meeting of 22 February 1939, in Cab. 23/97.
46. See minutes of Cabinet Committee meeting of 23 February 1939, in FO 371/23226.
47. For minutes of meeting of 23 February 1939, see FO 371/23225; present were Halifax, MacDonald, R. A. Butler (Parliamentary Under-Secretary at the Foreign Office), Weizmann, Ben-Gurion and Shertok; Aly Maher Pasha (Egypt), Gen. Nuri Said (Iraq), Taufiq Suweidi (Iraq), and Fuad Bey Hamza (Saudi Arabia).

48. MacDonald's reassurance to the Jews was given at a meeting with their delegation alone on the following day—see minutes of meeting of 24 February 1939, in FO 371/23227.
49. In 1939, there were approximately 450,000 Jews and 1,200,000 Arabs in Palestine.
50. Ibid. supra.
51. D.D., 26 February 1939, WA.
52. See Chaim Weizmann, *Trial and Error* (London 1950), p. 499, and D.D., 27 February 1939, WA.
53. MacDonald was at pains to distinguish between his own proposal—independent elected institutions after five years, with proper safeguards for minorities—and the Arab concept of an independent Arab State possessing full sovereignty. For the Jews, the distinction was purely academic.
54. MacDonald saw Weizmann on Sunday evening, 26 February 1939; see D.D., 27 February 1939, WA.
55. Ibid.
56. Ibid.
57. Weizmann told Butler this on 2 March 1939—see FO 371/23226. The Jewish statement was drawn up by Ben-Gurion, Namier, Mrs Dugdale, Dr N. Goldmann and Brodetsky on 26 February 1939—see D.D., 26 February 1939, WA.
58. See minutes of meeting of 27 February 1939 in FO 371/23226.
59. Meeting of 28 February 1939, in FO 371/23227.
60. Meeting with Arab delegation, 1 March 1939, in FO 371/23226.
61. MacDonald developed to a fine art the tactic of rebutting Zionist arguments with those of the Arabs, and vice versa.
62. Meeting of 2 March 1939, in Cab. 23/97.
63. Meeting with the Arabs on 6 March 1939, in FO 371/23227.
64. For following, see minutes of meeting of 7 March 1939 in FO 371/23228. The account is supplemented by Ben-Gurion, *Talks* ..., pp. 259–65. Ben-Gurion claims that the official British note of the meeting is in direct contradiction to notes taken by himself and Shertok.
65. The following is based largely on Ben-Gurion, ibid., who himself relies heavily on Shertok's Political Diary. There is no mention whatever of the closing dialogue in the official British Minutes of this meeting.
66. For following, see minutes of meeting between MacDonald, Aly Maher Pasha, Fuad Bey Hamza and Taufiq Suweidi on 8 March 1939, in FO 371/23228.
67. See Weizmann–MacDonald, 8 March 1939, WA.
68. See minutes of Cabinet meeting of 8 March 1939, in Cab. 23/97.
69. Yet on that very morning, MacDonald had proposed to the Arabs a figure of 70,000. See minutes in FO 371/23228.
70. MacDonald's original plan had envisaged 15–30,000 Jewish immigrants per annum for ten years, i.e. an immigration of 150–300,000. The White Paper figure was 75,000.
71. See minutes of Cabinet meeting of 8 March, Cab. 23/97. In retrospect, this remark is not without irony—on the next day, the Czechs deposed the Slovakian Government, and within a week the Germans had marched into Prague (15 March) and turned Bohemia into a German Protectorate.
72. See meetings of 9 and 11 March 1939, in FO 371/23228.
73. The Cabinet Committee on Palestine worked out the details on 13 March 1939 – see FO 371/23229; the Cabinet ratified the proposals on 15 March 1939. See minutes in Cab. 23/98.
74. See minutes in FO 371/23230, FO 371/23231.
75. Ibid.
76. See minutes of meetings of 21 and 23 March 1939, in FO 371/23232.

77. Meeting of 6 April 1939, in FO 371/23233.
78. MacDonald later claimed that he had been overruled on this point, which was naturally opposed vehemently by his High Commissioner in Palestine. See note on MacMichael–MacDonald, 16 June 1939, in 75872/85, CO 733/410.
79. See Lampson–FO, of 11 April 1939, in FO 371/23233.
80. See minutes of meeting of 20 April, in FO 371/23234. The delay was due to MacDonald's absence on convalescence in the south of France.
81. Ibid.
82. Ibid. My emphasis.
83. See Foreign Office–Lampson, 26 April 1939, in ibid.
84. See Lampson–Foreign Office, 30 April 1939, ibid.
85. See minutes of Cabinet meeting of 3 May 1939, in Cab. 23/99.
86. Shertok, with Dr Brodetsky met Shuckburgh on 13 April 1939. FO 371/23233. The Egyptian Ambassador in London had raised the alarm by flying off to Cairo on 6 April with the latest British proposals—instead of discreetly sending them by telegraph, as intended by the British.
87. Meeting of Shertok and A. Lourie with MacDonald on 27 April, 1939 in S25/9802, CZA.
88. Weizmann–J. R. MacDonald, 12 November 1930, WA.
89. MacDonald speech in Commons, 22 May 1939, *HC Deb. 5th series*, vol. 347, col. 1937.
90. Diary note of Blanche Dugdale (a Gentile), 23 January 1940, D.D. in WA.
91. See Lyttelton (Vt. Chandos, 1954), *Memoirs of Lord Chandos* (London 1962), p. 171: also MacDonald's own *Titans and Others* (London 1972), pp. 92–3.
92. MacDonald transferred first to the Ministry of Health, until February 1941, when he was appointed High Commissioner to Canada.
93. See memorandum by Wallace Murray (Chief of Division of Near Eastern Affairs), May 1939, in *Foreign Relations of the United States* (hereafter *FRUS*), 1939, iv (Washington 1955), pp. 752–7.
94. For text of the May 1939 White Paper, see Cmd 6019 (HMSO).
95. *Herbert Stanley Morrison*, 1888–1965: Minister of Supply, 1940; Home Secretary and Minister of Home Security, 1940–45; member of War Cabinet, 1942–5.
96. See *HC Deb., 5th Series*, vol. 347, cols. 1937–2056, 2129–98, 22–23 May 1939. A normal Government support of 413 was cut to 268 in the vote on the White Paper. 179 MPs voted against, 110 abstained.
97. See note of Chancellor–MacDonald interview of 17 September 1938, in Prem. 1/352.
98. See note by Downie, 'Government Policy at the London Conference', 28 August 1940 in 75872/85, CO 733/426.
99. MacDonald held two informal meetings with members of the Jewish Agency— on 12 and 16 March—devoted solely to the Agency's rejection of the British terms. Weizmann was not present at either meeting; he met MacDonald alone on 14 March, merely to tell him that Britain was betraying the Jews, and to ask for a meeting, alone, with the Prime Minister. See FO 371/23230.

6 BRITISH POLICY DURING THE CRITICAL PHASE, 1939–1942

1. See Y. Bauer, *From Diplomacy to Resistance* (Philadelphia 1970), p. 78.
2. For this and following, see minute by H. F. Downie of 4 June 1940, in CO 733/426, 75872/85. The 'constitutional' provisions are to be found in clause 10 (4), of the White Paper, Cmd 6019.
3. See Hirszowicz, op. cit.

4. For this and following, see MacMichael report of 27 June 1940, in FO 371/24563.
5. MacMichael Report of 31 December 1939, in ibid.
6. Ibid.
7. See minute by Bagallay of 18 January 1940, in ibid. My emphasis.
8. At the St James's Conference, the Government agreed to a demand by the Arabs that a committee (of Arabs and British only) examine the MacMahon–Hussein correspondence of 1915–16. The two sides failed to reach agreement on the nature of British promises to the Arabs. The Committee's report is to be found in Cmd 5974, of 16 March 1939.
9. Bagallay minute, 18 January 1940, ibid.
10. See Halifax–Lothian memorandum, 12 June 1940, for text of telegram sent to Lord Lothian, dated 17 February 1940, in WP (G) 149, in Cab. 67/7.
11. See minute in E2220/20/31, FO 371/24563.
12. See Bagallay minute of 16 February 1940, in ibid. For Cabinet decision of 28 February 1940 on Land Laws, see Cab. 65/11. The regulations were announced in the Commons on the same day, see *HC Deb.*, *5th series*, vol. 357, col. 2057. Under the new regulations the High Commissioner assumed control of all land transfers in Palestine except for those within a coastal strip between Tantura (near Haifa) and a point just south of Tel Aviv—an area already heavily populated by Jews—and in all municipal areas. All the hill country, together with the Gaza and Beersheba sub-districts, were prohibited to would-be Jewish purchasers. In the Plains of Esdraelon and Jezreel, in eastern Galilee and the Negev, Jews would be allowed to purchase land only in order to consolidate plots already held. See terms of regulations, in Cmd 6180.

    The regulations were seen by the Zionists, and indeed intended by the Colonial Office, as an attempt to restrict Jewish settlement in Palestine to those areas which might one day become a 'token' Jewish State.
13. Minutes in E2220/20/31, FO 371/24563. See Nuri Said letter of 25 May 1940, in E2077/20/31, FO 371/24563, quoted by *Sir Llewellyn Woodward, British Policy in the Second World War* (HMSO 1962), p. 559.
14. *Lord Lothian* (Philip Kerr), 1882–1940: Ambassador at Washington from 1939.
15. Bagallay minute, 3 June 1940, in FO 371/24563. My emphasis.
16. Bagallay minute, late June, in FO 371/24563.
17. See Halifax memorandum of 12 June 1940, WP (G) (40) 149, in Cab. 66/7.
18. Ibid.
19. For following, see meeting of 15 June 1940, in Cab. 65/7.
20. See Bagallay–Downie, 21 June 1940, in CO 733/426, 75872/85.
21. For this and following, see minutes of meeting of 3 July 1940, in Cab. 65/8.
22. For following, see Lampson–Foreign Office, of 13 July 1940, in CO 733/426, 75872/85.
23. The terms of Vichy's armistice with Germany included withdrawal of French colonies from the war.
24. See MacMichael–Colonial Office, 22 July 1940, in CO 733/426, 75872/85.
25. Ibid.
26. See Bagallay minute of 30 July 1940, in FO 371/24549.
27. Ibid.
28. See Lampson–Foreign Office, of 19 August 1940, in FO 371/24565.
29. MacMichael–Colonial Office, of 24 August 1940, ibid.
30. Ibid.
31. Bagallay–Lampson (draft) of 1 September 1940, ibid.
32. Lampson–Foreign Office, 16 September 1940, ibid.
33. See Colonial Secretary–MacMichael, 9 November 1940, in ibid.
34. See MacMichael–Colonial Secretary, 12 November 1940, ibid. The Zionists

opposed on principle any institutions upon which they were given minority representation, even though they, together with the British, constituted a majority over the Arabs.

35. See Downie minute of 15 November 1940, in CO 733/426, 75872/85; also minute by Baxter of 20 November 1940, in FO 371/24565.
36. See joint memorandum of 21 November 1940, in ibid.
37. See pp. 104–5.
38. Ibid. supra., my emphasis.
39. See C. Sykes, *Crossroads to Israel* (London 1965), p. 234.
40. Sir Llewellyn Woodward is also of the opinion that it was only the 'Patria' disaster that prevented implementation of the constitutional clauses at that juncture, op. cit., p. 560.
41. See MacMichael–Colonial Office of 24 February 1941, in FO 371/27137.
42. Colonial Secretary–MacMichael (draft), in ibid.
43. See for instance minute by Eyres of 11 April 1941, in ibid.
44. See memorandum by Eden of 27 May 1941, WP (41) 116, Cab. 66/16.
45. See Lampson–Seymour, of 26 April 1941, in FO 371/17043.
46. George Kirk, *Survey of International Affairs, 1939–1946, The Middle East in the War* (London 1952), p. 108.
47. See minute by S. E. V. Luke of 21 July 1941 in FO 371/27137.
48. For following, see MacMichael dispatch of 13 July 1941, ibid.
49. See minute by Luke of 21 July 1941, FO 371/27137.
50. *Sir G. A. Lloyd*, 1879–1941: High Commissioner for Egypt, 1925–9; Colonial Secretary, May 1940–February 1941.
51. Ibid. supra.
52. On 22 November 1940, Weizmann had written to Lord Lloyd informing him that the Zionist programme for an Arab–Jewish settlement after the war based itself on the establishment of a Jewish State of sufficient scope to absorb a considerable number of immigrants, adding that the Zionists were prepared for this State to enter a Federation with neighbouring Arab States, provided this Federation remained closely connected with the British Commonwealth. See WA.
53. See Baxter–Boyd (Colonial Office), 19 September 1941, in ibid.
54. See MacMichael–Foreign Office, 1 September 1941, in FO 371/27137.
55. Ibid.
56. See Baxter minute of 11 November 1941, ibid.
57. For report of meeting, see Luke minute of 22 December 1941, in 75872/115, CO 733/444.
58. See minute by Battershill of 6 April 1942, ibid.
59. Weizmann–Chamberlain, 29 August 1939, WA; also A. Eban, *Tragedy and Triumph*, in *Chaim Weizmann* (London 1962), pp. 253–4.
60. For the official Zionist record of the campaign to gain a Jewish Army under British auspices, see the not always reliable *Sefer Toldot Hahagana* (History of the Haganah), vol. iii, pt. 1, ed Yehuda Slutsky (Tel Aviv 1971) (in Hebrew), especially pp. 649–70. This volume, based on Zionist archives and foreign published works (but not British archives), makes several false assumptions— i.e. that the Government's initial agreement to a Jewish Division in October 1940 was postponed for six months (p. 655). On this subject, see p. 107.
61. See p. 8.
62. See Kirk, op. cit., p. 229.
63. The plan was forwarded to Churchill by Victor Cazalet, MP, on 14 October 1939. For details and comment, see Prem. 4/51/9. Cazalet was in that small circle of MPs who sympathized with Zionism and were in the Zionists' confidence. However, see his unexpected views on the Arab–Zionist conflict, p. 166.

He acted as British Liaison officer with the Polish leader, General Sikorski with whom he perished in an air crash on 4 July 1943.
64. *Brendan Bracken:* Parliamentary Private Secretary to Churchill, 1940–41: Minister of Information, 1941–45.
65. See Bracken minute of 31 October 1939, in Prem. 4.51/9.
66. For following, see minutes of Cabinet meeting of 19 October 1939, in Cab. 65/1.
67. See below, p. 103ff.
68. See MacDonald memorandum, WP (G) (40) 16, in Cab. 67/4, also minutes of Cabinet meeting on 12 February 1940, in Cab. 65/5.
69. Ibid. My emphasis.
70. For details of the defection of Arab members of the force in 1938, see p. 67.
71. See details of Jabotinsky's scheme of 12 May 1940, in Prem. 4/51/9; also minutes in E2044/187/31, FO 371/24566.
   Zeev Vladimir Jabotinsky, 1880–1940: Journalist, author. Founder of Zionist Revisionism, which broke away from the World Zionist Organization in 1935. The Revisionists persisted in claiming that Zionist rights extended to the area of the original Mandate, i.e. also to Transjordan, which had been partitioned off in 1922.
72. Minute by Lord Lloyd, 22 May 1940, in Prem. 4/51/9.
73. Ibid.
74. See Churchill minute of 23 May 1940, ibid.
75. Churchill–Lloyd, 23 May 1940, Appendix A, in W. Churchill, *The Second World War* (London 1949), ii, p. 559. The author was unable to trace this in Colonial Office records.
76. On 14 May the Dutch Army surrendered, and the German Army pierced French defences near Sedan.
77. Churchill note of 18 May 1940, COS (40) 364, in Cab. 80/11.
78. See COS (40) 365 of 18 May, ibid.
79. Churchill note of 23 May 1940, COS (40) 379, ibid.
80. See minutes of meeting of 25 May 1940, COS (40) 146, in Cab. 79/4.
81. See minutes of meeting in Cab. 65/7.
82. See Weizmann–Lloyd, 14 June 1940, in Z4/20.2801, CZA.
83. Ibid.
84. See Lloyd–Weizmann, 15 June 1940, WA. Eden, then Secretary of State for War, undoubtedly did have a 'tainted' record with the Zionists.
85. Ibid., my emphasis.
86. Lloyd–Churchill, 27 June 1940, in Prem. 4.51/9.
87. Churchill–Lloyd, 28 June 1940, in Prem. 3/348.
88. Lloyd–Churchill, 16 July 1940, in Prem. 4/51/9.
89. See minutes of meeting of Cabinet Committee on 29 July 1940, in Cab. 95/2. Both Eden and Moyne sat on the Committee. Moyne, a close friend of Churchill's, was at the time a Private Secretary (with the rank of Minister) at the Ministry of Agriculture and Fisheries—so one might assume that he was Churchill's own representative on the Committee. For minutes on decision, see also Milpal-Mideast HQ, 3 August 1940, in WO 201/185.
90. For following, see Martin–Eastwood, 10 August 1940, ibid.
91. The idea of sending recruits in excess of the quota to serve outside Palestine was Ernest Bevin's. See Weizmann–Bevin, 4 September 1940, WA.
92. See Martin–Eastwood, above.
93. Churchill–Ismay (for General Wavell), 12 August 1940, in Churchill, op. cit., ii, p. 377.
94. For Directive of 16 August 1940, see ibid., p. 380.
95. See report by Weizmann of 27 August 1940, in Z4/302/24, CZA.

96. *Ernest Bevin*, 1888–1951: Minister of Labour and National Service, 1940–45; Foreign Secretary, 1945–51.
97. Lord Bearsted (an oil expert at the War Office; had been a non-Zionist delegate to the St James's Conference) was mentioned.
98. For Weizmann record of meeting on 10 September 1940, see WA. As Weizmann remarked to an embarrassed Eden, the latter had never received him when he had been Foreign Secretary (December 1935–February 1938).
99. See above, Chapter 1.
100. See Colonial Office minute of 4 September 1940, in WO 32/9502.
101. On 3 September 1940, Weizmann had met with Churchill and handed him a memorandum summarizing Zionist proposals for the mobilization of Jewish forces; these included maximum recruitment of Jews in Palestine—with any in excess of Arab recruitment to be sent for training in Egypt or elsewhere in the Middle East; the training of an officer corps sufficient to lead a Jewish Division (10,000), to be chosen immediately from Palestinian Jewry; a 'Jewish Desert Unit' to be trained by Wingate; and the training of Jewish military units in England, to be formed from foreign Jews in England and volunteers from other countries, for service in the Middle East and elsewhere. Churchill gave his own approval, and gave Weizmann permission to take the scheme to the War Office. See Weizmann–Dill, 3 September 1940, WA.
102. See Weizmann's own report to the Jewish Agency Executive on 16 September 1940, in Z4/302/24, CZA. Also Eban, op. cit., pp. 259–60; Sykes, *Crossroads* ..., pp. 216–17.
103. On this, see Bauer, op. cit., p. 79.
104. The 'Anglo-saxons', called by Ben-Gurion 'Weizmann's Court', were Blanche Dugdale and Professors Namier and Brodetsky.
105. See Weizmann's report of 16 September 1940, above. On that same day, Italian forces reached Sidi Barrani.
106. For the following, see minutes of meeting of 18 September 1940 in Z4/302/24, CZA.
107. Ibid.
108. See for instance, Weizmann–Shertok, 22 September 1940, WA.
109. For minutes of Cabinet meeting 10 October 1940, see Cab. 65/9. Lloyd informed Weizmann orally on 14 October 1940, and confirmed officially on 17 October 1940, see Lloyd–Weizmann, 17 October 1940, in FO 371/27126; also WA.
110. Weizmann–Martin, 4 November 1940, in Prem. 4.51/9.
111. See minute by Martin of 4 November 1940, ibid.
112. See Eden–Churchill, 15 November 1940, in Prem. 4/51/9; also Weizmann–Eden interview of 15 November 1940, in WA.
113. Weizmann–Martin, 22 November 1940, WA. Haining was then Vice-CIGS.
114. See Weizmann–Sinclair, 3 February 1941, WA.
115. For following, see Weizmann report of his interview to Smaller Zionist Executive in London, 20 December 1940, in Z4/302/24, CZA.
116. See minute by Baxter of 29 January 1941, in FO 371/27126. The attack on Weizmann contains some irony, in view of later Foreign Office support for him in preference to the 'extremist' Ben-Gurion. See p. 119.
117. Ibid.
118. For this and following, see Weizmann–Lloyd, 6 January 1941, in WA.
119. See minutes of meeting between Eden, Weizmann and Namier, in WA.
120. The difference of views between Eden and the head of his own Eastern Department may be explained by the fact that Eden had been barely one month at the Foreign Office, and was undboutedly predominantly preoccupied with other issues.

121. For following, see account of interview at the Colonial Office of 19 February 1941, in Shuckburgh minute of 20 February 1941, in FO 371/27126.
122. See Rushbrook-Williams memorandum of 20 February 1941, ibid.
123. Comment by Eyres on Rushbrook-Williams memorandum, 28 February 1941, ibid.
124. MacMichael dispatch of 19 February, in ibid.
125. See Baxter minute of 24 February 1941, ibid.
126. Wavell–War Office, 26 February 1941, in Prem. 4.51/9.
127. For meeting of 28 February 1941, see Baxter minute of 3 March 1941, in FO 371/27126. The meeting was attended by the Secretary of State for War, Captain Margesson, by R. A. Butler on behalf of the Foreign Secretary, and by Lord Moyne.
128. *W. E. Guinness* (Lord Moyne, 1932), 1880–1944: Colonial Secretary, February 1941–February 1942; Deputy Minister of State, Cairo, until January 1944, when appointed Minister of State there.
129. Moyne–Churchill, 1 March 1941, in FO 371/27126.
130. Churchill refers here to the 'Patria' disaster, see above, p. 95. The emotional uproar following the tragedy forced London's hand to allow the survivors to remain in Palestine. For Wavell's objections, see minutes of Cabinet meeting of 2 December 1940, in Cab. 65/10.
131. Churchill–Moyne, 1 March 1941, in FO 371/27126; also in Churchill, op. cit., iii, p. 658. Churchill later told Weizmann that it had been very difficult to oppose Wavell, a victorious general then at the height of his powers. See Weizmann report to American Zionists on 28 June 1942, WA.
132. Weizmann–Shertok, 7 March 1941, WA.
133. i.e. as British Ambassador at Washington.
134. Weizmann–Judge Rosenmann (US Presidential Adviser), 22 May 1941, WA.
135. Sir Isaiah Berlin (attached to the Ministry of Information in New York, 1941–2; Press Attaché to the British Embassy, Washington, 1942–45) told Revisionist leaders in confidence—his letter on the subject was later intercepted by American Postal Censorship, and handed over to British Intelligence; see letter of 30 May 1941, in FO 371/27128.
136. See Bauer, op. cit., p. 142; also Hurevitz, op. cit., p. 128. The GOC Palestine had assumed his present position in February 1941. In June 1941 he was replaced by Lt.-General Sir H. M. Wilson.
137. See MacMichael–Moyne, 2 May 1941, in WO 32/9502.
138. See note of Moyne–Namier interview of 6 May 1941 in WA. The decision to waive the parity ruling seems to have been taken at Departmental level, not in Cabinet. It was mentioned in retrospect by Moyne in Cabinet, on 13 October 1941, see Cab. 65/19.
139. See Wavell–CIGS, 12 May 1941, in WO 216/121.
140. On 1 July 1941 Auchinleck was appointed by Churchill to replace Wavell, in whom Churchill had lost confidence, following his handling of the spring crises in Iraq and in the Balkans.
141. Auchinleck–War Office (repeated to MacMichael), 6 July 1941, in FO 371/27127.
142. MacMichael–Colonial Office, 2 July 1941, in ibid; repeated to War Office, in WO 201/185.
143. War Office–Middle East Command, 3 August 1941, in WO 201/185.
144. Minute by C. H. Bateman, 14 July 1941, in FO 371/27127.
145. See Kirk, op. cit., pp. 15–169.
146. See Lyttelton, op. cit., p. 228. Lyttelton was Minister of State from June 1941 to March 1942.
147. See Lampson–FO, 31 July 1941, and minutes in FO 371/27127.

148. Auchinleck–War Office, 5 August 1941, in FO 371/27128.
149. Auchinleck–Lampson, 5 August 1941, in WO 201/185.
150. See Lyttleton–Foreign Office, 9 August 1941, in FO 371/27128; for Lyttleton's negotiations with the Free French over the political future of Syria, see Kirk, op. cit., pp. 110–17.
151. Margesson–Eden, 15 August 1941, in E4866/60/31, ibid.
152. Eden–Lampson, 20 August 1941, ibid.; also in WO 201/185.
153. The meeting is reported on in Lampson–Foreign Office, 25 August 1941, in E5117/60/31, ibid. supra.
154. See Moyne–Eden, 2 July 1941, in FO 371/27127.
155. See minute by Eyres, 3 July 1941, in ibid.
156. See note of Weizmann–Moyne meeting 1 August 1941, in Prem. 4/51/9; also summary in Weizmann–Moyne, 1 December 1941, WA.
157. See note of Weizmann meeting with Brigadier Lee on 12 August 1941, WA.
158. Moyne–Weizmann, 28 August 1941, in FO 371/27128.
159. See Weizmann–Churchill, 1 October 1941, ibid. For text of Weizmann–Moyne of 1 September 1941, see his letter to Moyne of 1 December 1941 summarizing all the negotiations, WA.
160. Reference here to Lyttelton's telegram of 9 August (above, p. 114), which in fact referred to Auchinleck's demand for two thousand troops for Egypt.
161. Moyne–Eden, 12 September 1941, in FO 371/27128.
162. Minute by Baxter of 18 September 1941, in ibid.
163. See memorandum by Moyne of 30 September 1941, MSC (41) 17, in Cab. 95/8.
164. For meeting of Cabinet on 13 October, see Cab. 65/19; see also Moyne–Weizmann 15 October 1941, in FO 371/27129. Moyne informed the Cabinet that the parity rule had now been changed and that no limits were now imposed upon the enlistment of Jews, of whom some seventeen thousand were currently serving in Palestine's police and defence forces.
165. For this and following, see Moyne memorandum of 25 October 1941, WP (G) (41) 117 in Cab. 67/9.
166. MacMichael–Moyne, 4 November 1941, in FO 371/27129.
167. For this and following, see memorandum by Harold Beeley of 6 February 1942, in FO 371/31378; also memorandum by Isaiah Berlin, 23 February 1941, ibid.
168. For Eden memorandum WP (43) 200 of 10 May 1943, see Cab. 66/36; also Woodward, op. cit., p. 388.
169. See for instance Halifax–Eden, 15 January 1943, in FO 371/35031.
170. See page 161.
171. Weizmann–Law, 21 January 1942, in FO 371/31378.
172. Shertok memorandum of 17 April 1942, quoted by Bauer, op. cit., pp. 218–19. The Buffs had been restricted to static, defensive tasks. Bauer claims that in March 1942 the Palmach (a Jewish commando force formed on Jewish initiative in May 1941) was assigned the task of defending Palestine against possible invasion from the north.
173. For this and following, see Shertok report of 7 July 1942, WA.
174. See draft Cabinet paper by the Colonial and War Office, of 2 May 1942, in FO 371/31378. After several amendments, this appeared as a Cabinet memo in August. See below, p. 221, n. 183.
175. See Eyres' minute of 3 May 1942, ibid.
176. Weizmann–Churchill, 25 June 1942, in FO 371/31379; also in WA.
177. Halifax–Foreign Office, 27 June 1942, in ibid. My emphasis.
178. See Churchill–Cranborne of 5 July 1942, in Perm. 4.51/9.
179. Ibid.
180. Cranborne–Churchill, 6 July 1942, ibid.

181. For Cairo Conference, see Cairo–Foreign Office, 21 July 1942, in FO 921/8. Present were the Minister of State (Casey), MacMichael, Auchinleck, and General Scobie (GOC Palestine).
182. Ibid.
183. See WP (42) 332, of 1 August 1942, in Cab. 66/27.
184. For text of Commons announcement of 6 August 1942, see Colonial Secretary–Minister of State (Cairo), 5 August 1942, in FO 921/8; also *HC Deb.*, *5th series*, vol. 382, col. 1271.
185. See Grigg (Secretary of State for War, February 1942–July 1945)–Ismay, 20 October 1942, in Prem. 4.51/9.
186. For this and following, see minute of 21 October, in FO 371/31380.
187. War Office–Minister of State (Cairo), 1 October 1942, in FO 921/8.
188. For minutes of meeting on 7 October 1942, see ibid.
189. *General Sir Harold Alexander*, Commander-in-Chief, Middle East, 1942–43.
190. See Grigg memorandum of 26 November 1942, WP (42) 549, in Cab. 66/31.
191. See Grigg speech of 15 December 1942, in *HC Deb.*, *5th series*, vol. 387, cols. 1753–4.
192. Ibid.
193. Bauer, op. cit., p. 268.
194. Bauer, ibid., pp. 270–72; Kirk, op. cit., p. 310.
195. For following, see Shertok–Locker, 13 September 1943, WA.
196. See minutes of meeting of 23 February 1944, in Z4/302/28. Among those present were Weizmann, Shertok, N. Goldmann, Dugdale, Namier, Locker.
197. Weizmann–Churchill, 28 March 1944, in Prem. 4/51/9; also Weizmann–Grigg, 28 March 1944, in WA.
198. See WP (44) 344, of 26 June 1944, in Cab. 66/51.
199. See minutes of Cabinet meeting on 3 July 1944 in Cab. 65/47; also in Prem. 4/51/9.
200. Churchill minute of 10 July 1944 for Sir Edward Bridges (Secretary to the Cabinet), in ibid.; also in Churchill, op. cit., vi, p. 596.
201. Weizmann–Churchill, 4 July 1944, WA.
202. For this and following, see Grigg–Churchill, 21 July 1944, in Prem. 4.51/9. *General Paget:* C.-in-C. Middle East, February–December 1943; then became Supreme Allied Commander Mediterranean theatre; *General Wilson:* C.-in-C. Persia–Iraq.
203. Martin–War Office, 3 August 1944, ibid.
204. Churchill–Grigg, 26 July 1944, ibid.
205. Churchll–Grigg, 6 August 1944, ibid.
206. For following, see meeting of Cabinet on 9 August 1944, in Cab. 65/47; also in ibid.
207. See Churchill–Roosevelt, 23 August 1944 and Roosevelt–Churchill, 28 August 1944, in Prem. 4/51/9.
208. For minutes of Cabinet meetings, see Cab. 65/47; the brigade was forbidden to fly its own flag during transit through Egypt, but allowed to fly it only upon arrival in Italy.

7 ZIONIST LEADERSHIP IN CRISIS

1. See Hurevitz, op. cit., pp. 39–41.
2. This was the connotation given by the Peel Commission to the Arabs' Supreme Moslem Council.

3. For a pragmatical assessment of the motives behind the Balfour Declaration, see M. Vereté, 'The Balfour Declaration and its Makers', *Middle Eastern Studies*, vi, 1, 1970.
4. See, for instance, *Sefer Toldot Hahagana*, op. cit., p. 192.
5. *The Jewish Agency:* established in 1929 to finance, promote and supervise the development of the National Home. With its main offices in London and in Jerusalem, it soon became a form of quasi-Government.
6. For instance, Barnett Litvinoff, *The Road to Jerusalem* (London 1965), pp. 206–8.
7. Shertok to Mapai Central Committee, 9 July 1936, in Shertok, op. cit., p. 196.
8. Ibid.
9. Melchett–Shertok, 27 March 1936, WA.
10. Weizmann–Lourie, 28 July 1936, WA.
11. Shertok to Mapai Central Committee, 25 October 1936, in Shertok, op. cit., p. 347; my emphasis.
12. For an acute insight into the ambivalent relationships between Zionist leaders, see Josef Gorni, *Partnership and Conflict* (Tel Aviv 1976) (in Hebrew).
13. Weizmann–Weisgal, 13 April 1936, WA.
14. *Feisal ibn Hussein*, 1885–1933: commander of Arab Revolt, 1916–18; Head of Administration in Syria, 1918–20; King of Iraq from 1921. In January 1919, Feisal and Weizmann had signed a draft treaty, but it was abrogated by Feisal when he was ejected from Syria in July 1920.
15. Bauer, op. cit., p. 74.
16. *Toldot Hahagana*, op. cit., p. 141.
17. Ibid., p. 142.
18. Bauer, op. cit., p. 77, also *Toldot Hahagana*, op. cit., p. 144.
19. Ben-Gurion–Agency Executive (Jerusalem), 15 July 1940, quoted in Bauer, op. cit., p. 78.
20. *Toldot Hahagana*, op. cit., p. 145.
21. Bauer, op. cit., p. 93.
22. Weizmann–Wise, 20 June 1942, WA.
23. Issue of 17 January 1941.
24. Bauer, op. cit., pp. 236–7.
25. *Toldot Hahagana*, op. cit., p. 190.
26. Bauer, op. cit., pp. 236–7.
27. *Stephen Samuel Wise*, 1874–1949: Reform Rabbi, communal and Zionist leader; founding chairman, World Jewish Congress, 1936; president, American Zionist Emergency Council, 1940.
Nahum Goldmann, 1895– : Zionist statesman; represented Jewish Agency in New York during the war. *Louis Lipsky*, 1876–1963: vice-president and chairman, Governing Council of American Jewish Congress, 1934–45.
28. Bauer, op. cit., pp. 234–5; Hurevitz, op. cit., p. 158.
29. Ben-Gurion–Weizmann, 11 June 1942, WA.
30. Weizmann–Ben-Gurion, 15 June 1942, WA.
31. Ben-Gurion–Wise, 19 June 1942, WA.
32. Weizmann–Wise, 20 June 1942, WA.
33. Wise–Ben-Gurion, 22 June 1942, WA.
34. Meeting of 28 June 1942, WA. Present were Wise (Chairman), Weizmann, Ben-Gurion, N. Goldmann, Lipsky, Leventhal, Szold, Weisgal, Greenberg. The minutes are incomplete, and Ben-Gurion's remarks are deduced from Weizmann's reply.
35. My emphasis.
36. Weisgal–Agronsky, 29 July 1942, WA.
37. Draft proposal of 29 April 1942, WA. Also, Weizmann–Wise, 30 June 194, 2WA.

38. For account of meeting on 16 July 1942 between Weizmann, Ben-Gurion and N. Goldmann, see Weizmann–Locker, 27 July 1942, WA.
39. Weisgal–Agronsky, 29 July 1942, WA.
40. Eban, op. cit., p. 291.
41. Halifax–Eden, 1 July 1942, in FO 371/31379. My emphasis.
42. For following, see Wise–Ben-Gurion, 16 September 1942, WA.
43. For following, see Lourie–Brodetsky, 18 September 1942, WA. The meeting was held either on 17 or 18 September. Ben-Gurion, Lourie, and Szold were present, but it is uncertain who else—it may be presumed that Wise was not.
44. *Robert Szold*, 1889– : US lawyer, Zionist; later supported Weizmann.
45. Lourie–Brodetsky, 18 September 1942, WA.
46. Bauer, op. cit., pp. 238–43.
47. Reference to the programme of the first Zionist Congress, called by Herzl in 1897.
48. Weizmann–Dugdale, 8 January 1943, WA.
49. Kaplan appreciated the value of Biltmore as a slogan, but did not regard the resolutions as forming a practical basis of policy. Shertok thought the programme 'somewhat utopian'. Minutes of Agency Executive meeting at Jerusalem, on 11 November 1942, quoted by Bauer, op. cit., p. 245. On 12 November 1942, the Zionist Actions Committee in Palestine voted by a majority of 22 to 3, with 3 abstentions, in favour of the Biltmore resolutions, whereby they became official Zionist policy. *Toldot Hahagana*, op. cit., p. 192.
50. Agency Executive, Jerusalem–Agency Executive, New York, 26 November 1942, WA.
51. Report on Ben-Gurion speech by A. Giles (Inspector-General, Palestine CID), 12 October 1942, in FO 921/6.
52. Weizmann–Smuts interview, 23 November 1943, WA.
53. See p. 119.
54. Undated, but probably the beginning of 1943, in S25/10.134, CZA.
55. Weizmann–Shertok, 31 March 1943, WA, referring to a meeting of a few days earlier between Weizmann, Shertok, Wise and Goldmann.
56. Ibid.
57. Weisgal–Locker, February 1943, WA.
58. Shertok's visit on his own initiative caused a rift between him and Ben-Gurion. Shertok had gone primarily to torpedo Weizmann's plan to negotiate with Ibn Saud. But Ben-Gurion thought that the visit – at Weizmann's request – was treason to himself. Ben-Gurion cut off their previously intimate relationship, and ceased to call Shertok by his first name. See Shertok Diary entry for 23 November 1953, in *Maariv* (Israeli Evening Paper), 17 May 1974.
59. Jewish Agency Executive, 27 April 1943, CZA; reported by Intelligence, in E3689/87/31, FO 371/35035.
60. For this, and following, see Bauer, op. cit., pp. 263–4.
61. Weizmann–Shertok, 17 November 1943, WA.
62. Bauer, op. cit., p. 264.
63. Ibid., n. 10, p. 408.
64. For meetings of 14, 15 and 22 February 1944, see Z4/302/28.
65. Bauer, op. cit., p. 258.
66. Smaller Actions Committee, 11 May 1944, in S25/1772.
67. Bauer, op. cit., p. 265.
68. Bauer, ibid.
69. Meyer Weisgal, *So Far* . . . (London 1971), pp. 260–62.

8 PALESTINE AND ARAB FEDERATION

1. Report by Consul Ogden, 21 August 1936, in FO 371/20024. My emphasis.
2. For the following, see memorandum by Major Hawthorn, 9 February 1938, in FO 371/21873.
3. See memorandum by Bagallay, 28 September 1939, in FO 371/23239.
4. Ibid. My emphasis.
5. Eden memorandum on 'Arab Policy', WP (41) 116, of 27 May 1941, in Cab. 66/16.
6. Ibid. My emphasis.
7. Quoted by Kirk, op. cit., p. 334; also Hurevitz, op. cit., p. 117; for the Cabinet's post-facto approval of Eden's speech, see minutes of meeting of 2 June 1941, in Cab. 65/18.
8. Memorandum of 9 June 1941, in FO 371/27044. For the role of the Royal Institute of International Affairs, see Elie Kedourie, *The Chatham House Version* (London 1970).
9. See Eden–Jidda, 15 August 1941, in FO 371/27044.
10. See Amery–Churchill, 10 September 1941, in FO 371/27045; also Weizmann, op. cit., pp. 427–8.
11. See Elizabeth Monroe, *Philby of Arabia* (London 1973), pp. 221–5, also Kirk, op. cit., pp. 312–14. Also Chapter 9, note 56.
12. Minute by Baxter (First Secretary in Eastern Department), 25 September 1941, in FO 371/27045.
13. See the Committee's report of 9 January 1942, in Cab. 95/1.
14. Ibid.
15. *HC Deb.*, 5th series, vol. 387, col. 139.
16. Eyres minute, 21 March 1943, in FO 371/34956.
17. Ibid.
18. Eyres minute, 3 April 1943, in FO 371/34956.
19. For following, see Nuri Said–Casey, 14 January 1943, found in annexe to P (M) (43) 11 of 10 September 1943, in Cab. 95/14.
20. See Moyne memorandum of 1 November 1943, P (M) (43) 15, in Cab. 95/14; dealt with at greater length on pp. 169–70.
21. Minute by Baxter, 23 March 1943, in FO 371/34955.
22. Bullard (Jidda)–FO, 26 April, 1943, in FO 371/34957.
23. FO–Cairo, 2 March 1944, in FO 371/39987; also minute by R. M. A. Hankey, 1 June 1944, in FO 371/39988.
24. Minute by R. M. A. Hankey, 1 June 1944, in FO 371/39988.
25. Cornwallis–FO, 6 July 1944, ibid.
26. Minute by R. M. A. Hankey, 15 July 1944, ibid.
27. Kirk, op. cit., p. 339.
28. Killearn–FO, 3 September 1944, in FO 371/39990.
29. R. M. A. Hankey minute, 16 September 1944, ibid. The Palestinian Arabs chose Musa Alami as their delegate, at the very last minute.
30. For the text, see E6137/41/65, ibid.; also Kirk, op. cit., pp. 340–43.
31. See Cornwallis–Eden, 5 November 1944, also Moyne–Eden, 19 Ooctober 1944, in FO 371/3991.
32. Terence Shone (Minister at Cairo)–Eden, 10 October 1944, ibid.
33. *Musa el-Alami*, 1897– : Palestinian Arab politician. Private Secretary to High Commissioner in Palestine from 1931, and later Senior Assistant to Attorney-General; close adviser to Mufti until 1941; Palestinian representative on Arab League in 1945.
34. Cornwallis–Eden, 5 November 1944, FO 371/3991. My emphasis.

35. R. M. A. Hankey minute, 28 January 1945, in FO 371/45250.
36. Memorandum by Colonel de Gaury, 11 November 1945, in FO 371/45241.
37. Ibid. My emphasis.
38. Minutes in E2091/3/65, FO 371/45237.
39. R. M. A. Hankey minute, 30 March 1945, in FO 371/45237.

9 BRITISH POLICY IN PALESTINE, 1943–45

1. France had between the wars been very much a 'junior', even a 'sleeping' partner in the Middle East, posing no threat of expanding to the south, or east of its Syrian mandate.
2. A COS recommendation in June 1940 to withdraw the Mediterranean Fleet, following the French defeat, was not in fact implemented, because the Italian Fleet did not materialize into the menace anticipated. COS (40) 183, 17 June 1940, Cab. 79/5. Playfair, op. cit., i, pp. 145–64.
3. The German airlift to Iraq, via staging-posts in Vichy Syria, was on a limited scale and came too late. Hirszowicz, op. cit.
4. See COS (42) 357, of 29 July 1942, in Cab. 80/37.
5. Aide-memoire by Joint Planning Staff, JP (41) 580, of 23 July 1941, Cab. 95/1.
6. Ibid.
7. Playfair, op. cit., iii, p. 127.
8. COS (42) 90, 20 March 1942, in Cab. 79/19.
9. Churchill–Ismay, 5 January 1943, in Churchill, op. cit., iv, p. 823. Ismay was Chief of Staff to Churchill, in the latter's capacity as Minister of Defence.
10. I.e. W. R. Polk, *The United States and the Arab World* (Harvard 1965), p. 262; J. C. Hurevitz, *Middle East Dilemmas* (New York 1953), p. 1; and J. C. Campbell, *Defense of the Middle East* (New York 1958), p. 31.
11. See M. Howard, *The Mediterranean Strategy in the Second World War* (New York 1968), p. 24; also Gaddis Smith, *American Diplomacy in the Second World War* (New York 1967), p. 99.
12. John A. DeNovo, *American Interests and Policies in the Middle East, 1900–1939* (Minneapolis 1963), p. 208.
13. Cordell Hull, *Memoirs*, ii, (London 1948), p. 1517.
14. Ibid., pp. 1521–24.
15. WP (44) 102, of 11 February 1944, in Cab. 66/47.
16. By 1944, America controlled 42 per cent of the proved oil reserves of the Middle East, which had themselves increased 5.8 times by new discoveries since 1936. This compared with only 13 per cent control of the smaller amount in 1936 – an absolute increase of 1900 per cent. Kirk, op. cit., p. 25, n. 1.
17. Ibid., p. 24.
18. Minute by Sir M. Peterson, 5 April 1944, in FO 371/39984.
19. Minutes of meeting of 11 September 1945, in FO 371/45252.
20. Minute by Nevile Butler (formerly Minister at Washington Embassy), 14 July 1943, in FO 371/34975.
21. Minute of 13 August 1943, in FO 371/35040; also Woodward, op. cit., pp. 385–8; also M. J. Cohen, 'Anglo-American relations in the Middle East during World War Two', *American Jewish Historical Quarterly*, 1977.
22. P (M) (44) 11, 15 September 1944, in Cab. 95/14.
23. J. P. Mackintosh, in *Strategy and Tactics of Soviet Foreign Policy* (London 1962), pinpoints 1953–56; Adam B. Ulam, in *Expansion and Co-Existence: The History of Soviet Foreign Policy from 1917–67* (London 1968), pinpoints 1953; G·

Lenczowski, in *Soviet Advances in the Middle East* (Washington, DC 1972), sees 1955 as the turning-point.
24. E. A. Speiser, *The United States and the Near East* (London 1947), p. 177.
25. For following, see 'Probable post-war tendencies in Soviet foreign policy as affecting British interests', memorandum by the Cabinet Post-Hostilities Planning Sub-Committee of 29 April 1944, in FO 371/43335.
26. Ibid.
27. Ironically, at this very juncture, Britain was balking at the idea of a further share-out of Middle East oil with the United States.
28. Post-Hostilities Planning Sub-Committee memorandum of 29 April 1944, in FO 371/43335.
29. Minute by F. A. Warner (Counsellor at the Foreign Office since 1942) of 11 February 1944, in FO 371/39984.
30. Grigg memorandum, 'Imperial Security in the Middle East', CP (45) 55, of 2 July 1945, in Cab. 66/67.
31. Ibid.
32. Under the 1942 Tripartite Treaty, Russia had undertaken to withdraw its forces from Iran within six months of war's end. It did so finally two months after the deadline, following United States and United Nations' pressure.
33. Ivar Spectar, *The Soviet Union and the Muslim World, 1917–58* (Washington 1959), pp. 197–202.
34. For the following, see JP (42) 1025 of 20 December 1942, in Cab. 84/51.
35. Apart from his term as C.-in-C. Middle East, Wavell had been on active service in Palestine itself from 1936–39.
36. See minutes of Cabinet meeting on 2 July 1943, in Cab. 65/39.
37. See report on meetings of 10–13 May 1943, in WP (43) 247 of 19 May 1943, in Cab. 66/37.
38. For following, see appreciation by Post-Hostilities Sub-Committee of the COS, P (M) (43) 10 of 30 August 1943, in Cab. 95/14.
39. Ibid.
40. See Report on 'Strategic needs in the Levant States', P (M) (44) 6, 22 January 1944, in Cab. 95/14. My emphasis.
41. Even then, partition would have to be implemented at the expense of the redeployment of forces against Japan, or demobilization, or requirements for the occupation of Germany.
42. Churchill–Ismay, 25 January 1944, in Prem. 4/52/1.
43. COS–Churchill, 4 February 1944, in ibid.
44. See JP (44) 227 of 2 November 1944, annexe to COS (44) 359 of 6 November 1944, in Cab. 79/82.
45. For the following, see JP (44) 286 of 15 November 1944, in Cab. 79/83. The wholesale disarming of the Yishuv considered in this report was contemplated as a retaliatory measure for the assassination of Lord Moyne by Jewish terrorists on 6 November 1944.
46. Ibid.
47. See note of their meeting on 4 November 1944, in WA.
48. See for instance, COS (45) 582 of 21 September 1945, in Cab. 80/97.
49. See CP (45) 216 of 11 October 1945. This extract is from the draft found in E7637/15/31, FO 371/45381 and in AIR 20/4962 – but is missing from the final draft in Cab. 129/3.
50. Grigg likened his 'system' to the Quadrilateral in Italy upon which the Austrian Empire had based its rule there.
51. For following, see memorandum on 'Imperial Security in the Middle East', CP (45) 55 of 2 July 1945, in Cab. 66/67.

52. Ibid. My emphasis.
53. See E. Monroe, *Britain's Moment in the Middle East* (London 1963), pp. 157-8, 165-70.
54. See Churchill's objections, in minutes of Cabinet meeting of 12 February 1940, in Cab. 65/5; for details of Land Laws, see p. 215, n.12.
55. See Lampson-Eden, 4 January 1943, in FO 371/35031.
56. This scheme was initiated by St John 'Abdullah' Philby. At meetings with Weizmann in London in September and October 1939, Philby had claimed that Ibn Saud was prepared to agree to a Jewish State in all of Western Palestine, provided that the Arabs in other lands of the Middle East gained their independence, and in return for Jewish financial aid. Weizmann told Philby that he would be able to raise an estimated £20 millions. When Philby reported back to Ibn Saud in January 1940, the latter raised no objections, but swore Philby to secrecy, and suggested that the programme be 'imposed' upon him by Britain and the United States. When Philby reported back to Weizmann, the latter discussed the plan with Churchill, in March 1942. Churchill advised Weizmann to first gain the support of Roosevelt, so that the scheme might be implemented after the war. Weizemann discussed the scheme at the State Department in January and in March 1943. In July 1943 Roosevelt sent his expert on Middle Eastern affairs, Colonel Hoskins, to sound out Ibn Saud on the scheme. The latter now completely disowned the scheme and refused to negotiate with Weizmann, for whom he expressed a personal hatred for having impugned his honour with such a proposal. See Bauer, op. cit., pp. 224-7; Kirk, op. cit., pp. 312-14; see notes of Weizmann's meetings at the State Department in WA, and Hoskins' report in FO 371/35041; also Monroe, *Philby* . . . , pp. 221-5.
57. See, for instance, Weizmann-Berlin interview on 26 January 1943, in FO 371/35031.
58. *Sumner Welles*, 1892-1961: Under-Secretary of State, 1937-42.
59. Minute by H. A. Caccia, 17 February 1943, in FO 371/35031.
60. Minute by Sir M. Peterson (head of the Middle Eastern Department at the Foreign Office), 25 March 1943, in FO 371/34955.
61. Weizmann-Churchill, 2 April 1943, in FO 371/35033.
62. See speeches made by Lord Cranborne in this sense during a debate on refugees from German atrocities, on 23 March 1943; Parl. Debs, Lords, 5th series, col. 850.
63. Churchill minute of 18 April 1943, in FO 371/34955.
64. Col. Stanley (Colonial Secretary, 1943-45) in particular took personal offence.
65. For this, and following, see Churchill's memorandum of 28 April 1943, in WP (43) 178, Cab. 66/36. It included Weizmann's letter as an annexe.
66. Minute by Sir M. Peterson of 1 May 1943, in FO 371/35033.
67. See WP (43) 200 of 10 May 1943, in Cab. 66/36.
68. See Cranborne memorandum of 4 May 1943, WP (43) 187, in Cab. 66/36.
69. Ibid.
70. See report of 1 May 1943, prepared for a meeting of the Middle East War Council on 10 May; in FO 371/34975.
71. For minutes of the Council's meetings between 10-13 May 1943, see WP (43) 247 of 17 June 1943, in Cab. 66/37; also E3234/2551/65, ibid.
72. For this, and following, see Memorandum by R. G. Casey, WP (43) 246 of 17 June 1943, ibid. supra.
73. Minute by Sir M. Peterson of 25 June 1943, in FO 371/34975.
74. See minutes of meeting of 2 July 1943, in Cab. 65/39.
75. See minute by R. K. Law (Parliamentary Under-Secretary at the Foreign Office) of 10 August 1943, in FO 371/35036.

76. Churchill appointed the following: H. Morrison (Home Secretary) – Chairman; L. Amery (Secretary of State for India); Col. Stanley (Colonial Secretary); A. Sinclair (Secretary of State for Air); R. K. Law (Parliamentary Under-Secretary at the Foreign Office) – only after special appeal by Eden himself.
77. Churchill–Eden, 11 July 1943, in M458/3, Prem. 4/52/1.
78. Eden minute of 6 September 1943, in FO 371/35038.
79. For following, see Amery memorandum, P (M) (43) 3 of 31 July 1943, in Cab. 95/14.
80. See Cmd 5854, 9 November 1938.
81. For following, see Cazalet memorandum P (M) (43) 5 of 2 August 1943, in Cab. 95/14. The memorandum was evidently posthumous, for Cazalet, an officer MP who acted as British liaison with the Polish leader Gen. Sikorski, had perished together with the latter in an air crash on 4 July 1943.
82. For minutes of first meeting of 4 August 1943, see Cab. 95/14.
83. The Foreign Office referred to Weizmann's contacts with Stanley and Amery – see ibid. In fact, Weizmann met Amery on 2 September, and was informed by him that the partition then under discussion would include the Negev and Akaba, and the whole coastline up to the Lebanon, with the exception of Acre – see minutes of meeting, in Z4/302/27, CZA.
84. Peterson minute of 5 September, ibid. supra.
85. See minutes of meeting of 25 October 1943, in WA. The Commons announcement was made on 10 November 1943.
86. See minute by R. M. A. Hankey of 5 February 1944, in FO 371/40129.
87. For following, see memorandum by R. K. Law of 12 August 1943, P (M) (43) 7, in Cab. 95/14.
88. See Amery memorandum of 25 August 1943, P (M) (43) 9, in ibid.
89. Ibid.
90. For this and following, see Foreign Office memorandum of 1 November 1943, P (M) (43) 16, ibid.
91. Ibid.
92. See memorandum by R. Casey of 2 November 1943, P (M) (43), in Cab. 95/14.
93. Ibid.
94. For following, see Col. Stanley memorandum of 1 November 1943, P (M) (43) 14, in ibid.
95. See memorandum by Lord Moyne of 1 November 1943, P (M) (43) 15, in ibid.
96. For minutes of meeting of 4 November 1943, see Cab. 95/14.
97. See minutes of 18 October 1943, in FO 371/35040.
98. For minutes of meeting of 16 November 1943, see ibid.
99. See minute by Baxter of 7 December 1943, in FO 371/35042.
100. See minutes of meeting of 10 December 1943, in Cab. 95/14.
101. See P (M) (43) 28 of 10 December 1943, ibid.
102. See p. 172.
103. For following, see draft memorandum of 23 December 1943, in FO 371/35042.
104. See S. J. Conway, 'Between apprehension and indifference: Allied attitudes to the destruction of Hungarian Jewry', *The Wiener Library Bulletin*, 1973/4, vol. xxvii.
105. See minutes of meeting of 25 January 1944, in Cab. 65/45.
106. See Churchill minute of 16 January 1944, in Prem. 4/52/1.
107. Amery–Churchill, 22 January 1944, ibid.
108. For this and following, see Eden–Middle East Ambassadors, 1 February 1944, in ibid.
109. See Killearn–Eden, 16 February 1944, in ibid.
110. Cornwallis–Eden, 24 February 1944, ibid.

111. For following, see Eden–Middle East Ambassadors, ibid. supra. Also *FRUS*, 1945, viii (Washington 1969), pp. 683–7.
112. See Col. Stanley–Churchill, 10 June 1944, ibid.
113. Churchill–Stanley, 24 June 1944, ibid.
114. See MacMichael dispatch of July 1944, in WO 216/121.
115. See minutes of meeting of 9 August 1944, in Cab. 65/47.
116. See Colonial Office memorandum of 11 September 1944, P (M) (44) 10, in Cab. 95/14.
117. See Eden memorandum of 15 September 1944, P (M) (44) 11, ibid.
118. For minutes of meeting of 19 September 1944, see ibid.
119. For minutes of meeting of 26 September 1944, see ibid.
120. For following, see Second Report of Committee, P (M) (44) 14, in ibid.; also minute by Sir Edward Bridges (Secretary to the Cabinet) of 3 November 1944, in Prem. 4/52/1.
121. See report of Churchill's speech of 17 November 1944 in *The Times* of the following day.
122. See Morrison–Churchill, 26 February 1945, in Prem. 4/51/2.
123. See Y. Bauer, op. cit., pp. 323–31.
124. In his Commons announcement of 10 November 1943, Stanley announced that there remained some 31,078 of the 75,000 immigration certificates provided for under the 1939 White Paper.
125. See Morrison–Churchill, 26 February 1945, in Prem. 4/51/2.
126. For following see Stanley memorandum of 30 March 1945, in P (M) (45) 1, Cab. 95/14.
127. For this, and following, see Grigg memorandum of 4 April 1945, WP (45) 214, in Cab. 66/64.
128. See Grigg–Sir Edward Bridges, 4 April 1945, in FO 371/45377.
129. See P (M) (45) 2, 9 April 1945, in FO 371/45377.
130. See P (M) (45) 6, 4 May 1945, ibid.
131. See memorandum of 16 May 1945, ibid.
132. MacDonald was a possible exception in May 1940. But Churchill had not appointed him, nor did he remove him from the Cabinet until February 1941.
133. See *The Diaries of Alexander Cadogan, 1938–1945*, ed David Dilks (New York 1972), pp. 281, 300–01.
134. See Oskar K. Rabinowitz, *Winston Churchill on Jewish Problems* (London 1956), p. 119.
135. See W. H. Thompson, *I was Churchill's Shadow* (London 1954), p. 21.
136. See Harry Sacher, *The Establishment of a State* (London 1959), p. 30. MacMichael's belated conversion to partition, in July 1944, was the product of despair rather than of any conscious urge to nurture Zionism.
137. Ibid.
138. The new Foreign Secretary (Bevin), together with the Secretaries of State for War (Lawson) and Air (Viscount Stansgate), were members.
139. In May 1945, at the Labour Party's Election Conference, the National Executive reaffirmed the Palestine plank of its platform enunciated the previous year, which had called for the abrogation of the White Paper, unlimited Jewish immigration and Arab emigration, and the extension of Palestine's territory. Quoted by Hurevitz, op. cit., p. 227.
140. Rose, op. cit., pp. 5, 123, 132.
141. Ibid., p. 74ff.
142. See *Action This Day, Working with Churchill*, ed J. Wheeler-Bennett (London 1968), memoir by John Colville, p. 105.
   Lord Dalton, 1887–1962: Minister of Economic Warfare, 1940–41; President of

Board of Trade, 1942–45; Chancellor of Exchequer, 1945–47.
143. Dalton–Attlee, 25 September 1941, in *Dalton Papers* (held at the London School of Economics), quoted by Dilks, op. cit., p. 384.
144. For background to the Labour Party's Zionist policy, see the *Creech-Jones Papers*, ACJ 33/2, held in the Rhodes House Collection of the Bodleian Library, Oxford; also Richard Crossman, *Palestine Mission: A Personal Record* (New York 1947).
145. A sympathetic biographer wrote later than Bevin 'gave too much weight to the views of the military and Foreign Office advisers'. Francis Williams, *Ernest Bevin: Portrait of a Great Englishman* (London 1952), p. 259. A later biographical sketch is also revealing – 'He could not draft; he was not concerned with the meticulous details of presentation, or with the accurate recollection of precedents. What he liked to do, in his own phrase, was to get officials to "put clothes on his ideas". But he provided many of the ideas . . .' Roy Jenkins, in *Nine Men of Power* (London 1974), p. 78.
146. For Bevin's scheme, together with criticism, see Colonial Office memorandum, 7 September 1945, in FO 371/45382. For 'Provincial Autonomy' scheme, see P (M) (45) 11, 1 September 1945, in FO 371/45382.
147. On 24 September 1945, President Truman made public his earlier confidential request to Attlee that Britain make an immediate grant of 100,000 immigration certificates, to allow the transfer of that number of Jewish Displaced Persons from Europe.
148. See minute of Cabinet meeting of 4 October 1945, in Cab. 128/1. See also the author's 'The genesis of the Anglo-American Committee on Palestine, November 1945', forthcoming in *Historical Journal*, January 1979.
149. For the conflict over the terms of reference between the Foreign Office and the State Department, see FO 371/45384–85; also *Foreign Relations of the United States* 1945, V. VIII (Washington 1969).
150. Churchill minute, 6 July 1945, in FO 371/45378.

10 CONCLUSION
1. *British Security*, Royal Institute of International Affairs (London 1944), p. 118

Bibliography

UNPUBLISHED SOURCES

(i) *Public Records Office, London:*

a. Cabinet Papers
To 1939	Cab. 23	Minutes
	Cab. 24	Memoranda
War Cabinet	Cab. 65	Minutes
1939–45	Cab. 66	Memoranda – WP and CP series
	Cab. 67	Memoranda – WP (G) series
From August 1945	Cab. 128	Minutes
	Cab. 129	Memoranda

b. Cabinet Committees
To 1939	Cab. 51	Middle East Questions
	Cab. 53	COS Committee
	Cab. 54	Deputy COS Committee
	Cab. 55	Joint Planning Staff Committee
1939–45	Cab. 79	COS Meetings
	Cab. 80	COS Memoranda
1943–6	Cab. 95	Committee on Palestine

c. Prime Minister's Office
Prem. 1	Correspondence and Papers to 1940
Prem. 3	Operational
Prem. 4	Confidential Papers, 1940–5
Prem. 8	Correspondence and Papers, 1945–7

d. Foreign Office
FO 371	Political
FO 800	Private Papers (Lord Halifax: Viscount Cranborne)
FO 921	Minister of State, Cairo

e. Colonial Office
CO 733	Palestine Correspondence
CO 814	Minutes of Executive Council, Palestine

f. War Office
WO 32	Registered Papers, General Series
WO 33	Reports and Miscellaneous

WO 106 Directorate of Military Operations and Intelligence
WO 201 Middle East Forces
WO 216 Chief of Imperial General Staff, Unregistered Papers

g. *Air Ministry*

Air 20 Unregistered Papers

(ii) Archives in Israel:

Central Zionist Archives, Jerusalem
Israel State Archives, Jerusalem
Weizmann Archives, Rehovot
Mapai Party Archives, Bet Berl

(iii) Private Correspondence:

The Creech-Jones Papers, in the Rhodes House Library, Oxford
The Bowman and MacMichael Papers, in the Middle East Centre, St Antony's College, Oxford
The Lloyd George Papers, in the Beaverbrook Library, London
The Macleod Papers (GSO1 to CIGS Ironside in 1939), in the Centre for Military Archives, King's College, London

PRIMARY PUBLISHED SOURCES

a. Documents on foreign policy

British Documents on Foreign Policy (BDFP), Third Series, 1918–39
Foreign Relations of the United States (FRUS)
Documents on German Foreign Policy, 1918–1939, Series D

b. Hansard

Hansard, 5th Series, Parliamentary Debates, Lords and Commons

c. Command Papers

Cmd 5479 Report of Palestine Royal Commission, July 1937: The Peel Report
Cmd 5513 Palestine: A Statement of Policy, July 1937
Cmd 5854 The Palestine Partition (Woodhead) Report, October 1938
Cmd 5957 The text of the correspondence between Sir H. MacMahon and the Sherif of Mecca, July 1915–March 1916 (March 1939)
Cmd 6019 Palestine: A Statement of Policy, May 1939

BOOKS AND ARTICLES

Abdullah, *Memoirs* (London 1950)
Amery, L. S., *My Political Life* (London 1953), 3 vols
Antonious, G., *The Arab Awakening* (London 1938; New York 1965)

Arlosoroff, C., *Jerusalem Diary* (Jerusalem 1933 – in Hebrew)
Bar-Zohar, M., *Ben-Gurion: The Armed Prophet* (New Jersey 1967; London 1967)
Bauer, Y., *From Diplomacy to Resistance* (Philadelphia 1970)
——'From Co-Operation to Resistance: The Hagana, 1938–46' in *Middle Eastern Studies*, ii, 3, April 1966
Beigin, M., *The Revolt* (London 1951)
Ben-Gurion, D., *Letters to Paula* (Tel Aviv 1968 – in Hebrew; London 1971; Pittsburgh 1972)
——*Talks with Arab Leaders* (Tel Aviv 1967 – in Hebrew; New York 1973; London 1974)
——*Bama'aracha* (Tel Aviv 1947 – in Hebrew)
Bentwich, N., *My 77 Years* (London 1960; New York 1962)
Bentwich, N. and H., *Mandate Memories 1918–48* (London 1965; New York 1965)
Bentwich, N. and Kisch, M., *Brigadier Frederick Kisch* (London 1966)
Bowman, H., *Middle East Window* (London 1942)
Busch, B. C., *Britain, India and the Arabs, 1914–21* (Berkeley, Calif. 1971)
Byrnes, J. F., *Speaking Frankly* (New York and London 1947)
Campbell, J. C., *Defence of the Middle East* (New York and London 1960)
Casey, Lord, *Personal Experience 1939–46* (London and New York 1962)
Chandos, Viscount (Oliver Lyttelton), *Memoirs of Lord Chandos* (London 1962)
Churchill, W., *The Second World War* (London and New York 1948)
Cohen, A. H., *Israel and the Arab World* (London 1970; Boston 1976)
Cohen, M. J., 'Sir Arthur Wauchope, the Army and the Rebellion in Palestine, 1936' in *Middle Eastern Studies*, ix, 1, January 1973
——'British Strategy and the Palestine Question, 1936–39' in *Journal of Contemporary History*, vii, 3, October 1972
Colvin, I., *Vansittart in Office* (London 1965)
Confino, M. and Shamir, S., eds, *The USSR and the Middle East* (Jerusalem and New Brunswick 1973)
Crossman, R. H. S., *A Nation Reborn* (London 1960)
——*Palestine Mission: a personal record* (London 1946, New York 1947)
Crum, B., *Behind the Silken Curtain* (New York 1947)
Cunningham, Viscount, of Hyndhope, *A Sailor's Odyssey* (London 1951)
Dalton, H., *Memoirs 1945: High Tide and After* (London 1962)
Daniels, J., *Man of Independence: A Biography of Harry S. Truman* (Philadelphia 1950)
Debelot, R., *The Struggle for the Mediterranean, 1939–45* (New York 1951)
Denovo, J. A., *American Interests and Policies in the Middle East, 1900–39* (Minneapolis 1963)
Dilks, D., ed, *The Diaries of Sir Alex Cadogan, 1938–45* (London 1971; New York 1972)
Duff-Cooper, A., *Old Men Forget* (London 1953)
Eden, A., *Memoirs*, 2 vols (London and New York, 1962, 1964)
Esco Foundation, *Palestine: A study of Jewish, Arab and British Policies*, 2 vols (Yale 1947)
Evans, T. E., ed, *The Killearn Diaries, 1934–46* (London 1972)
Evron, Y., *The Middle East – Nations, Super-powers and Wars* (London and New York 1973)

Francis-Williams, Lord, *A Prime Minister Remembers* (London 1961)
——*Ernest Bevin – Portrait of a Great Englishman* (London 1952)
Furlonge, G., *Palestine is my Country* (London 1969)
Gabbay, R. E., *A Political Study of the Arab–Jewish Conflict* (Geneva 1959)
Glubb, Sir John, *A Soldier with the Arabs* (London 1957)
Goldmann, N., *Sixty Years of Jewish Life (Autobiography)* (New York 1969)
Gorni, J., *Partnership and Conflict* (Tel Aviv 1976 – in Hebrew)
Gott, R. and Martin, G., *The Appeasers* (London and Boston 1963)
Granott, E., *Land Settlement and Development in Palestine* (Jerusalem 1931)
Graves, P., ed, *Memoirs of King Abdullah of Transjordan* (London & New York 1950)
Halperin, S., *The Political World of American Zionism* (Detroit 1961)
Hancock, W. K. and Gowing, M. M., *The History of the Second World War, Civil Series: The British War Economy* (London 1949)
Hanna, P., *British Policy in Palestine* (Washington 1942)
Hirszowicz, L., *The Third Reich and the Arab East* (London and Buffalo, NY 1966)
Horowitz, D., *State in the Making* (New York 1953)
Hull, C., *Memoirs* (New York and London 1948)
Howard, M., *The Mediterranean Strategy in the Second World War* (New York and London 1968)
Hurevitz, J. C., *The Struggle for Palestine* (New York 1950)
——*Soviet–U.S. Rivalry in the Middle East* (New York and London 1969)
Hyamson, A. M., *Palestine under the Mandate* (London and Westport, Conn. 1950)
James, J. R., *Churchill – A Study in Failure, 1900–39* (London 1970)
Jeffries, J. M., *Palestine: The Reality* (London 1939; Westport, Conn. 1975)
Joseph, B., *British Rule in Palestine* (Washington 1948)
Katzburg, N., *British Policy in Palestine, 1936–40* (Jerusalem 1974 – in Hebrew)
Kedourie, E. 'Sir Herbert Samuel and the Government of Palestine', in *Middle Eastern Studies*, v, 1
——*In the Anglo-Arab Labyrinth* (Cambridge 1976)
——*The Chatham House Version* (London 1970)
Kirk, G. E., *Survey of International Affairs, 1939–46: The Middle East in the War* (London and New York 1952)
Kirkbride, A., *A Crackle of Thorns* (London 1956)
Kliemann, A., *Foundations of British Foreign Policy in the Arab World: The Cairo Conference, 1921* (Baltimore 1970)
Laqueur, W. Z., ed, *The Middle East in Transition* (London and New York 1958)
——*The Struggle for the Middle East: The Soviet Union and the Middle East, 1958–68* (London and New York 1969)
Lederer, I. J., *Russian Foreign Policy* (Yale and London 1962)
Lenczowski, G., *Soviet Advances in the Middle East* (Washington 1972)
Litvinoff, B., *The Road to Jerusalem* (London 1965)
Luke, H. C. and Keith-Roach, E., *Palestine Handbook* (London 1922)
Macdonald, M., *Titans and Others* (London 1972)
Manuel, F., *The Realities of American–Palestine Relations* (Washington 1949)
Marlowe, J., *Rebellion in Palestine* (London 1946)
——*The Seat of Pilate: An Account of the Palestine Mandate* (London 1959)
——*Arab Nationalism and British Imperialism – A Study in Power Politics* (London 1961)

Meinertzhagen, Col. R., *Middle East Diary, 1917–56* (London 1959)
Middlemas, K., and Barnes, J., *Baldwin, a Biography* (London 1969; New York 1970)
Millis, Walter, ed., *The Forrestal Diaries* (New York 1951)
Minney, J., *The Private Papers of Hore-Belisha* (London 1960)
Monroe, E., *The Mediterranean in Politics* (London 1935)
——*Britain's Moment in the Middle East* (London 1963)
Monsky, H. and Bisgyer, M., *H. Monsky, The Man and his Work* (New York 1947)
Namier, Sir L. B., *Conflicts* (London and New York 1942)
Parkinson, C., *The Colonial Office from Within, 1909–45* (London 1945)
Pearlman, W. M., *The Mufti of Jerusalem* (London 1947)
Perkins, F., *The Roosevelt I Knew* (New York 1946; London 1965)
Pinchuk, B. C., 'Soviet Penetration into the Middle East in Historical Perspective' in *The USSR and the Middle East*, eds M. Confino and S. Shamir (Jerusalem and New Brunswick 1973)
Playfair, Maj. Gen. I. S. O., *History of the Second World War, Military Series:* The Mediterranean and the Middle East (London 1956)
Polk, W. R., *The U.S. and the Arab World* (Harvard 1965)
Porath, Y., *The Emergence of the Palestinian Arab National Movement, 1918–29* (Jerusalem 1971; London 1974)
——*The Palestinian–Arab National Movement*, ii: *1929–39* (London 1977)
Preuss, W., *The Labour Movement in Israel* (Jerusalem 1965)
Proskauer, J. M., *A Segment of my Times* (New York 1950)
Rabinowicz, O. K., *Fifty Years of Zionism – A Historical Analysis of Dr Weizmann's 'Trial and Error'* (London 1950)
——*Winston Churchill on Jewish Problems* (London 1956; New York 1960)
Rendel, Sir G. W., *The Sword and the Olive* (London 1957)
Rose, N. A. *The Gentile Zionists* (London 1973)
Sachar, Howard, *Europe Leaves the Middle East* (New York 1972; London 1974)
——*The Emergence of the Middle East, 1914–24* (New York 1969)
Sacher, Harry, *Israel – the Establishment of a State* (London 1959; Westport. Conn. 1969)
Schechtman, J. B., *Rebel and Statesman*, 2 vols (New York and London 1951)
——*The United States and the Jewish State Movement, 1939–49* (New York and London 1966)
Schmidt, H., 'The Nazi Party in Palestine and the Levant' in *International Affairs* 1952
Shertok M., *Political Diary – 1936* (Tel Aviv 1968 – in Hebrew)
Shimoni, Y., *The Arabs of Palestine* (Jerusalem 1947)
Simson, H. J., *British Rule and Rebellion* (London 1937)
Smith, Gaddis, *American Diplomacy during the Second World War 1941–45* (New York and London 1965)
Spectar, I., *The Soviet Union and the Muslim World, 1917–58* (Washington 1959)
Speiser, E. A., *The United States and the Near East* (London 1947)
Stein, L., *The Balfour Declaration* (London 1961)
Stettinius, E., *Roosevelt and the Russians* (Garden City 1949)
Storrs, R., *Orientations* (London and New York 1937)
Sykes, C., *Crossroads to Israel* (London 1965; Bloomington, Indiana 1973)

——*Orde Wingate* (London 1959)
Trevor, D., *Under the White Paper* (Jerusalem 1948)
Truman, H. S., *Memoirs*, ii: *Years of Trial and Hope* (London and New York 1956)
Tuchman, B. W., *Bible and Sword* (New York 1956)
Vansittart, Lord, *The Mist Processiont The Autobiography of Lord Vansittart* (London 1958)
Voss, C. H., ed, *Stephen S. Wise, Servant of the People – Selected Letters* (Philadelphia 1969)
Watt, D. C., *Personalities and Politics* (London 1965)
Weisgal, M. W., *So Far . . .* (London 1971)
Weisgal, M. W. and Carmichael, J., ed, *Chaim Weizmann: A Biography by Several Hands* (London 1962)
Weizmann, C., *Trial and Error* (London 1950; New York 1966)
Wheeler-Bennett, J., ed, *Action This Day – Working with Churchill* (London 1968)
Wischnitzer, M., *To Dwell in Safety* (Philadelphia 1948)
Woodward, Sir L., *British Policy in the Second World War* (London 1962)
Woolbert, R. B., 'Pan-Arabism and the Palestine Problem' in *Foreign Affairs*, January 1938
Zeine, Z. N., *The Struggle for Arab Independence* (Beirut 1960; New York 1976)

Index

Abadan oil refinery, 152
Abdullah Ibn Husayn, Emir of Transjordan, 18, 21, 34, 41, 51–2, 146, 162, 178, 184, 196(n. 50)
Abyssinia, Italian invasion of (1935), 1, 16
Afghanistan, 58
Alexander, General Sir Harold, 121, 215(n. 189)
Alexandretta, ceded to Turkey by the French, 60, 141
Alexandria Protocol (October 1944), xi–xii, 148–9
Aly Maher Pasha, 77, 80, 81
al-Azmeh, Adel, 57
al-Azmeh, Nabih, 56, 203(n. 29)
al-Madi, Muin, 56, 203(n. 28)
American Presidential Committee on International Petroleum Policy, 153
American Zionist Emergency Council, 130, 132, 133
Amery, Leopold, 13, 35, 194(n. 13), 199(n. 21); his advocacy of Partition, 65, 167, 172, 177–8, 181, 183, 190
Amin el Husseini, Haj, Mufti of Jerusalem, xii, 11, 26, 31, 141, 145, 187–8, 189; seeks mediation by Arab States, 18, 28–9; and opposition to Partition, 41, 46; Nuri Said's meeting with, 47; British vacillation towards, 50–3, 65; his liaison with Germans, 65, 89, 205(n. 80); escapes to Beirut, 53–4, 202(n. 17); his exile in the Lebanon and Anglo-French attitudes towards, 54–62, 65; escapes to Iraq, 61–2; not invited to St James's Conference, 62–3, 65; Nashashibi revolt against authority of, 62–5, 204(n. 73); rejects 1939 White Paper, 64
Andrews, L. A., murder of, 51, 53
Anglo-American Commission on Palestine (1945), 159–60, 184
appeasement policy: in Europe, xi, 189; and in the Middle East, xi, 7–9, 15–16, 68, 85, 112, 153, 162, 189
Arab Club, Damascus, 58
Arab Federation *see* Arab States; Pan-Arabism

Arab League, 145, 180; formation of (1945), xii, 148–9, 190
Arab Rebellion, ix, 1, 5, 7, 65; 1936: 10–31 *passim*, 50, 140, 189; 1937: 11, 51, 62, 67; 1938: 51, 64, 69, 189; *see also* Palestinian Arabs
Arab States, xi–xii, 4, 8, 9; MacMahon–Hussein correspondence, x, 70, 71, 74, 192(n. 4); mediation by (1936), 18–22, 28–9; Rendel's views on, 32–3, 56–7; attitudes towards Partition, 38–9, 41, 42, 45–6, 67–8, 160, 173–5, 180; Mufti's disappointment at apathy of, 56; Palestinian Arab propaganda in, 58; British retreat from Partition and, 67–8, 70, 71, 72; MacDonald's plan for Middle East Federation, 73; St James's Conference, 74–5, 77, 79, 80, 86–7, 90; and post-Conference negotiations with British, 82–5; and publication of White Paper, 83–4, 85–6; and Constitutional clauses, 88–98; and implementation of Land Laws, 90, 91; Britain's 'Pan-Arab' policy, 140–4; Nuri Said's initiatives, 144–6; all-Arab Conference (Alexandria Protocol: 1944), 146–8; and formation of Arab League, 148–50, 190; reaction to Zionist publicity campaign in USA, 161; Churchill's views on, 162–3; Cairo Conference of Foreign Ministers, 179; *see also* individual countries
Arida, Maronite Patriarch of Lebanon, 33
arms smuggling/arms caches, 57, 122, 157, 159
Arslan, Shekib, 56, 203(n. 27)
Attlee, Clement, 14, 165, 184, 194(n. 16); his views on Partition, 35, 167; and on White Paper, 92; heads new Labour Government (1945), 159, 160, 182–3
Auchinleck, General, 113–14, 116, 118, 121, 152
Australian military forces, 101
Axis, x, xi, 151; Mufti's support for, 65, 89; Middle East propaganda of, 91, 110; and military successes, 92, 107; sympathy of Arabs for, 95; occupation of Greece by, 112; *see also* Germany; Italy

Bagallay, Lacy, 49, 90, 91, 93–4, 141, 203(n. 38)
Bahrein, 152; oil concessions in, 153
Baldwin, Stanley, 13, 14, 27, 194(n. 14), 197(n. 97)
Balfour, A. J., 193(n. 31)
Balfour Declaration (1917), x, xi, 15, 37, 39, 40, 42, 43, 47, 74, 75, 76, 125–6, 162, 187
Balkans, 107, 110, 151
Barker, Lt-General, 5, 192(n. 15)
Basle programme (of First Zionist Congress), 134
Bateman, Chargé d'Affaires, Baghdad, 28, 68
Battershill, Chief Secretary of the Palestine Government, 50, 55, 63, 67, 97–8
Baxter, Foreign Office official, 60, 204(n. 46)
Beaverbrook, Lord, 153
Ben-Gurion, David, 17, 32, 126, 195(n. 44); conflict between Weizmann and, 71, 70–1, 79, 80, 105–7, 126–39, 187; his attitude to Partition, 35, 37; and meetings with MacDonald, 70–1, 76; at St James's Conference, 77, 78, 79, 80–1, 82; his views on raising of Jewish Army, 105–6, 116, 129, 130, 131, 132; visits to USA, 106, 107, 129–30, 133–4; becomes Chairman of Agency Executive, 126; his policy towards Britain, 128–9, 134–5; and concept of Jewish States, 129–30, 134–5; attitude towards Biltmore Programme, 131, 134–5; and immigration, 134; resigns again from Executive, 137, 138; and withdraws resignation, 138; rift between Shertok and, 217(n. 58)
Berlin, Sir Isaiah, 112, 213(n. 135)
Bevin, Ernest, 104, 133, 139, 183, 184, 212(n. 96)
Biltmore Conference/Programme (May 1942), 119, 128, 130–1, 134–5, 137, 139, 158, 179, 217(n. 49)
Bracken, Brendan, 99, 182, 211(n. 64)
British Somaliland: British forces withdraw from, 94; Italian advances into, 103
Bushe, Sir Grattan, 60
Butler, R. A., 78, 82

Cabinet Committee on Arab federation (1941), 142
Cabinet Committee on Military Policy in the Middle East (1940), 103
Cabinet Committee(s) on Palestine, *1938–39:* 62–3, 72, 77, 83; *1943–44:* 142 145; establishment of, xi, 157, 165; 1st Report (1943), 158, 165–71, 172, 173, 177, 189–90; 2nd Report (1944), 154–5, 159, 175, 177–9, 180, 181; *1945:* 160, 183
Cairo Conference (1942), 120, 121

Campbell, Commissioner for Jerusalem District, 21
Casey, R. G., British Minister of State in Cairo, 145, 164, 168, 169
Cazalet, Victor, 99, 121, 166, 199(n. 21)
Chamberlain, Austen, 14, 194(n. 16)
Chamberlain, Neville, xi, 6, 43, 87, 92, 193(n. 22), 203(n. 34); Churchill's criticism of Palestine policy of, 99–100, 102, 162
Chancellor, Sir John, 86
Churchill, Winston Spencer, 14, 47, 86, 90, 108, 129, 136, 152–3, 155, 194(n. 16), 199(n. 21, 23); ambiguous attitude to Palestine problem, xi; and view of Peel Report, 34–5, 37; and animosity towards MacDonald, 85; forms Coalition Government (1940), 92, 100; his attitude towards Jewish Army, 99–102, 110–11, 115, 118–19, 122–4; issues General Directive to the War Office (16 August 1940), 103; his views on Arab federation, 142, 143, 144, 146; and on Partition, 158, 166–7, 171, 173, 174, 182, 183, 190; electoral defeat of (1945), 159, 182–3; his attitude to White Paper, 160–1, 162, 164, 165; and sponsors scheme for Jewish State 161–2; and his views on future of Palestine, 162–3; his reaction to Moyne's assassination, 179; and attitude to government officialdom, 182, 183
Columbani, M., 62, 204(n. 57)
Committee of Imperial Defence (CID), 3, 5; Sub-Committee on Middle Eastern problems (1938–39), 4; Middle East (Official) Committee (1942), 144
Commonwealth military forces, moved to Delta from Palestine, 103
Cornwallis, British Ambassador in Baghdad, 146–7, 148–9, 173–4
Cranborne, Viscount, Colonial Secretary, 45, 170; his attitude to Jewish Army, 119–20; and to Jewish immigration, 163, 201(n. 91)
Czechoslovakia, 66

Dalton, Hugh (later Lord Dalton), 183, 224(n. 142)
Dayan, Moshe, 194(n. 36)
Defence Party (Palestinian Arabs), 11, 63, 64, 79, 89
Dill, Lt-General (GOC Palestine), 5, 29, 50, 104, 192(n. 14)
Downie, First Secretary at the Colonial Office, 40, 43, 52, 86–7
Druse Revolt (1925), 203(n. 26)
Duff-Cooper, A., 26, 197(n. 96)
Dufferin, Lord, 63, 80

INDEX

Dugdale, Mrs Blanche ('Baffy'), 14, 35, 45, 47, 106, 134–5, 193(n. 31), 201(n. 88)

Eastern Mediterranean Fleet, 3
Edé, Emile, President of Lebanon, 33
Eden, Sir Anthony (later First Earl of Avon), 1, 26, 95, 162, 182, 192(n. 2), 201(n. 71); immigration issue and, 16, 17, 30; his reliance on Rendel for Palestine policy, 32; and attitude to Partition, 34, 38, 41, 42, 45, 154–5, 165, 172–3, 174, 177, 178; and to Mufti, 50, 55; and to Jewish Army, 102, 104–5, 107, 109, 114, 115, 116; and to Zionist propaganda in USA, 117, 154; his views on Arab federation, 142, 144
Egypt, 8, 11, 17, 20, 58, 60, 61, 68, 83, 84, 93, 95, 152, 160; British 'self-sufficiency' policy for (1936–39), 3, 4; St James's Conference, 74, 87; Middle East Reserve moved from Palestine to, 101, 103; Axis invasion, 105; Jewish companies for aerodrome defence in, 113–14; assassination of Lord Moyne in Cairo, 138, 179; Pan-Arabism and, 141, 144–5; Alexandria Protocol, 146–8; and formation of Arab League, 148–9; British post-war presence in, 160; opposition to Partition, 173, 175; Cairo Conference of Foreign Ministers of Arab States, 179
El Alamein, British retreat to, 118; and victory at, 144, 152
el-Alami, Musa, 148, 218(n. 32)
Elliott, Walter, 13, 47, 82, 193(n. 31), 194(n. 8), 201(n. 82)
Eritrea, 162
Executive Committee of Palestine High Commissioner, issue of Arab–Jewish representation on, 77, 82, 83, 88

Farouk, King, 6
Feisal ibn Hussein, Emir, 128, 143, 216(n. 14)
Foreign Affairs, Weizmann article in (January 1942), 130, 134, 145
France, French, 3, 98, 157, 164, 178; attitude to Palestine problem and relations with British, 54–62, 65; Alexandretta ceded to Turkey by, 60; negotiations for Treaty with Syria, 54, 55, 61, 91, 141, 203(n. 19); Munich crisis, 66; surrender of (June 1940), 91, 92; and wartime position in Syria, 92–3; declaration of Syrian independence (June 1941) by England and, 96; opposition to Pan-Arabism, 141, 146; Anglo–Free French invasion of Syria, 142
French North Africa, 54, 152
French Volunteer Unit, 103

Galilee, 41, 46, 48, 51, 166, 168, 170, 173, 175, 178, 200(n. 49), 202(n. 109)
de Gaulle, General Charles de, 146
Germany, 6, 46; Mufti's support during War for, 65, 205(n. 80); support for Arabs by, 70, 96; military advances by, 91, 101; Syria grants landing facilities to, 96; Rommel's offensives, 112, 117, 118; Allied invasion of Europe, 122; Jewish Brigade's action in, 124; retreat of military forces in North Africa, 144, 152; occupation of Greece by, 112, 151; invasion of USSR by, 151, 152; defeat of, 159, 182; seizure of power in Hungary, 172; *see also* Axis
Ghazi, King of Iraq, 19, 20, 28
Gibb, H. A. R., 143
Goldmann, Nahum, 130, 216(n. 27)
Gort, Viscount, 69, 180, 181
Greater Syria: Nuri Said's plan for federation of, 145–6; scheme for creation of, 169, 170, 171, 173, 174, 175, 178
Greece, 1, 191; British wartime operations in, 95, 151; and evacuation of, 112
Grigg, Sir Edward, 121, 122, 160, 180–1
Guinness, W. E., *see* Moyne, Lord
Gulf of Akaba, 6, 166, 167

Haganah, 120, 193(n. 25); British military co-operation with, 6, 9, 88; and anti-British feeling of, 122; strength of, 123, 159; secret arms-caches of, 159
Haifa, 6, 34, 37, 75, 157, 169; blowing up of 'Patria' in harbour, 95; Italian aircraft bombing of, 104; oil refineries at, 157, 159; British post-war strategic plans for, 157, 160
Haining, Major-General, 5, 7, 40, 69, 107, 192(n. 14)
Halifax Viscount (E. F. L. Wood), 19, 26, 60, 6,9, 80, 91, 153, 194(n.16), 196(n. 58); abortive visit to Hitler, 48; his views on White Paper's constitutional clauses, 91–2; and on Jewish Army, 100, 102, 104, 112, 119; Weizmann's relations with, 133, 136
Hall, J. H., 18, 21
Hamza, Fuad, 81
Hadi, Auni Abdul, 196(n. 78)
Harris, D. G., 202(n. 109)
Hashemite dynasty, 64
Hawes, Brigadier L. A., appointed commander for the Jewish force, 107–8
High Arab Committee, 52; formation of, 10–11, 52; National General Strike declared by, 10, 12, 14; Arab States' mediation sought by, 18–22, 28–9; and Nuri Said's intervention, 22–4; and

Palestine Post article, 25–6; strike called off by, 29; Peel Commission and, 32; arrest of members of, 53; *see also* Arab Rebellion; Palestinian Arabs
Histadruth, 126
Hitler, Adolf, xi, 8, 48, 106, 117, 129
Hoover, Senator, 161
Hore-Belisha, Leslie, 5, 193(n. 16), 201(n. 88)
Hoskins, Colonel, 174
Huleh salient, 168, 170, 171, 173, 174, 178
Hull, Cordell, 153
Hungary, German seizure of power in (1944), 172
Hussein ibn Ali, Sharif, Emir of Mecca, 192(n. 4)
Husseini family, 10–11, 12, 89; political conflicts between Nashashibis and, 51–2, 62–5; and transactions with Jews, 64; delegates to St James's Conference, 74; *see also* Amin el Husseini, Haj
Husseini, Jamal, 74, 148

Ibn Saud, Abdul Aziz, King of Saudi Arabia, 16, 42, 95, 128, 146, 162, 195(n. 40); mediation by (1936), 18, 19–20, 21, 22–3, 24, 26, 28, 29; Rendel's relations with, 32–3; and Peel Report, 34, 40; his view of Mufti, 64; and opposition to Partition, 67–8; attitude towards Pan-Arabism, 141, 142, 143, 146; his alleged agreement to scheme for Jewish State, 161, 221(n. 56); Sharif Hussein Ibn Ali defeated by (1924), 192(n. 4)
immigration, x, 6, 10, 12, 14, 34, 39, 68, 71, 73, 83, 188, 194(n. 1), 195(nn. 42, 46); 1936 discussions on suspension of, 16–18, 19–20, 21–2, 24, 25, 26, 27, 28, 30–1; political high level for, 30, 37, 73, 199(n. 22), 200(n. 44); reactions to 1937 schedule for, 32; Rendel's views, 39–40, 42; Ibn Saud's proposal for fixed numerical ratio, 42; British alternative schemes, 73–4, 76; discussed at St James's Conference, 76, 77, 78, 79, 80, 81–2; White Paper's provisions, 86, 91, 157, 163, 164, 170, 172, 179;illegal, 96, 111; Biltmore Programme's provisions, 131, 134, 179; Ben-Gurion's attitude towards, 134; and Cranborne's views, 163; new partition scheme and, 170, 177, 179; MacMichael's views, 174–5; and Grigg's views, 180; Joint Commission of Enquiry on (1945), 184
India, 1, 4, 69, 181, 191
Inskip, Minister for Co-ordination of Defence, 69
oil reserves in Middle East, 10, 151, 152, 153–4, 155–6, 157, 219(n. 16)

Iran, 58; oilfields, 152, 153; Anglo-Russian occupation (1941), 155; and Tripartite Treaty (Iran, 1942), 155, 220(n. 32); and Teheran Declaration, 155
Iraq, 6, 19, 20, 28, 58, 60, 64, 92, 93, 110, 160; Nuri Said's mediation (1936), 22–4, 25, 26, 28–9; and rivalry between Saudi Arabia and, 26; Rendel's views on, 33; attitude towards Partition, 34, 38–9, 53, 173–4, 175, 189; Mufti escapes to, 61, 62; MacDonald's view of, 68; St James's Conference, 74, 87; implementation of Constitutional clauses demanded by, 88, 95; Mufti organizes pro-Axis forces in, 89; Rashid Ali crisis, 89, 96, 112, 115, 142, 143, 151; Pan-Arabism and, 140, 141, 147; concerned at Zionist publicity campaign in USA, 161
Iraqi Petroleum Company (IPC), 153
Ironside, Field Marshal Sir Edmund, 9, 193(n. 35)
Ismay, Lord, 152–3
Italy, 6, 46, 70, 92; invasion of Abyssinia by, 1, 16; British strategy in Mediterranean and, 1, 3, 4; Saudi relations with, 32–3; declaration of War by, 91, 101, 103, 129; advances into British Somaliland, 103; bombing of Haifa by aircraft of, 104; Allied invasion of, 122; Jewish Brigade's action in, 124; Wavell's victories over forces of, 151; *see also* Axis

Jabotinsky, Zeev Vladimir, 100, 211(n. 71)
Jaffa, 52, 168, 169, 170; Arab attack on Jews in, 10
Jedda, 18, 19, 67
Jerusalem, 6, 11, 21, 22–4, 37, 200(n. 61)
Jerusalem State, plans for, 175, 178, 180
Jewish Agency, 77, 84, 97, 125, 216(n. 5); *see also* Zionist diplomacy
Jewish Agency Advisory Committee in London, 13
Jewish Agency Executive: delegation to St James's Conference, 8, 74, 75; negotiations for Jewish Army and, 98–9, 105, 108–9, 111, 112, 115, 120, 122, 123, 124; Ben-Gurion becomes Chairman of (1935), 126; and close 'supervision' of Weizmann by, 126–7; and conflict between Ben-Gurion and Weizmann, 127–8, 129–39; Ben-Gurion offers his resignation, 128–9; Zionist call for immigration to be controlled by, 131, 163, 179; Ben-Gurion resigns again, 137, 138; Shertok visits Weizmann in New York, 136–7; and Shertok heads delegation in London to negotiate with Weizmann, 137–8; Chiefs of Staff view of, 158–9

Jewish Agency Intelligence, 46, 55, 56, 57, 58, 59, 77
Jewish Agency London Executive, 17, 48, 102
Jewish Army, negotiations for (1939–44), 88, 95, 98–124, 127, 129, 130, 131, 132, 145, 161, 182, 212(n. 101); British and Zionist military needs (1939–40), 98–103; and parity principle, 99, 103, 112–13, 120, 121; Palestine Buffs (1940), 103–4; Jewish Division proposal (1940–41), 104–12; recruitment of Jews to guard aerodromes in Egypt and Palestine (1941), 113–15; rejection of Jewish Division scheme (1941), 115–17; campaign in USA for (1941–42), 117–18; Palestine Regiment (1942), 118–21; Jewish battalions shipped out of Palestine (1943), 122; Jewish Brigade (1944), 123–4; *see also* Haganah
Jewish Army Committee, New York, 117, 119
Jewish Brigade, 123–4, 182
Jewish Displaced Persons, 124
Jewish Home Guard, 106
Jewish Settlement Police, 112–13
Joint Planning Committee of the War Cabinet, 157

Kantara, 75
Kaplan, head of Jewish Agency Treasury, 126
Kawakji, Fawzi, 197(n. 87)
Keith-Roach, E., 61
Khaldi, Dr, Mayor of Jerusalem, 21, 196(n. 73)
Killearn, Lord *see* Lampson, Sir Miles
Kirkbride, British Resident at Amman, 18
Kol Israel (Voice of Israel), 129
Kuwait oil concessions, 153

Labour Government (1945), Palestine policy of, 133, 139, 182–6
Labour Party, 35, 37, 86, 167
Lampson, Sir Miles (later Lord Killearn), 20, 32, 33, 83, 147, 173, 196(n. 60); favours inviting Mufti to St James's Conference, 63; MacDonald's appraisal of, 68; opposed to a Jewish State, 68; his attitude to constitutional clauses, 92–3, 94, 96; and to Jewish Army, 113–14
land sales to Jews, x, 10, 12, 18, 20, 27, 64, 71, 73, 79, 84, 86, 204(n. 73); implementation of White Paper's Land Laws (1940), 90, 91, 128, 182, 209(n. 12)
Law, R. K., 169, 170
Lawrence, T. E., 32, 198(n. 5)
League of Nations, 41, 83, 86, 149
League of Nations Permanent Mandates Commission, 29–30, 34, 37, 38, 53

Lebanon, 98, 146, 157; Jewish state favoured by, 33; Mufti escapes to Beirut, 54; Anglo-French relations and attitudes towards Mufti's presence in, 54–62, 65; Arab federation and, 145, 147
Legislative Council scheme (1936), 12
Leigh, General, 107
Libya, 106, 95, 106, 152
Lipsky, Louis, 130, 137, 216(n. 27)
Lloyd, Sir G. A. (Lord Lloyd), Colonial Secretary, 94, 97, 182, 210(n. 50); his attitude towards Jewish Army, 100, 102–4, 105, 106, 108, 112
Lloyd George, David, 182
Loraine, Sir Percy (Ambassador to Turkey), 44
Lothian, Lord (Philip Kerr), 91, 205(n. 14)
Luke, Sir Harry, 29–30, 198(n. 112)
Lyttelton, Oliver, 114, 115, 214(n. 146)

McConnell, General, 120
MacDonald, Malcolm, 8, 15, 43, 60, 61, 189, 193(n. 33), 194(n. 16); appointed Colonial Secretary, 49, 66–7; and visits Palestine, 67, 68–9; and rejection of Partition by, 67, 69–72; Weizmann's meetings with, 67–8, 70, 78; his evaluation of Lampson, 68; and Woodhead Report, 69; Ben-Gurion's meetings with, 70–1, 76 recalls MacMichael for consultations, 71; formulates new policy for Palestine, 72–3; at St James's Conference, 74–82, 86, 88; and immigration issue, 76, 78, 79, 80, 81–2; and constitutional proposals, 76–7; tries to persuade Jews not to leave Conference, 78–9, 81; post-Conference negotiations with Arabs, 82–5; favours immediate publication of White Paper, 83–4; Zionists' reaction to negotiations with Arabs, 84–5; and their anger at his appeasement policy, 85; his attitude towards Jewish Army, 99, 100
MacDonnell, Sir Michael, 196(n. 64)
MacKereth, Colonel, 54, 55–6, 57, 59, 64, 204(n. 73)
MacMahon, Sir Henry, x, 192(n. 4)
MacMahon–Hussein correspondence, x, 70, 71, 74, 192(n. 4), 209(n. 8)
MacMichael, Sir Harold, High Commissioner for Palestine, 67, 170, 203(n. 39); his attitude towards Mufti, 58–9, 60; and towards Fakhri initiative, 63, 64; and views on Partition, 69, 174–5; requests military reinforcements, 69, 192(n. 10); recalled for consultations with MacDonald, 71; his attitude to White Paper's constitutional clauses, 93, 94–7; and to Jewish Army, 110, 113, 116–17, 121

Mapai, 126
Margesson, Capt. H. D. R., 114, 194(n. 16)
Martel, M. de, French High Commissioner, 33, 54
martial law in Palestine, threat of, 15, 26, 27, 29, 31, 34, 53, 54, 67
Mediterranean, 69; British strategy in (1936-39), 1-4; and during War, 101, 152; and Soviet threat, 156
Melchett, Lord (Henry Mond), 12, 13-14, 194(n. 12), 201(n. 88)
Middle East Reserve Brigade, 3, 69
Middle East Reserve Force, 66; moved from Palestine to Egypt (1940), 101, 103
Middle East Supply Centre, Cairo, 154
Middle East War Council, 114-15; May 1943 meetings, 157-8, 164
Mond, Henry *see* Melchett, Lord
Montgomery, Field-Marshal, 152
Montreux Convention (1936), 156
Morrison, Herbert, 86, 166, 172, 175, 178, 179, 183, 208(n. 95)
Mount Tabor, 175
Moyne, Lord (W. E. Guinness), Colonial Secretary, 145, 213(n. 128); his views on Jewish Army, 111, 112, 113, 115-16, 121; assassination of (1944), 138, 179, 190; his views on Partition, 169; and scheme for creation of Greater Syria, 169, 170, 175
Mufti *see* Amin el Husseini, Haj
Munich crisis (1938), 1, 4, 7, 51, 66, 189

Nablus, 52
Nahhas Pasha, Egyptian Prime Minister, 144-5; convenes all-Arab Conference (1944), 146-7
Namier, Sir Lewis, 14, 78, 113, 194(n. 22)
Nashashibi family, 10, 11-12; political conflicts with Husseini family, 51-2, 62-5; delegates to St James's Conference, 74
Nashashibi, Fakhri, 11-12, 62, 63, 204(n. 60)
Nashashibi, Regheb bey, 11, 12, 26, 52, 62
National General Strike (by Palestinian Arabs: 1936), 10, 12, 14, 21, 22, 24, 28, 29, 50
Negev, 166, 167, 169, 170, 171, 173, 178
Night Squads, 5, 7, 9, 51, 104, 193(n. 18)
Nuri Said, Iraqi Foreign Minister, 141, 148, 166, 180, 196(n. 73); mediation by (1936), 22-4, 26, 27, 28; and *Palestine Post* article, 25-6; abortive meeting of Samuel and Winterton with, 27-8; interview on Partition with Ormsby-Gore, 45-6, 48; and Mufti's meeting with, 47; demands guarantee of self-government in Palestine and Syria, 91, 92, 94, 96; Nahhas Pasha turns down his proposal for conference of Arab States, 144-5; and 'Greater Syria' federation plan of, 145-6; and all-Arab Conference in Alexandria, 147; protests at Zionist publicity campaign in USA, 161

Oliphant, L., Permanent Under-Secretary at Foreign Office, 19, 20, 34, 47
Ormsby-Gore, W. G. A. (later 4th Lord Harlech), 5, 13, 29, 189, 193(n. 17), 194(n. 16), 201(n. 93); his attitude towards Zionism, 14-15, 26, 198(n. 8); and policy on suspension of immigration, 17-18, 19, 21-2, 30; and Iraqi intervention, 23-4; *Palestine Post* article and, 25-6; his reaction to Rendel's views, 33, 47; favours Partition, 33, 38, 41-2, 43, 44, 45, 49; and Arab pressure on, 45-6, 48; replaced by MacDonald as Colonial Secretary, 49, 66; his attitude towards Mufti, 50, 53; and arrest of Mufti and members of Higher Arab Committee, 53

Paget, General, 123, 215(n. 202)
Palestine Arab Party, 11, 89
Palestine Buffs, 103-4, 113, 114, 116, 118, 120, 122, 214(n. 172)
Palestine Development Fund, proposal for, 180
Palestine Police, 52, 67, 157
Palestine Post, alleged text of Nuri Said-Higher Arab Committee agreement in (1936), 25-6
Palestine Regiment, 118, 120-1
Palestinian Arabs, 187-8; attitude towards Partition, 6, 11, 41, 51, 67; Jewish forces used against guerrillas, 6-7; Higher Arab Committee formed, 10-12; and National General Strike, 10, 12, 50; and taxes strike, 13; Arab States' mediation, 18-22, 28-9; and Nuri Said intervention, 22-7; and Samuel-Winterton initiative, 27-8; threat of martial law averted, 27, 29; and strike called off, 29; Peel Commission and, 32-4; British vacillation towards the Mufti, 50-4, 65; and Husseini-Nashashibi political conflicts, 51-2, 62-5; Mufti escapes to Beirut, 53-4; Anglo-French attitudes towards Mufti's presence in Lebanon and, 54-62; British retreat from Partition and, 66-72; at St James's Conference, 73-82; independent state demanded by, 74, 76-7, 79, 82, 83; MacDonald stresses Britain's moral obligation to, 74-5; and proposes representation on Executive Council of, 77, 82; veto on future immigration by, 78, 80, 81-2, 84, 86; reject idea of a further Conference, 79; demand for a Palestinian Ministry by, 84; terms of 1939 White Paper, 85-6; growth of militant, anti-British nationalism among, 87; pro-Axis activities of Mufti, 89; new

INDEX

Land Laws, 90, 91; recruitment during War of, 100; and Palestine Buffs, 103–4; and Palestine Regiment, 118; Alexandria Protocol, 147, 148–9; *see also* Arab Rebellion; Arab States; Pan-Arabism; White Paper (1939)
Palestinian Terrorists' Committee, 57
Palmach, 214(n. 172)
Pan-Arabism, ix, xii, 8, 24, 33, 64, 71, 94, 140–50, 188; British policy towards, 140–4, 148; Nuri Said's initiatives, 144–6; Nahhas Pasha convenes all-Arab Conference (Alexandria Protocol), 146–8; and formation of Arab League, 148–9; *see also* Palestinian Arabs
Parkinson, Sir Cosmo, Permanent Under-Secretary of State at Colonial Office, 44
Partition, ix, 1, 5, 11, 32–49, 143, 188–91; Cabinet approval and Foreign Office opposition (1937), 6; Peel Report on, 32–4, 165–6, 188–9; Zionist tactics in Commons debate on, 34–8; and Foreign Office sabotages, 38–41; Woodhead Commission, 39, 41–5, 48; Zionist evaluation of Government intentions, 45–9; Husseini–Nashashibi conflicts over, 51–2, 62–3; French attitude towards, 54; the retreat from (1938), 66–72; Cabinet Committee's consideration of and recommendations for (1943–4), 135–6, 137, 138, 154–5, 158, 159, 164–71, 177–9, 189–90; strategic aspects of, 151, 157–60; Foreign Office opposition to, 170–5, 177–8, 190; and Cabinet endorsement of (1944), 172; abandonment of, 179–82; Labour Cabinet's policy on, 183–6; *see also* Peel Commission; Woodhead Commission
Passfield White Paper (1930), 12, 47, 85
'Patria' (refugee ship), 95, 213(n. 130)
Peel Commission/Report (1936–7), 1, 5, 22, 23, 32–4, 42, 44, 46, 48, 50, 70, 72, 73, 96, 165–6, 168, 184, 188–9, 199(n. 27), 200; on power of the Mufti, 11; proposal for and opposition to, 12–14; and approved by Cabinet, 14; suspension of immigration and, 17–18, 19, 20, 21–2, 25, 26, 30–1; Zionist tactics in Commons debate on, 34–8; Foreign Office attacks Partition plan, 38–41
Peel, W. R. W., 1st Earl, 32, 198(n. 1)
Peirse, Air Vice-Marshal, 15
Percival, General, 101
Philby, Harry St John, 32, 128, 143, 198(n. 5), 221(n. 56)
Phipps, Sir Eric, British Ambassador at Paris, 60, 61
Polish Brigade, 103
Pound, Sir Dudley, 4

Pickthorne, Sir K., 38

Rashid Ali coup (1941), 89, 96, 112, 142, 143, 151
refugees, xii, 130, 134, 184; 'Patria' disaster, 95, 213(n. 130); *see also* immigration
Reid (member of Woodhead Commission), 48
Rendel, Sir George, 26, 90, 198(nn. 2, 4); advises Ibn Saud against mediation, 28; his attitude towards immigration, 30, 39–40; and memorandum on Arab views on Palestine, 32–3; opposes partition and establishment of Jewish State, 34, 39–40, 41–2, 43; and his attitude to Woodhead Commission, 46–7; and to Palestine Rebellion, 54, 55–6, 57, 58; and Arab countries' reactions, 56–7
Revisionists (Zionists), 100, 112, 211(n. 71); campaign in USA for Jewish Army by, 117, 119, 129, 179
Rommel, Field-Marshal, 112, 117, 118, 121, 151
Roosevelt, President F. D., 124, 143, 144, 155; proposes UN trusteeship for Palestine, 174, 177
Rushbrook-Williams, Professor, 109–10

St James's Conference (February 1939), 7, 8, 62–3, 65, 71, 72–82, 84, 85, 86–7, 88, 89, 189, 209(n. 8)
Samuel, Sir Herbert (Lord Samuel), 11, 27–8, 197(n. 101)
Saudi Arabia, 6, 40, 58, 161; mediation in Palestine by, 19–20, 21, 22–3, 28, 29; and rivalry between Iraq and, 26; Rendel's views on, 32–3; importance to Britain of, 67–8; St James's Conference, 74, 87; implementation of constitutional clauses demanded by, 88, 95; Pan-Arabism and, 140, 143–4, 147; US interests in, 153, 155
Schirach, Baldur von, 58
Scroll of Independence, 139
Shertok, Moshe (later Sharett), 35, 38, 84, 122, 200(n. 41); his attitude towards Woodhead Commission, 41, 48; at St James's Conference, 80, 82; meetings at Colonial Office, 84–5; his demands for Jewish fighting force, 118, 122; becomes head of Jewish Agency's Political Department, 126; against rift with Britain during War, 128; his visit to Weizmann in New York, 136–7, 217(n. 58); heads Agency Executive delegation to London to negotiate with Weizmann, 137–8
Shuckburgh, Sir John, 40, 84, 200(n. 53), 203(n. 46)
Shukri Quwatli, 147

Simon, Sir John, 27
Sinclair, Sir Archibald, 34, 86, 183, 199(n. 21)
Smaller Actions Committee (Zionist), 127–8
Smuts, General Jan, 5–6, 136, 193(n. 19)
Southern Syria, proposal for creation of, 175, 178–9
Soviet Union, xi, xii, 3, 178, 191; British wartime assistance to, 116; challenge to British hegemony in Middle East by, 151, 152, 153, 155–6; German invasion of, 151, 152, 153; Anglo-Russian occupation of Iran (1941), 155; and Tripartite Treaty, 155, 156, 220(n. 32); oil policy, 155, 156
Stalin, Josef, 155
Stanley, Colonel, Colonial Secretary, 166; his views on Partition, 168–9, 170, 175, 177, 178, 179, 181, 183, 227(n. 64)
Stern Group, 179
Stimson, Senator, 161
strategic considerations in Middle East: in Mediterranean (1936–39), 1–4; Zionist role in, 5–9; MacDonald's speech at St James's Conference on, 75; negotiations for Jewish Army and, 98–124 *passim*; Arab federation and, 140–50; wartime vulnerability, 151–2, 190; American and Soviet challenge to British hegemony, 152–7, 190–1; Partition and, 157–60; and Grigg's 'quadrilateral' security system, 160
Sudetan Germans, 66
Suez Canal, 1, 3, 4, 191
Supreme Moslem Council, 11, 52; dissolution of, 53, 65
Suweidi, Taufiq, 81
Swinton, Viscount (Sir Philip Cunliffe-Lister), 26, 194(n. 16), 197(n. 95)
Sykes–Picot Agreement (1916), 54, 65
Syria, 41, 68, 98, 115, 157, 178, 203(n. 19); Peel Commission and, 33; negotiations for Franco-Syrian Treaty, 54, 55, 61, 141, 203(n. 19); planning of Palestinian Arab rebellion in, 55, 56, 57, 58, 59; and Mufti's propaganda, 58; and Axis propaganda, 91, 110; Nuri Said demands guarantee of independence for, 91; France's wartime position in, 92–3; and Anglo-French declaration of independence for, 96; Pan-Arabism and, 140, 141, 143; Anglo-Free French invasion of, 142; Nuri Said's plan for 'Greater Syria' federation, 145–6; and all-Arab Conference in Alexandria, 147
Szold, Robert, 134, 217(n. 44)

taxes strike (by Palestinian Arabs), 13
Teheran Declaration (1943), 155
Tel Aviv, 168, 169

Thomas, J. H., 12, 13, 14, 194(n. 10)
Tobruk, fall of, 132
Transjordan, 33, 54, 55, 93, 160, 166, 173, 175, 176, 178; Mufti's plan to win over Bedouin tribes of, 51; St James's Conference, 74; Arab Federation and, 145, 147
Trans-Persian Railway, 155
Tripolitania, 162
Truman, President Harry S., xii, 184
Truman Doctrine, 191
Turkey, 1, 4, 8, 44, 101, 191; French cede Alexandretta to, 60, 141; neutrality of, 107; attitude to Pan-Arabism, 141; Soviet threat to British influence in, 155–6
'Tzahal' (Israel's defence forces), 124

United Nations, xii, 145, 164, 174, 177, 184, 186; Britain returns Palestine Mandate to (1947), 186, 191
United States, xi, 74, 82, 102, 128; opposition to 1939 White Paper, 83, 90; recruitment for Jewish force from, 105, 107; Presidential elections (1940), 107; influence of American Jews, 115–16, 154; and campaign for a Jewish Army, 117–18, 119, 127, 129, 133, 161; Biltmore Conference (1942), 119, 130–1, 134–5; Ben-Gurion in, 106, 107, 129–30, 133–4, 135, 136; Zionists' meetings to discuss Ben-Gurion–Weizmann conflict, 131–2; Shertok visits Weizmann in New York, 136; challenge to British hegemony in Middle East by, 151, 152, 153–5; and allocation of Middle East oil, 153–4; and role in operation of Middle East Supply Centre, 154; Zionist publicity campaign, 161; and scheme for Jewish State sponsored by Churchill, 161–2; possible effects of establishment of Jewish State on Jewish communities in, 171; Presidential elections (1944), 172; Roosevelt proposes UN trusteeship for Palestine, 174, 177; Anglo-American Joint Commission of Enquiry on Palestine, 184; Truman Doctrine, 191

Vansittart, Lord, 39, 55

Wahba, Sheikh Hafez, 19, 20
Wahhabi dynasty, 64
Wakf funds, 53; Mufti's alleged misappropriation of, 55, 64, 204(n. 74)
Wauchope, Lt-General Sir Arthur, 35, 194(n. 7); proposes Royal Commission (1936), 12, 13, 14; his attitude to Arabs, 15–16, 27, 28; and immigration, 18, 19, 21–2, 27, 30; and Nuri Said's mediation, 22, 23, 24, 25, 26, 27; Zionists' analysis of role of, 27; and threat to martial law averted, 29; his

INDEX

attitude to Partition, 38, 41; and to Mufti, 50–1, 52, 53
Wauchope Partition Plan, 48, 202(n. 109)
Wavell, General Sir Archibald (1st Earl), 5, 15–16, 103, 105, 151, 182, 192(n. 14); his attitude to Jewish Army, 110–11, 112, 113; and to Palestine problem, 157, 158, 181
Wedgwood, J., 199(n. 21)
Weisgal, Meyer, 130–1, 133, 193(n. 31)
Weizmann, Dr Chaim, xi, 6, 13, 15, 25, 26, 43, 85, 143, 193(n. 23); his views on immigration, 14, 16–17, 34; conflict between Ben-Gurion and, 17, 70–1, 79, 80, 105–7, 126–39, 187; meets Lebanese President and Patriarch in Paris, 33; his views on Partition, 34, 37–8, 40, 41, 46, 47–8, 67, 70, 158, 179; MacDonald's meetings with, 67–8, 70, 78; his 'weakness' for England, 70–1; at St James's Conference, 74, 76, 77, 78, 79, 80–1, 82; negotiations for Jewish Army and, 98, 102, 103–9, 111–12, 115–16, 117–19, 122–3, 131, 132, 212(nn. 101, 116); his meeting with Moyne, 116; position in Zionist movement, 125–6; and concept of Jewish State, 128, 130, 134, 145; Biltmore Programme and, 131, 134–5, 137, 179; illness of, 133; Shertok visits him in New York, 136–7; and Jerusalem Executive delegation visits him in London, 137–8; his first wartime visit to Palestine, 138–9; removed from Presidency of Zionist Movement (1946), 139; and his signature omitted from Scroll of Independence, 139; scheme for Jewish State, 161, 167, 221(n. 56); his attitude to White Paper, 162; Churchill's discussion on Partition with, 166–7
Weizmann, Michael, 132–3, 135, 137
Welles, Sumner, 161, 221(n. 58)
Western Desert campaigns, 112, 117, 151, 152–3; British retreat to El Alamein, 118; fall of Tobruk, 132; victory at El Alamein, 144, 152
White Paper (1922), 162
White Paper (1930: Passfield White Paper), 12, 47, 85
White Paper (January 1938), 47
White Paper (November 1938), 84
White Paper (May 1939), x, xi, xii, 8–9, 64, 72, 83–4, 87, 88, 110, 114, 157, 158, 159, 163–4, 173, 174, 181, 187; terms of, 85–6; and immigration provisions, 86, 91, 157, 163, 164, 170, 172, 173, 179; Constitutional clauses, 88–98; Land Laws, 90, 91, 128, 160; Ben-Gurion's attitude to, 128, 130; Arab federation and, 145, 146, 148, 149, 150; Churchill's views on, 160, 162, 164, 165; and Weizmann's, 162

Wilson, General, 123, 215(n. 202)
Wingate, Major-General Orde, 5, 9, 51, 99, 104, 105, 119, 120, 193(n. 18)
Winterton, Earl, 27–8, 197(n. 101)
Wise, Rabbi Dr Stephen Samuel, 130, 131, 132, 133–4, 216(n. 27)
Woodhead, Sir John, 45, 69, 201(n. 79)
Woodhead Commission (1938), 39, 40, 48, 66, 67, 69, 71, 72, 165, 168, 200(n. 47), 201(n. 79); significance of, 41–5; Zionist evaluation of Government intentions towards, 46–9
World Zionist Organization, 125, 132, 136, 139, 159, 187

Yasin Pasha, Iraqi Consul at Haifa, 28–9
Yemen, 74, 147
Yugoslavia, 1, 151

Zetland, Marquess of, 26
Zionist Actions Committee, 35, 134
Zionist Congresses: 1st (Basle: 1897), 134; *1931*: 125; *1933*: 126; *1939*: 127–8; *1946*: 139
Zionist diplomacy: role in British strategy (1936–39), 5–9; attitude to Peel Commission, 12–14, 189, 199(n. 27); and to suspension of immigration, 16–18, 30–1; responsible for *Palestine Post* article, 25–6; Samuel–Winterton initiative, 27–8; reaction to 1937 immigration schedule, 32; good relations with Lebanese Christians, 33; tactics in Commons debate on Partition, 34–8; reactions to Woodhead Commission, 41, 67, 72; evaluation of British Government intentions, 45–9; Weizmann's 'weakness' for England, 70–1; St James's Conference, 73–82; issue of Arab–Jewish representation on Executive Council, 77, 82; draft proposals to Arabs leaked in error to, 77; and Arab veto on future immigration, 78, 79, 80, 81–2; suggestion for further conference rejected by, 78–9, 80, 81; and post-Conference discussions, 84–5; implementation of Land Laws, 90; negotiations for a Jewish Army (1939–44), 98–124; and campaign in USA, 117–18, 119, 179; Weizmann's position in Zionist movement, 125–6; and Ben-Gurion–Weizmann conflict, 126–7, 129–39, 187; Ben-Gurion's wartime policy towards Britain, 128–9; Biltmore Programme, 130–1, 134, 179; Ben-Gurion challenges Weizmann's leadership, 131–9; attitude towards Arab federation, 143; and Nuri Said's 'Greater Syria' plan, 145–6; publicity campaigns in USA, 161; and scheme for Jewish state sponsored by Churchill, 161–2; *see also* Jewish Agency; Jewish Army